Theories of Personality:

Primary Sources and Research

Second Edition

Edited by

Gardner Lindzey
Harvard University

Calvin S. Hall
University of California, Santa Cruz

Martin Manosevitz
University of Texas, Austin

John Wiley & Sons, Inc.   New York   London   Sydney   Toronto

Library of Congress Cataloging in Publication Data:

Lindzey, Gardner, ed.
  Theories of personality.

  "Appropriate for use as a text in conjunction with
[Hall's and Lindzey's] Theories of personality . . .
[and for use] by itself."
  Includes bibliographies.
  1. Personality. I. Hall, Calvin Springer, 1909-
joint ed. II. Manosevitz, Martin, 1938-
joint ed. III. Title. [DNLM: 1. Personality. BF
698 L754t 1973]
BF698.L524 1973   155.2   72-6983
ISBN 0-471-53899-X
ISBN 0-471-53901-5 (pbk.)

Printed in the United States of America

10-9 8 7 6 5 4 3 2 1

Preface

This volume provides an organized and reasonably comprehensive view of the current status of personality theory and research. It is especially appropriate for use as a textbook in conjunction with *Theories of Personality*, but it can also be used as a textbook in combination with other books or, indeed, by itself.

The present collective is a thorough revision of the first edition. Approximately half of the articles are new. We have substantially reduced the length of the book and have introduced a soft-cover edition to further decrease the cost to the student. There are two new sections: one deals with Skinner's operant reinforcement theory and the other deals with existential psychology. The criteria used in choosing the selections are outlined in the preface to the first edition, which is reprinted here.

During the preparation of this edition, Gardner Lindzey was in residence at The Center for Advanced Study in the Behavioral Sciences. He is deeply grateful to O. Meredith Wilson and his staff for facilitating the work. The assistance of Dorothy Brothers and Lynne Johnson was of immeasurable value in preparing this book.

Gardner Lindzey
Calvin S. Hall
Martin Manosevitz

Preface
To The First Edition

It is now roughly seven years since we prepared a book (*Theories of Personality*) intended to provide a sympathetic and yet objective coverage of the major influential personality theories then existing. In the intervening years there have been changes both in the details of these theories and in the existing research that relates to them. The present volume is intended to provide a reasonable representation of contemporary theoretical contributions and at the same time to give a sample of the most interesting and pertinent empirical studies available. In addition, it seeks to enrich the original book by placing the reader in direct contact with the thinking and writing of many of the major personality theorists.

A systematic summary of the major ideas of important intellectual figures serves an essential didactic role, especially in view of the fact that the most creative and influential theorists have seldom devoted much of their energy to summarizing and systematizing their ideas; but it remains a matter of first importance that students be exposed directly to the original writings of these contributors. This is particularly necessary in an area where there is relatively little in the way of formal elegance and where much of the impact of any theory is indirect, heuristic, and mediated by complex processes that do not involve formal deductions and specific hypothesis testing.

Although the various theories showed considerable difference in the quantity of material that was available for inclusion, all offered many alternatives. Consequently, it was necessary to establish criteria for selection that would provide a rational basis for eliminating all but the few items that space permitted us to include.

In the selection of material written by the originator of the theory, that is, *primary sources*, we were guided by the following considerations:

1. The material included should be representative of the theorist both in regard to the content of his ideas and his usual style of thinking and writing.

2. The content of the paper should deal with one or more issues that are central to the position of the theorist.

3. If possible the paper should include not only theoretical statement and supporting reasoning but also empirical data of the sort that the theorist often used in developing or defending his conceptual position.

4. It should be relatively self-contained so that the reader can appreciate its message without exposure to other related papers.

5. It should be comprehensible to an advanced undergraduate or graduate student who has not had specialized training in this area of psychology.

6. Where feasible it should provide insight into changes that have been introduced by the theorist since the time that *Theories of Personality* was prepared.

The major considerations that influenced our selection of empirical studies were:

1. Where possible the article should provide clear evidence relevant to a hypothesis explicitly derived from the relevant theory. Just as our original book was focused on a statement of the positive aspects of the various theories, so here we were less interested in studies that provided negative results than those that provided confirmatory findings.

2. Where possible the research should be contemporary, objective, and quantitative.

3. Preferably the study should not have been discussed in *Theories of Personality*.

4. Reasonable diversity should be achieved so that as many varieties of different types of derivative research as possible could be represented.

5. Where possible we selected studies that deal with research topics that possess theoretical relevance and at the same time are of some intrinsic interest to persons interested in human behavior.

6. The paper should be comprehensible to an advanced undergraduate student or graduate student who has not had previous training in this area of psychology.

It is our conviction that these papers will be read with more comprehension and interest when they are coupled with the chapters contained in *Theories of Personality*. However, we do not consider them dependent on the other book so that they can be used independently.

Gardner Lindzey
Calvin S. Hall

March 1, 1965

Contents

Theories of Personality: Primary Sources and Research

Section I

Freud's Psychoanalytic Theory

In selecting articles to represent Freud's theory and the research which it has generated, one is confronted by a profusion of riches. For not only are there the twenty-three volumes of Freud's psychological writings which constitute the primary source but there are also a multitude of volumes written by his fellow workers which, in many cases, are substantial additions to the basic theory. As for the research, even if we limit ourselves only to that which is in accord with the positivistic tradition of American psychology, there is so much to choose from that the final selection becomes very difficult. Many worthy papers have had to be omitted for lack of space.

As one surveys this empirical literature, a luxuriant growth can be detected since the publication of Sears' (1943) rather bleak overview of psychoanalytically oriented research. The sophistication of investigators with respect both to methodology and to derivation of relevant hypotheses from Freudian theory has grown in recent years. No other theory, apart from behaviorism, has stirred up so many first-rate investigations; no other current theory aside from behaviorism has generated so many hypotheses that have been confirmed. Not the least of one's astonishment over this state of affairs arises from the fact that Freud's theory, which grew out of his observations of patients, is now being confirmed not only by studies using American psychologists' favorite species — college sophomores — as subjects, but also by experiments making use of infra-human primates and rodents.

The selections we have made from the primary sources are restricted to the works of Freud although, as intimated before, one could also have made selections from the writings of Abraham, Ferenczi, Roheim, Jones, Melanie Klein, Anna Freud, and a number of others.

The first paper, *Some Psychical Consequences of the Anatomical Distinction between the Sexes*, was chosen because it deals with a topic that engaged Freud's attention throughout his life. Libido theory and its applications, which were first developed at length in *Three Essays on Sexuality*, were topics that Freud returned to again and again. With each new discussion he brought new insights. In a number of publications using several different approaches Freud dealt with the facet of libido theory that was uniquely part of the psychology of women. The ideas set forth in our selection are Freud's final views regarding differences between the sexes.

Freud is seen in his work clothes in the second selection, which is taken from his long case history, "An infantile neurosis." The patient was a young Russian who was initially treated by Freud for approximately four and one-half years. The recent volume edited by Gardiner (1971) contains interesting follow-up data obtained from the wolf-man in his adult life. When one considers the development of psychoanalytic theory, this case history and that of "Little Hans" are probably the two most important that Freud published. The dream of the white wolves is probably the most thoroughly analyzed dream in all of Freud's writings including those in *The Interpretation of Dreams*. For, as Richard Jones has pointed out, no dream in that great volume is analyzed back to an infantile wish. The one presented here is. It is a magnificent *tour de force* of dream analysis and has been included so the student may see firsthand how Freud worked with the primary data of psychoanalysis.

The research reported in the papers by Hall and Levin is directly related to the first paper in this section. One should note in both papers the process by which the investigator derived from Freud's writings testable hypotheses and developed the necessary operational procedures to evaluate them.

Hall's paper uses the primary data of psychoanalysis—dreams. However, instead of an intensive analysis of a single or a few dreams using the free association method, an extensive and statistical analysis is made of the content of more than 3000 dream reports. Objective techniques for content analysis of dreams have been developed in the past few years. Application of these techniques has and should continue to produce a variety of interesting findings directly related to psychoanalytic theory.

A rarely investigated, but important, part of psychoanalytic theory—the castration complex in women—is the subject of the fourth paper. Levin assembled her subjects and collected her data with admirable care, and the eight components of the female castration complex identified by her would serve as an excellent starting point for additional experiments on the psychology of women.

References:

Gardiner, M. (Ed.) *The wolf-man by the wolf-man*. New York: Basic Books, 1971.

Sears, R. R. *Survey of objective studies of psychoanalytic concepts*. Social Science Research Council Bulletin, 1943, No. 51.

1. Some Psychical Consequences of the Anatomical Distinction between The Sexes

SIGMUND FREUD

In my own writings and in those of my followers more and more stress is laid on the necessity that the analyses of neurotics shall deal thoroughly with the remotest period of their childhood, the time of the early efflorescence of sexual life. It is only by examining the first manifestations of the patient's innate instinctual constitution and the effects of his earliest experiences that we can accurately gauge the motive forces that have led to his neurosis and can be secure against the errors into which we might be tempted by the degree to which things have become remodelled and overlaid in adult life. This requirement is not only of theoretical but also of practical importance, for it distinguishes our efforts from the work of those physicians whose interests are focused exclusively on therapeutic results and who employ analytic methods, but only up to a certain point. An analysis of early childhood such as we are considering is tedious and laborious and makes demands both upon the physician and upon the patient

which cannot always be met. Moreover, it leads us into dark regions where there are as yet no signposts. Indeed, analysts may feel reassured, I think, that there is no risk of their work becoming mechanical, and so of losing its interest, during the next few decades.

In the following pages I bring forward some findings of analytic research which would be of great importance if they could be proved to apply universally. Why do I not postpone publication of them until further experience has given me the necessary proof, if such proof is obtainable? Because the conditions under which I work have undergone a change, with implications which I cannot disguise. Formerly, I was not one of those who are unable to hold back what seems to be a new discovery until it has been either confirmed or corrected. My *Interpretation of Dreams* and my "Fragment of an Analysis of a Case of Hysteria" (the case of Dora) were suppressed by me—if not for the nine years enjoined by Horace—at all events for four or five years before I allowed them to be published. But in those days I had unlimited time before me— "oceans of time" as an amiable author puts it—and material poured in upon me in such quantities that fresh experiences

SOURCE. *Selection from Sigmund Freud, "Some psychical consequences of the anatomical distinction between the sexes" in* The Standard Edition, *Vol. XIX, pp. 248–258. London: The Hogarth Press, 1961 (First published 1925).*

were hardly to be escaped. Moreover, I was the only worker in a new field, so that my reticence involved no danger to myself and no loss to others.

But now everything has changed. The time before me is limited. The whole of it is no longer spent in working, so that my opportunities for making fresh observations are not so numerous. If I think I see something new, I am uncertain whether I can wait for it to be confirmed. And further, everything that is to be seen upon the surface has already been exhausted; what remains has to be slowly and laboriously dragged up from the depths. Finally, I am no longer alone. An eager crowd of fellow-workers is ready to make use of what is unfinished or doubtful, and I can leave to them that part of the work which I should otherwise have done myself. On this occasion, therefore, I feel justified in publishing something which stands in urgent need of confirmation before its value or lack of value can be decided.

In examining the earliest mental shapes assumed by the sexual life of children we have been in the habit of taking as the subject of our investigations, the male child, the little boy. With little girls, so we have supposed, things must be similar, though in some way or other they must nevertheless be different. The point in development at which this difference lay could not be clearly determined.

In boys the situation of the Oedipus complex is the first stage that can be recognized with certainty. It is easy to understand, because at that stage a child retains the same object which he previously cathected with his libido—not as yet a genital one—during the preceding period while he was being suckled and nursed. The fact, too, that in this situation he regards his father as a disturbing rival and would like to get rid of him and take his place is a straightforward consequence of the actual state of affairs. I have shown elsewhere how the Oedipus attitude in little boys belongs to the phallic phase, and how its destruction is brought about by the fear of castration—that is, by narcissistic interest in their genitals. The matter is made more difficult to grasp by the complicating circumstance that even in boys the Oedipus complex has a double orientation, active and passive, in accordance with their bisexual constitution; a boy also wants to take his *mother's* place as the love-object of his *father*—a fact which we describe as the feminine attitude.

As regards the prehistory of the Oedipus complex in boys we are far from complete clarity. We know that the period includes an identification of an affectionate sort with the boy's father, an identification which is still free from any sense of rivalry in regard to his mother. Another element of that stage is invariably, I believe, a masturbatory activity in connection with the genitals, the masturbation of early childhood, the more or less violent suppression of which by those in charge of the child sets the castration complex in action. It is to be assumed that this masturbation is attached to the Oedipus complex and serves as a discharge for the sexual excitation belonging to it. It is, however, uncertain whether the masturbation has this character from the first, or whether on the contrary it makes its first appearance spontaneously as an activity of a bodily organ and is only brought into relation with the Oedipus complex at some later date; this second possibility is by far the more probable. Another doubtful question is the part played by the bedwetting and by the breaking of that habit through the intervention of training measures. We are inclined to make the simple connection that continued bed-wetting is a result of masturbation and that its suppression is regarded by boys as an inhibition of their genital activity—that is, as having the meaning of a threat of castration; but whether we are always right in supposing this remains to be seen. Finally, analysis shows us in a shadowy way how the fact of a child at a very early age listening to his parents copulating may set up his first sexual excitation, and how that event may, owing to its after-effects, act as a starting-point for the child's whole sexual development. Masturbation, as well as the two attitudes in the Oedipus complex, later on become attached to this early experience, the child having subsequently interpreted its meaning. It is impossible, however, to suppose that these observations of coitus are of universal occurrence, so that at this point we are faced with the problem of "primal phantasies." Thus the prehistory of the Oedipus complex, even in boys, raises all of these questions for sifting and explanation; and there is the further problem of whether we are to suppose that the process invariably follows the same course, or whether a great variety of different preliminary stages may not converge upon the same terminal situation.

In little girls the Oedipus complex raises one problem more than in boys. In both cases the mother is the original object; and there is no cause for surprise that boys retain that object in the Oedipus complex. But how does it happen that girls abandon it and instead take their father as an object? In pursuing this question I have been able to reach some conclusions which may throw light precisely on the prehistory of the Oedipus relation in girls.

Every analyst has come across certain women who cling with especial intensity and tenacity to the bond with their father and to the wish in which it culminates of having a child by him. We have good reason to suppose that the same wishful phantasy was also the motive force of their infantile masturbation, and it is easy to form an impression that at this point we

have been brought up against an elementary and unanalysable fact of infantile sexual life. But a thorough analysis of these very cases brings something different to light—namely, that here the Oedipus complex has a long prehistory and is in some respects a secondary formation.

The old paediatrician Lindner once remarked that a child discovers the genital zones (the penis or the clitoris) as a source of pleasure while indulging in sensual sucking (thumb-sucking). I shall leave it an open question whether it is really true that the child takes the newly found source of pleasure in exchange for the recent loss of the mother's nipple—a possibility to which later phantasies (fellatio) seem to point. Be that as it may, the genital zone is discovered at some time or other, and there seems no justification for attributing any psychical content to the first activities in connection with it. But the first step in the phallic phase which begins in this way is not the linking-up of the masturbation with the object-cathexes of the Oedipus complex, but a momentous discovery which little girls are destined to make. They notice the penis of a brother or playmate, strikingly visible and of large proportions, at once recognize it as the superior counterpart of their own small and inconspicuous organ, and from that time forward fall a victim to envy for the penis.

There is an interesting contrast between the behaviour of the two sexes. In the analogous situation, when a little boy first catches sight of a girl's genital region, he begins by showing irresolution and lack of interest; he sees nothing or disavows what he has seen, he softens it down or looks about for expedients for bringing it into line with his expectations. It is not until later, when some threat of castration has obtained a hold upon him, that the observation becomes important to him: if he then recollects or repeats it, it arouses a terrible storm of emotion in him and forces him to believe in the reality of the threat which he has hitherto laughed at. This combination of circumstances leads to two reactions, which may become fixed and will in that case, whether separately or together or in conjunction with other factors, permanently determine the boy's relations to women: horror of the mutilated creature or triumphant contempt for her. These developments, however, belong to the future, though not to a very remote one.

A little girl behaves differently. She makes her judgment and her decision in a flash. She has seen it and knows that she is without it and wants to have it.

Here what has been named the masculinity complex of women branches off. It may put great difficulties in the way of their regular development towards feminity, if it cannot be got over soon enough. The hope of some day obtaining a penis in spite of everything and so of becoming like a man may persist to an incredibly late age and may become a motive for strange and otherwise unaccountable actions. Or again, a process may set in which I should like to call a "disavowal," a process which in the mental life of children seems neither uncommon nor very dangerous but which in an adult would mean the beginning of a psychosis. Thus a girl may refuse to accept the fact of being castrated, may harden herself in the conviction that she *does* possess a penis, and may subsequently be compelled to behave as though she were a man.

The psychical consequences of envy for the penis, in so far as it does not become absorbed in the reaction-formation of the masculinity complex, are various and far-reaching. After a woman has become aware of the wound to her narcissism, she develops, like a scar, a sense of inferiority. When she has passed beyond her first attempt at explaining her lack of a penis as being a punishment personal to herself and has realized that the sexual character is a universal one, she begins to share the contempt felt by men for a sex which is the lesser in so important a respect, and, at least in holding that opinion, insists on being like a man.

Even after penis-envy has abandoned its true object, it continues to exist: by an easy displacement it persists in the character-trait of *jealousy*. Of course, jealousy is not limited to one sex and has a wider foundation than this, but I am of opinion that it plays a far larger part in the mental life of women than of men and that that is because it is enormously reinforced from the direction of displaced penis-envy. While I was still unaware of this source of jealousy and was considering the phantasy "a child is being beaten," which occurs so commonly in girls, I constructed a first phase for it in which its meaning was that another child, a rival of whom the subject was jealous, was to be beaten. This phantasy seems to be a relic of the phallic period in girls. The peculiar rigidity which struck me so much in the monotonous formula "a child is being beaten" can probably be interpreted in a special way. The child which is being beaten (or caressed) may ultimately be nothing more nor less than the clitoris itself, so that at its very lowest level the statement will contain a confession of masturbation, which has remained attached to the content of the formula from its beginning in the phallic phase till later life.

A third consequence of penis-envy seems to be a loosening of the girl's relation with her mother as a love-object. The situation as a whole is not very clear, but it can be seen that in the end the girl's mother, who sent her into the world so insufficiently equipped, is almost always held responsible for her lack of a penis. The way in which this comes about historically is often that soon after the girl has discovered that her genitals are unsatisfactory she begins to show jealousy of another child on the ground that her mother is fonder of it than of her, which serves as a reason for her giving up her affectionate relation to her mother. It will fit in with this if the child which has been preferred by her mother is made into the first object of the beating-phantasy which ends in masturbation.

There is yet another surprising effect of penis-envy, or of the discovery of the inferiority of the clitoris, which is undoubtedly the most important of all. In the past I had often formed an impression that in general women tolerate masturbation worse than men, that they more frequently fight against it and that they are unable to make use of it in circumstances in which a man would seize upon it as a way of escape without any hesitation. Experience would no doubt elicit innumerable exceptions to this statement, if we attempted to turn it into a rule. The reactions of human individuals of both sexes are of course made up of masculine and feminine traits. But it appeared to me nevertheless as though masturbation were further removed from the nature of women than of men, and the solution of the problem could be assisted by the reflection that masturbation, at all events of the clitoris, is a masculine activity and that the elimination of clitoridal sexuality is a necessary precondition for the development of femininity. Analyses of the remote phallic period have now taught me that in girls, soon after the first signs of penis-envy, an intense current of feeling against masturbation makes its appearance, which cannot be attributed exclusively to the educational influence of those in charge of the child. This impulse is clearly a forerunner of the wave of repression which at puberty will do away with a large amount of the girl's masculine sexuality in order to make room for the development of her femininity. It may happen that this first opposition to auto-erotic activity fails to attain its end. And this was

in fact the case in the instances which I analysed. The conflict continued, and both then and later the girl did everything she could to free herself from the compulsion to masturbate. Many of the later manifestations of sexual life in women remain unintelligible unless this powerful motive is recognized.

I cannot explain the opposition which is raised in this way by little girls to phallic masturbation except by supposing that there is some concurrent factor which turns her violently against that pleasurable activity. Such a factor lies close at hand. It cannot be anything else than her narcissistic sense of humiliation which is bound up with penis-envy, the reminder that after all this is a point on which she cannot compete with boys and that it would therefore be best for her to give up the idea of doing so. Thus the little girl's recognition of the anatomical distinction between the sexes forces her away from masculinity and masculine masturbation on to new lines which lead to the development of femininity.

So far there has been no question of the Oedipus complex, nor has it up to this point played any part. But now the girl's libido slips into a new position along the line—there is no other way of putting it— of the equation "penis-child." She gives up her wish for a penis and puts in place of it a wish for a child: and *with that purpose in view* she takes her father as a love-object. Her mother becomes the object of her jealousy. The girl has turned into a little woman. If I am to credit a single analytic instance, this new situation can give rise to physical sensations which would have to be regarded as a premature awakening of the female genital apparatus. When the girl's attachment to her father comes to grief later on and has to be abandoned, it may give place to an identification with him and the girl may thus return to her masculinity complex and perhaps remain fixated in it.

I have now said the essence of what I had to say: I will stop, therefore, and cast an eye over our findings. We have gained some insight into the prehistory of the Oedipus complex in girls. The corresponding period in boys is more or less unknown. In girls the Oedipus complex is a secondary formation. The operations of the castration complex precede it and prepare for it. As regards the relation between the Oedipus and castration complexes there is a fundamental contrast between the two sexes. *Whereas in boys the Oedipus complex is destroyed by the castration complex, in girls it is made possible and led up to by the castration complex.* This contradiction is cleared up if we reflect that the castration complex always operates in the sense implied in its subject-matter: it exhibits and limits masculinity and encourages femininity. The difference between the sexual development of males and females at the stage we have been considering is an intelligible consequence of the anatomical distinction between their genitals and of the psychical situation involved in it; it corresponds to the difference between a castration that has been carried out and one that has merely been threatened. In their essentials, therefore, our findings are self-evident and it should have been possible to foresee them.

The Oedipus complex, however, is such an important thing that the manner in which one enters and leaves it cannot be without its effects. In boys the complex is not simply repressed, it is literally smashed to pieces by the shock of threatened castration. Its libidinal cathexes are abandoned, desexualized and in part sublimated; its objects are incorporated into the ego, where they form the nucleus of the super-ego and give that new structure its characteristic qualities. In normal, or, it is better to say, in ideal cases, the Oedipus complex exists no longer, even in the unconscious; the super-ego has become

its heir. Since the penis (to follow Ferenczi) owes its extraordinarily high narcissistic cathexis to its organic significance for the propagation of the species, the catastrophe to the Oedipus complex (the abandonment of incest and the institution of conscience and morality) may be regarded as a victory of the race over the individual. This is an interesting point of view when one considers that neurosis based upon a struggle of the ego against the demands of the sexual function. But to leave the standpoint of individual psychology is not of any immediate help in clarifying this complicated situation.

In girls the motive for the demolition of the Oedipus complex is lacking. Castration has already had its effect, which was to force the child into the situation of the Oedipus complex. Thus the Oedipus complex escapes the fate which it meets with in boys: it may be slowly abandoned or dealt with by repression or its effects may persist far into women's normal mental life. I cannot evade the notion (though I hesitate to give it expression) that for women the level of what is ethically normal is different from what it is in men. Their super-ego is never so inexorable, so impersonal, so independent of its emotional origins as we require it to be in men. Character-traits which critics of every epoch have brought up against women—that they show less sense of justice than men, that they are less ready to submit to the great exigencies of life, that they are more often influenced in their judgments by feelings of affection or hostility—all these would be amply accounted for by the modification in the formation of their super-ego which we have inferred above. We must not allow ourselves to be deflected from such conclusions by the denials of the feminists, who are anxious to force us to regard the two sexes as completely equal in position and worth; but we shall, of course, willingly agree that the majority of men are also far behind the masculine ideal and that all human individuals, as a result of their bisexual disposition and of cross-inheritance, combine in themselves both masculine and feminine characteristics, so that pure masculinity and femininity remain theoretical constructions of uncertain content.

I am inclined to set some value on the considerations I have brought forward upon the psychical consequences of the anatomical distinction between the sexes. I am aware, however, that this opinion can only be maintained if my findings, which are based on a handful of cases, turn out to have general validity and to be typical. If not, they would remain no more than a contribution to our knowledge of the different paths along which sexual life develops.

2. The Dream and The Primal Scene

SIGMUND FREUD

I have already published this dream elsewhere,[1] on account of the quantity of material in it which is derived from fairy tales; and I will begin by repeating what I wrote on that occasion:

"*'I dreamt that it was night and that I was lying in my bed. (My bed stood with its foot toward the window; in front of the window there was a row of old walnut trees. I know it was winter when I had the dream, and night-time.) Suddenly the window opened of its own accord, and I was terrified to see that some white wolves were sitting on the big walnut tree in front of the window. There were six or seven of them. The wolves were quite white, and looked more like foxes or sheep-dogs, for they had big tails like foxes and they had their ears pricked like dogs when they pay attention to something. In great terror, evidently of being eaten up by the wolves, I screamed and woke up. My nurse hurried to my bed, to see what had happened to me. It took quite a long while before I was convinced that it had only been a dream; I had had such a clear and life-*like picture of the window opening and the wolves sitting on the tree. At last I grew quieter, felt as though I had escaped from some danger, and went to sleep again.*

"'*The only piece of action in the dream was the opening of the window; for the wolves sat quite still and without making any movement on the branches of the tree, to the right and left of the trunk, and looked at me. It seemed as though they had riveted their whole attention upon me. I think this was my first anxiety dream. I was three, four, or at most five years old at the time. From then until my eleventh or twelfth year I was always afraid of seeing something terrible in my dreams.*'

"He added a drawing of the tree with the wolves, which confirmed his description. The analysis of the dream brought the following material to light.

"He had always connected this dream with the recollection that during these years of his childhood he was most tremendously afraid of the picture of a wolf in a book of fairy tales. His elder sister, who was very much his superior, used to tease him by holding up this particular picture in front of him on some excuse or other, so that he was terrified and began to scream. In this picture the wolf was standing upright, striding out with one foot, with its claws stretched out and its ears pricked. He thought this picture must have been an illustration to the story of Little Red Riding-Hood.

SOURCE. *Selection from Sigmund Freud, "The dream and the primal scene," section from "An infantile neurosis" in The Standard Edition, Vol. XVII, pp. 29–47. London: The Hogarth Press, 1955 (First published 1918).*

[1] The Occurrence in Dreams of Material from Fairy Tales.

"Why were the wolves white? This made him think of the sheep, large flocks of which were kept in the neighbourhood of the estate. His father occasionally took him with him to visit these flocks, and every time this happened he felt very proud and blissful. Later on — according to inquiries that were made it may easily have been shortly before the time of the dream — an epidemic broke out among the sheep. His father sent for a follower of Pasteur's, who inoculated the animals, but after the inoculation even more of them died than before.

"How did the wolves come to be on the tree? This reminded him of a story that he had heard his grandfather tell. He could not remember whether it was before or after the dream, but its subject is a decisive argument in the favour of the former view. The story ran as follows. A tailor was sitting at work in his room, when the window opened and a wolf leapt in. The tailor hit after him with his yard — no (he corrected himself), caught him by his tail and pulled it off, so that the wolf ran away in terror. Some time later the tailor went into the forest, and suddenly saw a pack of wolves coming towards him; so he climbed up a tree to escape from them. At first the wolves were in perplexity; but the maimed one, which was among them and wanted to revenge himself on the tailor, proposed that they should climb one upon another till the last one could reach him. He himself — he was a vigorous old fellow — would be the base of the pyramid. The wolves did as he suggested, but the tailor had recognized the visitor whom he had punished, and suddenly called out as he had before: 'Catch the grey one by his tail!' The tailless wolf, terrified by the recollection, ran away, and all the others tumbled down.

"In this story the tree appears, upon which the wolves were sitting in the dream. But it also contains an unmistakable allusion to the castration complex. The old wolf was docked of his tail by the tailor. The fox-tails of the wolves in the dream were probably compensations for this taillessness.

"Why were there six or seven wolves? There seemed to be no answer to this question, until I raised a doubt whether the picture that had frightened him could be connected with the story of Little Red Riding-Hood. This fairy tale only offers an opportunity for two illustrations — Little Red Riding-Hood's meeting with the wolf in the wood, and the scene in which the wolf lies in bed in the grandmother's nightcap. There must therefore be some other fairy tale behind his recollection of the picture. He soon discovered that it could only be the story of The Wolf and the Seven Little Goats. Here the number seven occurs, and also the number six, for the wolf only ate up six of the little goats, while the seventh hid itself in the clockcase. The white, too, comes into this story, for the wolf had his paw made white at the baker's after the little goats had recognized him on his first visit by his grey paw. Moreover, the two fairy tales have much in common. In both there is the eating up, the cutting open of the belly, the taking out of the people who have been eaten and their replacement by heavy stones, and finally in both of them the wicked wolf perishes. Besides all this, in the story of the little goats the tree appears. The wolf lay down under a tree after his meal and snored.

"I shall have, for a special reason, to deal with this dream again elsewhere, and interpret it and consider its significance in greater detail. For it is the earliest anxiety-dream that the dreamer remembered from his childhood, and its content, taken in connection with other dreams that followed it soon afterwards and with certain events in his earliest years, is of quite peculiar interest. We must confine ourselves here to the relation of the dream to the two fairy tales which have so much in common with each other, Little Red Riding-Hood and The Wolf and the Seven Little Goats. The effect produced by these stories was shown in the little dreamer by a regular animal phobia. This phobia was only distinguished from other similar cases by the fact that the anxiety-animal was not an object easily accessible to observation (such as a horse or a dog), but was known to him only from stories and picture books.

"I shall discuss on another occasion the explanation of these animal phobias and the significance attaching to them. I will only remark in anticipation that this explanation is in complete harmony with the principal characteristic shown by the neurosis from which the present dreamer suffered later in his life. His fear of his father was the strongest motive for his falling ill, and his ambivalent attitude towards every father-surrogate was the dominating feature of his life as well as of his behaviour during the treatment.

"If in my patient's case the wolf was merely a first father-surrogate, the question arises whether the hidden content in the fairy tales of the wolf that ate up the little goats and of Little Red Riding-Hood may not simply be infantile fear of the father.[2] Moreover, my patient's father had the characteristic, shown by so many people in relation to their children, of indulging in 'affectionate abuse'; and it is possible that during the patient's earlier years his father (though he grew severe later on) may more than once, as he caressed the little boy or played with him, have threatened in fun to 'gobble him up.' One of my patients told me that her two children could never get to be fond of their grandfather, because in the course of his affectionate romping with them he used to frighten them by saying he would cut open their tummies."

Leaving on one side everything in this quotation that anticipates the dream's remoter implications, let us return to its immediate interpretation. I may remark that this interpretation was a task that dragged on over several years. The patient related the dream at a very early stage of the analysis and very soon came to share my conviction that the causes of his infantile neurosis lay concealed behind it. In the course of the treatment we often came back to the dream, but it was

only during the last months of the analysis that it became possible to understand it completely, and only then thanks to spontaneous work on the patient's part. He had always emphasized the fact that two factors in the dream had made the greatest impression on him: first, the perfect stillness and immobility of the wolves, and secondly, the strained attention with which they all looked at him. The lasting sense of reality, too, which the dream left behind it, seemed to him to deserve notice.

Let us take this last remark as a starting-point. We know from our experience in interpreting dreams that this sense of reality carries a particular significance along with it. It assures us that some part of the latent material of the dream is claiming in the dreamer's memory to possess the quality of reality, that is, that the dream relates to an occurrence that really took place and was not merely imagined. It can naturally only be a question of the reality of something unknown; for instance, the conviction that his grandfather really told him the story of the tailor and the wolf, or that the stories of *Little Red Riding-Hood* and of *The Seven Little Goats* were really read aloud to him, would not be of a nature to be replaced by this sense of reality that outlasted the dream. The dream seemed to point to an occurrence the reality of which was very strongly emphasized as being in marked contrast to the unreality of the fairy tales. If it was to be assumed that behind the content of the dream there lay some such unknown scene—one, that is, which had already been forgotten at the time of the dream—then it must have taken place very early. The dreamer, it will be recalled, said: "I was three, four, or at most five years old at the time I had the dream." And we can add: "And I was reminded by the dream of something that must have belonged to an even earlier period." The parts of the manifest content of

---

[2] "Compare the similarity between these two fairy tales and the myth of Kronos, which has been pointed out by Rank."

the dream which were emphasized by the dreamer, the factors of attentive looking and of motionlessness, must lead to the content of this scene. We must naturally expect to find that this material reproduces the unknown material of the scene in some distorted form, perhaps even distorted into its opposite.

There were several conclusions, too, to be drawn from the raw material which had been produced by the patient's first analysis of the dream, and these had to be fitted into the collocation of which we were in search. Behind the mention of the sheep-breeding, evidence was to be expected of his sexual researches, his interest in which he was able to gratify during his visits with his father; but there must also have been allusions to a fear of death, since the greater part of the sheep had died of the epidemic. The most obtrusive thing in the dream, the wolves of the tree, led straight to his grandfather's story; and what was fascinating about this story and capable of provoking the dream can scarcely have been anything but its connection with the theme of castration.

We also concluded from the first incomplete analysis of the dream that the wolf may have been a father-surrogate; so that, in that case, this first anxiety-dream would have brought to light the fear of his father which from that time forward was to dominate his life. This conclusion, indeed, was in itself not yet binding. But if we put together as the result of the provisional analysis what can be derived from the material produced by the dreamer, we then find before us for reconstruction some such fragments as these:

A real occurrence — dating from a very early period — looking — immobility — sexual problems — castration — his father — something terrible.

One day the patient began to continue with the interpretation of the dream. He thought that the part of the dream which said that "suddenly the window opened of its own accord" was not completely explained by its connection with the window at which the tailor was sitting and through which the wolf came into the room. "It must mean: 'My eyes suddenly opened,' I was asleep, therefore, and suddenly woke up, and as I woke I saw something: the tree with the wolves." No objection could be made to this; but the point could be developed further. He had woken up and had seen something. The attentive looking, which in the dream was ascribed to the wolves, should rather be shifted on to him. At a decisive point, therefore, a transposition has taken place; and moreover this is indicated by another transposition in the manifest content of the dream. For the fact that the wolves were sitting on the tree was also a transposition, since in his grandfather's story they were underneath, and were unable to climb on to the tree.

What, then, if the other factor emphasized by the dreamer were also distorted by means of a transposition or reversal? In that case instead of immobility (the wolves sat there motionless; they looked at him, but did not move) the meaning would have to be: the most violent motion. That is to say, he suddenly woke up, and saw in front of him a scene of violent movement at which he looked with strained attention. In the one case the distortion would consist in an interchange of subject and object, of activity and passivity; being looked at instead of looking. In the other case it would consist in a transformation into the opposite; rest instead of motion.

On another occasion an association which suddenly occurred to him carried us another step forward in our understanding of the dream: "The tree was a Christmas-tree." He now knew that he had dreamt the dream shortly before Christmas and in expectation of it. Since Christmas Day was also his birthday, it now became possible to establish with certainty the date of the dream and of the change in him which proceeded from it. It was immediately before his fourth birthday. He had gone to sleep, then, in tense expectation of the day which ought to bring him a double quantity of presents. We know that in such circumstances a child may easily anticipate the fulfillment of his wishes. So it was already Christmas in his dream; the content of the dream showed him his Christmas box, the presents which were to be his were hanging on the tree. But instead of presents they had turned into—wolves, and the dream ended by his being overcome by fear of being eaten by the wolf (probably his father), and by his flying for refuge to his nurse. Our knowledge of his sexual development before the dream makes it possible for us to fill in the gaps in the dream and to explain the transformation of his satisfaction into anxiety. Of the wishes concerned in the formation of the dream the most powerful must have been the wish for the sexual satisfaction which he was at that time longing to obtain from his father. The strength of this wish made it possible to revive a long-forgotten trace in his memory of a scene which was able to show him what sexual satisfaction from his father was like; and the result was terror, horror of the fulfillment of the wish, the repression of the impulse which had manifested itself by means of the wish, and consequently a flight from his father to his less dangerous nurse.

The importance of this date of Christmas Day had been preserved in his supposed recollection of having had his first fit of rage because he was dissatisfied with his Christmas presents. The recollection combined elements of truth and of falsehood. It could not be entirely right, since according to the repeated declarations of his parents his naughtiness had already begun on their return in the autumn and

it was not a fact that they had not come on till Christmas. But he had preserved the essential connection between his unsatisfied love, his rage and Christmas.

But what picture can the nightly workings of his sexual desire have conjured up that could frighten him away so violently from the fulfillment for which he longed? The material shows that there is one condition which this picture must satisfy. It must have been calculated to create a conviction of the reality of the existence of castration. Fear of castration could then become the motive power for the transformation of the affect.

I have now reached the point at which I must abandon the support I have hitherto had from the course of the analysis. I am afraid it will also be the point at which the reader's belief will abandon me.

What sprang into activity that night out of chaos of the dreamer's unconscious memory-traces was the picture of copulation between his parents, copulation in circumstances which were not entirely usual and were especially favourable for observation. It gradually became possible to find satisfactory answers to all the questions that arose in connection with this scene; for in the course of the treatment the first dream returned in innumerable variations and new editions, in connection with which the analysis produced the information that was required. Thus in the first place the child's age at the date of the observation was established as being about one and a half years.[3] He was suffering at the time from malaria, an attack of which used to come on every day at a particular hour.[4] From his tenth year

---

[3] The age of six months came under consideration as a far less probable, and indeed scarcely tenable, alternative.

[4] Compare the subsequent metamorphoses of this factor during the obsessional neurosis. In the patient's dreams during the treatment it was replaced by a violent wind. "*Aria*" = "air." ("*Malaria*" = "bad air.")

onwards he was from time to time subject to moods of depression, which used to come on in the afternoon and reached their height at about five o'clock. This symptom still existed at the time of the analytic treatment. The recurring fits of depression took the place of the earlier attacks of fever or languor: five o'clock was either the time of the highest fever or of the observation of the intercourse, unless the two times coincided.[5] Probably for the very reason of this illness, he was in his parents' bedroom. The illness, the occurrence of which is also corroborated by direct tradition, makes it reasonable to refer the event to the summer, and, since the child was born on Christmas Day, to assume that his age was $n + 1\frac{1}{2}$ years. He had been sleeping in his cot, then, in his parents' bedroom, and woke up, perhaps because of his rising fever, in the afternoon, possibly at five o'clock, the hour which was later marked out by depression. It harmonized with our assumption that it was a hot summers' day, if we suppose that his parents had retired, half undressed [6] for an afternoon *siesta*. When he woke up, he witnessed a coitus *a tergo* (from behind), three times repeated;[7] he was able to see his mother's genitals as well as his father's organ; and he understood the process as well as its significance.[8] Lastly

he interrupted his parents' intercourse in a manner which will be discussed later.

There is at bottom nothing extraordinary, nothing to give the impression of being a product of an extravagant imagination, in the fact that a young couple who had only been married a few years should have ended a *siesta* on a hot summer's afternoon with a love-scene, and should have disregarded the presence of their little boy of one and a half, asleep in his cot. On the contrary, such an event would, I think, be something entirely commonplace and *banal*; and even the position in which we have inferred that the coitus took place cannot in the least alter this judgment—especially as the evidence does not require that the intercourse should have been performed from behind each time. A single time would have been enough to give the spectator an opportunity for making observations which would have been rendered difficult or impossible by any other attitude of the lovers. The content of the scene cannot therefore in itself be an argument against its credibility. Doubts as to its probability will turn upon three other points: whether a child at the tender age of one and a half could be in a position to take in the perceptions of such a complicated process and to preserve them so accurately in his unconscious; secondly, whether it is possible at the age of four for a deferred revision of the impression so received to penetrate the understanding; and finally, whether any procedure could succeed in bringing into consciousness coherently and convincingly the details of a scene of this kind which had been experienced and understood in such circumstances.[9]

---

[5] We may remark in this connection that the patient drew only *five* wolves in his illustration to the dream, although the text mentioned six or seven.

[6] In white underclothes: the *white* wolves.

[7] Why three times: He suddenly one day produced the statement that I had discovered this detail by interpretation. This was not the case. It was a spontaneous association, exempt from further criticism; in his usual way he passed it off on to me, and by this projection tried to make it seem more trustworthy.

[8] I mean that he understood it at the time of the dream when he was four years old, not at the time of the observation. He received the impressions when he was one and a half; his understanding of them was deferred, but became possible at the time of the dream owing to his development, his sexual excitations, and his sexual researches.

---

[9] The first of these difficulties cannot be reduced by assuming that the child at the time of his observation was after all probably a year older, that is to say *two* and a half, an age at which he may perhaps have been perfectly capable of talking. All the minor details of my patient's case almost ex-

Later on I shall carefully examine these and other doubts; but I can assure the reader that I am no less critically inclined than he towards an acceptance of this observation of the child's, and I will only ask him to join me in adopting a *provisional* belief in the reality of the scene. We will first proceed with the study of the relations between this "primal scene" and the patient's dream, his symptoms, and the history of his life; and we will trace separately the effects that followed from the essential content of the scene and from one of its visual impressions.

By the latter I mean the postures which he saw his parents adopt—the man upright, and the woman bent down like an animal. We have already heart that during his anxiety period his sister used to terrify him with a picture from the fairy-book, in which the wolf was shown standing upright, with one foot forward, with its claws stretched out and its ears pricked. He devoted himself with tireless perseverance during the treatment to the task of hunting in the second-hand bookshops till he found the illustrated fairy-book of his childhood, and had recognized his bogy in an illustration to the story of *The Wolf and the Seven Little Goats*. He thought that the posture of the wolf in this picture might have reminded him of that of his father during the constructed primal scene. At all events the picture became the point of departure for further manifestations of anxiety. Once when he was in his seventh or eighth year he was informed that next day a new tutor was coming for

him. That night he dreamt of this tutor in the shape of a lion that came towards his bed roaring loudly and in the posture of the wolf in the picture; and once again he awoke in a state of anxiety. The wolf phobia had been overcome by that time, so he was free to choose himself a new anxiety-animal, and in this late dream he was recognizing the tutor as a father-surrogate. In the later years of his childhood each of his tutors and masters played the part of his father, and was endowed with his father's influence both for good and for evil.

While he was at his secondary school the Fates provided him with a remarkable opportunity for reviving his wolf phobia, and of using the relation which lay behind it as an occasion for severe inhibitions. The master who taught his form Latin was called Wolf. From the very first he felt cowed by him, and he was once taken severely to task by him for having made a stupid mistake in a piece of Latin translation. From that time on he could not get free from a paralysing fear of this master, and it was soon extended to other masters besides. But the occasion on which he made his blunder in the translation was also to the purpose. He had to translate the word *filius*, and he did it with the French word *fils* instead of with the corresponding word from his own language. The wolf, in fact, was still his father.[10]

---

cluded the possibility of shifting the date in this way. Moreover, the fact should be taken into account that these scenes of observing parental intercourse are by no means rarely brought to light in analysis. The condition of their occurrence, however, is precisely that it should be in the earliest period of childhood. The older the child is, the more carefully, with parents above a certain social level, will the child be deprived of the opportunity for this kind of observation.

[10]After this reprimand from the schoolmaster-wolf he learnt that it was the general opinion of his companions that, to be pacified, the master expected money from him. We shall return to this point later. I can see that it would greatly facilitate a rationalistic view of such a history of a child's development as this if it could be supposed that his while fear of the wolf had really originated from the Latin master of that name, that it had been projected back into his childhood, and, supported by the illustration to the fairy tale, had caused the phantasy of the primal scene. But this is untenable; the chronological priority of the wolf phobia and its reference to the period of his childhood spent upon the first estate is far too securely attested. And his dream at the age of four?

The first "transitory symptom"[11] which the patient produced during the treatment went back once more to the wolf phobia and to the fairy tale of *The Seven Little Goats*. In the room in which the first sessions were held there was a large grandfather clock opposite the patient, who lay on a sofa facing away from me. I was struck by the fact that from time to time he turned his face towards me, looked at me in a very friendly way as though to propitiate me, and then turned his look away from me to the clock. I thought at the time that he was in this way showing his eagerness for the end of the hour. A long time afterwards the patient reminded me of this piece of dumb show, and gave me an explanation of it; for he recalled that the youngest of the seven little goats hid himself in the case of the grandfather clock while his six brothers were eaten up by the wolf. So what he had meant was: "Be kind to me! Must I be frightened of you? Are you going to eat me up? Shall I hide myself from you in the clock-case like the youngest little goat?"

The wolf that he was afraid of was undoubtedly his father but his fear of the wolf was conditional upon the creature being in an upright posture. His recollection asserted most definitely that he had not been terrified by pictures of wolves going on all fours or, as in the story of *Little Red Riding-Hood*, lying in bed. The posture which, according to our construction of the primal scene, he had seen the woman assume, was of no less significance; though in this case the significance was limited to the sexual sphere. The most striking phenomenon of his erotic life after maturity was his liability to compulsive attacks of falling physically in love which came on and disappeared again in the most puzzling succession. These attacks released a tremendous

energy in him even at times when he was otherwise inhibited, and they were quite beyond his control. I must, for a specially important reason, postpone a full consideration of this compulsive love; but I may mention here that it was subject to a definite condition, which was concealed from his consciousness and was discovered only during the treatment. It was necessary that the woman should have assumed the posture which we have ascribed to his mother in the primal scene. From his puberty he had felt large and conspicuous buttocks as the most powerful attraction in a woman; to copulate except from behind gave him scarcely any enjoyment. At this point a criticism may justly be raised: it may be objected that a sexual preference of this kind for the hind parts of the body is a general characteristic of people who are inclined to an obsessional neurosis, and that its presence does not justify us in referring it back to a special impression in childhood. It is part of the fabric of the anal-erotic disposition and is one of the archaic traits which distinguish that constitution. Indeed, copulation from behind — *more ferarum* (in the fashion of animals) — may, after all, be regarded as phylogenetically the older form. We shall return to this point too in a later discussion, when we have brought forward the supplementary material which showed the basis of the unconscious condition upon which this falling in love depended.

Let us now proceed with our discussion of the relations between his dream and the primal scene. We should so far have expected the dream to present the child (who was rejoicing at Christmas in the prospect of the fulfilment of his wishes) with this picture of sexual satisfaction afforded through his father's agency, just as he had seen it in the primal scene, as a model of the satisfaction that he himself was longing to obtain from his father. Instead of this picture, however, there

[11]Ferenczi.

appeared the material of the story which he had been told by his grandfather shortly before: the tree, the wolves, and the taillessness (in the over-compensated form of the bushy tails of the putative wolves). At this point some connection is missing, some associative bridge to lead from the content of the primal scene to that of the wolf story. This connection is provided once again by the postures and only by them. In his grandfather's story the tailless wolf asked the others *to climb upon him.* It was this detail that called up the recollection of the picture of the primal scene; and it was in this way that it became possible for the material of the primal scene to be represented by that of the wolf story, and at the same time for the *two* parents to be replaced, as was desirable, by *several* wolves. The content of the dream met with a further transformation, and the material of the wolf story was made to fit in with the content of the fairy tale of *The Seven Little Goats,* by borrowing from it the number seven.[12]

The steps in the transformation of the material, "primal scene—wolf story— fairy tale of *The Seven Little Goats,*" are a reflection of the progress of the dreamer's thoughts during the construction of the dream: "longing for sexual satisfaction from his father—realization that castration is a necessary condition of it—fear of his father." It is only at this point, I think, that we can regard the anxiety-dream of this four-year-old as being exhaustively explained.[13]

---

[12]It says "six or seven" in the dream. Six is the number of the children that were eaten; the seventh escaped into the clock-case. It is always a strict law of dream-interpretation that an explanation must be found for every detail.

[13]Now that we have succeeded in making a synthesis of the dream, I will try to give a comprehensive account of the relations between the manifest content of the dream and the latent dream-thoughts.

It was night, I was lying in my bed. The latter part

of this is the beginning of the reproduction of the primal scene. "It was night" is a distortion of "I had been asleep." The remark, "I know it was winter when I had the dream, and night-time," refers to the patient's recollection of the dream and is not part of its content. It is correct, for it was one of the nights before his birthday, that is, Christmas Day.

Suddenly the window opened of its own accord. That is to be translated: "Suddenly I woke up of my own accord," a recollection of the primal scene. The influence of the wolf story, in which the wolf leapt in through the window, is making itself felt as a modifying factor and transforms a direct expression into a plastic one. At the same time the introduction of the window serves the purpose of providing a contemporary reference for the subsequent content of the dream. On Christmas Eve the door opens suddenly and one sees before one the tree with the presents. Here, therefore, the influence of the actual expectation of Christmas (which comprises the wish for sexual satisfaction) is making itself felt.

The big walnut-tree. The representative of the Christmas tree, and therefore belonging to the current situation. But also the tree out of the wolf story, on which the tailor took refuge from pursuit, and under which the wolves were on the watch. Moreover, as I have often been able to satisfy myself, a high tree is a symbol of observing, of scopophilia. A person sitting on a tree can see everything that is going on below him and cannot himself be seen. Compare Boccaccio's well-known story, and similar *facetiae.*

The wolves. Their number: *six or seven.* In the wolf story there was a pack, and no number was given. The fixing of the number shows the influence of the fairy tale of *The Seven Little Goats,* six of whom were eaten up. The fact that the number two in the primal scene is replaced by a larger number, which would be absurd in the primal scene, is welcomed by the resistance as a means of distortion. In the illustration to the dream the dreamer brings forward the number five, which is probably meant to correct the statement "It was night."

They were sitting on the tree. In the first place they replace the Christmas presents hanging on the tree. But they are also transposed onto the tree because that can mean that they are looking. In his grandfather's story they were posted underneath the tree. Their relation to the tree has therefore been reversed in the dream; and from this is may be concluded that there are further reversals of the latent material to be found in the content of the dream.

They were looking at him with strained attention.

This feature comes entirely from the primal scene, and has got into the dream at the price of being turned completely round.

They were quite white. This feature is unessential in itself, but is strongly emphasized in the dreamer's narrative. It owes its intensity to a copious fusion of elemens from all the strata of the material, and it combines unimportant details from the other sources of the dream with a fragment of the primal scene which is more significant. This last part of its determination goes back to the white of his parents' bedclothes and underclothes, and to this is added the white of the flocks of sheep, and of the sheep-dogs, as an allusion to his sexual researches among animals, and the white in the fairy tale of *The Seven Little Goats*, in which the mother is recognized by the white of her hand. Later on we shall see that the white clothes are also an allusion to death. (There does not seem in fact to be any further clear reference to this point. The connection is perhaps with the episode of the winding-sheet.)

They sat there motionless. This contradicts the most striking feature of the observed scene, namely, its agitated movement, which, in virtue of the postures to which it led, constitutes the connection between the primal scence and the wolf story.

They had tails like foxes. This must be the contradiction of a conclusion which was derived from the action of the primal scene on the wolf story, and which must be recognized as the most important result of the dreamer's sexual researches: "So there really is such a thing as castration." The terror with which this conclusion was received finally broke out in the dream and brought it to an end.

The fear of being eaten up by the wolves. It seemed to the dreamer as though the motive force of this fear was not derived from the content of the dream. He said he need not have been afraid, for the wolves looked more like foxes or dogs, and they did not rush at him as though to bite him, but were very still and not at all terrible. We observe that the dream-work tries for some time to make the distressing content harmless by transforming it into its opposite. ("They aren't moving, and, only look, they have the loveliest tails.") Until at last this expedient fails, and the fear breaks out. It expresses itself by the help of the fairy tale, in which the goat-children are eaten up by the wolf-father. This part of the fairy tale may perhaps have acted as a reminder of threats made by the child's father in fun when he was playing with him; so that the fear of being eaten up by the wolf may be a reminiscence as well as a substitute by displacement.

That the wishes act as motive forces in this dream is obvious. First there are the superficial wishes of the day, that Christmas with its presents may already be here (a dream of impatience) and accompanying these is the deeper wish, now permanently present, for sexual satisfaction from the dreamer's father. This is immediately replaced by the wish to see once more what was then so fascinating. The mental process then proceeds on its way. Starting from the fulfilment of this last with the conjuring up of the primal scene, it passes on to what has now become inevitable — the repudiation of that wish and its repression.

The diffuseness and elaboration of this commentary have been forced on me by the effort to present the reader with some sort of equivalent for the convincing power of an analysis carried through by oneself; perhaps they may also serve to discourage him from asking for the publication of analyses which have stretched over several years.

After what has already been said I need only deal shortly with the pathogenic effect of the primal scene and the alteration which its revival produced in his sexual development. We will only trace that one of its effects to which the dream gave expression. Later on we shall have to make it clear that it was not only a single sexual current that started from the primal scene but a whole set of them, that his sexual life was positively splintered up by it. We shall further bear in mind that the activation of this scene (I purposely avoid the word "recollection") had the same effect as though it were a recent experience. The effects of the scene were deferred, but meanwhile it had lost none of its freshness in the interval between the ages of one and a half and four years. We shall perhaps find in what follows reason to suppose that it produced certain effects even at the time of its perception, that is from the age of one and a half onwards.

When the patient entered more deeply into the situation of the primal scene, he brought to light the following pieces of self-observation. He assumed to begin with, he said, that the event of which he was a witness was an act of violence, but the expression of enjoyment which he saw on his mother's face did not fit in with this; he was obliged to recognize that the experience was one of gratification.[14] What was essentially new for him in his observation of his parents' intercourse was the conviction of the reality of castration — a possibility with which his thoughts had already been occupied previously. (The sight of the two girls micturating, his Nanya's threat, the governess's interpretation of the sugar-sticks, the recollection of his father having beaten a snake to pieces.) For now he saw with his own eyes the wound of which his Nanya had spoken, and understood that its presence was a

---

[14]We might perhaps best do justice to this statement of the patient's by supposing that the object of his observation was in the first instance a coitus in the normal position, which cannot fail to produce the impression of being a sadistic act, and that only after this was the position altered, so that he had an opportunity for making other observations and judgments. This hypothesis, however, was not confirmed with certainty, and moreover does not seem to me indispensable. We must not forget the actual situation which lies behind the abbreviated description given in the text: the patient under analysis, at an age of over twenty-five years, was putting the impressions and impulses of his fourth year into words which he would never have found at that time. If we fail to notice this, it may easily seem comic and incredible that a child of four should be capable of such technical judgments and learned notions. This is simply another instance of *deferred action*. At the age of one and a half the child receives an impression to which he is unable to react adequately; he is only able to understand it and to be moved by it when the impression is revived in him at the age of four; and only twenty years later, during the analysis, is he able to grasp with his conscious mental processes what was then going on in him. The patient justifiably disregards the three periods of time, and puts his present ego into the situation which is so long past. And in this we follow him, since with correct self-observation and interpretation the effect must be the same as though the distance between the second and third periods of time could be neglected. Moreover, we have no other means of describing the events of the second period.

necessary condition of intercourse with his father. He could no longer confuse it with the bottom, as he had in his observation of the little girls.[15]

The dream ended in a state of anxiety, from which he did not recover until he had his Nanya with him. He fled, therefore, from his father to her. His anxiety was a repudiation of the wish for sexual satisfaction from his father — the trend which had put the dream into his head. The form taken by the anxiety, the fear of "being eaten by the wolf," was only the (as we shall hear, regressive) transposition of the wish to be copulated with by his father, that is, to be given sexual satisfaction in the same way as his mother. His last sexual aim, the passive attitude towards his father, succumbed to repression, and fear of his father appeared in its place in the shape of the wolf phobia.

And the driving force of this repression? The circumstances of the case show that it can only have been his narcissistic genital libido, which, in the form of concern for his male organ, was fighting against a satisfaction whose attainment seemed to involve the renunciation of that organ. And it was from his threatened narcissism that he derived the masculinity with which he defended himself against his passive attitude towards his father.

We now observe that at this point in our narrative we must make an alteration in our terminology. During the dream he had reached a new phase in his sexual organization. Up to then the sexual opposites had been for him *active* and *passive*. Since his seduction his sexual aim had been a passive one, of being touched on the genitals; it was then transformed, by regression to the earlier stage of the sadistic-anal organization, into the masochistic aim of being beaten or punished.

---

[15]We shall learn later on when we come to trace out his anal eroticism, how he further dealt with this portion of the problem.

It was a matter of indifference to him whether he reached this aim with a man or with a woman. He had travelled, without considering the difference of sex, from his Nanya to his father; he had longed to have his penis touched by his Nanya, and had tried to provoke a beating from his father. Here his genitals were left out of account; though the connection with them which had been concealed by the regression was still expressed in his phantasy of being beaten *on the penis*. The activation of the primal scene in the dream now brought him back to the genital organization. He discovered the vagina and the biological significance of masculine and feminine. He understood now that active was the same as masculine, while passive was the same as feminine. His passive sexual aim should now have been transformed into a feminine one, and have expressed itself as "being copulated with by his father" instead of being beaten by him on the genitals or on the bottom." This feminine aim, however, underwent repression and was obliged to let itself be replaced by fear of the wolf.

We must here break off discussion of his sexual development until new light is thrown from the later stages of his history upon these earlier ones. For the proper appreciation of the wolf phobia we will only add that both his father and mother became wolves. His mother took the part of the castrated wolf, which let the others climb upon it, was seized with fear as soon as it was reminded of the fact of its taillessness. It seems, therefore, as though he had identified himself with his castrated mother during the dream, and was now fighting against that fact. "If you want to be sexually satisfied by Father," we may perhaps represent him as saying to himself, "you must allow yourself to be castrated like mother; but I won't have that." In short, a clear protest on the part of his masculinity! Let us, however, plainly understand that the sexual development of the case that we are now examining has a great disadvantage from the point of view of research, for it was by no means undisturbed. It was first decisively influenced by the seduction, and was then diverted by the scene of observation of the coitus, which in its deferred action operated like a second seduction.

3. A Modest Confirmation of Freud's Theory of a Distinction between the Superego of Men and Women

CALVIN HALL

Freud observed that a woman's superego is "never so inexorable, so impersonal, so independent of its emotional origins as we require it to be in men." In other words, the female superego is not as fully internalized as that of the male. 2 testable hypotheses were derived from this theory. It was hypothesized that in their dreams (a) women would be more often the victim of aggression and (b) men would more often suffer a misfortune. The data for the study were obtained from the content analysis of 3,049 dreams. Both hypotheses were confirmed.

Freud (1925) observed that a woman's superego

"is never so inexorable, so impersonal, so independent of its emotional origins as we require it to be in men" [p. 257].

He accounts for this difference in male and female superego in terms of Oedipal theory.

"Under the influence of the danger of losing his penis, he the boy abandons his Oedipus-complex; it is repressed and in the most normal cases entirely destroyed, while a severe super-ego is set up as its heir. What happens in the case of the girl is almost the opposite. The castration-complex prepares the way for the Oedipus-complex instead of destroying it. . . .

The girl remains in the Oedipus situation for an indefinite period, she only abandons it late in life, and then incompletely. The formation of the super-ego must suffer in these circumstances; it cannot attain the strength and independence which gives it its cultural importance . . ." [Freud, 1933, pp. 176–177].

In other words, the distinction that Freud made between the male and the female superego is one of a more or less internalized superego. The less internalized superego is still dependent to some extent upon its sources in the external world. These sources are, in Freudian theory, the punishing and rewarding parents, or their surrogates. The fully internalized superego is one which has become independent of these parental sources. A person whose superego development is retarded so that it remains externalized tends to disown his guilt and to fear and to blame external enemies. A person whose superego development has attained a full measure of incorporation

SOURCE. Article by Calvin Hall, "A modest confirmation of Freud's theory of a distinction between the superego of men and women" in the Journal of abnormal and social psychology, Vol. 69, pp. 440–442, 1964. Copyright 1964 by the American Psychological Association and reproduced by permission.

in the personality acknowledges his own guilt and blames himself. For such a person the critical agent is his own conscience.

We think it is this distinction between *internalized* and *externalized* (the distinction is relative and not absolute) that Freud had in mind when he described the female superego as less inexorable, more personal, and more dependent on on its emotional origin than the superego of the male. The conscience of the woman is less inexorable because one can more easily evade an external authority than escape from an internalized conscience; more personal because the punitive agents are personified individuals rather than inner, impersonal feelings; and more dependent upon its emotional origins because the battle waged by an externalized superego is against the emotionally charged parental figures of early childhood.

Only a fully internalized superego can be of cultural importance because the stability of society depends more upon directives from the voice of conscience than from the sanctions and prohibitions of external authority.

So much then for the theory upon which this investigation is based. From the theory as stated, we have derived several propositions which can be tested on data secured from dreams. In order to make these propostions comprehensible it is necessary to present some introductory considerations.

Among the manuals which we have prepared for making content analyses of reported dreams is one for classifying aggressions and misfortunes in dreams (Institute of Dream Research, 1962). In the analysis of aggression, a distinction is made between those aggressive encounters in which the dreamer is the aggressor and those in which he is the victim of intentional aggression from another character or characters in the

dream. A third class of aggressive interactions in which there is no clearly defined aggressor or victim does not figure in the present investigation. In the analysis of misfortunes (which exclude, of course, any misfortune in connection with an aggressive encounter), a distinction is made between misfortunes to the dreamer and misfortune to other characters in the dream. A misfortune does not involve any social interaction, at least, of an intentional, premeditated, or motivated sort. A victim of misfortune is a victim of circumstance, accident, or of his own incapacities. Misfortunes include such items as illness, injury, adversity, loss or destruction of property, frustration, delay, encountering an obstacle, inability to do something, failure, and being lost.

The hypotheses to be tested in this investigation rest upon two assumptions. First, it is assumed that dreams in which the dreamer is the victim of aggression are expressions of an externalized superego. Second, it is assumed that dreams in which the dreamer is the victim of misfortune are expressions of an internalized superego.

Now we can state the hypotheses in data-oriented terms.

1. In female dreams, there will be a higher proportion of dreams in which the dreamer is the victim of aggression than in male dreams.

2. In male dreams, there will be a higher proportion of dreams in which the dreamer suffers a misfortune than in female dreams.

The data for this study were obtained from the analysis of more than 3,000 dreams which were collected primarily from young adults. They were written down by the dreamer on a standard report form which the writer has used for a number of years in collecting dreams.

The results are presented in Tables 1 and 2. The difference between the two proportions in Table 1 is significant at less than the 0.01 level. The difference between the two proportions in Table 2 is significant at less than the 0.01 level.

Both hypotheses are confirmed. Consequently, it is concluded that evidence from aggression and misfortune dreams supports Freud's view that the superego of the female is less internalized than is the superego of the male. This confirmation is considered to be a modest one because it involves only two hypotheses and because the data are derived from one type of material, namely, reported dreams. Complete confirmation of Freud's theory of the differences between the male superego and the female superego requires the testing of a number of hypotheses in a variety of situations with different populations.

Table 1 Proportion of Aggressions in Which the Dreamer Is the Victim

	Dreams	
	Male	Female
Number of dreams	1,494	1,555
Number of aggressions	534	492
Proportion of aggressions in which the dreamer is the victim	0.58	0.68

Table 2 Proportion of Misfortunes Which Happen to the Dreamer

	Dreams	
	Male	Female
Number of dreams	1,494	1,555
Number of misfortunes	410	397
Proportion of misfortunes to the dreamer	0.65	0.49

References

Freud, S. Some psychical consequences of the anatomical distinction between the sexes. In, *The standard edition*. Vol. 19. London: Hogarth Press, 1925. pp. 243–258.

Freud, S. *New introductory lectures on psychoanalysis*. New York: Norton, 1933.

Institute of Dream Research. *A manual for classifying aggressions, misfortunes, friendly acts, and good fortune in dreams*. Miami, Fla.: Author, 1962.

4. An Empirical Test of the Female Castration Complex

RACHEL B. LEVIN

This study investigated the psychoanalytic hypothesis that intensity of the female castration complex (FCC) is greater in women with a masculine social role than in those with a feminine social role. Ss were normal, college-educated women, ages 30–55, divided into 2 groups: 26 career women (CW), unmarried, and in masculine occupations; and 25 homemakers, married, with 2 or more children, and not employed outside the home. The CW scored significantly higher on an overall measure of the FCC based on the Rorschach. The hypothesis was thus supported. The CW also scored significantly higher on 3 of the 8 individual components of the FCC (Penis Envy, High Activity, and High Need for Achievement). Some theoretical implications are discussed.

The female castration complex (also called, among other things, "penis envy" and the "masculinity complex") has been offered by psychoanalytic theorists as a major explanatory concept in the psychology of women. In general terms, the complex refers to the woman's presumed discontent with her femininity and her modes of reacting to this discontent. The complex is seen as occurring in varying degrees in most women, along a continuum from the normal to the abnormal; as being a conspicuous feature of feminine neuroses and pathological character formations; and as motivating a wide variety of behavioral manifestations. As an intervening variable, the female castration complex is supposedly related to ob-servable clinical phenomena such as the feeling of having been castrated, envy of the penis, the desire to castrate men, or the wishfulfilling fantasy of possessing a penis. In addition to, or in place of, these sexual manifestations, the complex may also be related to more general social attitudes and behavior, such as a derogatory attitude toward women and their traditional social role, envious hostility toward men, and the attempt to emulate the masculine social role. Two frequently described clinical phenomena that cut across the sexual-nonsexual differentiation are "wish-fulfillment" and "revenge" behavior; while both may occur in the same individual, one generally predominates. The wish-fulfillment type of behavior is illustrated by homosexuality, the pursuit of an intellectual or professional career, the avoidance of marriage and/or motherhood, hypomanic activity in any sphere, and gynecological disturbances of a functional nature. Some examples of

SOURCE. *Article by Rachel B. Levin, "An empirical test of the female castration complex" in the* Journal of abnormal psychology, *Vol. 71, pp. 181–188, 1966. Copyright 1966 by the American Psychological Association and reproduced by permission.*

the revenge type are frigidity, vaginismus, and prostitution (Abraham, 1920; Deutsch, 1944; Fenichel, 1945; Freud, 1933; Menninger, 1939; Thompson, 1943).

In spite of the broad agreement that psychoanalytic writers have shown as to these clinical or descriptive aspects of the complex, there have been many theoretical differences with regard to its genesis and basic nature. The complex is conceded by all theorists to be related to both sexual and nonsexual behavior, but there remains an unresolved issue as to which of these two is primary, and which is secondary or derived. According to the biological approach (Abraham, 1920; Deutsch, 1944; Freud, 1925, 1931, 1933; Hayward, 1943), the origin of the complex is literal envy of the male anatomy. It is presumed that during the phallic stage every little girl falls victim to this envy, which in the course of normal feminine development is eventually resolved by being transformed into the wish for a child (equivalent to penis) from the father (the Oedipus complex). If, however, the girl's bisexual disposition is weighted in the direction of masculinity, her castration complex remains unresolved. In the adult woman the complex may take "rationalized" forms such as protests against the greater social freedom of men, or the pursuit of an intellectual or professional career, but its genetic roots and underlying motives are literally sexual and biological.

The culturally oriented theorists, on the other hand (Horney, 1937, 1939; Thompson, 1942, 1943), see the complex as stemming from social and family reactions to sexual differences. In the normal form in which it is believed to occur in most women in our culture, the complex is thought to represent a realistic wish for social equality with men. The complex may also be related to neurotic problems, such as deep feelings of inadequacy as a human being, which have become closely linked with the woman's sense of femininity. These problems arise from disturbed family relationships in which sexual differences play an important role, for example, the parents' preference for a male sibling. The complex may be symbolized in sexual forms such as literal penis envy, but its primary motives are nonsexual, for example, the needs for affection and self-esteem.

Notwithstanding the theoretical importance of the female castration complex, empirical studies of it have been few, both in the child and the adult (e.g., Blum, 1949; Eisenbud, 1951; Friedman, 1952; Landis, 1940; Levy, 1940; Schwartz, 1956). Most of the research has been characterized by methodological inadequacies such as the use of direct questions or the failure to demonstrate scorer reliability; and/or by conceptual oversimplification, such as the tendency to equate the female castration complex with the male castration complex (both often vaguely defined as "castration anxiety"). Other relevant studies have focused on limited areas such as masculine identification (e.g., Franck & Rosen, 1949), or have been more directly concerned with other topics (e.g., Bloomingdale, 1953).

In sum, there has been no systematic attempt to formulate a broad definition of the intervening variable of the female castration complex that would include its varied forms of expression in the adult woman; to design a reliable projective instrument for measuring these varied aspects or components; and, using this instrument, to test the validity of the construct by investigating its relationship to an independent, theoretically derived criterion. These were the general goals of the present research.

Since the complex has been assumed to be related to both literally sexual and more generalized nonsexual manifestations, it was decided to design a projective measure aimed at tapping both of these forms of expression. No hypothesis was formulated, however, with regard to the theoretical issue of the relative importance of the sexual as opposed to the nonsexual factors, since there was no way (evident to the author) of determining objectively which type of factor was basic and which was derived. In other words, sexual manifestations of the complex on the projective test might be symbolic expressions of generalized social attitudes (in the concrete language of the body), and conversely, nonsexual projective signs might be symbolic or derived representations of basically sexual factors. Our goal, then, was not to test the biological or cultural positions, but, very simply, to find out whether a group of women showing a type of overt behavior (the independent variable) theoretically related to the female castration complex, would show higher scores on a projective measure of the complex (the dependent variable) then a group of control women. The projective instrument was not designed to measure only the particular motivational factors that might be related to the specific behavioral criterion selected. It was devised with the more general aim of evoking as comprehensively as possible all the varied impulses and feelings, both sexual and nonsexual, both wish-fulfillment and revenge, that are common to most of the accounts of the complex.

The specific behavioral criterion that was selected was masculinity of social role or style of life. In broad terms, analytic theory proposes that the intensity of the woman's castration complex, an intervening motivational variable, is related to the degree of masculinity of her social role, an overt behavioral variable. The research hypothesis, derived from this general proposition, was as follows: *Intensity of the female castration complex as measured by a projective test is significantly greater in women with a masculine social role than in women with a feminine social role.* Of

course, masculinity of social role is only one of the many forms of behavior to which the complex has been theoretically related; this particular behavioral variable was selected on the basis of expediency, namely — the relative ease of obtaining research subjects. The hypothesis was not intended to imply that an overtly masculine style of life was the only way in which *the castration complex expressed itself.*

METHOD

Subjects

The research subjects consisted of 51 white, native-born, college-educated American women between the ages of 30 and 55, in good physical health, and with no history of psychiatric treatment. These subjects were selected from a pool of 499 women, local alumnae of various colleges, who responded to an innocuous questionnaire entitled "A Socio-Psychological Survey of American Women." The 51 women were divided into two groups: (*a*) 26 career women, who represented a masculine social role, and (*b*) 25 homemakers, who represented a feminine social role. Two criteria were used in determining masculinity or femininity of social role: (*a*) family status (marriage and children), and (*b*) occupation. The two research groups contrasted clearly with respect to both of these criteria. Thus, the career women were unmarried and employed in masculine occupations, while the homemakers were married, living with their husbands, mothers of two or more children, and not gainfully employed outside the home. Masculine occupations were defined by a high ratio of men to women in census statistics, or by a high level of status and responsibility; using these definitions, two psychologists showed strong agreement in assigning high ranks on masculinity of occupation to the career women ($\rho = 0.92$, $p < 0.001$). They included lawyers, physicians, research scientists, business executives, and university faculty members; 18 of them had higher degrees, including 9 doctorates. The homemakers had a median of 4 children each; none of them had higher degrees, although they were all college graduates.

Later, the two groups were compared with respect to Vocabulary subtest scores on the Wechsler Adult Intelligence Scale (WAIS); socioeconomic status of family of origin, as measured by father's education and occupation; and current socioeconomic status, as measured by the education and occupation of the subject herself in the case of the career women, and of the subject's husband in the case of the homemakers. Comparison by means of the chi-square test showed no significant differences between the two groups on any of these variables. In both groups, the median age was in the range of 35–39, and the majority were Protestant. The median Verbal IQ, as estimated by the WAIS Vocabulary scores, was 129 for the career women and 132 for the homemakers.

Procedure

All subjects were tested by the investigator in individual appointments that lasted about 2 hours each. Standard clinical procedures were used in administering first, the Rorschach test, and then, the Vocabulary subtest of the WAIS. These were followed by two especially designed instruments that the subjects filled out by themselves: an opinion questionnaire focusing on the social role of women (not reported on here), and a biographical questionnaire (used in the final equating of the groups). Cooperation by the subjects was excellent.

The Female Castration Complex Measure (FCCM)

The first step in constructing the measuring instrument was to delineate the major components (or modes of expression) of the female castration complex. On the basis of a survey of the psychoanalytic literature, 8 such specific components were selected (See Table 1). While these 8 were not assumed to be a comprehensive list of "pure" factors, they were felt to include most of the main features of the complex as described in the literature. The Rorschach was chosen as the most appropriate test upon which to base the measuring instrument. For each of the 8

components, a corresponding Rorschach measure consisting of one or more signs was formulated (Table 1); the 8 Rorschach measures together formed the FCCM. The individual signs were derived from the Rorschach literature and from common clinical usage with this test. They included both traditional Rorschach scores (such as form level) and thematic and stylistic features of the protocols that conventionally do not receive formal scoring. While these signs might, of course, reflect factors other than the female castration complex, they were assumed to have some degree of face validity as indicators of the various aspects of the complex as they are described in Table 1. For a detailed description of the FCCM, including the rationale for each of the signs, see Levin (1962).[1]

Since some of the FCCM signs consisted of conventional Rorschach scores, one person first scored the Rorschach protocols in the usual way. Then another person scored the protocols on the FCCM by deciding which, if any, FCCM signs were present in each Rorschach response. The FCCM scorer had first been trained in the application of the FCCM by the use of five protocols not included in the study. Neither of the two scorers had any knowledge of the design of the research. On 10 protocols (5 from each group of subjects) the first scorer (conventional Rorschach scores) showed percentages of agreement with another psychologist that ranged from 84 to 91. The FCCM scorer's percentage of agreement with a second psychologist on 20 protocols (10 from each group) was 91.

Nine main FCCM scores were computed for each subject: an overall FCCM score and eight specific measure scores. General Rorschach productivity (length of responses and total

---

[1]The complete manual of the Rorschach Female Castration Complex Measure, the instructions for its use, and the description of its rationale, have been deposited with the American Documentation Institute. Order Document No. 8532 from ADI Auxiliary Publications Project, Photoduplication Service, Library of Congress, Washington, D.C. 20540. Remit in advance $2.75 for microfilm or $7.50 for photocopies and make checks payable to: Chief, Photoduplication Service, Library of Congress.

Table 1   The Eight Components and Corresponding Rorschach Measures of the Female Complex

COMPONENT	RORSCHACH MEASURE[a]
1. *Castration Anxiety:* The woman's fear and rejection of her femininity in a specifically genital sense. Conception of the female genitals as castrated, damaged, and inferior.	1. *Female Sexual Disturbance:* Disturbance of structure, theme, or style in female sex (genital) percepts or in responses to popular female sex areas. For example, "Blood stain" in II D3.
2. *Penis Envy:* The woman's envy of the male genitals, in a literal sense. Wish to castrate men in revenge for her own castration. Projection of her hostility with consequent fear of the penis.	2. *Male Sexual Disturbance:* Disturbance of structure, theme, or style in male sex (genital) percepts or in responses to popular male sex areas. For example, any percept scored F- in II D4.
3. *Confused Body Image:* The woman's confusion about the male and female body images, stemming from her own ambivalent sexual identification. Blurring or denial of the physical distinctions between the sexes.	3. *Difficulty in Assigning Sex:* Avoidance, confusion, or misperception in assigning sex to human or human-like percepts. For example, "Two people, I can't tell if they're men or women."
4. *Penis Fantasy:* The woman's defense against her castration by denial and the wish-fulfilling fantasy of possessing a penis, in a literal sense.	4. *Phallic Symbolism:* Explicit reference to phallic characteristics of percepts. For example, "Person with a very long nose."
5. *Rejection of Femininity:* The woman's fear and rejection of her femininity in a general (not specifically sexual) sense. Image of women as weak, inferior, and victimized, or defensive conception of them as powerful and dangerous.	5. *Female General Disturbance:* Disturbance of structure, theme, or style in female general (nonsexual) percepts or in responses to popular female general areas. For example, any percept scored F- in I D4.
6. *Envy of Men:* The woman's envy of men in a general (not specifically sexual) sense. Conception of men as superior and powerful, or defensive image of them as inferior and weak. Projection of her hostility with consequent fear of men.	6. *Male General Disturbance:* Disturbance of structure, theme, or style in male general (nonsexual) percepts or in responses to popular male general areas. For example, "Scowling man."
7. *High Activity:* The woman's identification with "masculine activity." An active, energetic orientation to the world, and strong needs for independence and self-assertion.	7. *Active Human Movement:* Perception of human or humanlike percepts in active kinds of movement. For example, "Clowns doing tricks."
8. *High Need for Achievement:* The woman's identification with "masculine striving." Competitiveness, ambition, and strong needs for status and achivement, especially in masculine fields.	8. *Achievement Content:* Responses with content reflecting strong drives for achievement and prestige, especially in masculine fields. For example, "An emblem."

[a]For the derivation of the popular areas of Measures 1, 2, 5, and 6, see Levin (1962). Locations are those listed by Beck (1944).

number of responses), was controlled in these main scores by counting each response a maximum of once for each FCCM measure (even if it contained more than one sign of that measure), and by expressing each FCCM score as a percentage of the subject's total number of responses (Total R). Thus, the subject's main overall FCCM score consisted of the number of her responses containing one or more FCCM signs, divided by here Total R, and multiplied by 100; and each of her eight main measure scores consisted of the number of her responses containing one or more signs of that measure, divided by Total R, and multiplied by 100. In addition, a second set of scores was computed for six measures, controlling productivity in the special categories of Rorschach responses that were pertinent to those measures, that is, the categories that were potential carriers of signs. For example, the pertinent category of responses for Measure 7, Active Human Movement (human or human-like percepts in active kinds of movement), was the subject's total number of human movement (M) responses (both active and passive), since Measure 7 could occur only in M responses. Thus, the Measure-7 score controlling for productivity in the pertinent category of Rorschach responses consisted of the number of responses containing active

M, divided by the total number of responses scored M, and multiplied by 100; whereas in the main Measure-7 score, the number of active M was divided by Total R. Scores controlling for FCCM-pertinent productivity were not necessary in the case of Measures 4 and 8, since these measures could occur in any responses. For each FCCM measure, all scores (51 subjects) were dichotomized at the median, and the chi-square value (corrected for continuity) of the difference between the groups was determined. For the sake of consistency, all tests of significance were one-tailed. In order to obtain a measure of the degree of relationship between the homemakers-career women dichotomy and the FCCM scores, Φ coefficients were computed for all chi-square values.

Results

Main Findings. The main findings were the results for the overall FCCM scores, the measure for the overall intensity of the female castration complex, taking all the specific scores into account. As Table 2 (Scores controlling for Total R) in-

TABLE 2   *Relationship between The Homemakers–Career Women Dichotomy and The Individual FCCM Measures: Scores Controlling General Rorschach Productivity*

| Measure | MEDIAN | | χ^2 | Φ | p^a |
	Homemakers	Career women			
1. Female sex disturbance	0	0	0.04	0.03	*ns*
2. Male sex disturbance	1.8	5.4	3.36	0.26	< 0.05
3. Difficulty assigning sex	6.3	5.3	0.02	0.02	*ns*
4. Phallic symbolism	4.0	6.6	2.38	0.22	*ns*
5. Female general disturbance	5.3	8.9	4.43	0.30	< 0.05
6. Male general disturbance	9.1	13.0	0.97	0.14	*ns*
7. Active human movement	7.1	13.2	4.43	0.30	< 0.05
8. Achievement content	3.2	8.9	7.10	0.37	< 0.01
Overall FCCM	28.0	50.0	18.88	0.61	< 0.001

[a]One-tailed tests.

TABLE 3   *Relationship between The Homemakers–Career Women Dichotomy and the Individual FCCM Measures: Scores Controlling FCCM-Pertinent Rorschach Productivity*

| | MEDIAN | | | | |
Measure	Homemakers	Career women	χ^2	Φ	p^a
1. Female sex disturbance	0	0	0.04	0.03	ns
2. Male sex disturbance	25	100	5.66	0.33	< 0.01
3. Difficulty assigning sex	50	32	0.95	−0.14	ns
5. Female general disturbance	67	93	2.38	0.22	ns
6. Male general disturbance	75	100	2·38	0.22	ns
7. Active human movement	50	75	8.93	0.42	<0.01
Overall FCCM	80	122	19.15	0.61	<0.001

Note — Measures 4 and 8 were not affected by FCCM-pertinent productivity.
[a]One-tailed tests.

dicates, the career women were significantly higher in overall FCCM scores ($p < 0.001$). A second analysis using the FCCM scores controlling productivity in FCCM-pertinent responses yielded similar results (see Table 3). The research hypothesis was thus supported.

Although both groups of subjects were psychologically "normal" as defined by the criterion of never having received psychiatric treatment, this was obviously a very crude criterion. It was possible, therefore, that the two groups differed widely in general disturbance or maladjustment, and that it was this difference that accounted for the overall FCCM difference (since many FCCM signs were by definition signs of disturbance). In order to investigate this possibility, a measure of general disturbance, or disturbance independent of the female castration complex, was derived by considering only those responses that did not contain any FCCM signs and/or were not in the categories of responses pertinent to the FCCM. The percentage of these non-FCCM-pertinent responses that contained the same structural signs of disturbance used in the FCCM (such as F-) was the score for general disturbance. Comparison of the two groups on

these scores showed no significant difference ($\chi^2 = 1.62$, p ns). Also, the correlation between the overall FCCM scores and the general disturbance scores, although positive, was not significant ($\chi^2 = 2.38$, $\Phi = 0.22$, p ns). These findings do not exclude the possibility that disturbance of a general sort was manifesting itself only in the FCCM, especially since the measure of general disturbance, which included only structural signs, was probably not as sensitive as the FCCM, which contained also stylistic and thematic signs. Nevertheless, the findings with regard to general disturbance do suggest that the significant differences between the two groups on the FCCM probably could not be attributed to differences in overall level of adjustment.

Analysis of Specific Measures. When the eight individual measures were intercorrelated, only one of the resulting 28 intercorrelations (that between Difficulty in Assigning Sex and Male Sex Disturbance) was significant in the predicted (positive) direction ($\Phi = 0.25$, $p < 0.05$). Since one significant correlation out of a total of 28 could be due to chance, it was concluded that the eight measures were independent of each other.

Of the eight individual measures, four

were significantly higher in the career women when the main scores (controlling for Total R) were used (see Table 2). The results were essentially the same when scores controlling for productivity in FCCM-pertinent responses were analyzed, except that one significant measure no longer differentiated significantly between the groups, while the chi-square values of two other significant measures increased (see Table 3). If only the more conservative findings are selected from both analyses, these results may be summarized as follows: three measures differentiated significantly between the groups, one at the 0.01 level (Achievement Content) and two at the 0.05 level (Male Sex Disturbance and Active Human Movement); five measures failed to differentiate significantly between the groups (Female Sex Disturbance, Difficulty in Assigning Sex, Phallic Symbolism, Female General Disturbance, and Male General Disturbance).

Analysis of Structural, Thematic, and Stylistic signs. Since thematic and stylistic types of signs might be assumed to be more amenable to conscious control than structural ones, it was important to determine whether all three types of signs contributed to the significant findings. Therefore, within each of Measures 1, 2, 5, and 6, the signs within each type (structural, thematic, and stylistic, respectively) were combined, and each combination (with Total R controlled) was correlated with the homemakers-career women dichotomy. The mean correlation of the structural combinations over all four measures was then computed, and similarly, the mean correlations of the thematic and stylistic combinations. For each of these three types of combinations. For each of these three types of combinations, the mean correlation with the homemakers-career women dichotomy was significant ($p < 0.05$). All three types of signs, then, contributed significantly to the results.

Discussion

The major finding of this study was that a group of career women (not married, and in masculine occupations) showed significantly higher scores than a comparable group of homemakers (married, with children, and not employed) on a Rorschach measure for intensity of the female castration complex. On the assumption that the two groups of subjects represented two contrasting social roles or general styles of life, the one more masculine and the other more feminine, the study provides some support for the hypothesis that intensity of the female castration complex is significantly greater in women with a masculine social role than in those with a feminine social role. Also, some evidence is furnished for the validity of the Rorschach-based instrument that was developed to measure the complex.

In addition to the overall Rorschach measure of the complex, three of the eight individual components were also significantly higher in the group of career women: Penis Envy (envious, hostile, and/or fearful reactions to the male genitals); High Activity (energy, independence, and self-assertion); and High Need for Achievement (ambition and drive for status). In other words, the career women relative to the homemakers were found to be more active and assertive, more oriented towards status and achievement, and more disturbed in their reactions to male sexuality. These motivational variables seem quite consistent, in a common sense way, with the careers these women were engaged in as well as with their failure to marry.

The findings do not imply, of course, that a masculine social role is the only possible mode of expression of the female castration complex, or conversely, that all career women necessarily have a high intensity of the complex. The latter becomes clearly more doubtful, for ex- ample, in the case of career women who are married and/or working in feminine types of occupations. The ambition and vitality inherent in the pursuit of a career might, of course, be found in conflict- free femininity. Also, the failure to marry might stem from factors other than the castration complex, for example, over- dependence upon a parent, neurotic in- hibition, or a philosophical objection to the institution of marriage. Nevertheless, the study suggests that there is a rela- tionship between some motivational vari- ables that have been included in descrip- tions of the female castration complex, and a social role that involves remaining single and pursuing a masculine type of career.

The question might be asked, do the significant Rorschach differences between the two groups reflect factors that con- tributed to the different role choices, or consequences of those different social roles? The available data do not provide an answer to this question. It is possible, to mention only one example, that the career women failed to marry because of reasons irrelevant to the castration com- plex (e.g., rejection by the men of their choice), and then reacted with negative feelings about sex and a compensatory channeling of their energies into their careers (particularly since they were faced with the necessity of supporting them- selves). This study points only to a rela- tionship between certain motivational variables as measured by the Rorschach and the overt behavior of the research subjects.

Why did five of the eight components of the complex fail to differentiate be- tween the career women and the home- makers? First, it is possible that the Ror- schach measures of these five components were not as sensitive as the others, even though all eight Rorschach measures were derived in the same fashion. It is

also possible that all the Rorschach mea- sures were equally valid, but that no real differences obtained between the two groups of women with respect to the five nonsignificant components. That is, one might conclude that the masculine role behavior of the career women of the study (both with respect to their choice of occupation and their failure to be- come wives or mothers) is related only to the three significant components. Other groups of women such as homosexuals, women with functional gynecological dis- orders, discontented housewives, career women who are married or in feminine types of occupations, and neurotic or psychotic patients, might show higher scores on other specific measures of the complex.

This raises the question of whether the female castration complex can be viewed as a unitary variable. The absence of sig- nificant intercorrelations among the specific measures would argue against the idea of a unitary variable. If different aspects of the complex do not "hang to- gether," but are correlated with different types of behavior, then the phenomena under discussion may be unrelated to each other. The results of this study, for example, could be explained simply in terms of differences between the two groups of women in heterosexual adjust- ment, activity level, and achievement drive, without invoking the castration complex as an explanatory concept. It is possible, on the other hand, that the ab- sence of significant intercorrelations among the specific Rorschach measures might be due to the lack of precision of some or all of the measures. Further re- search would be necessary in order to investigate more fully whether and to what extent the various factors of the complex covary, and in order to deter- mine how useful or parsimonious the construct of the female castration com- plex might be.

References

Abraham, K. Manifestations of the female castration complex (1920). In *Selected papers of Karl Abraham*. New York: Basic Books, 1954. Pp. 338–369.

Beck, S. J. *Rorschach's Test*. Vol. I. New York: Grune & Stratton, 1944.

Bloomingdale, E. C. Psychological aspects of essential dysmenorrhea. Unpublished doctoral dissertation, Radcliffe Graduate School, 1953.

Blum, G. S. A study of the psychoanalytic theory of psychosexual development. *Genetic Psychology Monographs*, 1949, **39**, 3–99.

Deutsch, H. *The psychology of women*. Vol. I. New York: Grune & Stratton, 1944.

Eisenbud, R.-J. Factors influencing the repudiation of femininity: A comparison of professional and homemaking women. Unpublished doctoral dissertation, Radcliffe Graduate School, 1951.

Fenichel, O. *The psychoanalytic theory of neurosis*. New York: W. W. Norton, 1945.

Franck, K., & Rosen, E. A projective test of masculinity-femininity. *Journal of Consulting Psychology*, 1949, **13**, 247–256.

Freud, S. Some psychological consequences of the anatomical distinction between the sexes (1925). In *Collected papers*. Vol. V. New York: Basic Books, 1959. pp. 186–197.

Freud, S. Female sexuality (1931). In *Collected papers*. Vol. V. New York: Basic Books, 1959. Pp. 252–272.

Freud, S. The psychology of women. In *New introductory lectures on psychoanalysis*. New York: W. W. Norton, 1933. Pp. 153–185.

Friedman, S. An empirical study of the castration and Oedipus complexes. *Genetic Psychology Monographs*, 1952, **46**, 61–130.

Hayward, E. P. Types of female castration reaction. *Psychoanalytic Quarterly*, 1943, **12**, 45–66.

Horney, K. *The neurotic personality of our times*. New York: Norton, 1937.

Horney, K. Feminine psychology. In *New ways in psychoanalysis*. New York: W. W. Norton, 1939. Pp. 101–119.

Landis, C. *Sex in development*. New York: P. B. Hoeber, 1940.

Levin, R. B. The psychology of women: An empirical test of a psychoanalytic construct. Unpublished doctoral dissertation, Syracuse University, 1962.

Levy, D. M. "Control-situation" studies of children's responses to the differences in genitalia. *American Journal of Orthopsychiatry*, 1940, **10**, 755–762.

Menninger, K. A. Somatic correlations with the unconscious repudiation of femininity in women. *Journal of Nervous and Mental Disease*, 1939, **89**, 514–527.

Schwartz, B. J. An empirical test of two Freudian hypotheses concerning castration anxiety. *Journal of Personality*, 1956, **24**, 318–327.

Thompson, C. Cultural pressures in the psychology of women. *Psychiatry*, 1942, **5**, 331–339.

Thompson, C. "Penis envy" in women. *Psychiatry*, 1943, **6**, 123–135.

Jung's Analytic Theory

For Freud, there is an abundance of primary sources and research from which to choose. For Jung, there is only an abundance of primary sources. These primary sources, it is true, contain much that is empirical in nature, for Jung believed that all of his writings were factual rather than speculative. In one of his generous and characteristically outspoken comments on the first draft of the chapter on analytic theory that was written for the first edition of *Theories of Personality*, he expostulated, "Why don't you show the facts? *I am always talking of facts*. My concepts are merely names for *facts*. I have no system." (Jung's emphasis.) Many psychological readers are not likely to agree with Jung's own appraisal of his writings. Many of his *facts* appear to be speculations. Some of this difference of opinion arises out of contrasting views regarding the nature of research. Jung and many of his followers employ the comparative method. By this they mean a comparison of myths, symbols, and religions in various cultures and during different historical periods. They also include as research the presentation of case material from patients undergoing treatment. To the American psychologist, research demands controls against the operation of bias and chance factors and some measure of quantification, both of which are absent in Jung's research.

While Jung's influence on contemporary personality theory is still not very great, his ideas hold a fascination for many psychology students. Indeed there appears to be a growing interest in Jung's writings not only by psychology students, but also by students and scholars in literature, art, religion, and history. Among professional psychologists Jung's greatest influence at present appears to be on a relatively small group of Jungian analysts. However, there are a few investigators who have been concerned with systematic evaluation of Jungian personality theory, and their number is increasing.

Several Jungians were asked to suggest empirical studies to be included in the first edition of this volume. One replied, "In Jungian psychology today, the research studies that go on are simply within the laboratory of the individual personalities of the analyst and his case."

In view of this situation, it is paradoxical that Jung first attracted the attention of American psychology by quantitative, experimental studies using the word association test, a subject upon which he was asked to lecture at Clark University in 1909. His typology, especially the two major attitudes or orientations of personality, extraversion and introversion, also stimulated a good deal of paper-and-pencil testing in the United States and England. Within the last few years, a new test, the Myers-Briggs Type Indicator, which purports to measure not only the attitudes but also the four basic psychological functions of thinking, feeling, sensation, and intuition, has been published.

Jung's writings on personality theory can be found in the 18 volume series entitled *The Collected Works of C. G. Jung*, which have been edited by Read, Fordham, and Adler and published by the Princeton University Press. Our primary source selections have been chosen from two of these volumes, and they reveal the kind of empirical evidence from which Jung derived his concepts. The first selection displays the style and strategy of Jung's thinking about one of his fundamental concepts, the symbol. This paper contains many references to anthropology, mythology, and religion, and it demonstrates the wide range of material that Jung has at his command and used in developing his theory. An understanding of symbol formation is essential to understanding Jung's theory of personality development and dynamics. This selection should also provide the student with a glimpse into the differences between Freud and Jung with regard to the sexual instinct. The second selection shows how Jung interprets a dream. The reader may wish to compare his method of dream interpretation with that of Freud as presented in Section I.

The selection by Gorlow, Simonson, and Krauss is a factor analytic study of Jung's eight psychological types. In this study the Q-sort technique developed by Stephenson was used. This technique requires each subject, in this case undergraduate students, to sort 100 statements into 11 different categories. The 11 categories are arranged along a single dimension. In the present study it was "least like myself" to "most like myself." The statements are printed on individual cards, and after a thorough shuffling the subject sorts each card into one of the categories, so that the resultant distribution of cards provides a self-description. The development of the statements is a challenging task, and the authors of this paper clearly indicate how they proceeded in this part of the study. The Q-sort technique has also been used by a number of investigators who have studied various aspects of Rogerian theory (Section XII, Roger's Self Theory).

Although only two factors, extroverted-feeling type and extroverted-thinking type, accounted for sizable portions of the total variance, this study did provide some support for Jung's theory of psychological types. The sex differences in the factor loadings provide a theoretical as well as an empirical challenge. Additional research on sex differences in psychological types should be a fruitful line of inquiry.

1. Symbol Formation

C. G. JUNG

The psychological mechanism that transforms energy is the symbol. I mean by this a real symbol and not a sign. The Wachandi's hole in the earth is not a sign for the genitals of a woman, but a symbol that stands for the idea of the earth woman who is to be made fruitful. To mistake it for a human woman would be to interpret the symbol semiotically, and this would fatally disturb the value of the ceremony. It is for this reason that none of the dancers may look at a woman. The mechanism would be destroyed by a semiotic interpretation—would be like smashing the supply-pipe of a turbine on the ground that it was a very unnatural waterfall that owed its existence to the repression of natural conditions. I am far from suggesting that the semiotic interpretation is meaningless; it is not only a possible interpretation but also a very true one. Its usefulness is undisputed in all those cases where nature is merely thwarted without any effective work resulting from it. But the semiotic inter-

pretation becomes meaningless when it is applied exclusively and schematically—when, in short, it ignores the real nature of the symbol and debases it to a mere sign.

The first achievement wrested by primitive man from instinctual energy, through analogybuilding, is magic. A ceremony is magical so long as it does not result in effective work but preserves the state of expectancy. In that case the energy is canalized into a new object and produces a new dynamism, which in turn remains magical so long as it does not create effective work. The advantage accruing from a magical ceremony is that the newly invested object acquires a working potential in relation to the psyche. Because of its value it has a determining and stimulating effect on the imagination, so that for a long time the mind is fascinated and possessed by it. This gives rise to actions that are performed in a half-playful way on the magical object, most of them rhythmical in character. A good example is those South American rock-drawings which consist of furrows deeply engraved in the hard stone. They were made by the Indians playfully retracing the furrows again and again with stones, over hundreds of years. The content of the drawings is difficult to inter-

SOURCE. *Selection from C. G. Jung, "Symbol formation" in "The structure and dynamics of the psyche,"* The Collected Works, *Vol. 8, pp. 45–61. Edited by Sir Herbert Read, Michael Fordham, Gerhard Adler; translated from the German by R. F. C. Hull. New York: Pantheon, 1960. Copyright held by Bollingen Foundation, Inc.*

pret, but the activity bound up with them is incomparably more significant.[1]

The influence exerted on the mind by the magically effective object has other possible consequences. Through a sustained playful interest in the object, a man may make all sorts of discoveries about it which would otherwise have escaped him. As we know, many discoveries have actually been made in this way. Not for nothing is magic called the "mother of science." Until late in the Middle Ages what we today call science was nothing other than magic. A striking example of this is alchemy, whose symbolism shows quite unmistakably the principle of transformation of energy described above, and indeed the later alchemists were fully-conscious of this fact.[2] But only through the development of magic into science, that is, through the advance from the stage of mere expectation to real technical work on the object, have we acquired that mastery over the forces of nature of which the age of magic dreamed. Even the alchemist's dream of the transmutation of the elements has been fulfilled, and magical action at a distance has been realized by the discovery of electricity. So we have every reason to value symbol-formation and to render homage to the symbol as an inestimable means of utilizing the mere instinctual flow of energy for effective work. A waterfall is certainly more beautiful than a powerstation, but dire necessity teaches us to value electric light and electrified industry more highly than the superb wastefulness of a waterfall that delights us for a quarter of an hour on a holiday walk.

Just as in physical nature only a very small portion of natural energy can be converted into a usuable form, and by far the greater part must be left to work itself out unused in natural phenomena, so in our psychic nature only a small part of the total energy can be diverted from its natural flow. An incomparably greater part cannot be utilized by us, but goes to sustain the regular course of life. Hence the libido is apportioned by nature to the various functional systems, from which it cannot be wholly withdrawn. The libido is invested in these functions as a specific force that cannot be transformed. Only where a symbol offers a steeper gradient than nature is it possible to canalize libido into other forms. The history of civilization has amply demonstrated that man possesses a relative surplus of energy that is capable of application apart from the natural flow. The fact that the symbol makes this deflection possible proves that not all the libido is bound up in a form that enforces the natural flow, but that a certain amount of energy remains over, which could be called excess libido. It is conceivable that this excess may be due to failure of the firmly organized functions to equalize differences in intensity. They might be compared to a system of water-pipes whose diameter is too small to draw off the water that is being steadily supplied. The water would then have to flow off in one way or another. From this excess libido certain psychic processes arise which cannot be explained—or only very inadequately—as the result of merely natural conditions. How are we to explain religious processes, for instance, whose nature is essentially symbolical? In abstract form, symbols are religious ideas; in the form of action, they are rites or ceremonies. They are the manifestation and expression of excess libido. At the same time they are stepping-stones to new activities, which must be called cultural in order to distinguish them from the instinctual functions that run their regular course according to natural law.

I have called a symbol that converts

[1]Koch-Grünberg, *Südamerikanische Felszeichnungen.*
[2]Silberer, *Problems of Mysticism and Its Symbolism;* also Rosencreutz, *Chymische Hochzeit* (1616).

energy a "libido analogue."[3] By this I mean an idea that can give equivalent expression to the libido and canalize it into a form different from the original one. Mythology offers numerous equivalents of this kind, ranging from sacred objects such as *churingas*, fetishes, etc., to the figures of gods. The rites with which the sacred objects are surrounded often reveal very clearly their nature as transformers of energy. Thus the primitive rubs his *churinga* rhythmically and takes the magic power of the fetish into himself, at the same time giving it a fresh "charge."[4] A higher stage of the same line of thought is the idea of the totem, which is closely bound up with the beginnings of tribal life and leads straight up to the idea of the palladium, the tutelary tribal deity, and to the idea of an organized human community in general. The transformation of libido through the symbol is a process that has been going on ever since the beginnings of humanity and continues still. Symbols were never devised consciously, but were always produced out of the unconscious by way of revelation or intuition.[5] In view of the close connection between mythological symbols and dream-symbols, and of the fact that the dream is "le dieu des sauvages," it is more than probable that most of the historical symbols derive directly from dreams or are at least influenced by them.[6] We know that this is true of the choice of totem, and there is similar evidence regarding the choice of gods. This age-old function of the symbol is still present today, despite the fact that for many centuries the trend of mental development has been towards the suppression of individual symbol-formation. One of the first steps in this direction was the setting up of an official state religion, a further step was the extermination of polythesism, first attempted in the reforms of Amenophis IV. We know the extraordinary part played by Christianity in the suppression of individual symbol-formation. But as the intensity of the Christian idea begins to fade, a recrudescence of individual symbol-formation may be expected. The prodigious increase of Christian sects since the eighteenth century, the century of "enlightenment," bears eloquent witness to this. Christian Science, theosophy, anthroposophy, and "Mazdaznan" are further steps along the same path.

In practical work with our patients we come upon symbol-formations at every turn, the purpose of which is the transformation of libido. At the beginning of treatment we find the symbol-forming process at work, but in an unsuitable form that offers the libido too low a gradient. Instead of being converted into effective work, the libido flows off unconsciously along the old channels, that is, into archaic sexual fantasies and fantasy activities. Accordingly the patient remains at war with himself, in other words, neurotic. In such cases analysis in the strict sense is indicated, i.e., the reductive psychoanalytic method inaugurated by Freud, which breaks down all inappropriate symbolformations and reduces them to their natural elements. The power-station, situated too high and unsuitably

---

[3] *Symbols of Transformation*, par. 146.

[4] Spencer and Gillen, p. 277.

[5] "Man, of course, has always been trying to understand and to control his environment, but in the early stages this process was unconscious. The matters which are problems for us existed latent in the primitive brain; there, undefined, lay both problem and answer; through many ages of savagery, first one and then another partial answer emerged into consciousness; at the end of the series, hardly completed today, there will be a new synthesis in which riddle and answer are one." Crawley, *The Idea of the Soul*, p.11.

[6] "Dreams are to the savage man what the Bible is to us—the source of divine revelation." Gatschet, "The Klamath Indians of South-Western Oregon," cited in Lévy-Bruhl, p. 57.

constructed, is dismantled and separated into its original components, so that the natural flow is restored. The unconscious continues to produce symbols which one could obviously go on reducing to their elements *ad infinitum.*

But man can never rest content with the natural course of things, because he always has an excess of libido that can be offered a more favourable gradient than the merely natural one. For this reason he will inevitably seek it, no matter how often he may be forced back by reduction to the natural gradient. We have therefore reached the conclusion that when the unsuitable structures have been reduced and the natural course of things is restored, so that there is some possibility of the patient living a normal life, the reductive process should not be continued further. Instead, symbol-formation should be reinforced in a synthetic direction until a more favourable gradient for the excess libido is found. Reduction to the natural condition is neither an ideal state nor a panacea. If the natural state were really the ideal one, then the primitive would be leading an enviable existence. But that is by no means so, for aside from all the other sorrows and hardships of human life the primitive is tormented by superstitions, fears, and compulsions to such a degree that, if he lived in our civilization, he could not be described as other than profoundly neurotic, if not mad. What would one say of a European who conducted himself as follows? — A Negro dreamt that he was pursued by his enemies, caught, and burned alive. The next day he got his relatives to make a fire and told them to hold his feet in it, in order, by this apotropaic ceremony, to avert the misfortune of which he had dreamed. He was so badly burned that for many months he was unable to walk.[7]

Mankind was freed from these fears by

a continual process of symbol-formation that leads to culture. Reversion to nature must therefore be followed by a synthetic reconstruction of the symbol. Reduction leads down to the primitive natural man and his peculiar mentality. Freud directed his attention mainly to the ruthless desire for pleasure, Adler to the "psychology of prestige." These are certainly two quite essential peculiarities of the primitive psyche, but they are far from being the only ones. For the sake of completeness we would have to mention other characteristics of the primitive, such as his playful, mystical, or "heroic" tendencies, but above all that outstanding quality of the primitive mind, which is its subjection to suprapersonal "powers" be they instincts, affects, superstitions, fantasies, magicians, witches, spirits, demons, or gods. Reduction leads back to the subjection of the primitive, which civilized man hopes he had escaped. And just as reduction makes a man aware of his subjection to these "powers" and thus confronts him with a rather dangerous problem, so the synthetic treatment of the symbol brings him to the religious question, not so much to the problem of present-day religious creeds as to the religious problem of primitive man. In the face of the very real powers that dominate him, only an equally real fact can offer help and protection. No intellectual system, but direct experience only, can counterbalance the blind power of the instincts.

Over against the polymorphism of the primitive's instinctual nature there stands the regulating principle of individuation. Multiplicity and inner divisions are opposed by an integrative unity whose power is as great as that of the instincts. Together they form a pair of opposites necessary for self-regulation, often spoken of as nature and spirit. These conceptions are rooted in psychic conditions between which human consciousness fluctuates like the pointer on the scales.

---

[7]Lévy-Bruhl, p. 57.

The primitive mentality can be directly experienced by us only in the form of the infantile psyche that still lives in our memories. The peculiarities of this psyche are conceived by Freud, justly enough, as infantile sexuality, for out of this germinal state there develops the later, mature sexual being. Freud, however, derives all sorts of other mental peculiarities from this infantile germinal state, so that it begins to look as if the mind itself came from a preliminary sexual stage and were consequently nothing more than an offshoot of sexuality. Freud overlooks the fact that the infantile, polyvalent germinal state is not just a singularly perverse preliminary stage of normal and mature sexuality; it seems perverse because it is a preliminary stage not only of adult sexuality but also of the whole mental make-up of the individual. Out of the infantile germinal state there developes the complete adult man; hence the germinal state is no more exclusively sexual than is the mind of the grown man. In it are hidden not merely the beginnings of adult life, but also the whole ancestral heritage, which is of unlimited extent. This heritage includes not only instincts from the animal stage, but all those differentiations that have left hereditary traces behind them. Thus every child is born with an immense split in his make-up; on one side he is more or less like an animal, on the other side he is the final embodiment of an age-old and endlessly complicated sum of hereditary factors. This split accounts for the tension of the germinal state and does much to explain the many puzzles of child psychology, which certainly has no lack of them.

If now, by means of a reductive procedure, we uncover the infantile stages of the adult psyche, we find as its ultimate basis germs containing on the one hand the later sexual being *in statu nascendi*, and on the other all those complicated preconditions of the civilized being. This is reflected most beautifully in children's dreams. Many of them are very simple "childish" dreams and are immediately understandable, but others contain possibilities of meaning that almost makes one's head spin, and things that reveal their profound significance only in the light of primitive parallels. This other side is the mind *in nuce*. Childhood, therefore, is important not only because various warpings of instinct have their origin there, but because this is the time when, terrifying or encouraging, those far-seeing dreams and images appear before the soul of the child, shaping his whole destiny, as well as those retrospective intuitions which reach back far beyond the range of childhood experience into the life of our ancestors. Thus in the child-psyche the natural condition is already opposed by a "spiritual" one. It is recognized that man living in the state of nature is in no sense merely "natural" like an animal, but sees, believes, fears, worships things whose meaning is not at all discoverable from the conditions of his natural environment. Their underlying meaning leads us in fact far away from all that is natural, obvious, and easily intelligible, and quite often contrasts more sharply with the natural instincts. We have only to think of all those gruesome rites and customs against which every natural feeling rises in revolt, or of all those beliefs and ideas which stand in insuperable contradiction to the evidence of the facts. All this drives us to the assumption that the spiritual principle (whatever that may be) asserts itself against the merely natural conditions with incredible strength. One can say that this too is "natural," and that both have their origin in one and the same "nature." I do not in the least doubt this origin, but must point out that this "natural" something consists of a conflict between two principles, to which you can give this or that name according to taste, and that this opposition is the expression, and perhaps also the basis, of the tension we call psychic energy.

For theoretical reasons as well there must be some such tension of opposites in the child, otherwise no energy would be possible, for, as Heraclitus has said, "war is the father of all things." As I have remarked, this conflict can be understood as an opposition between the profoundly primitive nature of the newborn infant and his highly differentiated inheritance. The natural man is characterized by unmitigated instinctuality, by his being completely at the mercy of his instincts. The inheritance that opposes this condition consists of mnemonic deposits accruing from all the experience of his ancestors. People are inclined to view this hypothesis with scepticism, thinking that "inherited ideas" are meant. There is naturally no question of that. It is rather a question of inherited *possibilities* of ideas, "paths" that have gradually been traced out through the cumulative experience of our ancestors. To deny the inheritance of these paths would be tantamount to denying the inheritance of the brain. To be consistent, such sceptics would have to assert that the child is born with the brain of an ape. But since it is born with a human brain, this must sooner or later begin to function in a human way, and it will necessarily begin at the level of the most recent ancestors. Naturally this functioning remains profoundly unconscious to the child. At first he is conscious only of the instincts and of what opposes these instincts—namely, his parents. For this reason the child has no notion that what stands in his way may be within himself. Rightly or wrongly it is projected on to the parents . This infantile prejudice is so tenacious that we doctors often have the greatest difficulty in persuading our patients that the wicked father who forbade everything is far more inside than outside themselves. Everything that works from the unconscious appears projected on

others. Not that these others are wholly without blame, for even the worst projection is at least hung on a hook, perhaps a very small one, but still a hook offered by the other person.

Although our inheritance consists of psychological paths, it was nevertheless mental processes in our ancestors that traced these paths. If they came to consciousness again in the individual, they can do so only in the form of other mental processes; and although these processes can become conscious only through individual experience and consequently appear as individual acquisitions, they are nevertheless pre-existent traces which are merely "filled out" by individual experience. Probably every "impressive" experience is just such a break-through into an old, previously unconscious river-bed.

These pre-existent paths are hard facts, as indisputable as the historical fact of man having built a city out of his original cave. This development was made possible only by the formation of a community, and the latter only by the curbing of instinct. The curbing of instinct by mental and spiritual processes is carried through with the same force and the same results in the individual as in the history of mankind. It is a normative or, more accurately, a "nomothetical"[8] process, and it derives its power from the unconscious fact of the inherited disposition. The mind, as the active principle in the inheritance, consists of the sum of the ancestral minds, the "unseen fathers"[9] whose authority is born anew with the child.

The philosophical concept of mind as "spirit" has still not been able to free itself, as a term in its own right, from the overpowering bond of identity with the other connotation of spirit, namely "ghost."

[8]("Ordained by law."—Editors.)
[9]Söderblom, *Das Werden des Gottesglaubens*, pp. 88ff. and 175ff.

Religion, on the other hand, has succeeded in getting over the linguistic association with "spirits" by calling the supreme spiritual authority "God." In the course of the centuries this conception came to formulate a spiritual principle which is opposed to mere instinctuality. What is especially significant here is that God is conceived at the same time as the Creator of nature. He is seen as the maker of those imperfect creatures who err and sin, and at the same time he is their judge and taskmaster. Simple logic would say: if I make a creature who falls into error and sin, and is practically worthless because of his blind instinctuality, then I am manifestly a bad creator and have not even completed my apprenticeship. (As we know, this argument played an important role in Gnosticism.) But the religious point of view is not perturbed by this criticism; it asserts that the ways and intentions of God are inscrutable. Actually the Gnostic argument found little favour in history, because the unassailability of the God-concept obviously answers a vital need before which all logic pales. (It should be understood that we are speaking here not of God as a *Ding an sich*, but only of a human conception which as such is a legitimate object of science.)

Although the God-concept is a spiritual principle *par excellence*, the collective metaphysical need nevertheless insists that it is at the same time a conception of the First Cause, from which proceed all those instinctual forces that are opposed to the spiritual principle. God would thus be not only the essence of spiritual light, appearing as the latest flow on the tree of evolution, not only the spiritual goal of salvation in which all creation culminates, not only the end and aim, but also the darkest, nethermost cause of Nature's blackest deeps. This is a tremendous paradox which obviously reflects a profound psychological truth. For it asserts the essential contradictoriness of one and the same

being, a being whose innermost nature is a tension of opposites. Science calls this "being" energy, for energy is like a living balance between opposites. For this reason the God-concept, in itself impossibly paradoxical, may be so satisfying to human needs that no logic however justified can stand against it. Indeed the subtlest cogitation could scarcely have found a more suitable formula for this fundamental fact of inner experience.

It is not, I believe, superfluous to have discussed in considerable detail the nature of the opposites that underlie psychic energy.[10] Freudian theory consists in a casaul explanation of the psychology of instinct. From this standpoint the spiritual principle is bound to appear only as an appendage, a by-product of the instincts. Since its inhibiting and restrictive power cannot be denied, it is traced back to the influence of education, moral authorities, convention, and tradition. These authorities in their turn derive their power, according to the theory, from repression in the manner of a vicious cycle. The spiritual principle is not recognized as an equivalent counterpart of the instincts.

The spiritual standpoint, on the other hand, is embodied in religious views which I can take as being sufficiently known. Freudian psychology appears threatening to this standpoint, but it is not more of a threat than materialism in general, whether scientific or practical. The one-sidedness of Freud's sexual theory is significant at least as a symptom. Even if it has no scientific justification, it has a moral one. It is undoubtedly true that instinctuality conflicts with our moral views most frequently and most conspicuously in the realm of sex. The conflict between infantile instinctuality and ethics

---

[10] I have treated this same problem under other aspects and in another way in *Symbols of Transformation*, pars. 253, 680; and *Psychological Types* (1923 ed., p. 240).

can never be avoided. It is, it seems to me, the *sine qua non* of psychic energy. While we are all agreed that murder, stealing, and ruthlessness of any kind are obviously inadmissible, there is nevertheless what we call a "sexual question." We hear nothing of a murder question or a rage question; social reform is never invoked against those who wreak their bad tempers on their fellow men. Yet these things are all examples of instinctual behaviour, and the necessity for their suppression seems to us self-evident. Only in regard to sex do we feel the need of a question mark. This points to a doubt — the doubt whether our existing moral concepts and the legal institutions founded on them are really adequate and suited to their purpose. No intelligent person will deny that in this field opinion is sharply divided. Indeed, there would be no problem at all if public opinion were united about it. It is obviously a reaction against a too rigorous morality. It is not simply an outbreak of primitive instinctuality; such outbreaks, as we know, have never yet bothered themselves with moral laws and moral problems. There are, rather, serious misgivings as to whether our existing moral views have dealt fairly with the nature of sex. From this doubt there naturally arises a legitimate interest in any attempt to understand the nature of sex more truly and deeply, and this interest is answered not only by Freudian psychology but by numerous other researches of the kind. The special emphasis, therefore, that Freud has laid on sex could be taken as a more or less conscious answer to the question of the hour, and conversely, the acceptance that Freud has found with the public proves how well-timed his answer was.

An attentive and critical reader of Freud's writings cannot fail to remark how wide and flexible his concept of sexuality is. In fact it covers so much that one often wonders why in certain places the author uses a sexual terminology at all. His concept of sexuality includes not only the physiological sexual processes but practically every stage, phase, and kind of feeling or desire. This enormous flexibility makes his concept universally applicable, though not always to the advantage of the resulting explanations. By means of this inclusive concept you can explain a work of art or a religious experience in exactly the same terms as an hysterical symptom. The absolute difference between these three things then drops right out of the picture. The explanation can therefore be only an apparent one for at least two of them. Apart from these inconveniences, however, it is psychologically correct to tackle the problem first from the sexual side, for it is just there that the unprejudiced person will find something to talk about.

The conflict between ethics and sex today is not just a collision between instinctuality and morality, but a struggle to give an instinct its rightful place in our lives, and to recognize in the instincts a power which seeks expression and evidently may not be trifled with, and therefore cannot be made to fit in with our well-meaning moral laws. Sexuality is not mere instinctuality; it is an indisputably creative power that is not only the basic cause of our individual lives, but a very serious factor in our psychic life as well. Today we know only too well the grave consequences that sexual disturbances can bring in their train. We could call sexuality the spokesman of the instincts, which is why from the spiritual standpoint sex is the chief antagonist, not because sexual indulgence is in itself more immoral than excessive eating and drinking, avarice, tyranny, and other extravagances, but because the spirit senses in sexuality a counterpart equal and indeed akin to itself. For just as the spirit would press sexuality, like every other instinct, into its service, so sexuality has an ancient claim upon the spirit, which it once—in procreation, pregnancy, birth, and childhood—contained within itself, and whose passion the spirit can never dispense with in its creations. Where would the spirit be if it had no peer among the instincts to oppose it? It would be nothing but an empty form. A reasonable regard for the other instincts has become for us a self-evident necessity, but with sex it is different. For us sex is still problematical, which means that on this point we have not reached a degree of consciousness that would enable us to do full justice to the instinct without appreciable moral injury. Freud is not only a scientific investigator of sexuality, but also its champion; therefore, having regard to the great importance of the sexual problem, I recognize the moral justification of his concept of sexuality even though I cannot accept it scientifically.

This is not the place to discuss the possible reasons for the present attitude to sex. It is sufficient to point out that sexuality seems to us the strongest and most immediate instinct,[11] standing out as *the* instinct above all others. On the other hand, I must also emphasize that the spiritual principle does not, strictly speaking, conflict with instinct as such but only with blind instinctuality, which really amounts to an unjustified preponderance of the instinctual nature over the spiritual. The spiritual appears in the psyche also as an instinct, indeed as a real passion, a "consuming fire," as Nietzsche once expressed it. It is not derived from any other instinct, as the psychologists of instinct would have us believe, but is a principle *sui generis*, a specific and necessary form of instinctual power. I have gone into this problem in a special study, to which I would refer the reader.[12]

Symbol-formation follows the road

offered by these two possibilities in the human mind. Reduction breaks down all inappropriate and useless symbols and leads back to the merely natural course, and this causes a damming up of libido. Most the alleged "sublimations" are compulsory products of this situation, activities cultivated for the purpose of using up the unbearable surplus of libido. But the really primitive demands are not satisfied by this procedure. If the psychology of this dammed-up condition is studied carefully and without prejudice, it is easy to discover in it the beginnings of a primitive form of religion, a religion of an individual kind altogether different from a dogmatic, collective religion.

Since the making of a religion or the formation of symbols is just as important an interest of the primitive mind as the satisfaction of instinct, the way to further development is logically given: escape from the state of education lies in evolving a religion of an individual character. One's true individuality then emerges from behind the veil of the collective personality, which would be quite impossible in the state of reduction since our instinctual nature is essentially collective. The development of individuality is also impossible, or at any rate seriously impeded, if the state of reduction gives rise to forced sublimations in the shape of various cultural activities, since these are in their essence equally collective. But, as human beings are for the most part collective, these forced sublimations are therapeutic products that should not be underestimated, because they help many people to bring a certain amount of useful activity into their lives. Among these cultural activities we must include the practice of a religion within the framework of an existing collective religion. The astonishing range of Catholic symbolism, for instance, has an emotional appeal which for many natures is absolutely satisfying. The immediacy of the relationship to God

---

[11]This is not the case with primitives, for whom the food question plays a far greater role.
[12]See "Instinct and the Unconscious," infra.

in Protestantism satisfies the mystic's passion for independence, while theosophy with its unlimited speculative possibilities meets the need for pseudo-Gnostic intuitions and caters for lazy thinking.

These organizations or systems are "symbola" which enable man to set up a spiritual counterpole to his primitive instinctual nature, a cultural attitude as opposed to sheer instinctuality. This has been the function of all religions. For a long time and for the great majority of mankind the symbol of a collective religion will suffice. It is perhaps only temporarily and for relatively few individuals that the existing collective religions have become inadequate. Wherever the cultural process is moving forward, whether in single individuals or in groups, we find a shaking off of collective beliefs. Every advance in culture, is, psychologically, an extension of consciousness, a coming to consciousness that can take place only through discrimination. Therefore an advance always begins with individuation, that is to say with the individual, conscious of his isolation, cutting a new path through hitherto untrodden territory. To do this he must first return to the fundamental facts of his own being, irrespective of all authority and tradition, and allow himself to become conscious of his distinctiveness. If he succeeds in giving collective validity to his widened consciousness, he creates a tension of opposites that provides the stimulation which culture needs for its further progress.

This is not to say that the development of individuality is in all circumstances necessary or even opportune. Yet one may well believe, as Goethe has said, that "the highest joy of man should be the growth of personality." There are large numbers of people for whom the development of individuality is the prime necessity, especially in a cultural epoch like ours, which is literally flattened out by collective norms, and where the newspaper is the real monarch of the earth. In my naturally limited experience there are, among people of maturer age, very many for whom the development of individuality is an indispensable requirement. Hence I am privately of the opinion that it is just the mature person who, in our times, has the greatest need of some further education in individual culture after his youthful education in school or university has moulded him on exclusively collective lines and thoroughly imbued him with the collective mentality. I have often found that people of riper years are in this respect capable of education to a most unexpected degree, although it is just those matured and strengthened by the experience of life who resist most vigorously the purely reductive standpoint.

Obviously it is in the youthful period of life that we have most to gain from a thorough recognition of the instinctual side. A timely recognition of sexuality, for instance, can prevent that neurotic suppression of it which keeps a man unduly withdrawn from life, or else forces him into a wretched and unsuitable way of living with which he is bound to come into conflict. Proper recognition and appreciation of normal instincts leads the young person into life and entangles him with fate, thus involving him in life's necessities and the consequent sacrifices and efforts through which his character is developed and his experience matured. For the mature person, however, the continued expansion of life is obviously not the right principle, because the descent towards life's afternoon demands simplification, limitation, and intensification — in other words, individual culture. A man in the first half of life with its biological orientation can usually, thanks to the youthfulness of his whole organism, afford to expand his life and make something of value out of it. But the man in the second half of life is oriented towards culture, the diminishing powers of his organism allowing him to subordinate his instincts to cultural goals. Not a few are wrecked during the transition from the biological to the cultural sphere. Our collective education makes practically no provision for this transitional period. Concerned solely with the education of the young, we disregard the education of the adult, of whom it is always assumed — on what grounds who can say? — that he needs no more education. There is an almost total lack of guidance for this extra-ordinarily important transition from the biological to the cultural attitude, for the transformation of energy from the biological form into the cultural form. This transformation process is an individual one and cannot be enforced by general rules and maxims. It is achieved by means of the symbol. Symbol-formation is a fundamental problem that cannot be discussed here. I must refer the reader to Chapter V in my *Psychological Types*, where I have dealt with this question in detail.

2. *An Interpretation of a Dream*

C. G. JUNG

First I must acquaint the reader in some measure with the personality of the dreamer, for without this acquaintance he will hardly be able to transport himself into the peculiar atmosphere of the dreams. There are dreams that are pure poems and can therefore only be understood through the mood they convey as a whole. The dreamer is a youth of a little over twenty, still entirely boyish in appearance. There is even a touch of girlishness in his looks and manner of expression. The latter betrays a very good education and upbringing. He is intelligent, with pronounced intellectual and aesthetic interests. His aestheticism is very much in evidence: we are made instantly aware of his good taste and his fine appreciation of all forms of art. His feelings are tender and soft, given to the enthusiasms typical of puberty, but somewhat effeminate. There is no trace of adolescent callowness. Undoubtedly he is too young for his age, a clear case of retarded development. It is

SOURCE. *Selection from C. G. Jung, "An interpretation of a dream" in "Two essays on analytical psychology," The* Collected Works, *Vol. 7, pp. 100–109. Edited by Sir Herbert Read, Michael Fordham, Gerhard Adler; translated from the German by R. F. C. Hull, New York:* Pantheon, 1953. Copyright held by Bollingen Foundation, Inc.

quite in keeping with this that he should have come to me on account of his homosexuality. The night preceding his first visit he had the following dream: *"I am in a lofty cathedral filled with mysterious twilight. They tell me that it is the cathedral at Lourdes. In the centre there is a deep dark well, into which I have to descend."*

The dream is clearly a coherent expression of mood. The dreamer's comments are as follows: "Lourdes is the mystic fount of healing. Naturally I remembered yesterday that I was going to you for treatment and was in search of a cure. There is said to be a well like this at Lourdes. It would be rather unpleasant to go down into this water. The well in the church was ever so deep."

Now what does this dream tell us? On the surface it seems clear enough, and we might be content to take it as a kind of poetic formulation of the mood of the day before. But we should never stop there, for experience shows that dreams are much deeper and more significant. One might almost suppose that the dreamer came to the doctor in a highly poetic mood and was entering upon the treatment as though it were a sacred religious act to be performed in the mystical half-light of some awe-inspiring sanctuary. But this does not fit the facts at all. The patient merely came to the doctor to be treated for that unpleasant matter, his homosexuality, which is anything but poetic. At any rate we cannot see from the mood of the preceding day why he should dream so poetically, if we were to accept so direct a causation for the origin of the dream. But we might conjecture, perhaps, that the dream was stimulated precisely by the dreamer's impressions of that highly unpoetical affair which impelled him to come to me for treatment. We might even suppose that he dreamed in such an intensely poetical manner just because of the unpoeticalness of his mood on the day before, much as a man who has fasted by day dreams of delicious meals at night. It cannot be denied that the thought of treatment, of the cure and its unpleasant procedure, recurs in the dream, but poetically transfigured, in a guise which meets most effectively the lively aesthetic and emotional needs of the dreamer. He will be drawn on irresistibly by this inviting picture, despite the fact that the well is dark, deep, and cold. Something of the dream-mood will persist after sleep and will even linger on into the morning of the day on which he has to submit to the unpleasant and unpoetical duty of visiting me. Perhaps the drab reality will be touched by the bright, golden after-glow of the dream feeling.

Is this, perhaps, the purpose of the dream? That would not be impossible, for in my experience the vast majority of dreams are compensatory.[1] They always stress the other side in order to maintain the psychic equilibrium. But the compensation of mood is not the only purpose of the dream picture. The dream also provides a *mental corrective*. The patient had of course nothing like an adequate understanding of the treatment to which he was about to submit himself. But the dream

gives him a picture which describes in poetic metaphors the nature of the treatment before him. This becomes immediately apparent if we follow up his associations and comments on the image of the cathedral: "Cathedral," he says, "makes me think of Cologne Cathedral. Even as a child I was fascinated by it. I remember my mother telling me of it for the first time, and I also remember how, whenever I saw a village church, I used to ask if that were Cologne Cathedral. I wanted to be a priest in a cathedral like that."

In these associations the patient is describing a very important experience of his childhood. As in nearly all cases of this kind, he had a particularly close tie with his mother. By this we are not to understand a particularly good or intense *conscious* relationship, but something in the nature of a secret, subterranean tie which expresses itself consciously, perhaps, only in the retarded development of character, i.e., in a relative infantilism. The developing personality naturally veers away from such an unconscious infantile bond; for nothing is more obstructive to development than persistence in an unconscious—we could also say, a psychically embryonic—state. For this reason instinct seizes on the first opportunity to replace the mother by another object. If it is to be a real mother-substitute, this object must be, in some sense, an analogy of her. This is entirely the case with our patient. The intensity with which his childish fantasy seized upon the symbol of Cologne Cathedral corresponds to the strength of his unconscious need to find a substitute for the mother. The unconscious need is heightened still further in a case where the infantile bond threatens injury. Hence the enthusiasm with which his childish imagination took up the idea of the Church; for the Church is, in the fullest sense, a mother. We speak not only of Mother Church, but even of the Church's womb. In the ceremony known

---

[1]The idea of comprensation has already been extensively used by Alfred Adler.

as the *benedictio fontis*, the baptismal font is apostrophized as "immaculatus divini fontis uterus" — the immaculate womb of the divine fount. We naturally think that a man must have known this meaning consciously before it could get to work in his fantasy, and that an unknowing child could not possibly be affected by these significations. Such analogies certainly do not work by way of the conscious mind, but in quite another manner.

The Church represents a higher spiritual substitute for the purely natural, or "carnal," tie to the parents. Consequently it frees the individual from an unconscious natural relationship which, strictly speaking, is not a relationship at all but simply a condition of inchoate, unconscious identity. This, just because it is unconscious, possesses a tremendous inertia and offers the utmost resistance to any kind of spiritual development. It would be hard to say what the essential difference is between this state and the soul of an animal. Now, it is by no means the special prerogative of the Christian Church to try to make it possible for the individual to detach himself from his original, animal-like condition; the Church is simply the latest, and specifically Western, form of an instinctive striving that is probably as old as mankind itself. It is a striving that can be found in the most varied forms among all primitive peoples who are in any way developed and have not yet become degenerate: I mean the institution or rite of initiation into manhood. When he has reached puberty the young man is conducted to the "men's house," or some other place of consecration, where he is systematically alienated from his family. At the same time he is initiated into the religious mysteries, and in this way is ushered not only into a wholly new set of relationships, but, as a renewed and changed personality, into a new world, like one reborn (*quasi modo genitus*). The initiation is often attended

by all kinds of tortures, sometimes including such things as circumcision and the like. These practices are undoubtedly very old. They have almost become instinctive mechanisms, with the result that they continue to repeat themselves without external compulsion, as in the "baptisms" of German students or the even more wildly extravagant initiations in American students' fraternities. They are engraved in the unconscious as a primordial image.

When his mother told him as a little boy about Cologne Cathedral, this primordial image was stirred and awakened to life. But there was no priestly instructor to develop it further, so the child remained in his mother's hands. Yet the longing for a man's leadership continued to grow in the boy, taking the form of homosexual leanings — a faulty development that might never have come about had a man been there to educate his childish fantasies. The deviation towards homosexuality has, to be sure, numerous historical precedents. In ancient Greece, as also in certain primitive communities, homosexuality and education were practically synonymous. Viewed in this light, the homosexuality of adolescence is only a misunderstanding of the otherwise very appropriate need for masculine guidance. One might also say that the fear of incest which is based on the mother-complex extends to women in general; but in my opinion an immature man is quite right to be afraid of women, because his relations with women are generally disastrous.

According to the dream, then, what the initiation of the treatment signifies for the patient is the fulfilment of the true meaning of his homosexuality, i.e., his entry into the world of the adult man. All that we have been forced to discuss here in such tedious and long-winded detail, in order to understand it properly, the dream has condensed into a few vivid metaphors, thus creating a picture which works far more effectively on the imagination, feeling, and understanding of the dreamer than any learned discourse. Consequently the patient was better and more intelligently prepared for the treatment than if he had been overwhelmed with medical and pedagogical maxims. (For this reason I regard dreams not only as a valuable source of information but as an extraordinarily effective instrument of education.)

We come now to the second dream. I must explain in advance that in the first consultation I did not refer in any way to the dream we have just been discussing. It was not even mentioned. Nor was there a word said that was even remotely connected with the foregoing. This is the second dream: "*I am in a great Gothic cathedral. At the altar stands a priest. I stand before him with my friend, holding in my hand a little Japanese ivory figure, with the feeling that it is going to be baptized. Suddenly an elderly woman appears, takes the fraternity ring from my friend's finger and puts it on her own. My friend is afraid that this may bind him in some way. But at the same moment there is a sound of wonderful organ music.*"

Here I will only bring out briefly those points which continue and supplement the dream of the preceding day. The second dream is unmistakably connected with the first: once more the dreamer is in church, that is, in the state of initiation into manhood. But a new figure has been added: the priest, whose absence in the previous situation we have already noted. The dream therefore confirms that the unconscious meaning of his homosexuality has been fulfilled and that a further development can be started. The actual initiation ceremony, namely the baptism, may now begin. The dream symbolism corroborates what I said before, namely that it is not the prerogative of the Christian Church to bring about such transitions and psychic transformations, but

that behind the Church there is a living primordial image which in certain conditions is capable of enforcing them.

What, according to the dream, is to be baptized is a little Japanese ivory figure. The patient says of this: "It was a tiny, grotesque little manikin that reminded me of the male organ. It was certainly odd that this member was to be baptized. But after all, with the Jews circumcision is a sort of baptism. That must be a reference to my homosexuality, because the friend standing with me before the altar is the one with whom I have sexual relations. We belong to the same fraternity. The fraternity ring obviously stands for our relationship."

We know that in common usage the ring is the token of a bond or relationship, as for example the wedding ring. We can therefore safely take the fraternity ring in this case as symbolizing the homosexual relationship, and the fact that the dreamer appears together with his friend points in the same direction.

The complaint to be remedied is homosexuality. The dreamer is to be led out of this relatively childish condition and initiated into the adult state by means of a kind of circumcision ceremony under the supervision of a priest. These ideas correspond exactly to my analysis of the previous dream. Thus far the development has proceeded logically and consistently with the aid of archtypal images. But now a disturbing factor appears to enter. An elderly woman suddenly takes possession of the fraternity ring; in other words, she draws to herself what has hitherto been a homosexual relationship, thus causing the dreamer to fear that he is getting involved in a new relationship with obligations of its own. Since the ring is now on the hand of a woman, a marriage of sorts has been contracted, i.e., the homosexual relationship seems to have passed over into a heterosexual one, but a heterosexual relationship of a peculiar kind since it concerns an elderly woman. "She is a friend of my mother's," says the patient. "I am very fond of her, in fact she is like a mother to me."

From this remark we can see what has happened in the dream: as a result of the initiation the homosexual tie has been cut and a heterosexual relationship substituted for it, a platonic friendship with a motherly type of woman. In spite of her resemblance to his mother, this woman is not his mother any longer, so the relationship with her signifies a step beyond the mother towards masculinity, and hence a partial conquest of his adolescent homosexuality.

The fear of the new tie can easily be understood, firstly as fear which the woman's resemblance to his mother might naturally arouse—it might be that the dissolution of the homosexual tie has led to a complete regression to the mother—and secondly as fear of the new and unknown factors in the adult heterosexual state with its possible obligations, such as marriage, etc. That we are in fact concerned here not with a regression but with a progression seems to be confirmed by the music that now peals forth. The patient is musical and especially susceptible to solemn organ music. Therefore music signifies for him a very positive feeling, so in this case it forms a harmonious conclusion to the dream, which in its turn is well qualified to leave behind a beautiful, holy feeling for the following morning.

If you consider the fact that up to now the patient had seen me for only one consultation, in which little more was discussed than a general anamnesis, you will doubtless agree with me when I say that both dreams make astonishing anticipations. They show the patient's situation in a highly remarkable light, and one that is very strange to the conscious mind, while at the same time lending to the banal medical situation an aspect that is uniquely attuned to the mental peculiarities of

the dreamer, and thus capable of stringing his aesthetic, intellectual, and religious interests to concert pitch. No better conditions for treatment could possibly be imagined. One is almost persuaded, from the meaning of these dreams, that the patient entered upon the treatment with the utmost readiness and hopefulness, quite prepared to cast aside his boyishness and become a man. In reality, however, this was not the case at all. Consciously he was full of hesitation and resistance; moreover, as the treatment progressed, he constantly showed himself antagonistic and difficult, every ready to slip back into his previous infantilism. Consequently the dreams stand in strict contrast to his conscious behavior. They move along a progressive line and take the part of the educator. They clearly reveal their special function. This function I have called compensation. The unconscious progressiveness and the conscious regressiveness together form a pair of opposites which, as it were, keeps the scales balanced. The influence of the educator tilts the balance in favour of progression.

In the case of this young man the images of the collective unconscious play an entirely positive role, which comes from that fact that he has no really dangerous tendency to fall back on a fantasy-substitute for reality and to entrench himself behind it against life. The effect of these unconscious images has something fateful about it. Perhaps—who knows?—these eternal images are what men mean by fate.

The archetypes are of course always at work everywhere. But practical treatment, especially in the case of young people, does not always require the patient to come to close quarters with them. At the climacteric, on the other hand, it is necessary to give special attention to the images of the collective unconscious, because they are the source from which hints may be drawn for the solution of the problem of opposites. From the conscious elaboration of this material the transcendent function reveals itself as a mode of apprehension mediated by the archetypes and capable of uniting the opposites. By "apprehension" I do not mean simply intellectual understanding, but understanding through experience. An archetype, as we have already said, is a dynamic image, a fragment of the objective psyche, which can be truly understood only if experienced as a living opposite.

A general account of this process, which may extend over a long period of time, would be pointless — even if such a description were possible — because it takes the greatest imaginable variety of forms in different individuals. The only common factor is the emergence of certain definite archetypes. I would mention in particular the shadow, the animal, the wise old man, the anima, the animus, the mother, the child, besides an indefinite number of archetypes representative of situations. A special position must be accorded to those archetypes which stand for the goal of the developmental process. The reader will find the necessary information on this point in my *Psychology and Alchemy*, as well as in *Psychology and Religion* and the volume produced in collaboration with Richard Wilhelm, *The Secret of the Golder Flower*.[2]

The transcendent function does not proceed without aim and purpose, but leads to the revelation of the essential man. It is in the first place a purely natural process, which may in some cases pursue its course without the knowledge or assistance of the individual, and can sometimes forcibly accomplish itself in the face of opposition. The meaning and purpose of the process is the realization, in all its aspects, of the personality originally hidden away in the embryonic germ-plasm; the production and unfolding of the original, potential wholeness. The symbols used by the unconscious to this end are the same as those which mankind has always used to express wholeness, completeness, and perfection: symbols, as a rule, of the quaternity and the circle. For these reasons I have termed this the *individuation process*.

This natural process of individuation served me both as a model and guiding principle for my method of treatment. The unconscious compensation of a neurotic conscious attitude contains all the elements that could effectively and healthily correct the one-sidedness of the conscious mind, if these elements were made conscious, i.e., understood and integrated into it as realities. It is only very seldom that a dream achieves such intensity that the shock is enough to throw the conscious mind out of the saddle. As a rule dreams are too feeble and too unintelligible to exercise a radical influence on consciousness. In consequence, the compensation runs underground in the unconscious and has no immediate effect. But it has some effect all the same; only, it is indirect in so far as the unconscious opposition will, if consistently ignored, arrange symptoms and situations which irresistibly thwart our conscious intentions. The aim of the treatment is therefore to understand and to appreciate, so far as practicable, dreams and all other manifestations of the unconscious, firstly in order to prevent the formation of an unconscious opposition which becomes more dangerous as time goes on, and secondly in order to make the fullest possible use of the healing factor of compensation.

These proceedings naturally rest on the assumption that a man is capable of attaining wholeness, in other words, that he has it in him to be healthy. I mention this assumption because there are with-

---

[2]Respectively, in Vols. 11, 12, and (i.e., my commentary) 13 of the *Collected Works*.

out doubt individuals who are not at bottom altogether viable and who rapidly perish if, for any reason, they come face to face with their wholeness. Even if this does not happen, they merely lead a miserable existence for the rest of their days as fragments or partial personalities, shored up by social or psychic parasitism. Such people are, very much to the misfortune of others, more often than not inveterate humbugs who cover up their deadly emptiness under a fine outward show. It would be a hopeless undertaking to try to treat them with the method here discussed. The only thing that "helps" here is to keep up the show, for the truth would be unendurable or useless.

3. An Empirical Investigation of the Jungian Typology

LEON GORLOW, NORMAN R. SIMONSON, AND HERBERT KRAUSS

The study examines the hypothesis that in the domain of self-report individuals will order themselves into the types postulated by Jung. It also examines the usefulness of inverse factor analysis as a technique for studying typologies. The analysis of a Q-sort of 100 self regarding propositions yielded a number of interpretable factors. In this fashion five of the eight types postulated by Jung were identified. These factors were correlated with other characteristics of the subjects.

The present study represents another effort to examine the typology developed by Jung (1923). It is directed toward an examination of the hypothesis that within the domain of self-report, individuals will order themselves into the types postulated by Jung.

Jung, it will be recalled, postulated two attitudes—extroversion and introversion—and four functions: thinking, feeling, sensing, and intuiting. The four functions interact with the two attitudes to produce eight psychological types. The basic reference for his ideas regarding types, as well as a description of the types, is *Psychological Types* (1923).

Thus far, empirical evaluations of the Jungian typology have not been particularly successful in verifying the existence of these types. A well-known early study was conducted by Stephenson (1939). In this study, however, the Jungian personality typology was employed to represent Stephenson's position regarding correlation between persons as contrasted with correlations between tests. It was primarily a procedural rather than a substantive study.

In addition to Gray's (1948) research which examined the applicability of questionnaires for the assessment of types, there have been the notable efforts of Eysenck (1953) whose research led to the identification of an introversion–extroversion factor. His work, however, has been limited to this single dimension, and his efforts have not been directed toward the verification of the general Jungian hypothesis about types.

Recently Myers-Briggs (1962) developed a self-report instrument which was designed to classify people within the Jungian typology. The instrument consists of four scales: extroversion–introversion, sensing–intuiting, thinking–feeling, and judging–perceiving. In a recent study, Stricker & Ross (1964) examined some of the structural properties of the Jungian typology by employing the Myers-Briggs instrument. For example, they argued that as a logical consequence of

SOURCE. *Article by Leon Gorlow, Norman R. Simonson, and Herbert Krauss, "An empirical investigation of the Jungian typology" in the* British journal of social and clinical psychology, *Vol. 5, pp. 108–117, 1966.*

the Jungian typology defining individuals as qualitatively different, bi-modality should be observed in the distributions of scores in each scale. They concluded that the results of their investigation offered little support for many of the properties attributed to the Jungian typology. However, they acknowledged that their negative findings make it impossible to decide whether it is Jung's hypothesis regarding the structure of typology which is incorrect or whether the Myers-Briggs Type Indicator fails to represent the typology in an adequate way. In discussing their results Stricker and Ross endorse the use of a wide variety of approaches for examining the Jungian typology hypothesis. One of these suggested was the factor analytic study of correlations between persons.

The present investigation is in accord with this latter suggestion. The availability of modern electronic computers allowed an examination of Jungian typology using the method of inverse factor analysis on a scale not possible heretofore.

The study inspects the hypothesis that individuals in their self-reports will order themselves into types postulated by Jung. It was anticipated that self-report Q-sorts of self-regarding propositions generated from *Psychological Types* would yield factors (clusters of persons) congruent with those postulated within the typology.

METHOD

Subjects

The *Ss* for the study were 99 male and female volunteers from an introductory psychology course at The Pennsylvania State University who routinely volunteer and receive extra credit in their psychology course work for their participation as subjects in research studies. There was a total of 64 males and 35 females. They were between the ages of 17 and 22, and came from a wide variety of curricula in the University.

The Q-Sort

One hundred self-regarding propositions were selected from a larger number generated from *Psychological Types* by three psychologists who studied Jung's description of a type and then formulated statements which they considered to be in accord with the type characterization. The following material, taken from Jung's volume, is given to illustrate the basis for writing self-regarding proposition of an introverted-thinking type.

His judgment appears cold, obstinate, arbitrary, and inconsiderate simply because he is related less to the object than the subject. (Jung, 1923, p. 485).

Hardly ever will he go out of his way to win anyone's appreciation especially if it be anyone of influence... In his own special province there are usually awkward experiences with his colleagues, he never knows how to win their favor; as a rule he only succeeds in showing them how entirely superfluous they are to him. (*ibid.*, p. 486).

He lets himself be brutalized and exploited in the most ignominious way, if only he can be left undisturbed in the pursuit of his ideas. (*ibid.*, p. 487).

In thinking out his problems to the utmost of his ability, he also complicates them, and constantly becomes entangled in every possible scruple. (*ibid.*, p. 487).

To people who judge him from afar, he appears prickly, inaccessible, haughty; frequently he may even seem soured as a result of his anti-social prejudices. (*ibid.*, p. 488).

That he's a poor teacher, because while teaching his thought is engaged with the actual material, and will not be satisfied with its mere presentation. (*ibid.*, p. 488).

With the intensification of his type, his convictions become all the more rigid and unbending. Foreign influences are eliminated; he becomes more unsympathetic to his peripheral world and therefore more dependent upon his intimates. (*ibid.*, p. 488.)

External facts are not the aim and origin of this thinking, although the introvert would often like to make it appear so. It begins in the subject and returns to the subject, although it may undertake the widest flights into the territory of the real and the actual. Hence, in the statement of new facts, its chief value is indirect, because new views rather than perception of new facts are its main concern. It formulates questions and creates theories; it opens up prospects and yields insights, but in the presence of facts it exhibits a reserved demeanor. Facts are collected as evidence or examples of a theory but never for their own sake . . . what apparently is of absolute paramount importance is the development and presentation of the subjective idea; that primordial symbolic image standing more or less darkly before the inner vision. Its aim, therefore is never concerned with an intellectual reconstruction of concrete actuality, but with the reshaping of their dim image into a resplendent idea. Its desire is to reach reality; its goal is to see how external facts fit into and fulfil, the framework of the idea; its actual creative power is proved by the fact that this thinking can also create that idea which, was not present in the external facts, is yet the best suitable abstract expression of them. Its task is accomplished when the idea it has fashioned seems to emerge so inevitably from the external facts that they actually prove its validity. (*ibid.*, p. 481).

Careful study of Jung's representations about the introverted-thinking type, part of which are given above, led to the construction of self-regarding propositions, some of which are presented as examples. 'I would enjoy being a logician'; 'I think clearest when left to myself'; 'I am more interested in theory than facts'; 'I would prefer to work on a job which allows me to work on my own ideas.' This general procedure was followed to produce propositions for each of Jung's types.

The 100 final propositions were selected from a larger pool of statements by two *E*s who agreed that these items best represented those discussed by Jung. The 100 statements in the Q-sort were made up of 12 statements representing the extroverted-thinking person, 12 statements representing the introverted-thinking person, 13 statements representing the introverted-feeling person, 12 statements representing the introverted-feeling person, 13 statements representing the extroverted-sensing person, 12 statements representing the introverted-sensing person, 13 statements representing the introverted-sensing person, 13 statements representing the extroverted-intuiting person, and 13 statements representing the introverted-intuiting person.[1]

Procedure

*S*s were gathered in groups of about 20 and assured about the confidentiality of their responses. Each *S* was given the 100 self-regarding propositions which were reproduced on cards. They were instructed to sort them into 11 piles along the dimension 'least like myself' to 'most like myself'. These 11 piles represented a forced normal distribution.

In addition to the Q-sort task, *S*s were also instructed to respond to some items providing demographic data. In this fashion *S*'s sex, birth-order, religion, family income and size of home community were recorded.

Statistical Procedure

The Q-sort data for 98 *S*s were transferred to data cards and a matrix of correlations between persons was generated. A principal components factor analysis was carried out and was rotated by a Varimax solution on an IBM 7074 computer.[2] While the Varimax solution imposes orthogonality on the factor structure which on Jung's hypothesis probably would not be orthogonal, the decision to seek an orthogonal rather than an oblique solution arose from the intent at first to seek uncorrelated clusters of persons (types) in the domain of *self-report*. That is, the effect was directed towards the identification of separate and distinct types.

In order to identify the characteristics of persons clustering together (types), correlations between factor scores and placements of 100 self-regarding propositions were computed. The identification of propositions

---

[1]The items are available from the authors.

[2]The original matrix of correlations, the unrotated and rotated matrices are available from the authors.

significantly related to the factors enabled an identification of the characteristics of the clusters of persons yielded in the factor analysis. While an *r* of 0.20 is required for significance at the 0.05 level, the relevant tables will include only those propositions correlating beyond 0.30.

Results and Discussion

The factor analysis accounted for 46.03 per cent of the total variance. In general, the criteria ordinarily given for attaining the simple structure were met: each row of the factor matrix had at least one zero; each column had a number of zeros exceeding the number of common factors; and for pairs of columns, there are adequate numbers of variables vanishing in one column but not in the other.

Eight factors were extracted which accounted for a total of 92 per cent of the common variance. The following discussion offers an analysis of the characteristics of each of the identifiable factors.

Factor I, Extroverted-feeling Type. This factor accounts for 19 per cent of the common variance. The items significantly related to Factor I are reported in Table

TABLE 1   *Self-Regarding Propositions Significantly Correlated With Factor I*

PROPOSITION	*r*	PROPOSITION	*r*
I think of myself as a person who is drawn to pretty displays	0.300	I think of myself as a person whose feelings about what is right and wrong differ from that of the majority	−0.303
I think of myself as a person who is a regular guy	0.324	I think of myself as a person who would prefer a job that allows me to develop new applications for things	−0.429
I think of myself as a person who is attracted to those people everybody likes.	0.400	I think of myself as a person who has a great respect for logical thinking	−0.373
I think of myself as a person who would enjoy reading warm human stories	0.550	I think of myself as a person who would enjoy being a logician	−0.349
I think of myself as a person who enjoys being with people who are enjoying themselves.	0.344	I think of myself as a person who has had a religious or mystical experience	−0.494
I think of myself as a person who would characterize myself as being warm and outgoing.	0.337	I think of myself as a person who likes games with complex rules which allow complicated manoeuvres	−0.362
I think of myself as a person who goes out of my way not to offend people	0.510	I think of myself as a person who would enjoy being a scientist	−0.470
I think of myself as a person who believes that people should be more concerned with enjoying life than trying to change it	0.376	I think of myself as a person who has some ideas which are so unique that it is hard to convey them to others	−0.343
I think of myself as a person who would enjoy social work	0.645	I think of myself as a person who believes that my life has symbolic meaning that transcends everyday activity	−0.407
I think of myself as a person who is very sensitive to how others are feeling	0.446		
I think of myself as a person who would enjoy being an inventor.	−0.515		

1. An examination of the table suggests that individuals clustering in Factor I report themselves as warm and outgoing, responding to feelings, enjoying warm stories, and interacting with people. These items suggest a correspondence with the extroverted-feeling type. The rejection of propositions requiring interest in problem-solving, logical thinking, working with ideas, and scientific careers support this interpretation.

Factor II, Introverted-thinking Type, A. This factor accounted for 11 per cent of the common variance. The items significantly related to Factor II are reported in Table 2. Individuals clustering on this factor report themselves as enjoying research, making new applications, problem solving, logical thinking, and science. The negative correlations suggest a rejection of interest in being sensitive to others' feelings. These individuals reject feelings as guides to behaviour and identify themselves as having little interest in pomp and pageantry or mystical and religious experiences. This factor suggests a person who can be characterized as being primarily the thinking-introverted type. Since another cluster of individuals is also identified further on as belonging to the thinking introverted type, this factor uses the additional designation, A.

It is of interest to note that Factors I and II appear to be, in part, reciprocals of

TABLE 2   *Self-Regarding Propositions Significantly Correlated With Factor II*

PROPOSITION	r	PROPOSITION	r
I think of myself as a person who would enjoy a job that allowed me to develop my inner intuitions.	0.442	I think of myself as a person who has some ideas which are so unique that it is hard to convey them to others	0.320
I think of myself as a person who would like to work on a research team so that I could share my ideas	0.388	I think of myself as a person who goes out of my way not to offend people	−0.356
I think of myself as a person who would enjoy being a trouble-shooter	0.434	I think of myself as a person who believes that some of the greatest truths of the world have been arrived at by revelation	−0.342
I think of myself as a person who would prefer a job that allows me to develop new applications for things.	0.402	I think of myself as a person who enjoys pomp and pageantry	−0.367
I think of myself as a person who prefers innovation to tradition.	0.306	I think of myself as a person who likes to experience beauty when I'm not in the company of others	−0.339
I think of myself as a person who believes that beauty is truth	0.390	I think of myself as a person who is deeply moved by religious services.	−0.484
I think of myself as a person who would prefer to work at a job which allows me to work on my own ideas	0.507	I think of myself as a person who is drawn to pretty displays	−0.485
I think of myself as a person who enjoys science fiction	0.439	I think of myself as a person for whom the effect of events upon myself is very important to me	−0.379
I think of myself as a person who would enjoy being a scientist	0.505	I think of myself as a person for whom simple landscape can trigger a picture of something very much more powerful inside of me	−0.351

each other. Many of the items accepted in one factor are rejected in the other.

Factor III, Extroverted-thinking Type.

This factor accounted for 16 per cent of the common variance. The propositions significantly related to Factor III are reported in Table 3. Individuals clustering on this factor endorse items reflecting interest in research and the sharing of ideas, enjoying other people, being warm and outgoing, and they reject items re-flecting general subjective experiences and self-examination. This cluster of individuals may be identified as the extroverted-thinking type.

It is of interest to note that there is a general pattern of extroversion reflected in Factors I and III which together account for the largest share of the common variance. These two types may represent the characteristics of the largest group in the population under examination here. Both Factors represent outgoing, other-directed orientations. They differ only in

TABLE 3   *Self-Regarding Propositions Significantly Correlated With Factor III*

PROPOSITION	r	PROPOSITION	r
I think of myself as a person who would like to work on a research team so that I could share my ideas .	-0.327	I think of myself as a person who enjoys a work of art that portrays an artistic inner life more than one which portrays realistic scenes . .	-0.435
I think of myself as a person who enjoys being with people who are enjoying themselves. . . .	0.307	I think of myself as a person whose feelings about what is right and wrong differ from that of the majority	-0.374
I think of myself as a person who would characterize myself as being warm and outgoing	0.373	I think of myself as a person who works in bursts rather than steadily	-0.382
I think of myself as a person who goes out of my way not to offend people	0.302	I think of myself as a person who finds it very difficult to convey my sudden insights to others and expect them to really understand	
I think of myself as a person who likes the sensation of participating in group sports.	0.500	them	-0.309
I think of myself as a person who is deeply moved by religious services.	0.440	I think of myself as a person who is more interested in theory than facts.	-0.421
I think of myself as a person who, although I do not show it well, strongly love my (wife; children; parents)	0.337	I think of myself as a person who would like to be a prophet or a seer	-0.315
I think of myself as a person who is a regular guy . . .	0.348	I think of myself as a person who often sees an inner meaning to events and things	-0.341
I think of myself as a person who would enjoy being a scientist . .	0.386	I think of myself as a person who enjoys observing my reations to drink	-0.420
I think of myself as a person who feels that if I were a painter I'd be an abstractionist (impressionist) .	-0.425	I think of myself as a person who has some ideas which are so unique that it is hard to convey them to	
I think of myself as a person who enjoys music which corresponds to my mood	-0.390	others	-0.36

that one operates through the thinking mode while the other operates through the feeling mode.

Factor IV, Introverted-thinking Type, B.

This factor accounted for 10 per cent of the common variance. The items significantly related to Factor IV are reported in Table 4. These individuals endorse items which reflect difficulty and lack of productivity in communicating with others. They seem to feel that their experiences cannot be conveyed to others, nor do they find it worthwhile to let others know how they feel. They also endorse interest in invention, trouble-shooting, and facts. These together with the rejection of subjective sensitivities suggest that this factor reflects a second kind

TABLE 4 *Self-Regarding Propositions Significantly Correlated With Factor IV*

PROPOSITION	r	PROPOSITION	r
I think of myself as a person who would enjoy being an inventor.	0.301	I think of myself as a person who feels that there is much more to a painting than that which meets the eye	−0.407
I think of myself as a person who would enjoy being a trouble-shooter	0.305	I think of myself as a person who would characterize myself as being warm and outgoing	−0.373
I think of myself as a person whose moods aren't affected by the behaviour of others	0.301	I think of myself as a person who feels that half the fun of thinking is in communicating my ideas to others	−0.335
I think of myself as a person who finds that conversation with others rarely generates any of my new thoughts	0.439	I think of myself as a person who believes that beauty is truth	−0.370
I think of myself as a person who feels that my mental life would not be seriously affected if I have no sense organs (eyes, ears, etc.)	0.366	I think of myself as a person whose perception of detail is marked	−0.311
I think of myself as a person who feels strongly about things but does not often communicate those feelings to others	0.481	I think of myself as a person who would enjoy studying philosophy	−0.304
I think of myself as a person who believes that an individual's sensual experiences cannot really be conveyed to others.	0.395	I think of myself as a person who often sees an inner meaning to events and things	−0.567
I think of myself as a person who doesn't often find it worthwhile to let others know how I feel about things	0.458	I think of myself as a person who enjoys music which corresponds to my mood	−0.355
I think of myself as a person who enjoys science fiction	0.373	I think of myself as a person who believes that my life has a symbolic meaning that transcends everyday activity	−0.454
I think of myself as a person who would enjoy being a scientist	0.310		
I think of myself as a person who enjoys a work of art that portrays an artistic inner life more than one which portrays realistic scenes	−0.405	I think of myself as a person for whom simply landscape can trigger a picture of something very much more powerful inside of me	−0.334

of introverted thinking. They, however, differ from those individuals clustering in Factor II in that the latter appear to direct their activity toward abstract events while those who are represented in this factor appear to be more practically oriented. Individuals clustering in Factor II seem to have a more aesthetic satisfaction in their thinking activities, while individuals clustering in Factor IV might view their own thinking in a more pragmatic fashion.

who characterizes himself as a warm and sensitive person; the other theme is one of an orientation towards sensation in endorsing interest in pomp and pageantry, pleasurable activities, convivial drinking, and perception for detail. These themes seem to correspond with the extroverted-sensing type. It is of further interest to note that the negative correlations with this factor seem to explicitly reject thinking, feeling, and intuitive ways of experiencing.

Factor V, Extrovered-sensing Type.

This factor accounted for 10 per cent of the common variance. The propositions significantly related to Factor V are reported in Table 5. They consist of two themes: one is of the extroverted individual who enjoys being with others, who feels that the personal factor is important,

Factor VI, Extroverted-intuitive Type.

This factor account for 6 per cent of the common variance. The items significantly related to Factor VI are reported in Table 6. This type of person endorses items which suggest that some of his ideas are very unique, that he relies on insight, that he has a knack for solving problems,

TABLE 5 *Self-Regarding Propositions Significantly Correlated With Factor V*

PROPOSITION	r	PROPOSITION	r
I think of myself as a person who enjoys drinking with a convivial group	0.617	I think of myself as a person who enjoys science fiction . . .	0.307
I think of myself as a person who is attracted to those people everybody likes.	0.345	I think of myself as a person who enjoys observing my reactions to drink	0.463
I think of myself as a person who enjoys being with people who are enjoying themselves. . .	0.492	I think of myself as a person who seeks out activities which give me pleasure	0.337
I think of myself as a person who believes that the personal factor is the most important in any plan .	0.386	I think of myself as a person who has a knack for solving problems that others can't	−0.320
I think of myself as a person who would characterize myself as being warm and outgoing	0.306	I think of myself as a person who feels strongly about things but does not often communicate those feelings to others	−0.320
I think of myself as a person whose perception of detail is marked . .	0.302	I think of myself as a person who thinks most clearly when left to myself	−0.444
I think of myself as a person who enjoys pomp and pageantry . .	0.321	I think of myself as a person who doesn't often find it worthwhile to let others know how I feel about things	−0.385
I think of myself as a person who would enjoy social work . . .	0.326		
I think of myself as a person who is a regular guy.	0.520		

TABLE 6   *Self-Regarding Propositions Significantly Correlated With Factor VI*

PROPOSITION	r	PROPOSITION	r
I think of myself as a person who has some ideas which are so unique that it is hard to convey them to others	0.301	I think of myself as a person who has a knack for solving problems that others can't	0.406
I think of myself as a person who feels it's better to act quickly if an idea occurs rather than thinking about it too much	0.304	I think of myself as a person whose mood depends upon my surroundings	−0.631
I think of myself as a person who would enjoy being a trouble-shooter	0.325	I think of myself as a person who feels strongly about things but does not often communicate those feelings to others	−0.510
I think of myself as a person who would characterize myself as being warm and outgoing	0.378	I think of myself as a person who doesn't often find it worthwhile to let others know how I feel about things	−0.367
I think of myself as a person who feels that half the fun of thinking is in communicating my ideas to others	0.307	I think of myself as a person for whom the effect of events upon myself is very important to me . . .	−0.307

enjoys communicating ideas to others, and is warm and outgoing. The items correlating negatively on this factor suggests that this type of person is not dependent on his surroundings for his mood, and who enjoys communicating with other people. It seems as if we have a primarily extroverted person who has an intuitive approach to problems of the real world which he has been able to solve and would like to communicate to others.

Factor VII and Factor VIII.   Factor VII accounts for 8 per cent of the common variance and Factor VIII accounts for 10 per cent of the common variance. Neither of these factors seemed to present a clearcut or readily identifiable type. In fact, there were mixtures of types and contradictory themes. In terms of the Jungian typology then, these factors were uninterpretable.

An analysis of the demographic variables was conducted by correlating the responses on each variable with each of the six interpretable factors. The correlations between sex of S and factor scores was the only set of correlations that seemed to be significant. These correlations are presented in Table 7.

The high correlation between sex and Factor I suggests that a large proportion of Ss loading on this factor were female. This finding is in accord with Jung's assertion that the feeling-extrovert person is

TABLE 7   *Correlations Between Sex and Factor Loadings*

FACTOR	r
I	−0.58[1]
II	−0.54
III	−0.02
IV	0.25
V	−0.16
VI	−0.03

[1]An r of 0.16 is required for significance at the 0.05 level; and when the r is negative it indicates that a high proportion of females are in the group.

more commonly a woman than a man (Jung, 1923, p. 448).

Factors II and IV, both of which are introverted-thinking types are more commonly males while the extroverted-thinking type does not seem to be correlated with sex.

There were some significant correlations between curricula and factor scores though these are spurious because there are very high correlations between sex and curricula. Almost all of these subjects majoring in science, for example, were male and this made it impossible to examine the correlations between sex and factor scores and curriculum and factor scores in a differential fashion. Though it cannot be argued from these findings that sex is a more basic variable than curricula in a correlation with factor scores it does seem reasonable to make this assumption and correlations between curricula and factor scores will not be reported.

The results of this study offer support for the hypothesis that individuals in their self-reports order themselves into types postulated by Jung. Five types clearly emerged. Those types postulated to exist which did not emerge in the population under study here were the introverted-feeling type, the introverted sensing type, and the introverted-intuiting type. There are a number of ways of accounting for the absence of these three types. One possibility is that these types do not exist in the population under study. That is, clusters of these kinds of young persons are not found in a large state university in rural surroundings attended heavily by members of the middle class. Further work on other campuses serving other sectors of the population might well identify these absent types. Another reason for the non-emergence of all of Jung's postulated types might be the fact that individuals in their self-reports might be reluctant or unable to identify themselves with the introverted side in the feeling, sensing and intuiting modes. It may be the case that personality description at a level different from self-report would yield such clusters of persons. A further possibility is that the instrument which was employed was not adequate for the identification and discrimination of these absent types. The self-regarding propositions might not have included a sample of statements which adequately reflected them.

On the whole, the results offer support for Jung's typology and for the utilization of Q-sort methodology representing clusters of persons within the Jungian system. These results provide an opportunity for further research in associating extent of membership in types with a wide range of other variables of interest to psychologists.

References

Eysenck, H. J. (1953). *The structure of human personality.* New York: Wiley.

Gray, H. (1948). Jung's psychological types: meaning and consistency of the question-naire. *J. gen. Psychol.* **37**, 177–185.

Jung, C. G. (1923). *Psychological types.* London: Kegan Paul, Trench, Trubner & Co.

Myers, I. B. (1962). Inferences as to the dichotomous nature of Jung's types. *Amer. Psychologist*, **17**, 364. (Abstract)

Stephenson, W. (1939). Methodological consideration of Jung's typology. *J. ment. Sci.* **85**, 185–205.

Stricker, L. & Ross, J. (1964). An assessment of some structural properties of the Jungian personality typology, *J. abnormal soc. Psychol.* **68**, 62–71.

Social Psychological Theories: Adler, Fromm, Horney, and Sullivan

Before Alfred Adler, the founder of individual psychology, came to the United States to live in 1935, he had been asked by Carl Murchison to summarize his viewpoint in a volume entitled *Psychologies of 1930*. This succinct piece written for an audience of psychologists is reprinted here because it reveals almost better than any of his longer writings the full range of Adler's thought.

It was Adler who emphasized order of birth as a determiner of personality. He believed that the oldest, middle, and youngest children in a family will develop different personalities because they have different social experiences. Although this thesis was tested many times in the past, it was not until Stanley Schachter's work was published that impressive positive confirmations of the hypothesis were obtained. Stimulated by Schachter's findings many other psychologists have investigated correlates of birth order, and it has been shown that a wide variety of personality dispositions and abilities are associated with birth order. It is almost certain that this will continue to be an area of active research in personality. The as yet unanswered but important question is what are the childhood experiences and parental behaviors that are differentially associated with each birth order and how do they affect personality and social development?

Fromm continues to be a prolific and popular writer on many topics relating to his version of psychoanalysis. He is one of the most able of those theoreticians who have attempted to broaden orthodox psychoanalytic theorizing to encompass more fully the role of society and social organization. A selection from one of his earlier writings is reprinted here because it demonstrates as clearly and eloquently as anything that Fromm has written how society shapes a person so that he gets personal satisfaction from doing what is good for society. The nature of social character, a key concept in Fromm's thinking, is delineated in this paper. In addition, the emphasis Fromm places on society and the interrelationship between the individual and society as a factor in social change is clearly presented.

Horney consistently maintained that neurosis is geared to society, and that different types of societies will produce different types of neurosis. The selection from her writings that is presented here makes this point very clearly. She selects, as an example to show the nature of the relationship between culture and neurosis, the problem of competition in American society. From the emphasis on competition, success, failure, and rivalry develops neurotic feelings of inferiority that Horney says ". . . is one of the most common psychic disorders of our time and culture." The ideas presented in this paper stem from her clinical experience and should be studied using evidence collected in nonclinical settings.

Sullivan's writings are characterized by being discursive, polemical, and colloquial. These characteristics may be due to the fact that much of what appears in print under his authorship was not written but spoken. The writings, for the most part, are edited transcriptions of tape recordings of lectures. Almost any selection from Sullivan's "writings" conveys to the reader the style of his thought and expression. The chapter that has been reprinted here deals with a critical period in the life of the individual. How he gets through this period of adolescence pretty much determines, in Sullivan's opinion, how he will get along in society the rest of his life.

It will also be noted in this selection that Sullivan assumes the role of social critic. This is a typical role for him. Sullivan was forthright in condemning what he regarded as inhuman in society. Like other social psychological theorists, he believed that an imperfect society breeds imperfect people—ergo, in order to improve man's character it is necessary to improve the society in which his character develops.

1. Individual Psychology

ALFRED ADLER

The point of departure upon this line of research seems to me to be given in a work entitled ("The aggression drive in life and in neurosis"), published in 1908 and included in a collective volume, *To Cure and Form* (1). Even at that time I was engaged in a lively controversy with the Freudian school, and in opposition to them, I devoted my attention in that paper to the *relation* of the child and the adult to the demands of the external world. I tried to present, howbeit in a very inadequate fashion, the multifarious forms of attack and defense, of modification of the self and of the environment, effected by the human mind, and launched on the momentous departure of repudiating the sexual aetiology of mental phenomena as fallacious. In a vague way I saw even then that the impulsive life of man suffers variations and contortions, curtailments and exaggerations, *relative to the kind and degree of its aggressive power.* In accordance with the present outlook of individual psychology, I should rather say: relative to the way the power of co-operation has developed in childhood. The Freudian school, which at that time was purely sexual psychology, has accepted this primitive-impulse theory without any reservations, as some of its adherents readily admit.

I myself was too deeply interested in the problem of what determined the various forms of attack upon the outer world. From my own observations, and supported by those of older authors, also perhaps guided by the concept of a place of least resistance, I arrived at the notion that inferior organs might be responsible for the feeling of psychic inferiority, and in the year 1907 recorded my studies concerning this subject in a volume entitled *Study of organ inferiority and its psychical compensation* (2). The purpose of the work was to show that children born with hereditary organic weaknesses exhibit not only a physical necessity to compensate for the defect, and tend to overcompensate, but that the entire nervous system, too, may take part in this compensation; especially the mind, as a factor of life, may suffer a striking exaggeration in the direction of the defective function (breathing, eating, seeing, hearing, talking, moving, feeling, or even thinking), so that this overemphasized function may

We are grateful to H. L. Ansbacher for his help in translating and editing the references.

become the mainspring of life, in so far as a *"successful* compensation" occurs. This compensatory increase, which, as I showed in the above-mentioned book, has originated and continued the development of a human race blessed with inferior organs, may in favourable cases affect also the endocrine glands, as I have pointed out, and is regularly reflected in the condition of the sexual glands, their inferiority and their compensation—a fact which seemed to me to suggest some connection between individual traits and physical heredity. The link between organic inferiority and psychic effects, which to this day cannot be explained in any other way, but merely assumed, was evident to me in the mind's experience of the inferior organ, by which the former is plunged into a *constant feeling of inferiority*. Thus I could introduce the body and its degree of excellence as a factor in mental development.

Experts will certainly not fail to see that the whole of our psychiatry has tended in this direction, both in part before that time and quite definitely thereafter. The works of Kretschmer, Jaensch, and many others rest upon the same basis. But they are content to regard the psychic minus quantities as congenital epiphenomena of the physical organic inferiority, without taking account of the fact that it is the *immediate* experience of physical disability which is the key to the failures of performance, as soon as the demands of the outer world and the creative power of the child lead it into "wrong" alleys and force upon it a one-sided interest. What I treated there as failure appeared to me later as a premature curtailment of the cooperative faculty, the social impulse, and a greatly heightened interest for the self.

This work also furnished a test for organic inferiority. As proofs of inferiority it mentions insufficient development of physical form, of reflexes, of functions, or retardation of the latter. Defective development of the nerves in connection with the organ and of the brain-centers involved was also considered. But the sort of compensation which would under favorable circumstances occur in any one of these parts was always insisted upon as a decisive factor. A valuable by-product of this study, and one which has not yet been sufficiently appreciated, was the discovery of the significance of the birthmark for the fact that the embryonic development at that point or in that segment had not been quite successful. Schmidt, Eppinger, and others have found this insight correct in many respects. I feel confident that in the study of cancer, too, as I suggested in this connection, the segmental naevus will someday furnish a clue to the aetiology of carcinoma.

In trying thus to bridge the chasm between physical and mental developments by a theory that vindicated in some measure the doctrine of heredity, I did not fail to remark explicitly somewhere that the stresses engendered by the relation between the congenitally inferior organ and the demands of the external world, though, of course, they were greater than those which related to approximately normal organs, were none the less mitigated, to some degree, by the variability of the world's demands; so that one really had to regard them as merely relative. I repudiated the notion of the hereditary character of psychological traits, in that I referred their origin to the various intensities of organic functions in each individual. Afterwards I added to this the fact that children, in cases of abnormal development, are without any guidance, so that their activity (aggression) may develop in unaccountable ways. The inferior organs offer a temptation but by no means a necessity for neuroses or other mental miscarriages. Herewith I established the problem of the education of such children, with prophylaxis as its aim, on a perfectly sound footing. Thus the family history, with all its plus and minus factors, became an index to the serious difficulties which might be expected and combatted in early childhood. As I said at that time, a hostile attitude toward the world might be the result of excessive stresses which must express themselves somehow in specific characteristics.

In this way I was confronted with the problem of character. There had been a good deal of nebulous speculations on this subject. Character was almost universally regarded as a congenital entity. My conviction that the doctrine of congenital mental traits was erroneous helped me considerably. I came to realize that characters were guiding threads, *ready attitudes* for the solution of the problems of life. The idea of an "arrangement" of all psychical activities became more and more convincing. Therewith I had reached the ground which to this day has been the foundation of individual psychology, the belief that *all psychical phenomena originate in the particular creative force of the individual, and are expressions of his personality.*

But who is this driving force behind the personality? And why do we find mostly individuals whose psychological upbuilding was not successful? Might it be that, after all, certain congenitally defective impulses, i.e., congenital weaknesses, decided the fate of our mental development, as almost all psychiatrists supposed? Is it due to a divine origin that an individual, that the human race may progress at all?

But I had realized the fact that children who were born with defective organs or afflicted by injuries early in life, go wrong in the misery of their existence, constantly deprecate themselves, and, usually, to make good this deficiency, behave differently all their lives from what might be expected of normal people. I took another step, and discovered that children may be artificially placed in the same straits as if their organs were defective. If we make their work in very early life so hard that even their relatively normal organs are not equal to it, then they are in the same distress as those with defective physique, and from the same unbearable condition of stress they will give wrong answers as soon as life puts their preparation to any test. Thus I found two further categories of children who are apt to develop an abnormal sense of inferiority—*pampered children and hated children.*

To this period of my complete defection from Freud's point of view, and absolute independence of thought, date such works as *The psychic root of trigeminal neuralgia* (3) in which I attempted to show how, besides cases of organic origin, there were also certain ones in which excessive partial increase of blood-pressure, caused by emotions such as rage, may under the influence of severe inferiority feelings give rise to physical changes. This was followed by a study, decisive for the development of individual psychology, entitled *The problem of distance* (4), wherein I demonstrated that every individual, by reason of his degree of inferiority feeling, hesitated before the solution of one of the three great problems of life, stops or circumvents, and preserves his attitude in a state of exaggerated tension through psychological symptoms. As the three great problems of life, to which everyone must somehow answer by his attitude, I named: (*a*) society, (*b*) vocation, (*c*) love. Next came a work on *The unconscious* (5), wherein I tried to prove that upon deeper inspection there appears no contrast between the conscious and the unconscious, that both cooperate for a higher purpose, that our thoughts and feelings become conscious as soon as we are faced with a difficulty, and unconscious as soon as our personality-value requires it. At the same time I tried to set forth the fact that that which other authors had used for their explanations under the name of *conflict, sense of guilt,* or *ambivalence* was to be regarded as symptomatic of a *hesitant attitude*, for the purpose of evading the solution of one of the problems of life. Ambivalence and polarity of emotional or moral traits present themselves as an attempt at a multiple solution or rejection of a problem.

This and some other works dating from the time of the self-emancipation of individual psychology have been published in a volume bearing the title *The practice and theory of individual psychology* (6). This was also the time when our great Stanley Hall turned away from Freud and ranged himself with the supporters of individual psychology, together with many other American scholars who popularized the "inferiority and superiority complexes" throughout their whole country.

I have never failed to call atention to the fact that the whole human race is blessed with deficient organs, deficient for coping with nature; that consequently the whole race is constrained ever to seek the way which will bring it into some sort of harmony with the exigencies of life; and that we make mistakes along the way, very much like those we can observe in pampered or neglected children. I have quoted one case especially, where the errors of our civilization may influence the development of an individual, and that is the case of the underestimation of women in our society. From the sense of female inferiority, which most people, men and women alike, possess, both sexes have derived an overstrained desire for masculinity, a superiority complex which is often extremely harmful, a will to conquer all difficulties of life in the masculine fashion, which I have called the *masculine protest*.

Now I began to see clearly in every psychical phenomenon the *striving for superiority*. It runs parallel to physical growth. It is an intrinsic necessity of life itself. It lies at the root of all solutions of life's problems, and is manifested in the way in which we meet these problems. All our functions follow its direction; rightly or wrongly they strive for conquest, surety, increase. The impetus from minus to plus is never-ending. The urge from "below" to "above" never ceases. Whatever premises all our philosophers and psychologists dream of—self-preservation, pleasure principle, equalization—all these are but vague representations, attempts to express the great upward drive. The history of the human race points in the same direction. Willing, thinking, talking, seeking after rest, after pleasure, learning, understanding, work and love, betoken the essence of this eternal melody. Whether one thinks or acts more wisely or less, one always moves along the lines of that upward tendency. In our right and wrong conceptions of life and its problems, in the successful or the unsuccessful solution of any question, this striving for perfection is uninterruptedly at work. And even where foolishness and imbecility, inexperience, seem to belie the fact of any striving to conquer some defect, or tend to depreciate it, yet the will to conquer is really operative. From this net-work which in the last analysis is simply given with the relationship "man-cosmos," no one may hope to escape. For even if anyone wanted to escape, yet, even if he *could* escape, he would still find himself in the general system, striving "upward," from "below." This does not only fix a fundamental category of thought, the structure of our reason, but what is more, it yields *the fundamental fact of our life.*

The origin of humanity and the ever repeated beginning of infant life rubs it in with every psychic act: "Achieve! Arise! Conquer!" This feeling is never absent, this longing for the abrogation of every imperfection. In the search for relief, in Faustian wrestling against the forces of nature, rings always the basic chord: "I relinquish thee not, thou bless me withal." The unreluctant search for truth, the ever unsatisfied longing for solution of the problems of life, belongs to this hankering after perfection of some sort.

This, now, appeared to me as the fundamental law of all spiritual expression: that the total melody is to be found again in every one of its parts, as a greatest common measure—in every individual craving for power, for victory over the difficulties of life.

And therewith I recognized a further premise of my scientific proceeding, one which agreed with the formulations of older philosophers, but conflicted with the standpoint of modern psychology: *the unity of the personality*. This, however, was not merely a premise, but could to a certain extent be demonstrated. As Kant has said, we can never understand a person if we do not presuppose his unity. Individual psychology can now add to that: this unity, which we must presuppose, is the work of the individual, which must always continue in the way it once found toward victory.

These were the considerations which led me to the conviction that early in life, in the first four or five years, a *goal* is set for the need and drive of psychical development, a goal toward which all its currents flow. Such a goal has not only the function of determining a direction, of promising security, power, perfection, but it is also of its essence and of the essence of the mind that this portentous goal should awaken feelings and emotions through that which it promises them. Thus the individual mitigates its sense of weakness in the anticipation of its redemption.

Here again we see the meaninglessness of congenitial psychic traits. Not that we could deny them. We have no possible way of getting at them. Whoever would draw conclusions from the results is making matters too simple. He overlooks the thousand and one influences after birth, and fails to see the power that lies in the necessity of acquiring a goal.

The staking of a goal compels the unity of the personality in that it draws the stream of all spiritual activity into its definite direction. Itself a product of the common, fundamental sense of inferiority—a sense derived from genuine weakness, not from any comparison with others—the goal of victory in turn forces the direction of all powers and possibilities toward itself. Thus every phase of psychical activity can be seen within one frame, as though it were the end of some earlier phase and the beginning of a succeeding one. This was a further contribution of individual psychology to modern psychology in general—that it insisted absolutely on the indispensability of *finalism* for the understanding of all psychological phenomena. No longer could causes, powers, instincts, impulses, and the like serve as explanatory principles, but the final goal alone. Experiences, traumata, sexual-development mechanisms could not yield us an explanation, but the perspective in which these had been regarded, the individual way of seeing them, which subordinates all life to the ultimate goal.

This final aim, abstract in its purpose of assuring superiority, fictitious in its task of conquering all the difficulties of life, must now appear in concrete form in order to meet its task in actuality. Deity in its widest sense, it is apperceived by the childish imagination, and under the exigencies of hard reality, as victory over men, over difficult enterprises, over social or natural limitations. It appears in one's attitude toward others, toward one's vocation, toward the opposite sex. Thus we find concrete single purposes, such as:

to operate as a member of the community or to dominate it, to attain security and triumph in one's chosen career, to approach the other sex or to avoid it. We may always trace in these special purposes *what sort of meaning the individual has found in his existence*, and how he proposes to realize that meaning.

If, then, the final goal established in early childhood exerts such an influence for better or worse upon the development of the given psychical forces, our next question must be: What are the sources of the individuality which we find in final aims? Could we not quite properly introduce another causal factor here? What brings about the differences of individual attitudes, if one and the same aim of superiority actuates everyone?

Speaking of this last question, let me point out that our human language is incapable of rendering all the qualities within a superiority goal and of expressing its innumerable differences. Certainty, power, perfection, deification, superiority, victory, etc., are but poor attempts to illumine its endless variants. Only after we have comprehended the partial expressions which the final goal effects, are we in any position to determine specific differences.

If there is any causal factor in the psychical mechanism, it is the common and often excessive sense of inferiority. But this continuous mood is only activating a drive, and does not reveal the way to compensation and overcompensation. Under the pressure of the first years of life there is no kind of philosophical reflection. There are only impressions, feelings, and a desire to renew the pleasurable ones and exclude those which are painful. For this purpose all energies are mustered, until motion of some sort results. Here, however, training or motion of any sort forces the establishment of an end. There is no motion without an end. And

so, in this way, a final goal becomes fixed which promises satisfaction. Perhaps, if one wanted to produce hypotheses, one might add: Just as the body approximates to an ideal form which is posited with the germ plasm, so does the mind, as a part of the total life. Certainly it is perfectly obvious that the soul ((mind— *The psychic organ*) exhibits some systematic definite tendency.

From the time of these formulations of individual psychology dates my book, *The neurotic constitution* (7), which introduced *finalism* into psychology with especial emphasis. At the same time I continued to trace the connection between organic inferiority and its psychological consequences, in trying to show how in such cases the goal of life is to be found in the type of overcompensation and consequent errors. As one of these errors I mentioned particularly the *masculine protest*, developed under the pressure of a civilization which has not yet freed itself from its overestimation of the masculine principle nor from an abuse of antithetic points of view. The imperfection of childish modes of realizing the fictitious ideal was also mentioned here as the chief cause for the differences in style of living—the unpredictable character of childish expression, which always moves in the uncontrollable *realm of error*.

By this time, the system of individual psychology was well enough established to be applied to certain special problems. *The problem of homosexuality* (8) exhibited that perversion was a neurotic construct erroneously made out of early childhood impressions, and recorded researches and findings which are published at greater length in *The handbook of normal and pathological physiology* (9). Uncertainty in the sexual rôle, overestimation of the opposite sex, fear of the latter, and a craving for easy, irresponsible successes proved to be the inclining but by no means constraining factors. Uncertainty in the solution of the erotic problem and fear of failure in this direction lead to wrong or abnormal functioning.

More and more clearly I now beheld the way in which the varieties of failure could be understood. In all human failure, in the waywardness of children, in neurosis and neuropsychosis, in crime, suicide, alcoholism, morphinism, cocainism, in sexual perversion, in fact in all nervous symptoms, we may read lack of the proper degree of *social feeling*. In all my former work I had employed the idea of the individual's attitude toward society as the main consideration. The demands of society, not as of a stable institution but as of a living, striving, victory-seeking mass, were always present in my thoughts. The total accord of this striving and the influence it must exert on each individual had always been one of my main themes. Now I attained somewhat more clarity in the matter. However we may judge people, whatever we try to understand about them, what we aim at when we educate, heal, improve, condemn—we base it always on the same principle: social feeling! cooperation! Anything that we estimate as valuable, good, right, and normal, we estimate simple in so far as it is "virtue" from the point of view of an ideal society. The individual, ranged in a community which can preserve itself only through cooperation as a human society, becomes a part of this great whole through socially enforced division of labor, through association with a member of the opposite sex, and finds his task prescribed by this society. And not only his task, but also his preparation and ability to perform it.

The unequivocally given fact of our organic inferiority on the face of this earth necessitates social solidarity. The need of protection of women during pregnancy and confinement, the prolonged helplessness of childhood, gains the aid of others. The preparation of the child for a complicated, but protective and therefore necessary civilization and labor requires the cooperation of society. The need of security in our personal existence leads automatically to a cultural modification of our impulses and emotions and to our individual attitude of friendship, social intercourse, and love. The social life of man emanates inevitably from the man-cosmos relation, and makes every person a creature and a creator of society.

It is a gratuitous burden to science to ask whether the social instinct is congenital or acquired, as gratuitous as the question of congenital instincts of any sort. We can see only the results of an evolution. And if we are to be permitted a question at all concerning the beginnings of that evolution, it is only this— whether anything can be evolved at all for which no possibilities are in any way given before birth. This possibility exists, as we may see through the results of development, in the case of human beings. The fact that our sense organs behave the way they do, that through them we may acquire *impressions* of the outer world, may combine these physically and mentally in ourselves, shows our connection with the cosmos. That trait we have in common with all living creatures. What distinguishes man from other organisms, however, is the fact that he must conceive his superiority goal in the social sense as a part of a total achievement. The reasons for this certainly lie in the greater need of the human individual and in the consequent greater mobility of his body and mind, which forces him to find a firm vantage point in the chaos of life.

But because of this enforced sociability, our life presents only such problems which require *ability to cooperate* for their solution. To hear, see, or speak "correctly," means to lose one's self completely in another or in a situation, to become *identified* with him or with it. The capacity for identification, which alone makes us capable of friendship, human love, pity, vocation, and love, is the basis of the social sense and can be practiced and exercised only in conjunction with others. In this intended assimilation of another person or of a situation not immediately given, lies the whole meaning of comprehension. And in the course of this identification we are able to conjure up all sorts of feelings, emotions, and affects, such as we experience not only in dreams but also in waking life, in neurosis and psychosis. It is always the fixed style of life, the ultimate ideals, that dominates and selects. The style of life is what makes our experiences reasons for our attitude, that calls up these feelings and determines conclusions in accordance with its own purposes. Our very identification with the ultimate ideal makes us optimistic, pessimistic, hesitant, bold, selfish, or altruistic.

The tasks which are presented to an individual, as well as the means of their performance, are conceived and formulated within the framework of society. No one, unless he is deprived of his mental capacities, can escape from this frame. *Only within this framework is psychology possible at all.* Even if we add for our own time the aids of civilization and the socially determined pattern of our examples, we still find ourselves confronted with the same unescapable conditions.

From this point of vantage we may look back. As far as we can reasonably determine, it appears that after the fourth or fifth year of life the style of life has been fashioned as a prototype, with its particular way of seizing upon life, its strategy for conquering it, its degree of ability to cooperate. These foundations of every individual development do not alter, unless perchance some harmful errors of construction are recognized by the subject and corrected. Whoever has not acquired in childhood the necessary degree of social sense, will not have it

later in life, except under the abovementioned special conditions. No amount of bitter experience can change his style of life, *as long as he has not gained understanding.* The whole work of education, cure, and human progress can be furthered only along lines of better comprehension.

There remains only one question: What influences are harmful and what beneficial in determining differences in the style of life, i.e., in the capacity for cooperation?

Here, in short, we touch upon the matter of preparation for cooperation. It is evident, of course, that deficiences of the latter become most clearly visible when the individual's capacity to cooperate is put to the test. As I have shown above, life does not spare us these tests and preliminary trials. We are always on trial, in the development of our sense organs, in our attitude toward others, our understanding of others, in our morals, our philosophy of life, our political position, our attitude toward the welfare of others, toward love and marriage, in our aesthetic judgments, in our whole behavior. As long as one is not put to any test, as long as one is without any trials or problems, one may doubt one's own status as a fellow of the community. But as soon as a person is beset by any problem of existence, which, as I have demonstrated, always involves cooperative ability, then it will unfailingly become apparent—as in a geographical examination—how far his preparation for cooperation extends.

The first social situation that confronts a child is its relation to its mother, from the very first day. By her educational skill the child's interest in another person is first awakened. If she understands how to train this interest in the direction of cooperation, all the congenital and acquired capacities of the child will converge in the direction of social sense. If she binds the child to herself exclusively, life will bear for it the meaning that all other persons are to be excluded as much as possible. Its position in the world is thereby rendered difficult, as difficult as that of defective or neglected children. All these grow up in a hostile world and develop a low degree of cooperative sense. Often in such cases there results utter failure to adjust to the father, brothers and sisters, or more distant persons. If the father fails to penetrate the circle of the child's interest, or if by reason of exaggerated rivalry the brothers and sisters are excluded, or if because of some social short-coming or prejudice the remoter environment is ruled out of its sphere, then the child will encounter serious trouble in acquiring a healthy social sense. In all cases of failure later in life it will be quite observable that they are rooted in this early period of infancy. The question of responsibility will naturally have to be waived there, since the debtor is unable to pay what is required of him.

Our findings in regard to these errors and erroneous deductions of early childhood, which have been gathered from a contemplation of this relation complex which individual psychology reveals, are exceedingly full. They are recorded in many articles in the *International journal of individual psychology* (10), *Individual psychology in the school* (11), and in *Science of Living* (12). These works deal with problems of waywardness, neurosis and psychosis, criminality, suicide, drunkenness, and sexual perversion. Problems of society, vocation, and love have been included in the scope of these studies. In *The technique of individual psychology* (13) I have published a detailed account of a case of fear and compulsion neurosis.

Individual psychology considers the essence of therapy to lie in making the patient aware of his lack of cooperative power, and to convince him of the origin of this lack in early childhood maladjustments. What passes during this process is no small matter; his power of cooperation is enhanced by collaboration with the doctor. His "inferiority complex" is revealed as erroneous. Courage and optimism are awakened. And the "meaning of life" dawns upon him as the fact that proper meaning must be given to life.

This sort of treatment may be begun at any point in the spiritual life. The following three points of departure have recommended themselves to me, among others: (*a*) to infer some of the patient's situation from his place in the order of births, since each successive child usually has a somewhat different position from the others; (*b*) to infer from his earliest childhood recollections some dominant interest of the individual, since the creative tendency of the imagination always produces fragments of the life ideal (*Lebensstl*); (*c*) to apply the individualistic interpretation to the dream-life of the patient, through which one may discover in what particular way the patient, guided by the style-of-life ideal, conjures up emotions and sensations contrary to common sense, in order to be able to carry out his style of life more successfully.

If one seems to have discovered the guiding thread of the patient's life, it remains to test this discovery through a great number of expressive gestures on his part. Only a perfect coincidence of the whole and all the parts gives one the right to say: I understand. And then the examiner himself will always have the feeling that, if he had grown up under the same misapprehensions, if he had harbored the same ideal, had the same notions concerning the meaning of life, if he had acquired an equally low degree of social sense, he would have acted and lived in an "almost" similar manner.

References

1. Adler, A. Der Aggressionstrieb im Leben und in der Neurose. (The aggression drive in life and in neurosis.) *Fortschr. Med.*, 1908, **26**, 577–584. Reprinted in *Heilen und Bilden*. 3rd ed. Munich: Bergmann, 1928. Pp. 33–42. Partial transl. & comments in *The individual psychology of Alfred Adler*. New York: Basic Books, 1956. Pp. 30–39.

2. _____. *Studie über Minderwertigkeit von Organen*. Vienna: Urban & Schwarzenberg, 1907. Transl.: *Study of organ inferiority and its psychical compensation*. New York: Nerv. Ment. Dis. Publ. Co., 1917.

3. _____. Die psychische Behandlung der Trigeminusneuralgie. (The psychic treatment of trigeminal neuralgia.) *Zbl. Psychoanal.*, 1910, **1**, 10–29. Transl. in *The practice and theory of individual psychology*. Totowa, N. J.: Littlefield, Adams & Co., 1968. Pp. 78–99.

4. _____. Das Problem der Distanz. (The problem of distance.) *Z. Indiv. Psychol.*, 1914, **1**, 8–16. Transl. in *The practice and theory of individual psychology*. Totowa, N. J.: Littlefield, Adams & Co., 1968. Pp. 100–108.

5. _____. Zur Rolle des Unbewussten in der Neurose. (On the role of the unconscious in neurosis.) *Zbl. Psychoanal.*, 1913, **3**, 169–174. Transl. in *The practice and theory of individual psychology*. Totowa, N. J.: Littlefield, Adams & Co., 1968. Pp. 227–234.

6. _____. *Praxis und Theorie der Individualpsychologie*. 2nd ed. Munich: Bergmann, 1924. Transl. *The practice and theory of individual psychology*. Totowa, N. J.: Littlefield, Adams & Co., 1968.

7. _____. *Ueber den nervösen Charakter: Grundzüge einer vergleichenden Individual-Psychologie und Psychotherapie*. Wiesbaden: Bergmann, 1912. Transl. *The neurotic constitution: outline of a comparative individualistic psychology and psychotherapy*. New York: Moffat, Yard, 1917.

8. _____. *Das Problem der Homosexualität: erotisches Training und erotischer Rückzug*. (The problem of homosexuality: erotic training and erotic retreat.) 2nd ed. Leipzig: Hirzel, 1930.

9. _____. Various. In A. Bethe *et al.* (Eds.), *Handbuch der normalen und pathologischen Physiologie*. Vol. 14(1). Berlin: Springer, 1926. Pp. 802–807, 808–812, 842–844, 881–886, 887–894, 895–899. These six contributions are included in Item 8 above.

10. _____. *Menschenkenntnis*. Leipzig: Hirzel, 1927. Transl. *Understanding human nature*. New York: Fawcett World Libr., 1965.

11. _____. *Individualpsychologie in der Schule: Vorlesungen für Lehrer und Erzieher*. (individual psychology in the school: lectures for teachers and educators.) Leipzig: Hirzel, 1929.

12. _____. *The science of living* (1929). Garden City N.Y.: Doubleday Anchor Books, 1969.

13. _____. *Die Technik der Individualpsychologie.* Vol. 1. *Die Kunst, eine Lebensund Krankengeschichte zu lesen.* Munich: Bergmann, 1928. Transl. *The case of Miss R.: the interpretation of a life story.* New York: Greenberg, 1929.

14. _____. *Problems of neurosis* (1929). New York: Harper Torchbooks, 1964.

2. *Ordinal Position and Fighter Pilot Effectiveness*

STANLEY SCHACHTER

So far, we have examined real-life analogies to the experimentally demonstrated relationship of birth rank to the affiliative reaction to anxiety. But what about anxiety itself? In the experiments, first-born subjects when faced with a standard anxiety-provoking situation responded with considerably more fright and anxiety than later-born subjects. Does this result have any explanatory power outside of the immediate experimental situation?

Let us consider first the relationship between anxiety or fright and performance. It is fairly well accepted that there is a non-monotonic relationship between these variables, that is, performance improves with small amounts of anxiety and deteriorates with excessive anxiety. It should be anticipated, then, that under really frightening conditions first-born individuals will be less effective than later-born individuals. Combat would seem the ideal locus for testing this expectation; if this line of reasoning is correct, later-born soldiers should make better fighters than early-born soldiers.

The only data available for testing these

propositions derives from a study of fighter pilot effectiveness conducted by Paul Torrance. In a way, the situation of the fighter pilot is almost ideal for purposes of this test: first, there is a clear, unambiguous criterion of fighter pilot effectiveness—the number of enemy planes downed; second, the fighter pilot fights alone and his performance is relatively uncontaminated by the multitude of variables affecting performance in group combat. This isolation of the fighter pilot does, however, raise one new question. When the individual faces an anxiety-provoking situation alone, does ordinal position have a differential effect on anxiety? No data has yet been presented on the question, but in terms of what is already known about the effects of ordinal position on the arousal of affiliative needs under anxiety, it is conceivable that being alone in such a situation magnifies the fears of the first-born far more than the fears of the later-born individual. If this is correct, it would imply that the anxiety differential between first and later-born individuals is even greater in solitary combat than in group combat and, again, it should be anticipated that the later-born will be more effective fighter pilots than the early-born individuals.

The purpose and procedure of Tor-

SOURCE. *Stanley Schachter, "Ordinal position and fighter pilot effectiveness" in* The Psychology of Affiliation. *Stanford: Stanford University Press, 1959.*

rance's study are best explained in his own words:

"The major purpose of the larger study was to discover why pilots with backgrounds comparable with those of the more successful pilots were not themselves equally successful in combat with the MIG's over Korea. The 38 Air Force aces (pilots with 5 or more MIG-15 kills) accounted for 38.2 percent of the total claims, although they represented less than 5 percent of the pilots completing fighter interceptor tours in Korea. Furthermore, 53.5 percent made no kills at all. . . . The subjects of the study are 31 of the 38 aces in air-to-air combat over Korea. Of the seven aces not studied, one was killed in action, one is reported to be held in Manchuria, one was killed in an accident after returning to the States, and the other four were unavailable because of release from the Air Force or the like. Their ages ranged from 24 to 39 years and averaged about 30. Six of those studied are colonels; 3, lieutenant colonels; 6, majors, 13, captains; and 3, first lieutenants. Similar studies were also made of pilots with one to four kills and pilots with no kills, matched for rank, age, and World War II combat experience.

There are, then, three matched groups which we will call aces (5 or more kills), near-aces (1 to 4 kills), and non-aces (0 kills). The distribution of these categories as they relate to ordinal position is presented in Table 1, where it will be noted that the data conform to expectations. Some 67.7 percent of the aces, 54.6 percent of the near-aces and 41.0 percent of

the non-aces are later-borns. It does appear that later-born flyers are more effective fighter pilots. The overall differences in this table are significant at the 0.08 level of confidence. Comparing the two extreme groups (aces vs. nonaces) yields a chi-square of 4.95, significant with one degree of freedom at the 0.03 level of confidence.

The experimental result which stimulated this particular analysis was the finding that ordinal position affected the degree of anxiety or fear. Since it is known, from previous analyses that family size also affects the magnitude of anxiety, it is obvious that the effects of family size must again be evaluated before any unequivocal conclusions can be drawn. Fortunately, the data are available to permit such an evaluation and they are presented in Table 2, where the cases in each of the three groups are distributed according to ordinal position and family size. Ignoring, momentarily, the data on only children, examination of the sub-table for aces reveals that for each family size the number of first-borns who are aces is below chance expectations. Chance expectancies are simply computed by dividing the total number of cases falling in families of a given size by family size; e.g., there are 6 aces originating from 3-child families, if chance alone were operating these 6 cases should be equally distributed among the three ordinal positions with 2 cases at each position. For all of the sub-tables, the figure 5 may be used

TABLE 1 Ordinal Position and Fighter Pilot Effectiveness

	ACE (5 + Kills)	NEAR-ACE (1 − 4 Kills)	NON-ACE (0 Kills)
First-Born and Only	10	15	23
Later	21	18	16
Overall $\chi^2 = 5.12$	Aces vs. Non-Aces		$\chi^2 = 4.95$
d.f. = 2			d.f. = 1
p = 0.08			p = 0.03

TABLE 2 *Effects of Ordinal Position and Family Size on Fighter Pilot Effectiveness*

a. ACES

Family size (Number children)

Ordinal Position	1	2	3	4+
1	6	3	0	1
2		6	4	1
3			2	4
4+				4

b. NEAR-ACES

Family size (Number children)

Ordinal Position	1	2	3	4+
1	3	9	2	1
2		4	1	4
3			3	4
4+				2

c. NON-ACES

Family size (Number children)

Ordinal Position	1	2	3	4+
1	7	7	6	3
2		2	5	1
3			4	2
4+				2

as a convenient and close approximation to the average number of children in families in the combined category used for families with 4 or more children. For this group of aces, then, family size does not appear to be a confounding variable; for all family sizes there are fewer first-borns than would be expected by chance. The data in the sub-table for non-aces reveal quite the opposite trend. For all family sizes, first-borns occur with greater than chance frequency. There are good indications, then, that the effects noted are a function of ordinal position independent of family size.

The data on only children are of special interest, for they do seem to deviate somewhat from the pattern for the first-born flyers. Six of the 10 first-born aces are only children, and these 6 constitute 37.5 percent of the total number of only children in these three groups of pilots. Should this be considered contrary to expectations? Perhaps, but the reader will recall from the discussion of differences between only and first-born subjects in the preceding chapter that there are indications that only children are less fearful than first-born children. In the high-anxiety conditions of the experiments 35 percent of all first-born subjects wanted to drop out of the experiment, while none of the only subjects wanted to drop out. In terms of the differential anxiety explanation of the relationship between fighter pilot effectiveness and ordinal position, these two sets of data can be considered consistent.

If this differential anxiety interpretation is an appropriate explanation of these data on fighter pilots, it should be anticipated that there will be further consistencies with the experimental data. Virtually the sole remaining item for which there is sufficient data to allow meaningful comparison is the effect of family size. In previously reported experiments subjects from small families were more frightened than subjects from large families. Consistency demands, then, that there be proportionately fewer pilots from small families among the aces than among non-aces. The reverse trend might be expected to obtain for pilots from large families. And the data do tend to conform to these expectations. Pilots from small families (2–3) children) compose 48.4 percent of the group of aces, 57.6 percent of near-aces, and 61.5 percent of non-aces. Pilots from large families (4+ children) make up 32.3 percent of the aces, 33.3 percent of near-aces, and 20.5 percent of non-aces.

It would be intriguing to compare these data with similar data on bomber pilots. Since the bomber pilot is a member of a crew, such a comparison might permit evaluation of the effect that being a member of a group has on the relationship of ordinal position to pilot effectiveness. If being a member of a group has little or no effect on anxiety level, precisely the same relationships should be expected for bomber pilots as for fighter pilots. If, as earlier speculation suggested, being a member of a group has differential effects on the anxiety levels of first- and later-born individuals, the relationship between ordinal position and pilot effectiveness should be considerably weaker for bomber pilots than for fighter pilots. In any case, the matter must remain unresolved, for discussion with those who have worked extensively on the criterion problem of bomber pilot effectiveness indicates that the highly interdependent nature of bomber crew action has so far made it impossible to hit upon any satisfactory criterion of bomber pilot effectiveness in comabt conditions.

3. Character and The Social Process

ERICH FROMM

Through this book we have dealt with the interrelation of socio-economic, psychological and ideological factors by analyzing certain historical periods like the age of the Reformation and the contemporary era. For those readers who are interested in the theoretical problems involved in such analysis I shall try, in this appendix, to discuss briefly the general theoretical basis on which the concrete analysis is founded.

In studying the psychological reactions of a social group we deal with the character structure of the members of the group, that is, of individual persons; we are interested, however, not in the peculiarities by which these persons differ from each other, but in that part of their character structure that is common to most members of the group. We can call this character the *social character*. The social character necessarily is less specific than the individual character. In describing the latter we deal with the whole of the traits on which in their particular configuration form the personality structure of this or that individual. The social character comprises only a selection of traits, *the essen-*

tial nucleus of the character structure of most members of a group which has developed as the result of the basic experiences and mode of life common to that group. Although there will be always "deviants" with a totally different character structure, the character structure of most members of the group are variations of this nucleus, brought about by accidental factors of birth and life experience as they differ from one individual to another. If we want to understand one individual most fully, these differentiating elements are of the greatest importance. However, if we want to understand how human energy is channeled and operates as a productive force in a given social order, then the social character deserves our main interest.

The concept of social character is a key concept for the understanding of the social process. Character in the dynamic sense of analytic psychology is the specific form in which human energy is shaped by the dynamic adaptation of human needs to the particular mode of existence of a given society. Character in its turn determines the thinking, feeling, and acting of individuals. To see this is somewhat difficult with regard to our thoughts, since we all tend to share the conventional belief that thinking is an exclusively intellectual act and independent of the

SOURCE. *Selection from Erich Fromm, "Character and the social process" Appendix to* Escape from Freedom, *pp. 277–299. New York: Rinehart, 1941.*

psychological structure of the personality. This is not so, however, and the less so the more our thoughts deal with ethical, philosophical, political, psychological or social problems rather than with the empirical manipulation of concrete objects. Such thoughts, aside from the purely logical elements that are involved in the act of thinking, are greatly determined by the personality structure of the person who thinks. This holds true for the whole of a doctrine or of a theoretical system as well as for a single concept, like love, justice, equality, sacrifice. Each such concept and each doctrine has an emotional matrix and this matrix is rooted in the character structure of the individual.

We have given many illustrations of this in the foregoing chapters. With regard to doctrines we have tried to show the emotional roots of early Protestantism and modern authoritarianism. With regard to single concepts we have shown that for the sado-masochistic character, for example, love means symbiotic dependence, not mutual affirmation and union on the basis of equality; sacrifice means the utmost subordination of the individual self to something higher, not assertion of one's mental and moral self; difference means difference in power, not the realization of individuality on the basis of equality; justice means that everybody should get what he deserves, not that the individual has an unconditional claim to the realization of inherent and inalienable rights; courage is the readiness to submit and to endure suffering, not the utmost assertion of individuality against power. Although the word which two people of different personality use when they speak of love, for instance, is the same, the meaning of the word is entirely different according to their character structure. As a matter of fact, much intellectual confusion could be avoided by correct psychological analysis of the meaning of these concepts,

since any attempt at a purely logical classification must necessarily fail.

The fact that ideas have an emotional matrix is of the utmost importance because it is the key to the understanding of the spirit of a culture. Different societies or classes within a society have a specific social character, and on its basis different ideas develop and become powerful. Thus, for instance, the idea of work and success as the main aims of life were able to become powerful and appealing to modern man on the basis of his aloneness and doubt; but propaganda for the idea of ceaseless effort and striving for success addressed to the Pueblo Indians or to Mexican peasants would fall completely flat. These people with a different kind of character structure would hardly understand what a person setting forth such aims was talking about even if they understood his language. In the same way, Hitler and that part of the German population which has the same character structure quite sincerely feel that anybody who thinks that wars can be abolished is either a complete fool or a plain liar. On the basis of their social character, to them life without suffering and disaster is a little comprehensible as freedom and equality.

Ideas often are consciously accepted by certain groups, which, on account of the peculiarities of their social character, are not really touched by them; such ideas remain a stock of conscious convictions, but people fail to act according to them in a critical hour. An example of this is shown in the German labor movement at the time of the victory of Nazism. The vast majority of German workers before Hitler's coming into power voted for the Socialist or Communist Parties and believed in the ideas of those parties; that is, the *range* of these ideas among the working class was extremely wide. The *weight* of these ideas, however, was in no proportion to their range. The onslaught of Nazism did not meet with political opponents, the majority of whom were ready to fight for their ideas. Many of the adherents of the leftist parties, although they believed in their party programs as long as the parties had authority, were ready to resign when the hour of crisis arrived. A close analysis of the character structures of German workers can show one reason—certainly not the only one— for this phenomenon. A great number of them were of a personality type that has many of the traits of what we have described as the authoritarian character. They had a deep-seated respect and longing for established authority. The emphasis of socialism on individual independence versus authority, on solidarity versus individualistic seclusion, was not what many of these workers really wanted on the basis of their personality structure. One mistake of the radical leaders was to estimate the strength of their parties only on the basis of the range which these ideas had, and to overlook their lack of weight.

In contrast to this picture, our analysis of Protestant and Calvinist doctrines has shown that those ideas were powerful forces within the adherents of the new religion, because they appealed to needs and anxieties that were present in the character structure of the people to whom they were addressed. In other words, *ideas can become powerful forces, but only to the extent to which they are answers to specific human needs prominent in a given social character.*

Not only thinking and feeling are determined by man's character structure but also his actions. It is Freud's achievement to have shown this, even if his theoretical frame of reference is incorrect. The determinations of activity by the dominant trends of a person's character structure are obvious in the case of neurotics. It is easy to understand that the compulsion to count the windows of houses and the number of stones on the pavement is an activity that is rooted in certain drives of the compulsive character. But the actions of a normal person appear to be determined only by rational considerations and the necessities of reality. However, with the new tools of observation that psychoanalysis offers, we can recognize that so-called rational behavior is largely determined by the character structure. In our discussion of the meaning of work for modern man we have dealt with an illustration of this point. We saw that the intense desire for unceasing activity was rooted in aloneness and anxiety. This compulsion to work differed from the attitude toward work in other cultures, where people worked as much as it was necessary but where they were not driven by additional forces within their own character structure. Since all normal persons today have about the same impulse to work and, furthermore, since this intensity of work is necessary if they want to live at all, one easily overlooks the irrational component in this trait.

We have now to ask what function character serves for the individual and for society. As to the former the answer is not difficult. If an individual's character more or less closely conforms with the social character, the dominant drives in his personality lead him to do what is necessary and desirable under the specific social conditions of his culture. Thus, for instance, if he has a passionate drive to save and an abhorrence of spending money for any luxury, he will be greatly helped by this drive—supposing he is a small shopkeeper who needs to save and to be thrifty if he wants to survive. Besides this economic function, character traits have a purely psychological one which is no less important. The person with whom saving is a desire springing from his personality gains also a profound psychological satisfaction in being able to act accordingly; that is, he is not only benefited practically when he saves, but he also feels satisfied psychologically. One can easily convince oneself of this if one observes, for instance, a woman of the lower middle class shopping in the market and being as happy about two cents saved as another person of a different character may be about the enjoyment of some sensuous pleasure. This psychological satisfaction occurs not only if a person acts in accordance with the demands springing from his character structure but also when he reads or listens to ideas that appeal to him for the same reason. For the authoritarian character an ideology that describes nature as the powerful force to which we have to submit, or a speech which indulges in sadistic descriptions of political occurrences, has a profound attraction and the act of reading or listening results in psychological satisfaction. To sum up: the subjective function of character for the normal person is to *lead him to act according to what is necessary for him from a practical standpoint and also to give him satisfaction from his activity psychologically.*

If we look at social character from the standpoint of its function in the social process, we have to start with the statement that has been made with regard to its function for the individual: that by adapting himself to social conditions man develops those traits that make him desire to act as he has to act. If the character of the majority of people in a given society — that is, the social character — is thus adapted to the objective tasks the individual has to perform in this society, the energies of people are molded in ways that make them into productive forces that are indispensable for the functioning of that society. Let us take up once more the example of work. Our modern industrial system requires that most of our energy be channeled in the direction of work. Were it only that people worked because of external necessities, much friction be-

tween what they ought to do and what they would like to do would arise and lessen their efficiency. However, by the dynamic adaptation of character to social requirements, human energy instead of causing friction is shaped into such forms as to become an incentive to act according to the particular economic necessities. Thus modern man, instead of having to be forced to work as hard as he does, is driven by the inner compulsion to work which we have attempted to analyze in its psychological significance. Or, instead of obeying overt authorities, he has built up an inner authority — conscience and duty — which operates more effectively in controlling him than any external authority could ever do. In other words, *the social character internalizes external necessities and thus harnesses human energy for the task of a given economic and social system.*

As we have seen, once certain needs have developed in a character structure, any behavior in line with these needs is at the same time satisfactory psychologically and practical from the standpoint of material success. As long as a society offers the individual those two satisfactions simultaneously, we have a situation where the psychological forces are cementing the social structure. Sooner or later, however, a lag arises. The traditional character structure still exists while new economic conditions have arisen, for which the traditional character traits are no longer useful. People tend to act according to their character structure, but either these actions are actual handicaps in their economic pursuits or there is not enough opportunity for them to find positions that allow them to act according to their "nature." An illustration of what we have in mind is the character structure of the old midle classes, particularly in countries with a rigid class stratification like Germany. The old middle class virtues — frugality, thrift, cautiousness, suspiciousness — were of diminishing value in modern business in comparison with new virtues, such as initiative, a readiness to take risks, aggressiveness, and so on. Even inasmuch as these old virtues were still an asset—as with the small shopkeeper—the range of possibilities for such business was so narrowed down that only a minority of the sons of the old middle class could "use" their character traits successfully in their economic pursuits. While by their upbringing they had developed character traits that once were adapted to the social situation of their class, the economic development went faster than the character development. This lag between economic and psychological evolution resulted in a situation in which the psychic needs could no longer be satisfied by the usual economic activities. These needs existed, however, and had to seek for satisfaction in some other way. Narrow egotistical striving for one's own advantage, as it had characterized the lower middle class, was shifted from the individual plane to that of the nation. The sadistic impulses, too, that had been used in the battle of private competition were partly shifted to the social and political scene, and partly intensified by frustration. Then, freed from any restricting factors, they sought satisfaction in acts of political persecution and war. Thus, blended with the resentment caused by the frustrating qualities of the whole situation, the psychological forces instead of cementing the existing social order became dynamite to be used by groups which wanted to destroy the traditional political and economic structure of democratic society.

We have not spoken of the role which the educational process plays with regard to the formation of the social character; but in view of the fact that to many psychologists the methods of early childhood training and the educational techniques employed toward the growing child appear to be the cause of character de-velopment, some remarks on this point seem to be warranted. In the first place we should ask ourselves what we mean by education. While education can be defined in various ways, the way to look at it from the angle of the social process seems to be something like this. The social function of education is to qualify the individual to function in the role he is to play later on in society; that is, to mold his character in such a way that it approximates the social character, that his desires coincide with the necessities of his social role. The educational system of any society is determined by this function; therefore we cannot explain the structure of society or the personality of its members of the educational process; but we have to explain the educational system by the necessities resulting from the social and economic structure of a given society. However, the methods of education are extremely important in so far as they are the mechanisms by which the individual is molded into the required shape. They can be considered as the means by which social requirements are transformed into personal qualities. While educational techniques are not the cause of a particular kind of social character, they constitute one of the mechanisms by which character is formed. In this sense, the knowledge and understanding of educational methods is an important part of the total analysis of a functioning society.

What we have just said also holds true for one particular sector of the whole educational process: the *family*. Freud has shown that the early experiences of the child have a decisive influence upon the formation of its character structure. If this is true, how then can we understand that the child, who—at least in our culture—has little contact with the life of society, is molded by it? The answer is not only that the parents—aside from certain individual variations—apply the educational patterns of the society they live in, but also that in their own personalities they represent the social character of their society or class. They transmit to the child what we may call the psychological atmosphere or the spirit of a society just by being as they are — namely representatives of this very spirit. *The family thus may be considered to be the psychological agent of society.*

Having stated that the social character is shaped by the mode of existence of a given society, I want to remind the reader of what has been said in the first chapter on the problem of dynamic adaptation. While it is true that man is molded by the necessities of the economic and social structure of society, he is not infinitely adaptable. Not only are there certain physiological needs that imperatively call for satisfaction, but there are also certain psychological qualities inherent in man that need to be satisfied and that result in certain reactions if they are frustrated. What are these qualities? The most important seems to be the tendency to grow, to develop and realize potentialities which man has developed in the course of history — as, for instance, the faculty of creative and critical thinking and of having differentiated emotional and sensuous experiences. Each of these potentialities has a dynamism of its own. Once they have developed in the process of evolution they tend to be expressed. This tendency can be suppressed and frustrated, but such suppression results in a new reaction, particularly in the formation of destructive and symbiotic impulses. It also seems that this general tendency to grow — which is the psychological equivalent of the identical biological tendency — results in such specific tendencies as the desire for freedom and the hatred against oppression, since freedom is the fundamental condition for any growth. Again, the desire for freedom can be repressed, it can disappear from the awareness of the individual; but even then it does not cease to exist as a potentiality, and indicates its existence by the conscious or unconscious hatred by which such suppression is always accompanied.

We have also reason to assume that, as has been said before, the striving for justice and truth is an inherent trend of human nature, although it can be repressed and perverted like the striving for freedom. In this assumption we are on dangerous ground theoretically. It would be easy if we could fall back on religious and philosophical assumptions which explain the existence of such trends by a belief that man is created in God's likeness or by the assumption of a natural law. However, we cannot support our argument with such explanations. The only way in our opinion to account for this striving for justice and truth is by the analysis of the whole history of man, socially and individually. We find then that for everybody who is powerless, justice and truth are the most important weapons in the fight for his freedom and growth. Aside from the fact that the majority of mankind throughout its history has had to defend itself against more powerful groups which could oppress and exploit it, every individual in childhood goes through a period which is characterized by powerlessness. It seems to us that in this state of powerlessness traits like the sense of justice and truth develop and become potentialities common to man as such. We arrive therefore at the fact that, *although character development is shaped by the basic conditions of life and although there is no biologically fixed human nature, human nature has a dynamism of its own that constitutes an active factor in the evolution of the social process.* Even if we are not yet able to state clearly in psychological terms what the exact nature of this human dynamism is, we must recognize its existence. In trying to avoid the errors of biological and metaphysical concepts we must not succumb to an equally grave error, that of a socio-logical relativism in which man is nothing but a puppet, directed by the strings of social circumstances. Man's inalienable rights of freedom and happiness are founded in inherent human qualities: his striving to live, to expand and to express the potentialities that have developed in him in the process of historical evolution.

4. *Culture and Neurosis*

KAREN HORNEY

In the psychoanalytic concept of neuroses a shift of emphasis has taken place: whereas originally interest was focussed on the dramatic symptomatic picture, it is now being realized more and more that the real source of these psychic disorders lies in character disturbances, that the symptoms are a manifest result of conflicting character traits and that without uncovering and straightening out the neurotic character structure we cannot cure a neurosis. When analyzing these character traits, in a great many cases one is struck by the observation that, in marked contrast to the divergency of the symptomatic pictures, character difficulties invariably center around the same basic conflicts.

These similarities in the content of conflicts present a problem. They suggest to minds open to the importance of cultural implications, the question of whether and to what extent neuroses are moulded by cultural processes in essentially the same way as "normal" character formation is determined by these influences; and, if so, how far such a concept would necessitate certain modifications in Freud's views of the relation between culture and neurosis.

In the following remarks I shall try to outline roughly some characteristics typically recurring in all our neuroses. The limitations of time will allow us to present neither data—good case histories—nor method, but only results. I shall try to select from the extremely complex and diversified observational material the essential points.

There is another difficulty in the presentation. I wish to show how these neurotic persons are trapped in a vicious circle. Unable to present in detail factors leading up to the vicious circle, I must start rather arbitrarily with one of the outstanding features, although this in itself is already a complex product of several interrelated, developed mental factors. I start, therefore, with the problem of competition.

The problem of competition, or rivalry, appears to be a never-failing center of neurotic conflicts. How to deal with competition presents a problem for everyone in our culture; for the neurotic, however, it assumes dimensions which generally surpass actual vicissitudes. It does so in three respects:

(1) There is a constant measuring-up with others, even in situations which do

SOURCE. *Article by Karen Horney, "Culture and neurosis" in* American sociological review, *Vol. 1, pp. 221–230, 1936.*

not call for it. While striving to surpass others is essential for all competitive situations, the neurotic measures up even with persons who are in no way potential competitors and have no goal in common with him. The question as to who is the more intelligent, more attractive, more popular, is indiscriminately applied towards everyone.

(2) The content of neurotic ambitions is not only to accomplish something worth while, or to be successful, but to be absolutely best of all. These ambitions, however, exist in fantasy mainly—fantasies which may or may not be conscious. The degree of awareness differs widely in different persons. The ambitions may appear in occasional flashes of fantasy only. There is never a clear realization of the powerful dramatic role these ambitions play in the neurotic's life, or of the great part they have in accounting for his behavior and mental reactions. The challenge of these ambitions is not met by adequate efforts which might lead to realization of the aims. They are in queer contrast to existing inhibitions towards work, towards assuming leadership, towards all means which would effectually secure success. There are many ways in which these fantastic ambitions influence the emotional lives of the persons concerned: by hypersensitivity to criticism, by depressions or inhibitions following failures, etc. These failures need not necessarily be real. Everything which falls short of the realization of the grandiose ambitions is felt as failure. The success of another person is felt as one's own failure.

This competitive attitude not only exists in reference to the external world, but is also internalized, and appears as a constant measuring-up to an ego-ideal. The fantastic ambitions appear on this score as excessive and rigid demands towards the self, and failure in living up to these demands produces depressions and irri-

tations similar to those produced in competition with others.

(3) The third characteristic is the amount of hostility involved in neurotic ambition. While intense competition implicitly contains elements of hostility— the defeat of a competitor meaning victory for oneself, the reactions of neurotic persons are determined by an insatiable and irrational expectation that no one in the universe other than themselves should be intelligent, influential, attractive, or popular. They become infuriated, or feel their own endeavors condemned to futility, if someone else writes a good play or a scientific paper or plays a prominent role in society. If this attitude is strongly accentuated, one may observe in the analytical situation, for example, that these patients regard any progress made as a victory on the part of the analyst, completely disregarding the fact that progress is of vital concern to their own interests. In such situations they will disparage the analyst, betraying, by the intense hostility displayed, that they feel endangered in a position of paramount importance to themselves. They are as a rule completely unaware of the existence and intensity of this "no one but me" attitude, but one may safely assume and eventually always uncover this attitude from reactions observable in the analytical situation, as indicated above.

This attitude easily leads to a fear of retaliation. It results in a fear of success and also in a fear of failure: "If I want to crush everyone who is successful, then I will automatically assume identical reactions in others, so that the way to success implies exposing me to the hostility of others. Furthermore: if I make any move towards this goal and fail, then I shall be crushed." Success thus becomes a peril and any possible failure becomes a danger which must at all costs be avoided. From the point of view of all these dangers it appears much safer to stay in the corner, be modest and inconspicuous. In other and more positive terms, this fear leads to a definite recoiling from any aim which implies competition. This safety device is assured by a constant, accurately working process of automatic self-checking.

This self-checking process results in inhibitions, particularly inhibitions towards work, but also towards all steps necessary to the pursuit of one's aims, such as seizing opportunities, or revealing to others that one has certain goals or capacities. This eventually results in an incapacity to stand up for one's wishes. The peculiar nature of these inhibitions is best demontrated by the fact that these persons may be quite capable of fighting for the needs of others or for an impersonal cause. They will, for instance, act like this:

When playing an instrument with a poor partner, they will instinctively play worse than he, although otherwise they may be very competent. When discussing a subject with someone less intelligent than themselves, they will compulsively descend below his level. They will prefer to be in the rank and file, not to be identified with the superiors, not even to get an increase in salary, rationalizing this attitude in some way. Even their dreams will be dictated by this need for reassurance. Instead of utilizing the liberty of a dream to imagine themselves in glorious situations, they will actually see themselves, in their dreams, in humble or even humiliating situations.

This self-checking process does not restrict itself to activities in the pursuit of some aim, but going beyond that, tends to undermine the self-confidence, which is a prerequisite for any accomplishment, by means of self-belittling. The function of self-belittling in this context is to eliminate onself from any competition. In most cases these persons are not aware of actually disparaging themselves, but are aware of the results only as they feel themselves inferior to others and take for granted their own inadequacy.

The present of these feelings of inferiority is one of the most common psychic disorders of our time and culture. Let me say a few more words about them. The genesis of inferiority feelings is not always in neurotic competition. They present complex phenomena and may be determined by various conditions. But that they do result from, and stand in the service of, a recoiling from competition, is a basic and everpresent implication. They result from a recoiling inasmuch as they are the expression of a discrepancy between high pitched ideals and real accomplishment. The fact, however, that these painful feelings at the same time fulfill the important function of making secure the recoiling attitude itself, becomes evident through the vigor with which this position is defended when attacked. Not only will no evidence of competence or attractiveness ever convince these persons, but they may actually become scared or angered by any attempt to convince them of their positive qualities.

The surface pictures resulting from this situation may be widely divergent. Some persons appear thoroughly convinced of their unique importance and may be anxious to demonstrate their superiority on every occasion, but betray their insecurity in an excessive sensitivity to every criticism, to every dissenting opinion, or every lack of responsive admiration. Others are just as thoroughly convinced of their incompetence or unworthiness, or of being unwanted or unappreciated; yet they betray their actually great demands in that they react with open or concealed hostility to every frustration of their unacknowledged demands. Still others will waver constantly in their self-estimation between feeling themselves all important and feeling, for instance, honestly amazed that anyone pays any attention to them.

If you have followed me thus far, I can now proceed to outline the particular vicious circle in which these persons are moving. It is important here, as in every complex neurotic picture, to recognize the vicious circle, because, if we overlook it and simplify the complexity of the processes going on by assuming a simple cause-effect relation, we either fail to get an understanding of the emotions involved, or attribute an undue importance to some one cause. As an example of this error, I might mention regarding a highly emotion-charged rivalry attitude as derived directly from rivalry with the father. Roughly, the vicious circle looks like this:

The failures, in conjunction with a feeling or weakness and defeat, lead to a feeling of envy towards all persons who are more successful, or merely more secure or better contented with life. This envy may be manifest or it may be repressed under the pressure of the same anxiety which led to a repression of, and a recoiling from, rivalry. It may be entirely wiped out of consciousness and represented by the substitution of a blind admiration; it may be kept from awareness by a disparaging attitude towards the person concerned. Its effect, however, is apparent in the incapacity to grant to others what one has been forced to deny himself. At any rate, no matter to what degree the envy is repressed or expressed, it implies an increase in the existing hostility against people and consequently an increase in the anxiety, which now takes the particular form of an irrational fear of the envy of others.

The irrational nature of this fear is shown in two ways: (1) it exists regardless of the presence or absence of envy in the given situation; and (2) its intensity is out of proportion to the dangers menacing

from the side of the envious competitors. This irrational side of the fear of envy always remains unconscious, at least in nonpsychotic persons, therefore it is never corrected by a reality-testing process, and is all the more effective in the direction of reinforcing the existing tendencies to recoil.

Consequently the feeling of own insignificance grows, the hostility against people grows, and the anxiety grows. We thus return to the beginning, because now the fantasies come up, with about this content: "I wish I were more powerful, more attractive, more intelligent than all the others, then I should be safe, and besides, I could defeat them and step on them." Thus we see an ever-increasing deviation of the ambitions towards the stringent, fantastic, and hostile.

This pyramiding process may come to a standstill under various conditions, usually at an inordinate expense in loss of expansiveness and vitality. There is often some sort of resignation as to personal ambitions, in turn permitting the diminution of anxieties as to competition, with the inferiority feelings and inhibitions continuing.

It is now time, however, to make a reservation. It is in no way self-evident that ambition of the "no-one-but-me" type must necessarily evoke anxieties. There are persons quite capable of brushing aside or crushing everyone in the way of their ruthless pursuit of personal power. The question then is: Under what special condition is anxiety invoked in neurotically competitive people?

The answer is that they at the same time want to be loved. While most persons who pursue an asocial ambition in life care little for the affection or the opinion of others, the neurotics, although possessed by the same kind of competitiveness, simultaneously have a boundless craving for affection and appreciation. Therefore, as soon as they make any move towards self-assertion, competition, or success, they begin to dread losing the affection of others, and must automatically check their aggressive impulses. This conflict between ambition and affection is one of the gravest and most typical dilemmas of the neurotics of our time.

Why are these two incompatible strivings so frequently present in the same individual? They are related to each other in more than one way. The briefest formulation of this relationship would perhaps be that they both grow out of the same sources, namely, anxieties, and they both serve as a means of reassurance against the anxieties. Power and affection may both be safeguards. They generate each other, check each other, and reinforce each other. These interrelations can be observed most accurately within the analytic situation, but sometimes are obvious from only a casual knowledge of the life history.

In the life history may be found, for instance, an atmosphere in childhood lacking in warmth and reliability, but rife with frightening elements—battles between the parents, injustice, cruelty, oversolicitousness—generation of an increased need for affection—disappointments—development of an outspoken competitiveness—inhibition—attempts to get affection on the basis of weakness, helplessness, or suffering. We sometimes hear that a youngster has suddenly turned to ambition after an acute disappointment in his need for affection, and then given up the ambition on falling in love.

Particularly when the expansive and aggressive desires have been severely curbed in early life by a forbidding atmosphere, the excessive need for reassuring affection will play a major role. As a guiding principle for behavior this implies a yielding to the wishes or opinions of others rather than asserting one's own wishes or opinions; an overvaluation of the significance for one's own life of ex-

pressions of fondness from others, and a dependence on such expressions. And similarly, it implies an overvaluation of signs of rejection and a reacting to such signs with apprehension and defensive hostility. Here again a vicious circle begins easily and reinforces the single elements: in diagram it looks somewhat like this:

Anxiety plus repressed hostility
   ↘ Need for reassuring affection
      ↘ Anticipation of, sensitivity to, rejection
        ↘ Hostile reactions to feeling rejected

These reactions explain why emotional contact with others that is attained on the basis of anxiety can be at best only a very shaky and easily shattered bridge between individuals, and why it always fails to bring them out of their emotional isolation. It may, however, serve to cope with anxieties and even get one through life rather smoothly, but only at the expense of growth and personality development, and only if circumstances are quite favorable.

Let us ask now, which special features in our culture may be responsible for the frequent occurence of the neurotic structures just described!

We live in a competitive, individualistic culture. Whether the enormous economic and technical achievements of our culture were and are possible only on the basis of the competitive principle is a question for the economist or sociologist to decide. The psychologist, however, can evaluate the personal price we have paid for it.

It must be kept in mind that competition not only is a driving force in economic activities, but that it also pervades our personal life in every respect. The character of all our human relationships is moulded by a more or less outspoken competition. It is effective in the family between siblings, at school, in social relations (keeping up with the Joneses), and in love life.

In love, it may show itself in two ways: the genuine erotic wish is often overshadowed or replaced by the merely competitive goal of being the most popular, having the most dates, love letters, lovers, being seen with the most desirable man or woman. Again, it may pervade the love relationship itself. Marriage partners, for example, may be living in an endless struggle for supremacy, with or without being aware of the nature or even of the existence of this combat.

The influence on human relations of this competitiveness lies in the fact that it creates easily aroused envy towards the stronger ones, contempt for the weaker, distrust towards everyone. In consequence of all these potentially hostile tensions, the satisfaction and reassurance which one can get out of human relations are limited and the individual becomes more or less emotionally isolated. It seems that here, too, mutually reinforcing interactions take place, so far as insecurity and dissatisfaction in human relations in turn compel people to seek gratification and security in ambitious strivings, and vice versa.

Another cultural factor relevant to the structure of our neurosis lies in our attitude towards failure and success. We are inclined to attribute success to good personal qualities and capacities, such as competence, courage, enterprise. In re ligious terms this attitude was expressed by saying that success was due to God's grace. While these qualities may be effective—and in certain periods, such as the pioneer days, may have represented the only conditions necessary—this ideology omits two essential facts: (1) that the possibility for success is strictly limited; even external conditions and personal qualities being equal, only a comparative few can possibly attain success; and (2) that other

factors than those mentioned may play the decisive role, such as, for example, unscrupulousness or fortuitous circumstances. Inasmuch as these factors are overlooked in the general evaluation of success, failures, besides putting the person concerned in a factually disadvantageous position, are bound to reflect on his self-esteem.

The confusion involved in this situation is enhanced by a sort of double moral. Although, in fact, success meets with adoration almost without regard to the means employed in securing it, we are at the same time taught to regard modesty and an undemanding, unselfish attitude as social or religious virtues, and are rewarded for them by praise and affection. The particular difficulties which confront the individual in our culture may be summarized as follows: for the competitive struggle he needs a certain amount of available aggressiveness; at the same time, he is required to be modest, unselfish, even self-sacrificing. While the competitive life situation with the hostile tensions involved in it creates an enhanced need of security, the chances of attaining a feeling of safety in human relations—love, friendship, social contacts—are at the same time diminished. The estimation of one's personal value is all too dependent on the degree of success attained, while at the same time the possibilities for success are limited and the success itself is dependent, to a great extent, on fortuitous circumstances or on personal qualities of an asocial character.

Perhaps these sketchy comments have suggested to you the direction in which to explore the actual relationship of our culture to our personality and its neurotic deviations. Let us now consider the relation of this conception to the views of Freud on culture and neurosis.

The essence of Freud's views on this subject can be summarized, briefly, as follows: Culture is the result of a sublimation of biologically given sexual and aggressive drives—"sexual" in the extended connotation Freud has given the term. Sublimation presupposes unwitting suppression of these instinctual drives. The more complete the suppression of these drives, the higher the cultural development. As the capacity for sublimating is limited, and as the intensive suppression of primitive drives without sublimation may lead to neurosis, the growth of civilization must inevitably imply a growth of neurosis. Neuroses are the price humanity has to pay for cultural development.

The implicit theoretical presupposition underlying this train of thought is the belief in the existence of biologically determined human nature, or, more precisely, the belief that oral, anal, genital, and aggressive drives exist in all human beings in approximately equal quantities.[1] Variations in character formation from individual to individual, as from culture to culture, are due, then, to the varying intensity of the suppression required, with the addition that this suppression can affect the different kinds of drives in varying degrees.

This viewpoint of Freud's seems actually to encounter difficulties with two groups of data. (1) Historical and anthropological findings[2] do not support the assumption that the growth of civilization is in a direct ratio to the growth of instinct suppression. (2) Clinical experience of the kind indicated in this paper suggests that neurosis is due not simply to the quantity of suppression of one or the other instinctual drives, but rather to difficulties caused by the conflicting character of the demands which a culture imposes on its individuals. The differences in neuroses typical of different cultures may be understood to be conditioned by the amount and quality of conflicting demands within the particular culture.

In a given culture, those persons are likely to become neurotic who have met these culturally determined difficulties in accentuated form, mostly through the medium of childhood experiences; and who have not been able to solve their difficulties, or have solved them only at great expense to personality.

---

[2] Ruth Benedict, *Patterns of Culture;* Margaret Mead, *Sex and Temperament in Three Savage Societies.*

---

[1] I pass over Freud's recognition of individual constitutional difference.

5. *Malevolence, Hatred, and Isolating Techniques*

HARRY STACK SULLIVAN

Required Behavior and the Necessity to Conceal and Deceive

I now want to discuss further the very interesting phenomenon of one's becoming malevolent, and we will see if we can approach a consensus. The gross pattern of a great many things that happen in childhood, as compared with the infantile phase of personality, includes two conspicuous elements. One, as has been emphasized, is the acquisition of not only private but communicative language, with the great returns which the learning of this vitally important human tool always carries with it. But the second element, so far as actual development of interpersonal relations goes, is the more significant difference between the two epochs; it can be stated in terms of required behavior. At birth the infant can do practically nothing to assure his own survival. During infancy, he learns only the grossest culture patterns about zonal and general needs. But throughout the era of child-

hood there is an increasing demand for his cooperation. The child is expected to do things which are brought to his attention or impressed on him as requirements for action by the authority-carrying environment—the mother, increasingly the father, and perhaps miscellaneous siblings, servants, and what not.

In childhood—in contradistinction to at least the first two-thirds of the infantile period, and, one rather hopes, the whole infantile period—a new educative influence, *fear*, is brought to bear; we touched on this earlier, but we have not given it very much attention, since it has not so far had remarkable significance with respect to personality development. The discrimination between fear and anxiety is a vital one. Very severe fear and very severe anxiety, so far as I know, feel the same—that is, the felt component is identical—but the discrimination between these two powerful disjunctive processes in life is at times vital. Anxiety is something which I believe is acquired by an empathic linkage with the significant older persons, whereas fear is that which appears when the satisfaction of general needs is deferred to the point where these needs become very powerful. And of these general needs, the need which we particularly want to deal with here is the

SOURCE. *Harry Stack Sullivan, "Malevolence, hatred, and isolating techniques" in* The Interpersonal Theory of Psychiatry. *Edited by Helen Swick Perry and Mary Ladd Gawell. New York: Norton, 1953. Copyright held by W. A. White Psychiatric Fund.*

need to be free from painful sensations. Pain is here defined, not figuratively, but in its most obvious central meaning, hurt—that which occurs, for instance, as a result of sufficient pressure on, or incision into, the actual physical organization, or from misadventures in the internal function of some of the vital organs.

In childhood, perhaps not universally nowadays, but still with great frequency in almost all cultures I think, the child, in contradistinction to the infant, is presumed, at certain times, to deserve or require punishment; and the punishment I am talking about is the infliction of pain. Such punishment can be practically free from anxiety, or it can be strongly blended with anxiety. A parent who very methodically feels that a certain breach of the rules calls for a certain more or less specified form and amount of pain can administer it with no particular anxiety, although possibly with some regret, or possibly with singular neutral feelings as one might have in training a pet. Many parents, however, for a variety of reasons subject the child to anxiety as well as pain. But insofar as punishment, the causing of pain, is used in its own right as an educative influence, this means a new type of learning—namely, learning enforced by a growing discrimination of the connection between certain violations of imposed authority and pain.

Frequently the child is subjected to punishment—pain with or without anxiety, but almost always with anxiety in this case—where he could have foreseen it except that the pressure of a need, zonal or otherwise, made the foresight ineffective in preventing the behavior. In a much more significant, although necessarily quite infrequent, group of circumstances, there comes punishment—pain with, almost invariably in this case, plenty of anxiety—under circumstances which are such that the child could not possibly have foreseen such an outcome from the be-

havior. This is particularly likely to happen with irritable, ill-tempered parents who are afflicted by many anxiety-producing circumstances in their own lives, and who tend rather strikingly to take it out on the dog or the child or what not.

Thus we see in childhood a new educative influence which shows up very definitely as actual fear of the capacity of the authority-carrying figure to impose pain. It is a peculiarity of the difference between anxiety and fear that, under fortunate circumstances, the factors in the situation in which one was hurt can be observed, analyzed, identified, and incorporated in foresight for the future, while in the case of anxiety that is only relatively true, at best; and if anxiety is very severe, it has, as I have said before, almost the effect of a blow on the head. Thus one has very little data on which to work in the future—we might almost say there is nothing in particular to be elaborated into information and foresight.

In childhood, the increased effort of the parents to teach, to discharge their social responsibility, and—I regret to say—to discharge a good many of the more unfortunate peculiarities of their personality produces, in many cases, a child who is "obedient" or a child who is "rebellious," and this outcome may appear fairly early. Of course the pattern may alternate in the same child, and have a very definite relationship to the existent personifications of good-me and bad-me; in reasonably healthy circumstances, good-me tends fairly definitely to be associated with obedience—but still with a considerable measure of freedom to play and so on—and rebelliousness tends to be part of the personification of bad-me.

In this stage of development—when the parents are making increasing efforts to teach the child, when his abilities are maturing, and when he is organizing past experiences and exercising his fantasy, his covert processes in play and make-believe—there is invariably, from very early, a beginning discrimination by the child among the authority-carrying figures, and later, but still quite early, a beginning discrimination of authority situations. In other words, almost all children learn certain indices that stand them in reasonably good stead as to when it is extremely unsafe to violate authority and when there is some chance of "getting away with it." This is, I think, a healthy discrimination which provides useful data, although under certain circumstances, of course, when the parental figures are overloaded with inappropriate and inadequate ways of life, it can be very unfortunate in the way of experience for later life. As the presumed relationship of more-or-less complete dependence of the infant on the mothering one is suspended and the father gets more and more significant, this discrimination by the child of different authority figures and authority situations, insofar as it succeeds —that is, gives information that proves reasonably dependable in foreseeing the course of events—contributes definitely to the growth of and importance of foresight in interpersonal relations. But insofar as the authority figures are confusing to the child and insofar as the authority situations are incongruous from time to time so that, according to the measure of the child's maturing abilities and experience, there is no making sense of them — then, even before the end of the thirtieth month, let us say, we see instances in which the child is already beginning to suffer a deterioration of development of high-grade foresight. In such cases it is quite probable that, in later stages of development, conscious exercise of foresight, witting study of how to get to a more-or-less recognized goal, will not be very highly developed.

Among the things that almost always attend the training of the child to take part in living, to "cooperate" with the parent, to carry out instructions, to do chores and so on, is very frequently the imposition on the child of the concepts of duties and responsibilities. That is certainly good preparation for life in a social order; but again in cases where the parents are uninformed or suffering from unfortunate peculiarities of personality, this training in concepts and responsibilities includes as a very important adjunct (adulterant perhaps) a great deal of training—that is, experience which is presumed, erroneously I think in a great many cases, to be educational—in which the idea of *ought* is very conspicuous.

When it comes to putting into words an adequate statement of the cultural prescriptions which are generally required in the socialization of the young, one really is confronted by a task which requires most remarkable genius. Had culture grown as the work of a single person or a small group of greatly gifted people, almost crushed under their responsibility for their fellow man, then it is quite possible that one could build up a great structure of statements of what principles govern under all sorts of situations, and the result would be a coherent and rationally understandable social system. But that has been nowhere on earth, that I know of, very strikingly the case; possibly the nearest approach to such a social order is to be found in the regimented groups which have characterized various people at various times. For example, there is at least an attempt to embody often subtly contradictory requirements in such things as army regulations; but people who are really diligent students of army regulations frequently discover that it requires only a minor effort to discover a little conflict in authority, and such a conflict provides room for interpreting a situation according to which of the conflicting authoritative statements apply. But, as I was saying, such regulations do provide a rough approximation to this ideal of a rational culture, in that pretty ingenious people, many of them actively interested in maintaining the peculiar social organization of the military, have done their damndest to put plain statements of *ought* and *must* into words which could be understood by the comparatively uninitiated.

But when it comes to imposing the prescriptions of the culture on the child, these prescriptions are often most glaringly contradictory on different occasions, so that they require complex discrimination of authority situations. Moreover the child is incapable for a good many years of comprehending the prescriptions in terms of their possible reasonableness. And more important than anything else, out of the irrational and impulse-driven type of education by anxiety, and by reward and punishment—that is, tenderness and fear—a great many children quite early begin to develop the ability to conceal what is going on in them, what actually they have been doing behind someone's back, and thus to deceive the authoritative figures. Some of this ability to conceal and to deceive is literally taught by the authority-carrying figures, and some of it represents trial-and-error learning from human example—that is, by observing and analyzing the performances, the successes and failures, of siblings, servants, and the like.

Verbalisms and "As If" Performances

Now these growing abilities to conceal and to deceive tend very early to fall into two of the important patterns of inadequate and inappropriate behavior—considered from the broad point of view—which become troublesome in later life and get themselves called mental disorders or processes in mental disorder. I hope that I have communicated by this time a very firm conviction that no pattern of mental disorder which is purely functional, as it is called—that is, which is an inadequate and inappropriate way of living with other people and with one's personifications—includes anything which is at all novel as to human equipment. Everything that we see in the symptomatology of these nonorganic—that is, nondefect—situations has its reflection in kind, if not in degree, in the developmental history of every one of us. And so, when we get to, let us say, mid-childhood, it is not uncommon to discover that the child has become fairly skillful at concealing what might otherwise bring anxiety or punishment—at deceiving the authority-carrying figures as to the degree or nature of his compliance with their more-or-less recognized demands.

The first of these two patterns we touched on previously—namely, verbalisms which are often called rationalizations, in which a plausible series of words is offered, regardless of its actual, remarkable irrelevancy, which has power to spare one anxiety or punishment. The degree to which verbalisms constitute elements in inadequate and inappropriate living which we call mental disorder, whether mild or severe, is truly remarkable. If you think that this is not a very powerful tool, you overlook its amazing significance in the service of the self-system, in the very striking characteristic of the self-system, which makes favorable change so difficult—namely, the self-system's tendency to escape from experience not congruent to its current directions.

But the second pattern is even more impressive than verbalisms: it is the unfortunate—in the sense of being concealing and deceptive—learning of the value of *as if* performances. There are two grand divisions of these. One of them, far from being necessarily troublesome in personality development, is an absolutely inevitable part of everybody's maturing through childhood; and this is the group which perhaps may be called *dramatizations*. A great deal of the learning which the child achieves is on the basis of human examples, and these examples are at this phase authority-invested. The child will inevitably learn in this fashion a good deal about the mother, and, as the father personification becomes more conspicuous, about the father; and this trial-and-error learning by human example can be observed in the child's playing at *acting-like* and *sounding-like* the seniors concerned, and, in fact, playing at *being* them. Probably the progression literally is that one tries first to *act like* and one tries then to act *as if one were*.

In the earlier half of childhood, this inevitable part of one's learning to be a human being becomes a rather serious concern—in terms of what may show up later—only when these dramatizations become particularly significant in concealing violations of cooperation and in deceiving the authority-invested figures. In these latter cases, for a variety of reasons, some of which we will touch on briefly, these dramatizations tend to become what I could perhaps safely call sub-personifications. The roles which are acted in this way that succeed in avoiding anxiety and punishment, or that perhaps bring tenderness when there was no performance based on previous experience to get tenderness, are organized to the degree that I think we can properly call them *personae*; they are often multiple, and each one later on will be found equally entitled to be called *1*. To describe this type of deviation from the ideal personality development, I long since set up the conception of me-you patterns, by which I mean often grossly incongruent ways of behaving, or roles that one plays, in interpersonal relations with someone else. And all of them, or most of them, seem just as near the real thing—the personification of the self—as can be, although

there is no more making sense of them from the standpoint of their representing different aspects of durable traits than there is of translating Sanskrit before you understand language. While these dramatizations are very closely related to learning to be human, they can even in these early days begin to introduce a very strikingly irrational element in the personification of the self.

The other group of these *as if* performances to which I wish to refer is perhaps best considered under the rubric of *preoccupations*. I would like to say a few words about one of my cocker spaniels, because it perhaps makes the point better than anything else I can think of now. This particular dog has always been the most diminutive in a litter of six; she has been kept with two others in this litter to the present time. The two others are a rather large male and a very shrewd and, shall I say, domineering female. The little bitch whom I am attempting to discuss was quite often the butt of the unquestionably painful vigor of the male and the unquestionably clever domineering of the female. Probably as a result of this, this little dog very conspicuously indeed took to remaining apart from her brother and sister, and could be observed very diligently digging great holes and trenches in the environment. This was literally quite a complex performance, in that each scoop of dirt that was flung out between her hind legs had to be examined carefully lest it contain something edible or otherwise interesting; the little dog would dig furiously in one of these mammoth excavations, rush around, examine the dirt thrown out, go down and get another shovel full—a tremendous activity for literally hours at a time. Somehow there seemed to be a stipulation that as long as she was so hard at work, the other two would leave her alone most of the time. But time has passed; she has been rescued from her unhappy submersion in the bigger siblings; and nowadays she treats them very roughly when she meets them. Now the trash man is outstanding around our place as a stimulus for provoking fear in the dogs — they are all quite upset when he shows up and to some extent are afraid of the mammoth truck and the din and so on that goes on about it. But when he is around, this little dog, alone out of the whole family, goes out and barks furiously at him. But she stops, after almost every third bark, to dig frantically, and to rush around and examine the dirt again, and then she goes back and roars furiously at him again. It is not, I think, too much to infer that this dog is really very timid, having had excellent reasons for being afraid in the past, but that she became so accustomed to being saved in the past by being preoccupied with her digging that the excess of fear in this situation leads to the reappearance of her preoccupation with digging.

In the human being, preoccupation as a way of dealing with fear-provoking situations or the threat of punishment, and of avoiding or minimizing anxiety appears quite early in life. And quite often the irrational and, shall I say, emotional way in which parental authority is imposed on the child, teaches the child that preoccupation with some particular onetime interesting and probably, as it turns out, profitable activity is very valuable to continue, not because it is any longer needed for the maturation of abilities or for satisfaction in new abilities, but as a preoccupation to ward off punishment and anxiety. Now if these performances are not only successful in avoiding unpleasantness, but also get positive reward by the child's being treated tenderly and approved, that naturally sets him on what will later be a strikingly complex way of life — that to which we refer as the *obsessional*.

Section IV

Murray's Personology

In recent years Henry Murray has continued to reshape and modify his theoretical formulations, and at the same time he has pursued his ingenious attempts to uncover central aspects of personality through various measures or instruments. In addition to the papers reprinted here, the interested reader will wish to consult his chapter entitled "Preparations for the Scaffold of a Comprehensive System" (Murray, 1959) and his autobiography (Murray, 1967). Both contain a wealth of information concerning the origin of his theoretical ideas as well as the introduction of new concepts and formulations.

We have selected the first paper *In Nomine Diaboli*, for inclusion here in spite of the fact that it was discussed at some length in *Theories of Personality*. Our willingness to override this consideration provides a good index of our admiration for this sensitive psychological analysis of a great American novel *Moby Dick*. The paper reveals clearly Murray's depth of psychological understanding as well as the richness of his general scholarship.

Murray made a fundamental contribution in his distinction between complementary and supplementary projection, and this distinction has played an important part in most theories of projection. The two types of projection were first identified in his 1933 study of the effect of fear upon ratings of photographs. The second paper in this section is related to this early experiment. In the studies by the Feshbachs the stimuli shown to the subjects were controlled in an effort to determine more precisely the type of projection used and the degree of its use. It was observed that boys who had been exposed to an experimental manipulation designed to arouse fear would tend to perceive pictures of boys as fearful (supplementary projection) and pictures of adults as malicious (complementary projection). The results of a second experiment supported the Feshbachs' expectation that one of the important variables influencing the use of supplementary and complementary projection is the relationship between the perceiver and the stimulus person.

The third paper, "Studies of stressful interpersonal disputations," was presented by Murray following his receiving the Distinguished Scientific Award of the American Psychological Association. It provides a glimpse of the research with which he has been occupied recently. In this investigation a small number of persons in a social setting are appraised by multiple methods and observers (the multiform method) in an effort to expand our understanding of an important affect — anger. The paper also includes a number of recommendations in regard to how to conduct personological research.

References

Murray, H. A. Preparations for the scaffold of a comprehensive system. In S. Koch (Ed.) *Psychology: A study of a science.* Vol. 3, New York: McGraw-Hill, 1959, pp. 7–54.

Murray, H. A. Autobiography. In E. G. Boring and G. Lindzey (Eds.), *A history of psychology in autobiography*, Vol. V, New York: Appleton-Century-Crofts, 1967, pp. 283–310.

1. In Nomine Diaboli

HENRY A. MURRAY

Next to the seizures and shapings of creative thought—the thing itself—no comparable experience is more thrilling than
being witched, illumined, and transfigured by the magic of another's art. This is a
trance from which one returns refreshed
and quickened, and bubbling with unen-
vious praise of the exciting cause, much
as Melville bubbled after his first reading
of Hawthorne's *Mosses*. In describing *his*
experience Melville chose a phrase so
apt—"the shock of recognition"—that in
the thirties Edmund Wilson took it as the
irresistibly perfect title for his anthology
of literary appreciations. Acknowledging
a shock of recognition and paying homage to the delivering genius is singularly
exhilarating, even today—or especially
today—when every waxing enthusiasm
must confront an outgoing tide of culture.

In our time, the capacities for wonder
and reverence, for generous judgments
and trustful affirmations, have largely
given way, though not without cause
surely, to their antipathies, the humors of
a waning ethos: disillusionment, cynicism,
disgust, and gnawing envy. These states
have bred in us the inclination to dissect
the subtlest orders of man's wit with ever-
sharper instruments of depreciation, to
pour all values, the best confounded by
the worst, into one mocking-pot, to sneer
"realistically," and, as we say today,
"assassinate" character. These same
humors have disposed writers to spend
immortal talent in snickering exhibitions
of vulgarity and spiritual emptiness, or in
making delicate picture-puzzles out of the
butt-ends of life.

In the face of these current trends and
tempers, I, coming out of years of brim-
ming gratefulness for the gift of *Moby-
Dick*, would like to praise Herman Melville
worthily, not to bury him in a winding-
sheet of scientific terminology. But the
odds are not favorable to my ambition. A
commitment of thirty years to analytic
modes of thought and concepts lethal to
emotion has built such habits in me that
were I to be waked in the night by a cry
of "Help!" I fear I would respond in the
lingo of psychology. I am suffering from
one of the commonest ailments of our
age—trained disability.

The habit of a psychologist is to break
down the structure of each personality
he studies into elements, and so in a few
strokes to bring to earth whatever merit
that structure, as a structure, may possess.

SOURCE. *Article by Henry A. Murray, "In nomine
diaboli" in the* New England Quarterly, *Vol. 24, pp.
435–452, 1941.*

Furthermore, for reasons I need not mention here, the technical terms for the majority of these elements have derogatory connotations. Consequently, it is difficult to open one's professional mouth without disparaging a fellow-being. Were an analyst to be confronted by that much heralded but still missing specimen of the human race—the normal man—he would be struck dumb, for once, through lack of appropriate ideas.

If I am able to surmount to some extent any impediments of this origin, you may attribute my good fortune to a providential circumstance. In the procession of my experiences *Moby-Dick* anteceded Psychology, that is, I was swept by Melville's gale and shaken by his appalling sea dragon before I had acquired the all-leveling academic oil that is poured on brewed-up waters, and before I possessed the weapons and tools of science—the conceptual lance, harpoons, cutting irons, and what-nots—which might have reduced the "grand hooded phantom" to mere blubber. Lacking these defenses I was whelmed. Instead of my changing this book, this book changed me.

To me, *Moby-Dick* was Beethoven's *Eroica* in words: first of all, a masterly orchestration of harmonic and melodic language, of resonating images and thoughts in varied metres. Equally compelling were the spacious sea-settings of the story, the cast of characters and their prodigious common target, the sorrow, the fury, and the terror, together with all those frequent touches, those subtle interminglings of unexampled humor, quizzical and, in the American way, extravagant, and finally the fated closure, the crown and tragic consummation of the immense yet firmly-welded whole. But still more extraordinary and portentous were the penetration and scope, the sheer audacity of the author's imagination. Here was a man who did not fly away with his surprising fantasies to some unbelievable dreamland, pale or florid, shunning the stubborn objects and gritty facts, the prosaic routines and practicalities of everyday existence. Here was a man who, on the contrary, chose these very things as vessels for his procreative powers—the whale as a naturalist, a Hunter or a Cuvier, would perceive him, the business of killing whales, the whale-ship running as an oil-factory, stowing-down, in fact, every mechanism and technique, each tool and gadget, that was integral to the money-minded industry of whaling. Here was a man who could describe the appearance, the concrete matter-of-factness, and the utility of each one of these natural objects, implements, and tools with the fidelity of a scientist, and, while doing this, explore it as a conceivable repository of some aspect of the human drama; then, by an imaginative tour de force, deliver a vital essence, some humorous or profound idea, coalescing with its embodiment. But still more. Differing from the symbolists of our time, here was a man who offered us essences and meanings which did not level or depreciate the objects of his contemplation. On the contrary, this loving man exalted all creatures—the mariners, renegades, and castaways on board the *Pequod*—by ascribing to them "high qualities, though dark" and weaving round them "tragic graces." Here, in short, was a man with the myth-making powers of a Blake, a hive of significant associations, who was capable of reuniting what science had put asunder—pure perception and relevant emotion—and doing it in an exultant way that was acceptable to skepticism.

Not at first, but later, I perceived the crucial difference between Melville's dramatic animations of nature and those of primitive religion-makers: both were spontaneous and uncalculated projections, but Melville's were in harmony, for the most part, with scientific knowledge, because they had been recognized as projections, checked, and modified. Here, then, was a man who might redeem us from the virtue of an incredible subjective belief, on the one side, and from the virtue of a deadly objective rationality, on the other.

For these and other reasons the reading of *Moby-Dick*—coming before Psychology—left a stupendous reverberating imprint, too lively to be diminished by the long series of relentless analytical operations to which I subsequently subjected it. Today, after twenty-five years of such experiments, *The Whale* is still *the Whale*, more magnificent, if anything, than before.

Before coming to grips with the "mystery" of *Moby-Dick* I should mention another providential circumstance to which all psychologists are, or should be, forever grateful, and literary critics too, since without it no complete understanding of books like *Moby-Dick* would be possible today. Ahead of us were two greatly gifted pioneers, Freud and Jung, who, with others, explored the manifold vagaries of unconscious mental processes and left for our inheritance their finely-written works. The discoveries of these adventurers advantaged me in a special way: they gave, I thought, support to one of Santayana's early convictions, that in the human being imagination is more fundamental than perception. Anyhow, adopting this position, some of us psychologists have been devoting ourselves to the study of dreams, fantasies, creative productions, and projections—all of which are primarily and essentially emotional and dramatic, such stuff as myths are made of. Thus, by chance or otherwise, this branch of the tree of psychology is growing in the direction of Herman Melville.

To be explicit: psychologists have been recognizing in the dream figures and fantasy figures of today's children and adolescents more and more family like-

nesses of the heroes and heroines of primitive myths, legends, and fables—figures, in other words, who are engaged in comparable heroic strivings and conflicts, and experiencing comparable heroic triumphs or fatalities. Our ancestors, yielding to an inherent propensity of the mind, projected the more relevant of these figures into objects of their environment, into sun, moon, and stars, into the unknown deeps of the sea and of the earth, and into the boundless void of heaven; and they worshipped the most potent of these projected images, whether animal or human, as super-beings, gods, or goddesses. On any clear night one can see scores of the more luminous of such divinities parading up and down the firmament. For example, in Fall and Winter, one looks with admiration on that resplendent hero Perseus and above him the chained beauty, Andromeda, whom he saved from a devouring monster, ferocious as Moby Dick. Now, what psychologists have been learning by degrees is that Perseus is in the unconscious mind of every man and Andromeda in every woman, not, let me hasten to say, as an inherited fixed image, but as a potential set of dispositions which may be constellated in the personality by the occurrence of a certain kind of situation. Herman Melville arrived at this conclusion in his own way a hundred years ago, sooner and, I believe, with more genuine comprehension than any other writer.

An explanation of all this in scientific terms would require all the space permitted me and more. Suffice it to say here that the psychologists who are studying the elementary myth-makings of the mind are dealing with the germy sources of poetry and drama, the fecundities out of which great literature is fashioned. Furthermore, in attempting to formulate and classify these multifarious productions of the imagination, the psychologist uses modes of analysis and synthesis very similar to those that Aristotle used in setting forth the dynamics of Greek tragedy. In these and other trends I find much encouragement for the view that a rapprochement of psychology and literary criticism is in progress, and that it will prove fruitful to both callings. As an ideal meeting ground I would propose Melville's world of "wondrous depths."

To this Columbus of the mind, the great archetypal figures of myth, drama, and epic were not pieces of intellectual Dresden china, heirlooms of a classical education, ornamental bric-a-brac to be put here and there for the pleasure of genteel readers. Many of the more significant of these constellations were inwardly experienced by Melville, one after the other, as each was given vent to blossom and assert itself. Thus, we are offered a spectacle of spiritual development through passionate identifications. Only by proceeding in this way could Melville have learnt on his pulses what it was to be Narcissus, Orestes, Oedipus, Ishmael, Apollo, Lucifer. "Like a frigate," he said, "I am full with a thousand souls."

This brings me to the problem of interpreting *Moby-Dick*. Some writers have said that there is nothing to interpret: it is a plain sea story marred here and there by irrelevant ruminations. But I shall not cite the abundant proof for the now generally accepted proposition that in *Moby-Dick* Melville "meant" something— something, I should add, which he considered "terrifically true" but which, in the world's judgment, was so harmful "that it were all but madness for any good man, in his own proper character, to utter or even hint of." What seems decisive here is the passage in Melville's celebrated letter to Hawthorne: "A sense of unspeakable security is in me this moment, on account of your having understood the book." From this we can conclude that there *are* meanings to be understood in *Moby-Dick*, and also—may we say for our own encouragement?—that Melville's ghost will feel secure forever if modern critics can find them, and, since Hawthorne remained silent, set them forth in print. Here it might be well to remind ourselves of a crucial statement which follows the just quoted passage from Melville's letter: "I have written a wicked book." The implication is clear: all interpretations which fail to show that *Moby-Dick* is, in some sense, wicked have missed the author's avowed intention.

A few critics have scouted all attempts to fish Melville's own meaning out of *The Whale*, on the ground that an interpretation of a work of art so vast and so complex is bound to be composed in large measure of projections from the mind of the interpreter. It must be granted that preposterous projections often do occur in the course of such an effort. But these are not inevitable. Self-knowledge and discipline may reduce projections to a minimum. Anyhow, in the case of *Moby-Dick*, the facts do not sustain the proposition that a critic can see nothing in this book but his own reflected image. The interpretations which have been published over the last thirty years exhibit an unmistakable trend towards consensus in respect to the drama as a whole as well as many of its subordinate parts. Moreover, so far as I can judge, the critics who, with hints from their predecessors, applied their intuitions most recently to the exegesis of *The Whale*, can be said to have arrived, if taken together, at Melville's essential meaning. Since one or another of these authors has deftly said what I clumsily thought, my prejudices are strongly in favor of their conclusions, and I am whole-hearted in applauding them, Mr. Arvin's[1] most especially, despite their having left me with nothing fresh to say. Since this is how things stand, my version of the main theme of *Moby-Dick* can be

[1]Newton Arvin, *Herman Melville* (New York, 1950.)

presented in a briefer form, and limited to two hypotheses.

The first of them is this: Captain Ahab is an embodiment of that fallen angel or demi-god who in Christendom was variously named Lucifer, Devil, Adversary, Satan. The Church Fathers would have called Captain Ahab "Antichrist" because he was not Satan himself, but a human creature possessed of all Satan's pride and energy, "summing up within himself," as Irenaeus said, "the apostasy of the devil."

That it was Melville's intention to beget Ahab in Satan's image can hardly be doubted. He told Hawthorne that his book has been boiled in hell-fire and secretly baptized not in the name of God but in the name of the Devil. He named his tragic hero after the Old Testament ruler who "did more to provoke the Lord God of Israel to anger than all the Kings of Israel that were before him." King Ahab's accuser, the prophet Elijah, is also resurrected to play his original rôle, though very briefly, in Melville's testament. We are told that Captain Ahab is an "ungodly, god-like" man who is spiritually outside Christendom. He is a well of blasphemy and defiance, of scorn and mockery for the gods—"cricket-players and pugilists" in his eyes. Rumor has it that he once spat in the holy goblet on the altar of the Catholic Church at Santa. "I never saw him kneel," says Stubb. He is associated in the text with scores of references to the Devil. He is an "anaconda of an old man." His self-assertive sadism is the linked antithesis of the masochistic submission preached by Father Mapple.

Captain Ahab-Lucifer is also related to a sungod, like Christ, but in reverse. Instead of being light leaping out of darkness, he is "darkness leaping out of light." The *Pequod* sails on Christmas Day. *This* new year's sun will be the god of Wrath rather than the god of Love. Ahab does

not emerge from his subterranean abode until his ship is "rolling through the bright Quito spring" (Easter-tide, symbolically, when the all-fertilizing sun-god is resurrected). The frenzied ceremony in which Ahab's followers are sworn to the pursuit of the White Whale—"Commend the murderous chalices!"—is suggestive of the Black Mass; the lurid operations at the try-works is a scene out of Hell.

There is some evidence that Melville was rereading *Paradise Lost* in the summer of 1850, shortly after, let us guess, he got the idea of transforming the captain of his whale-ship into the first of all cardinal sinners who fell by pride. Anyhow, Melville's Satan is the spitting image of Milton's hero, but portrayed with deeper and subtler psychological insight, and placed where he belongs, in the heart of an enraged man.

Melville may have been persuaded by Goethe's Mephistopheles, or even by some of Hawthorne's bloodless abstracts of humanity, to add Fedallah to his cast of characters. Evidently he wanted to make certain that no reader would fail to recognize that Ahab had been possessed by, or had sold his soul to, the Devil. Personally, I think Fedallah's rôle is superfluous and I regret that Melville made room for him and his unbelievable boat-crew on the ship *Pequod*. Still, he is not wholly without interest. He represents the cool, heartless, cunning, calculating, intellectual Devil of the Medieval myth-makers, in contrast, to the stricken, passionate, indignant, and often eloquent rebel angel of *Paradise Lost*, whose rôle is played by Ahab.

The Arabic name "Fedallah" suggests "dev(il) Allah," that is, the Mohammedans' god as he appeared in the mind's eye of a Crusader. But we are told that Fedallah is a Parsee—a Persian fire-worshipper, or Zoroastrian, who lives in India. Thus, Ahab, named after the Semitic apostate who was converted to the orgiastic cult of Baal, or Bel, originally a Babylonian fertility god, has formed a compact with a Zoroastrian whose name reminds us of still another Oriental religion. In addition, Captain Ahab's whale-boat is manned by a crew of unregenerate infidels, as defined by orthodox Christianity, and each of his three harpooners, Queequeg, Tastego, and Daggoo, is a member of a race which believed in other gods than the one god of the Hebraic-Christian Bible.

Speaking roughly, it might be said that Captain Ahab, incarnation of the Adversary and master of the ship *Pequod* (named after the aggressive Indian tribe that was exterminated by the Puritans of New England), has summoned the various religions of the East to combat the one dominant religion of the West. Or, in other terms, that he and his followers, Starbuck excepted, represent the horde of primitive drives, values, beliefs, and practices which the Hebraic-Christian religionists rejected and excluded, and by threats, punishments, and inquisitions, forced into the unconscious mind of Western man.

Stated in psychological concepts, Ahab is captain of the culturally repressed dispositions of human nature, that part of personality which psychoanalysts have termed the "Id." If this is true, his opponent, the White Whale, can be none other than the internal institution which is responsible for these repressions, namely the Freudian Superego. This then is my second hypothesis: Moby-Dick is a veritable spouting, breaching, sounding whale, a whale who, because of his whiteness, his mighty bulk and beauty, and because of one instinctive act that happened to dismember his assailant, has received the projection of Captain Ahab's Presbyterian conscience, and so may be said to embody the Old Testament Calvinistic conception of an affrighting

Deity and his strict commandments, the derivative puritan ethic of nineteenth-century America, and the society that defended this ethic. Also, and most specifically, he symbolizes the zealous parents whose righteous sermonizings and corrections drove the prohibitions in so hard that a serious young man could hardly reach outside the barrier, except possibly far away among some tolerant, gracious Polynesian peoples. The emphasis should be placed on that unconscious (and hence inscrutable) wall of inhibitions which imprisoned the puritan's thrusting passions. "How can the prisoner reach outside," cries Ahab, "except by thrusting through the wall? To me, the White Whale is that wall, shoved near to me . . . I see in him outrageous strength, with an inscrutable malice sinewing it." As a symbol of a sounding, breaching, white-dark, unconquerable New England conscience what could be better than a sounding, breaching, white-dark, unconquerable sperm whale?

Who is the psychoanalyst who could resist the immediate inference that the *imago* of the mother as well as the *imago* of the father is contained in the Whale? In the present case there happens to be a host of biographical facts and written passages which support this proposition. Luckily, I need not review them, because Mr. Arvin and others have come to the same conclusion. I shall confine myself to one reference. It exhibits Melville's keen and sympathetic insight into the cultural determinants of his mother's prohibiting dispositions. In *Pierre*, it is the "high-up, and towering and all-forbidding . . . edifice of his mother's immense pride . . . her pride of birth . . . her pride of purity," that is the "wall shoved near," the wall that stands between the hero and the realization of his heart's resolve. But instead of expending the fury of frustration upon his mother, he directs it at Fate, or, more specifically, at his mother's God and the society that shaped her. For he saw "that not his mother had made his mother; but the Infinite Haughtiness had first fashioned her; and then the haughty world had further molded her; nor had a haughty Ritual omitted to finish her."

Given this penetrating apprehension we are in a position to say that Melville's target in *Moby-Dick* was the upper middle-class culture of his time. It was *this* culture which was defended with righteous indignation by what he was apt to call "the world" or "the public," and Melville had very little respect for "the world" or "the public." The "public," or men operating as a social system, was something quite distinct from "the people." In *White Jacket* he wrote: "The public and the people! . . . let us hate the one, and cleave to the other." "The public is a monster," says Lemsford. Still earlier Melville had said: "I fight against the armed and crested lies of Mardi (the world)." "Mardi is a monster whose eyes are fixed in its head, like a whale." Many other writers have used similar imagery. Sir Thomas Browne referred to the multitude as "that numerous piece of monstrosity"; Keats spoke of "the dragon world." But closest of all was Hobbes: "By art is created that great Leviathan, called a commonwealth or state." It was in the laws of this Leviathan, Hobbes made clear, that the sources of right and wrong reside. To summarize: the giant mass of Melville's whale is the same as Melville's man-of-war world, the *Neversink*, in *White Jacket*, which in turn is an epitome of Melville's Mardi. The Whale's white forehead and hump should be reserved for the world's heavenly King.

That God is incarnate in the Whale has been perceived by Mr. Stone,[2] and, as far as I know, by every other Catholic critic of Melville's work, as well as by several Protestant critics. In fact, Mr. Chase[3] has marshalled so fair a portion of the large bulk of evidence on this point that any more from me would be superfluous. Of course, what Ahab projects into the Whale is not the image of a loving Father, but the God of the Old Dispensation, the God who brought Jeremiah into darkness, hedged him about, and made his path crooked; the God, adopted by the fire-and-brimstone Puritans, who said: "With fury poured out I will rule over you." "The sword without and the terror within, shall destroy both the young man and the virgin." "I will also send the teeth of beasts upon them." "I will heap mischiefs upon them." "To me belongeth vengeance and recompense."

Since the society's vision of deity, and the society's morality, and the parents and ministers who implant these conceptions, are represented in a fully socialized personality by an establishment that is called the Superego—Conscience as Freud defined it—, and since Ahab has been proclaimed "Captain of the Id," the simplest psychological formula for Melville's dramatic epic is this: an insurgent Id in mortal conflict with an oppressive cultural Superego. Starbuck, the First Mate, stands for the rational realistic Ego which is overpowered by the fanatical compulsiveness of the Id and dispossessed of its normally regulating functions.

If this is approximately correct, it appears that while writing his greatest work Melville abandoned his detached position in the Ego from time to time, hailed "the realm of shades," as his hero Taji had, and, through the mediumship of Ahab, "burst his hot heart's shell" upon the sacrosanct Almighty and the sacrosanct sentiments of Christendom. Since in the world's judgment, 1851, nothing could be more reproachable than this, it would

[2]Geoffrey Stone, *Melville* (New York, 1949).

[3]Richard Volney Chase, *Herman Melville: A Critical Study* (New York, 1949).

be unjust, if not treacherous, of us to reason *Moby-Dick* into some comforting morality play for which no boldness was required. This would be depriving Melville of the ground he gained for self-respect by having dared to abide by his own subjective truth and write a "wicked book," the kind of book that Pierre's publishers, Steel, Flint, and Asbestos, would have called "a blasphemous rhapsody filched from the vile Atheists, Lucian and Voltaire."

Some may wonder how it was that Melville, a fundamentally good, affectionate, noble, idealistic, and reverential man, should have felt impelled to write a wicked book. Why did he aggress so furiously against Western orthodoxy, as furiously as Byron and Shelley, or any Satanic writer who preceded him, as furiously as Nietzsche or the most radical of his successors in our day?

In *Civilization and its Discontents* Freud, out of the ripeness of his full experience, wrote that when one finds deep-seated aggression — and by this he meant aggression of the sort that Melville voiced — one can safely attribute it to the frustration of Eros. In my opinion this generalization does not hold for all men of all cultures of all times, but the probability of its being valid is extremely high in the case of an earnest, moralistic, nineteenth-century American, a Presbyterian to boot, whose anger is born of suffering, especially if this man spent an impressionable year of his life in Polynesia and returned to marry the very proper little daughter of the Chief Justice of Massachusetts, and if, in addition, he is a profoundly creative man in whose androgynic personality masculine and feminine components are integrally blended.

If it were concerned with *Moby-Dick*, the book, rather than with its author, I would call *this* my third hypothesis: Ahab-Melville's aggression was directed against the object that once harmed Eros with apparent malice and was still thwarting it with presentiments of further retaliations. The correctness of this inference is indicated by the nature of the injury — a symbolic emasculation — that excited Ahab's ire. Initially, this threatening object was, in all likelihood, the father, later, possibly, the mother. But, as Melville plainly saw, both his parents had been fashioned by the Hebraic-Christian, American Calvinist tradition, the tradition which conceived of a deity in whose eyes Eros was depravity. It was the first Biblical mythmakers who dismissed from heaven and from earth the Great Goddess of the Oriental and primitive religions, and so rejected the feminine principle as a spiritual force. Ahab, protagonist of these rejected religions, in addressing heaven's fire and lightning, what he calls "the personified impersonal," cries: "But thou art my fiery father; my sweet mother I know not. Oh, cruel! What has thou done with her? He calls this god a foundling, a "hermit immemorial," who does not know his own origin. Again, it was the Hebraic authors, sustained later by the Church Fathers, who propagated the legend that a woman was the cause of Adam's exile from Paradise, and that the original sin was concupiscence. Melville says that Ahab, spokesman of all exiled princes, "piled upon the whale's white hump the sum of all the general rage and hate felt by his whole race from Adam down. Remember also that it was the lure of Jezebel that drew King Ahab of Israel outside the orthodoxy of his religion and persuaded him to worship the Phoenician Astarte, goddess of love and fruitful increase. "Jezebel" was the worst tongue-lash a puritan could give a woman. She was Sex, and sex was Sin, spelled with a capital. It was the Church periodicals of Melville's day that denounced *Typee*, called the author a sensualist, and influenced the publisher to delete suggestive passages from the second edition. It was this long heritage of aversion and animosity, so accentuated in this country, which banned sex relations as a topic of discourse and condemned divorce as an unpardonable offense. All this has been changed, for better and for worse, by the moral revolutionaries of our own time who, feeling as Melville felt but finding the currents of sentiment less strongly opposite, spoke out, and with their wit, indignation, and logic, reinforced by the findings of psychoanalysis, disgraced the stern-faced idols of their forebears. One result is this: today an incompatible marriage is not a prison-house, as it was for Melville, "with wall shoved near."

In *Pierre* Melville confessed his own faith when he said that Eros is god of all, and Love "the loftiest religion of this earth." To the romantic Pierre the image of Isabel was "a silent and tyrannical call, challenging him in his deepest moral being, and summoning Truth, Love, Pity, Conscience to the stand." Here he seems to have had in mind the redeeming and inspiring Eros of Courtly Love, a heresy which the Medieval Church has done its utmost to stamp out. *This*, he felt convinced, was *his* "path to God," although in the way of it he saw with horror the implacable conscience and worldly valuations of his revered mother.

If this line of reasoning is as close as I think it is to the known facts, then Melville, in the person of Ahab, assailed Calvinism in the Whale because it blocked the advance of a conscience beneficent to evolutionary love. And so, weighed in the scales of its creator, *Moby-Dick* is not a wicked book but a *good* book, and after finishing it Melville had full reason to feel as he confessed, "spotless as the lamb."

But then, seen from another point, *Moby-Dick* might be judged a wicked book, not because its hero condemns an entrenched tradition, but because he is completely committed to destruction. Although Captain Ahab manifests the basic

stubborn virtues of the archprotestant and the rugged individual carried to their limits, *this* god-defier is no Prometheus, since all thought of benefiting humanity is foreign to him. His purpose is not to make the Pacific safe for whaling, nor, when blasting at the moral order, does he have in mind a more heartening vision for the future. The religion of Eros which might once have been the secret determinant of Ahab's undertaking is never mentioned. At one critical point in *Pierre* the hero-author, favored by a flash of light, exclaims, "I will gospelize the word anew"; but he never does. Out of light comes darkness: the temper of Pierre's book is no different from the temper of *Moby-Dick.* The truth is that Ahab is motivated solely by his private need to avenge a private insult. His governing philosophy is that of nihilism, the doctrine that the existing system must be shattered. Nihilism springs up when the imagination fails to provide the redeeming solution of an unbearable dilemma, when "the creative response," as Toynbee would say, is not forthcoming, and a man reacts out of a hot heart—"to the dogs with the head" —and swings to an instinct—"the same that prompts even a worm to turn under the heel." This is what White Jacket did when arraigned at the mast, and what Pierre did when fortune deserted him, and what Billy Budd did when confronted by his accuser. "Nature has not implanted any power in man," said Melville, "that was not meant to be exercised at times, though too often our powers have been abused. The privilege, inborn and inalienable, that every man has, of dying himself and inflicting death upon another, was not given to us without a purpose. These are last resources of an insulted and unendurable existence."

If we grant that Ahab is a wicked man, what does this prove? It proves that *Moby-Dick* is a *good* book, a parable in epic form, because Melville makes a great spectacle of Ahab's wickedness and shows through the course of the narrative how such wickedness will drive a man on iron rails to an appointed nemesis. Melville adhered to the classic formula for tragedies. He could feel "spotless as the lamb," because he had seen to it that the huge threat to the social system, imminent in Ahab's two cardinal defects—egotistic self-inflation and unleashed wrath—was, at the end, fatefully exterminated, "and the great shroud of the sea rolled on as it rolled five thousand years ago." The reader has had his catharsis, equilibrium has been restored, sanity is vindicated.

This is true, but is it the whole truth? In point of fact, while writing *Moby-Dick* did Melville maintain aesthetic distance, keeping his own feelings in abeyance? Do we not hear Ahab saying things that the later Pierre will say and that Melville said less vehemently in his own person? Does not the author show marked partiality for the "mighty pageant creature" of his invention, put in *his* mouth the finest, boldest language? Also, have not many interpreters been so influenced by the abused Ahab that they saw nothing in his opponent but the source of all malicious agencies, the very Devil? As Mr. Mumford has said so eloquently, Ahab is at heart a noble being whose tragic wrong is that of battling against evil with "power instead of love," and so becoming "the image of the thing he hates." With this impression imbedded in our minds, how can we come out with any moral except this: evil wins. We admit that Ahab's wickedness has been cancelled. But what survives? It is the much more formidable, compacted wickedness of the group that survives, the world that is "saturated and soaking with lies," and their man-of-war God, who is hardly more admirable than a primitive totem beast, some oral-aggressive, child-devouring Cronos of the sea. Is this an idea that a man of good-will can rest with?

Rest with? Certainly not. Melville's clear intention was to bring not rest, but *unrest* to intrepid minds. All gentle people were warned away from his book "on the risk of a lumbago or sciatica." "A polar wind blows through it," he announced. He had not written to soothe, but to kindle, to make men leap from their seats, as Whitman would say, and fight for their lives. Was it the poet's function to buttress the battlements of complacency, to give comfort to the enemy? There is little doubt about the nature of the enemy in Melville's day. It was the dominant ideology, that peculiar compound of puritanism and materialism, of rationalism and commercialism, of shallow, blatant optimism and technology, which proved so crushing to creative evolutions in religion, art, and life. In such circumstances every "true poet," as Blake said, "is of the Devil's party," whether he knows it or not. Surveying the last hundred and fifty years, how many exceptions to this statement can we find? Melville, anyhow, knew that *he* belonged to the party, and while writing *Moby-Dick* so gloried in his membership that he baptized his work *In Nomine Diaboli*. It was precisely under these auspices that he created his solitary masterpiece, a construction of the same high order as the Constitution of the United States and the scientific treaties of Willard Gibbs, though huge and wild and unruly as the Grand Canyon. And it is for this marvel chiefly that he resides in our hearts now among the greatest in "that small but high-hushed world" of bestowing geniuses.

Here ends this report of my soundings in *Moby-Dick*. The drama is finished. What became of its surviving author?

Moby-Dick may be taken as a comment on the strategic crisis of Melville's allegorical life. In portraying the consequences of Ahab's last suicidal lunge, the hero's umbilical fixation to the Whale and his death by strangling, the author signalized not only his permanent attachment to the *imago* of the mother, but the submission he had forseen to the binding power of the parent conscience, the Superego of middle-class America. Measured against the standards of *his* day, then, Melville must be accounted a *good* man.

But does this entitle him to a place on the side of the angels? He abdicated to the conscience he condemned and his ship *Pequod*, in sinking, carried down with it the conscience he aspired to, represented by the sky-hawk, the bird of heaven. With his ideal drowned, life from then one was load and time stood still. All he had denied to love he gave throughout a martyrdom of forty years, to death.

But "hark ye yet again—the little lower layer." Melville's capitulation in the face of overwhelming odds was limited to the sphere of action. His embattled soul refused surrender and lived on, breathing back defiance, disputing "to the last gasp" of his "earthquake life" the sovereignty of that inscrutable authority in him. As he wrote in *Pierre*, unless the enthusiast "can find the talismanic secret, to reconcile this world with his own soul, then there is no peace for him, no slightest truce for him in this life." Years later we find him holding the same ground. "Terrible is earth" was his conclusion, but despite all, "no retreat through me." By this dogged stand he bequeathed to succeeding generations the unsolved problem of the talismanic secret.

Only at the very last, instinct spent, earthquake over, did he fall back to a position close to Christian resignation. In his Being, was not this man "a wonder, a grandeur, and a woe?"

2. Influence of The Stimulus Object upon the Complementary and Supplementary Projection of Fear

SEYMOUR FESHBACH AND NORMA FESHBACH

2 studies were conducted bearing on the hypothesis that frightened boys attribute malice to male adults but attribute fear to other boys.
In the 1st experiment, a Halloween setting was used to elicit fear. The experimental group, in comparison to a matched control group, manifested a reliable increment in attribution of maliciousness to pictures of men and boys but no significant change in attribution of fear. Because of possible complications due to hostility arousal, a 2nd experiment was carried out in which judgments were elicited from boys who thought they were going to participate in a study involving frightening equipment. Under these conditions, the experimental Ss attributed reliably more maliciousness to men and reliably more fear to boys.

Clinical observation as well as experimental studies (Feshbach & Singer, 1957; Murray, 1933; Singer & Feshbach, 1962) indicate that a frightened individual tends to distort his judgments of other people. The factors that determine the degree and type of distortion that will take place have yet to be specified. The present study proposes to investigate the influence of the stimulus person upon the projective process under conditions in which fear has been aroused and in which social interaction between the perceiver and the stimulus is minimized.

SOURCE. Article by Seymour Feshbach and Norma Feshbach "Influence of the stimulus object upon the complementary and supplementary projection of fear" in the Journal of abnormal and social psychology, Vol. 66, pp. 498–502, 1963. Copyright 1966 by the American Psychological Association and reprinted by permission.

At least two different kinds of changes in social judgment have been observed in response to fear arousal. Murray (1933), in his pioneer study, found that frightened girls perceived pictures of adults, primarily male, as malicious and threatening. Murray described this effect as "complementary projection" to distinguish it from the more classic form of "supplementary projection" in which characteristics of the perceiver are directly attributed to the stimulus. In a study by Feshbach and Singer (1957), using college males who were subjected to electric shocks as the subjects and a film of an adult male taking some psychological tests as the stimulus, evidence of supplementary projection was obtained; that is, under conditions of fear arousal, the subjects tended to attribute both fear and hostility to the stimulus person.

Although the above cited studies are concerned with the problem of projection, the processes involved are probably quite distinct from that mediating psychoanalytic projection (Murstein, 1959). In the case of the latter, the attributed trait is unacceptable and the function of the projection is the reduction of anxiety. In the case of the fear arousal studies, one appears to be dealing with a process which is more akin to stimulus generalization in that the perceiver generalizes from his own state to that of the person being judged. In terms of this process which has been previously labeled "infusion" (Feshbach & Singer, 1957), the degree of "projection" will be a function of the degree of similarity between the perceiver and the stimulus person. From this point of view, egocentricity of the perceiver or the extent to which he is preoccupied with his own feelings should exaggerate the influence of his feelings upon his judgment.

While these assumptions can account for the phenomenon of supplementary projection, they do not explain the attribution of maliciousness found by Murray (1933) under conditions of fear arousal. A comparison of the differences between the Murray and the Feshbach and Singer studies provides some suggestions as to the conditions which elicit a particular type of "projection." There are a number of differences in procedure and subject population between these two experiments which may have been responsible for the differences in results including the very obvious fact that Murray had not obtained ratings of the degree to which the stimuli appeared anxious or fearful. However, we suggest that even if Murray had obtained judgments of fearfulness, changes in the ratings of this dimension would have been less marked than the observed changes in the ratings of maliciousness, because the children judged only adults. It is the principal contention of this paper that a critical variable determining the kind of distortion in judgment that is likely to take place under conditions of fear arousal is the relationship between the perceiver and the stimulus person.

More specifically, a frightened child who is observing an adult, in the absence of information about the adult, is likely to attribute to him those feelings and attitudes which adults displayed in previous situations in which he had been frightened. If the past experience of fear has been associated with a punitive adult, then, under subsequent conditions of fear arousal, the child will tend to attribute maliciousness to similar adults; that is, he will manifest complementary projection. However, when a child judges another child, the psychological situation is markedly different. The similarity of the stimulus person to the perceiver is likely to foster the direct attribution of the affect of the perceiver to the stimulus. Also, the variable of past experience, although less clear in its consequences than in the case of interaction with adults, would probably facilitate the direct attribution of the child's feelings to the stimulus child; that is, when children judge others who are similar to them in age and sex, supplementary projection should be manifested.

On the basis of these considerations, it is hypothesized that frightened boys tend to perceive other boys as fearful and tend to perceive adults, particularly males, as malicious. The prediction regarding adult males is based upon Murray's previous findings and upon the assumption that, in general, boys in our culture are likely to be more frightened of male figures, particularly their fathers, than female figures. This assumption receives some support from Kagan's (1956) finding that 6–10 year old children view their mothers as friendlier and less punitive than their fathers.

EXPERIMENT I

Method

The first experiment to be described which bears upon these hypotheses is essentially a replication of various features of Murray's (1933) original study with some important modifications. Ten neighborhood boys, ranging in age from 9 to 12, were invited to a Halloween party at the home of the experimenters. The parents of the children had previously been informed of the purpose of this "party" and had consented to their children participating, being reassured by the fact that the experimenters' son was also to be a subject in the study.

When the boys arrived, they found themselves in a completely darkened house except for one room which was illuminated by a jack-o'-lantern. The eeriness of the atmosphere was further enhanced by having the children form a circle and relate ghost stories to each other. The second author sat in the center of the circle and initiated the stories. (Although the diameter of the circle was about 11 feet at the beginning of the story telling, by the time the last ghost story was completed, it had been spontaneously reduced to approximately 3 feet.) After the ghost stories, she introduced the boys to a game called "murder" in which they were required to hide alone and conceal themselves from the individual who, without their knowledge, was designated as the murderer. Immediately after he was caught, the child was taken to the "testing" room where he was presented a series of 16 pictorial stimuli consisting of an equal number of men, women, boys, and girls, arranged in a random sequence with the restriction that no two pictures within the same age-sex category should follow each other. Three such random sequences were employed. The pictures were first rated for fearfulness and then for maliciousness. Each rating scale consisted of seven alternatives which in the case of fearfulness ranged from "fearless" to "extremely scared" and in the case of maliciousness ranged from "extremely good and kind" to "extremely bad and cruel."

A control group of 10 boys was obtained from the same school which the experimental subjects attended. The controls and experimental subjects were matched on the basis of age, intelligence, school performance, religion, and race. Each control subject was seen individually and after rapport was established, the subject rated the standard set of stimuli. Both control and experimental subjects were subsequently retested under relaxed conditions with the same stimuli after an interval of 4 weeks.

Results

Scores ranging from one to seven were assigned to each judgment of a photograph, a higher score reflecting a higher rating of maliciousness or fearfulness, according to the scale being used. Ratings of a particular characteristic for each set of four photographs within an age-sex grouping were separately summed for each child. For every subject, then, judgments of men, women, boys, and girls were determined for each of the two testing sessions. Change scores were obtained by subtracting the second set of ratings from the corresponding initial set so that for the experimental group, for example, a positive score reflects a greater degree of attribution of the trait or affect in question under conditions of fear arousal than under relaxed conditions. Mean changes in attribution of maliciousness and fear by the experimental and control groups are reported in Table 1. With respect to attribution of fear, although the experimental group displays larger positive increments than does the control group, the differences are not significant. However, there are marked, statistically significant differences in the attribution of maliciousness. The increments in perception of maliciousness are significantly greater for the experimental than for the control group in response to male stimuli, but are not

TABLE 1 *Mean Change Scores in Attribution of Maliciousness and Fearful-*
ness as a Function of Experimental Treatment and Sex and Age of
the Stimulus

(Experiment I)

Group	Attribution of maliciousness				Attribution of fear			
	BOYS	MEN	GIRLS	WOMEN	BOYS	MEN	GIRLS	WOMEN
Experimental	+0.9	+2.6	+0.4	−1.0	+2.3	+2.6	+0.9	+1.3
Control	−2.7	−2.3	−2.3	−3.5	+0.9	+0.5	+1.7	−0.4
p^a	< 0.01	< 0.02	< 0.10	< 0.10	—	—	—	—

[a]All *p* values presented in the tables are based on a two-tailed Mann-Whitney *U*
test. Dash entry indicates *p* value greater than 0.10.

significant for the judgments of girls and women.

The data then provide evidence of complementary projection only and fail to support the pediction of supplementary projection when judging similar age boys. In addition, the results are not consistent with a simple model of complementary projection since distortions of this type were evidenced in judgments of boys as well as adult males. The data can be accounted for within the proposed theoretical framework if one assumes that the experimental situation aroused hostile impulses as well as fear. The telling of ghost stories and the murder game may well have aroused aggressive fantasies. As an incidental but pertinent note, the boys were rather aggressive and unrestrained when dessert was served following completion of the experiment. (The experimenters, at least, interpreted as aggressive the use of the white dining room walls as targets for chocolate ice cream balls fired from improvised sling shots.) The attribution of malice to the male stimuli may then have been a function of generalization of hostile impulses as well as, in the case of the adult males, the redintegration of negative percepts associated with previous fear arousal situations.

EXPERIMENT II

Method

Because of the ambiguous nature of the findings in this initial study, it was felt desirable to obtain similar data but under conditions in which fear arousal would be maximized and hostility arousal minimized. This second study was conducted in a YMCA setting. Twenty-seven volunteers from several boys' clubs were assigned at random to an experimental or control condition. These boys ranged in age from 8 to 12. The subjects in the experimental or fear arousal condition entered a room in which in one corner was situated a black stool to which were attached a number of metallic extensions. Several wires led from the stool to an adjacent black box which had elaborate dials and a series of flickering colored lights. A long hypodermic needle placed on a white napkin near the box was also visible to the subjects. Midway in the experiment, a male assistant dressed in a white coat entered the room and conspicuously filled the hypodermic with a milky white fluid. The experimental subjects were initially told by the senior author that there were two phases to the experiment, the first consisting of judgments of a series of pictures and the second having "something to do with the equipment in the corner." As in the first study, the subjects were given a series of stimuli to rate on scales of fearfulness and then maliciousness, except that in this second experiment, the photographs were projected onto a screen. The photographs used in this second study were the same as those initially employed except that a new, male adult photograph was substituted for one used in the Halloween study. There was an additional variation in procedure: before either of the ratings was made, the subjects were asked to select an adjective from the following list—relaxed, mean, pleased, scared, kind, unhappy—which best fitted the person in the picture. Thus, the photographs were presented three times—once for the adjective description, and once for the ratings of fearfulness, and finally once more for the ratings of maliciousness. It is important to note that the judgments of the experimental group were elicited while the fear arousing stimuli were in clear view. The "second part" of the experiment involving these stimuli was, of course, never carried out and a party was substituted instead. The control group followed the same procedure as the experimental group except for the absence of the fear inducing objects that were present in the experimental room.

Results. The ratings obtained in the YMCA study were summed and analyzed according to the age and sex of the stimulus person. The pertinent data are presented in Table 2. These results are much more consistent with the experimental hypotheses than was the case for the Halloween data. As Table 2 indicates, the experimental subjects attributed significantly more maliciousness to the adult male photographs than did the control subjects. The attribution of maliciousness to adult males is quite specific since in no other instance did the differences in ratings of maliciousness approach statistical significance. One notes that under control conditions, a markedly greater degree of malice was attributed to boys than to any of the other stimuli. While it is possible that the absence of an experimental effect in the judgment of boys is due to these high ratings, the fact that the Halloween subjects who also attributed greater maliciousness to boys under control conditions manifested a reliable increment under experimental conditions argues against this possibility.

When the fearfulness ratings are examined, a quite different pattern emerges. The experimental group perceives boys as more frightened, the *p* value of the difference being 0.053. In addition, the experimental subjects tend to attribute more fear to women than do the controls, the difference being significant at the 0.10 level.

Inspection of the adjective choice data revealed that the only substantial differences occurred in the attribution of the adjectives "scared" and "unhappy" to boys. The experimental subjects used these adjectives significantly more frequently than did the controls, a finding which supports the difference obtained in the direct ratings of fearfulness of boys. The mean frequency with which "scared"

TABLE 2   *A Comparison of Experimental and Control Mean Ratings of Fearfulness and Maliciousness as a Function of Sex and Age of the Stimulus (Experiment II)*

Group	Attribution of maliciousness				Attribution of fear			
	BOYS	MEN	GIRLS	WOMEN	BOYS	MEN	GIRLS	WOMEN
Experimental	19.0	17.6	13.2	14.1	14.8	12.1	10.8	15.1
Control	18.0	13.4	12.4	13.5	11.6	10.1	9.1	12.0
p	—	<0.01	—	—	0.053	—	—	<0.10

TABLE 3 *A Comparison of Mean Frequencies of Attribution of "Scared" and "Unhappy" Descriptions to Stimuli of Varying Age and Sex by the Experimental and Control Groups*
(Experiment II)

Group	BOYS	MEN	GIRLS	WOMEN
Experimental	2.4	1.2	1.2	2.1
Control	1.4	1.1	1.5	1.6
p	< 0.05	—	—	—

and "unhappy" were employed for the various age and sex groups is presented in Table 3. Although the difference is unreliable, one notes that the experimental subjects tend to attribute more of these same adjectives to women than do the controls, a trend consistent with the rating results.

Discussion. The data of the YMCA study conform rather well to the experimental predictions. Fear arousal is seen to result in qualitatively different distortions depending upon characteristics of the stimulus being judged. Complementary projection is observed in the judgments of adult males; that is, the frightened boys tended to perceive men as malicious. Supplementary projection is observed in the judgments of the young males similar in age to the perceiver; that is, the frightened boys tended to perceive other boys as similarly frightened and unhappy. The greater attribution of fear to boys was reflected by both the adjective choice measure and the ratings of fearfulness. Significant differences in the attribution of malice to men were obtained for ratings of maliciousness but not for adjective choice. The lack of sensitivity of the adjective choice measure in the latter instance may have been due to the fact that only one adjective — "mean" — out of six provided could be used as an index of complementary projection while two adjectives — "scared" and "unhappy" — were available as indices of supplementary projection, thus providing a more reliable datum.

Although an attempt was made in the second experiment to maximize fear arousal and reduce hostility arousal, the conditions for arousing fear are so similar to the conditions under which hostility is elicited that one cannot be certain that the boys, in addition to being frightened, were not also aggressive. However, the possibility that the complementary projection observed was actually a case of supplementary projection — namely, the boys directly attributing their aggressive impulses to the adult male figures — seems unlikely for the following reason. If supplementary projection of aggressive impulses was the essential process, then one might have expected the attribution of maliciousness to boys as well as to men. In contrast to the results from the Halloween study, this effect did not take place. The results of the YMCA study are more readily accounted for by the predicted interaction of fear arousal with the type of stimulus person being judged.

The interpretation of this interaction which is offered here stresses past rather than current sources of threat. The latter may also be a relevant variable and, under some circumstances could override the influence of past experience. A child recently frightened by a very hostile female may tend to generalize and attribute malice to other females rather than to males. One could argue that the perception of male adults as malicious by the experimental subjects in the YMCA experiment was due to the fact that while a female associate was present during part of the experimental session, a male acted as the primary experimenter. The force of this argument is weakened when one considers that the primary experimenter in the Halloween experiment was female and yet there was an increase in attribution of maliciousness to males and not to females.[1]

Still another interpretation of the data could be offered in terms of Heider's (1958) balance theory. From this point of view, the primary mechanism would be the need to maintain cognitive consistency. The child's perception of other children and adults balances as it were his perception of his own emotional state. Since what constitutes an appropriate match for the child's affective state may well depend upon past experience, the implications drawn from balance theory could be quite similar to those based upon the redintegration hypothesis.

The tendency of the frightened boys to attribute a greater degree of fear to women, while never reaching the 0.05 level, seems sufficiently consistent to warrant some comment. It may be that

---

[1]The issue could be readily resolved by repeating the YMCA study, using a female as the primary experimenter. However, it is the opinion of the present authors that the procedure used in the YMCA study may be too disturbing for some children. The authors feel rather fortunate in that they were readily able to reduce the anxiety of two boys who were quite upset by the experimental situation. In investigating future problems in this area, one could take advantage of natural fear producing situations such as children awaiting a polio shot or some form of surgery.

women, particularly mothers, are more likely than men to have occasion in which they share dysphoric feelings of their children; that is, in the past, when a child has been frightened and upset he has perceived similar affects in his mother. If the present analysis is correct, it should be possible by obtaining prior information as to the perception by the child of his parents—whether he perceives his mother as more sympathetic than his father, whether he views his father as a more severe punitive agent than his mother—to predict more precisely the specific kind of distortion that a particular child will manifest when he is frightened.

In conclusion, perhaps the most significant implication that one can draw from this study is that the influence of fear upon the cognitive functions involved in judging the motives and feelings of other people is specific and ordered, rather than pervasive and erratic. Under conditions of fear arousal the perception of only certain classes of people reflect the influence of complementary and supplementary projection. The subjects' perception of girls, for instance, in both the Halloween and YMCA studies was unaffected by the experimental conditions. These results point up the importance of the role of the stimulus in determining the influence of subjective factors upon social judgments. The subject's judgment represents the outcome of the interaction of so-called subjective and objective variables and both must be considered in order to adequately predict his behavior.

References

Feshbach, S., & Singer, R. The effects of fear arousal and suppression of fear upon social perception. *J. abnorm. soc. Psychol.*, 1957, **55**, 283–288.

Heider, F. *The psychology of interpersonal relations*. New York: Wiley, 1958.

Kagan, J. The child's perception of the parent. *J. abnorm. soc. Psychol.*, 1956, **53**, 257–258.

Murray, H. A. The effect of fear on the estimates of the maliciousness of other personalities. *J. soc. Psychol.*, 1933, **4**, 310–329.

Murstein, B. I. The concept of projection: A review. *Psychol. Bull.*, 1959, **56**, 353–371.

Singer, R., & Feshbach, S. The effects of anxiety arousal in psychotics and normals upon the perception of anxiety in others. Paper read at Western Psychological Association, San Francisco, April 1962.

3. Studies of Stressful Interpersonal Disputations

HENRY A. MURRAY

Between me and the substance of all that I can say in the allotted time are several pages of writing, the contents of which may be summarized as follows:

1. A short introduction with a barely discernible thread of humor;

2. A prosaic survey of the seven major components of what some of us have called the "multiform system of assessment" which is old hat to most of you;

3. A passage in which it is pointed out that two of the essential components of this system have been grievously neglected by most psychologists in their investigations of normal personalities, one being the collection by various means of an abundance of experimental, biographical data from each subject, and the other being a serious systematic attempt to construct a coherent formulation of each personality;

4. The Jeremiad of an aging psychologist who views with sorrow and misgivings the apparent accentuation of certain powerful forces that are keeping a multiplicity of his colleagues dissociated from the nature and experiences of actual peo-

ple by binding their energies to an enthralling intellectual game played with abstract counters of dubious importance and of spurious relevance to human life.

Integration Plan

Having been led to the belief that this dissociation, if prolonged, would seriously impede the full future development of psychology, I am eager to propose a remedy which could be instituted at numerous centers in this country on a scale that might be just sufficient to make a decisive, vital difference in the evolution of our discipline. The suggested remedy consists of integrating the endeavors of experimental specialists with those of personologists engaged in a multiform assessment program. That is, instead of choosing either to learn a lot about a single area of human activity or to learn a little about a lot of areas, everybody chooses both, and can attain both by a division of interrelated labors.

There are only two rules to this integration plan, as I shall call it, the first being that all experimenters will use the same population of thoroughly assessed subjects, no matter how many other sub-

SOURCE. Article by Henry A. Murray, "Studies of stressful interpersonal disputations" in American Psychologist, Vol. 18, pp. 28–36, 1963.

jects they may need. The enormous advantage of this arrangement is that each experimenter, without any expenditure of his own time, will have at his disposal to help him in interpreting his findings, not only the results of other experiments, but the massive collection of data (several hundred rank orders, for example) obtained by the assessment process. The second rule—with even greater potentialities for a sophisticated science of psychology as well as for broadening the horizon of every student—calls for two series of meetings of experimentalists and personologists: one series to formulate the personality of each subject as a unit, and another series to attempt plausible explanations of the variant individual responses in each experiment taken as a unit. The aim would be to test the most promising of these plausible explanations, and in due course to attain the enviable position of being able to predict the critical reactions of each individual subject with a fair measure of accuracy and precision.

To be a little more specific, let me outline one possible version of the integration plan. First there will be four variously trained and variously experienced personologists (members or research associates of a department of psychology) who are engaged in a three-year program of intensive study of 25 preselected subjects. They will be assisted in the assessment process by second-year graduate students who will administer, as part of their technical training course, some of the simpler tests and questionnaires. Then there will be several graduate students of more advanced standing, seven in number, let us say, each of whom is planning an experiment to be performed for a PhD degree. Their interests may vary all the way from those of a physiological-psychologist in search of more precise knowledge respecting the temporal correlates of marked changes in the heart rate to those of an investigator of higher mental processes who wishes to test certain propositions as to the power of a subject to recall different parts of a dyadic conversation in which he has actively participated.

Now, as it happens, a few of us at Harvard—research fellows for the most part—found that these two experimental aims and five others could be pursued in unison as interdependent parts of a single chain of linked procedures. The topics of the other five studies, each concerned with a different aspect of a stressful, two-person disputation, were as follows: (*a*) the determinants of variations among judges in estimating degree of anxiety and of anger; (*b*) personological and situational determinants of degree of anxiety and of anger; (*c*) personological correlates of variations of mentational and linguistic style under stress; (*d*) typological differences as manifested in restrospectively experiencing and reporting a stressful, verbal interaction; and (*e*) apperceptions and evaluations of an alter before and after meeting him and being exposed to his insulting criticisms.

Now, as partial demonstration of how researches such as these can be readily coordinated, let me outline as briefly as possible the series of techniques that was carried out by a number of us at the Annex (as I shall call our workshop in Cambridge, Massachusetts), first in 1957 with the compliance of 23 comprehensively assessed college sophomores, and then, in a more refined way, in 1960 with a comparable aggregate of 21 subjects. Imagine that you are one of these volunteer subjects.

Experimental Procedures. First, you are told you have a month in which to write a brief exposition of your personal philosophy of life, an affirmation of the major guiding principles in accord with which you live or hope to live.

Second, when you return to the Annex with your finished composition, you are informed that in a day or two you and a talented young lawyer will be asked to debate the respective merits of your two philosophies. You are given a copy of his philosophy and he is given a copy of your philosophy. You are told that a moving picture will be taken of this debate.

Third, on arriving at the Annex on the appointed day, you are given these directions: The debate will be limited to three 6-minute periods separated by two shorter silent periods, in which to rest or collect your thoughts. The first period will be for mutual orientation, for asking and answering questions, clarifying certain points. In the second period the young lawyer will present his criticisms of your philosophy and your task will be to defend it as logically as possible. In the third and final period it will be your turn to call attention to whatever weaknesses you have noted in the lawyer's philosophy. At this point you are introduced to the young lawyer, and in his company escorted to the brilliantly lighted room where the debate will take place in front of a one-way mirror and a hole in the wall for the lens of a moving picture camera with sound track. Before sitting down next to each other, the leads of a cardiotachometer (which records instantaneous heart rates and respirations) are strapped to your chest and to the lawyer's chest by Paul Gross.

Fourth, a signal is given and the discussion starts, continuing through three differentiated periods as you were told it would. In the second period, however, the lawyer's criticism becomes far more vehement, sweeping, and personally abusive than you were led to expect. The directions given to the lawyer were the same as you received, except that he was told to anger you and, adhering to a rehearsed and more or less standardized mode of attack, he will almost certainly

succeed in doing this, having been successful in all the dyads we have witnessed. Dyad is the convenient four-letter word we use to refer to each of these 18-minute two-person interactions, plus four inactive periods amounting to 9 minutes, i.e, about 27 minutes in all.

Fifth, after the termination of the debate, you are taken to a room where you are left alone with the instruction to write down as much as you are able to recall of what was said by the lawyer and by yourself, word for word if possible and in proper sequence.

Sixth, as soon as you have reached the end of your memories of the verbal interactions, you are escorted to the room of an interviewer (Alden Wessman), where you are encouraged to relax, and to say what comes to mind while you relive in your imagination the dyad as you experienced it, chronologically from start to finish. When you are through with this— about 30 minutes later, let us say—you are asked certain questions designed to obtain as valid estimates as you both *can* give and *will* give of the intensity of certain variables, such as felt anxiety, felt anger, involvement in the task, liking or disliking the lawyer, respecting or disrespecting his ability or views. A final short questionnaire covering these and other points completes your set of exercises for that day. The interviewer is left with a tape recording of the whole proceeding.

At four appointed times subsequent to your participation in the stressful dyad, you will be called back to the Annex. On two occasions there will be another verbal memory test similar to the one I have described, the aim of which is to measure the percentage of different classes of speech units in the dyad that are recalled by each subject after 2 weeks and after 8 weeks. In addition to these sessions there will be two interviews, in one of which you will again be asked to relive the experience of the dyad and to report it as you go along. In the other interview, the plan of which was both conceived and executed with extraordinary cleverness by Gerhard Nielsen, you will witness and become involved in two or three showings of the sound film of your own dyad. You will see yourself making numerous grimaces and gestures of which you were unconscious at the time, and you will hear yourself uttering incongruent, disjunctive, and unfinished sentences. You are likely to be somewhat shocked by your performance and will be moved to identify with yourself as you were feeling and thinking during those stressful moments; and when the experimenter, *this* experimenter, stops the film at critical points, and asks you what you associate with this and that physiognomic movement or with this and that verbal expression, you are likely to become uncommonly communicative and your free associations may lead you back to childhood memories. Counting the other two reliving interviews and the three memory sessions, you will spend about 8 hours all told trying to recapture various aspects of those 18 minutes under stress.

I have devoted more minutes than I can well afford to this account of how we secured reports of your subjective experience of the dyad as a whole and in detail, because nothing more about the phenomenology of it all will be said this morning, and I wanted to assure you that we considered the covert, inner aspect of that event as essential and revealing as its overt, outer aspect.

Raw Data. The dyad in which you participated has perished as an event in time and you are through with it and we with you, in a sense and for a while. But we are in no sense through with the imperishable data pertinent to that event which you have left behind with us, the nature of which I have already briefly indicated: (*a*) a cardiotachometric tracing of your heart and respiration rates, (*b*) a sound film portraying your physical expressions and your verbal interactions with the lawyer, (*c*) a typed record of the exchange of words, (*d*) a tape recording of the debate giving both voice and words, and (*e*) a series of typed protocols of everything that you said about the dyad as you retrospectively relived it. So far as I know, these interrelated temporal records of your discussion are more precise and more complete than those of any other dyadic event in human history. But *cui bono*? As they stand they are nothing but raw data, meaningless as such; and the question is what meaning, what intellectual news, can be extracted from them?

Certain Methodological Principles

Besides presenting a plan for coordinating the aims and efforts of experimental specialists and personological generalists, and besides describing a series of procedures as an example of how seven different experimental projects can be coordinated, I had another purpose for this paper to which I shall now attend, namely, to set forth a few of the strategic methodological principles, or aims, which guided the ordination (designing, planning) of our interlocked techniques. These principles will be illustrated by references to what we have learned so far regarding the determinants of variations of the heart rate during a dyadic verbal transaction of varying stressor potency.

1. *Make the experimental conditions as natural as possible.* Although some degree of artificiality is unavoidable in the design of an experiment, we have assumed (without unequivocal evidence) that the wanted range of emotional, conational, and mentational involvement of the subjects (and hence sufficient elevations of

the heart rate) is more frequently obtained when the experimental conditions (the directions if any, the setting, the successive stimulus situations, etc.) are naturalistic (i.e., comparable to those that occur, commonly or exceptionally, in everyday life) and, conversely, that the degree of such involvement is generally less when artificiality is conspicuous and a subject has reason to say to himself, "this is nothing but an experiment, an attempt to show that I can be excited by these means." We have also assumed that the reactions of a subject (including changes of his heart rate) will be less natural (less representative of those that occur in everyday life) if his freedom of action is impeded, either, say, by strapping him to an array of instruments and telling him not to move, or by providing him with no opportunity for effective mental action, no problem to solve, or no way of altering the course of events by verbal means; or by limiting each of the subject's responses to a mere choice between two or more predetermined alternatives, instead of expecting him to *compose* adequate responses. It is not unlikely that the change of the heart rate after stimulation varies in direction or degree according to whether a subject is set (*a*) to inhibit or (*b*) to actuate, either all impulses or impulses of a certain class.

As to the naturalness of our experimental conditions, it may be said that heated arguments are common in the ordinary course of social events and dyadic discussions before a camera are daily occurrences on TV programs; but that an unwanted and unnecessary degree of artificiality was introduced in most of the dyads by the suddenness, intensity, and irrationality of the lawyer's criticisms in the second of the active phases of the dyad.

2. *Aim at a temporal, holistic model of the observed event by obtaining synchronized recordings of the occurrence and intensity of each of the most influential participating variables.* "Holistic model" in this sentence means (*a*) a sufficiently complete model *of* the whole (entire) event, one which includes all parts (variables) that are of noteworthy relevance and significance, and (*b*) a model of the even *as* a whole, one which represents the interdependence of the parts (variables) and in so doing exhibits whatever degree of unity or disunity may prevail. Pertinent to this principle is our assumption that variations in the heart rate are determined by the interaction of several different variables. The importance of synchronized temporal records of the occurrence and intensity of each of the relevant variables is obvious, since only in this way can one discover what intrasubject, sequential (cause and effect), or concomitant relationships among the variables recur with dependable regularity. Furthermore, we should not lose sight of the basic tenet that time is an inherent component or attribute of every process and that the history of an event *is* the event.

In charting changes in the intensity of a variable, such as anxiety or anger, or changes in the heart rate or speech rate, a good deal may depend on the duration of the time unit that is represented by a single figure (the average of all measures obtained during that temporal segment). In representing changes in heart rate, for example, the choice of a short micro time unit of 5 seconds (with one point indicating the average interval between six successive beats if the rate is 60 beats per minute) will generally eliminate the effects of respiration (occuring at the rate of roughly 12 a minute); and a choice of a large micro time unit of 30 seconds will generally result in the obliteration of the effects of gross muscular motility if the frequency and magnitude of these movements remain constant; and the choice of a large macro time unit of 6 minutes will obliterate the effects of changes of stimulation during the course of that phase, and so forth. Some of these points will be demonstrated later.

3. *Assume that every psychological variable is a hypothetical (theoretical) construct, the activity of which can be inferred only on the basis of one or more of its subjective and/or objective manifestations.* For centuries every psychological variable was conscious by definition; but within the last half century most psychologists have come round to Freud's conception of unconscious psychic processes; and a host of psychologists have been persuaded, first of all, by Pavlov and Watson, to study organisms who are unable to report whatever awareness of interior mental experiences they may have. As a result many psychologists are now accustomed to the practice of inferring (on the basis of more or less rigorously defined criteria) the operation of imperceptible central (psychic) variables. In view of the prevalent American bias in favor of "behavioral" psychology I am strongly disposed to stress the understanding to be gained from the development of a sophisticated "experimental" psychology.

4. *Attempt to explain the reactions, especially the variant reactions of every individual subject.* We do not say that every person is unique, but say, instead, that every person is in certain very general respects like *all* other persons, in certain less general respects like *some* other persons (persons of this or that sex, age, culture, status, vocation, type, etc.), and in certain particular respects like no other person. As usually, we take note of whatever is common to all subjects, and then of whatever is common to this and to that aggregate or class of subjects, and, finally, we investigate in great detail whatever eccentric or hitherto unknown particularities are manifested by different individuals. From endeavors to understand these unique features have come the greater portion of our "new ideas." But these endeavors, I believe, would have had little chance of bearing fruit if we had had to deal with subjects whose lives and personalities were unexplored to us. Here, then, is another good reason for adhering to the practice of performing experiments only on thoroughly assessed persons.

Now, to illustrate the application of the third principle (variables as theoretical constructs), I shall present an outline of our conception of anger, and then to illustrate the second principle (synchronized temporal tracings) I shall describe one of our ways of estimating the degree of anger.

Theoretical and Operational Definition of Anger. Anger was defined as an hypothetical state of excitation in certain not-yet-definitely-localized, subcortical regions of the brain (say, in the hypothalamus and limbic systems) which, if sufficiently intense, produces various manifestations of which the following could be discriminated in our data:

1. Covert manifestations: (*a*) experienced, or felt, anger, (*b*) aggressive words or images of aggressive actions invading the stream of consciousness, and (*c*) certain "emotional" qualities of the temporal structure of mentation; the avowals of all of which by the subject (at various times in the three postdyadic interviews) are ordinarily but not always modulated by some degree of inhibition (suppression).

2. Physiological manifestations: autonomic excitations, including changes of the heart rate and respiration rate as recorded on the polygraph by the cardiotachometer, the nature of which changes seems to depend on the character of the situation.

3. Overt manifestations: (*a*) physiognomic and motoric phenomena which can be seen in the silent moving picture and analyzed in great detail by means of a perceptoscope projecting one frame at

a time; (*b*) verbal productions of an oppositional, rude, critical, aggressive, or insulting nature which can be read in the typed protocol; (*c*) vocal qualities, such as louder and more rapid speech which, in conjunction with the verbal productions, can be heard in the playback of the magnetic tape recording of the dyad; and, finally, (*d*) temporal patterns of these motoric, verbal, and vocal manifestations, which can be synchronously seen and heard in the sound movie in conjunction with the behavior of the alter, or lawyer; all of which manifestations of central processes are modulated to some degree by the subject's efforts to control and to conceal them.

To be complete, this scheme would have to be supplemented by the addition of physical (muscular) endeavors, such as fighting, and by further specifications here and there, for example as to the qualities of voice and flow of speech which may be recorded instrumentally, or discriminated without instruments even when one does not understand the language spoken by the subject. But these supplementations are not pertinent to our data which allow for only four completely independent sources of information (cf. 1, 2, 3a, and 3b) which may be compared in respect to their dependability as indices of central anger.

Here I shall limit myself to estimations of anger based on observations of the sound movie which combines the vocal qualities of speech with two of the independent sources of information (physiognomic movements and verbal productions). These estimates were made from moment to moment independently and simultaneously by six psychologists (Arthur Couch, Paul Gross, Kenneth Keniston, David Ricks, Bernard Rosenthal, and myself), each of whom held a dial whose movements produced tracings on a polygraph, that could be synchronized with the tracings of the heart rate, as well as

with the speech units produced by the two debaters.

The overt manifestations of five other preselected psychological variables (the subject's level of anxiety, gross motility, vocal-verbal intensity, and task involvement, and the potency of the lawyer's criticisms and insults) were estimated, one by one, in a similar fashion, two of these variables by six judges and three by two judges. I shall not discuss, at this time, the question of the determinants of the unrealiability of these estimates, but return to the second methodological principle that I mentioned, which calls for a temporal record of each variable, and illustrates the difference in amount of information gained between choosing a macro or a meso time unit for each point that is represented in a graph by showing two records of the heart rate, before, during, between, and after dyadic interactions.

Figure 1 shows first, the average basal heart rate (74) for all subjects and then seven average dyadic heart rates plotted against time. (The average of about 12 afternoon pulse rates, as counted by each

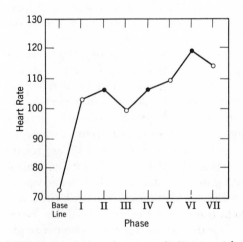

Figure 1. *Average heart rate during stressful dyad (with seven points).*

subject on different days under resting conditions, was taken as that subject's basal heart rate.) The three black circles give the average HR (absolute heart rate) for each of the periods of active verbal interchanges (a 6-minute time segment). The white circles give the average HR for each of the verbally inactive periods: pre-dyadic first, post-dyadic last, and two intradyadic rest periods. Time units of this percentage of total time (about four to six minutes in this case) are called by us macro units and each cycle is called a macro figure. What can we learn from this macro-temporal chart?

1. Note the relatively great elevation of the heart rate (above the average basal rate of 74) before the start of the dyad, an index of a high degree of anticipatory central excitation, and then note a similar anticipatory rise before Phase 6, the phase in which the subject had been instructed to criticize the lawyer's views.

2. Note the increase of heart rate during the transition from an overtly inactive state to an overtly active state in all three instances. Micro analyses show that this occurred in 18 of our 21 subjects.

3. Note that the average heart rate in the sixth phase, when most of the subjects were criticizing the lawyer, was considerably higher than it was in Phase 4, when they were *being* criticized.

4. Note the surprising and in-this-graph-unexplainable fact that the average heart rate in the fourth phase (when the subjects were insulted) was no higher than it was in the second phase during which the interpersonal atmosphere was friendly.

Figure 2 is a *meso*temporal chart which exhibits 17 successive figures, one for the first, or predyadic, phase, then one for each of 15 subphases (9 active and 6 inactive) of the dyad proper, and finally one for the seventh, or post-dyadic, phase. Each black circle is the average for a 2-

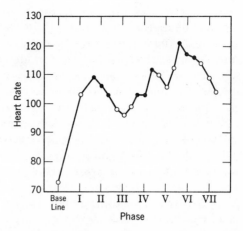

Figure 2. *Average heart rate during stressful dyad (with 17 points).*

minute time unit (instead of for a 6-minute time unit), a choice of temporal segment which certainly gives you a more intelligible picture of what generally occurred during those stressful proceedings.

1. Take note of some new information: first, the fall of the heart rate during Phase 2 and again during Phase 6, one reasonable explanation of which would be in terms of homeostatic principles, namely that an elevated heart rate always tends to fall as the person becomes habituated to the existing situation, provided the stressor potency of the situation does not increase. During the first two-thirds of Phase 4 the subjects were confronted by a series of unexpected provocations in the form of personally offensive criticisms from the lawyer, and consequently the existing HR level did not fall, but was sustained during the middle subphase and in the last phase ascended sharply. The low HR level during the first subphase of Phase 4 as compared to the level during the initial but unaggressive subphase of Phase 2 might be partly explained by the low level in the middle of resting

Phase 3 (the level from which the heart rate had to rise) as compared to the higher level of Phase 1, the predyadic phase. And the lower HR level during the middle subphase of Phase 4 as compared to the level in the third subphase might be partly explained by the fact that subjects talked far less in the first two subphases of Phase 4 than they did during any other period of the dyad; since, according to our micro findings, the HR level is lower, as a rule, when subjects are listening than it is when they are talking. Another possible explanation that needs to be explored through micro analyses is that the eruption of covert anger (which came suddenly in the first subphase of Phase 4 when conditions more or less prohibited its ample expression) produced momentary increase in blood pressure (the noradrenalin effect) and a consequent decrease in the heart rate in some subjects.

2. Again note that the heart rate was high at the end of Phase 4, by which time most subjects had become engaged in self-defensive refutations and still higher in Phase 6 when they were both most talkative and most offensively aggressive. Taking this covariation of heart rate and vigorous verbal activity in conjunction with the fall in level during the first two-thirds of each resting period, as well as with the other pertinent facts that I have mentioned (e.g., the rise of the heart rate at the end of each of three inactive periods, and the additional rise beyond this point, in all instances, as the subject went from inaction to interaction), the data exhibited in our graphs all point to a positive correlation of the heart rate with (*a*) anticipated interactivity of a certain sort and (*b*) with the first phase of actual interactivity. After that, if the intensity level of the interactivity decreases or remains constant, the heart rate will decline; but if the intensity level increases the heart rate will rise or remain constant. Viewing these facts within a functional frame of reference, we might say that the circula-

tory system of the majority of our subjects was over-prepared (by nervous excitement) for Phase 2 and for Phase 6 (i.e., the subjects anticipated, consciously or unconsciously, more stressors, more demands for quick, difficult, and effective responses, than they subsequently encountered), and as they came to the realization that the situational demands were not so pressing (less than they were physiologically prepared to meet), their heart rates fell to a level that was appropriate to the apperceived current state of affairs. This well-known habituational, or homeostatic, fall of the heart rate, particularly in Phase 2, was the cause of numerous negative intrasubject correlations between heart rate and anxiety (nervous excitement); because, since the subjects were not filmed during any of the inactive periods, the judges had no grounds for inferring a high level of anxiety at the very start of the interaction. Generally speaking, the judges started Phase 2 (the first phase to be observed in the movie) at zero and moved up as signs of nervousness appeared and reappeared and their confidence in the significance of these signs became less wavering. Therefore, while the judges' tracings for anxiety were mounting ("catching up" to the subject's current emotional state) the subject's heart rate was declining. This was but one of many unexpected complications we encountered.

My first reason for showing the two graphs of average heart rate changes during the dyad was to illustrate the general principle (which applies to data such as ours) that, above an ascertainable low limit, the shorter the time segment which is represented by a single figure, the greater will be the amount of usable information to be gained by mere inspection. My second reason was to point out the suitability of the synchronized mesotemporal graphs of our major variables: They present nine opportunities for intersubject correlations between the rank orders of the average subphase intensities of the variables and eight opportunities for intrasubject correlations of their concurrently changing intensities between subphases. Besides these we have the opportunity afforded by the macrotemporal graphs for three more sets of intersubject intercorrelations and finally a set of intercorrelations based on average variable intensities for the total dyad, yielding in all 13 intersubject correlation coefficients for each pair of variables. Finally, to end this paper with a little meat to chew on, it was my intention to summarize the unexpected results of the execution, by Paul Gross and others, of some of the just-enumerated possible correlations for comparison with the information gained through a close inspection of the mesotemporal graph (Figure 2.)

The first surprise, if not distress, was occasioned by the finding that the elevated heart rate, calculated in the manner I described earlier, was correlated to a significant degree with *none* of our major variables, in *contrast* to the absolute heart rate which correlated positively with all our "activity" variables, in two instances at the 5% level of significance. This result, which at first blush runs counter to accepted principles of measurement in physiology, constitutes a riddle for which I have no ready answer, except to report that the correlation of -0.78 between basal heart rate and elevated heart rate might conceivably be the key to its solution. In any case, the average of 13 rank order correlations were significantly positive between absolute heart rate and both of our two measures of manifest drive, or need achievement, in the dyad (the apparent degree of continuous concentration and emotional-mentational-verbal energy devoted to the accomplishment of the assigned task): (*a*) *vocal-verbal intensity*, aver. $+0.45$ (range from $+0.19$ to $+0.59$, with all but one over $+0.34$); and (*b*) *task-involvement*, aver. $+0.42$ (range from $+0.31$ to $+0.56$). The fact that these

correlations are all positive, that they are consonant with all the data presented by the graphs, and that they make functional sense, suggests that individual differences among our subjects in respect to basal heart rate and degree of sensitivity of the neurocardiac system were not so great or influential as to cancel the possibility of demonstrating a consistent relationship between motivation and heart rate under the stressful conditions that existed in the dyads. The comparably high heart rates of surgeons while performing major operations could likewise be attributed to this functional relationship. Also positive, but to no significant degree, are the correlations between HR and (*c*) *manifest anger*, aver. $+0.30$ (range from $+0.11$ to $+0.49$), and (*d*) *gross muscular motility*, aver. $+0.29$ (range from $+0.16$ to $+0.35$). Most surprising was the absence of any correlation with (*e*) *anxiety*, aver. -0.03 (range $+0.15$ to -0.28), and a not-yet-explained, slightly negative correlation with *press* (the alter's *vocal-verbal* intensity and *aggressiveness*), aver. -0.26 (range $+0.04$ to -0.58). The averages of the intrasubject correlations were also significantly positive for absolute heart rate and vocal-verbal intensity, gross muscular motility, and task-involvement, in that order, and insignificantly positive for press and anger. The correlation with anxiety was in this slightly negative.

As to anxiety, we might first of all raise the question of whether this is the most appropriate term to apply, say, to a surgeon at the start of a difficult emergency operation. His nervousness is not morbid anxiety in the Freudian sense (fear of conscience), nor is it associated with any tendency to escape, to withdraw, or to avoid, in the usual sense: Surgery is his chosen profession and here is his opportunity to save a life and thus to achieve an all-important result. It might be said, however, that he is bent on avoiding disaster for both his patient and himself. But, regardless of these and other objections, I shall continue to use the term "anxiety" for the duration of this paper to stand for a nervous apprehension of the forthcoming possibility of experiencing some sort of acute pain, distress, failure, exposure, shame, or disgrace. Now, despite the fact that none of our rank order correlations between heart rate and anxiety were positive, it is clear from the graph that the effect of predyadic anxiety (nervous excitement) on the heart rate (elevating it 33 points on the average) is greater than that of any other definable variable, that is to say, heart rate and anxiety *are* in fact positively correlated, as effect and cause, or cause and effect, in all subjects. The contradiction can be explained, in functional terms, by assuming that anxiety (situational fear) is a mobilization of energy for emergency action in a situation that is apprehended as perilous. If the anxiety is high and a resulting drive to overt action is correspondingly high, particularly if the drive is combined with anger as well as an increase of gross motility, the heart rate will be in the highest range, and since the signs of anxiety

will be largely obscured or inhibited by the vigorous and focused ongoing activity (verbal in our experiments), the subject will be given a rather low rating on anxiety and a very high rating on both vocal-verbal intensity and task involvement (see the curve of Tandy in Figure 3). If, on the other hand, an equally high degree of anxiety results in a form of action which may be termed "surrender and submission," with extrapunitiveness replaced by a mild intrapunitiveness, the heart rate will fall and remain at a low level, as one can see in the case of Keeper, also represented in Figure 3. Keeper will receive low ratings on vocal-verbal intensity and high ratings on manifest anxiety. This, in brief, is a partial explanation of the absence of positive correlations between heart rate and anxiety.

And now I have come to the end of my allotted time, with only a few seconds in which to show one last figure (Figure 4) in which the average heart rates of seven subjects with the highest drive ratings are compared with the average heart rates of seven subjects with the lowest drive ratings.

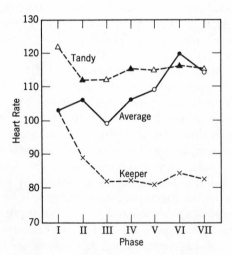

Figure 3. *Average heart rate of two deviant cases compared to group average.*

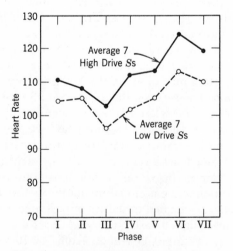

Figure 4. *Average heart rate for seven subjects with highest drive and seven subjects with lowest drive.*

Section V

Lewin's Field Theory

Although many of Lewin's concepts of personality have been incorporated into the mainstream of psychology and continue to stimulate research, the theory itself has not been expanded or modified to any significant extent since Lewin's death. This is in sharp contrast to his other major contribution to modern psychology: the formulation of a theory of group dynamics. Group dynamics both as a theory and as a field of research is one of the most viable areas in present-day psychology.

We have chosen from Lewin's many writings, as our first selection, an article that is particularly far-ranging in scope. In it Lewin relates how his theory developed out of observation and experiment. He discusses such constructs as tension systems, needs and quasi needs, and field forces in the context of methodology and research. He sets forth his views on the rate at which formalization and quantification should take place in psychology. And finally he answers some of the criticisms that have been made of his work.

The empirical papers represent experiments on various facets of Lewin's theory of personality. Gordon and Thurlow's study is a sequel of Mary Henle's monograph, which is discussed at length in *Theories of Personality*. Their study was aimed at clarifying Henle's results by controlling for several previously uncontrolled factors. It also represents an extension of Henle's work since the present experiment used young children and the earlier experiment used college student subjects. They found that a completed task of medium valence could serve as a substitute for an incompleted task that was either high or low in valence.

Barthol and Ku's experiment is a clever test of Lewin's formulation of the psychoanalytic concept of regression. It is the human counterpart of a number of animal studies. The reader who has tried to learn to tie a bowline knot will identify sympathetically with the task set for the subjects by Barthol and Ku. The data from this experiment strongly supported the hypothesis. The students searching for a little psychology project could replicate this experiment, but an independent assessment of the level of stress for each subject should be included. This could be done with paper and pencil self-report data or various psychophysiological measures.

The paper by Weiner, Johnson, and Mehrabian is an interesting study of Lewin's well known Zeigarnik effect. Unlike many of the studies selected for this volume, this study was conducted in a natural field setting and not in a laboratory. Of course, in the process of developing a robust data base for personality theory, both types of studies are necessary. However, personality psychologists probably have not made as much use of natural settings as they could.

The Weiner et al. study is a direct test of Atkinson's suggestion that individual differences in achievement motivation should influence recall of completed and incompleted tasks. Each subject was enrolled in an introductory psychology personality course, and the entire class took several personality tests at the second meeting of the class. These tests provided scores for each subject on achievement motivation, test anxiety, and resultant achievement motivation. At the end of the course, after completing the final examination each student was asked to write down on a piece of paper as many examination items as he could remember. The examination results were used to calculate the number of completed and incompleted items. The authors assumed that every item a student answered incorrectly was an incompleted item. It would be interesting to see what the results would be if the authors had scored as incompleted items not all items missed, but only those items in which the student did not fill in the missing word in the blank space. For that truly would be an incompleted task! The student should note that the crucial data for assessing the Zeigarnik effect was obtained from males only. This is due to the fact that one of the independent variables, achievement motivation, is measured very imprecisely in women. In this natural setting the Zeigarnik effect was again demonstrated, and the additional factor of resultant achievement motivation as an important determinant of the Zeigarnik effect was identified.

1. Formalization and Progress in Psychology

KURT LEWIN

I

In recent years there has been a very marked change in the attitude of American psychology. During the 1920's and early 1930's psychologists were, on the whole, rather adverse to theory. Governed by a naive metaphysical belief, they were apt to consider "fact finding" the only task of "scientific" psychology, and were particularly skeptical of the idea of psychological laws in the fields of needs, will, and emotion, that is, in fields other than perception and memory.

Today, a definite interest in psychological theory has emerged, due partly to the efforts of a few psychologists (particularly Tolman and Hull in animal psychology). The need for a closer fusion of the various branches of psychology demands tools which permit better integration. The practical tasks of mental hygiene and education demand conceptual tools which permit prediction. Neither demand can be met without theory.

Now, however, it seems necessary to point to certain dangers of theorizing.

Enthusiasm for Theory? Yes! Psychology can use much of it. However, we will produce but an empty formalism, if we forget that mathematization and formalization should be done only to the degree that the maturity of the material under investigation permits at a given time.

Philosophically, there seems to exist only an "either-or": if scientific "facts" and particularly all so-called dynamic facts are not merely "given data," but inseparably interwoven with theoretical assumptions, there seems to be no choice other than to base every statement in psychology on theoretical assumptions.

For the psychologist, as an empirical scientist, the situation looks rather difficult. He finds himself in the midst of a rich and vast land full of strange happenings: there are men killing themselves; a child playing; a child forming his lips trying to say his first word; a person who having fallen in love and being caught in an unhappy situation is not willing or not able to find a way out; there is the mystical state called hypnosis, where the will of one person seems to govern another person; there is the reaching out for higher, and more difficult goals; loyalty to a group; dreaming; planning; exploring the world; and so on without end. It is an immense continent full of fascina-

SOURCE. *Selection from Kurt Lewin, "Formalization and progress in psychology" in* Field Theory in Social Science: Selected Theoretical Papers, *Chapter 1. Edited by Darwin Cartwright. New York: Harper, 1951.*

tion and power and full of stretches of land where no one ever has set foot.

Psychology is out to conquer this continent, to find out where its treasures are hidden, to investigate its danger spots, to master its vast forces, and to utilize its energies.

How can one reach this goal? At first, in what might be called the "speculative epoch," the attempt was made to dig down deep into the ground. A peculiar something was reported to lie underground as the hidden source of energy. One gave it the name "association." New investigators drove their shafts down at somewhat different places. They found something different which they called "instinct." A third group of explorers reported a different entity, "libido." And all claimed to have found *the* foundation on which the land rested. By this time, psychologists has become rather tired of the various claims. It had become clear that the continent was much larger than was suspected at first. Perhaps there was more than one source of energy. The whole depth-sounding process had become rather open to suspicion, particularly since no explorer seemed able to bring his material up to the surface for inspection in broad daylight. How was one ever to prove a real connection between the entities supposedly existing underground and what was going on at the surface? There, open to all eyes, and unquestionable, interesting phenomena, presented themselves. The psychologist now turned to extensive traveling over the surface of the continent, eager to find new phenomena, to describe them exactly, to count and to measure them, to register their growth.

This procedure, however, did not prove altogether satisfactory either. After all, what the psychologist observed were human beings. Children needed help and education; delinquent people needed guidance; people in distress wanted cure.

Counting, measuring, and classifying their sorrows did not help matters much. Obviously one had to go to the facts "behind," "below the surface." How to accomplish this without the fallacies of the speculative epoch? That is the dominant methodological question of psychology today, at the beginning of its "Galilean period."

The answer is something like this: to make oneself master of the forces of this vast scientific continent one has to fulfill a rather peculiar task. The ultimate goal is to establish a network of highways and superhighways, so that any important point may be linked easily with any other. This network of highways will have to be adapted to the natural topography of the country and will thus itself be a mirror of its structure and of the position of its resources.

The construction of the highway system will have to be based partly upon assumptions which cannot be expected to be fully correct. The test drilling in exploring the deposits will not always lead to reliable results. Besides, there is a peculiar paradox in the conquering of a new continent, and even more so in that of a new scientific field. To make the proper tests, some machinery has to be transported, and such transportation presupposes more or less the same road, the construction of which is contingent upon the outcome of the test. In other words, to find out what one would like to know one should, in some way or other, already know it.

What should science do to resolve this paradox? If it is wise, it follows the same procedure used in a systematic exploration of the resources of a new land: small paths are pushed out through the unknown; with simple and primitive instruments, measurements are made; much is left to assumption and to lucky intuition. Slowly certain paths are widened; guess and luck are gradually replaced by experience and systematic exploration with more elaborate instruments. Finally highways are built over which the streamlined vehicles of a highly mechanized logic, fast and efficient, can reach every important point on fixed tracks.

By and large, the actual development of a science seems to follow this general pattern. Yet frequently somebody, thinking he knows where an important treasure lies, tries to build a superhighway straight to this point without regard for the natural structure of the country. Much enthusiasm and work are put into such road-building, but after some time it becomes apparent that this superhighway is a dead end leading nowhere.

Formalization and mathematization in psychology, if prematurely done, may lead us to the building of such logical superhighways. Formalization will have to be achieved if psychology is to become an acceptable science, and psychology can and must take definite steps in that direction now. However, the promising beginning and the growing interest for such undertaking will soon turn into disappointment if certain dangers, arising partly from recent trends in philosophy and logic, are not frankly discussed and avoided.

I feel somewhat obliged to take this matter up, because two of my books[1] deal mainly with the conceptual tools of psychology. Some of the critics, who did not realize that these conceptual tools have been used for several years in a great number of investigations in a variety of fields, seem to have concluded that my main interest in psychology is formalization or mathematization. Nothing can be more erroneous. As psychologists we are interested in finding new knowledge about, and deeper insight into, psychological processes. That is, and always has been, the guiding principle. Theory, mathematization, and formalization are tools for this purpose. Their value for psychology exists only in so far as they serve as a means to fruitful progress in its subject matter, and they should be applied, as complex tools always should, only when and where they help and do not hinder progress.

II

Some psychologists interested in "strict logical derivations" have criticized our experimental work for not being written in the form: (*a*) definition, (*b*) assumption, (*c*) conclusion. On the other hand, French[2] writes:

"In the course of fifty years [psychoanalysis] has developed an extensive system of scientific concepts but the concepts have grown step by step as a necessary and inevitable product of Freud's attempt to orient himself in a bewildering chaos of psychological facts that no one previously had been able to understand. Due to close contact of these new concepts with the facts, one set of concepts was devised to explain one set of facts and a new problem would give rise to an entirely new set of concepts . . . . Topological psychology on the other hand starts with a self-consistent mathematical discipline and then goes to look for facts to fit it" (p. 127).

As an answer I may be permitted to survey the actual historical development. My work in psychology began with experiments on association and the *determinier-*

[1]*Principles of Topological Psychology* (New York: McGraw-Hill Book Co., 1936); The conceptual representation and the measurement of psychological forces, *Contr. psychol. theor.*, 1938, **1**, No. 4, Duke University Press.

[2]Thomas M. French: A review of *A Dynamic Theory of Personality* and *The Principles of Topological Psychology*, by Kurt Lewin. In *Psychoanalytic Quarterly*, 1937, **6**, 122–128.

ende Tendenz.[3] The intention was not to criticize associationism but rather to refine the measurement of the "strength of the will" as developed by Ach. His work at that time, I believe, was the most precise theoretically in the field of will and association. After three years of experimentation with hundreds of series of nonsense syllables, and after thousands of measurements of reaction times (at that time one had to measure in 1/1000 seconds) I became convinced that there was no point in trying to improve the exactness of this measurement. The attempts were all based on the assumption of the classical law of association as stated, e.g., by G. E. Müller. The experiments however seemed to prove conclusively, contrary to my expectation, that this assumption had to be abandoned or decidedly modified. It was necessary to distinguish two rather different types of habits (associations): "need habits" (like alcoholism) and "execution habits" (like pulling a lever up rather than down). The first types represents a "tension" (source of energy), a need such as hunger, which demands satisfaction either directly or through substitution. The execution habit, on the other hand, is in itself no source of action. It is equivalent to a pattern of restraining forces determining a certain path. Without a need or quasi-need the execution habit does not lead to action.

After an interruption due to the first World War, a systematic attempt was made to test the positive assumption growing out of this criticism of the law of association. The first step was an attempt to achieve a more precise conceptual analysis. Dynamically, an "association" is something like a link in a chain, i.e., a pattern of restraining forces without

intrinsic tendency to create a change. On the other hand, the tendency to bring about action is basic to a need. This property of a need or quasi-need can be represented by coordinating it to a "system in tension." By taking this construct seriously and using certain operational definitions, particularly by correlating the "release of tension" to a "satisfaction of the need" (or by the "reaching of the goal") and the "setting up of tension" to an "intention" or to a "need in a state of hunger," a great number of testable conclusions were made possible.

After these basic conclusions had been proved valid, mainly through the experiments of Zeigarnik[4] and Ovsiankina,[5] the theory was expanded to include problems like psychological satiation, substitution on the reality and irreality level and in play situations, the measurement of substitute value, the level of aspiration, its shift after success and failure, the effect of distance from the goal upon the strength of psychological forces; in short, the pattern of goals and needs, their interrelation, and the ways of satisfying them, were studied. Today, a multitude of problems including personality and personality development, cognitive structure, social and cultural relations are being attacked with a set of related concepts.

If one looks through our publications in the order that they have been published one will, I think, agree that the various theoretical assumptions and constructs have been developed rather slowly step by step. The assumptions were made rather tentatively at first and with a fair amount of hestitation. Only to the degree that more and more empirical facts could

[3]Kurt Lewin. Die psychische Tätigkeit bei der Hemmung von Willensorgängen und das Grundgesetz der Assoziation, *Ztschr. f. Psychol.*, 1917, **77**, 212–247.

[4]B. Zeigarnik: Über das behalten von erledigten and unerledigten Handlungen, *Psychol. Forsch.*, 1927, **9**, 1–85.

[5]M. Ovsiankina: Die Wiederaufnahme von unterbrochenen Handlungen, *Psychol. Forsch.*, 1928, **11**, 302–389.

be brought together experimentally, the theory gained in firmness and more specific statements emerged.

This gradual elaboration based on empirical facts and a great variety of experiments holds true particularly for the mathematical aspects of the theory. The application of topological and vector concepts was first made in a way which left it open whether we had to deal merely with a pedagogical device or rather with a real scientific representation. Only to the extent that these conceptual tools proved to be valuable in formulating problems, and permitting derivations which could be tested experimentally, did they become essential parts of the theory and of its dynamic constructs.

French's criticisms of the *Principles of Topological Psychology* overlook the fact that this first attempt at a systematic survey of the conceptual tools used in our research was not made till after many years of empirical work with them. What French says about the gradual growth of psychoanalytic concepts out of psychological facts can as well be said in regard to the use of topological and vector concepts in field theory. As a matter of fact, the feeling for the necessity of rather slow and careful theorization was the main reason which restrained us from using strict, so-called formalistic derivations in those early experimental studies. That does not mean that I considered those derivations to be not fully stringent or that I did not esteem the value of a mathematical logical language which I had found very helpful when treating problems of comparative theory of science.[6] However, it would have been premature to present certain ideas *"more geometrico,"* i.e., by setting forth so-called formal definitions, assumptions, and deductions without being able to do so in well-

defined mathematical symbols, in the form of equations or similar representations of functional dependence. If one uses terms of everyday language such as "frustration," "need," "earning," without being able to coordinate mathematical entities to them, one might as well use the normal form of reasoning. To present statements employing a mathematical constructs *"more geometrica"* suggests a degree of exactness of derivation which, I am afraid, cannot generally be reached with those types of constructs. This holds true even when these conceptually rather vague constructs are operationally well defined. We will come back to this point later.

One can go even one step further. The dynamic constructs used for example in the study of Zeigarnik may be said to be already of that type which readily lends itself to a strict mathematical representation. However, we felt that it would be wiser to wait with the formalistic representation until these constructs had proved more thoroughly to be empirically fruitful. A too high degree of formalization is likely to endanger this plasticity.

Psychology cannot try to explain everything with a single construct, such as association, instinct, or gestalt. A variety of constructs has to be used. These should be interrelated, however, in a logically precise manner. Moreover, every theoretical statement brought forth to explain certain empirical data should be carefully examined not only in the light of these data but in the light of the totality of empirical data and theoretical statements of psychology. In other words *ad hoc* theories should be avoided. Bringing together the total field of psychology and doing that in a logically consistent manner might well be viewed as one of the basic purposes of our approach. The demand for a new level of precision in regard to the conceptual properties of the constructs, with a view to an ultimately strict-

---

[6]Kurt Lewin: *Der Begriff der Genese in Physik, Biologie, und Entwicklungsgeschichte* (Berlin: Springer, 1922).

ly mathematical representation, is but a means to this end. On the other hand, it has been realized that without such mathematization the development of a consistent scientific psychology is impossible in the long run.

III

Occasionally criticisms have been made that the number of subjects in some of our experiments was not sufficiently large. It is probable that, in one or the other experiment, a greater number of cases would have added to the reliability; and, of course, additional confirmation is always desirable. But, where other investigators have repeated our experiments in a competent manner, our results have stood up very well on the whole. Besides, different types of confirmation are most desirable for different types of questions. For instance, if one wishes to find out how the frequency of resumption depends upon the point at which an activity has been interrupted one will have to use a relatively great number of cases to get reliable results, for the problem involved is how within one situation a gradual quantitative change of one factor changes another factor quantitatively. In such cases the problem of the exactness of measurement is paramount and therefore a great number of cases is important.

Take, on the other hand, such questions as whether the effect of an intention is that of a link (association) or the creation of a quasi-need (equivalent to a tension system). If the latter theory is correct, one should expect a fair number of resumptions after interruption. The study of about one hundred interruptions by Ovsiankina shows indeed 80 per cent of resumption. There is some merit in trying another group of one hundred interruptions. If, however, this group again shows about 80 per cent of resumption, one can follow two lines. Either one tries

to determine the actual percentage of resumption as accurately as possible, or one is mainly interested in the question whether the effect of an intention can be adequately understood as the creation of a tension system. For the latter question it is at present of minor importance whether the percentage of resumption is 75, 80, or 85, because any of these figures would be in line with the general assumption. To prove or disprove the theory of tension systems, it seems much more important to find a variety of derivations from this theory which should be as different as possible from each other, and to test as many as possible of these derivations, even if this test should be rather crude quantitatively at the beginning.

V

Psychologists agree that the value of constructs and theories in an empirical science depends in the last analysis on their fruitfulness in "explaining" known facts and predicting unknown ones. Not infrequently it has been stated that theories which merely explain known facts are of no particular value. I cannot agree with this view. Particularly if the theory combines into one logical system known facts which previously had to be treated by separate theories; it would have a definite advantage as an organizational device. Besides, agreement with the known facts proves the adequacy of this theory at least to a certain degree. It is true, however, that it is a clearer test of the adequacy of the theory if one can make predictions from it and prove these predictions experimentally. The reason for this difference seems to be that empirical data generally allow for quite a range of different interpretations and classifications and that therefore it is usually easy to invent a variety of theories covering them.

Most of the proofs used in the study of Zeigarnik have had the character of predicting unknown facts. These facts are generally not of a nature which one would have expected from everyday experience. As a matter of fact, at the time the experiments were carried out one would have had to predict the opposite results for the main experiment according to the laws of association and emotion accepted at that time. And these predictions are the more significant as they deal with a wide range of psychological data: they link problems of memory with problems of fatigue; with momentary emotional states; with attitudes such as ambition, which are generally considered to belong to the field of personality; with perceptual structurization (seeing the tasks separately or as one series); with problems of development and personality constancy. In what single experimental study do a few constructs and theorems allow for a greater manifold of experimentally testable predictions in different fields of psychology? Zeigarnik's study, to my mind, sufficiently demonstrated the fruitfulness of constructs and theories to warrant continued investigation. There have since been a great number of studies about satiation, level of aspiration, success and failure, substitution, habits, emotion, environmental structure and forces, social power fields, social pressure, feeblemindedness, development and regression —all of which have been based on this field theoretical approach. They have been carried out partly by my co-workers, but to a considerable extent by independent investigators. They have confirmed and elaborated these results and thus indirectly shown the value of the constructs used. Nearly all of this experimentation was quantitative in character in the sense that this is used in psychology today. Of course, difficulties have arisen, and more serious difficulties may still arise later. Until now, however, the contradictions have been minor ones and generally could be clarified quite simply. To hold

that all these results could have been predicted without these constructs and theorems might be logically possible; actually, it was these constructs which first led to the predictions. Besides, to my knowledge, there is not yet any other theory formulated which actually would account for the totality of these results.

The attempt to develop a field theory on the basis of mathematically defined constructs and theorems is, however, very much at an early stage. Thus, in spite of what seems to be an astonishingly wide range of consistent applications, one will have to be ready for major changes. As Hull[7] most appropriately points out, it should be the virtue of an empirical theory not to refrain from making definite assumptions which might later turn out to be wrong. That no major change has had to be made until now I mainly attribute to one aspect of our methodological procedure, viz., the method of gradual approximation. We have tried to avoid developing elaborate "models"; instead, we have tried to represent the dynamic relations between the psychological facts by mathematical constructs at a sufficient level of generality. Only gradually, and hand in hand with experimental work, was the specification of the constructs attempted.

To my mind, such a method of gradual approximation, both in regard to the constructs used and the technical measurement in experiments, is by far the most cautious and "empirical." In this way a minimum of assumption is made.

The mathematician too easily forgets that the problem of mathematics in psychology is one of applied mathematics. It cannot be the task of the psychologist to develop new mathematical propositions, nor to look for particularly com-

---

[7]C. Hull: The problem of intervening variables in molar behavior theory, *Psychol. Rev.*, 1943, **50**, 273–291.

plicated mathematical laws. Instead, he will have to be interested in using as simple mathematical tools as possible. The mathematician will have to realize, in addition, that to apply a system of mathematical concepts in an empirical field one does not necessarily have to prove directly the adequacy of the basic mathematical axioms of this system one by one. It is as well to prove the fruitfulness of some of the derived propositions of this mathematical system for the representation of the empirical properties of the field in question. If the representation of spatial relations in physics by Euclidean geometry had not been permitted until its axioms (such as the divisibility *ad infinitum* of any part of the space) were proved one by one to hold also for the physical space, physics could never have used Euclidean geometry. All one can say is this: if one coordinates certain physical processes to certain geometrical entities one can make certain physical predictions. Such a fruitfulness of coordinating certain physical processes to entities of one rather than of another kind of geometry is all that one can mean by saying that a certain type of geometry holds or does not hold for the physical space. Exactly the same procedure is followed if certain psychological processes (such as social locomotion) are coordinated to certain entities of topological or hodological geometry (such as path). There can be no other meaning and no other proof of the applicability of these geometrics to psychology than the fruitfulness of predictions based on such coordination.

The nonmathematician, on the other hand, has accused us of using highbrow mathematical or physical concepts. In several places it has been explained that using spatial geometrical concepts does not necessarily mean using physical concepts. In regard to logico-mathematical deduction there is no difference in principle between numerical and geometrical concepts. It seems necessary to emphasize two points which should warn us against a too early formalization and may be helpful in describing with greater precision the purpose of mathematization in an empirical science like psychology.

VI

In recent years it has been much emphasized, particularly by Hull and his students, that a psychological theory should be presented in the form of definitions, assumptions, and conclusions. This argumentation should be carried out step ty step so that its logical stringency can be easily checked. We, too, have emphasized for quite a while that psychology will have to depend on strictly logical derivations and that a step in this direction is at present one of the most urgent tasks. Hull has attempted to fulfill this task, as far as I can see, mainly by retaining the traditional concepts of conditioned reflex and by elaborating them and presenting them in the order of definitions, assumptions, and conclusions.

One should recognize the value of a presentation of psychological argumentation in the form of such a strict scheme because it might help to discover shortcomings of a less formal reasoning. I feel, however, that we are not dealing here with the most essential aspect of the development of psychology towards a science which uses logical derivations based on well-defined constructs. The terms conditioned reflex, inhibition, excitatory tendency, frustrations, etc., as used in such derivations are operationally more or less well defined. However, little attempt has been made to clarify the conceptual properties of these constructs. One does not ask whether any of these constructs has mathematically the properties of a vector, or a scalar, or a tensor, whether it is a region in a field, a pattern of regions, or a change occurring within a region. No attempt is made to approach what is called in physics the dimension of a construct. In short, the conceptual properties of the constructs, i.e., their logical interdependence as opposed to their empirical interdependence as discovered by experiments, are left entirely vague. An outstanding example is the construct *intelligence* which is very well defined operationally but so poorly defined conceptually that practically no logical derivation seems possible. In the long run, it seems hopeless to approach a satisfactory logical level in psychology and, at the same time, to leave conceptually vague the dynamic constructs which play an outstanding part within the framework of derivation.

The necessary conceptualization of psychology cannot be reached by merely repeating, in a more formalistic manner, the statements of an existing psychological school like that of conditioned reflex or of psychoanalysis. Logical form and content are closely interwoven in any empirical science. Formalization should include the development of constructs every one of which is considered from the start both as a carrier for formal implication and as an adequate representation of empirical data. This implies that the operational and the conceptual definitions are not arbitrarily related but show an internal coherence (e.g., the possibility of coordinating psychological force operationally to locomotion and conceptually to a vector is mainly based on their common feature of directedness). It further implies that the various constructs should be built up in such a way as to be parts of one logically consistent and empirically adequate system.

Without the development of such a type of dynamic constructs the mere formalization of the traditional constructs might hamper progress in psychology, in spite of a possible gain in precision. One psychologist believes that association is something real, libido or gestalt but a magic word; another is equally convinced that libido or instinct is something real. Which psychological constructs are accepted and which are repudiated depends mainly upon the system-language in which the individual psychologist has been taught to think. It is clear that the formalization of such a language into an elaborate system is apt to have a freezing effect. Even after conceptually well-defined concepts have been found, it may be well to postpone formalization until their empirical fruitfulness has been well established.

This is the reason why the original presentation of Zeigarnik's derivations and results was not given in a formalistic system. Similar caution is advisable in new psychological fields such as experimental social psychology. The further the conceptual development proceeds in psychology as a whole, the quicker will it be possible to apply formalistic representation even to new fields.

VII

What is accomplished in regard to representing psychological relations by means of topological and vector concepts, and what should be the next objectives? If I may express my own feeling about this question, which will be answered properly, of course, only by the future development of psychology, I would stress the following points:

1. The possibilities of a field theory in the realm of action, emotion, and personality are firmly established. The basic statements of a field theory are that (*a*) behavior has to be derived from a totality of coexisting facts, (*b*) these coexisting facts have the character of a "dynamic field" insofar as the state of any part of this includes the statement that we have to deal in psychology, too, with a manifold, the interrelations of which cannot be represented without the concept of space. In fact all psychological schools

implicitly agree with this statement by using concepts like approach or withdrawal, social position, and so forth in their descriptions. It is more and more recognized, although there are still some exceptions, that the spatial relations of psychological data cannot be adequately represented by means of the physical space, but have to be treated, at least for the time being, as a psychological space. It is everywhere accepted that this "life space" includes the person and the psychological environment.

In regard to proposition (b) the situation is similar. Even theories originally based on a coordination of isolated stimuli to isolated reactions have developed in a direction which brings them at least very close to (b). A good example of this is the theory of Hull, which does not correlate a reaction to a single stimulus such as an optical one, but to a "pattern of stimuli" which includes goal and drive stimuli. In principle it is everywhere accepted that behavior (B) is a function of the person (P) and the environment (E), $B = F(P, E)$, and that P and E in this formula are interdependent variables.

2. The first prerequisite for a scientific representation of the psychological field is the finding of a geometry adequate to represent the spatial relations of psychological facts. We know from the history of physics that an empirical space might be represented by different geometries: at first physics used Euclidean, more recently Riemannian geometry. It is to be expected that for psychology, too, more than one geometry might be found useful. Today, one will be more satisfied to find at least one geometry which permits a mathematical interpretation of terms like "approach" and "withdrawal" without being psychologically meaningless. The hodological space[8] is supposed to be

such a geometry. The hodological space is a finitely structured space, that is, its parts are not infinitely divisible but are composed of certain units or regions. Direction and distance are defined by "distinguished paths" which can easily be coordinated to psychological locomotion. Such a geometry permits an adequate representation of the step-by-step character of most psychological processes. It permits furthermore an adequate answer to the puzzling necessity to ascribe different psychological directions to locomotions in the same physical direction if the goal of these locomotions is different. This is particularly important for the problem of the roundabout route. The hodological space permits the description of the structural relations within the person as well as in his psychological environment. For instance, the degree of differentiation of the person and the peripheral and central layers can thus be defined. Hodological space is no less useful for describing the structure of groups and their changes. Its greatest value, however, becomes apparent when we deal with problems of dynamics.

3. During the latter part of the last century the development of dynamic concepts in scientific psychology was governed by the fear of slipping into the "metaphysics of teleology." The idea that not the future but the past has to be considered as the "cause" of behavior was one of the major motives in developing associationism. At that time anything connected with the concept of direction was considered to be a teleological approach. The concept of goal was suspect and had to be replaced by something which did not imply the concept of direction. Other aspects of teleology looked upon with no less suspicion were: "foresight," which permits the avoiding of obstacles, and "consciousness," which takes into account the total setting. Associationism tried hard to avoid these allegedly un-

---

[8]Kurt Lewin: The conceptual representation and the measurement of psychological forces, *Contr. Psychol. Theor.*, 1938, **1**, No. 4, Duke University Press.

scientific elements. It tried to develop a concept of association devoid of the logical element of direction. Association should be "blind" and based entirely on the past (that meant that the theory of association had to be based on the concept of repetition).

Of course the facts of goals, needs and will were too important simply to be neglected. With psychology under the spell of the dichotomy "teleology" or "causation by the past," nothing else seemed to be left for those psychologists who were impressed by the importance of goal-seeking and directedness than to resort to a definite teleological theory. McDougall is a classic representative of this approach. The associationists, too, could not entirely neglect goal-directed and meaningful behavior. They tried to take goals, intentions, and will into their system, and it is interesting to see how by doing this the character of the associationistic theory was changed. Thorndike's law of effect and Ach's concept of *determinierende Tendenz* ascribe to those types of repetition which are connected with certain aspects of a goal (reaching the goal, or setting up an intention) the creation of particularly strong associations. Hull recognized the importance of goals and needs by including goal- and need-stimuli as important elements into those "stimulus patterns," which are assumed as the cause of a reaction. More and more, the theory of associationism (conditioned reflex) has been influenced by the attempt to derive directed activities without assuming directed dynamic factors.

According to field theory, behavior depends neither on the past nor on the future, but on the present field. (This present field has a certain time-depth. It includes the "psychological past," "psychological present," and "psychological future" which constitute one of the dimensions life space existing at a given time.) This is in contrast both to the belief of teleology that the future is the cause of behavior, and that of associationism that the past is the cause of behavior. Furthermore, it is an error to consider the assumption of directed factors as characteristic of teleology. The causal explanations in physics certainly do not avoid such assumptions: physical force is a direct entity, a vector. Psychology, too, becomes in no way metaphysical by resorting to constructs of vectorial character such as psychological forces. This permits a direct attack on the problems of directed action. In addition, by defining direction in terms of hodological space, an adequate representation is possible of what has been meaningful in some of the other claims of teleology. The puzzling relation between knowledge and dynamics which had a mystical character in teleology is made understandable at least in one fundamental point: it becomes clear why lack of knowledge has the effect of a barrier. The mysterious ability of animals to make round-about routes can be rationally related to the fact that equilibria in the hodological space depends upon the totality of relations in the field.

4. A variety of psychological processes, I feel, can be treated with relative adequacy with the conceptual tools at hand.[9] These include the basic *characteristics of needs* and the various ways of their gratification, including substitution. The *substitute value* of one activity for another can be measured, and the general conditions for substitute value can be derived. Substitution involves the basic problems of *setting up new goals* and of the *level of aspiration*. In this field an important step forward has been made by the derivation of the somewhat paradoxical tendency to prefer difficult goals to easy ones, (a tendency which seems to contradict the

---

[9]For a more detailed description of the research mentioned here, See Chapter X.

"law of parsimony"). We have already mentioned that many problems related to the process of *striving for a given goal* can be attacked, particularly the relation between the *cognitive structure* (learning, insight, round-about route) and the direction and the strength of the psychological forces. The same holds for many problems connected with *conflict situations*. The treatment of problems of *atmospheres* might be specifically mentioned. It is possible to derive the effect of pressure of different degrees upon the degree of the momentary *personality differentiation*. The predictions concerning the effect of *frustration* upon *productivity* and *regression* have been borne out by experiment. The degree of *rigidity* or dynamic communication between the subparts of the person (one of the basic factors in personality besides its degree of differentiation) has been measured. Finally, one result which seems to me of great consequence: the size of those regions which, at a given time, have the character of undifferentiated *units in the life space* has become measurable, at least in certain cases.[10] A number of predictions about the effect of the size of these units on animal behavior have been verified.[11]

As to the next tasks, it is hoped that the quantitative measurement of psychological forces will be accomplished soon. This will provide the answer for the laws of the composition of forces (resultant forces) and aid in the measurement of tension. One of the fields which most urgently requires improvements is that of social psychology. To my mind, it is possible today to define *groups* and group goals operationally and with the type of constructs referred to. With their help predictions have been made, and experimentally confirmed, about the effect of certain *social atmospheres* on group life. However, a number of basic constructs in social psychology, including that of inducing fields (power fields), need refinement.

The progress thus far made in the conceptual development of psychology warrants much optimism. The idea that such phenomena as hope or friendship could ever be represented by geometrical or other mathematical concepts would have seemed beyond any realistic expectation a few years ago. Today such representation is possible and of great help in dealing with these phenomena. I have no doubt that the concepts of topology and hodological space, or concepts of a similar nature, will prove fruitful for representation and prediction in every field of psychology. On the other hand, one of the most important factors for steady progress in any science is good judgment in deciding which problems are ready for attack and which are better delayed until a more mature state of that science has been reached.

---

[10]Dorwin Cartwright: Relation of decision-time to the categories of response, *Am. J. Psychol.*, 1941, **54**, 174–196.

[11]Claude Buxton: Latent learning and the goal gradient hypothesis, *Contr. Psychol. Theor.*, 1940, **2**, No. 2, Duke University Press.

2. *Substitution with Interrupted Tasks of Differing Valence*

ANITRA GORDON AND WILLARD THURLOW

Introduction

Tendency to complete an interrupted task has been related by Lewin to the operation of a system under tension (3, p. 184). Completion of the interrupted task presumably releases the tension of the system corresponding to it. Completion of a second task may result in a decreased tendency for the subject to complete a prior incomplete task. In this case, *substitution* is said to have taken place. Henle (1, p. 73–81; 2) reported experiments on the influence of valence on substitution, utilizing both objectively similar and dissimilar tasks. In her results it is not completely clear which valence (that of Task 1 or Task 2) was chiefly responsible for the results. The present experiment was designed to overcome these difficulties of interpretation by including suitable control conditions. These experiments, run with children, utilized objectively dissimilar tasks, and aimed to answer the following questions: (*a*) Will substitution occur when a low valence task is followed by an objectively dissimilar medium valence task? (*b*) Will substitution fail to occur when a high valence task is followed by an objectively dissimilar medium valence task?

Procedure

The following general conditions were used: (*a*) *LM*: Low valence task, interrupted, followed by medium valence task, completed. (*b*) *L* − : Low valence task, interrupted, followed by simple questions ("How old are you?" etc.), taking up the same average time as *M* in the *LM* condition. Questions were kept constant for all subjects. (*c*) *HM* : High valence condition corresponding to *LM*. (*d*) *H* − : High valence condition corresponding to *L* −. In all conditions, the main interest was to see whether resumption of the interrupted task would occur. One minute was allowed for resumption. (Preliminary experimentation indicated that resumption — and completion — tended to occur within one minute if it occurred at all.)

The subjects, 32 children (age $4\frac{1}{2}$–$6\frac{1}{2}$ years), were each run in all conditions. Conditions *LM* and *L* − (or *HM* and *H* −)

SOURCE: *Article by Anitra Gordon and Willard Thurlow, "Substitution with interrupted tasks of differing valence" in* The Journal of genetic Psychology, *Vol. 93, pp. 303–305, 1958.*

were administered first; then after a pause of 15 minutes the other pair of conditions was administered. Order of conditions within pairs, and also tasks used for each valence condition were counterbalanced among subjects. The following six tasks were used: (*a*) cutting out animal, (*b*) putting together puzzle (11 pieces), (*c*) building wall, 12 blocks, (*d*) coloring in picture, (*e*) stringing 12 beads, (*f*) putting together simple form board. The six tasks were first demonstrated to the subject; then his order of preference for the tasks was determined. Tasks ranked 1 and 2 were designated high valence tasks; 3 and 4, medium valence tasks; 5 and 6, low valence tasks. Valences determined from initial rankings were used for the first pair of experimental conditions. Valences were redetermined after the 15-minute pause, and these redetermined valences were used for the second pair of conditions.

Results

Percentage resumption (and completion) for the interrupted task was as follows: $H-$, 100; HM, 78; $L-$, 72; LM, 50. The hypothesis (derived from Henle) that LM should be significantly less than $L-$ was confirmed (beyond 0.05 level, using test for correlated proportions). The hypothesis (also derived from Henle) that HM should not be significantly different from $H-$ was not confirmed (difference significant beyond 0.05 level). Thus significant substitution was demonstrated when a medium valence task followed both a high valence and low valence interrupted task.

Discussion

It should be noted that although substitution occurred significantly, a large number of the subjects did not show a substitution effect. This may well be a function of the subjects we used. The difference in subjects used must be remembered in comparing our results to those of Henle, who used college students.

This experiment is considered to be only a first step in the investigation of the influences of valence on substitution. There are a number of further questions to be answered. For instance we need to know to what extent degree of completion of the second task influences substitution.

Summary

"Substitution" is said to have taken place when completion of a second task results in a decreased tendency for a subject to complete a prior incomplete task. The present experiment was designed to determine the degree of substitution obtained when a medium valence task followed a high valence or low valence incompleted task. Tasks, used were objectively dissimilar. Subjects were 32 children whose ages ranged from $4\frac{1}{2}$ years to $6\frac{1}{2}$ years.

Statistically significant degrees of substitution were found. It is concluded that a medium valence task can provide significant substitution for an incomplete high or low valence task. It has also been pointed out that a large number of the children did not show a substitution effect under the conditions of this experiment.

References

1. Henle, M. An experimental investigation of dynamic and structural determinants of substitution. *Contrib. Psychol. Theo.*, 1942, **2**, No. 3.
2. ———. The influence of valence on substitution. *J. of Psychol.*, 1944, **17**, 11–19.
3. Lewin, K. A. Dynamic Theory of Personality. New York: McGraw-Hill, 1935.

3. Regression under Stress to First Learned Behavior

RICHARD P. BARTHOL AND NANI D. KU

In a report on studies of frustration in young children, Barker, Dembo, and Lewin (1941) and Barker, Dembo, Lewin, and Wright (1947) state that "... strong frustration causes tension which leads to emotionality and restlessness, to de-differentiation of the person, and hence to behavioral regression." They described behavior changes in children when faced with a frustrating situation, indicating less "constructiveness of play," a deterioration of social interaction, and "intellectual regression." Other studies (Hamilton & Krechevsky, 1933; Kleemeier, 1942; O'Kelly: 1940a, 1940b) have accumulated evidence showing that there is regression in behavior following stress or frustration.

This paper describes a study designed to test the hypothesis that under stress or frustration the person regresses to the *earliest* learned behavior that is appropriate to the situation. In other words, if a person has learned two or more responses to a simulus situation, he will respond

with the first learned of these when placed under stress. Mowrer (1940), among others, has shown that frustrating a particular learned behavior causes the organism to revert to earlier learned behavior. Maier (1949, p. 66) has pointed out some of the problems inherent in these earlier studies:

"*Hamilton and Krechevsky, Everall, Sanders, Martin, O'Kelly, and Mowrer believe that frustration causes a return to a former response (historical regression), but in their studies adequate controls were not present for distinguishing between the return to a former response and the abandoning of the prevailing response for a new one that just happened to correspond to an earlier response. The above authors used punishment for disrupting a prevailing response and demonstrated that some animals persisted in this response whereas others did not. That frustration tends to make animals return to a former response, however, is open to question.*"

In the view advocated here, the source of stress may be entirely unrelated to the behavior, and the person may have a free choice among behaviors that were learned at various times. The terms "stress" and "frustration" are used interchangeably

SOURCE: *Article by Richard P. Barthol and Nani D. Ku, "Regression under stress to first learned behavior" in* The Journal of abnormal and social Psychology, *Vol. 59, No. 1, July 1959. Copyright held by American Psychological Association.*

under the assumption that frustration, fatigue, and conflict are specific cases of the more generalized state of stress

METHOD

The tying of a bowline knot was selected for study because there are two quite dissimilar methods of achieving the end result. Eighteen Ss were randomly divided into two groups. Both groups were taught both methods of tying the knots but in different order. In a later stressful situation Ss were asked to "tie a knot." Whether the S used the method learned first or second was then noted.

The details are as follows. The Ss. 4 men and 14 women undergraduates at the Pennsylvania State University, were told that they were participating in two separate studies. One was an investigation of training methods, and the other was the validation of a new intelligence test. Ostensibly as part of the former study they met with the second author to learn how to tie a bowline. Each S learned both methods of tying the knot. There is a simple straightforward way of tying a bowline, Method A, that includes a story which makes it easy to learn. Method B is more elegant and faster but harder to learn. Most Ss seemed to prefer tying the knot by Method B once they had mastered it. The motions used for the two methods are quite dissimilar; until the final product is achieved there is no apparent relation between the two methods.

Group I learned Method A first; Group II, Method B. The training sessions were conducted informally and there was no evidence of stress or anxiety. The criterion for training was five consecutive perfect trials, each trial under four seconds. After a lapse of time ranging from one to four days, each S was trained in the second method of tying the knot. Time between training periods was determined by the mutual convenience of E and the Ss. All Ss completed training no later than three days prior to the stress situation.

The stress situation consisted of the taking of a difficult intelligence test late at night under restrictive conditions. The first eight Ss, all women, reported to E at 1:00 A.M. on a Sunday morning immediately after returning from a dance. The remaining ten, four men and six women, reported to E immediately after finishing a final examination at 9:00 P.M. on a Thursday evening.[1] The Ss were told that they were to take a simple intelligence test designed for high school students, and that the average college student would be able to answer most of the questions without difficulty. Actually the test used was the Lepley Synonym Vocabulary Test (Lepley, 1955; Lepley & Zeigler, 1956), which is designed to discriminate at the upper levels of intelligence as well as at the normal range. The average college student would find many words in the test that he would not have encountered before. The test has 16 parts, each of which requires the S to match each of 30 words with one of five common words. The test usually requires between 40 minutes and one hour for completion. The Ss were required to spend 12 minutes on each part and were not allowed to proceed to the next section until the time had elapsed. The total time was thus $3\frac{1}{2}$ hours. The Ss had time after each section during which they had nothing to do. They were not allowed to smoke, talk, leave the room, or direct any overt activity toward anything but the test proper. Notes made by Es indicate that the experience was stressful. Seven of the Ss had to be kept awake by constant reminders. One S burst into tears. In spite of the admonitions for silence many comments were made such as "how many more minutes to go" or "can't I smoke just one cigarette?" At the end of the time the group was extremely irritable and restless. It should be pointed out that the Ss knew that they would be kept up late and that they were to take the test. After the conclusion of the experiment a complete explanation was given, and the Ss departed quite amicably.

At the end of the $3\frac{1}{2}$-hour test, the Ss were called out of the room individually in random order, handed a cord, and told "tie a knot."

As a check on the importance of the stress situation in determining the response, all Ss had been asked to tie a knot under conditions that were considered to be without stress. The

---

[1]Separate analyses of the results for the first eight and the last ten Ss support the same conclusions as the pooled analysis. Only the latter will therefore be reported in this paper.

results were that nine tied the knot by the method learned first and nine by the method learned second. Method B was slightly preferred, ten to eight. These results indicate that the fact of primacy was not the determining one in a non-stress situation.

RESULTS

Sixteen of the 18 *S*s tied a bowline by the method learned first. The remaining two tied a bowline by the method learned second. Using the binomial test (Siegel, 1956, p. 39), the null hypothesis was rejected at the 0.001 level.

All of the nine *S*s in Group I used Method A; seven of the nine in Group II used Method B. One of the two who used Method A volunteered the fact that he had belatedly remembered that he had learned to tie the knot in this way while a Boy Scout. (All volunteers had been screened for this information before the training period; two had been rejected because they had already learned the knot.) The other *S* in Group II who used Method A started to tie the knot by Method B but stopped midway and used the other, simpler, method.

Discussion and Conclusion

The initial hypothesis was clearly supported for the case of *two* learned responses: if a person has learned two alternate responses to a stimulus and is placed under stress unrelated to the behavior being observed, he responds to the stimulus with the earlier learned behavior pattern. The more general formulation that regression occurs to the *first* learned behavior appropriate to the situation was not adequately tested, since there were only two responses available to the *S*s; a study allowing three or more alternatives would serve to decide whether the response pattern is the first learned or merely an earlier learned response.

The stimulus, "tie a knot," was deliberately chosen to allow the *S*s the opportunity of tying a knot that had been learned under different conditions and much earlier than the bowline. The second author, who had trained all of the *S*s in the knot tying, and who therefore was presumably identified with the bowline, gave the *S*s the stimulus instructions. All of the *S*s were familiar with the simple overhand knot, usually learned at a very early age while learning to tie shoes. Not only was this response learned earlier, but it had received much more practice over the years and had the advantage of recency, since the *S*s had all tied their shoes subsequent to the training on the bowline. No *S* tied an overhand knot or any other knot except the bowline. This result was predicted on the grounds that tying the bowline would be seen as the only appropriate behavior under the circumstances.

The concept of specific regression suggests that under stress the person does not simply go back along some time dimension and produce more "primitive" behavior as if he were younger, but instead responds in a way that gave him his first taste of success under similar conditions. Lepley (1954) has stated that variability in behavior is decreased under disturbed and excited states, a statement that fits with the concept of regression under stress. He also indicated that variability has high survival value and is related to intelligence. If regression is not adaptive because it tends to reduce variability of behavior, one might ask why the evolutionary processes have not weeded out this characteristic. Perhaps it is because at times of stress the organism does not have time to consider what it is going to do, but instead must act immediately. Other factors then determine whether the response is adequate to meet the needs of the situation. Thus, even stereotyped or regressive behavior allowed

Aesop's cat to escape the hunters, since it was not necessary for him to take the time to select one of several responses. The fox, with many available responses, was caught and killed while making up his anthropomorphic mind.

References

Barker, R. G., Dembo, T., & Lewin, K. Frustration and regression: An experiment with young children. *Univ. Ia. Stud. Child Welf.*, 1941, **18**, No. 1.

Barker, G. R., Dembo, T., Lewin, K., & Wright, M. E. Experimental studies of frustration in young children. In T. M. Newcomb & E. L. Hartley (Ed.), *Readings in social psychology*. New York: Holt, 1947, Pp. 283–290.

Hamilton, J. A., & Krechevsky, I. Studies in the effect of shock upon behavior plasticity in the rat. *J. comp. Psychol.*, 1933, **16**, 237–253.

Kleemeier, R. W. Fixation and regression in the rat. *Psychol. Monogr.*, 1942, **54**, No. 4 (Whole No. 246).

Lepley, W. M. Variability as a variable. *J. Psychol.*, 1954, **37**, 19–25.

Lepley, W. M. The rationale, construction, and preliminary try-out of the Synonym Vocabulary Test. *J. Psychol.*, 1955, **39**, 215–225.

Lepley, W. M., & Zeigler, M. L. The Synonym Vocabulary Test: Standardization and validation. *J. Psychol.*, 1956, **41**, 419–425.

Maier, N. R. F. *Frustration: The study of behavior without a goal*. New York: McGraw-Hill, 1949.

Mowrer, O. H. An experimental analogue of "regression" with incidental observations on "reaction formation." *J. abnorm. soc. Psychol.*, 1940, **35**, 56–87.

O'Kelly, L. I. An experimental study of regression. I. Behavioral characteristics of the regressive response. *J. comp. Psychol.*, 1940, **30**, 41–53. (a)

O'Kelly, L. I. An experimental study of regression. II. Some motivational determinants of regression and perseveration. *J. comp. Psychol.*, 1940, **30**, 56–95. (b)

Sears, R. R. Survey of objective studies of psychoanalytic concepts. *Social Sci. Res. Council*, 1943, **51**, 76–104.

Siegel, S. *Nonparametric statistics for the behavioral sciences*. New York: McGraw-Hill, 1956.

4. *Achievement Motivation and the Recall of Incompleted and Completed Exam Questions*

BERNARD WEINER, PATRICK B. JOHNSON, AND
ALBERT MEHRABIAN

Male students indicated their level of aspiration on a final exam, and subsequently were asked to recall the exam items. 2 measures of resultant achievement motivation, 1 objective and 1 in part projective, were employed to classify Ss into motive groups. For both measures Ss high in resultant achievement motivation recalled a greater percentage of failed than passed questions (the Zeigarnik effect). In addition, they exhibited a greater Zeigarnik effect than Ss low in resultant achievement motivation. The differential recall was due to greater remembrance of the failed items by the high achievement-oriented Ss. It is hypothesized that these students covertly rehearse and think about the missed questions more than students low in achievement motivation. Therefore, it is contended that the Zeigarnik effect is a learning rather than a memory phenomenon. Only the projective measure revealed group differences in level of aspiration.

The interrupted task paradigm was introduced into psychology by Zeigarnik in 1927. Individuals receive a number of tasks to complete, and are interrupted before finishing some of them. Following this activity, they unexpectedly are asked to recall the tasks. Zeigarnik found greater recall of the incompleted (I) than completed (C) tasks (the Zeigarnik effect). The differential recall was believed to support Lewin's (1935) conception of enduring tension systems.

There was a partial reversal of Zeigarnik's results when studies of task recall were conducted in America. Many investigators (e.g., Glixman, 1949; Rosenzweig, 1943) found greater recall of the C than I tasks in "ego-involved" situations. It was reasoned that it is "threatening" to remember failure (I) experiences; the material associated with failure therefore is "repressed."

Atkinson (1953) in part resolved the apparent contradiction between the findings of Zeigarnik and Rosenzweig. He demonstrated that individuals classified as high in need for achievement (n Ach) remember more I than C tasks in achievement-oriented contexts. Conversely, subjects (Ss) who are low in n Ach

SOURCE: *Article by Bernard Weiner, Patrick B. Johnson, and Albert Mehrabian, "Achievement motivation and the recall of incompleted and completed exam questions"* in the Journal of educational psychology, *Vol. 59, pp. 181–185, 1968. Copyright 1968 by the American Psychological Association and reproduced by permission.*

and considered relatively anxious about failure remember more C than I tasks. Analysis of Ss used by Rosenzweig indicated that they were receiving services from the psychological clinic, and presumably would be characterized as relatively anxious. This was not true of the population used by Zeigarnik. Atkinson argues that the different S populations were responsible for the contradictory results of Zeigarnik and Rosenzweig. Atkinson also found that the differential Zeigarnik effect was attributable to differences in the recall of I, rather than C, tasks. He reasons that the remembrance of I tasks is instrumental to the attainment of achievement-related goals; these goals are strived for by individuals high in n Ach, but avoided by individuals relatively low in n Ach. (The reader is directed to Butterfield, 1964, and Weiner, 1966a, for a more detailed review of experimentation in this area.)

In the present study Atkinson's suppositions are investigated in a real-life achievement setting. Following a final examination students were asked to recall the exam items. These circumstances should maximize aroused achievement motivation and task involvement, and therefore magnify previous findings (Atkinson, 1953; Zeigarnik, 1927). Two measures of *resultant* achievement motivation (n Ach minus anxiety) were employed to classify Ss into motive groups. One classification method included a Thematic Apperception Test (TAT) to measure n Ach, and a Test Anxiety Questionnaire (TAQ) to assess level of anxiety. Subtracting the z score on the TAQ from the z score on the TAT yields a measure of resultant achievement motivation. This method of grouping individuals is used most extensively in current studies of achievement motivation (Atkinson, 1964). The second measure of resultant achievement motivation was devised by Mehrabian (in press), and is similar in principle to a self-report measure constructed by O'Connor (1962). The O'Connor scale has been used with some success (e.g., Weiner, 1966b) to classify Ss into motive groups.

METHOD

The Ss were 205 students enrolled in the undergraduate personality course at the University of California, Los Angeles. On the second day of class a TAT, picture series 2, 8, 4, 48 (Atkinson, 1958) was administered under neutral conditions (McClelland, Atkinson, Clark, & Lowell, 1953). All pictures were highly cued for achievement. The story protocols were scored for n Ach by a trained rater according to a reliable method of content analysis (Atkinson, 1958).[1] Evidence suggests that the TAT measure of n Ach is not a valid indicator of achievement strivings for all females (Atkinson, 1958; French & Lesser, 1964). Only the male sample ($N = 82$) was used in the final data analysis. Following the administration of the TAT, the TAQ was distributed (Mandler & Sarason, 1952). This is a self-report measure of situationally aroused anxiety. The items were scored on a 5-point Likert Scale. As previously indicated, z scores on the TAT and TAQ were computed, and an index of resultant achievement motivation derived by subtracting z score on the TAQ from the z score on the TAT. The Ss in the top and bottom 25% of the distribution were respectively classified as high or low in resultant achievement motivation, while the remaining 50% of the sample comprised the middle group.

The final test administered was a measure of resultant achievement motivation devised by Mehrabian (in press). The test, labeled the Resultant Achievement Motivation Scale (RAM), includes 34 items primarily derived from a theory of achievement motivation formulated by Atkinson in 1957 and from data supporting that conception. Atkinson and other investigators have demonstrated that individuals high in resultant achievement motivation engage in achievement-related ac-

---

[1]The protocols were scored by Patrick Johnson. Interrater reliability with the senior author had been established to be $r = 0.86$.

tivities, anticipate success, and prefer tasks of intermediate difficulty. The test items tap the direction of behavior, approach or avoidance exhibited in achievement contexts; the kind of affect, hope or fear, associated with achievement situations; and the degree of risk, intermediate versus easy or difficult odds, preferred. Sample items are:

1. In my spare time I would rather learn a game to develop skill than for recreation.
2. I worry more about getting a good grade than I worry about getting a bad grade.
3. I would prefer a job which is important, difficult, and involves a 50% chance of failure, to a job which is somewhat important but not difficult.

Items were rated +3 (very strong agreement) to −3 (very strong disagreement). The 10-week test-retest reliability of the measure is $r = 0.78$; the item-total correlations range between 0.2–0.5.[2] Again Ss high or low in resultant achievement motivation comprised the top and bottom 25% of the distribution.

Ten weeks after the individual difference test administrations, the students were given a 58-question final examination. At the top of the test the following question was written:

I am trying to get_____correct out of 58.

The responses to this question provide an index of level of aspiration on the exam (Lewin, Dembo, Festinger, & Sears, 1943). The test format was "fill in the blanks." When the students handed in their exams, they were given a paper with the following written instructions:

Please start at the top of the space below and write, as they occur to you, the items on the exam. Do not worry about spelling or how exact your memory of each question is. You do not have to write the whole question, but just enough for us to be able to identify it. The questions need not be written in the order in which they appeared on the exam. Look at the clock and take three minutes to do this. At the end of that time turn in the paper.

[2]Further details of test construction, reliability, and validity will be presented in a forthcoming paper by Mehrabian.

To provide an objective index of task completion, test items missed were considered incomplete or failed, while correct items were considered complete or successful. Some failed items undoubtedly were subjective successes, and some solved questions subjective failures. These occurences should attenuate the expected results (Marrow, 1938). Because of the nature of the examination situation, it was decided not to ask the students to indicate their perceived performance on each question during the exam.

Results

The correlation between the two indexes of resultant achievement motivation was positive and significant, but relatively low, $r = 0.30$, $p < 0.01$. The mean number of correct answers on the exam was 46. Therefore, there were many more C than I items. Exam performance was virtually identical for the three motive groups when classified with either resultant motivation index ($F < 1$).

Table 1 gives the percentage of I-percentage of C recall and percentage of Ss exhibiting a Zeigarnik effect for the three motive groups. The table indicates that the likelihood of a Zeigarnik effect is monotonically related to the strength of resultant achievement motivation. This occurs when either the TAT-TAQ or RAM is used as the motive measure. Among Ss high on the TAT-TAQ index, 15 out of 20 ($p < 0.05$) exhibit a Zeigarnik effect, while of the 21 Ss high on the RAM, 17 recall a greater percentage of I than C items ($p < 0.01$). The difference between the proportion of Ss in the extreme groups recalling a greater percentage of I than of C questions approaches statistical significance with the TAT-TAQ index, ($z = 1·67$, $p < 0.10$), and is significant when the RAM is the motive measure ($z = 2.26$, $p < 0.05$). The prediction for the differential recall is best sub-

TABLE 1   *Recall of Incorrect Minus Correct Items and Level of Aspiration for Groups Differing in Strength of Resultant Achievement Motivation*

	MOTIVE MEASURE					
ITEM	TAT-TAQ			RAM		
	High	Mid	Low	High	Mid	Low
N	20	42	20	21	40	21
Percentage of *Ss* with percentage of I > percentage of C recall	75	57	50	81	60	48
Percentage of I-percentage of C recall	10.0	5.3	−2.3	8.8	6.5	−2.8
Aspiration level	54.9	51.9	48.9	51.1	51.7	52.6

stantiated when both indexes are employed simultaneously to classify *Ss* into motive groups. Of the 9 *Ss* high on both measures, 8 show a Zeigarnik effect; only 2 of the 6 *Ss* low on both resultant measures recall a greater percentage of I than C test items ($p < 0.05$, Fisher Exact Test).

Figure 1 separately illustrates the percentage recall of the I and C questions for the motive groups when classified according to TAT-TAQ score. The figure reveals clearly that the Zeigarnik effect shown in Table 1 is primarily due to the differential recall of I items. The *Ss* high in resultant achievement motivation recall a greater percentage of I questions than *Ss* low in resultant achievement motivation ($z = 1.82$, $p < 0.10$). The pattern of results is identical when *Ss* are classified according to score on the RAM ($z = 1.68$, $p < 0.10$).

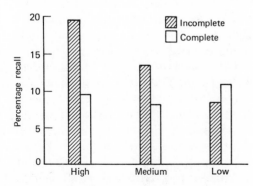

Figure 1. *Percentage recall of correct and incorrect items when Ss are classified according to strength of resultant achievement motivation (TAT-TAQ).*

Level of Aspiration. Table 1 also shows the level of aspiration for the three motive groups. When the TAT-TAQ is employed to classify *Ss*, there is a monotonic relationship between aspiration level and strength of resultant achievement motivation. The difference in aspiration level between the extreme motive groups is significant, $t = 2.35$, $df = 38$, $p < 0.01$. However, when the RAM is the motive measure, there are no differences in aspiration level between the extreme groups, $t < 1$.

Discussion

The data indicated that assessment instruments which supposedly measure the same personality dimension only correlate moderately with one another. However, the measures were equally valid in their prediction of task recall. It appears that the objective resultant measure complemented, rather than supplemented, the partly projective assessment technique. Yet only the TAT-TAQ index significantly differentiated the motive groups in terms of aspiration level. Level of aspiration in the present context denoted an imaginative achievement goal. Many students indicated that their goal was to answer all the questions correctly. The responses were similar to those of Ss asked what they are "hoping" for, as opposed to what level they actually are attempting to reach (Lewin et al., 1943). Recently, Wallace (1966) has argued that: "the closer the approximation of the role-playing situation to the predictive situation, the greater ... the accuracy of the prediction [p. 136]." In the present experiment the partial fantasy measure predicted fantasy behavior better than the objective index. It is conceivable that the objective and fantasy indexes of resultant achievement motivation will, at times, successfully predict different achievement behaviors. In sum the data presented here do provide validity for the RAM as a motive measure, and suggest that this is a promising instrument for the prediction of some achievement strivings. In addition, because the RAM items were derived from a theory of achievement motivation, the positive results tend to validate both the theory and the measure (Cronbach & Meehl, 1955).

The findings concerning task recall replicate results reported previously by Atkinson (1953). The Zeigarnik effect is predominantly manifested in Ss high in resultant achievement motivation, and

is caused by the differential recall of I tasks. But differential recall does not necessarily reflect memory disparities. Retention is conceptualized as a multi-stage process. The first stage is learning, or trace formation. The temporally subsequent stages are trace storage and trace retrieval. Only the latter two stages are adjudged to be memory processes. To show differences in the memory of events, there must be equality in the degree of original learning of the material. If Ss learn I tasks to a greater degree than C tasks, then one also would expect differential recall of those tasks. Caron and Wallach (1957) have demonstrated that the Zeigarnik effect is due to differential learning rather than to differential retention. In their study Ss were told that the I tasks were insoluble after the initial recall period was completed. Therefore, there was no persisting source of motivation for relatively anxious Ss to repress the tasks, nor any instrumental inducement for Ss striving for success to retain the material. Following this information about the insolubility of the I tasks the differential retention found at the end of the first recall period should dissipate. However, customary differences in the pattern of recall between the motive groups were observed after the feedback. Caron and Wallach therefore concluded that the recall differences must be attributed to differential learning, rather than to differential memory.

The results of the study by Caron and Wallach, combined with the present data, suggest that Ss high in resultant achievement motivation learn I tasks to a greater extent than Ss low in resultant achievement motivation. Learning is in part a function of the number of repetitions of the stimulus. It is hypothesized that Ss high in resultant achievement motivation covertly repeat and rehearse questions which they have missed more than low-achievement individuals. Weiner (1965) has summarized a number of studies which reveal that *S*s high in achievement motivation are attracted toward tasks which they have initially failed. Conversely, *S*s low in achievement motivation especially avoid tasks which they have not been able to complete. Because students low in resultant achievement motivation avoid failed or incompleted test items, they are less likely covertly to repeat and remember those items than the high resultant achievement motivation students. This analysis implies that if students are not allowed to return to the failed tasks, then the differential Zeigarnik effect would not be exhibited. The differential persistence at failed tasks also might be responsible for the disparate grade point averages that are, at times, manifested by the groups (see McClelland, et al., 1953).

References

Atkinson, J. W. The achievement motive and recall of interrupted and completed tasks. *Journal of Experimental Psychology*, 1953, **46**, 381–390.

Atkinson, J. W. Motivational determinants of risk-taking behavior. *Psychological Review*, 1957, **64**, 359–372.

Atkinson, J. W. (Ed.) *Motives in fantasy, action, and society*. Princeton: Van Nostrand, 1958.

Atkinson, J. W. *An introduction to motivation*. Princeton: Van Nostrand, 1964.

Butterfield, E. C. The interruption of tasks: Methodological, factual, and theoretical issues. *Psychological Bulletin*, 1964, **62**, 309–322.

Caron, A. J., & Wallach, M. A. Personality determinants of repressive and obsessive reactions to failure stress. *Journal of Abnormal and Social Psychology*, 1957, **55**, 372–381.

Cronbach, L. J., & Meehl, P. E. Construct validity in psychological test. *Psychological Bulletin*, 1955, **52**, 281–302.

French, E. G., & Lesser, G. S. Some characteristics of the achievement motive in women. *Journal of Abnormal and Social Psychology*, 1964, **68**, 119–128.

Glixman, A. F. Recall of completed and incompleted activities under varying degrees of stress. *Journal of Experimental Psychology*, 1949, **39**, 281–295.

Lewin, K. *A dynamic theory of personality*. New York: McGraw-Hill, 1935.

Lewin, K., Dembo, T., Festinger, L., & Sears, P. S. Level of aspiration. In J. McV. Hunt (Ed.), *Personality and the behavioral disorders*. New York: Ronald, 1943.

McClelland, D. C., Atkinson, J. W., Clark, R. W., & Lowell, E. L. *The achievement motive*. New York: Appleton-Century-Crofts, 1953.

Mandler, G., & Sarason, S. B. A study of anxiety and learning. *Journal of Abnormal and Social Psychology*, 1952, **47**, 166–173.

Marrow, A. J. Goal tension and recall. II. *Journal of General Psychology*, 1938, **19**, 37–64.

Mehrabian, A. Male and female scales of the tendency to achieve. *Educational and Psychological Measurement*, in press.

O'Connor, P. An achievement risk preference scale: A preliminary report. *American Psychologist*, 1962, **17**, 317 (Abstract).

Rosenzweig, S. An experimental study of "repression" with special reference to need-persistive and ego-defensive reactions to frustration. *Journal of Experimental Psychology*, 1943, **32**, 64–74.

Wallace, J. An abilities conception of personality: Some implications for personality measurement. *American Psychologist*, 1966, **21**, 132–138.

Weiner, B. The effects of unsatisfied achievement motivation on persistence and subsequent performance. *Journal of Personality*, 1965, **33**, 428–442.

Weiner, B. Effects of motivation on the availability and retrieval of memory traces. *Psychological Bulletin*, 1966, **65**, 24–37. (a)

Weiner, B. Achievement motivation and task recall in competitive situations. *Journal of Personality and Social Psychology*, 1966, **3**, 693–696. (b)

Zeigarnik, B. Das Behalten erledigter und unerlidigter Handlungen. *Psychologische Forschung*, 1927, **9**, 1–85.

Allport's Psychology of The Individual

The topics dealt with in the papers presented here are a blend of the familiar and the novel—of themes that Allport has dealt with for decades and of approaches that appeared late in his theoretical writings. His preference for a discriminating eclecticism in his approach to personality made it easy for him over time to expand the range of events or determinants of behavior to which his systematic position directed specific attention. Some of these changes are depicted here.

The first paper, *The General and the Unique in Psychological Science*, was selected as providing the best and most representative example of Allport's position in regard to the importance of uniqueness or individuality as a key to understanding personality. What he says here is obviously consistent with his initial position, but at the same time he employs concepts that were first introduced in his 1961 book, *Pattern and Growth in Personality*, and he provides an extended discussion of those methods of study that are particularly appropriate for the study of individual (morphogenic) traits.

In the second paper we find Professor Allport in the familiar role of provocative and historically oriented teacher. The occasion was an invited address to the American Psychological Association Convention following his being awarded a Distinguished Scientific Contribution Award from the Association. Of special interest is the fact that Allport, nearing the end of his career, returned to a problem that he addressed in his dissertation and was the subject of his first article.

In *Traits Revisited* Allport defends his conception of the trait against many criticisms that have been made over the years. It is important to note that Allport's definition of a trait is undoubtedly the most widely used among psychologists, and it is one of his major contributions to personality psychology. In this paper he deals with the fundamental issue of the degree to which variability in behavior can be accounted for by the situation or external stimulus factors as opposed to internal behavioral disposition. His comments on "heuristic realism" should provide an important guide to the student considering research in personality. The three research examples he discusses cover a broad range of topics and research methodologies, and all represent questions that interested Allport for long periods of time.

The final paper in this section reports one of the last investigations that Allport conducted. The article provides a further assessment of the relationship between prejudice and religious orientation. The research is closely related to some of the issues Allport raises in his discussion of traits. One can obtain a clear illustration of one way in which knowledge progresses by viewing the initial results bearing on the relationship between religion and prejudice, the interpretations of those data, the suggestion for further research and, finally in the Allport and Ross study, the collection and analysis of relevant data to test the ideas (or hypotheses) generated by the previous studies. The authors' interpretation in terms of cognitive style opens the door to still further research.

1. *The General and The Unique in Psychological Science*

GORDON W. ALLPORT

Let me take my text from the opening sentence of *Ethical Standards of Psychologists*, the official code set forth by the American Psychological Association (1959). This sentence defines a psychologist as a person "committed to increasing man's understanding of man." The code itself makes it abundantly clear that both *man in general* and *man in particular* are the objects of our concern. Thus the psychologist, as psychologist, can properly make two sorts of statement; he can say:

1. the problem of human personality concerns me deeply;
2. the problem of Bill's personality concerns me deeply.

Although superficially similar the two statements are poles apart. In the second we are speaking of one and only one person; in the first we are abstracting elusive properties from all of the three billion inhabitants of the earth. Both statements are true; both appropriate; and both fall squarely within the domain of psychological science.

SOURCE. *Article by Gordon W. Allport, "The general and the unique in psychological science" in* Journal of Personality, *Vol. 30, pp. 405–422, 1962.*

Some people, to be sure, object to this broad coverage. Artists, literati, some psychiatrists, perhaps a few clinical psychologists, would say that to generalize about personality is to lose it. Bill, as an integral datum, we are told, cannot belong to scientific psychology. He can be represented only by the methods of biography, drama, or other artistic portraiture. Bill himself might say to the psychologist, "If you think those pockmarks on your silly IBM card represent *me*, you have another guess coming."

Among scientific psychologists the objection takes a somewhat different form. Usually we repress one half of the APA definition, and say that our job is to reach only generalized formulae — propositions that hold across the board for all mankind, or at least for some identifiable section of the population. We recognize the single case as a useful source of hunches — and that is about all. We pursue our acquaintance with Bill long enough to derive some hypothesis, and then spring like a gazelle into the realm of abstraction, drawing from Bill a "testable proposition" but carrying with us no coordinated knowledge of him as a structural unit. We tolerate the single case only as a take-off point. We forgive Ebbinghaus for performing 163 experiments on himself, since almost immediately his findings were confirmed on other subjects. Luckily these subjects, like him, displayed a logarithmic relationship between the percentage of material forgotten and the time elapsing after the original act of learning. We forgive Köhler and Wallach for intensive work on their own figural after-effects, for it was soon confirmed that others too show a displacement of the percept, after long stimulation, away from the retinal area stimulated.

But imagine the consternation if some deviant psychologist (perhaps I myself) were to say, "Can't we linger longer with Ebbinghaus and discover in his life what relationships might exist between his memory functions and *his* motives and *his* cognitive style and *his* aspirations?" The objection would be: "Of what use is that? Even if we find the relationship we'd have to generalize to other people or else we'd have nothing of any scientific value."

Such is the prevailing "response set" of our specialty. The intricacy of internal structure in concrete lives seldom challenges or detains us. Our concern is with commonalities and comparabilities across individuals.

This response set is undoubtedly derived from our submissiveness to the goals and procedures of natural science. And this submissiveness is not in itself a bad thing. Up to now it has taught us much. The question is whether we have become so enslaved that we overlook an important half of our particular professional assignment which is "increasing man's understanding of man."

It does no good to argue that every individual system in nature is unique; every rat, every porpoise, every worm; and that it is only the general laws of their functioning that lead to comprehension.

No, we can't take this easy way out of the dilemma. The human system, unlike all others, possesses a degree of openness to the world, a degree of foresight and self-awareness, a flexibility and binding of functions and goals that present a unique structural challenge far more insistent than that presented by any other living system. It is because of their essential stereotypy and lack of variation that psychologists like to draw their generalizations from lower animals. But for my part I venture the opinion that all of the infrahuman vertebrates in the world differ less from one another in psychological functioning and in complexity of organization, then one human being does from any other.

And so I wonder whether the time has not come for students of personality to shake themselves loose from a too-rigid response set, and perhaps even to reverse it. Instead of growing impatient with the single case and hastening on to generalization, why should we not grow impatient with our generalizations and hasten to the internal pattern? For one thing we should ask, are our generalizations really relevant to the case we are studying? If so, do they need modification? And in what ways is this individual the asymptote of all our general laws?

Or to state the procedure more simply: Why should we not start with individual behavior as a source of hunches (as we have in the past), and then seek our generalizations (also as we have in the past), but finally come back to the individual— not for the mechanical application of laws (as we do now), but for a fuller, supplementary, and more accurate assessment than we are now able to give? I suspect that the reason our present assessments are now so often feeble and sometimes even ridiculous, is because we do not take this final step. We stop with our wobbly laws of personality and seldom confront them with the concrete person.

The Dimensional and the Morphogenic

The issue before us is not new. More than a hundred years ago John Stuart Mill proposed that we distinguish sharply between psychology, the science of mind-in-general, and ethology, a science of character (having no relation to what is called ethology today). To his mind ethology should trace the operation of psychological laws in specifically individual combinations — such as the pattern of the single person or of a single culture or nation. Somewhat similar was Dilthey's proposal to distinguish between "explanatory" and "understanding" psychology. Said Dilthey, "We explain nature, but we understand human beings," Windelband too would recognize two classes of science: the nomothetic (seeking general laws) and the diographic (dealing with structured pattern).

In confronting this same problem William James almost threw up his hands in despair. It is well known that after writing his textbook, he concluded that general psychological laws are poor stuff. He declared that psychology has not produced "a single law in the sense in which physics shows us laws. . . . This is no science, it is only the hope of a science" (1961 ed., p. 335). Perhaps the ensuing half-century of intensive research would have strengthened his faith in general laws; but I doubt it. At any rate he not only questioned the validity of general laws but, champion of the individual though he was, he seemed to feel that the concrete person must also inevitably elude psychology. In his *Memories and Studies* (1912) he wrote,

". . . in every concrete individual, there is a uniqueness that defies all formulation. We can feel the touch of it and recognize its taste, so to speak, relishing or disliking, as the case may be, but we can give no ultimate account of it, and have in the end simply to admire the Creator" (pp. 109 f.).

And so at the end of his career James seems to despair of psychology as a science of either the general or the concrete.

The problem has not yet been solved, but I for one detect signs of progress. For one thing it increasingly haunts us, in our dual roles as experimenter and clinician, as theorist and practitioner. A decade ago Meehl (1954) wrote a distinguished treatise on the subject entitled *Clinical vs. Statistical Prediction*. His own position he declared to be "ambivalent." Some called it middle-of-the-road (but only those, I think, whose own adaptation level was somewhere to the right of Sarbin and Lundberg).

Meehl's book draws an important distinction. It points out that in comparing so-called clinical with so-called statistical procedures we may be talking about (*a*) the methods we employ and the type of data we use, or (*b*) about the way we piece together these data and reach a final assessment. Thus the data, on the one hand, may be percentile scores or other quantifiable dimensional data; or they may be looser types of information, case records, free associations, and the like. Further, in reaching a conclusion from these data we may use statistical procedures with mechanical regularity, or we may — as Dilthey advises — simply try to "understand" the pattern. Meehl's chief concern is with the latter issue. Does one handle the data (whatever they be) more successfully through using the statistical cookbook, or through global comprehension? While this issue is surely central, it is not the focus of my interest in the present paper. Here I am concerned rather more with Meehl's first problem: the type of data that should go into our assessments.

More recently a German author (Graumann, 1960) puts the problem this way:

shall our units of analysis in the study of personality be derived from general psychological concepts, or from lives as actually lived? Another statement of the issue is found in the presidential address of L. S. Hearnshaw (1956) to the British Psychological Society. He first calls attention to the strain that exists between the demands of conventional scientific method and "the appreciation of the richness of human individuality." He pleads for "a constant search for concepts which while capable of scientific definition and employment, nevertheless possess humanistic implications" and reflect patterned structure accurately.

It would serve no good purpose here to review the long-standing debate between partisans of the nomothetic and idiographic methods, between champions of explanation and understanding. Indeed, to insure more rapid progress I think it best to avoid traditional terms altogether. For the purposes of our present discussion I shall speak of "dimensional" and "morphogenic" procedures. Let me explain the latter term.

The science of molecular biology shows us that life-substances are identical across species. The building blocks of life— vegetable and animal—turn out to be strikingly uniform in terms of nucleic acids, protein molecules, and enzymatic reactions. Yet an antelope differs from an ash tree, a man from an antelope, and one man is very unlike another. The challenge of morphogenesis (accounting for pattern) grows more rather than less acute as we discover the commonalities of life. Yet biologists admit that morphogenic biology lags far behind molecular (or dimensional) biology. So too does morphogenic psychology lag far behind dimensional psychology.

The commonalities in personality are the horizontal dimensions that run through all individuals. We focus our attention chiefly upon these commonali-

ties: for example, upon the common traits of achievement, anxiety, extraversion, dominance, creativity; or upon the common processes of learning, repression, identification, aging. We spend scarcely one per cent of our research time discovering whether these common dimensions are in reality relevant to Bill's personality, and if so, how they are patterned together to compose the Billian quality of Bill. Ideally, research should explore both horizontal and vertical dimensions.

I have already rejected the easy solution that assigns the general to science and the unique to art. I should like also to dispose of another proposed solution. Some psychologists would say that Bill, our individual, is known primarily by his conformity to, or deviation from, universal norms or group norms. His private and unique qualities are only the residual peculiarities left over when we have accounted for most of his behavior in terms of general norms. My colleagues, Professors Kluckhohn, Murray, and Schneider (1953, p. 53) have expressed the thought by saying every man is in certain respects:

a. like all other men (universal norms)
b. like some other men (group norms)
c. like no other men (idiosyncratic norms).

Now it is certainly true that we often wish to use universal and group norms. We want to know whether Bill, relative to others, is high or low in intelligence, in dominance, in affiliativeness. But although Bill can be compared profitably on many dimensions with the average human being or with his cultural group, still he himself weaves all these attributes into a unique idiomatic system. His personality does not contain three systems, but only one. Whatever individuality is, it is not the residual ragbag left over after general dimensions have been exhausted. The organization of Bill's life is first, last, and all the time, the primary fact of his human nature.

Since we cannot brush our problem aside we do well to ask how a truly morphogenic psychology (sadly neglected up to now) can become a scientific asset. To become such it will have to learn certain lessons from dimensional empiricism, and from positivism—most of all the lesson of observer reliability. It is not sufficient to "intuit" the pattern of Bill or Betty. All of their friends do this much, with greater or less success. A science, even a morphogenic science, should be made of sterner stuff. The morphogenic interpretations we make should be testable, communicable, and have a high measure of predictive power.

My purpose is to suggest certain procedures that seem to me to be morphogenic in nature, or at least semi-morphogenic, and yet to be at the same time controlled, repeatable, reliable. Before I do so, let us look more closely at the question of successful prediction, which, we are told, is the acid test of a valid science.

Prediction: Dimensional and Morphogenic

Prediction based on general or dimensional information is called actuarial. For many purposes it is surprisingly accurate. One marvels, for example, at the correctness with which insurance companies predict the number of deaths that will occur by highway accidents, from cancer, or from suicide. The chances of a hypothetical average man for survival or death are all the insurance business wants to know. Whether Bill himself will be one of the fatal cases it cannot tell—and that is what Bill wants to know.

The situation is exactly the same in psychology. Actuarial prediction enables us,

with fair success, to predict what proportions of boys, having a certain type of physique and family history, will become delinquent; what percentage of engaged couples, having various types of background, will enjoy successful marriage. Actuarial prediction can tell approximately what the average student's university record will be on the basis of his elementary school record or I.Q. It can advise industry concerning crucial cutting points on psychological tests by designating the score below which most applicants would probably fail on the job.

Note please that these actuarial predictions are far more useful to insurance companies, school authorities, police, and industrial management than to Bill himself. As a person he is frozen out, for although statistical generalizations hold with small error for large populations they do not hold for any given individual. And as practitioners we have fully as much responsibility to Bill as to his employers or to the public. Nay, if we follow our own professional code of ethics, we have more.

Suppose we take John, a lad of 12 years, and suppose his family background is poor; his father was a criminal; his mother rejected him; his neighborhood is marginal. Suppose that 70 per cent of the boys having a similar background become criminals. Does this mean that John himself has a 70 per cent chance of delinquency? Not at all. John is a unique being, with a genetic inheritance all his own; his life-experience is his own. His unique world contains influences unknown to the statistician: perhaps an affectionate relation with a certain teacher, or a wise word once spoken by a neighbor. Such factors may be decisive and may offset all average probabilities. There is no 70 per cent chance about John. He either will or will not become delinquent. Only a complete understanding of his personality, of his present and future circumstances, will give us a basis for sure prediction.

It was this line of argument, I believe, that led Meehl (1954) to say, "Let us see what the research evidence is regarding the relative success of dimensional and morphogenic prediction." Surveying such relevant studies as were available, Meehl concludes that morphogenic (what he calls "clinical") prediction seems to be actually inferior. More successful are predictions made mechanically with the aid of a standard formula. Best to keep strictly to our Rorschach diagnostic signs, to our I.Q. measures, to our profile on the Minnesota Multiphasic Personality Inventory, and to other standard predictive indexes. We can, of course, weight the signs, but we must do so according to rule. We may give one sign twice as much weight as another, just as a cook uses two cups of flour but only one of sugar. Meehl appropriately calls the procedure he advocates the "cookbook" method.

The point is that whenever we deal with well-defined variables, possessing a known relation to a pathological type, or to success in occupation or in school, we are usually safer in following the cookbook method of combining scores according to a formula known to have a good average validity. If strictly followed the logical outcome of this procedure would be the early elimination of the clinician or practitioner as assessor or diagnostician. A computing machine could handle the data more accurately than a fallible psychologist. In coming years we shall, no doubt, increasingly encounter IBM diagnoses and IBM predictions in psychological practice. It does no good to shudder at such a *lèse majesté* to human dignity. It will surely come to pass. But already we can sense its limitations.

Limitations of the Cookbook

In the first place, as Meehl (1957) himself has pointed out, the cookbook is usable only under restricted circumstances. The dimensions studied must be objectively defined, reliably measured, validly related to the target of prediction (e.g., to vocational success), clearly normed for a population to which the subject belongs. Most of the dimensions we employ have not attained this level of objective perfection.

The question of weighting signs gives us special difficulty. Suppose John has a good engineering profile, but also scores high in aesthetic interests; suppose he is introverted, but has high egostrength; and with all this suffers some physical disability—what then does the final pattern signify? Cookbook enthusiasts might say a computer could tell us. But could it? In all the world there are not enough cases of this, or of any other, personal pattern to warrant assured actuarial prediction.

Again, by keeping within a previously established dimensional frame the cookbook procedure rules out insights peculiarly relevant to the individual. True, the computer can tell whether Sam should be diagnosed as schizophrenic. But whether Sam's love for his sister and her way of dealing with him are such as to effect his recovery, the computer cannot tell. A dimensional frame is a rigid thing. It is like giving to the cook ingredients that will produce only dumplings while imagining that she has the freedom to produce a cake.

Further, the dimensions imposed on the individual are dimensions of interest to the investigator, or to the hospital, school, or firm. For this reason they may not be relevant in guiding John. The most salient features of his life—his aspirations, his sense of duty, his existential pattern, may be left untouched. In every dimensional analysis there are inevitably many "empty cells."

Finally, as for the discovery that clinical or morphogenic predictions are in fact poorer than cookbook predictions, I can only say, "What a pitiful reflection on the inventiveness and sensitivity of psychologists!" The findings — which, by the way, are not necessarily the last word on the matter — prove only that we do not yet know how to maximize clinical skill through training. I suspect that our present emphasis on tests and cookbooks may actually be damaging the potential skill of young clinicians and advisers. There are studies that indicate that clinicians grow confused when they have too many data concerning an individual life, and that for this reason their predictions are better when they fall back on a mere formula (Sarbin, Taft, & Bailey, 1960, pp. 262–274). But this finding, too, points chiefly to our neglect in inventing and training in sensitive morphogenic methods.

Recently, Meehl (1959) has shown that under certain circumstances a combined actuarial and clinical — a kind of "configural" — procedure is superior in predictive power to either method used alone. This is progress indeed. But I would raise two objections: (1) the level of success achieved is still too low; (2) the diagnostic instruments employed in the first instance are too one-sided. The original instruments on which the predictions are based are nearly always of a dimensional or horizontal order (extending across people) and seldom of an intensive vertical order (within the person).

My point is that while dimensional diagnostic methods are an indispensable half of the psychologist's tools of trade, the other half of the tool box is, up to now, virtually empty. I recall that a few years before his death I was discussing this matter with the beloved psychologist, Edward Tolman. He said to me with his characteristic twinkle, employing the then-current terminology, "I know I should be more idiographic in my research, but I just don't know how to be." My reply now, as then, is, "Let's learn!"

Morphogenic Methods

To start simply: it is worth asking whether we ought to seek only objective validation for our measuring instruments. Why not demand likewise, where possible, subjective validation by asking our subject what he himself thinks of the dimensional diagnosis we have made? (If the subject is a child, a psychotic, or manifestly defensive, this step, of course, has no point). Too often we fail to consult the richest of all sources of data, namely, the subject's own self-knowledge. During the war psychiatrists were assigned the task of screening candidates for the armed services. While they employed various dimensional tests, it is said that the best predictive question turned out to be, "Do you feel that you are emotionally ready to enter military service?" The men themselves were often the best judges — although, of course, not infallible.

One might think that the existential outlook in psychology (now spreading at considerable speed) could logically be expected to bring a revolution in methods of psychological assessment. Its basic emphasis is upon the individual as a unique being-in-the-world whose system of meanings and value-orientations are not precisely like anyone else's. Hence an existential psychologist, be he conducting research, assessment, or therapy, would seem to need procedures tailored to each separate case. But up to now followers of this school of thought have not been as inventive as their own basic postulate requires. There is a methodological lag.

It is true that psychiatrists and clinical psychologists have long known that they should take the patient's own story as a starting point. But almost immediately they redact this story into general categories, dismembering the complex pattern of the life into standard dimensions (abilities, needs, interest inventories, and the like), and hasten to assign scores on their favorite variables. One notes too that therapists who claim to be existential in their orientation also tend to employ standard procedures in treatment. Their techniques and even their interpretations are sometimes indistinguishable from orthodox psychoanalysis (G. W. Allport, 1961a).

Our conceptual flexibility is greater than our methodological flexibility. Let me illustrate the point by reference to the valuable and extensive bibliography of nearly 500 items prepared by Ruth Wylie (1961). Most of these items deal with empirical studies of the self concept. (The very fact that the self in recent years has been readmitted to good standing in psychology is proof of our conceptual flexibility.) A close inspection, however, shows that virtually all the studies approach the self concept only via general dimensions. We encounter such descriptions as the following: "this test infers self-esteem from scores on an anxiety questionnaire"; or "nine bipolar semantic differential scales are employed"; or "self ratings of 18 trait words on a five-point scale from which self-acceptance is inferred." I am not objecting to these studies but point out that they are methodologically stereotyped.

But let us turn now to what at present lies available in the morphogenic half of our tool box. My inventory will be illustrative rather than exhaustive. I shall be brief in describing each method, hoping that the array as a whole will help to make clear what I mean by morphogenic method, and, best of all, may stimulate

further invention.

1. Familiar is the method of matching, used with profit by both German and American investigators (see G. W. Allport, 1961 (b), pp. 387 f. and 446 f.). This method invites us to fit together any record of personal expression, however complex, with any other record. We test our skill in seeing that this case record must fit such-and-such a test profile; or that this handwriting goes with that voice. It is a good way to discover how much of a perceptible form-quality saturates separate performances. Although the method gives us no insight into causal relationships it is, so far as it goes, a good example of a 100 per cent morphogenic procedure.

2. Another wholly morphogenic technique was devised by Baldwin (1942) who made use of a long series of personal letters written by one woman, Jenny by name. Her unique thought-structure, i.e., associative complexes, was the object of interest. If she talked about women, money, or nature, with what feeling-tone did she mention them? If she mentioned her son what else did she mention in the same context? This technique, called by Baldwin "personal structure analysis," is highly revealing, and is carried through without reference to any general or dimensional norms.

3. Somewhat similar, and wholly morphogenic, is the procedure recommended by Shapiro (1961) for psychiatrists. On the basis of a five-hour intensive interview with a patient he constructs a questionnaire which from that time on is standard for this patient but not directly relevant to any other patient. Administered over intervals of months or years, the instrument will show the course of development, including improvement or deterioration in health.

4. A somewhat more ambitious attempt, still wholly morphogenic, would be to attempt to discover the number and range of all the major structural foci a

given life possesses. Many years ago in his *Experiment in Autobiography*, H. G. Wells, asserted that there were only two major themes in his life: interest in world government and in sex. Elsewhere I have explored the possibility that a life may be understood almost completely by tracing only a few major themes or intentions. Probably two is too few for most lives (perhaps especially for H. G. Wells), although it is said that Tolstoy after his conversion had only one major theme: viz., the simplification of life. More typical, I believe, would be the case of William James, who, according to his biographers, R. B. Perry (1936, chaps. 90–91), had eight dominant trends. In some preliminary explorations with my students (G. W. Allport, 1958), I find that they regard it possible to characterize a friend adequately on the average with 7.2 essential characteristics, the range falling for the most part between 3 and 10.

What to call these central motifs I do not exactly know. They are "essential characteristics," for the most part motivational in type although some seem to be stylistic. F. H. Allport (1937) has proposed the term "teleonomic trends" and suggest that we proceed to regard them as life-hypotheses held by the individual, and count carefully how many of his daily acts can accurately be ordered to one or more of these trends. The idea has merit but it has not yet been systematically tried out. One question is whether we can obtain sufficiently high observer-reliability (i.e., reliable judgments of the fit of specific acts to the hypothesized trend). At present it is only one of the avenues of research needing exploration.

5. Suppose we are interested in an individual's value system. Direct questioning is useful, of course. "What would you rather have than anything else in the world?" "What experiences give you a feeling of completeness, of fully functioning, or of personal identity?" "What," in Maslow's terms, "are your peak experiences of life?" Elsewhere I have argued strongly for the use of such direct questions as these, for in important matters we should grant our client the right to be believed. Projective methods should never be used without direct methods, for we cannot interpret the results of projective testing unless we know whether they confirm or contradict the subject's own self-image (see G. W. Allport, 1960, chap. 6).

But how can we grow more precise in this type of work, benefitting from lessons learned from objective dimensional procedures? One such technique is the "self-anchoring scale," devised by Kilpatrick and Cantril (1960). It consists of a simple diagram of a ladder, having 10 rungs. The subject is asked first to describe in his own terms the "very best or ideal way of life" that he can imagine. Then he is told that rung 10 at the top of the ladder represents this ideal. Similarly he is asked to describe the "worst possible way of life" for himself. This he is told is the bottom of the ladder. Now he is asked to point to the rung on the ladder where he thinks he stands today—somewhere between the bottom and top rungs. He can also be asked, "Where on this scale were you two years ago? Five years ago? Where do you think you will be five years hence?"

This device has considerable value in personal counselling. It is also used by the authors to study rising or falling morale in different countries, e.g., in those having undergone recent revolution as compared with those living in a static condition. In this case, a curious thing happens, a completely morphogenic instrument is adapted for use as a tool for nomothetic research. Ordinarily, of course, the situation is reversed: it is a nomothetic mold that is forced upon the individual.

All these various examples suffice to

show that it is possible to examine the internal and unique pattern of personal structure without any dependence whatsoever on universal or group norms. All the methods I have mentioned up to now are completely morphogenic, although they are seldom explicitly recognized as such.

Semi-Morphogenic Methods

Let us turn our attention to certain procedures that are highly useful for exploring individuality even though they are in part also dimensional.

6. First, there is the common dimensional instrument, the rating scale. Many years ago Conrad (1932) asked teachers to rate pupils on 231 common traits. The teachers were thus forced to make the assumption that all children did in fact possess all 231 traits in some degree. Proceeding on this assumption the teachers agreed poorly, as reflected in a median reliability coefficient of 0.48. After this nomothetic orgy, the same teachers were asked to star *only* those traits that they considered to be of "central or dominating importance in the child's personality." On this part of their task the teacher's agreed almost perfectly, their judgment correlating 0.95. This result shows that low reliability may be due to the essential irrelevance of many of the dimensions we forcibly apply to an individual. On well-configurated prominent dispositions there is likely to be good agreement.

A related method is the simple adjective check list. Here the rater is confronted with perhaps hundreds of common trait-names (which are, of course, common linguistic dimensions). But he is required to use only those that seem to him appropriate to the primary trends in the individual life.

Both the method of starring and the use of the check list have the advantage of permitting us to discard irrelevant dimensions—a feature lacking in most other dimensional procedures.

7. Another half-way method is the Role Construct Repertory Test, devised by Kelly (1955). The method asks the subject to tell in what way two concepts are alike and how they differ from a third. The concepts might, for example, be *mother, sister, wife*. The subject could, for instance, reply that mother and sister are alike because both are comforting; and the wife different because she is demanding. Not only is the particular response revealing of his family attitudes, but over a long series of comparisons it may turn out that the subject has a characteristic cognitive style in which the polarity of comfortableness vs. demandingness may recur time and time again. This method is not wholly morphogenic since it prescribes for the subject what "significant others" he shall characterize, and in other ways limits his spontaneous choices, but it allows none the less for a certain amount of morphogenic discovery.

8. Certain other devices for approaching cognitive style likewise move in a desirable direction. I have in mind Broverman (1960) who employs standard tests with his subjects, but makes his interpretations entirely in terms of the subject's tendency to do well or poorly on a given type of test relative to his own mean for all tests. By the use of such ipsative scores he is able to determine which responses are strong or weak with respect to other responses within the same individual.

If this line of thought were extended we would be moving toward a psychophysics of one person—a desirable advance indeed. We would at last know, so to speak, the relation between Bill's sensory acuity and his interests, between his cognitive style and his tempo, between his respiration and extraversion. To what extent it is necessary to start, as Broverman does, with standard dimensional measures, is a question for the future. I doubt that we can answer it a priori.

9. Another mixed method is the Allport-Vernon-Lindzey *Study of Values* (1960), devised to measure the relative prominence of each of the six Spranger *Lebensformen* within a particular person. The resulting profile does not tell how high or low a given person stands on the economic, theoretic, or religious value in the population at large, but only which value is relatively most, or next most, or least prominent in his own life. This type of profile is semidimensional, semi-morphogenic.

10. Sometimes the *Q* sort (Stephenson, 1953) is said to be an idiographic technique. Yet it, like other devices we are now considering, goes only part way. It has the merit of making use of self-report, and can be used for measuring changes in the self-concept. As ordinarily used, however, only a standard set of propositions is employed, thus creating for the subject little more than a standard rating scale. And if the subject is forced, as he often is, to produce a quasi-normal distribution among his sorts he is further restricted. In short, the method can be rigidly dimensional. Yet it is a flexible method, and some variants are highly promising, perhaps especially when combined with inverse factor analysis.

11. For example, Nunnally (1955) studied one therapy case over a two-year period, using 60 statements selected for their unique relevance to this person (and this, I think, is a great improvement over the use of uniform lists). The patient made her sorts under many different sets of instructions on many occasions. Using an inverse factor analysis it was possible to find three fairly independent factors that comprised her total self concept. During

therapy these factors showed only a moderate change.

It strikes me as curious that out of the thousands and thousands of factor-analytic studies that smother us today, scarcely any are carried through in such a manner as to discover the internal, unique, organizational units that characterize a single life. Even inverse factor analysis does not fully achieve this goal unless the initial information employed is selected for its morphogenic relevance. A good deal of creative work still lies ahead for factor analysis. It has potentiality, I think, for discovering the main foci of organization in a given life, but has not yet moved far enough in this direction.

Final Word

This survey of possible relevant methods is not complete, but may indicate that by a deliberate shift of procedures we can bring the laggard end of our science up to a more flourishing level. To effect the shift we shall have to restrain to some extent our present dimensional debauch.

In this paper I have introduced the term "morphogenic psychology," borrowed from, but not identical with the usage in biology. It is, I think, a good term, better than "idiographic" which so many students of personality misuse and misspell. I hope the concept "morphogenic" catches on, but even more do I hope that the types of research to which I have ventured to apply the label will flourish and spread. Already we know that personality (in general) is an interesting topic for study. But only when morphogenic methods are more highly developed shall we be able to do justice to the fascinating individuality that marks the personalities of Bill, John, and Betty.

References

Allport, F. H. Teleonomic description in the study of personality. *Char. & Pers.*, 1937, **6**, 202–214.

Allport, G. W. What units shall we employ? Chap. 9 in G. Lindzey, (Ed.), *Assessment of human motives.* New York: Rinehart, 1958. Also chap. 7 in G. W. Allport, *Personality and social encounter.* Boston: Beacon, 1960.

Allport, G. W. The trend in motivational theory. Chap. 6 in *Personality and social encounter.* Boston: Beacon, 1960.

Allport, G. W., Vernon, P. E., Lindzey, G. *A Study of Values.* (3rd ed.) Boston: Houghton Mifflin, 1960.

Allport, G. W. Comment. In R. May, (Ed.), *Existential psychology.* New York: Random House, 1961. Pp. 94–99. (a).

Allport, G. W. *Pattern and growth in personality.* New York: Holt, Rinehart & Winston, 1961. (b).

Allport, G. W. Das Allgemeine und das Eigenartige in der psychologischen Praxis. *Psycholog. Beitr.*, 1962, **6**, 630–650. Also: The unique and the general in psychological science. In J. A. Ross, & R. Thompson, (Eds.), *Proceedings of the Summer Conference*, Western Washington State College, 1961, Pp. 25–37.

American Psychological Association. Ethical standards of psychologists. *Amer. Psychologist*, 1959, **14**, 279–282.

Baldwin, A. L. Personal structure analysis: A statistical method for investigation of the single personality. *J. abnorm. soc. Psychol.*, 1942, **37**, 163–183.

Broverman, D. M. Cognitive style and intra-individual variation in abilities. *J. Pres.*, 1960, **28**, 240–256.

Conrad, H. H. The validity of personality ratings of preschool children. *J. educ. Psychol.*, 1932, **23**, 671–680.

Graumann, C. F. Eigenschaften als Problem der Persönlichkeits-Forschung. Chap. 4 in P. Lersch, and H. Thomae (Eds.), *Persönlichkeitstheorie.* Gottingen: Hogrefe, 1960.

Hearnshaw, L. S. *Bull. Brit. Psychol. Soc.*, 1956, **1**, No. 36. See also, G. W. H. Leytham, Psychology and the individual. *Nature*, 1961, **189**, No. 4763, pp. 435–438.

James, W. *Memories and studies.* New York: Longmans, Green, 1912.

James, W. *Psychology: The briefer course.* G. W. Allport, (Ed.) New York: Harper, Torchbooks, 1961.

Kelly, G. A. *The psychology of personal constructs.* Vol. 1. New York: Norton, 1955.

Kilpatrick, F. P., & Cantril, H. Self-anchoring scale: A measure of the individual's unique reality world. *J. indiv. Psychol.*, 1960, **16**, 158–170.

Kluckhorn, C. M., Murray, H. A., & Schneider, D. M. (Eds.), *Personality in nature, society, and culture*. New York: Knopf, 1953.

Meehl, P. E. *Clinical vs. statistical prediction*. Minneapolis: Univ. Minn. Press, 1954.

Meehl, P. E. When shall we use our heads instead of a formula? *J. counsel. Psychol.*, 1957, **4**, 268–273.

Meehl, P. E. A comparison of clinicians with five statistical methods of identifying psychotic MMPI profiles. *J. counsel. Psychol.*, 1959, **6**, 102–109.

Nunnally, J. C. An investigation of some propositions of self-conception: The case of Miss Sun. *J. abnorm. soc. Psychol.*, 1955, **50**, 87–92.

Sarbin, T. R., Taft R., & Bailey, D. E. *Clinical inference and cognitive theory*. New York: Holt, Rinehart & Winston, 1960.

Shapiro, M. B. The single case in fundamental clinical psychological research. *Brit. J. med. Psychol.*, 1961, **34**, 255–262.

Stephenson, W. *The study of behavior*. Chicago: Univ. Chicago Press, 1953.

Wylie, Ruth C. *The self concept: A critical survey of pertinent research literature*. Lincoln: Univ. Nebraska Press, 1961.

2. Traits Revisited

GORDON W. ALLPORT

Years ago I ventured to present a paper before the Ninth International Congress at New Haven (G. W. Allport, 1931). It was entitled "What Is a Trait of Personality?" For me to return to the same topic on this honorific occasion is partly a sentimental indulgence, but partly too it is a self-imposed task to discover whether during the past 36 years I have learned anything new about this central problem in personality theory.

In my earlier paper I made eight bold assertions. A trait, I said,

1. Has more than nominal existence.
2. Is more generalized than a habit.
3. Is dynamic, or at least determinative, in behavior.
4. May be established empirically.
5. Is only relatively independent of other traits.
6. Is not synonymous with moral or social judgment.
7. May be viewed either in the light of the personality which contains it, or in the light of its distribution in the population at large.

SOURCE. *Article by Gordon Allport, "Traits revisited" in the* American Psychologist, *Vol. 21, pp. 1–10, 1966. Copyright 1966 by the American Psychological Association and reproduced by permission.*

To these criteria I added one more:

8. Acts, and even habits, that are inconsistent with a trait are not proof of the nonexistence of the trait.

While these propositions still seem to me defensible they were originally framed in an age of psychological innocence. They now need reexamination in the light of subsequent criticism and research.

Criticism of the Concept of Trait

Some critics have challenged the whole concept of trait. Carr and Kingsbury (1938) point out the danger of reification. Our initial observation of behavior is only in terms of adverbs of action: John behaves aggressively. Then an adjective creeps in: John has an aggressive disposition. Soon a heavy substantive arrives, like William James' cow on the doormat: John has a trait of aggression. The result is the fallacy of misplaced concreteness.

The general positivist cleanup starting in the 1930s went even further. It swept out (or tried to sweep out) all entities, regarding them as question-begging redundancies. Thus Skinner (1953) writes:

"When we say that a man eats because he is hungry, smokes a great deal because he has the tobacco habit, fights because of the instinct of pugnacity, behaves brilliantly because of his intelligence, or plays the piano well because of his musical ability, we seem to be referring to causes. But on analysis these phrases prove to be merely redundant descriptions [p. 31].

It is clear that this line of attack is an assault not only upon the concept of trait, but upon all intervening variables whether they be conceived in terms of expectancies, attitudes, motives, capacities, sentiments, or traits. The resulting postulate of the "empty organism" is by now familiar to us all, and is the scientific credo of some. Carried to its logical extreme this reasoning would scrap the concept of personality itself—an eventuality that seems merely absurd to me.

More serious, to my mind, is the argument against what Block and Bennett (1955) called "traitology" arising from many studies of the variability of a person's behavior as it changes from situation to situation. Every parent knows that an offspring may be a hellion at home and an angel when he goes visiting. A businessman may be hardheaded in the office and a mere marshmallow in the hands of his pretty daughter

Years ago the famous experiment by La Piere (1934) demonstrated than an innkeeper's prejudice seems to come and go according to the situation confronting him.

In recent months Hunt (1965) has listed various theories of personality that to his mind require revision in the light of recent evidence. Among them he questions the belief that personality traits are the major sources of behavior variance. He, like Miller (1963), advocates that we shift attention from traits to interactions among people, and look for consistency in behavior chiefly in situa-

tionally defined roles. Helson (1964) regards traits as the residual effect of previous stimulation, and thus subordinates it to the organism's present adaptation level.

Scepticism is likewise reflected in many investigations of "person perception." To try to discover the traits residing within a personality is regarded as either naive or impossible. Studies, therefore, concentrate only on the *process* of perceiving or judging, and reject the problem of validating the perception and judgment. (Cf. Tagiuri & Petrullo, 1958.)

Studies too numerous to list have ascribed chief variance in behavior to situational factors, leaving only a mild residue to be accounted for in terms of idiosyncratic attitudes and traits. A prime example is Stouffer's study of *The American Soldier* (Stouffer et al., 1949). Differing opinions and preferences are ascribed so far as possible to the GI's age, marital status, educational level, location of residence, length of service, and the like. What remains is ascribed to "attitude." By this procedure personality becomes an appendage to demography (see G. W. Allport, 1950). It is not the integrated structure within the skin that determines behavior, but membership in a group, the person's assigned roles—in short, the prevailing situation. It is especially the sociologists and anthropologists who have this preference for explanations in terms of the "outside structure" rather than the "inside structure" (cf. F. H. Allport, 1955, Ch. 21).

I have mentioned only a few of the many varieties of situationism that flourish today. While not denying any of the evidence adduced I would point to their common error of interpretation. If a child is a hellion at home, an angel outside, he obviously has two contradictory tendencies in his nature, or perhaps a deeper genotype that would explain the opposing phenotypes. If in studies of person perception the process turns out to be complex and subtle, still there would be no perception at all unless there were something out there to perceive and to judge. If, as in Stouffer's studies, soldiers' opinions vary with their marital status or length of service, these opinions are still their own. The fact that my age, sex, social status help form my outlook on life does not change the fact that the outlook is a functioning part of me. Demography deals with distal forces — personality study with proximal forces. The fact that the inn-keeper's behavior varies according to whether he is, or is not, physically confronted with Chinese applicants for hospitality tells nothing about his attitude structure, except that it is complex, and that several attitudes may converge into a given act of behavior.

Nor does it solve the problem to explain the variance in terms of statistical interaction effects. Whatever tendencies exist reside in a person, for a person is the sole possessor of the energy that leads to action. Admittedly different situations elicit differing tendencies from my repertoire. I do not perspire except in the heat, nor shiver except in the cold; but the outside temperature is not the mechanism of perspiring or shivering. My capacities and my tendencies lie within.

To the situationist I concede that our theory of traits cannot be so simpleminded as it once was. We are now challenged to untangle the complex web of tendencies that constitute a person, however contradictory they may seem to be when activated differentially in various situations.

On the Other Hand

In spite of gunfire from positivism and situationism, traits are still very much alive. Gibson (1941) has pointed out that the "concept of set or attitude is nearly universal in psychological thinking." And in an important but neglected paper — perhaps the last he ever wrote — McDougall (1937) argued that *tendencies* are the "indispensable postulates of all psychology." The concept of *trait* falls into this genre. As Walker (1964) says trait, however else defined, always connotes an enduring tendency of some sort. It is the structural counterpart of such functional concepts as "expectancy," and "goal-directedness."

After facing all the difficulties of situational and mood variations, also many of the methodological hazards such as response set, halo, and social desirability, Vernon (1964) concludes, "We could go a long way towards predicting behavior if we could assess these stable features in which people differ from one another [p. 181]." The powerful contributions of Thurstone, Guilford, Cattell, and Eysenck, based on factor analysis, agree that the search for traits should provide eventually a satisfactory taxonomy of personality and of its hierarchical structure. The witness of these and other thoughtful writers helps us withstand the pessimistic attacks of positivism and situationism.

It is clear that I am using "trait" as a generic term, to cover all the "permanent possibilities for action" of a generalized order. Traits are cortical, subcortical, or postural dispositions having the capacity to gate or guide specific phasic reactions. It is only the phasic aspect that is visible; the tonic is carried somehow in the still mysterious realm of neurodynamic structure. Traits, as I am here using the term, include long-range sets and attitudes, as well as such variables as "perceptual response dispositions," "personal constructs," and "cognitive styles."

Unlike McClelland (1951) I myself would regard traits (i.e., some traits) as motivational (others being merely stylistic). I would also insist that traits may be studied at two levels: (*a*) dimensionally, that is as an aspect of the psychology of individual differences, and (*b*) individually, in terms of *personal dispositions*. (Cf. G. W. Allport, 1961, Ch. 15.) It is the latter approach that brings us closest to the person we are studying.

As for factors, I regard them as a mixed blessing. In the investigations I shall soon report, factorial analysis, I find, has proved both helpful and unhelpful. My principal question is whether the factorial unit is idiomatic enough to reflect the structure of personality as the clinician, the counselor, or the man in the street apprehends it. Or are factorial dimensions screened so extensively and so widely attenuated—through item selection, correlation, axis manipulation, homogenization, and alphabetical labeling—that they impose an artifact of method upon the personal neural network as it exists in nature?

A Heuristic Realism

This question leads me to propose an epistemological position for research in personality. Most of us, I suspect, hold this position although we seldom formulate it even to ourselves. it can be called a *heuristic realism*.

Heuristic realism, as applied to our problem, holds that the person who confronts us possesses inside his skin generalized action tendencies (or traits) and that it is our job scientifically to discover what they are. Any form of realism assumes the existence of an external structure ("out there") regardless of our shortcomings in comprehending it. Since traits, like all intervening variables, are never directly observed but only inferred, we must expect difficulties and errors in

the process of discovering their nature.

The incredible complexity of the structure we seek to understand is enough to discourage the realist, and to tempt him to play some form of positivistic gamesmanship. He is tempted to settle for such elusive formulations as: "If we knew enough about the situation we wouldn't need the concept of personality"; or "One's personality is merely the way other people see one"; or "There is no structure in personality but only varying degrees of consistency in the environment."

Yet the truly persistent realist prefers not to abandon his commitment to find out what the other fellow is really like. He knows that his attempt will not wholly succeed, owing partly to the complexity of the object studied, and partly to the inadequacy of present methods. But unlike Kant who held that the *Ding an Sich* is doomed to remain unknowable, he prefers to believe that it is at least partly or approximately knowable.

I have chosen to speak of *heuristic* realism, because to me special emphasis should be placed on empirical methods of discovery. In this respect heuristic realism goes beyond naive realism.

Taking this epistemological point of view, the psychologist first focuses his attention on some limited slice of personality that he wishes to study. He then selects or creates methods appropriate to the empirical testing of his hypothesis that the cleavage he has in mind is a trait (either a dimensional trait or a personal disposition). He knows that his present purposes and the methods chosen will set limitations upon his discovery. If, however, the investigation achieves acceptable standards of validation he will have progressed far toward his identification of traits. Please note, as with any heuristic procedure the process of discovery may lead to important corrections of the hypothesis as originally stated.

Empirical testing is thus an important aspect of heuristic realism, but it is an empiricism restrained throughout by rational considerations. Galloping empiricism, which is our present occupational disease, dashes forth like a headless horseman. It has no rational objective; uses no rational method other than mathematical; reaches no rational conclusion. It lets the discordant data sing for themselves. By contrast heuristic realism says, "While we are willing to rest our case for traits on empirical evidence, the area we carve out for study should be rationally conceived, tested by rational methods; and the findings should be rationally interpreted."

Three Illustrative Studies

It is now time for me to illustrate my argument with sample studies. I have chosen three in which I myself have been involved. They differ in the areas of personality carved out for study, in the methods employed, and in the type of traits established. They are alike, however, in proceeding from the standpoint of heuristic realism. The presentation of each study must of necessity be woefully brief. The first illustrates what might be called *meaningful dimensionalism*; the second *meaningful covariation*; the third *meaningful morphogenesis*.

Dimensions of Values. The first illustration is drawn from a familiar instrument, dating almost from the stone age, *The Study of Values* (Allport & Vernon, 1931). While some of you have approved it over the years, and some disapproved, I use it to illustrate two important points of my argument.

First, the instrument rests on an a priori analysis of one large region of

human personality, namely, the region of generic evaluative tendencies. It seemed to me 40 years ago, and seems to me now, that Eduard Spranger (1922) made a persuasive case for the existence of six fundamental types of subjective evaluation or *Lebensformen*. Adopting this rational starting point we ourselves took the second step, to put the hypothesis to empirical test. We asked: Are the six dimensions proposed—the *theoretic*, the *economic*, the *esthetic, social, political,* and *religious*—measurable on a multidimensional scale? Are they reliable and valid? Spranger defined the six ways of looking at life in terms of separate and distinct ideal types, although he did not imply that a given person belongs exclusively to one and only one type.

It did not take long to discover that when confronted with a forced-choice technique people do in fact subscribe to all six values, but in widely varying degrees. Within any pair of values, or any quartet of values, their forced choices indicate a reliable pattern. Viewed then as empirical continua, rather than as types, the six value directions prove to be measurable, reproducible, and consistent. But are they valid? Can we obtain external validation for this particular a priori conception of traits? The test's *Manual* (Allport & Vernon, 1931) contains much such evidence. Here I would add a bit more, drawn from occupational studies with women subjects. (The evidence for men is equally good.) The data in Table 1 are derived partly from the *Manual*, partly from Guthrie and McKendry (1963) and partly from an unpublished study by Elizabeth Moses.

For present purposes it is sufficient to glance at the last three columns. For the *theoretic* value we note that the two groups of teachers or teachers in preparation select this value significantly more often than do graduate students of business administration. Conversely the young

TABLE 1   *Mean Scores for Occupational Groups of Women: Study of Values*

	FEMALE COLLEGIATE NORMS N = 2,475	GRADUATE NURSES TRAINING FOR TEACHING N = 328	GRADUATE STUDENTS OF BUSINESS ADMINISTRATION N = 77	PEACE CORPS TEACHERS N = 131
Theoretical	36.5	40.2	37.3	40.6
Economic	36.8	32.9	40.4	29.9
Esthetic	43.7	43.1	46.8	49.3
Social	41.6	40.9	35.0	41.2
Political	38.0	37.2	41.8	39.7
Religious	43.1	45.7	38.7	39.2

ladies of business are relatively more *economic* in their choices. The results for the *esthetic* value probably reflect the higher level of liberal arts background for the last two groups. The *social* (philanthropic) value is relatively low for the business group, whereas the *political* (power) value is relatively high. Just why nurses should more often endorse the *religious* value is not immediately clear.

Another study of external validation, showing the long-range predictive power of the test is an unpublished investigation by Betty Mawardi. It is based on a follow-up of Wellesley graduates 15 years after taking the Study of Values.

Table 2 reports the significant deviations (at the 5% level or better) of var-ious occupational groups from the mean scores of Wellesley students. In virtually every case we find the deviation meaningful (even necessary) for the occupation in question. Thus women in business are significantly high in *economic* interests; medical, government, and scientific workers in *theoretical*; literary and artistic workers in *esthetic*; social workers in *social*; and religious workers in *religious* values.

One must remember that to achieve a relatively high score on one value, one must deliberately slight others. For this reason it is interesting to note in the table the values that are systematically slighted in order to achieve a higher score on the occupationally relevant value. (In the case

TABLE 2   *Significant Deviations of Scores on the Study of Values for Occupational Groups of Wellesley Alumni from Wellesley Mean Scores*

OCCUPATIONAL GROUPS	N	THEOR-ETICAL	ECONOMIC	ESTHETIC	SOCIAL	POLITICAL	RELIGIOUS
Business workers	64	Lower	Higher				
Medical workers	42	Higher	Lower			Lower	
Library workers	40	Higher	Lower	Higher			
Artistic workers	37			Higher	Lower		
Scientific workers	28	Higher		Lower			
Government workers	24	Higher			Lower		Lower
Social workers	26				Higher		
Religious workers	11					Lower	Higher

of social workers it appears that they "take away" more or less uniformly from other values in order to achieve a high social value.)

Thus, even at the college age it is possible to forecast in a general way modal vocational activity 15 years hence. As Newcomb, Turner, and Converse (1965) say, this test clearly deals with "inclusive values" or with "basic value postures" whose generality is strikingly broad. An evaluative posture toward life saturates, or guides, or gates (choose your own metaphor) specific daily choices over a long expanse of years.

One reason I have used this illustration of trait research is to raise an important methodological issue. The six values are not wholly independent. There is a slight tendency for theoretic and esthetic values to covary; likewise for economic and political values; and so too with social and religious. Immediately the thought arises, "Let's factor the whole matrix and see what orthogonal dimensions emerge." This step has been taken several times (see *Manual*); but always with confusing results. Some investigators discover that fewer than six factors are needed — some that we need more. And in all cases the clusters that emerge seem strange and unnamable. Here is a case, I believe, where our empiricism should submit to rational restraint. The traits as defined are meaningful, reliably measured, and validated. Why sacrifice them to galloping gamesmanship?

Covariation: Religion and Prejudice. Speaking of covariation I do not mean to imply that in restraining our empirical excesses we should fail to explore the patterns that underlie covariation when it seems reasonable to do so.

Take, for example, the following problem. Many investigations show conclusively that on the broad average church attenders harbor more ethnic prejudice than nonattenders. (Some of the relevant studies are listed by Argyle, 1959, and by Wilson, 1960.) At the same time many ardent workers for civil rights are religiously motivated. From Christ to Gandhi and to Martin Luther King we note that equimindedness has been associated with religious devoutness. Here then is a paradox: Religion makes prejudice; it also unmakes prejudice.

First we tackle the problem rationally and form a hypothesis to account for what seems to be a curvilinear relation. A hint for the needed hypothesis comes from *The Authoritarian Personality* (Adorno, Frenkel-Brunswik, Levinson, & Sanford, 1950) which suggests that acceptance of institutional religion is not as important as the *way* in which it is accepted. Argyle (1959) sharpens the hypothesis. He says, "It is not the genuinely devout who are prejudiced but the conventionally religious [p. 84]."

In our own studies we have tentatively assumed that two contrasting but measurable forms of religious orientation exist. The first form we call the *extrinsic* orientation, meaning that for the church-goer religious devotion is not a value in its own right, but is an instrumental value serving the motives of personal comfort, security, or social status. (One man said he went to church because it was the best place to sell insurance.) Elsewhere I have defined this utilitarian orientation toward religion more fully (G. W. Allport, 1960, 1963). Here I shall simply mention two items from our scale, agreement with which we assume indicates the extrinsic attitude:

What religion offers me most is comfort when sorrows and misfortune strike.

One reason for my being a church member is that such membership helps to establish a person in the community.

By contrast the *intrinsic* orientation regards faith as a supreme value in its own right. Such faith strives to transcend self-centered needs, takes seriously the commandment of brotherhood that is found in all religions, and seeks a unification of being. Agreement with the following items indicates an intrinsic orientation:

My religious beliefs are what really lie behind my whole approach to life.

If not prevented by unavoidable circumstances, I attend church, on the average (more than once a week) (once a week) (two or three times a month) (less than once a month).

This second item is of considerable interest, for many studies have found that it is the irregular attenders who are by far the most prejudiced (e.g., Holtzmann, 1956; Williams, 1964). They take their religion in convenient doses and do not let it regulate their lives.

Now for a few illustrative results in Table 3. If we correlate the extrinsicness of orientation with various prejudice scales we find the hypothesis confirmed.

TABLE 3   *Correlations between Measures of Religious Orientation among Churchgoers and Various Prejudice Scales*

DENOMINATIONAL SAMPLE	N	r
Unitarian	50	
Extrinsic — anti-Catholicism		0.56
Intrinsic — anti-Catholicism		−0.36
Extrinsic — anti-Mexican		0.54
Intrinsic — anti-Mexican		−0.42
Catholic	66	
Extrinsic — anti-Negro		0.36
Intrinsic — anti-Negro		−0.49
Nazarene	39	
Extrinsic — anti-Negro		0.41
Intrinsic — anti-Negro		−0.44
Mixed[a]	207	
Extrinsic — anti-Semitic		0.65

[a]From Wilson (1960).

Likewise, as predicted, intrinsicness of orientation is negatively correlated with prejudice.

In view of the difficulty of tapping the two complex traits in question, it is clear from these studies that our rationally derived hypothesis gains strong support. We note that the trend is the same when different denominations are studied in relation to differing targets for prejudice.

Previously I have said that empirical testing has the ability to correct or extend our rational analysis of patterns. In this particular research the following unexpected fact emerges. While those who approach the intrinsic pole of our continuum are on the average less prejudiced than those who approach the extrinsic pole, a number of subjects show themselves to be disconcertingly illogical. They accept both intrinsically worded items and extrinsically worded items, even when these are contradictory, such as:

My religious beliefs are what really lie behind my whole approach to life.

Though I believe in my religion, I feel there are many more important things in my life.

It is necessary, therefore, to inspect this sizable group of muddleheads who refuse to conform to our neat religious logic. We call them "inconsistently proreligious." They sample like religion; for them it has "social desirability" (cf. Edwards, 1957).

The importance of recognizing this third mode of religious orientation is seen by comparing the prejudice scores for the groups presented in Table 4. In the instruments employed the lowest possible prejudice score is 12, the highest possible, 48. We note that the mean prejudice score rises steadily and significantly from the intrinsically consistent to the inconsistently proreligious. Thus subjects with an undiscriminated pro-

TABLE 4   *Types of Religious Orientation and Mean Prejudice Scores*

	MEAN PREJUDICE SCORES			
	Consistently intrinsic	Consistently extrinsic	Moderately inconsistent (proreligion)	Extremely inconsistent (proreligion)
Anti-Negro	28.7	33.0	35.4	37.9
Anti-Semitic	22.6	24.6	28.0	30.1

Note.—$N = 309$, mixed denominations. All differences significant at 0.01 level.

religious response set are on the average most prejudiced of all.

Having discovered the covariation of prejudice with both the extrinsic orientation and the "pro" response set, we are faced with the task of rational explanation. One may, I think, properly argue that these particular religious attitudes are instrumental in nature; they provide safety, security, and status—all within a self-serving frame. Prejudice, we know, performs much the same function within some personalities. The needs for status, security, comfort, and a feeling of self-rightness are served by both ethnic hostility and by tailoring one's religious orientation to one's convenience. The economy of other lives is precisely the reverse: It is their religion that centers their existence, and the only ethnic attitude compatible with this intrinsic orientation is one of brotherhood, not of bigotry.

This work, along with the related investigations of Lenski (1963), Williams (1964), and others, signifies that we gain important insights when we refine our conception of the nature of the religions sentiment and its functions. Its patterning properties in the economy of a life are diverse. It can fuse with bigotry or with brotherhood according to its nature.

As unfinished business I must leave the problem of nonattenders. From data available it seems that the unchurched are less prejudiced on the average than either the extrinsic or the inconsistent church-judiced on the average than those whose religious orientation is intrinsic. Why this should be so must form the topic of future research.

Personal Dispositions: An Idiomorphic Approach. The final illustration of heuristic realism has to do with the search for the natural cleavages that mark an individual life. In this procedure there is no reference to common dimensions, no comparison with other people, except as is implied by the use of the English language. If, as Allport and Odbert (1936) have found, there are over 17,000 available trait names, and if these may be used in combinations, there is no real point in arguing that the use of the available lexicon of a language necessarily makes all trait studies purely nomothetic (dimensional).

A series of 172 published *Letters from Jenny* (G. W. Allport, 1965) contains enough material for a rather close clinical characterization of Jenny's personality, as well as for careful quantitative and computational analysis. While there is no possibility in this case of obtaining external validation for the diagnosis reached by either method, still by employing both procedures an internal agreement is found which constitutes a type of empirical validation for the traits that emerge.

The *clinical* method in this case is close to common sense. Thirty-nine judges listed the essential characteristics of

TABLE 5   Central Traits in Jenny's Personality as Determined by Two Methods

COMMON-SENSE TRAITS	FACTORIAL TRAITS
Quarrelsome-suspicious ⎫ Aggressive ⎬	Aggression
Self-centered (possessive)	Possessiveness
Sentimental	⎧ Need for affiliation ⎨ Need for family acceptance
Independent-autonomous	Need for autonomy
Esthetic-artistic	Sentience
Self-centered (self-pitying)	Martyrdom
(No parallel)	Sexuality
Cynical-morbid	(No parallel)
Dramatic-intense	("Overstate")

Jenny as they saw them. The result was a series of descriptive adjectives, 198 in number. Many of the selected trait names were obviously synonymous; and nearly all fell readily into eight clusters.

The *quantitative* analysis consisted of coding the letters in terms of 99 tag words provided by the lexicon of the General Inquirer (Stone, Bales, Namenwirth, & Ogilvie, 1962). The frequency with which these basic tag words are associated with one another in each letter forms the basis for a factor analysis (see G. W. Allport, 1965, p. 200).

Table 5 lists in parallel fashion the clusters obtained by clinical judgment based on a careful reading of the series, along with the factors obtained by Jeffrey Paige in his unpublished factorial study.

In spite of the differences in terminology the general paralleling of the two lists establishes some degree of empirical check on both of them. We can say that the direct common-sense perception of Jenny's nature is validated by quantification, coding, and factoring. (Please note that in this case factor analysis does not stand alone, but is tied to a parallel rational analysis.)

While this meaningful validation is clearly present, we gain (as almost always) additional insights from our attempts at empirical validation of the traits we initially hypothesize. I shall point to one instance of such serendipity. The tag words (i.e., the particular coding system employed) are chiefly substantives. For this reason, I suspect, *sexuality* can be identified by coding as a minor factor; but it is not perceived as an independent quality by the clinical judges. On the other hand, the judges, it seems, gain much from the running style of the letters. Since the style is constant it would not appear in a factorial analysis which deals only with variance within the whole. Thus the common-sense traits *cynical-morbid* and *dramatic-intense* are judgments of a pervading expressive style in Jenny's personality and seem to be missed by factoring procedure.

Here, however, the computer partially redeems itself. Its program assigns the tag "overstate" to strong words such as *always, never, impossible,* etc., while words tagged by "understate" indicate reserve, caution, qualification. Jenny's letters score exceedingly high on overstate and exceedingly low on understate, and so in a skeletonized way the method does in part detect the trait of dramatic intensity.

One final observation concerning this essentially idiomorphic trait study. Elsewhere I have reported a small investigation (G. W. Allport, 1958) showing that when asked to list the "essential characteristics" of some friend, 90% of the judges employ between 3 and 10 trait names, the average number being 7.2. An "essential characteristic" is defined as "any trait, quality, tendency, interest, that you regard as of major importance to a description of the person you select." There is, I submit, food for thought in the fact that in these two separate studies of Jenny, the common-sense and the factorial, only 8 or 9 central traits appear. May it not be that the essential traits of a person are few in number if only we can identify them?

The case of Jenny has another important bearing on theory. In general our besetting sin in personality study is irrelevance, by which I mean that we frequently impose dimensions upon persons when the dimensions fail to apply. (I am reminded of the student who was told to interview women patients concerning their mothers. One patient said that her mother had no part in her problem and no influence on her life; but that her aunt was very important. The student answered, "I'm sorry, but our method requires that you tell about your mother." The *method* required it, but the *life* did not.)

In ascribing a list of traits to Jenny we may seem to have used a dimensional method, but such is not the case. Jenny's traits emerge from her own personal structure. They are not imposed by predetermined but largely irrelevant schedules.

Conclusion

What then have I learned about traits in the last 4 decades? Well, I have learned that the problem cannot be avoided — neither by escape through positivism or situationism, nor through statistical interaction effects. Tendencies, as McDougall (1937) insisted, remain the "indispensable postulates of all psychology."

Further, I have learned that much of our research on traits is overweighted with methodological preoccupation; and that we have too few restraints holding us to the structure of a life as it is lived. We find ourselves confused by our intemperate empiricism which often yields unnamable factors, arbitrary codes, unintelligible interaction effects, and sheer flatulence from our computers.

As a safeguard I propose the restraints of "heuristic realism" which accepts the common-sense assumption that persons are real beings, that each has a real neuropsychic organization, and that our job is to comprehend this organization as well as we can. At the same time our profession uniquely demands that we go beyond common-sense data and either establish their validity or else — more frequently — correct their errors. To do so requires that we be guided by theory in selecting our trait slices for study, that we employ rationally relevant methods, and be strictly bound by empirical verification. In the end we return to fit our findings to an improved view of the person. Along the way we regard him as an objectively real being whose tendencies we can succeed in knowing — at least in part — beyond the level of unaided common sense. In some respects this recommended procedure resembles what Cronbach and Meehl (1955) call "construct validation," with perhaps a dash more stress on external validation.

I have also learned that while the major foci of organization in a life may be few in number, the network of organization, which includes both minor and contradictory tendencies, is still elusively complex.

One reason for the complexity, of course, is the need for the "inside" system to mesh with the "outside" system—in other words, with the situation. While I do not believe that traits can be defined in terms of interaction effects (since all tendencies draw their energy from within the person), still the vast variability of behavior cannot be overlooked. In this respect I have learned that my earlier views seemed to neglect the variability induced by ecological, social, and situational factors. This oversight needs to be repaired through an adequate theory that will relate the inside and outside systems more accurately.

The fact that my three illustrative studies are so diverse in type leads me to a second concession: that trait studies depend in part upon the investigator's own purposes. He himself constitutes a situation for his respondents, and what he obtains from them will be limited by his purpose and his method. But this fact need not destroy our belief that, so far as our method and purpose allow, we can elicit real tendencies.

Finally, there are several problems connected with traits that I have not here attempted to revisit. There are, for example, refinements of difference between trait, attitude, habit, sentiment, need, etc. Since these are all inside tendencies of some sort, they are for the present occasion all "traits" to me. Nor am I here exploring the question to what extent traits are motivational, cognitive, affective, or expressive. Last of all, and with special restraint, I avoid hammering on the distinction between common (dimensional, nomothetic) traits such as we find in any standard profile, and individual traits (personal dispositions) such as we find in single lives, e.g., Jenny's. (Cf. G. W. Allport, 1961, Ch. 15, also 1962.) Nevitt Sanford (1963) has written that by and large psychologists are "unimpressed" by my insisting on this distinction. Well, if this is so in spite of 4 decades of labor on my part, and in spite of my efforts in the present paper—I suppose I should in all decency cry "uncle" and retire to my corner.

References

Adorno, T. W., Frenkel-Brunswik, Else, Levinson, D. J., & Sanford, R. N. *The authoritarian personality* New York: Harpers, 1950.

Allport, F. H. *Theories of perception and the concept of structure.* New York: Wiley, 1955.

Allport, G. W. What is a trait of personality? *Journal of Abnormal and Social Psychology,* 1931, **25**, 368–372.

Allport, G. W. Review of S. A. Stouffer et al., *The American Soldier. Journal of Abnormal and Social Psychology,* 1950, **45**, 168–172.

Allport, G. W. What units shall we employ? In G. Lindzey (Ed.), *Assessment of human motives.* New York: Rinehart, 1958.

Allport, G. W. Religion and prejudice. In, *Personality and social encounter*. Boston: Beacon Press, 1960. Ch. 16.

Allport, G. W. *Pattern and growth in personality*. New York: Holt, Rinehart & Winston, 1961.

Allport, G. W. The general and the unique in psychological science. *Journal of Personality*, 1962, **30**, 405–422.

Allport, G. W. Behavioral science, religion and mental health. *Journal of Religion and Health*, 1963, **2**, 187–197.

Allport, G. W. (Ed.) *Letters from Jenny*. New York: Harcourt, Brace & World, 1965.

Allport, G. W., & Odbert, H. S. Trait-names: A psycholexical study. *Psychological Monographs*, 1936, **47** (1, Whole No. 211).

Allport, G. W., & Vernon, P. E. *A study of values*. Boston: Houghton-Mifflin, 1931. (Reprinted: With G. Lindzey, 3rd ed., 1960.)

Argyle, M. *Religious behaviour*. Glencoe, Ill.: Free Press, 1959.

Block, J., & Bennett, Lillian. The assessment of communication. *Human Relations*, 1955, **8**, 317–325.

Carr, H. A., & Kingsbury, F. A. The concept of trait. *Psychological Review*, 1938, **45**, 497–524.

Cronbach, L. J., & Meehl, P. E. Construct validity in psychological tests. *Psychological Bulletin*, 1955, **52**, 281–302.

Edwards, A. L. *The social desirability variable in personality assessment and research*. New York: Dryden Press, 1957.

Gibson, J. J. A critical review of the concept of set in contemporary experimental psychology. *Psychological Bulletin*, 1941, **38**, 781–817.

Guthrie, G. M., & McKendry, Margaret S. Interest patterns of Peace Corps volunteers in a teaching project. *Journal of Educational Psychology*, 1963, **54**, 261–267.

Helson, H. *Adaptation-level theory*. New York: Harper & Row, 1964.

Holtzman, W. H. Attitudes of college men toward nonsegregation in Texas schools. *Public Opinion Quarterly*, 1956, **20**, 559–569.

Hunt, J. McV. Traditional personality theory in the light of recent evidence. *American Scientist*, 1965, **53**, 80–96.

La Piere, R. Attitudes *vs*. actions. *Social Forces*, 1934, 230–237.

Lenski, G. *The religious factor*. Garden City, N.Y.: Doubleday, 1961.

McClelland, D. C. *Personality*. New York: Dryden Press, 1951.

McDougall, W. Tendencies as indispensable postulates of all psychology. In, *Proceedings of the XI International Congress on Psychology: 1937*. Paris: Alcan, 1938. Pp. 157–170.

Miller, D. R. The study of social relationships: Situation, identity, and social inter-action. In S. Koch (Ed.), *Psychology: A study of a science.* Vol. 5. *The process areas, the person, and some applied fields: Their place in psychology and the social sciences.* New York: McGraw-Hill, 1963. Pp. 639–737.

Newcomb, T. M., Turner, H. H., & Converse, P. E. *Social psychology: The study of human interaction.* New York: Holt, Rinehart & Winston, 1965.

Sanford, N. Personality: Its place in psychology. In S. Koch (Ed.), *Psychology: A study of a science.* Vol. 5. *The process areas, the person, and some applied fields: Their place in psychology and in science.* New York: McGraw-Hill, 1963. Pp. 488–592.

Skinner, B. F. *Science and human behavior.* New York: Macmillan, 1953.

Spranger, E. *Lebensformen.* (3rd ed.) Halle: Niemeyer, 1922. (Translated: P. Pigors. *Types of men.* Halle: Niemeyer, 1928.)

Stone, P. J., Bales R. F., Namenwirth, J. Z., & Ogilvie, D. M. The general inquirer: A computer system for content analysis and retrieval based on the sentence as a unit of information. *Behavioral Science,* 1962, **7** (4), 484–498.

Stouffer, S. A., et al. *The American soldier.* Princeton: Princeton Univer. Press, 1949. 2 vols.

Tagiuri, R., & Petrullo, L. *Person perception and interpersonal behavior.* Stanford: Stanford Univer. Press, 1958.

Vernon, P. E. *Personality assessment: A critical survey.* London: Methuen, 1964.

Walker, E. L. Psychological complexity as a basis for a theory of motivation and choice. In D. Levine (Ed.), *Nebraska symposium on motivation: 1964.* Lincoln: Univer. Nebraska Press, 1964.

Williams, R. M., Jr. *Strangers next door.* Englewood Cliffs, N. J.: Prentice-Hall, 1964.

Wilson, W. C. Extrinsic religious values and prejudice. *Journal of Abnormal and Social Psychology,* 1960, **60**, 286–288.

3. Personal Religious Orientation and Prejudice

GORDON W. ALLPORT AND J. MICHAEL ROSS

3 generalizations seem well established concerning the relationship between subjective religion and ethnic prejudice: (a) On the average churchgoers are more prejudiced than nonchurchgoers; (b) the relationship is curvilinear; (c) people with an extrinsic religious orientation are significantly more prejudiced than people with an intrinsic religious orientation. With the aid of a scale to measure extrinsic and intrinsic orientation this research confirmed previous findings and added a 4th: people who are indiscriminately proreligious are the most prejudiced of all. The interpretations offered are in terms of cognitive style.

Previous psychological and survey research has established three important facts regarding the relationship between prejudiced attitudes and the personal practice of religion.

1. On the average, church attenders are more prejudiced than nonattenders.

2. This overall finding, if taken only by itself, obscures a curvilinear relationship. While it is true that most attenders are *more* prejudiced than nonattenders, a significant minority of them are *less* prejudiced.

3. It is the casual, irregular fringe members who are high in prejudice; their religious motivation is of the extrinsic order. It is the constant, devout, internalized members who are low in prejudice; their religious motivation is of the *intrinsic* order.

The present part will establish a fourth important finding—although it may properly be regarded as an amplification of the third. *The finding is that a certain cognitive style permeates the thinking of many people in such a way that they are indiscriminately proreligious and, at the same time, prejudiced.*

But first let us make clear the types of evidence upon which the first three propositions are based and examine their theoretical significance.

Churchgoers Are More Prejudiced

Beginning the long parade of findings demonstrating that churchgoers are more intolerant of ethnic minorities than nonattenders is a study by Allport and Kramer (1946). These authors discovered that

SOURCE. Article by Gordon Allport and J. Michael Ross, "Personal religious orientation and prejudice" in the Journal of personality and social psychology, Vol. 5, pp. 432–443, 1967. Copyright 1967 by the American Psychological Association and reprinted by permission.

students who claimed no religious affiliation were less likely to be anti-Negro than those who declared themselves to be protestant or Catholic. Furthermore, students reporting a strong religious influence at home were higher in ethnic prejudice than students reporting only slight or no religious influence. Rosenblith (1949) discovered the same trend among students in South Dakota. *The Authoritarian Personality* (Adorno, Frenkel-Brunswik, Levinson, & Sanford, 1950, p. 212) stated that scores on ethnocentricism (as well as on authoritarianism) are significantly higher among church attenders than among nonattenders. Gough's (1951) findings were similar. Kirkpatrick (1949) found religious people in general to be slightly less humanitarian than nonreligious people. For example, they had more punitive attitudes toward criminals, delinquents, prostitutes, homosexuals, and those in need of psychiatric treatment. Working with a student population Rokeach (1960) discovered nonbelievers to be consistently less dogmatic, less authoritarian, and less ethnocentric than believers. Public-opinion polls (as summarized by Stember, 1961) revealed confirmatory evidence across the board.

Going beyond ethnic prejudice, Stouffer (1955) demonstrated that among a representative sample of American church members those who had attended church within the past month were more intolerant of nonconformists (such as socialists, atheists, or communists) than those who had not attended. It seems that on the average religious people show more intolerance in general — not only toward ethnic but also toward ideological groups.

Is this persistent relationship in any way spurious? Can it be due, for example, to the factor of educational level? Many studies show that people with high education tend to be appreciably less prejudiced

than people with low education. Perhaps it is the former group that less often goes to church. The reasoning is false. Sociological evidence has shown conclusively that frequent church attendance is associated with high socioeconomic status and with college education (Demerath, 1965). Furthermore, Stouffer's study found that the intolerant tendency among churchgoers existed only when educational level was held constant, Struening (1963), using as subjects only faculty members of a large state university (all highly educated), discovered that nonattenders were on the average less prejudiced than attenders. These studies assure us that the association between churchgoing and prejudice is not merely a spurious product of low education.

Turning to the theoretical implications of these findings, shall we say that religion in and of itself makes for prejudice and intolerance? There are some arguments in favor of such a conclusion, especially when we recall that certain powerful *theological* positions — those emphasizing revelation, election (chosen people), and theocracy (Allport, 1959, 1966) — have throughout history turned one religion against another. And among *sociological* factors in religion we find many that make for bigotry. One thinks of the narrow composition of many religious groups in terms of ethnic and class membership, of their pressure toward conformity, and of the competition between them (see Demerath, 1965; Lenski, 1961). It does seem that religion as such makes for prejudice.

And yet it is here that we encounter the grand paradox. One may not overlook the teachings of equality and brotherhood, of compassion and humanheartedness, that mark all the great world religions. Nor may one overlook the precept and example of great figures whose labors in behalf of tolerance were and are religiously motivated — such as Christ himself, Tertullian, Pope Gelasius I, St. Ambrose, Cardinal Cusa, Sebastian Castellio, Schwenckfeld, Roger Williams, Mahatma Gandhi, Martin Luther King, and many others, including the recently martyred clergy in our own South. These lives, along with the work of many religious bodies, councils, and service organizations would seem to indicate that religion as such *unmakes prejudice.* A paradox indeed.

The Curvilinear Relationship

If religion as such made *only* for prejudice, we would expect that churchgoers who expose themselves most constantly to its influence would, as a result, be more prejudiced than those who seldom attend. Such is not the case.

Many studies show that frequent attenders are less prejudiced then infrequent attenders and often less prejudiced even than nonattenders. Let us cite one illustrative study by Struening (1963). The curvilinear trend is immediately apparent in Table 1. In this particular study nonattenders had lower prejudice

TABLE 1   *Church Attendance and Prejudice among Faculty Members of a Midwestern University*

FREQUENCY OF ATTENDANCE (times per mo.)	N	PREJUDICE SCORE
0	261	14.7
1	143	25.0
2	103	26.0
3	84	23.8
4	157	22.0
5–7	94	19.9
8–10	26	16.3
11 or more	21	11.7

Note. — From Struening (1957).

TABLE 2   *Church Attendance and Prejudice among Students in The Border States*

	1956 study % intolerant	MEAN SCORE ON D SCALE	
		1958 study	1960 study
Nonattenders	37	41.3	38.1
Once a mo.	66	48.5	51.4
Twice a mo.	67	50.6	48.4
Once a wk. or oftener	49	44.5	44.3

Note. — Adapted from Holtzman (1956), Kelley, Ferson, and Holtzman (1958), Young, Benson, and Holtzman (1960).

scores than any group, save only those devotees who managed to attend 11 or more times a month. Without employing such fine time intervals other studies have shown the same curvilinear trend. Thus, in *The Authoritarian Personality* (p. 212) we learned that in 12 out of 15 groups "regular" attenders (like nonattenders) were less prejudiced then "seldom" or "often" attenders. Employing a 26-item Desegregation Scale in three separate studies, Holtzman (1956) found the same trend as shown in Table 2. If more evidence for the curvilinear relationship is needed, it will be found in community studies made in New Jersey (Friedrichs, 1959), North Carolina (Tumin, 1958), New England (Pettigrew, 1959), and Ohio and California (Pinkney, 1961). One could almost say there is a unanimity of findings on this matter. The trend holds regardless of religion, denomination, or target of prejudice (although the case seems less clear for anti-Semitism than for prejudice against other ethnic groups).

What are the theoretical implications? To find that prejudice is related to frequency of church attendance is scarcely explanatory, since it may reflect only formal behavior, not involvement or commitment to religious values. And yet it seems obvious that the regular attenders who go to church once a week or oftener (and several studies indicate that oftener than once a week is especially significant) are people who receive something of special ideological and experiential meaning. Irregular, casual fringe members, on the other hand, regard their religious contacts as less binding, less absorbing, less integral with their personal lives.

At this point, therefore, we must pass from external behavioral evidence into the realm of experience and motivation. Unless we do so we cannot hope to understand the curvilinear relationship that has been so clearly established.

Extrinsic versus Intrinsic Motivation

Perhaps the briefest way to characterize the two poles of subjective religion is to say that the extrinsically motivated person *uses* his religion, whereas the intrinsically motivated *lives* his religion. As we shall see later, most people, if they profess religion at all, fall upon a continuum between these two poles. Seldom, if ever, does one encounter a "pure" case. And yet to clarify the dimension it is helpful to characterize it in terms of the two ideal types.

Extrinsic Orientation. Persons with this orientation are disposed to use religion for their own ends. The term is borrowed from axiology, to designate an interest that is held because it serves other, more ultimate interests. Extrinsic values are always instrumental and utilitarian. Persons with this orientation may find religion useful in a variety of ways—

to provide security and solace, sociability and distraction, status and self-justification. The embraced creed is lightly held or else selectively shaped to fit more primary needs. In theological terms the extrinsic type turns to God, but without turning away from self.

Intrinsic Orientation. Persons with this orientation find their master motive in religion. Other needs, strong as they may be, are regarded as of less ultimate significance, and they are, so far as possible, brought into harmony with the religious beliefs and prescriptions. Having embraced a creed the individual endeavors to internalize it and follow it fully. It is in this sense that he *lives* his religion.

A clergyman was making the same distinction when he said,

> *"Some people come to church to thank God, to acknowledge His glory, and to ask His guidance. . . . Others come for what they can get. The interest in the church is to run it or exploit it rather than to serve it."*

Approximate parallels to these psychological types have been proposed by the sociologists Fichter (1954) and Lenski (1961). The former, in studying Catholic parishioners, classified them into four groups: the dormant, the marginal, the modal, and the nuclear. Omitting the dormant, Fichter estimated in terms of numbers that 20% are marginal, 70% modal, and less than 10% nuclear. It is, of course, the latter group that would most closely correspond to our conception of the "intrinsic." Lenski distinguished between church members whose involvement is "communal" (for the purpose of sociability and status) and those who are "associational" (seeking the deeper values of their faith).

These authors see the significance of

their classifications for the study of prejudice. Fichter has found less prejudice among devout (nuclear) Catholics than among others (see Allport, 1954, p. 421). Lenski (1961, p. 173) reported that among Detroit Catholics 59% of those with a predominantly "communal" involvement favored segregated schools, whereas among those with predominantly an "associational" involvement only 27% favored segregation. The same trend held for Detroit Protestants.

The first published study relating the extrinsic-intrinsic dimension directly to ethnic prejudice was that of Wilson (1960). Limiting himself to a 15-item scale measuring an extrinsic (utilitarian-institutional) orientation, Wilson found in 10 religious groups a median correlation of 0.65 between his scale and anti-Semitism. In general these correlations were higher than he obtained between anti-Semitism and the Religious-Conventionalism Scale (Levinson, 1954). From this finding Wilson concluded that orthodoxy or fundamentalism is a less important factor than extrinsicness of orientation.

Certain weaknesses may be pointed out in this pioneer study. Wilson did not attempt to measure intrinsicness of orientation, but assumed without warrant that it was equivalent to a low score on the extrinsic measures. Further, since the items were worded in a unidirectional way there may be an error of response set. Again, Wilson dealt only with Jews as a target of prejudice, and so the generality of his finding is not known.

Finally, the factor of educational level plays a part. Wilson used the California Anti-Semitism scale, and we know that high scores on this scale go with low education (Christie, 1954; Pettigrew, 1959; Titus & Hollander, 1957; Williams, 1964). Further, in our own study the extrinsic subscale is negatively correlated with degree of education ($r = -0.32$). To an appreciable extent, therefore, Wilson's high correlations may be "ascribed" to educational level.

At this point, however, an important theoretical observation must be made. Low education may indeed predispose a person toward an exclusionist, self-centered, extrinsic, religious orientation and may dispose him to a stereotyped, fearful image of Jews. This fact does not in the least affect the functional relationship between the religious and the prejudiced outlooks. It is a common error for investigators to "control for" demographic factors without considering the danger involved in doing so. In so doing they are often obscuring and not illuminating the functional (i.e., psychological) relationships that obtain (see Allport, 1950).

Following Wilson the task of direct measurement was taken up by Feagin (1964) who used a more developed scale— one designed to measure not only extrinsic orientation but also the intrinsic. His scales are essentially the same as those discussed in a later section of this paper. In his study of Southern Baptists Feagin reached four conclusions: (*a*) Contrary to expectation, extrinsic and intrinsic items did not fall on a unidimensional scale but represented two independent dimensions; (*b*) only the extrinsic orientation was related to intolerance toward Negroes; (*c*) orthodoxy as such was not related to the extrinsic or intrinsic orientation; (*d*) greater orthodoxy (fundamentalism of belief) did, however, relate positively to prejudice.

Taking all these studies together we are justified in assuming that the inner experience of religion (what it means to the individual) is an important causal factor in developing a tolerant or a prejudiced outlook on life.

Yet, additional evidence is always in place, and new insights can be gained by a closer inspection of the rather coarse relationships that have been established up to now.

The Present Study

We wished to employ an improved and broader measure of prejudice than had previously been used. And since direct measures of prejudice (naming the target groups) have become too sensitive for wide use, we wished to try some abbreviated indirect measures. Further, we wished to make use of an improved Extrinsic-Intrinsic scale, one that would give reliable measures of both extrinsic and intrinsic tendencies in a person's religious life. For these reasons the following instruments were adopted.

Social Problems Questionnaire. This scale, devised by Harding and Schuman (unpublished[1]; see also Schuman & Harding, 1963, 1964), is a subtly worded instrument containing 12 anti-Negro, 11 anti-Jewish, and 10 anti-other items (pertaining to Orientals, Mexicans, and Puerto Ricans). The wording is varied so as to avoid an agreement response set.

Indirect Prejudice Measures. Six items were taken from Gilbert and Levinson's (1956) Custodial Mental Illness Ideology Scale (CMI). Example: "We should be sympathetic with mental patients, but we cannot expect to understand their odd behavior. (*a*) I definitely disagree. (*b*) I tend to disagree. (*c*) I tend to agree. (*d*) I definitely agree."

Four items are related to a "jungle" philosophy of life, suggesting a generalized suspiciousness and distrust. Example: "The world is a hazardous place in which men are basically evil and dangerous. (*a*) I definitely disagree. (*b*) I tend

TABLE 3 *Intercorrelations between five measures of prejudice*

	ANTI-JEWISH	ANTI-OTHER	JUNGLE	CMI
Anti-Negro	0.63	0.70	0.20	0.25
Anti-Jewish		0.67	0.24	0.31
Anti-Other			0.33	0.36
Jungle				0.43

Note.—$N = 309$.

to disagree. (*c*) I tend to agree. (*d*) I definitely agree."

In all cases the most prejudiced response receives a score of 5 and the least prejudiced response, 1. No response was scored 3.

From Table 3 we see that while the indirect measures have a positive correlation with each other and with direct measures the relationship is scarcely high enough to warrant the substitution of the indirect for the direct. The high correlations between prejudice for the three ethnic target groups once again illustrate the well-established fact that ethnic prejudice tends to be a broadly generalized disposition in personality.

Religious Orientation Measure. The full scale, entitled "Religious Orientation," is available from ADI.[2] It separates the intrinsically worded items from the extrinsic, gives score values for each item, and reports on item reliabilities. In all

---

[1] J. Harding and H. Schuman, "Social Problems Questionnaire," Cornell University.

[2] The full Religious Orientation scale has been deposited with the American Documentation Institute. Order Document No. 9268 from ADI Auxilary Publications Project, Photoduplication Service, Library of Congress, Washington, D. C. 20540. Remit in advance $1.25 for microfilm or $1.25 for photocopies and make checks payable to: Chief, Photoduplication Service, Library of Congress.

cases a score of 1 indicates the most intrinsic response, a score of 5, the most extrinsic. While it is possible to use all 20 items as one continuous scale, it will soon become apparent that it is often wise to treat the two sub-scales separately. A sample item from the extrinsic subscale follows: "What religion offers me most is comfort when sorrows and misfortune strike. (*a*) I definitely disagree, 1. (*b*) I tend to disagree, 2. (*c*) I tend to agree, 4. (*d*) I definitely agree, 5." A sample item from the intrinsic subscale: "My religious beliefs are what really lie behind my whole approach to life. (*a*) this is definitely not so, 5. (*b*) probably not so, 4. (*c*) probably so, 2. (*d*) definitely so, 1.

SAMPLE

While our sample of six groups of churchgoers shows some diversity of denomination and region, it is in no sense representative. Graduate-student members of a seminar collected the 309 cases from the following church groups: Group A, 94 Roman Catholic (Massachusetts); Group B, 55 Lutheran (New York State); Group C, 44 Nazarene (South Carolina); (Group D, 53 Presbyterian (Pennsylvania); Group E, 35 Methodist (Tennessee); Group F, 28 Baptist (Massachusetts).

We labeled the groups alphabetically since such small subsamples could not possibly lead to valid generalizations concerning denominations as a whole. All subjects knew that they were invited to participate as members of a religious group, and this fact may well have introduced a "proreligious" bias.

Gross Results

If we pool all our cases for the purpose of correlating religious orientation with prejudice, we discover that while the findings are in the expected direction they are much less impressive than those of previous studies, especially Wilson's.

Correlations with Extrinsic Subscale. Since Wilson employed an extrinsic scale similar to ours, we first present in Table 4 our findings using this subscale and the various measures of prejudice. Whereas Wilson found a correlation of 0.65 between his extrinsic and anti-Semitic measures, our correlation falls to 0.21. In part the reason no doubt lies in certain features of Wilson's method which we have criticized.

Correlations with Combined Extrinsic-Intrinsic Scale. From the outset it was our intention to broaden Wilson's unidirectional (extrinsic) measure to see whether our hypothesis might hold for the total scale (combined scores for the 11 extrinsic and 9 intrinsic items). As Table 5 shows, matters do not improve but seem to worsen. The logic of combining the two subscales is of course to augment the continuum in length and presumably enhance the reliability of the total measure. It soon became apparent, however, that subjects who endorse extrinsically worded items do not necessarily reject those worded intrinsically, or vice versa. It turns out that there is only a very low correlation in the expected direction between the two subscales ($r = 0.21$). Obviously at this point some reformulation is badly needed.

TABLE 4 *Correlations between Extrinsic Subscale and Prejudice*

Anti-Negro	0.26
Anti-Jewish	0.21
Anti-Other	0.32
Jungle	0.29
CMI	0.44

Note.—$N = 309$.

TABLE 5   Correlations between Total Ex-
           trinsic-Intrinsic Scale and Pre-
           judice

Anti-Negro	0.26
Anti-Jewish	0.18
Anti-Other	0.18
Jungle	0.21
CMI	0.17

Note.—N = 309.

Reformulation of the approach

Examination of the data reveals that some subjects are indeed "consistently intrinsic," having a strong tendency to endorse intrinsically worded. Correspondingly others are "consistently extrinsic." Yet, unfortunately for our neat typology, many subjects are provokingly inconsistent. They persist in endorsing any or all items that to them seem favorable to religion in any sense. Their responses, therefore, are "indiscriminately proreligious."

The problem is essentially the same as that encountered by the many investigators who have attempted to reverse the wording of items comprising the F scale, in order to escape an unwanted response-set bias. Uniformly the effort has proved to be frustrating, since so many subjects subscribe to both the positive and negative wording of the same question (see Bass, 1955; Chapman & Bock, 1958; Chapman & Campbell, 1959; Christie, 1954; Jackson & Messick, 1957).

An example from our own subscales would be: "My religious beliefs are what really lie behind my whole approach to life" (intrinsic). "Though I believe in my religion, I feel there are many more important things in my life" (extrinsic).

The approach used by Peabody (1961) offers us a model for analyzing our data in a meaningful way. Peabody adminis-

tered both positive and negative F-scale items to subjects at two different testing sessions. By comparing each individual's responses to the same question stated positively at one time and in reverse at another he was able to separate out those who were consistently pro or anti toward the content of authoritarian items. But he found many who expressed double agreement (or disagreement) with both versions of the same question. Table 6 applies Peabody's paradigm to our data.

In assigning our 309 cases to these categories we employed the following criteria.

Intrinsic type includes individuals who agree with intrinsically worded items on the intrinsic subscale, and who disagree with extrinsically stated items on the extrinsic subscale. By the scoring method employed these individuals fall below the median scores on both subscales.

Extrinsic type includes individuals who agree with extrinsically stated items on the extrinsic subscale, and who disagree with items on the intrinsic subscale. By our scoring method these individuals all fall above the median scores on both subscales.

Indiscriminately proreligious includes those who on the intrinsic subscale score at least 12 points less than on the extrinsic

TABLE 6   Four Patterns of Religious Orientation

	AGREES WITH INTRINSIC CHOICE	DISAGREES WITH INTRINSIC CHOICE
Agrees with extrinsic choice	Indiscriminately proreligious	Consistently extrinsic in type
Disagrees with extrinsic choice	Consistently intrinsic in type	Indiscriminately antireligious or nonreligious*

*Not found in present sample.

TABLE 7 *Percentage of Each Religious Type in Each Subsample*

RELIGIOUS GROUP	N	CONSISTENTLY INTRINSIC	CONSISTENTLY EXTRINSIC	INDISCRIMINATELY PRORELIGIOUS
A	(94)	36	34	30
B	(55)	35	36	29
C	(44)	36	39	25
D	(53)	32	30	38
E	(35)	31	29	40
F	(28)	39	39	22

subscale. (This figure reflects the fact that a subject gives approximately 50% more intrinsic responses on the intrinsic subscale than we should expect from his extrinsic responses to the extrinsic subscale.)

Indiscriminately antireligious or nonreligious includes those who would show a strong tendency to disagree with items on both subscales. Since nonchurchgoers are excluded from our samples, such cases are not found. (Some pilot work with markedly liberal groups indicates that this type does exist, however, even among members of "religious" organizations.)

Table 7 gives the percentage of the three types.

Results of the Reformulation

The five measures of prejudice were analyzed by a 6 (Groups) × 3 (Religious Types) analysis of variance. Table 8 presents the overall effects for religious types for each of the five measures of prejudice. The multivariate analysis of variance indicates that there is both a significant difference between the three types of religious orientation and between the six subsamples in the level of prejudice.[3]

Examination of the means shows two trends: (*a*) The extrinsic type is more prejudiced than the intrinsic type for both direct and indirect measures; (*b*) the indiscriminate type of religious orientation is more prejudiced than either of the two consistent types. Statistically all these trends are highly significant.

We note especially that the scores of the indiscriminate type are markedly higher on all measures than the scores of the intrinsic type. Corresponding F ratios for paired comparisons range from 8.4 for the jungle scale to 20.4 for the CMI scale. The differences between the indiscriminate and extrinsic types are smaller. For the anti-Jewish and CMI scales these differences are, however, beyond the 0.005 level; for the anti-other and jungle scales, at the 0.05 level. For the anti-Negro the difference falls below significance.

The relationship between the indiscriminately proreligious orientation and prejudice receives support (see Table 9) when we compare subjects who are *moderately* indiscriminate with those who are *extremely* indiscriminate. (In the first group the scores on the intrinsic subscale average 16 points lower than on the extrinsic subscale, whereas the extreme

---

[3]The multivariate F reported here is Wilk's lambda (Anderson, 1958). Statistical computations are summarized by Bock (1963) and programmed for

the IBM 7090 by Hall and Cramer (1962). The univariate tests to be reported are adjusted for unequal Ns to obtain orthogonal estimates according to mathematical procedures described in Hall and Cramer.

TABLE 8   *Prejudice and Religious Orientation*

Target of prejudice	MEAN PREJUDICE SCORE			F ratio
	Intrinsic type $N = 108$	Extrinsic type $N = 106$	Inconsistent type $N = 95$	
Anti-Negro	28.7	33.0	36.0	8.6†
Anti-Jewish	22.6	24.6	28.9	11.1†
Anti-Other	20.4	23.3	26.1	10.9†
Jungle	7.9	8.7	9.6	9.4†
CMI	10.2	11.8	13.4	20.4†

Multivariate analysis of variance

Source of variation	F ratio	df
Religious type (A)	5.96‡	10.574
Sample groups (B)	3.19‡	25.668
A × B	1.11*	50.1312

*$p > 0.25$.
†$p > 0.001$.
‡$p > 0.0005$.

cases average 23 points less on the intrinsic than on the extrinsic subscale.)

The discovery that the degree of indiscriminateness tends to relate directly to the degree of prejudice is an important finding. It can only mean that some functional relationship obtains between religious muddleheadedness (for that is what indiscriminate scores imply) and antagonism toward ethnic groups. We shall return to this interpretation in the concluding section of this paper.

Results for Subsamples

It would not be correct to assume that the variance is distributed equally over all the subsamples, for it turns out that the denominational groups differ appreciably in prejudice scores and in religious type, as Tables 10 and 11 indicate.

It is true that when we combine subsamples all the trends are in the expected direction, but troublesome exceptions occur for single groups as indicated by

TABLE 9   *Degrees of Indiscriminateness and Average Prejudice Scores*

TARGET OF PREJUDICE	MODERATELY INDISCRIMINATE $N = 56$	EXTREMELY INDISCRIMINATE $N = 39$	F RATIO
Anti-Negro	35.4	37.9	0.97
Anti-Jewish	28.0	30.1	0.90
Anti-Other	24.9	28.2	3.25*
Jungle	9.5	10.2	1.11
CMI	10.2	14.6	3.99*

*$p > 0.05$.

TABLE 10   *Anti-Negro Prejudice: Mean Scores on Social Problems Scale*

RELIGIOUS GROUP	INTRINSIC TYPE	EXTRINSIC TYPE	INDISCRIMINATE TYPE	GROUP M
A	27.4 (34)	34.8 (32)	32.2 (28)	31.4 (94)
B	27.2 (19)	32.3 (20)	31.9 (16)	30.4 (55)
C	22.4 (16)	36.2 (17)	35.0 (11)	30.9 (44)
D	35.5 (17)	28.7 (16)	42.5 (20)	36.1 (53)
E	40.5 (11)	35.5 (10)	43.0 (14)	40.1 (35)
F	22.6 (11)	27.9 (11)	28.7 (6)	26.0 (28)
Type M	28.7 (108)	33.0 (106)	36.0 (95)	32.5 (309)

Analysis of Variance

SOURCE OF VARIATION	df	MS	F RATIO
Religious type (A)	2	1077.8	8.6†
Religious group (B)	5	952.2	7.6†
A × B	10	251.1	2.0*
Error (w)	291	125.6	

*$p > 0.10$.
†$p > 0.001$.

TABLE 11   *Indirect (CMI) Measure of Prejudice*

RELIGIOUS GROUP	INTRINSIC TYPE	EXTRINSIC TYPE	INDISCRIMINATE TYPE	GROUP M
A	11.2 (34)	12.4 (32)	13.6 (28)	12.3 (94)
B	10.1 (19)	10.8 (20)	13.4 (16)	11.3 (55)
C	9.5 (16)	12.2 (17)	12.6 (11)	11.3 (44)
D	10.6 (17)	11.4 (16)	14.8 (20)	12.4 (53)
E	8.6 (11)	12.9 (10)	13.6 (14)	11.8 (35)
F	9.2 (11)	10.7 (11)	9.2 (6)	9.8 (28)
Type M	10.2 (108)	11.8 (106)	13.4 (95)	11.9 (309)

Analysis of Variance

SOURCE OF VARIATION	df	MS	F RATIO
Religious type (A)	2	255.0	20.4†
Religious group (B)	5	36.5	2.9*
A × B	10	15.3	1.2
Error (w)	291	12.5	

*$p > 0.05$.
†$p > 0.001$.

the nearly significant interaction effects. The most troublesome contradictions appear in relation to the anti-Negro measures based on the Harding-Schuman scale. Table 10 discloses certain sore points, even though the average trend over all the subsamples is in the predicted direction.

For Groups A, B, and C we note that the indiscriminate type is slightly less prejudiced then the extrinsic type, and for Groups D and E the extrinsic type seems actually less prejudiced than the intrinsic. (Groups D and E are consistently more troublesome than other subsamples, perhaps because of some salient racial issue in the local community. It will be noted that both these groups are considerably more anti-Negro than the other subsamples.)

By way of contrast we present in Table 11 the results for the short (five-item) CMI scale. With the exception of the indiscriminate type in Group F, the progression of scores is precisely as expected. Each subsample shows that the intrinsic type is less prejudiced toward the mentally ill than the extrinsic type, and the extrinsic type is less prejudiced than the indiscriminately proreligious.[4]

Returning in a different way to the original question of whether consistent extrinsic and intrinsic orientations make for prejudice and for tolerance, respectively, we shall now examine this matter

in each subsample separately. Inspection of the mean scores and variance for the total scale indicates that we are dealing with a relatively narrow range of variation. To minimize the effect of a narrow range of scores and skewed distributions, we used Kendal's (1955) tau as a measure of degree of relationship between prejudice and consistent religious orientation. The results are given in Table 12. While the correlations are not high (14 are significant in the expected direction), only one (in the troublesome Group E) is significant in the reverse direction.

Educational Differences

Computing the actual years of schooling for all groups we find that the indiscriminate type has significantly less formal education than the intrinsic cases ($p > 0.005$, $F = 18.29$), and somewhat less than the extrinsic type ($p > 0.10$, $F = 2.89$). Comparing extrinsic with intrinsic types we find that the former has finished fewer years of schooling ($p > 0.10$, $F = 3.45$). (Oddly enough the groups with highest average education are D and E, which also displayed the highest anti-Negro and anti-Semitic prejudice — perhaps because of particular local conditions.)

In our survey of earlier studies we saw that educational level is often a factor in the various relationships discovered between religion and prejudice. We have also argued that demographic factors of this sort should not be allowed to obscure the functional (psychological) analysis that the data call for. Granted that low education makes for indiscriminate thinking, the mental confusion that results from low education may have its own peculiar effects on religious and ethnic attitudes.

---

[4]If we apply a more severe test, asking whether *all* differences between groups are significant, we find the following results. In four of the six groups (in both Tables 10 and 11) the extrinsic type is significantly more prejudiced than the intrinsic. Likewise in four out of six groups (Table 10) and five out of six (Table 11), the indiscriminate type is significantly more prejudiced than the intrinsic. However, in only two of the six groups (in both Tables 10 and 11) is the indiscriminate type significantly more prejudiced than the extrinsic.

TABLE 12   Correlations   between   Combined   Extrinsic-Intrinsic   Religious
Scores (for consistent subjects) and Prejudice (Kendal's Tau)

RELIGIOUS GROUP	ANTI-NEGRO	ANTI-JEWISH	ANTI-OTHER	JUNGLE	CMI
A	0.31†	0.26†	0.24†·	0.14*	0.19†
B	0.19*·	0.13	0.15	−0.05	0.03
C	0.32†	0.17*	0.35†	0.14*	0.28†
D	−0.12	0.05	−0.09	0.03	0.11
E	−0.24*	−0.11	−0.13	0.26*	0.46†
F	0.39†	0.13	0.25*	−0.01	0.24*

*$p > 0.10$.
†$p > 0.01$.

Summary and Interpretations

At the outset we stated three propositions that seem to be firmly established:
(*a*) Churchgoers on the broad average
harbor more ethmic prejudice than nonchurchgoers; (*b*) in spite of this broad
tendency a curvilinear relationship in fact
exists; (*c*) the intrinsically motivated
churchgoers are significantly less prejudiced than the extrinsically motivated.
Our present research supplies additional
strong support for the second and third
of these propositions.

To these propositions we add a fourth:
*churchgoers who are indiscriminately pro-
religious are more prejudiced than the consistently extrinsic, and very much more prejudiced than the consistently intrinsic types.*

The psychological tie between the intrinsic orientation and tolerance, and
between the extrinsic orientation and
prejudice, has been discussed in a series
of papers by Allport (1959, 1963, 1966). In
brief the argument holds that a person
with an extrinsic religious orientation
is using his religious views to provide
security, comfort, status, or social support for himself—religion is not a value
in its own right, it serves other needs,
and it is a purely utilitarian formation.
Now prejudice too is a "useful" formation: it too provides security, comfort,

status, and social support. A life that is
dependent on the supports of extrinsic
religion is likely to be dependent on the
supports of prejudice, hence our positive
correlations   between   the   extrinsic
orientation and intolerance. Contrari-
wise, the intrinsic religious orientation
is not an instrumental device. It is not a
mere mode of conformity, nor a crutch,
nor a tranquilizer, nor a bid for status.
All needs are subordinated to an over-
arching religious commitment. In inter-
nalizing the total creed of his religion
the individual necessarily internalizes
its values of humility, compassion, and
love of neighbor. In such a life (where
religion is an intrinsic and dominant
value) there is no place for rejection,
contempt,   or   condescension   toward
one's fellow man. Such is our explanation
for the relationship between extrinsic
religion and prejudice, and between
intrinsic religion and tolerance.

Our present task is to discover, if we
can, some similar functional tie between
prejudice (as measured both directly
and indirectly) and the indiscriminately
proreligious orientation. The common
factor seems to be a certain cognitive
style. Technically it might be called
"undifferentiated thinking," or excessive "category width," as defined by
Pettigrew (1958). Rokeach (1960) notes

the inability of the "dogmatic" mind to perceive differences; thus, whereas some people distinguish in their thinking and feeling between Communists and Nazis, the undifferentiated dogmatist has a global reaction (cognitive and emotional) toward "Communazis."

We have no right, of course, to expect all our subjects to make discriminations exactly corresponding to our own logic. Nor should we expect them to read and respond to every item on the Extrinsic-Intrinsic scale according to its full meaning as intended by the investigators. Perhaps we should be gratified that two-thirds of our cases can be safely classified as "consistent" (i.e., having about the same strength of disposition toward an extrinsic or intrinsic orientation across most of the items). These consistent cases, as we have seen, support the hypothesis with which we started. It is the remaining (indiscriminate) one-third of the cases which obscure the trend (or diminish its statistical significance).

In responding to the religious items these individuals seem to take a superficial or "hit and run" approach. Their mental set seems to be "all religion is good." "My religious beliefs are what really lie behind my whole life" — Yes! "Although I believe in my religion, I feel there are many more important things in my life" — Yes! "Religion is especially important to me because it answers many questions about the meaning of life" — Yes! "The church is most important as a place to formulate good social relationships" — Yes!

There seems to be one wide category — "religion if OK." From the way in which the scale is constructed this undifferentiated endorsement can be the product of an aggrement response set. Our inconsistently proreligious may be "yea-sayers" (Cough & Keniston, 1960). But if so, we are still dealing with an undifferentiated cognitive disposition. We recall

likewise that the inconsistent cases have a lower level of formal education than the consistent cases. This factor also is relevant to the formation and holding of overwide categories.

But why should such a disposition, whatever its source, be so strongly related to prejudice, in such a way that the *more* undifferentiated, the *more* prejudiced — as Table 9 shows?

The anser is that prejudice itself is a matter of stereotyped overgeneralization, a failure to distinguish members of a minority group as individuals (Allport, 1954, Chaps. 2, 10). It goes without saying that if categories are overwide the accompanying feeling tone will be undifferentiated. Thus, religion as a whole is good; a minority group as a whole is bad.

It seems probable that people with undifferentiated styles of thinking (and feeling) are not entirely secure in a world that for the most part demands fine and accurate distinctions. The resulting diffuse anxiety may well dispose them to grapple onto religion and to distrust strange ethnic groups. The positive correlation between the jungle items and other prejudice scales (Table 3) is evidence for this interpretation.

Our line of reasoning, readers will recognize, is compatible with various previous contributions to the theory of prejudice. One thinks here of Rokeach's concept of dogmatism; of Schuman and Harding's (1964) discovery of a "confused" type in their study of the relation between rational consistency and prejudice; of the same authors' work on sympathetic identification (1963); of studies on the dynamics of scapegoating, the role in insecurity, of authoritarian submission, of intolerance for ambiguity, and of related concepts.

All in all we conclude that prejudice, like tolerance, is often embedded deeply in personality structure and is reflected in a consistent cognitive style. Both states of mind are enmeshed with the individual's religious orientation. One definable style marks the individual who is bigoted in ethnic matters and extrinsic in his religious orientation. Equally apparent is the style of those who are bigoted and at the same time indiscriminately proreligious. A relatively small number of people show an equally consistent cognitive style in their simultaneous commitment to religion as a dominant, intrinsic value and to ethnic a tolerance.

One final word: our research argues strongly that social scientists who employ the variable "religion" or "religiosity" in the future will do well to keep in mind the crucial distinction between religious attitudes that are *intrinsic, extrinsic*, and *indiscriminately pro*. To know that a person is in some sense "religious" is not as important as to know the role religion plays in the economy of his life. (The categories of *nonreligious* and *indiscriminately antireligious* will also for some purposes be of central significance, although the present research, confined as it is to churchgoers, does not employ them.)

References

Adorno, T. W., Frenkel-Brunswik, E., Levinson, D. J., & Sanford, R. N. *The authoritarian personality*. New York: Harper, 1950.

Allport, G. W. Review of S. A. Stouffer, E. A. Suchman, L. C. De Vinney, S. A. Star, & R. W. Williams, Jr., *The American soldier*. Vol. 1. *Adjustment during Army life. Journal of Abnormal and Social Psychology*, 1950, **45**, 168–173.

Allport, G. W. *The nature of prejudice*. Reading Mass.: Addison-Wesley, 1954.

Allport, G. W. Religion and prejudice. *The Crane Review*, 1959, **2**, 1–10.

Allport, G. W. Behavioral science, religion, and mental health. *Journal of Religion and Health*, 1963, **2**, 187–197.

Allport, G. W. Religious context of prejudice. *Journal for the Scientific Study of Religion*, 1966, **5**, 447–457.

Allport, G. W., & Kramer, B. M. Some roots of prejudice. *Journal of Psychology*, 1946, **22**, 9–39.

Anderson. T. W. *An introduction to multivariate statistical analysis*. New York: Wiley, 1958.

Bass, B. M. Authoritarianism or acquiescence. *Journal of Abnormal and Social Psychology*, 1955, **56**, 616–623.

Bock, R. D. Programming univariate and multivariate analysis of variance. *Technometrics*, 1963, **5**, 95–117.

Chapman, L. J., & Bock, R. D. Components of variance due to acquiescence and content in the F-scale measure of authoritarianism. *Psychological Bulletin*, 1958, **55**, 328–333.

Chapman, L. J., & Campbell, D. T. The effect of acquiescence response-set upon relationships among the F-scale, ethnocentrism, and intelligence. *Sociometry*, 1959, **22**, 153–161.

Christie, R. C. Authoritarianism re-examined. In R. C. Christie & M. Jahoda (Eds.), *Studies in the scope and method of the authoritarian personality*. New York: Free Press of Glencoe, 1954. Pp. 123–196.

Couch, A., & Keniston, K. Yeasayers and naysayers: Agreeing response set as a personality variable. *Journal of Abnormal and Social Psychology*, 1960, **60**, 151–174.

Demerath, N. J., III. *Social class in American Protestantism*. Chicago: Rand McNally, 1965.

Feagin, J. R. Prejudice and religious types: A focused study of southern fundamentalists. *Journal for the Scientific Study of Religion*, 1964, **4**, 3–13.

Fichter, J. H. *Social relations in the urban parish*. Chicago: University of Chicago Press, 1954.

Friedrichs, R. W. Christians and residential exclusion: An empirical study of a northern dilemma. *Journal of Social Issues*, 1959, **15**, 14–23.

Gilbert, D. C., & Levinson, D. J. Ideology, personality, and institutional policy in the mental hospital. *Journal of Abnormal and Social Psychology*, 1956, **53**, 263–271.

Gough, H. G. Studies in social intolerance: IV. *Journal of Social Psychology*, 1951, **33**, 263–269.

Hall, C. E., & Cramer, E. *General purpose program to compute multivariate analysis of variance on an IBM 7090*. Washington, D. C.: George Washington University Biometric Laboratory, 1962.

Holtzman, W. H. Attitudes of college men toward non-segregation in Texas schools. *Public Opinion Quarterly*, 1956, **20**, 559–569.

Jackson, D. H., & Messick, S. J. A note on ethnocentrism and acquiescence response sets. *Journal of Abnormal and Social Psychology*, 1957, **54**, 132–134.

Kelly, J. G. Ferson, J. E., & Holtzman, W. H. The measurement of attitudes toward the Negro in the South. *Journal of Social Psychology*, 1958, **48**, 305–317.

Kendal, M. G. *Rank correlation methods*. (2nd ed.) London: Griffin, 1955.

Kirkpatrick, C. Religion and humanitarianism: A study of institutional implications. *Psychological monographs*, 1949, **63**(9, Whole No. 304).

Lenski, G. *The religious factor*. Garden City, N.Y.: Doubleday, 1961.

Levinson, D. J. The inter-group workshop: Its psychological aims and effects. *Journal of Psychology*, 1954, **38**, 103–126.

Peabody, D. Attitude content and agreement set in scales of authoritarianism, dogmatism, anti-Semitism, and economic conservatism. *Journal of Abnormal and Social Psychology*, 1961, **63**, 1–11.

Pettigrew, T. F. The measurement and correlates of category width as a cognitive variable. *Journal of Personality*, 1958, **26**, 532–544.

Pettigrew, T. F. Regional differences in anti-Negro prejudice. *Journal of Abnormal and Social Psychology*, 1959, **49**, 28–36.

Pinkney, A. The anatomy of prejudice: Majority group attitudes toward minorities in selected American cities. Unpublished doctoral dissertation, Cornell University, 1961.

Rokeach, M. *The open and closed mind: Investigations into the nature of belief systems and personality systems.* New York: Basic Books, 1960.

Rosenblith, J. F. A replication of "Some roots of prejudice." *Journal of Abnormal and Social Psychology*, 1949, **44**, 470–489.

Schuman, H., & Harding, J. Sympathetic identification with the underdog. *Public Opinion Quarterly*, 1963, **27**, 230–241.

Schuman, H., & Harding, J. Prejudice and the norm of rationality. *Sociometry*, 1964, **27**, 353–371.

Stember, H. C. *Education and attitude change.* New York: Institute of Human Relations Press, 1961.

Stouffer, S. A. *Communism, civil liberties, and conformity.* Garden City, N.Y.: Doubleday, 1955.

Struening, E. L. Antidemocratic attitudes in a Midwest university. In H. H. Remmers (Ed.), *Anti-democratic attitudes in American schools.* Evanston: Northwestern University Press, 1963. Ch. 9.

Titus, H. E., & Hollander, E. P. The California F scale in psychological research: 1950–1955. *Psychological Bulletin*, 1957, **54**, 47–64.

Tumin, M. *Desegregation: Resistance and readiness.* Princeton: Princeton University Press, 1958.

Williams, R. M. *Strangers next door: Ethnic relations in American communities.* Englewood Cliffs, N. J.: Prentice-Hall, 1964.

Wilson, W. C. Extrinsic religious values and prejudice. *Journal of Abnormal and Social Psychology*, 1960, **60**, 286–288.

Young, R. K., Benson, W. M., & Holtzman, W. H. Changes in attitudes toward the Negro in a southern university. *Journal of Abnormal and Social Psychology*, 1960, **60**, 131–133.

Section VII

Organismic Theory

An important influence on the thinking of the present generation of psychologists was a book with the simple title, *The Organism*, by Kurt Goldstein. Not himself a psychologist by training—he was trained as a medical doctor—Goldstein's book appeared in 1939 at a time when it seemed to many psychologists that the individual had all but disappeared in a fission of reflexes and segmental responses. *The Organism* put Humpty-Dumpty, fragmented by behaviorism, together again, and once more psychologists were asked to view man as a whole. It is, perhaps, ironical that this picture of the man emerged out of Goldstein's researches on brain-injured soldiers of the First World War, but irony became insight when Goldstein demonstrated that even in the brain-injured, the drive to maintain the integrity of the organism is a transcendental drive. Coupled with Gestalt psychology that had already made an impact upon American psychology, and firmly rooted in a philosophical tradition that was eloquently reiterated by the South African Jan Smuts in *Holism and Evolution*, *The Organism* provided many psychologists with an antidote for the atomistic analysis of behavior. It is altogether fitting, therefore, that a selection from this influential book should introduce this chapter. It reads with the same freshness and relevance today that it did when it was first published more than 30 years ago.

Goldstein's viewpoint as stated in his various writings is more of a posture and a program than it is a theory. Although the organismic attitude permeates contemporary research, it is not easy to point to any large area of investigation that has been generated specifically by Goldstein. An exception is the problem of abstract versus concrete behavior that was formulated by Goldstein and that has been widely investigated.

A paper by Milgram on this topic is the second selection. In this study, using schizophrenic, brain-damaged, and normal males, it was demonstrated that the schizophrenic and brain-damaged subjects chose the abstract word less frequently than normal males. These results clearly support Goldstein's distinction between concrete and abstract verbal behavior.

When Andreas Angyal died he left as a legacy at least two unpublished works on personality. One of these books has been published post-humously under the title *Neurosis and Treatment—a Holistic Theory*, and the third paper is from this book. It is an updated version of Angyal's position regarding the dualistic organization of personality.

Since the publication of the second edition of *Theories of Personality*, Maslow has died (1970). Throughout his entire career he was a prolific writer. His early research on dominance relationships in monkeys was far afield—both methodologically and substantively—of his more recent interests. Maslow was one of the leaders of the "third force" movement in psychology. With a humanistic orientation, he wrote on diverse topics such as education, therapy, personality theory, and philo-sophy of science. It should surprise no one that he wrote critically of much of contemporary psychology, including clinical and personality psychology. The paper that has been selected was originally an address he gave in 1964 at a workshop for training counselors. In this paper Maslow clearly reveals his attitude toward experimental research as a source of data that might lead to modification of his theory. One is reminded of Freud's rather pessimistic attitude about the contribution of experimental research to psychoanalysis. Maslow's conception of the self-actualized person is one contribution that is inextricably tied to his name. Thus, of special significance in this paper is the discussion of the eight ways in which one may become self-actualized.

1. The Organism

KURT GOLDSTEIN

As our starting point, we are taking phenomena exhibited in man when the brain cortex is damaged. This, for two reasons: First, because, with some justification, we attribute a particular, dominating significance to the cortex; and thereby, phenomena appearing during its injury will be especially relevant for our *understanding of the essential nature of man.* Second, because the analysis of these phenomena enables us to demonstrate certain *general laws of the disintegration of function*; and thereby these laws in turn, will be especially relevant for our understanding of the organism's functions.

A study of most of the former publications may convey the impression that cortical injury is usually followed by a loss of circumscribed functions, such as speech, visual perception, or motor performance. Writers on the subject actually assumed this to be so. According to this conception, they distinguished and designated various disease syndromes by such terms as aphasia in its various forms, visual agnosia, apraxia, etc. They assumed also that circumscribed centers controlled those particular functions.

In recent years, however, improved observation has led to a change of this view. It has been found that, even in cases of circumscribed cortical damage, the disturbances are scarcely ever confined to a single field of performance. In such intricate syndromes, we deal not only with a simple combination of disparate disturbances, but also with a more or less unitary, basic change which affects different fields homolously, and expresses itself through different symptoms. It has also become apparent that the relationship between mental performances and definite areas in the brain, constitutes a far more complicated problem than the so-called localization theory has assumed.

This difference in observations should not lead us to believe that the more recent investigators are more competent than the earlier ones. The early investigations were those of experts who were highly esteemed and real masters in their field. Rather, a difference in the methodology was responsible for the emergence of other facts.

The problem of methodology has the greatest significance for psycho-pathology, and for biological research in general. For example, in the descriptions of symptoms given by the so-called "classicists"

SOURCE. *Selection from Kurt Goldstein, "The organism" in* The Organism, *Chapter 1, pp. 15–49, 51–52, 55–58, 59, 61. Boston: Beacon Press, 1963.*

on the subject of aphasia—we choose these because they demonstrate the general procedure particularly well—we find that their characteristic tendency, their reference to a hypothetical "primary symptom," renders a given symptomatology plausible. In motor-speech disturbance, for instance, an impairment of the "motor-speech images" was regarded as the "primary" symptom. Where this speech defect was found associated with a disturbance of the writing function, the latter was likewise interpreted as a consequence of the impairment of the "motor-speech images." In word deafness, an impairment of the sensory speech images was assumed to be the primary symptom. From this primary symptom, they also attempted to explain the further symptoms found in such cases, for instance, paraphasia.

The fundamental principle of this procedure is, of course, reasonable. We shall see later that we cannot obtain direct proof of a functional disturbance. To define the latter, we are dependent upon conclusions derived from changes in performances as exhibited in the symptoms. Such procedure can be conclusive, only if we ascertain, by accurate analyses of every disturbed performance, the one functional disturbance which really does account for the appearance of the various changes. This exactness can hardly be expected from pioneer work in an unknown field, where obviously one must begin by examining the most striking features. And this is not dangerous as long as one bears in mind that the phenomena which first attract attention are not necessarily essential, or basic, not necessarily the key to all subsequent phenomena. Such phenomena stand out only by virtue of certain circumstances; and while they may appear to be characteristic, they do not necessarily support a theoretical foundation for understanding the genesis of the whole symptomatological structure. The danger arises only when this discrimination between essential and incidental phenomena is neglected, and when the scientist forgets that he bases his theory upon such a defective foundation. The incidental phenomena may have value only for preliminary orientation, and may, at best, merit the position of a crude working hypothesis. The real crisis arises when, even in the face of new findings, the investigator cannot free himself from the former theory; rather he attempts to preserve it, and by constant emendations, to reconcile it with these new facts, instead of replacing it by a new theory fit to deal with both the old and new facts. This error has not been avoided in the evolution of the classical doctrine.

The Problem of Determination of Symptoms

The basic error in the procedure under consideration was the failure to recognize the complex problem involved in the method of symptoms. We have become so accustomed to regard symptoms as direct expressions of the damage in a part of the nervous system that we tend to assume that, corresponding to some given damage, definite symptoms must inevitably appear. We do so, because we forget that normal as well as abnormal reactions ("symptoms") are only expressions of the organism's attempt to deal with certain demands of the environment. Consideration of this makes it evident that symptoms are by no means certain to become self-apparent. Symptoms are answers, given by the modified organism, to definite demands: They are attempted solutions to problems derived on the one hand from the demands of the natural environment, and on the other from the special tasks imposed on the organism in the course of the examination. We shall see that in the everyday life of the patient, a certain transformation of the environment goes hand-in-hand with each defect, and tends to prevent certain disturbances from manifesting themselves. It is of primary interest that the *appearance of symptoms depends on the method of examination*, although the significance of this fact has been largely overlooked. By focusing attention only upon certain phenomena, or upon a selected few, the investigator comes to isolate "symptoms." Phenomena, more striking than others, are registered first, and so give the impression of being *the* dominant symptom. Most likely to attract attention, of course, are the atypical reactions to a normal situation, and especially, the *complete* absence of any reaction when one is expected.

In this way, complete loss of a special function tends to be the outstanding symptom, and conceals the real or basic defect. On other occasions, those phenomena appear, more or less accidentally, as outstanding symptoms, which are answers elicited by specific questions presented by the examiner.

Of course, these "questions" are not fortuitous, but are dictated by the investigator's fundamental ideas about the phenomena he is studying. It is true, these ideas themselves may have been suggested by the data; but frequently a theory has been evolved on the basis of symptoms that have gained their apparent preeminence purely by chance. This bias has often resulted in delaying the understanding of the symptoms and the advance of research. Of course, if one tried to include *all* symptoms in the construction of a theory, no theory could ever be elaborated. Obviously, such theorizing presumes that one has grouped the symptoms into the more and less relevant—the primary and secondary—and has tried to build only upon the so-called primary symptoms. In making this distinction, the investigator is commonly prejudiced by theoretical viewpoints which have proved useful in other fields of research, and which he judges—usually without testing their qualifications—to be adequate for the material at hand.

Heretofore, psycho-pathological symptoms were explained in the light of concepts borrowed from reflexology and the prevailing association psychology. The theory that the structure of the nervous system is based on a number of separate mechanisms, each functioning independently, led to the supposition that circumscribed injuries would result in disorders specific to the mechanisms involved. Consequently, the investigator looked for the latter and found them, because he noticed only the disorders which best corresponded to the theory, i.e., disorders which could be regarded as changes resulting from the failure of a hypothetically independent and separate function. Just as normal events had been explained as composites of *elementary* processes, so also, symptoms were interpreted as changes of similar mechanisms of mental elements. When the investigator assumed that an impairment of motor speech images was the cause of the motor aphasia, or an impairment of visual images the cause of alexia, he believed that his deductions were genuinely based upon the symptoms. Actually, such explanations were merely the outcome of a theoretical preconception, merely an *interpretation of the phenomena* in terms of a special theory, i.e., association psychology.

The correctness of the basic assumption was accepted so implicitly, that no attempt was made to prove that the images in question really played the part in *normal* speech which it was assumed they did. Neither was any attempt made to ascertain whether these images were actually defective in patients.

Once the basic concept of the importance of specific areas for certain functions was formulated, and seemingly confirmed, it now determined all subsequent investigations, especially because of its applicability to practice. Thereafter, the question was confined to the decision as to whether the supposed individual centers and pathways functioned in a "normal" or "abnormal" manner. Still more serious was the fact that this concept became the criterion for determining whether or not individual phenomena belonged in the given syndrome resulting from injury to a certain area. If, besides the phenomena which had been regarded as essential symptoms, others were found, these were pushed aside as "complications" that disturbed the "purity" of the case, and were considered the result of some injury incurred simultaneously in another area. Or, if this were not done, an attempt was made to explain them as merely secondary effects contingent upon the hypothetically primary disturbance. Yet not even the growing necessity for the most diverse modifications of the basic conception and for the most daring theoretical constructions has deterred theorists from building such auxiliary hypotheses.

Three Methodological Postulates. Clearly such reasoning in circles has necessarily delayed the realization that the basic concept is untenable. Yet this procedure can be regarded as characteristic of the majority of clinical, physiological, and biological research of the older school. In what respect does our procedure differ from that described? Simply, in that we have endeavored to record, in an open-minded fashion, *all* phenomena. Pursuing this aim, there result three methodological postulates equally valid for the examination of patients or animals.

(1) The first methodological postulate is: Consider initially all the phenomena presented by the organism (in this case it may be a patient), *giving no preference, in the description, to any special one.* At this stage no symptom is to be considered of greater or less importance. Only under these conditions is the description correct. It must be left for future investigation to determine how far one symptom, rather than another, is essential for understanding the underlying changes of a function.

Every unbiased and exhaustive examination of a case repeatedly teaches us that alteration of a given performance, even if at first sight it appears to be very prominent, is not necessarily of primary significance for understanding the underlying functional disturbance. On the other hand, a trifle which barely attracts notice may be of the utmost importance. For example, as long as the most prominent symptom of amnesic aphasia, namely, the difficulty in finding words, was allowed to suggest the plantation of this disease, the theory that the basic disturbance consisted in a reduced evocability of speech images, appeared perfectly satisfactory. But as soon as a subtle and formerly neglected alteration in the total behavior of the patient was taken into consideration, there resulted not only an entirely different conception of the underlying functional disturbance, but a new insight into the meaning of the aphasic phenomena was made possible. The difficulty in finding words, formerly regarded as the main symptom, retreated into the background. The theory of the reduced evocability of speech images became obsolete, because it could be sustained only by means of auxiliary hypothese — hypotheses not required in *our* explanation — since the patients are quite capable of using the words under specific circumstances. They have not lost the use of words per se, but the ability of employing words as bearers of *meaning*. Under circumstances where the latter is not demanded, and the words "belong" to an action or concrete situation, the patient "has the words." The inability to find and use words voluntarily is not due to the primary defect of the speech mechanism, but to a change in their total personality which bars them from the situation where meaning is required.

(2) The second methodological postulate concerns the correct description of the observable phenomena themselves. It was a frequent methodological error to accept what amounted to a mere description of the effect; but an effect might be *ambiguous* with respect to its underlying function. Therefore, only a thorough analysis of the causes of such effects, of success or failure in a given task, for example, can provide clarification. The older psychopathological investigations usually confined themselves to the question of whether a patient actually gave, or failed to give, the correct response in a task. This "plus or minus method," however, is inadequate, no matter whether we are dealing with positive or negative results. If we regard a reaction only from the standpoint of the actual solution of a task, we may overlook the deviation from normality, because the individual completes the task by a detour which may not be evident in the solution. Only accurate analysis, through an examination which makes it impossible for the patient to achieve a result in a roundabout way, can disclose the defect. If our capacity to observe were not so imperfect, closer attention would show that the patient has reached the goal in an abnormal manner, for of course, under such conditions the results cannot correspond, in *all* details, to the normal. Once we become alive to this fact, diagnosis is often simplified by noting small and hitherto unobserved deviations. We may use an example to illustrate this.

Patients with loss of "categorical behavior" find it difficult, for instance, to consider an individual color according to a category such as redness, greenness, etc. When we ask patients to select all red color skeins of the Holmgren wool samples, they often place the colors "in a row": the lightest to the darkest red. On the basis of this we might assume that they have proceeded categorically, since they have apparently selected the shades according to a concept—in this case that of brightness, and therewith have placed them in a row. This assumption, however, is based on an *error of observation*, namely, a disregard for the slight differences which distinguish the patient behavior from a behavior determined by the categorical attitude. It can easily be shown that they have not proceeded and cannot proceed categorically: they are not able to arrange the colors in a row as to their brightness, if *asked* to do so. They also fail in the task of putting together all the reds in a heap—activities which presuppose the categorical attitude.

These observations make it rather doubtful whether the patient originally selected the skeins according to the category of brightness. Actually, if one more carefully examines the manipulations of the patient, one discovers that he has not really laid down a *row* according to brightness. What he did, was to place *one shade beside another, one at a time*. In this way, single pairs of similar shades were formed under the guidance of the concrete sensory cohesion between the *last* skein and the *next* similar one. By this procedure of "successive pairs," he finally came to an arrangement which *in toto* *looked like* a scale of brightness, but really was not. In selecting a new skein the patient was entirely and solely dependent on the skein which immediately preceded it. This accounts for the pairing of, and the *intervals* between the skeins. That his procedure was determined by this "piece to piece" performance, could be shown by the fact that when the examiner removed the skein the patient had last placed in position, he was unable to continue with his "series." This showed that he depended on the immediately preceding skein for the selection of the new one. We mention this example to show how vital it is, for an accurate interpretation, that description of phenomena be minute and exact. And, in order that the description be correct, how careful must be the attention given to those small matters all too easily overlooked through theoretical bias.

Equally ambiguous are the negative results of a medical examination. The *wrong* response is too often judged to be a simple failure, whereas actually, under careful analysis, it may throw considerable light upon the mental functions of the patient. Only by this means can we discover whether there is really a defect in the ability demanded by the task, or whether the patient has failed only because of special circumstances induced by the task situation. Furthermore, in the wrong response, analysis often uncovers a detour which the patient has used, perhaps because the normal way was not practicable. Such facts may have an important bearing on the explanation of the capacities of the organism.

(3) The third methodological postulate we wish to stress is that no phenomenon should be considered without reference to the organism concerned, and to the situation in which it appears. We shall have to refer to this point so often that it is not worth further elaboration at this time. Little as this requirement has been observed in the past, because of theoretical bias, it should nonetheless become a matter of course in the future. Many an error would have been avoided in psychopathology if this postulate, quite deliberately stated by Hughlings Jackson

decades ago, had not been so completely neglected. The same postulate holds to no less a degree for animal behavior observations. Later on we shall deal in detail with the fundamental difficulties following from the application of this precept, since it necessitates taking into account the organism as a whole.

We wish to refute briefly two possible objections to our methodological postulates. The first concerns the charge that, according to our postulates, one can never really determine *at what point an examination can be regarded as completed*. As a matter of fact, it never is, But there is still a great difference between the two forms of procedure: between the usual description and enumeration of separate disturbances, such as those of visual or linguistic performances, etc., and our procedure, which is primarily directed toward the cognition of the whole, and, within this frame of reference, seeks to analyze as many individual performances as possible. This technique will certainly obviate the grossest errors, *even though it may not lead to absolutely incontestable results*. Bearing in mind this aim of completeness, it will be possible to avoid precipitate theoretical conclusions and the rigid maintenance of any hypothesis preventing us from radically revising our theories, on the strength of new experience. In the course of the examination, one comes to a point when one feels that the analysis can be terminated without risk of gross errors in the interpretation. The examination must be carried far enough at least to insure that (on the basis of facts) a theory can be developed which will *render understandable all observed phenomena in question*, and which will make it possible to predict how the organism will react, even in such tasks hitherto not investigated. Only such an analysis is to be considered adequate.

The procedure of investigating the patient, which Gelb and I have described as a case of visual agnosia, may provide an example. On the basis of our first examinations, which were not sufficiently exhaustive, we had formed a hypothesis which was not quite adequate. Further examinations drove us to the formulation of a new hypothesis which did justice to both old and new facts. The further we advanced with the examinations, the more clearly delineated did the functional disturbance in this case become. Finally, we have progressed so far toward constructing the total picture of the patient that we can predict with relatively great certainty how he will behave in any situation, even in respect to tasks which we have not yet examined. Only cases which have been investigated with such thoroughness should be used in the formation of a theory. *One single extensive analysis of this sort is much more valuable than many examinations involving many patients, but yielding only imperfect conclusions.*

This leads to the second objection to our postulates. Our procedure necessarily enforces *a limit upon the number of cases investigated.* To examine many cases so thoroughly would be patently impossible. It is argued that this may vitiate the conclusiveness of the statements, since we may have encountered a special instance which cannot serve as pattern for the explanation of others. This objection completely misses the point:-

First: The accumulation of even a myriad of imperfectly investigated cases can in no way guide us toward recognition of the true facts. There is no alternative to carrying the examination of each case to the extent we have indicated.

Second: Important though it may be to seek repeated confirmation of our findings through new case material, such *confirmation adds nothing essential to our knowledge.* Those patients must be subjected to investigation who offer a guarantee of unequivocal statements of fact, as well as

of theoretical interpretation. Under such conditions, the conclusions drawn from one case will likewise have validity for others. Since the basic laws are the same, the multiplicity encountered in various instances will be readily understood, once these basic laws are recognized. True, a new observation may induce us to modify somewhat our original assumptions; but if the analysis of the first observation was sufficient, this modification can be made without conflict, whereas imperfect analysis of ever so many cases may be very misleading—as the literature bears witness only too clearly.

If patients with cortical injuries are examined according to these methodological principles (I am thinking primarily of patients whose "central" cortical region has been injured), an extraordinarily intricate picture results, a systematic account of which has been given in a number of papers.

Disintegration of Performances and the Hierarchy within the Organism

Before outlining the features which all these cases have in common, we must define the term "performances." We call performance of an organism any kind of behavior, activity, or operation as a whole or in part, which expresses itself overtly, and bears reference to the *environment.* Hence physiological processes, events within the nervous system, mental activities, attitudes, affectivities are *not* performances as long as they do not manifest themselves in some overt action —any *disclosable* outward behavior. More specifically, a performance is a coming to terms of the organism with environmental stimuli by a behavioral act, be this eyelid-closure under stimulation or a total movement like running towards a goal, or hearing, seeing, etc. The afore-mentioned outline may now be presented:

(1) A single performance or perform-ances in a specific field (e.g., visual, motor)[1] will never drop out alone. In-variably *all* performance fields are affect-ed, although the degree to which the individual field is involved, varies.

(2) *A single performance field will never drop out completely. Some individual per-formances are always preserved.* Responses to the apparently equal demands of equal tasks do not drop out indiscriminately under all circumstances. There is a pecul-iar and, at first, subtle variation of reac-tion, even when the demand remains constant. This inconsistency is usually explained as the effect of some disturb-ances of "general functions," such as fatigue, etc., or it is argued away. Actually, it indicates to us the need for further analysis.

(3) The modification of performances manifested by a patient in different fields is in principle of the same nature. The different symptoms can be regarded as expressions of *one and the same basic dis-turbance.* In spite of this, we are con-fronted with various syndromes having to do with the question of localization.

(4) The basic disturbance can be char-acterized either as a *change of behavior,* or as an *impairment of the functions of the brain matter.* The discussion of the latter, we have to postpone. Here we shall merely confine ourselves to a characterization of the change in behavior. We venture to remark that whenever the patient must transcend concrete (immediate) experi-ence in order to act—whenever he must refer to things in an imaginary way—then he fails. On the other hand, whenever the result can be achieved by manipulation of concrete and tangible material, he per-forms successfully. Each problem which

forces him beyond the sphere of im-mediate reality to that of the "possible" or to the sphere of representation, insures his failure. This manifests itself in all responses such as action, perception, thinking, volition, feeling, etc. The patient acts, perceives, thinks, has the right impulses of will, feels like others, cal-culates, pays attention, retains, etc., as long as he is provided with the oppor-tunity to handle objects concretely and directly. He fails when this is impossible. This is the reason why he does not suc-ceed in intelligence tests. This is also the reason why he can grasp a little story as long as it concerns a familiar situation in which he, himself, has participated. But he will not understand a story—certainly no more difficult for the average person—requiring him to place himself, in imagina-tion, in the position of someone else. He does not comprehend metaphors or puzzles. He can manipulate numbers in a practical manner, but has no concept of their value. He can talk if there is some concrete subject matter present for him to depend upon, but he cannot recount material unrelated to him, or report it purely conceptually. He is incapable of representation of direction and localities in objective space, nor can he estimate distances; but he can find his way about very well, and can execute actions which are dependent upon perception of dis-tance and size.

Depending on which of these mani-festations of the basic disturbance has been brought into focus, they have been named respectively: disturbance of *"sym-bolic expression"* (Head), of the *"repre-sentational function"* (Woerkom), of *"cate-gorical behavior"* (Gelb and Goldstein). With regard to the effect of the change, one may, in emphasizing the disturbance of that capacity which is prerequisite for the performance in question, talk of impairment of the capacity to *comprehend the essential features of an event.*

---

[1]Hereafter, we shall speak in this context of a "per-formance field."

Or we might point to the patient's inability to emancipate and withhold himself from the world, the shrinkage of his freedom, and his greater bondage to the demands of environment. The most general formula to which the change can be reduced is probably: The patient has lost the capacity to deal with *that which is not real—with the* possible.

Inquiring now into the question of how the various performances reveal the impairment, we find that voluntary performances are particularly affected, while activities directly determined by the situation remain relatively intact. Adapting a performance so that it corresponds to the changing demands of the situation requires a voluntary attitude. Therefore, all those performances which require, for their proper execution, such a voluntary shifting, must suffer, e.g., all "choice reactions." *The isolated performances are affected to a greater degree than the so-called total responses.* This shows itself in a greater loss of isolated movements than of integrated movements, as well as in the inability to distinguish the details of a picture (the whole of which may yet be recognized), or in the inability to pronounce a single word or single letters out of context. The disintegration of a familiar function *proceeds from the highly differentiated and articulated state to a more amorphous total behavior.*

The symptoms vary with the severity of impairment, and the degree to which one area or another is affected. The *basic disturbance, however, remains the same.* I cannot produce proof of this assertion here. I might emphasize at the same time, however, that for our particular purposes, the differences of opinion are unimportant. One thing is agreed upon: cortical injury does not result in the loss of isolated performances, but in *systematic disintegration following the principle that certain forms of behavior will be impaired while others remain intact.* Only

with this in mind, will it be possible to make a distinct classification of the performances which the patient can and cannot carry out, as well as to provide a meaningful description of the symptoms.

Is our characterization of the change after cortical injury satisfactory? Are we really dealing exclusively with the impairment of certain kinds of behavior? *Have not "contents" also dropped out?* Certainly! Yet it must be admitted that many of these losses are secondary, since it is true that certain contents appear only within certain kinds of behavior. The impairment of the behavior entails the loss of numerous contents. This is perhaps most clearly demonstrable in cases of what are known as "amnesic aphasia." Patients suffering in this way have lost the ability to call objects by their *names. Seemingly, they lack the "content":* names. The analysis, however, indicates that, in such cases, we are dealing with a disturbance of "categorical" behavior, an impairment of the capacity to experience and to handle "meaning," which is requisite for "naming" objects. This explains why the patients cannot find the words in those situations where the words have to function as symbols— as representations for something. The loss of "contents" is therefore secondary.

But contents can also be embedded in other forms of behavior, namely, those which belong to acquired faculties; for example, words memorized in foreign languages. Such contents may be preserved, in spite of a disturbance of the aforementioned behavior. To illustrate: Some individuals, with a good command of language, of superior linguistic knowledge, are able to name certain objects, even when they are afflicted with "amnesic aphasia." Under other conditions, these acquired performances may be lost when the substratum is damaged. Only exact analysis can show whether, in any particular case where "contents" are lacking, we are dealing with a *consequence of behavior disturbance, or of loss of these acquisitions.* Only in the case of these acquired faculties are we entitled to speak of contents. The distinction is of fundamental importance for accurate diagnosis of a disturbance, as well as for any attempt to prescribe therapeutic exercises, because only correct diagnosis of the change can provide the correct procedure. These comments apply equally well to the interpretation of content losses in operated animals, and to all experiments of relearning after injury, etc.

Accurate observation of many cases teaches us that disintegration of function always results in the *same pattern of distribution of the intact and affected modes of behavior.* The behavior we have characterized as categorical behavior always suffers first. We are well justified in crediting the intact organism with a greater performance capacity than the injured one, and in admitting that the "higher" or more complex performances require a more intact substratum than the simpler ones. Therefore, we speak of a hierarchy or descending scale of disintegration, in which the higher performances are more disturbed than the simpler ones. Study of the phenomena in progressive and regressive brain processes most clearly reveals such a hierarchy in the *regular* succession of the onset of the various symptoms, and their abatement in recovery.

We might venture to say that the most complicated performances, those first to be impaired, are probably the ones most essential and most vital to the existence of the organism, and further, with respect to the nature of the organism, they have the highest functional significance. Through the deterioration of those performances, the organism loses its most characteristic properties. We may become particularly

conscious of this fact by contrasting an individual suffering from brain injuries with a normal person. Those behavioral forms which are earliest and most markedly affected express the main characteristics of man, and bring to the fore his unique place in nature

In this way, the order manifested in the disintegration may provide us with the idea of a hierarchy of capacities and performances—a stratified structure of the organism. Of course, it is not hierarchical in the sense that the individual forms of behavior represent performances existing in isolation, side by side, and only linked one to the other. It is not so simple as that.

Characterization of Performances According to Their Functional Significance or Value and Their Survival Importance

Our use of the terms "higher" and "lower" functional significance or "value," requires clarification. If, from one standpoint, we characterize certain forms of behavior as *intrinsically valuable* because of their significance for the nature of the organism, we might, from another standpoint, characterize other performances as *most important* because they resist the effect of injury. Without doubt, the survival of "automatic" performances, in contrast to that which we have characterized as "higher," more conscious, or more voluntary, is of special importance for the organism, inasmuch as they are those which *insure mere existence.* In this sense, we would be justified in speaking of performances which have *greater or less importance for survival.* This is what is implied in the expression "the instinct of self preservation." If this means preservation only in the sense of continued survival, we may ask the questions: Does such an "instinct" exist in the normal organism? More specifically, can it be regarded as belonging to the highest level of functioning or is not the appearance of such a "drive," as the predominant feature in an individual, itself a symptom of abnormality — a pathological phenomenon? As we shall see, the normal organism is characterized as a "Being" in a temporal succession of definite form. For the realization of this "Being," the existence, the "mere being alive," plays, of course, a prominent, but by no means the essential role. Under extreme circumstances, it can be compatible with the "nature" of an organism to renounce life, i.e., to give up its bodily existence, in order to save its most essential characteristics — for example, a man's ethical convictions. *Preservation of material existence becomes "essential" only after defect sets in*, and possibly in certain emergencies. In the latter case, the body achieves the position of supreme importance, since all the other possibilities of self-realization are bound to it. Regarding the defective organism, the scale of performance values is likely to differ from that of the normal. In order to preclude any misunderstanding, we shall differentiate in the future, between *functional significance* or value — by which we shall mean "essential to the nature of the organism," — and "survival importance" by which we shall mean "paramount in the preservation of its life." In the normal organism, the two usually go hand in hand inasmuch as here preservation also means preservation of the intrinsic nature so far as that is possible. In the pathologically changed organism, the preservation of existing potentialities, the survival importance, comes to the fore. At present we only wish to stress the importance of the principle of hierarchy indicated in the laws of disintegration, and will subsequently return to this question with special reference to the structure of the organism.

2. *Preference for Abstract versus Concrete Word Meanings in Schizophrenic and Brain-damaged Patients*

NORMAN ALVIN MILGRAM

It is generally held that of the recognized cognitive abilities, vocabulary fund is least susceptible to disturbance and is, therefore, the most stable index of premorbid functioning in disturbed persons (1, 11, 13). It is also generally held that schizophrenic and brain-damaged patients differ from normals in the use and understanding of words (6, 8, 12, 14, 15). There is, however, no necessary contradiction between these statements. Yacorzynski (16), Goldstein (5, pp. 11–12), Rapaport (10, p. 149), and others have suggested that the stability of word usage in clinical populations is more apparent than real. As Yacorzynski stated the issue, "It appears reasonable to assume that the reason why the vocabulary of the deteriorated individual remains relatively unchanged is because easier methods of reaching the same end results are left to the organism even if the more difficult solutions are no longer available" (16, p. 265). Several experimental studies

SOURCE. *Article by Norman Alvin Milgram, "Preference for abstract versus concrete word meanings in schizophrenic and brain-damaged patients" in* Journal of clinical Psychology, *Vol. 15, pp. 207–212, 1959.*

(2, 3, 7) have confirmed "Yacorzynski's hypothesis" and have shown that while gross word definitions are adequately retained, the more subtle, conceptual usages of words are impaired.

The present study enlarges upon an earlier investigation by Flavell (4) who found that in a special test situation in which S is asked to select the one of two choice words which is "closest in meaning" to a given stimulus word, normals selected words bearing an abstract or essential meaning relationship to the stimulus word more often than schizophrenics. Flavell's investigation, like the majority of others in this area, dealt with the verbal performance of schizophrenics alone. An investigation of the verbal performance of brain-damaged patients and a comparison of their performance with that of schizophrenics appear warranted both from empirical and theoretical points of view.

METHOD

The present study compares the preferences of schizophrenic, brain-damaged, and normal Ss for abstract or essential versus concrete or non-essential word meaning relationships. Although the three groups will be equated on vocabulary fund, systematic difference in word usage are expected to emerge, *i.e.*, normals will select abstract meaning relationships more often than schizophrenics or brain-damaged patients. In Flavell's study significant differences between schizophrenics and normals were found only for the total abstract score, but not for the separate abstract or concrete categories. Certain changes from Flavell's procedure are being introduced in the present study to accentuate the preferential weight given each of the separate abstract and concrete word meaning categories by the three groups.

Subjects. Three male groups consisting of 32 schizophrenics, 30 brain-damaged patients, and 20 normals were used. The criteria for selection of the schizophrenic group included (*a*) a psychiatric diagnosis of schizophrenia (paranoid, 24; hebephrenic, 2; catatonic, 2; and chronic, undifferentiated, 2) and (*b*) no neurological involvement, no somatic therapy (insulin coma or electric shock) within the past six months, and no history of lobotomy.

The criteria for the selection of the brain-damaged group included (*a*) a neurological diagnosis of damage to the cerebral cortex (vascular disease, 9; degenerative disease, 12; chronic brain syndrome, 9) and (*b*) no previous history of severe mental disturbance and no evidence of psychosis at time of testing.

A final criterion for inclusion in any subject group was the willingness and ability of S to attend to instructions and to follow through with the demands of the testing situation (of which the data reported in the present paper are a small portion). Excluded from this study were litigious paranoid patients and mute catatonic patients who refused to cooperate; also excluded were grossly impaired brain-damaged patients, especially patients with severe aphasia.

The two clinical groups were drawn from the psychiatric and neurological wards of two hospitals of the Veterans Administration. The normals were drawn from the medical wards of one hospital and from the general population outside the hospital. The three groups were equated on age and vocabulary fund as measured by the Vocabulary Subtest of the Wechsler-Bellevue; the vocabulary

scores are reported as IQ scores. Data on age, years of formal education, and IQ are shown in Table 1. A statistically significant, but small, difference between normals and the two clinical groups in years of formal education was observed.

PROCEDURE

This test (Figure 1) was taken from Flavell (4) with some modifications in procedure and new word items, and consisted of 40 items each containing a stimulus word and two choice words. All the stimulus words were nouns; the choice words were nouns, adjectives, or verbs. On a given item, the stimulus word was related to one of the response words in one of three *abstract* ways and to the other response word in one of four *concrete* ways. The seven different types of relationship between stimulus and response words were as follows:

1. *Synonym (Syn)*, e.g., "car"-"auto."
2. *Supraordinate (Supra)*, e.g., "car"-"vehicle."
3. *Subordinate (Sub)* e.g., "car"-"Ford."
4. *Part-Whole (PW)*, e.g., "car"-"fender"
5. *Adjective (A)*, e.g., "car"-"flashy."
6. *Verb (V)*, e.g., "car"-"drive."
7. *Concrete Context (CC)*, e.g., "car"-"garage."

Of the above seven categories, the first three are considered abstract, essential meaning relationships; the last four are concrete, non-essential meaning relationships. Each of the abstract categories was paired with each of the concrete categories four times, to make a

TABLE 1 *Age, IQ and Years of Formal Education*

GROUP		AGE	IQ	EDUCATION
N	M	44.6	116.2	12.0
	SD	(15.2)	(10.0)	(2.7)
S	M	43.1	114.9	10.8
	SD	(13.4)	(15.7)	(3.2)
BD	M	45.6	110.5	11.5
	SD	(15.2)	(17.7)	(3.2)

1. Tune	*melody* (S) — sing (V)	24. Stove	*oven*(S) — hot(A)
2. Electricity	dynamo (CC) — *energy* (SP)	25. Boat	*canoe*(SB) — row(V)
3. Parcel	*package*(S) — wrapper (PW)	26. Violin	strings(PW) — *fiddle* (S)
4. Book	page (PW) — *novel*(SB)	27. Flower	garden(CC) — *rose*(SB)
5. Salt	*spice*(SP) — sprinkle (V)	28. Water	*liquid*(SP) — drink(V)
6. Hobby	interesting(A) — *stamps*(SB)	29. Eggs	hen(CC) — *food*(SP)
7. Harbor	ships(CC) — *bay*(S)	30. King	crown(CC) — *monarch* (S)
8. Hour	*time*(SP) — minute (PW)	31. Tree	*Pine*(SB) — branch (PW)
9. Rabbit	ears(PW) — *bunny*(S)	32. Camera	*equipment*(SP) — lens (PW)
10. Knife	*dagger*(SB) — blade (PW)	33. Weight	heavy(A) — *ton*(SB)
11. Blanket	warm(A) — *cover*(S)	34. Winter	*season*(SP) — cold(A)
12. Dog	*poodle*(SB) — bark(V)	35. Wagon	wheel(PW) — *cart*(S)
13. Sickness	hospital(CC) — *illness* (S)	36. Candy	*gumdrop*(SB) — sweet (A)
14. Mother	*parent*(SP) — dear(A)	37. String	tie(V) — *twine*(S)
15. Bird	nest(CC) — *robin*(SB)	38. Breakfast	morning(CC) — *meal* (SP)
16. Stairs	*steps*(S) — climb(V)	39. Saloon	*tavern*(S) — noisy(A)
17. Hat	head(CC) — *clothing* (SP)	40. River	*Mississippi*(SB) — flow (V)
18. Dream	*nightmare*(SB) — sleep (CC)	41. World	*globe*(S) — round(A)
19. Mountain	high(A) — *Rockies*(SB)	42. Bureau	drawer(PW) — *furni-ture*(SP)
20. Shirt	*garment*(SP) — sleeve (PW)	43. Lake	swim(V) — *pond*(S)
21. Silk	smooth(A) — *material* (SP)	44. Pocketbook	*purse*(S) — money(CC)
22. Bacon	*meat*(SP) — fry(V)	45. Moon	shine(V) — *planet*(SP)
23. Auto	drive(V) — *ford*(SB)	46. Container	*box*(SB) — top(PW)
		47. Grandmother	old(A) — *relative*(SP)
		48. Direction	*north*(SB) — compass (CC)

Figure 1. *Word meaning test (the Abstract responses are italicized)*

total of 48 items. In a given item, the stimulus word is related abstractly to one choice word and concretely to the other.[1]

[1]This represents a departure from Flavell who paired each of the eight categories (he used a Homonym category which I discarded in the present study) to each of the other seven, e.g., some items were *Syn-Supra* and *PW-CC*. As a result in his study *Ss* chose between two abstract or two concrete reponse alternatives on over 40% of the items. In the present study *Ss* chose only between an abstract and a concrete response alternative on all items. This change was made to maximize the hypothesized deficit of the experimental groups in choosing responses from each of the separate abstract and concrete categories.

Subjects were tested individually and were instructed to read aloud the stimulus word and to select from the two choice words the "one that means most nearly the same" as the stimulus word. The maximum score for any one abstract category was 16; for a concrete category, 12. Thus, for example, if a *S* chose only abstractly related choice words, his abstract score was 48.

Results and Discussion

The results summarized in Table 2 confirm the hypothesis that normals

TABLE 2   Means and Standard Deviations of Scores of Abstract and Concrete Categories

CATEGORY		NORMALS	SCHIZ.	BRAIN-DAM.	*P* N > SCHIZ.	*P* SCHIZ. > BD
Total Abstract Score	M	42.60	38.38	31.84	<0.01*	<0.001
	SD	3.21	7.56	7.07		
Synonym	M	15.35	13.97	11.47	<0.001	<0.001
	SD	0.81	2.28	2.68		
Supraordinate	M	14.50	13.22	11.07	<0.05	<0.02
	SD	1.50	2.97	3.20		
Subordinate	M	12.75	11.19	9.30	<0.05	<0.02
	SD	1.86	3.18	2.76		
Part-Whole	M	1.75	2.00	3.30	ns.	<0.05
	SD	1.65	1.69	2.44		
Adjective	M	1.60	3.19	4.77	<0.01	<0.02
	SD	1.47	2.65	2.38		
Verb	M	0.55	2.09	3.90	<0.001	<0.01
	SD	1.00	1.96	2.34		
Concrete Context	M	1.50	2.34	4.30	ns.	<0.01
	SD	1.28	2.44	2.04		

*The t Test with Snedecor's Correction was used because the assumption of homogeneity was untenable
for the eight comparisons made above.

select abstract word meaning relationships more than schizophrenics and brain-damaged patients. It is also observed that schizophrenics are significantly superior to the brain-damaged patients in this regard. The total mean scores for the groups were 42.60, 38.38, and 31.74, respectively. With respect to the separate response categories, normals and schizophrenics chose significantly more abstract and fewer concrete words than did brain-damaged patients; significant differences between normals and schizophrenics were obtained on all but two categories, PW and CC. It is concluded that a person may retain the ability to summon up creditable definitions to words without retaining the ability to discriminate the abstract-concrete or essential-nonessential continuum of word meaning. This con-

clusion applies to both experimental groups, but more especially to the brain-damaged group. Only five of the 30 brain-damaged patients received scores as high or higher than the lowest score obtained by a normal; the overlap between schizophrenics and normals was considerably greater with 19 of 32 schizophrenics scoring higher than the lowest normal.

Rank-order correlation coefficients were computed for the three groups between age and abstract scores and were significant only for the schizophrenic group (0.30, significant at 0.05 level, one tail test). The explantion for this inverse relationship between verbal age and abstractive ability may lie in the fact that chronicity of illness and hospitalization in the schizophrenics are a direct function of age. The older schizophrenics have had lengthy hospitalizations, while the younger schizophrenics have suffered from disturbances of relatively recent onset. Hence, the older, more chronically ill and deteriorated patients failed to do as well in the conceptual use of words as the younger, more acute patients. This explanation is consistent with Flavell's finding of a positive relationship between abstractive ability and adequacy of everyday social interaction. While no measures of social interaction were made in this study, clinical observation showed the older, more chronically ill schizophrenics to be in less adequate social contact and interaction than the younger schizophrenics. Rabin, King, and Ehrmann (9) have also showed that long-term schizophrenics were significantly lower than normals and short-term schizophrenics on three measures of vocabulary performance.

Rank-order correlation coefficients between IQ and abstractive ability were also computed. These correlations were highly significant (0.001 level) for the normals and the schizophrenics (0.67 and 0.77 respectively), but were not for the brain-damaged group (0.25). These findings further highlight the discrepancy in the brain-damaged group between the ability to retain the approximate definitions to words and the ability to use words conceptually. For the normals and schizophrenics, a high vocabulary score is generally associated with a high abstract score; for the brain-damaged patients a high score in vocabulary may be earned by a person with considerable deficit in cognitive abilities as a result of which he earns a low score on a verbal conceptual task.

When a comparison is made of the response hierarchy of each group, it is noted that *Syn*, *Supra*, and *Sub* were chosen in descending order of frequency by the three groups, except that the difference between *Syn* and *Supra* did not reach significance for the two clinical groups. Whether this represents the hierarchy of meaning relationships in the general population of adult thinkers is unanswered. It should be noted, however, that Flavell observed the same hierarchy with his groups, although his items and scoring procedure[2] differed from those used in the present study.

Turning to the concrete categories, no such hierarchy prevailed. *V* was chosen least frequently by normals, of the four concrete categories. *A* was chosen most frequently by the two clinical groups and *CC* was chosen second in frequency to *A* by the brain-damaged group. All other differences were not significant. A possible explanation of the preference for *A* is that adjectives have a strong sensory stimulus value; normal adults are able to inhibit the tendency to respond to this stimulus and are able to follow the logically determined habits of word meaning; schizophrenics and brain-damaged patients are less able to inhibit this tendency, hence they are more likely to choose an adjective over an abstractly related word than they are to choose one of the other types of concretely related word categories.

Summary

The present study compared the preferences of schizophrenics, brain-damaged patients, and normals for abstract or essential versus concrete or nonessential

---

[2]For Flavell, a category score represented the preference of items of that category over items of all other categories, abstract or concrete. In the present study an abstract category score represents the preference of items of that category over items of the four concrete categories only; conversely concrete items were matched only with abstract items.

word meaning relationships. Although these three groups were presumably equated in ability for defining words (Vocabulary Subtest scores), both schizophrenic and brain-damaged patients chose fewer abstractly related words than normals. This disturbance in the abstract-concrete continuum of word meaning was greater and more consistently observed in the brain-damaged group than in the schizophrenic group. Results were interpreted as supporting "Yacorzynski's hypothesis."

References

1. Babcock, Harriet. An experiment in the measurement of mental deterioration. *Arch. Psychol.*, 1930, No. 117.

2. Chodorkoff, B. and Mussen, P. Qualitative aspects of the vocabulary responses of normals and schizophrenics. *J. consult. Psychol.*, 1952, **16**, 43–48.

3. Feifel, H. Qualitative differences in the vocabulary responses of normals and abnormals. *Genet. Psychol. Monogr.*, 1949, **39**, 151–204.

4. Flavell, J. Abstract thinking and social behavior in schizophrenia. *J. abn. soc. Psychol.*, 1956, **52**, 208–211.

5. Goldstein, K. and Scheerer, M. Abstract and concrete behavior: an experimental study with special tests. *Psychol. Monogr.*, 1941, **53**, No. 2.

6. Goldstein, K. Methodological approach to the study of schizophrenic thought disorder. In J. S. Kasanin (Ed.) *Language and thought in schizophrenia.* Berkeley, Calif.: Univ. of Calif. Press, 1944, 17–40.

7. Harrington, R. and Ehrmann, J. C. Complexity of response as a factor in the vocabulary performance of schizophrenics, *J. abn. soc. Psychol.*, 1954, **49**, 362–364.

8. Moran, L. J. Vocabulary knowledge and usage among normal and schizophrenic subjects. *Psychol. Monogr.*, 1953, **67**, No. 20.

9. Rabin, A. L., King, G. F. and Ehrmann, J. C. Vocabulary performance of short-term and long-term schizophrenics. *J. consult. Psychol.*, 1955, **50**, 255–258.

10. Rapaport, D. *Diagnostic psychological testing.* Chicago: Year Book Publishers, 1945, Vol. I.

11. Schwartz, R. Mental deterioration in dementia praecox. *Amer. J. Psychiat.*, 1932, **12**, 555–560.

12. Vigotsky, L. S. Thought in schizophrenia. *Arch. Neurol. Psychiat.*, 1934, **31**, 1063–1077.

13. Wechsler, D. *The measurement of adult intelligence.* (3rd Ed.) Baltimore: Williams & Wilkins, 1944.

14. Werner, H. *Comparative psychology of mental development*. Chicago: Follett, 1948.

15. White, W. A. The language of schizophrenia. *Arch. Neurol. Psychiat.*, 1926, **16**, 395–413

16. Yacorzynski, G. K. An evaluation of the postulates underlying the Babcock Deterioration Test. *Psychol. Rev.*, 1941, **48**, 261–267.

3. The Theory of Universal Ambiguity

ANDRAS ANGYAL

In discussing integration, I have described how richness and range are achieved in personality through a multiple utilization of a relatively small number of components, through their successive reordering into a variety of patterns. Because of this mode of functioning, personality must be viewed as a multivalent, pluralistic organization. Such a description, however, is not sufficient since it side steps the main issue. Man is to be understood not in terms of any specific traits he possesses, or any specific patterns they form, but in terms of the overall pattern that organizes these traits and their multiple interconnections. In the course of my work with neurotic patients I have been searching for a conceptualization of personality adequate for the practical tasks of education and therapy. The most significant general statement I am able to make as a result of this search is that while personality is pluralistic in the detail of its functioning, in its broad outline it is a *dualistic* organization.

There is no life course in which every developmental experience has been traumatic nor one from which all deleterious influences have been absent. There are both healthy and traumatic features in every child's environment and in his relations with it; the early attempts at relating oneself to the world succeed in part, and in part fail. As a result, the personality of the child develops simultaneously around two nuclei, forms two patterns. One of them may be underdeveloped but it is never absent. One pattern is based on isolation and its derivatives: feelings of helplessness, unlovableness, and doubts about one's prospects. The other is based on the confidence that a modicum of one's autonomous and homonomous strivings may be realized more or less directly. The overall system principle of the human personality, the guiding pattern of life composed of the two basic tendencies, does not change when the neurotic orientation comes into being. Whether in health or in neurosis, our life is guided by the same unalterable superordinate trends, autonomy and homonomy. But when two opposite sets of convictions have been formed about the nature of the world and the self, these trends function in a setting of very different expectations.

One outlook, while not indiscriminate optimism, reflects the confidence that

SOURCE. *Andras Angyal, "The theory of universal ambiguity," in* Neurosis and Treatment: A Holistic Theory, *Chapter 8, pp. 99–115. Edited by E. Hanfmann and R. M. Jones. New York: Wiley, 1965.*

the "supplies" for one's basic needs exist in the world and that one is both adequate and worthy of obtaining these "supplies." The neurotic belief is that these conditions are not available or that they can be made available only by extremely complicated and indirect methods. Thus, in one way of life, the two basic human propensities function in an atmosphere of hope, confidence, trust, or faith, if you like. In the other, the propelling forces are the same, but they function in an atmosphere of diffidence, mistrust, and lack of faith. Phenomenological concepts such as hope, trust, and faith have not yet achieved a clear position in systematic theorizing, but no one can doubt that these states, as well as their opposites, do exist and are extraordinarily potent irrespective of whether or not they can be translated into current psychological concepts. Confidence and diffidence, conviction and doubt that human life is livable in this world, mark the "great divide," the point at which our path bifurcates and our life acquires its dual organization and its basic existential conflict.

The differences between the two ways of life, or the two "worlds" that are elaborated from the two nuclear convictions, have been stated, by implication, in the description of the main features of neurosis. They shall be briefly recapitulated here. The two patterns differ not only in their system principle but also in their integrational features. Although each can be tightly organized, the organization of the neurotic system bears the imprint of its origin in the state of isolation and anxiety; several of its features represent defects or integration along the dimensions of depth, progression, and breadth.

One of the two worlds is real, the other fictitious. This is not, strictly speaking, due to the truth or falsehood of the assumptions governing each system; both of them are expressions of faith and neither can be validly proved. But doubt and anxiety have the effect of making the images developed to elaborate or to disguise the basic neurotic assumptions ever more compelling and indiscriminate, so that reality easily falls victim to fantasy. In the healthy system, the basic assumptions do not call for disguises, and the confidence in one's ability to manage in the world as it is permits a realistic perception of the negative aspects of life.

The world visualized in the healthy pattern feels like one's home; it is rich in opportunities, lawfully ordered, and meaningfully related to the person. The world of neurosis is foreign and threatening, full of obstacles and dangers, lawless, capricious, a chaos rather than a cosmos. The consequences of this difference are many. In the "good" world it is possible and rewarding to pursue positive goals which one desires and enjoys; in the threatening world the main concern and joy must be to escape danger. The difference between working for and working against something is reflected in the fixed predominance of fear and anger in the neurotic as against the more positive feeling tone and the wider range of normal emotions. Communication and the absence of it are crucial for contact both with people and things. Love and community formation are easy in the one pattern, difficult or impossible in the other. In the healthy orientation it is possible to perceive wholes, to see things in a wide perspective, to receive impressions which point beyond the datum itself; continuity and intentionality make the world meaningful. In the neurotic orientation, the things and events of the world appear as isolated items or fragments. The long view is replaced by short sightedness; the fresh outlook yields to a stereotyped and biased one. Impressions cannot be fully valued and enjoyed, because their pointing quality, their "message character," is lost; the result is a truncated experience.

The person himself is also transformed by the negative fantasies about himself and by assuming poses and characteristics that are not genuine to him and are meant to disguise his imagined lack of worth. While in the confident orientation the person feels, thinks, and speaks as he is and not as he is "supposed" to be, the neurotic, having settled for appearances, acts for the sake of effect. He is not in touch with his real wishes, and the main function of his thoughts and acts is more often to "prove" than to enjoy. Since the connection between the expression and that which is expressed has been multiply twisted, neurotic behavior has no depth; it is superficial and inexpressive. A vivid example of settling for appearances is one patient's boyhood memory of how frustrated he was when a swimming instructor wanted him to take his feet off the ground. The boy finally cried in exasperation, "But *it looks like* swimming with just my arms, and nobody can see my legs under the water." He was genuinely nonplussed when the instructor did not accept his solution. This patient's adult life was, to all outward appearances, filled with exemplary achievements. It was only in his sex life that he was faced with the insufficiency of merely "looking" successful.

Integration along the dimension of progression is also disturbed in neurosis. In the healthy orientation the means are an organic part of the total activity and are positively valued both as a way to the goal and in their own right as part of a whole. In the neurotic system everything is a means towards some vague end which is secretely believed to be unreachable. Means activities are thereby devalued, and so is the present as such, because everything is merely preliminary. If the neurotic is not dreaming about some value lost in the past, he is con-

stantly hurrying and expecting. The present is related to his future no more organically than the means are related to his goals or his personal trends to expression. Both in experience and in his actions the neurotic leads an impoverished disintegrated existence. Many of his actions conflict with his other impulses and take no account of the surrounding realities; such incongruous, disharmonious actions are necessarily self-defeating.

Personality as an Ambiguous Gestalt

In the psychoanalytic theory of complexes these interfering unconscious forces are not thought of as single repressed impulses; complexes are partial organizations. The hypothesis of duality which I propose extends the use of the organizational principle by assuming the existence, not of discrete complexes, but of more inclusive systems competing for influence on the person's conduct of his life.

We live, all of us, in two worlds, not in one, but we don't live in these worlds simultaneously. Health and neurosis are not segments of personality so that one might be neurotic in some aspects of one's life and healthy in others at the same time. The two patterns which are almost mirror reversals of each other, two alternate ways in which our basic trends can seek expression, are both total organizations. Health and illness are determined by the dominance of one of the two systems. When one system becomes dominant, it tends to organize the total field, the total life of the person, since every Gestalt tends toward a complete realization of its system principle. The healthy aspects do not remain healthy, and the neurotic ones do not remain neurotic when the opposite organization gains dominance. The parts in a system function as such not through their imminent qualities but through their positional values; they change their mode of functioning when they become parts of a different system. Health and neurosis are to be thought of as two organized processes, two dynamic Gestalts organizing the same material, so that each item has a position within two different patterns. There can be shifts between the two, lasting or short lived, in either direction, but at any given moment the person is either healthy or neurotic, depending on which system is dominant.

This mode of coexistence of the two systems cannot be represented by depicting them side by side or by picturing one as enclosed in the other (as complexes or repressed conflicts are sometimes represented). They coexist, as it were, within each other. The dynamic aspect of the relationship, the coexistence of two fields of forces, can be expressed through the following metaphor: If a straight elastic rod is bent to form a loop, it retains its resiliency, a molecular arrangement that will straighten it out again as soon as the constraining force is removed. While it is bent, two organizations are present: the one that keeps it bent and the one that could straighten it out. Depending on which system is stronger the arrangement of the parts will be straight or crooked. This metaphor expresses quite well the simultaneous existence of two competing dynamic factors and the primacy of the ever-present factor of health, but it does justice neither to the complex articulation of the two systems, nor to the all-or-none character of their dominance.

In these respects the dual personality organization is represented much more adequately by being likened to a visual *ambiguous Gestalt* of the kind you find reproduced in treatises on visual perception. In the one most frequently seen the spatial arrangement is such that the picture may be perceived as representing either a black vase on a white background or two white faces in profile, turned toward each other. The basis for both organizations is there, but only one of the two can be perceived at any given moment. When a shift occurs, what was seen as the figure becomes the background, and each item of the spatial arrangement acquires a new meaning as part of a representation of a different object; the two images never mix. Because of its dual organization human life similarly is an ambiguous Gestalt, each part process having a different function and meaning, depending on whether it takes place within the Gestalt of health or the Gestalt of neurosis. Everything in life has a double meaning—hence universal ambiguity.

The theory of universal ambiguity has far-reaching consequences for the theory and therapy of neurosis. It precludes the conception of neurosis as a rotten part of a healthy apple, or a limited segregated growth within the person, a plant that can be pulled out by the roots without disturbing or changing the rest of the personality. The neurotic person is neurotic throughout, in every area of his life, in all the crannies and crevices of his existence. Conversely, one cannot say that there is in anyone only an element or segment of personality that is healthy. One is healthy throughout and this health extends over one's entire existence, down to the most distorted forms of behavior and the most troublesome symptoms. The so-called "healthy core," the patient's real self, will not be found stuck away in some distant or hidden region of his personality; it is to be found right there, where it is least expected. Health is present potentially in its full power in the most destructive, most baneful, most shameful behavior.

"As a boy, one patient felt compelled to drink his own urine. Later he managed, with the aid

of a contraption of his own invention, the difficult feat of performing fellatio on himself. The most agonizing paroxysms of shame accompanied these revelations, which demonstrated his isolation, his morbid preoccupation with himself, and the fantastic indirections he felt were necessary to achieve gratification. Yet the same behavior expressed diverse "completion" and "fulfillment" motives: "I could have belonged in the family circle only if I had given up the right to be alone; still the circle had to be completed, so I made my own." These distortions also expressed the tendency to experience sensuality to its fullest and a determined wish to affirm his uniqueness in the face of tempting conventional compromises."

In an ambiguous Gestalt, the parts do not belong independently to one pattern or another. All parts belong to both patterns and have their function assigned to them by the currently dominant system principle. There is therefore no motivational force that the person has to discard in therapy. If the pattern of health becomes dominant, the problematic factors will find their places within it in a system-consistent fashion. I do not mean that, for instance, a neurotic headache as such can find a comfortable niche in a healthy organization. I mean that whatever attitude the headache is expressing will fit constructively into the healthy pattern, filling a vital role and not being merely tolerated, and then this attitude will not be expressed through headaches. One of the frequent obstacles to therapy is that the patient conceives of the process of getting well as getting rid of something within him. This is like tearing away a part of himself, and he cannot wish it wholeheartedly. Alternately he may conceive of the therapeutic goal as becoming reconciled to an irremovable handicap or defect and learning to live with it, not a very inspiring prospect. Both conceptions are based on the idea of a segmental disturbance which can be removed or kept but not changed. Viewing neurosis as an organization provides a basis for a different conception of therapy, which will be discussed later.

The dual organization of human life, with one or the other pattern predominating, is often obscured from view because it is overlaid with what might be called the surface or social personality. In this stratum some manifestations of the two basic patterns may form a spurious kind of apparent synthesis. This surface patterning of personality, however, can hardly be considered an organization in its own right. Even in many healthy people this phenomenal level is superficial and devoid of personal roots. Since it is determined largely by compliance or compromise with conventions, such patterning is sometimes almost entirely verbal or composed of routine actions. It serves as a front for others and in part for oneself.

For the neurotic, the existence of this superficial structure provides easy proof that his life is no different from that of anyone else and blunts the secret impact of his feelings on futility. He may climb on a streetcar like anyone else and, even though he feels pushed, competitive, and on the alert, he may carry on a "perfectly normal" conversation all the while with another whose outward behavior is no different from his. The blandness of this culturally accepted cover is in strong contrast to the underlying organizations. In almost all styles of psychotherapy the patient is encouraged to abandon the superficial level; that is why therapy is the situation of choice for observing the workings of the principle of universal ambiguity.

Shifts of Dominance

The dual patterning of personality cannot become clearly visible, even to observation that penetrates beyond the surface, as long as one system maintains a strong dominance. The coexistence of two incompatible all-inclusive structures can be clearly and strikingly demonstrated only when a shift takes place between two patterns both of which are well developed and strongly articulated—much as the visual ambiguous Gestalts are revealed only through shifts. Such dramatic, seemingly sudden shifts are rare, but they do happen. Foremost among them are the phenomena of conversion, such as religious conversions exemplified by the reports collected by W. James, those described in some case histories of Alcoholics Anonymous, and the less well-known, spontaneous radical changes which are not formulated by the person in religious terms. No less clear cut is the evidence provided by sudden sweeping personality changes after an accumulation of traumata or an accumulation of insights in therapy. Similarly, some cases of traumatic neurosis and relapse after successful therapy represent shifts from health to neurosis. Cases of hysterical dual personality, though not founded in the basic dual pattern we have described, also demonstrate the possibility of complex alternate organizations coexisting in the same person. Some people, in whom both the healthy and the neurotic systems are strongly organized, report vivid experiences of periodic change of mood and behavior, each mood incorporating one of the two basic orientations.

Shifts cannot be expected to occur if or as long as, the nondominant pattern is underdeveloped and has a low degree of organization. Consequently the best opportunity for observation of shifts is afforded the therapist at that time in therapy when, the neurotic pattern having been weakened and the healthy one strengthened, both are approximately equal in strength and give marked indications of competing for the patient's alle-

giance. The strongest empirical support for the hypothesis of the dual organization of personality comes from the observations made at this stage of the therapeutic process. The dynamic effects exerted by each Gestalt as it struggles toward a complete realization of its system principle by eliminating or refitting system-inconsistent elements can be best observed at this time. The resulting shifts are well exemplified by the experience of a patient who visualized his former way of life as a Roman circus arena where he had become very skillful in avoiding the lions, and in nothing else. He felt that in therapy he had learned to spot and reach the exits from the arena, but once he was outside, the doors looked to him "just as inviting in a devilishly compelling way; from the outside they are not exits, they are entrances—and before I know it, there I am right back dodging the lions."

Universal Ambiguity

The ambiguity created by the dual organization of human life is reflected in the fact that, taken outside of its context, every item of human experience and behavior has a double meaning. Language sometimes assigns different terms to the two meanings and sometimes combines them under one term, but regardless of the verbal formulation and its evaluative connotation, the two discernible meanings of any human trait are commonly evaluated in diametrically opposite ways. In the chapter on homonomy we have discussed how the healthy wish to be needed, to be of help, acquires its neurotic counterpart in a compulsive assumption of obligations and how "love" can mean possessiveness. These examples could be multiplied. Dependence, though the term has taken on a perjorative meaning, actually is one aspect of every community formation, an expression of the homonomous trend. Only the dependence that expresses the neurotic feeling of helplessness, and consequently far exceeds the objective necessity for support, merits negative evaluation. Pride is highly throught of when it expresses self-respect and pleasure in real achievement; in some dialects, "proud" is the equivalent of "glad." Yet "pride goes before a fall," and Horney uses the term "pride system" to designate an essential component of neurosis. Submission and surrender both refer to a state of non-assertion of individuality, of losing oneself in something else, but the difference is momentous. One submits to the alien and becomes diminished through submission; one surrenders one's isolation to enter into a larger unit and enlarges one's life.

These examples do not imply that each personal manifestation has only two psychological meanings, only two fixed contexts. Since personality is a multiple organization, each item of behavior can serve as an expression of a variety of motives and be a part of a multitude of subsystems even within the same person. All these multiple meanings, however, are subsystems of one of the two major patterns. This grouping is not an arbitrary classification in terms of the "good-bad" polarity; rather the fact that a linguistic formulation of any human phenomenon can be given positive and negative connotations reflects the ambiguity created by the dual patterning of personality. This ambiguity often functions as an obstacle to communication in the theoretical discussion of human issues. The participants may disagree because in using identical or similar terms they assign to them not only different but practically opposite meanings.

An instructive example of both the dual and plural meanings of an attitude for which our language has but one name is afforded by the analysis of curiosity as it appears in healthy and in unhealthy contexts. Normal curiosity arises from the person's wish to broaden out, to learn about people and things for the sake of increased mastery and participation. Neurotic curiosity has entirely different goals and an entirely different emotional coloring. In one of its forms it is born of a feeling of helplessness; one feels that one does not know how to live and looks enviously at others who seem to be "successful" at it. The purpose of watching them is to find out "how they do it" in order to copy their methods; one does this without any reference to one's own inclinations and competencies, so that the borrowed methods remain inorganic accretions. Success is viewed as being achieved by some trick, not as growing out of one's total conduct of life. Much of the popular "adjustment" literature capitalizes on this neurotic trait; one reads it not to straighten out one's life but to learn the "techniques." The goal of curiosity in this pattern is the appropriation of something belonging to others; it is a method of stealing and one goes about it stealthily. It may well happen that the patient attempts to "steal" something which he actually possesses without knowing it, but this does not change the meaning of his act.

A more striking form of neurotic curiosity is directed defensively and aggressively against the assumed dangerous world. One seeks to "dig up the dirt" to alleviate one's own assumed worthlessness through comparison with the shortcomings of others but even more to protect oneself by storing up ammunition for an attack. One is gathering information that can be used against others, whether or not one is aware of this goal. Some go about it quite openly and make themselves disliked by asking personal questions that are "none of their business." More often, however, even publicly available information is gathered stealthily, and the person may engage in fantasies of the type "if he only knew that I know," a kind of secret psychological black mailing. He feels both maliciously triumphant and extremely guilty and fearful for having broken into another's privacy and stolen his secrets. This aggressive pattern is an essential component of voyeurism. Yet, in a perverted form the normal wish for human contact is present even in this aggressive form of curiosity. In all such cases that I have known there was an enormous craving to be loved.

"Amalgamation"

When a healthy motive and a neurotic one, each occupying an important position in the system to which it belongs, are aroused or expressed by an identical or strongly analogous behavior pattern, the two meanings of this pattern may coalesce or amalgamate. The pattern can then no longer function alternately now as a part of one organization and now as a part of the other. When the pattern is being utilized in the service of the dominant organization, it activates the meaning which attaches to it in the latent one and an inhibiting stalemate may result. An example of such a situation is provided by some types of fear of success. This fear can arise from a variety of neurotic motives, such as the boy's fear that his father will punish his attempts to become an active adult male. These motives, however, can amalgamate with others having strong roots in the healthy organization. In certain contexts, individual success may be seen by the person as separating him from his "universal background" of which the parents are representatives, thus condemning

him to an isolated lonely existence. If this meaning of success is prominent for the person, the force of the neurotic motives is increased by that of the healthy ones and, in therapy, the fear will not yield until *both* its roots have been laid bare. Amalgamation can also take place between two distinct neurotic meanings of a pattern. However, the strength and persistence of some of the most destructive damaging symptoms—of which fear of success is one—often have their source in the amalgamation of the two meanings that represent health and neurosis.

"Such was the case of a brilliant and dedicated young scientist whose career was on the verge of being eclipsed when he developed a circumscribed inability to prepare for his doctoral examination. As a child he had suffered from a deep uncertainty about what was expected of him. His father seemed to wish only to be left alone by his son and punished all attempts to attract his attention. The boy embarked early on various research pursuits, an effective and creative way of cultivating certainty and courting expectations. These activities brought gratification and success, but they skirted the issue of the needs and expectations of the loved ones. As he put it, "It was all for me." The examination in which he had to meet the expectations of his teachers in order to obtain the degree, a confirmation of his "right to success," brought the issue to a head. The study block, while neurotically self-destructive, was expressive of healthy impulses as well. It reintroduced an element of uncertainty into a pattern that had become excessively centered on establishing certainty, and it covertly expressed his wish to give up his too willful control which permitted no sharing with others."

Defense Mechanisms as Types of System Action

The theory of universal ambiguity represents a radical departure from the customary ways of viewing neurosis and health. It requires a reappraisal and a reformulation of those major concepts which have previously proved useful in the study of personality dynamics, and it makes some of these concepts appear in a new light.

The point can be best illustrated by a consideration of the defense mechanisms. I see the defense mechanisms as processes taking place not between the conscious and unconscious, or between ego, and superego, and id, but between the two major organizations of personality which struggle for dominance. The conflict of these two incompatible orientations, these two ways of adapting to life, is the basic conflict of human existence. Within this framework the processes referred to as defense mechanisms acquire a new significance. They are organizational devices, specific types of system action, through which each system seeks to complete itself in a manner consistent with its system principle and to maintain this organization, thereby preventing the alternative system from reaching a position of dominance.

This conception has two implications. First, it implies that the "defense mechanisms" have two functions: the internal organization of the system and its defense against the alternate one. Both functions can be fulfilled by means of one process. The organizing function is in the forefront when the given system is in a position of dominance; the defensive function becomes prominent when the two systems are in strong competition. Second, this conception implies an essential symmetry in the organizational-defensive maneuvers of the two systems; they maintain themselves and thereby ward off each other with identical or similar means. This symmetry is not complete, for several reasons. The system based on confidence, when it is securely dominant, can maintain this position with a minimum of special devices. It is a relatively self-consistent stable system. The neurotic system, with its double focus on fear and on hope, is not stable even when it is entrenched. It must continue to use many devices to achieve at least a semblance of consistency. Some of these defense mechanisms—those that result in a crass distortion of facts—are not compatible with the principles governing the system of health. Furthermore, the traditional formulation of some of the defense mechanisms obscures those components that are capable of functioning bilaterally, on behalf of either health or neurosis. Reformulations are required to make these components obvious. In spite of these qualifications the proposition stands that defense mechanisms are part and parcel of the dynamics of systems and as such are utilized both by the system of health and by the system of neurosis. I shall demonstrate this proposition with examples of two dynamic processes for only one of which a traditional formulation is available.

In the original formulation of *repression* certain impulses are considered to be made incompatible with the person's sense of self-esteem by parental reflection of socio-cultural sanctions and are therefore excluded from consciousness. According to my theory, the repressed is that which is inconsistent with the dominant organization, whichever it be. Repression remains a very useful concept, but it takes on new properties. It is no longer a one-way affair but a two-way affair. Not only the neurotic feelings and trends but the healthy ones too may be repressed, in this case by the neurotic organization. Both organizations are repressive, in the general sense of the term, because they are incompatible Gestalts, two total patterns struggling for dominance. If one system gains dominance, the other is *eo ipse* subdued or submerged, and this may take the form of excluding it from consciousness, i.e., of repression in the technical sense of the word. This conception is borne out by numerous observations that one can and does repress feelings and wishes that are in no way socially tabooed and are even considered laudable.

One of the mechanisms that come to light in analysis becomes very prominent at the stage when an intensive struggle takes place between neurosis and health. Like many dynamic devices, it has no traditional name. I would call it perversion if this term did not connote sexual perversions, which are unrelated to the process in question. It would also be described as annexation or *appropriation*.

Let us picture a patient who is considered a very warm-hearted person, and let us say that in analysis he discovers in himself a strong tendency to exploit people. He can then say, "My kindness is phony; when I get a person well buttered up I exploit him. I have no real warmth." He may, however, be wrong. His warmth may not be a pretense but a genuine trait that has developed within the context of the health system but is used at times within a neurotic context, for a neurotic purpose. Figuratively speaking, it is unlawfully appropriated by the competing organization and perverted to its uses. This process can take place in reverse as well. A misgiving about therapy frequently expressed by people who feel that they are creative is that they may lose their originality, that they will become flattened out and turn into ordinary John Does. Usually this does not happen, but such misgivings are not entirely unfounded; the energy of the tension created by the neurosis *can* serve socially valuable purposes. If it does happen, the question may be asked whether such an outcome is healthy or neurotic.

In the psychoanalytic literature this question has been much, and inconclusively, debated in relation to sublimation, a concept which can be made to coincide with *one* of the two directions appropriation can take. In terms of my theory, the neurotic pattern appropriated by the healthy system remains neurotic unless its inner structure is changed. Yet it is used for a good purpose. We do not have to assume that all philanthropists are sincere lovers of mankind. People do good in this world out of quite unrespectable motives. The neurotic's wish to escape from doubt and turmoil can on occasion facilitate constructive decisions. A striking example of a neurotically founded impulse being made to serve health is a suicidal attempt that turns into a plea for help. The very thought of suicide can serve as protection if the person feels that he can bear his suffering because he knows he can stop it at any moment.

I see appropriation, or "perversion," as a very important mechanism, and, like repression, it is clearly a two-way street. It is used to a different extent by different people; those who use it extensively are extremely confusing to others. When in therapy the submerged healthy pattern comes more and more to the fore and the two systems struggle for dominance, each appropriates features that belong to the other and utilizes them for its own purpose.

Id and Ego in the Light of the Theory of Duality

The hypothesis of dual organization of personality establishes a distinction which I consider more basic than the ones between conscious and unconscious or between id, ego, and superego. It cuts across the other divisions and seems to me to make for greater clarity, especially in ordering one's observations of the therapeutic process. Needless to say, the distinction between the conscious and the unconscious remains important; no adequate description of personality dynamics and of the process of therapy can be given without taking into account the consequences of vital processes reaching consciousness, or remaining unsymbolized. However, as I tried to show in discussing repression, the dynamic factors reside in the two systems qua systems; both of them are organizations of the total personality process and consequently both include conscious and unconscious factors.

With regard to the structural division of personality, though I can see good reasons to justify it, I have found that the more I made use in my thinking of the idea of dual organization, the less I had occasion to think in terms of id, ego, and superego. In therapeutic work it is a great advantage for the therapist to be able to talk to his patients essentially in the language of concepts in which the therapist actually thinks, even though translated into the vernacular. I have found that formulations based on my theory made very good sense to the patients, meeting, as it were, their own concepts. On the other hand, I have found the concepts underlying the traditional structural division to be useless in therapeutic conversation, and sometimes worse than useless.

In trying to see how the psychoanalytic concepts could be meaningfully fitted into the cross-cutting framework of my hypothesis so as to retain their theoretical usefulness, I did not have much success with the concepts of id and ego. Since each of the two systems in terms of which I think organizes the total content of personality, id, ego, and superego would have to be present in each. Such doubling of concepts would make sense only if one could ascribe clear-cut differences to each of these three structures, depending on whether each forms a part of the system organized by the confident or by the pessimistic and uncertain expectations. This cannot be done in the case of id and ego without violating their conceptual properties. But if one does not change its properties, the concept of id is altogether incompatible with the holistic point of view. In thinking about personality in terms of its most general trends, which ramify down to specifics, I do not assign a special position to those functions that are physiologically fixed, and even less do I consider them the basis from which all other functions derive. These functions are dynamically important, particularly because of the absolute necessity of satisfying these vital needs, but still they are only a few of the many manifestations of personality. Consequently I can only think of the id as either this special group of functions, or as a totality of functions in a very primitive early state of organization.

The question of how the concept of ego could be related to my system is the most obscure. Ego seems to be, first, the embodiment of the organizational principle as such, the totality of the organizational aspects of all human functions. In this meaning ego participates equally in the two systems I postulate. Both the system of health and the system of neurosis can be strongly and articulately organized, and in both this organization functions also as a defense against the other system. On the other hand, the function of reality testing, also ascribed to the ego, finds a greater development in the system of health than in that of neurosis. Finally, as a source of motivation ego seems to embody the trend to increased autonomy.

Superego: Duality of Conscience

The concept of superego has a more concrete and coherent content; I can think of this structure as a special subsystem of personality without violating either the concept of superego or that of a system. Within the framework I have outlined, the concept of superego would have to be doubled, and I feel that there is a sound empirical basis for doing just that. There is a healthy conscience without which the person is sick, a psychopathic personality, and there is an unhealthy one which makes the person spend his life worrying whether he has stepped on the cracks in the pavement.

It seems to me that in the classical psychoanalytic formulation of the superego, the problem of the healthy conscience is not touched upon. The superego appears as a central accident, a necessary evil; it is not inherent in human nature as such but is an extraneous result of social development, something required not by the individual but only by society. Actually it boils down to fear of punishment or ostracism. The assumption is that, except for this ever-present fear, everyone would break the Ten Commandments and obey the 11th: Thou shalt not get caught. Even when the commands and the punishment for breaking them have been internalized, the superego still represents an external factor, the society as mediated by the parents; it is not an organic growth. In its extreme forms this kind of conscience which fluorishes in neurosis and never is totally absent in health, implies the conception of a power that represents the *mythical enemy*, an alien and arbitrary force, an irrational authority. The "superego rules" that emanate from this power become idols or frightening demons.

There is no doubt that fear of punishment lives in all of us and that many of the "moral principles" we feel to be our own originate in this fear, but that is not all there is to conscience. There is another aspect which does not depend on swallowing something that has been forced down one's throat by society, but expresses certain value attitudes inherent in human nature. I derive this factor from the trend toward homonomy, from the need to belong and to identify with persons, groups, or causes. Guilt generated by this conscience may be termed "real guilt," It is not fear but an emotional reaction to having acted against somebody or something with which one is genuinely identified; such an act of disloyalty is also an offense against one's own integrity. The pattern that underlies the experience of real guilt, in spite of the wide cultural variation of its content, is a universal expression of a universal human trend. When acceptance of the "Superego rules" is founded in the homonomous trend, they function (no matter how nonsensical their content) as expressions of the person's own ethical attitudes, and any offense against them is guilt laden.

A patient told me of a childhood event about which he felt most ashamed and guilty. He was Jewish and lived in a neighborhood where he was exposed to some very painful scenes in the street. There was an old man in the neighborhood who made his living by teaching Hebrew and who was apparently intellectually limited or peculiar in some other way. He was the target of non-Jewish children who often made fun of him. Once my patient was caught in a crowd of these children as they were shouting, "Jew, Jew" and throwing stones at the old man, who was running away crying. My patient panicked and in his anxiety started running and shouting with the children. He was closely identified with the Jewish group and with certain features of Judaism, but on this occasion his fear got the better of him and he acted against the things he was devoted to."

This anecdote illustrates the central phenomenon of real guilt: the betrayal of somebody or something one loves. This is also a self-betrayal, because one acts not in line with one's genuine values but out of one's weakness, one's fear. Usually hate is also involved—in the case I have described there was not only love but also anger against the community which exposed its members to threat—but the presence of a positive tie is the necessary precondition of real guilt. An act directed against somebody who is an enemy, and nothing but an enemy, would not arouse guilt. But real people rarely live up to the qualifications of the mythical enemy. Even in those whom we hate we can usually see something that represents a possibility for human contact, and we can consequently feel a measure of guilt toward them.

Guilt based on love is radically different from guilt based on fear of retaliation, but in many instances the two are so closely interwoven that it is useful to have a term which covers the whole complex. Both kinds of guilt feelings can be called superego functions; the term conscience, however should be reserved for the pattern which underlies the experience of real guilt. To disentangle the different roots of guilt feelings is not simple. In every course of therapy a great deal of effort must be devoted to this task and to working out the problems of conscience and guilt. Even if someone feels guilty because he engages in masturbation, it is not enough to try and reassure him, e.g., by giving him statistics of its incidence or other pertinent information. The correct information should be given, and it does bring relief, but that is not the end of the story. Before getting this information the patient was convinced that he was doing something evil and yet he continued doing it, so there is still the issue of guilt to deal with, the issue of having acted against the wishes and beliefs of those whom one loved.

In therapy it is necessary to disentangle the various aspects of guilt because one cannot treat all guilt indiscriminately by assuaging it, passing it off as unimportant, or citing extenuating circumstances. We have the double task of freeing the patient from pangs of "conscience" which are ultimately based on irrational fears, and of awakening and strengthening his real conscience, making him feel real guilt. This second goal is fully as important as the first, if not more so. The patient's insight, accompanied by a feeling of guilt, into the nature of his neurosis as a self-betrayal and a betrayal is a necessary step in the development of his motivation for reconstructing his life.

The Dual Source of Anxiety

In conclusion a word about the position of anxiety within the dual organization of personality. Anxiety arises not only out of the state of isolation but also out of anticipating such a state. Consequently anxiety will appear whenever the dominant organization is threatened with dissolution, regardless of whether the threat is directed against the pattern of neurosis or health. This is not as paradoxical as it may sound, if one recalls that both systems aim at fulfilling the basic human trends and are perceived as ways toward that goal. Although only in the healthy pattern are human purposes actually being realized, the entrenched neurotic pattern nurses the dim hope that they may be realized yet. A threat to the position of dominance of either pattern by its underdeveloped or subordinated alter-system is a threat to the only known path away from isolation and toward fulfillment. Hence anxiety, though phenomenologically undistinguishable, can arise from either of the two opposite camps. Freud's hesitancy and change in his formulation of anxiety is significant in this connection: there is good empirical basis for equating anxiety both with the (transformed) repressed content and with the reaction of the repressor to the threat of the repressed.

Anxiety signals the existence of a threat to whichever system is dominant, and leads to the enhancement of its self-protective measures. Thus it serves indiscriminately as a safeguard of the status quo. Those for whom the dominance of the pattern of health has been a hard-won position often find that sensitivity to anxious feelings is the best sentinel against the re-encroachment of the neurosis and an effective reminder that only challenges husband confidence. When the issue is to exchange neurosis for health, little progress can be made if anxiety is quickly allowed to initiate defensive measures which serve to protect and consolidate the old pattern. To collaborate with anxiety in this case means to make our first enemy our last ally.

4. *Self-actualizing and Beyond*

ABRAHAM H. MASLOW

In this chapter, I plan to discuss ideas that are in midstream rather than ready for formulation into a final version. I find that with my students and with other people with whom I share these ideas, the notion of self-actualization gets to be almost like a Rorschach ink blot. It frequently tells me more about the person using it than about reality. What I would like to do now is to explore some aspects of the nature of self-actualization, not as a grand abstraction, but in terms of the operational meaning of the self-actualizing process. What does self-actualization mean in moment-to-moment terms? What does it mean on Tuesday at four o'clock?

The Beginnings of Self-actualization Studies. My investigations on self-actualization were not planned to be research and did not start out as research. They started out as the effort of a young intellectual to try to understand two of his teachers whom he loved, adored, and admired and who were very, very

SOURCE: *Abraham H. Maslow, "Self-actualization and beyond,"* in Challenges of Humanistic Psychology, *pp. 279–286. Edited by James F. T. Bugental. New York: McGraw-Hill, 1967.*

wonderful people. It was a kind of high-IQ devotion. I could not be content simply to adore, but sought to understand why these two people were so different from the run-of-the-mill people in the world. These two people were Ruth Benedict and Max Wertheimer. They were my teachers after I came with a Ph.D. from the West to New York City, and they were most remarkable human beings. My training in psychology equipped me not at all for understanding them. It was as if they were not quite people but something more than people. My own investigation began as a pre-scientific or nonscientific activity. I made descriptions and notes on Max Wertheimer, and I made notes on Ruth Benedict. When I tried to understand them, think about them, and write about them in my journal and my notes, I realized in one wonderful moment that their two patterns could be generalized. I was talking about a kind of person, not about two noncomparable individuals. There was wonderful excitement in that. I tried to see whether this pattern could be found elsewhere, and I did find it elsewhere, in one person after another.

By ordinary standards of laboratory research, that is of rigorous and controlled research, this simply was not research at all. My generalizations grew out of *my* selection of certain kinds of people. Obviously, other judges are needed. So far, one man has selected perhaps two dozen people whom he liked or admired very much and thought were wonderful people and then tried to figure them out and found that he was able to describe a syndrome—the kind of pattern that seemed to fit all of them. These were people only from Western cultures, people selected with all kinds of built-in biases. Unreliable as it is, that was the only operational definition of self-actualizing people as I described them in my first publication on the subject.

After I published the results of my investigations, there appeared perhaps six, eight, or ten other lines of evidence that supported the findings, not by replication, but by approaches from different angles. Carl Rogers' findings (1961, etc.) and those of his students add up to corroboration for the whole syndrome. Bugental (1965, pp. 266–275) has offered confirmatory evidence from psychotherapy. Some of the new work with LSD,[1] some of the studies on the effects of therapy (good therapy, that is) some test results—in fact everything I know adds up to corroborative support, though not replicated support, for that study. I personally feel very confident about its major conclusions. I cannot conceive of any research that would make major changes in the pattern, though I am sure there will be minor changes. I have made some of those myself. But my confidence in my rightness is not a scientific datum. If you question the kind of data I have from my researches with monkeys and dogs, you are bringing my competence into doubt or calling me a liar, and I have a right to object. If you question my findings on self-actualizing

people (Maslow, 1954, pp. 203–205; Maslow, 1962), you may reasonably do so because you don't know very much about the man who selected the people on whom all the conclusions are based. The conclusions are in the realm of prescience, but the affirmations are set forth in a form that can be put to test. In that sense, they are scientific.

The people I selected for my investigation were older people, people who had lived much of their lives out and were visibly successful. We do not yet know about the applicability of the findings to young people. We do not know what self-actualization means in other cultures, although studies of self-actualization in China and in India are now in process. We do not know what the findings of these new studies will be, but of one thing I have no doubt: When you select out for careful study very fine and healthy people, strong people, creative people, saintly people, sagacious people—in fact, exactly the kind of people I picked out—then you get a different view of mankind. You are asking how tall can people grow, what can a human being become? These are the Olympic gold-medal winners—the best we have. The fact that somebody can run 100 yards in less than ten seconds means that potentially any baby that is born into the world is, in theory, capable of doing so too. In that sense, any baby that is born into the world can in principle reach the heights that actually exist and can be described.

Intrinsic and Extrinsic Learning. When you look at mankind this way, your thinking about psychology and psychiatry changes radically. For example, 99 percent of what has been written on so-called learning theory is simply irrelevant to a grown human being. "Learning theory" does not apply to a human being growing as tall as he can. Most of the literature on learning theory deals with

---

[1]See, for example, Chap. 16 in this volume, by Robert Mogar. (Editor).

what I call "extrinsic learning," to distinguish it from "intrinsic learning." Extrinsic learning means collecting acquisitions to yourself like keys in your pocket or coins that you pick up. Extrinsic learning is adding another association or another craft. The process of learning to be the best human being you can be is another business altogether. The far goals for adult education, and any other education, are the processes, the ways in which we can help people to become all they are capable of becoming. This I call intrinsic learning, and I am confining my remarks here entirely to it. That is the way self-actualizing people learn. To help the client achieve such intrinsic learning is the far goal of counseling.

These things I *know* with certainty. There are other things that I feel very confident about—"my smell tells me," so to speak. Yet I have even fewer objective data on these points than I had on those discussed above. Self-actualization is hard enough to define. How much harder it is to answer the question: Beyond self-actualization, what? Or, if you will: Beyond authenticity, what? Just being honest is, after all, not sufficient in all this. What else can we say of self-actualizing people?

B-values. Self-actualizing people are, without one single exception, involved in a cause outside their own skin, in something outside of themselves. They are devoted, working at something, something which is very precious to them —some calling or vocation in the old sense, the priestly sense. They are working at something which fate has called them to somehow and which they work at and which they love, so that the work-joy dichotomy in them disappears. One devotes his life to the law, another to justice, another to beauty or truth. All, in one way or another, devote their lives to the search for what I have called (1962)

the "being" values ("B," for short), the ultimate values which are intrinsic, which cannot be reduced to anything more ultimate. There are about fourteen of these B-values, including the truth and beauty and goodness of the ancients and perfection, simplicity, comprehensiveness, and several more. These B-values are described in the appendix to my book *Religions, Values and Peak Experiences* (1964). They are the values of being.

Meta-needs and Meta-pathologies. The existence of these B-values adds a whole set of complications to the structure of self-actualization. These B-values behave like needs. I have called them *meta-needs*. Their deprivation breeds certain kinds of pathologies which have not yet been adequately described but which I call *meta-pathologies*—the sicknesses of the soul which come, for example, from living among liars all the time and not trusting anyone. Just as we need counselors to help people with the simpler problems of unmet needs, so we may need *meta-counselors* to help with the soul-sicknesses that grow from the unfulfilled meta-needs. In certain definable and empirical ways, it is necessary for man to live in beauty rather than ugliness, as it is necessary for him to have food for an aching belly or rest for a weary body. In fact, I would go so far as to claim that these B-values are the meaning of life for most people, but many people don't even recognize that they have these meta-needs. Part of our job as counselors may be to make them aware of these needs in themselves, just as the classical psychoanalyst made his patients aware of their instinctoid basic needs. Ultimately, perhaps, we shall come to think of ourselves as philosophical or religious counselors.

We try to help our counselees move and grow toward self-actualization. These people are often all wrapped up in value problems. Many are youngsters who are, in principle, very wonderful people, though in actuality they often seem to be little more than snotty kids. Nevertheless, I assume (in the face of all behavioral evidence sometimes) that they are, in the classical sense, idealistic. I assume that they are looking for values and they would love to have something to devote themselves to, to be patriotic about, to worship, adore, love. These youngsters are making choices from moment to moment of going forward or retrogressing, moving away from or moving toward self-actualization. As counselors, or as meta-counselors, what can we tell them about becoming more fully themselves?

Behaviors Leading to Self-actualization

What does one do when he self-actualizes? Does he grit his teeth and squeeze? What does self-actualization mean in terms of actual behavior, actual procedure? I shall describe eight ways in which one self-actualizes.

First, self-actualization means experiencing fully, vividly, selflessly, with full concentration and total absorption. It means experiencing without the self-consciousness of the adolescent. At this moment of experiencing, the person is wholly and fully human. This is a self-actualization moment. This is a moment when the self is actualizing itself. As individuals, we help clients to experience them more often. We can encourage them to become totally absorbed in something and to forget their poses and their defenses and their shyness—to go at it whole hog. From the outside, we can see that this can be a very sweet moment. In those youngsters who are trying to be very tough and cynical and sophisticated, we

can see the recovery of some of the guilelessness of childhood; some of the innocence and sweetness of the face can come back as they devote themselves fully to a moment and throw themselves fully into the experiencing of it. The key word for this is "selflessly," and our youngsters suffer from too little selflessness and too selfconsciousness, self-awareness.

Second, let us think of life as a process of choices, one after another. At each point there is a progression choice and a regression choice. There may be a movement toward defense, toward safety, toward being afraid; but over on the other side, there is the growth choice. To make the growth choice instead of the fear choice a dozen times a day is to move a dozen times a day toward self-actualization. Self-actualization is an ongoing process; it means making each of the many single choices about whether to lie or be honest, whether to steal or not to steal at a particular point, and it means to make each of these choices as a growth choice. This is movement toward self-actualization.

Third, to talk of self-actualization implies that there is a self to be actualized. A human being is not a *tabula rasa*, not a lump of clay or plastocene. He is something which is already there, at least a "cartilaginous" structure of some kind. A human being is, at minimum, his temperament, his biochemical balances, and so on. There is a self, and what I have sometimes referred to as "listening to the impulse voices" means letting the self emeremerge. Most of us, most of the time (and especially does this apply to children, young people), listen not to ourselves but to Mommy's introjected voice or Daddy's voice or to the voice of the Establishment, of the Elders, of authority, or of tradition.

As a simple first step toward self-actualization, I sometimes suggest to my students that when they are given a glass of wine and asked how they like it, they try a different way of responding. First, I suggest that they *not* look at the label on the bottle. Thus they will not use it to get any cue about whether or not they *should* like it. Next, I recommend that they close their eyes if possible and that they "make a hush." Now they are ready to look within themselves and try to shut out the noise of the world so that they may savor the wine on their tongues and look to the "Supreme Court" inside themselves. Then, and only then, they may come out and say, "I like it" or "I don't like it." A statement so arrived at is different from the usual kind of phoniness that we all indulge in. At a party recently, I caught myself looking at the label on a bottle and assuring my hostess that she had indeed selected a very good Scotch. But then I stopped myself: What was I saying? I know little about Scotches. All I knew was what the advertisements said. I had no idea whether this one was good or not; yet this is the kind of thing we all do. Refusing to do it is part of the ongoing process of actualizing oneself. Does *your* belly hurt? Or does it feel good? Does this taste good on *your* tongue? Do *you* like lettuce?

Fourth, when in doubt, be honest rather than not. I am covered by that phrase "when in doubt," so that we need not argue too much about diplomacy. Frequently, when we are in doubt we are not honest. Our clients are not honest much of the time. They are playing games and posing. They do not take easily to the suggestion to be honest. Looking within oneself for many of the answers implies taking responsibility. That is in itself a great step toward actualization. This matter of responsibility has been little studied. It doesn't turn up in our textbooks, for who can investigate responsibility in white rats? Yet it is an almost tangible part of psychotherapy. In psychotherapy, one can see it, can feel it, can know the moment of responsibility.

Then there is a clear knowing of what it feels like. This is one of the great steps. Each time one takes responsibility, this is an actualizing of the self.

Fifth, we have talked so far of experiencing without self-awareness, of making the growth choice rather than the fear choice, of listening to the impulse voices, and of being honest and taking responsibility. All these are steps toward self-actualization, and all of them guarantee better life choices. A person who does each of these little things each time the choice point comes will find that they add up to better choices about what is constitutionally right for him. He comes to know what his destiny is, who his wife or husband will be, what his mission in life will be. One cannot choose wisely for a life unless he dares to listen to himself, *his own self*, at each moment in life, and to say calmly, "No, I don't like such and such."

The art world, in my opinion, has been captured by a small group of opinion and taste makers about whom I feel suspicious. That is an *ad hominem* judgment, but it seems fair enough for people who set themselves up as able to say, "You like what I like or else you are a fool." We must teach people to listen to their own tastes. Most people don't do it. When standing in a gallery before a puzzling painting, one rarely hears, "That is a puzzling painting." We had a dance program at Brandeis not too long ago—a weird thing altogether, with electronic music, tapes, and people doing surrealistic and Dada things. When the lights went up everybody looked stunned, and nobody knew what to say. In that kind of situation most people will make some smart chatter instead of saying, "I would like to think about this." Making an honest statement involves daring to be different, unpopular, nonconformist. If we cannot teach our clients, young or old, about being prepared to be unpopular, we might just as well give up right now. To be courageous rather than afraid is another version of the same thing.

Sixth, self-actualization is not only an end state but also the process of actualizing one's potentialities at any time, in any amount. It is, for example, a matter of becoming smarter by studying if one is an intelligent person. Self-actualization means using one's intelligence. It does not mean doing some far-out thing necessarily, but it may mean going through an arduous and demanding period of preparation in order to realize one's possibilities. Self-actualization can consist of finger exercises at a piano keyboard. Self-actualization means working to do well the thing that one wants to do. To become a second-rate physician is not a good path to self-actualization. One wants to be first-rate or as good as he can be.

Seventh, peak experiences (Maslow, 1962; Maslow, 1964) are transient moments of self-actualization. They are moments of ecstasy which cannot be bought, cannot be guaranteed, cannot even be sought. One must be, as C. S. Lewis wrote, "surprised by joy." But one can set up the conditions so that peak experiences are more likely, or he can perversely set up the conditions so that they are less likely. Breaking up an illusion, getting rid of a false notion, learning what one is not good at, learning what his potentialities are *not*—these are also part of discovering what one is in fact.

Practically everyone does have peak experiences, but not everyone knows it. Some people wave these small mystical experiences aside. Helping people to recognize these little moments of ecstasy[2] when they happen is one of the jobs of the counselor or meta-counselor. Yet, how does one's psyche, with nothing external in the world to point at—there is no blackboard there—look into another person's secret psyche and then try to communicate? We have to work out a new way of communication. I have tried one. It is described in another appendix in that same book (*Religions, Values and Peak Experiences*) under the title "Rhapsodic Communications." I think that kind of communication may be more of a model for teaching, and counseling, for helping adults to become as fully developed as they can be, than the kind we are used to when we see teachers writing on the board. If I love Beethoven and I hear something in a quartet that you don't, how do I teach you to hear? The noises are there, obviously. But I hear something very, very beautiful, and you look blank. You hear the sounds. How do I get you to hear the beauty? That is more our problem in teaching than making you learn the ABC's or demonstrating arithmetic on the board or pointing to a dissection of a frog. These latter things are external to both people; one has a pointer, and both can look at the same time. This kind of teaching is easy; the other kind is much harder, but it is part of our job as counselors. It is meta-counseling.

Eighth, finding out who one is, what he is, what he likes, what he doesn't like, what is good for him and what bad, where he is going and what his mission is—opening oneself up to himself—means the exposure of psychopathology. It means identifying defenses, and after defenses have been identified, it means finding the courage to give them up. This is painful because defenses are erected against something which is unpleasant. But giving up the defenses is worthwhile. If the psychoanalytic literature has taught us nothing else, it has taught us that repression is not a good way of solving problems.

Desacralizing. Let me talk about one defense mechanism that is not mentioned

---

[2]See Chap. 14, by Herbert Otto. (Editor)

in the psychology textbooks, though it is a very important defense mechanism to the snotty and yet idealistic youngster of today. It is the defense mechanism of *desacralizing*. These youngsters mistrust the possibility of values and virtues. They feel themselves swindled or thwarted in their lives. Most of them have, in fact, dopey parents whom they don't respect very much, parents who are quite confused themselves about values and who, frequently, are simply terrified of their children and never punish them or stop them from doing things that are wrong. So you have a situation where the youngsters simply despise their elders—often for good and sufficient reason. Such youngsters have learned to make a big generalization: They won't listen to anybody who is grown up, especially if the grown-up uses the same words which they've heard from the hypocritical mouth. They have heard their fathers talk about being honest or brave or bold, and they have seen their fathers being the opposite of all these things.

The youngsters have learned to reduce the person to the concrete object and to refuse to see what he might be or to refuse to see him in his symbolic values or to refuse to see him or her eternally. Our kids have desacralized sex, for example. Sex is nothing; it is a natural thing, and they have made it so natural that it has lost its poetic qualities in many instances, which means that it has lost practically everything. Self-actualization means giving up this defense mechanism and learning or being taught to resacralize.[3]

Resacralizing. Resacralizing means being willing, once again, to see a person "under the aspect of eternity," as Spinoza says, or to see him in the medieval Christian unitive perception, that is, being able to see the sacred, the eternal, the symbolic. It is to see Woman with a capital "W" and everything which that implies, even when one looks at a particular woman. Another example: One goes to medical school and dissects a brain. Certainly something is lost if the medical student isn't awed but, without the unitive perception, sees the brain only as one concrete thing. Open to resacralization, one sees a brain as a sacred object also, sees its symbolic value, sees it as a figure of speech, sees it in its poetic aspects.

Resacralization often means an awful lot of corny talk—"very square," the kids would say. Nevertheless, for the counselor, especially for the counselor of older people, where these philosophical questions about religion and the meaning of life come up, this is a most important way of helping the person to move toward self-actualization. The youngsters may say that it is square, and the logical positivists may say that it is meaningless, but for the person who seeks our help in this process, it is obviously very meaningful and very important, and we had better answer him, or we're not doing what it is our job to do.

Put all these points together, and we see that self-actualization is not a matter of one great moment. It is not true that on Thursday at four o'clock the trumpet blows and one steps into the pantheon forever and altogether. Self-actualization is a matter of degree, of little accessions accumulated one by one. Too often our clients are inclined to wait for some kind of inspiration to strike so that they can say, "At 3:23 on this Thursday I became self-actualized!" People selected as self-actualizing subjects, people who

---

[3]I have had to make up these words because the English language is rotten for good people. It has no decent vocabulary for the virtues. Even the nice words get all smeared up. "Love," for instance.

fit the criteria, go about it in these little ways: They listen to their own voices; they take responsibility; they are honest; and they work hard. They find out who they are and what they are, not only in terms of their mission in life, but also in terms of the way their feet hurt when they wear such and such a pair of shoes and whether they do or do not like eggplant or stay up all night if they drink too much beer. All this is what the real self means. They find their own biological natures, their congenital natures, which are irreversible or difficult to change.

The Therapeutic Attitude

These are the things people do as they move toward self-actualization. Who, then, is a counselor? How can he help the people who come to him to make this movement in the direction of growth?

Seeking a Model. I have used the words "therapy," "psychotherapy," and "patient." Actually, I hate all these words, and I hate the medical model that they imply because the medical model suggests that the person who comes to the counselor is a sick person, beset by disease and illness, seeking a cure. Actually, of course, we hope that the counselor will be the one who helps to foster the self-actualization of people, rather than the one who helps to cure a disease.

The helping model has to give way, too; it just doesn't fit. It makes us think of the counselor as the person or the professional who knows and reaches down from his privileged position above to the poor jerks below who don't know and have to be helped in some way. Nor is the counselor to be a teacher, in the usual sense, because what teachers have

specialized in and gotten to be very good at is the "extrinsic learning" I described above. The process of growing into the best human being one can be is, instead, intrinsic learning, as we saw.

The existential therapists have wrestled with this question of models, and I can recommend Bugental's book, *The Search for Authenticity* (1965), for a discussion of the matter. Bugental suggests that we call counseling or therapy "ontogogy," which means trying to help people to grow to their fullest possible height. Perhaps that's a better word than the one I once suggested, a word derived from a German author, "psychogogy," which means the education of the psyche. Whatever the word we use, I think that the concept we will eventually have to come to is one that Alfred Adler suggested a long, long time ago when he spoke of the "older brother." The older brother is the loving person who takes responsibility, just as one does for his young, kid brother. Of course, the older brother knows more; he's lived longer, but he is not qualitatively different, and he is not in another realm of discourse. The wise and loving older brother tries to improve the younger, and he tries to make him better than he is, in the younger's own style. See how different this is from the "teaching somebody who doesn't know nothin'" model!

Counseling is not concerned with training or with molding or with teaching in the ordinary sense of telling people what to do and how to do it. It is not concerned with propaganda. It is a Taoistic uncovering and *then* helping. Taoistic means the noninterfering, the "letting be." Taoism is not a laissez-faire philosophy or a philosophy of neglect or of refusal to help or care. As a kind of model of this process we might think of a therapist who, if he is a decent therapist and also a decent human being, would never dream of imposing himself upon his patients or propagandizing in any way or of trying to make a patient into an imitation of himself.

What the good clinical therapist does is to help his particular client to unfold, to break through the defenses against his own self-knowledge, to recover himself, and to get to know himself. Ideally, the therapist's rather abstract frame of reference, the textbooks he has read, the schools that he has gone to, his beliefs about the world—these should never be perceptible to the patient. Respectful of the inner nature, the being, the essence of this "younger brother," he would recognize that the best way for him to lead a good life is to be more fully himself. The people we call "sick" are the people who are not themselves, the people who have built up all sorts of neurotic defenses against being human. Just as it makes no difference to the rosebush whether the gardener is Italian or French or Swedish, so it should make no difference to the younger brother how his helper learned to be a helper. What the helper has to give is certain services that are independent of his being Swedish or Catholic or Mohammedan or Freudian or whatever he is.

These basic concepts include, imply, and are completely in accord with the basic concepts of Freudian and other systems of psychodynamics. It is a Freudian principle that unconscious aspects of the self are repressed and that the finding of the true self requires the uncovering of these unconscious aspects. Implicit is a belief that truth heals much. Learning to break through one's repressions, to know one's self, to hear the impulse voices, to uncover the triumphant nature, to reach knowledge, insight, and the truth—these are the requirements.

Lawrence Kubie (1953–1954), in "The Forgotten Man in Education," some time ago made the point that one, ultimate goal of education is to help the person become a human being, as fully human as he can possible be.

Especially with adults we are not in a position in which we have nothing to work with. We already have a start; we already have capacities, talents, directions, missions, callings. The job is, if we are to take this model seriously, to help them to be more perfectly what they already are, to be more full, more actualizing, more realizing in fact what they are in potentiality.

References

Bugental, J. F. T. *The Search for Authenticity.* New York: Holt, Rinehart and Winston, 1965.

Kubie, L. The forgotten man in education, *Harvard Alumni Bulletin,* 1953–1954, **56,** 349–353.

Maslow, A. H. *Motivation and Personality.* New York: Harper & Row, 1954.

_____. *Toward a Psychology of Being.* Princeton, N. J.: Van Nostrand, 1962.

_____. *Religions, Values and Peak Experiences*. Columbus, Ohio: Ohio State University Press, 1964.

Rogers, C. R. *On Becoming a Person*. Boston: Houghton Mifflin, 1961.

Sheldon's Constitutional Psychology

In spite of the fact that William Sheldon has continued to conduct research relevant to his earlier investigations and also has modified and made more objective his method of somatotyping, he has produced only one significant publication in recent years (Sheldon, Lewis, and Tenney, 1969). In this important paper a new somatotyping technique, called the Trunk Index, is described in full detail and a number of very interesting findings employing it are presented.

In the past several years, investigators other than Sheldon have been working on physique and behavior relationships. Much of this work has been done in England where somewhat different methods and formulations have been used. An examination of the literature of the past two decades suggests a growing incident of significant investigations — many of which have provided strong confirmation of some of Sheldon's most interesting results. Some documentation for this statement is provided in the following papers.

As the psychobiological foundations of behavior receive more attention in contemporary psychological research, the formulations of personality psychologists are beginning to reflect this. One result is that constitutional and temperamental components of personality are being studied with renewed interest and frequency. Thus one may expect continued concern with the questions posed by Sheldon's research and thinking, and an increasing amount of relevant research.

The study by Walker is primarily of interest because virtually all possibility of experimenter bias has been removed. Thus, whatever association is observed between body build and behavior is largely independent of contamination of data of the sort that may have operated strongly in the case of Sheldon's major study of physique and temperament. One important feature of this study is the demonstration of associations that correspond to those reported by Sheldon, although of lower magnitude, in young children. Thus, whatever the determinants of these relationships may be, they begin to operate early in the individual's life.

The second paper in this section is a report by McNeill and Livson of longitudinal data collected as part of a larger study conducted at

Berkeley, and is particularly interesting because it employs Sheldon's recently devised Trunk Index. The purpose of this study was to see if linearity of body build was associated with adolescent maturation rate. Photographs were taken of these girls over a period of years and provided the data for establishing somatype measures. The results of the investigation demonstrate a relationship between body type and significant aspects of development. Another important finding is that the association between body type and rate of maturation persists over a considerable period of time.

Cortes and Gatti have investigated physique and personality factors in a series of studies. In the paper chosen for this section the authors report the results of an investigation of the relationship between a well-known personality variable, the need for achievement, and body type. They hypothesized that persons who are high "need achievers" would also tend to have mesomorphic body types. Using a sample of high school boys and a sample of delinquents, the general hypothesis was substantiated. Similar findings from the two groups of subjects, in spite of the many differences between them, suggest the generality of the findings.

The final paper is an attempt by one of the editors, Gardner Lindzey, to examine the position of morphological or physique variables in modern psychology and to evaluate their potential contribution to selected areas of psychological investigation. One of the principal reasons for its inclusion is that it discusses much of the relatively recent and interesting work that has been done in this area and also clearly identifies the relative reluctance of American psychologists to give serious attention to this important area of research.

Reference

Sheldon, W. H., Lewis, N. D. C., and Tenney, A. M. "Psychotic patterns and physical constitution: A thirty-year follow-up of thirty-eight hundred psychiatric patients in New York State." In D. V. Siva Sankar (Ed.) *Schizophrenia: current concepts and research*. New York: PJD Publications, 1969, pp. 838–912.

1. Body Build and Behavior in Young Children: Body Build and Nursery School Teacher's Ratings

RICHARD N. WALKER

This study, part of a larger research project, investigates some relations between children's physique and their behavior in a nursery school setting. It tests the adequacy of certain predictions based on the work of William Sheldon and explores additional areas of possible physique-behavior interrelations.

Sample

The main subjects were 73 boys and 52 girls, all the children attending the Gesell Institute Nursery School during one or both of two consecutive years, with the exception of (a) children having physical handicaps, (b) children falling clearly outside the intelligence distribution of the rest of the group, (ac) children of nonwhite racial background, (d) children whose stay in school was too short to permit teacher ratings, and (e) children who refused to be photographed. At the time

of photographing, the children ranged in age from 2–6 to 2–11, 3–6 to 3–11, or 4–6 to 4–11. Socioeconomic status of the sample was biased upward and along academic lines: 95 per cent of the children's fathers held college degrees and over half held a degree at the doctoral level. As judged from the PARI scores of a subgroup, the children's mothers were relatively homogeneous in disagreeing with statements endorsing punitiveness and authoritarian control. The children formed a sample of well cared for, well nourished, healthy, bright subjects.

PROCEDURE

Each child was photographed in the nude in standard pose in front, side, and back position. The physique evaluations were made from these photographs by three judges, two of whom never saw the subjects and one of whom was acquainted with the children. Each judge rated each child for manifest level of three physique dimensions: endomorphy (roughly speaking, fatness), mesomorphy (muscle and bone development), and ectomorphy (slenderness).

A set of 63 rating scales was assembled for appraising the children's nursery school be-

SOURCE. *Selection from Monograph by Richard N. Walker, "Body build and behavior in young children: body build and nursery school teacher's ratings" in* Child Development Monograph, *pp. 75–79, 1962.*

havior. Before any ratings were made, a set of predictions was drawn up concerning the probable direction of correlation of each behavior item with each physique variable. These predictions were based on Sheldon's report of physique-behavior relations in college men.

The children were then rated on the behavior scales. Each was rated independently by four or five teachers. Of the 15 teachers who contributed ratings, three knew that these were to be used for physique-behavior comparisons. At least three naive judges' ratings were averaged with each rating by an informed judge. From the 63 individual items of the inventory, nine more general scales were developed, each composed of two to six intercorrelated items.

THE MEASURING INSTRUMENTS

Physique Ratings

Along with the 125 photographs of children whose behavior was rated, the judges evaluated an additional 249 photographs of children in the same age range who had attended the nursery school in previous years. Standard scores were computed for endomorphy, mesomorphy, and ectomorphy for each judge's ratings at each age and these were averaged for the three judges. These mean scores were transformed into somatotype-like scores with a mean of 3.5, a standard deviation of 1.0, and an interval of 0.5. Each physique component at each age then ranged by half steps from 1 or $1\frac{1}{2}$ to $6\frac{1}{2}$ or 7, with a mean of $3\frac{1}{2}$. Coefficients of reliability for the average of the standard scores of the three judges fell near 0.90 for endomorphy and ectomorphy at each age. Interjudge agreement in rating mesomorphy was lower, represented by coefficients of around 0.85 for the boys and around 0.70 for the girls. For a subsample of children rated at more than one age (two judges did not know which were repeats), all retest correlations for a one-year-interval reached or exceeded 0.90, when corrected for attenuation. The small group of children rated at 2 and 4 years showed lower values, though all exceeded 0.70.

Behavior Ratings

A rating of the child's compliance-resistance in the photographing situation was made by the photographer and, during the second year of the study, by the teacher assisting. Correlations between the two were 0.93 for the 31 boys rated by both, 0.80 for the 32 girls.

For the individual items of the nursery school behavior scale, Horst's index of reliability of the average of scores of multiple judges was computed for the first year's ratings. Median reliability indices for the different age groups ranged from 0.71 to 0.81. Reliability coefficients for the cluster scores for the total sample were higher, ranging from 0.75 to 0.92 and with two thirds of the coefficients exceeding 0.85.

RESULTS

Reaction to the Photographing Situation

While no age differences appeared in compliance ratings, marked differences appeared between the sexes, boys being the more resistant. Children of endomorphic physique tended to be resistant to the situation, while mesomorphs and ectomorphs tended to be compliant, in the case of both boys and girls. (Three of the six coefficients were significant.) Multiple correlations between the three physique variables and compliance reached 0.42 for boys, 0.67 for girls.

Outcome of the Predictions

Of the total of 292 predictions made for boys and girls for the three physique variables, 73 per cent were confirmed in direction and 21 per cent were confirmed beyond the 0.05 level while 3 per cent were disconfirmed beyond the 0.05 level. Sex differences in success of prediction were clear: over a third of predictions made for boys were significantly confirmed, less than 10 per cent for girls. The three physique components also showed differences in success ratios. Relations with mesomorphy were best predicted; for boys close to half the predictions made were confirmed at a significant level. Relations with ectomorphy were intermediate in success, though nearly as many predictions were confirmed significantly for boys. Relations with endomorphy were predicted with little better than chance success for the girls and slightly less than chance success for the boys.

Nursery School Behavior and Individual Physique Components

Endomorphy. For boys, only one cluster score, aggressiveness, correlated significantly with endomorphy, and this evidently by virtue of the correlation of both with mesomorphy. Ten individual behavior items were associated with endomorphy, six of them in a direction opposite to that which had been predicted. Together with nine items significant only at the 0.10 level, these give a picture of assertive aggressiveness (self-assertive, revengeful, easily angered, inconsiderate, quarrelsome, etc.), high energy level (ambitious, daring, noisy, boyish), extraversion (does not daydream, social in play), and low sensitivity (insensitive to pain, feelings not easily hurt, few nervous habits). For girls also one cluster score, cooperativeness, correlated significantly with endomorphy. Only a single individual rating item was significantly associated with endomorphy, though together with the four items significant at the 0.10 level it contributed to a consistent picture of good personal-social adjustment (recovers quickly from upsets, not tense, does not daydream, direct in solving social problems, social in play).

Mesomorphy. For boys, all but one of the nine cluster scores showed significant relation with mesomorphy, as did 24 of the individual rating items. The girls showed just three significant correlations between mesomorphy and the cluster scores, eight between mesomorphy and the individual rating items. Characteristic of both boys and girls high in mesomorphy is a dominating assertiveness (leader in play, competitive, self-assertive, easily angered, attacks others, etc.), high energy output, openness of expression, and fearlessness. The girls combine this assertiveness with socialness, cheerfulness, and warmth. The boys' items give more suggestion of

hostility (quarrelsome, revengeful, inconsiderate) and of an impulsive, headlong quality to their activity (daring, noisy, quick, accident prone, self-confident, etc.).

Ectomorphy. Boys and girls each showed two cluster scores which correlated with ectomorphy, but 27 individual items showed significant association with ectomorphy for the boys, just eight for the girls. In common for both sexes are items suggesting a certain aloofness (not social in play, does not attack others, daydreams, indirect in solving problems). Different items for boys and girls suggest an emotional restraint in both (boys: not easily angered, not expressive in movements, not talkative, etc.; girls: not dramatic, not open in expressing feelings, low verbal interests). For boys, the items in general define a cautious, quiet child, not self-assertive, hesitant to give offence, looking to adults rather than to children for approval, sensitive, slow to recover from upsets. He appears lacking in energy reserves (not energetic, dislikes gross motor play, enjoys hand activities, has few accidents). For girls, the composite picture is similar but tends more to indicate a somberness of outlook — unfriendly, tense, not gay or cheerful, irritable.

Total physique pattern. Combination of the three physique components in multiple regression correlation with the cluster scores gave little increase over the highest single-component coefficients for the boys, somewhat greater increase for the girls. The multiple correlations ranged from 0.20 to 0.52.

A graphic technique of analysis suggests higher relations, particularly for the boys. In this method, the physique rating of each individual is plotted on a somatotype distribution chart, the plotted point indicating whether the subject is below or above average on the cluster score in question. A single, straight cutting line is then drawn which separates the total distribution of subjects into (approximately) equal halves and which gives a maximum of above-average subjects in one half. For this dichotomy a tetrachoric correlation can be computed. For a majority of the nine traits, the cutting lines chosen by inspection closely approximated a single, common cutting line. For boys, a dichotomy contrasting mesomorphs and mesomorphic endomorphs with ectomorphs and ectomorphic endomorphs produced differences in rates of aggressiveness, energy level, and sensitivity corresponding to tetrachoric correlations in the 0.60's. The traits of fearfulness, cheerfulness, and cooperativeness showed less striking separation by this common cutting line. Two other cutting lines showed some suggestion of association with behavior differences in boys, though the evidence was weaker. A line separating endomorphs and ectomorphs appears to separate boys more oriented to peer approval from boys more oriented to adult approval. And a line separating endomorphs from mesomorphs separates boys resistant in the photographing situation from boys compliant in that setting.

For girls, only a single cutting line was found which appeared associated with behavior differences. Girls plotted in the mesomorphic area of the chart differ from other girls in showing greater aggressiveness, cheerfulness, socialness, and energy, as well as less fearfulness and less sensitivity.

Conclusions

It is concluded that in this group of preschool children important associations do exist between individuals' physiques and particular behavior characteristics. Further, these associations show considerable similarity to those described by Sheldon for college-aged men, though the strength of association is not as strong as he reports. It is suggested that the relations are multiply determined, arising from primary bodily conditions (e.g., strength, energy, sensory thresholds), from direct learnings concerning the efficacy of different modes of behavior and adjustment techniques, and from less direct learnings regarding expectations and evaluations accorded to different physiques by others. Other factors, possibly innate, as well as opportunity for and encouragement of particular behaviors, appear important in directing the physique-associated behavior. This is suggested by the mesomorphic girls' channeling of their energies more into social activities, the mesomorphic boys' more into physical, gross-motor activity. The young ages of the subjects would seem to give some weight to constitutional and direct-learning factors as contrasted with reputation variables, which others have pointed out as important at later ages. In particular, variations in physical energy, in bodily effectiveness for assertive or dominating behavior, and in bodily sensitivity appear as important mediating links between physique structure and general behavior.

2. *Maturation Rate and Body Build in Women*

DAVID McNEILL and NORMAN LIVSON

Three general statements may be made, with varying degrees of confidence, about female physique in relation to maturation: (*a*) becoming a woman, morphologically speaking, is in large part a matter of decreasing linearity in body build during adolescence; but (*b*) women who mature early are less slender at maturity than their later maturing peers. However, (*c*) this outcome is not attributable to differential growth during adolescence since such a difference in body build between these groups is apparent from childhood. For the first assertion the evidence of our senses should suffice although definitive data exist (2, 10). On the other two points, the literature can be seen to yield substantial consensus. However, because of the diversity of anthropometric ratios employed to measure linearity (various transverse diameters, as well as weight, in relation to height), an unequivocal synthesis of the available data is difficult.

Assessing adolescent maturation rate by remembered age at menarche, Stone and Barker(13) found very low, but

reliable, positive correlations of height/weight with menarcheal age in a group of physically mature women. This suggestion of lesser linearity in build for earlier maturing women is further supported in an analysis of extreme maturation groups by their significantly greater pelvic width/height. A later study led these same authors to conclude that, at maturity, "...women with later menarcheal ages tend toward the longitudinal (leptosomic) type, whereas those with early menarcheal ages tend toward the lateral (pyknic) type" (1, p. 221).

Both Richey and Shuttleworth used longitudinal growth data, hence had the advantage of contemporaneously determined maturation rate indices. Richey's (8) data permit the inference, from a rather indirect technique of comparing deviations over maturity subgroups of mean of true weights from height-predicted weights, that weight/height at maturity systematically increases with earlier menarche. Shuttleworth confirmed this relation (10) and extended it to age of maximum growth (11). In none of these studies has the statistical significance of the relation been evaluated but, in all, the relations have persisted throughout adolescence and, what is more to our third point, are clearly

SOURCE. *Article by David McNeill and Norman Livson, "Maturation rate and body build in women" in* Child development, *Vol. 34, pp. 25–32, 1963. Copyright by the Society for Research in Child Development, Inc., 1963.*

evident as early as age 6, well before the onset of the growth spurt.

Other longitudinal data tend to support such a relation of linearity of build in preadolescence with subsequent menarcheal age, but also indicate that the regression may be curvilinear. Reynolds and Wines(7) found that, at age 8, "very early" maturing girls are slightly *lower* in weight/height³, hence more linear than "somewhat early" girls, but both show more weight for height than "late" maturers. Since even the latest maturing girl in the "somewhat early" group achieves menarche before the mean age for the total sample, a combining of these groups establishes a clear difference on an early-late dichotomy. Also, using age 8 data and with menarche again as the maturation index, Simmons and Greulich(12) found a somewhat different result; their "early" maturing group does show most weight for height but, in this instance, the "late" group is less linear than the "middle" maturers.

From these studies the outlines of a generalization may be sketched: earlier maturing girls are more broadly built, whether by bodily proportions or weight/height ratios, well before their adolescence and maintain this differential through the growth spurt into maturity. However, due to the almost exclusive use of menarche as the measure of maturation rate, this conclusion suffers some loss in generality, and, perhaps because of the diversity of indices used to describe linearity, the precise form of the relation is very much in question. Were these limitations insufficient justification in themselves for a reconsideration of the question, Bayley's(2) unmistakable dissent would be an adequate challenge. She argues that the apparent relation is artifactual and that, in fact, there is none when proper account is taken of differential timing of development during adolescence. Later on, following

the presentation of our own findings, we will undertake a detailed analysis of this hypothesis and of the data adduced in its support.

In the present report, we intend to re-examine the relation of linearity of build to adolescent maturation rate. And, since somatotyping provides our primary assessment of physique, we also shall evaluate the contributions of other aspects of body build. A highly general measure of maturation rate in women is employed, and, through correlational techniques, its relation to the several indices of body build, considered separately and in conjunction, will be determined over their full normal ranges. Our final purpose is to carry out parallel analyses at maturity and preadolescence in order to provide data, collected within the context of a single longitudinal investigation, on the relevance of growth patterns *during* adolescence to the relations that may exist between maturation rate and body build.

METHOD

Sample

The sample ($N = 68$) includes all females from the Guidance Study of the Institute of Human Development for whom somatotypes and adequate longitudinal growth data were both available. The maximum allowable gap in measurement was three years (two years during adolescence) but, for the most part, the program of semiannual physical examinations until physical maturity insured more continuous records, with gaps of over one year being quite rare in the present data. A detailed description of the sample (born in the years 1928–1929) and of the anthropometric measures employed is to be found elsewhere (5, 14).

Index of Maturation Rate

The index of maturation rate is based on the Nicolson and Hanley(6) factor analysis of 14 indicators of adolescent maturation rate in Guidance Study females, which finds a single general factor sufficient to account for all reliable covariation. Since all indices were not present for all cases, separate regression equations were derived for every necessary combination so that each girl was assigned a Maturity Factor Score (MFS) which represented the best possible estimate which could be made from her available growth data. Most efficient ($R = 0.99$) and possible for a majority of the cases, was an equation employing age of reaching 90 per cent of mature height, skeletal age 12.75, and Reynolds and Wines hair stage II. In no instance did an estimator correlate less than 0.96 with the general factor.

Assignment of Somatotypes

A series of body photographs, starting at age 8 and, with few exceptions taken at half-yearly intervals, was available for each girl through to physical maturity. In most cases a photograph at about age 30 was also included. From these, and assisted by various anthropometric data, somatotypes were assigned. The procedure differs somewhat from the most recently published method(9), and a comparison of results from the two methods is presented in an earlier publication (4).[1]

Results

For the present sample, the mean values (and standard deviations) for the somatotype components are: endomorphy, 5.2 (0.84); mesomorphy, 3.1 (0.62); ectomorphy, 3.1 (0.95). These means coincide

---

[1]Dr. William Sheldon and his staff, particularly Ann Turner, are responsible for the somatotype data in this study. The ratings employed here are based upon his recent revision in procedure wherein three anthropometric indices completely determine somatotype in most cases. These are: minimum ponderal index (height/cube root of weight), trunk index (ratio of cross-sectional areas, upper torso/lower torso), and mature height.

with the modal female somatotype reported by Sheldon (9). The intercorrelations of the three components are: endomorphy $\times$ mesomorphy, -0.21; endomorphy $\times$ ectomorphy, -0.51; mesomorphy $\times$ ectomorphy, -0.42.

Both endomorphy and ectomorphy are significantly related to MFS, and in the expected directions; mesomorphy is essentially unrelated (*see* Table 1). In no case is there an indication of curvilinear regression. The multiple R between MFS and the three components is 0.49 ($p < 0.001$).

An examination of the *beta* coefficients and second-order partial correlations yields some surprises. Mesomorphy, which has a negligible first-order relation to MFS, nevertheless is significantly weighted in the prediction of maturation rate variance and, were the other two components to be held constant, would predict the remaining variance quite well. On the other hand, the substantial first-order contribution of ectomorphy vanishes entirely in multiple prediction and, with the influence of the other components removed, ectomorphy is still unrelated to maturation rate. Endomorphy apparently absorbs this variance since, when it is partialled out of the ectomorphy $\times$ MFS relationship, the remaining correlation (-0.12) is not significant.

This failure of ectomorphy to make a unique contribution to the relation of body build and maturational rate suggests a speculation as to the specific morphological basis of its first-order relation. Evidently there is a characteristic of physique common to the endomorphy and ectomorphy components which is responsible for their first-order correlation with MFS while whatever is unique to ectomorphy is unrelated to maturational rate. Among the three parameters on which our somatotypes are based (*see* footnote 2), endomorphy and ectomorphy are both substantially related to

Table 1   Relations of Somatotype Components to Maturity Factor Scores (MFS)

(N = 68)

	r	BETA COEFFICIENT	SECOND-ORDER PARTIAL r
Endomorphy	0.43†	0.53‡	0.40‡
Mesomorphy	0.14	0.28*	0.36†
Ectomorphy	−0.31†	0.08	0.06

*$p \leqslant 0.05$.
†$p \leqslant 0.01$.
‡$p \leqslant 0.001$.

only one of them, the minimum ponderal index (PI_{min}) with which they correlate, respectively, −0.90 and 0.75. Since these values are so high and since PI_{min} relates about as strongly to MFS (−0.40) as do either of the components, we may hazard the conclusion that this index accounts for their common relation to maturation rate. Further, mature height, another somatotype parameter, correlates 0.62 with ectomorphy and not at all (0.06) with endomorphy, being thus a unique attribute of ectomorphic physique and, presumably, unrelated to maturation rate. This proves to be the case; mature height is insignificantly (−0.09) correlated with MFS. It is clear, then, that the relation of ectomorphy—and, for that matter, endomorphy—to maturation rate is largely mediated by PI_{min}, a common index of linearity.

Do these relations predate adolescence and survive into maturity? Somatotyping —as it is assessed in this study and, for that matter, as its theoretical rationale would insist—is intended to be a description of the enduring nature of the physique. Therefore, we must turn to age-dated body build indices in order to consider the question. Since, as we have just seen, PI_{min} accounts for most, if not all, of the relation between somatotype and maturation rate, good estimates of this parameter from anthropometric data obtained at preadolescence and at

maturity would serve our purpose. These data were available: ponderal indices computed from measurements at age 8 (PI_8)—well before the onset of pubescence for even our earliest maturers— and at maturity (PI_{mat}) correlate 0.80 and 0.90, respectively, with PI_{min}. In turn, both of these indices have correlations of −0.40 with MFS, identical with the value obtained for PI_{min} (and for endomorphy). Thus, it is clear that the relations between body build and maturational rate—at least as determined by the present indices—are enduring ones in the sense that they are certainly not a product of growth patterns during adolescence.

Discussion

The present findings accord well with the previous literature, confirming a negative association, for women, of slenderness of build with earliness of maturation in adolescence. However, the suggestion that the relation may be a curvilinear one finds no support in our data. Further, almost one third of the variability in maturation rate can be predicted from physique, as it is described by somatotype, but, to the extent that this method affords a comprehensive assessment of body build, considerable reliable variance remains independent of morphology in women. This contrasts with the result for males where, in a study of similar design, none of the somatotype components was significantly correlated with maturation rate (4).

Interestingly enough, the ponderal index (height/cube root of weight), which can account for the bulk of the association in our data, refers to very much the same aspect of body build — some variant of a height/weight ratio — for which maturational relations have been reported by several earlier investigators. In fact, with the ponderal index (PI_{min}) partialled out, not one of the components remains significantly correlated with MFS so that this single anthropometric index is, by itself, a fully sufficient measure[2]. And, since the ponderal index at age 8 is as highly correlated with MFS as is the minimum value, PI_8 can serve as a very easily obtained *predictor* of adolescent maturation rate, used alone or, by a multiple regression equation, in conjunction with a skeletal age determination. A further implication of this result is that a complete somatotype description of physique provides no more information on the present question than can be derived from but one of the anthropometric indices upon which it depends.

As to Bayley's (2) claim that any apparent relation between body build and maturation rate is an artifact of differential growth patterns during adolescence, our results, like those of others, are in disagreement. Yet she does present data in support of her argument, and these either must be reconciled or, failing in this, be left to stand in apparent contradiction to the general finding. Perhaps a review of her rationale will help. Linear-

ity of build, she would maintain, *seems* to be associated with later maturation simply because all girls grow less slender as they approach maturity. Later maturing girls, at any point of development and especially during adolescence, are relatively less mature, hence appear more slender. Thus, she reasons, girls differing in maturation rate would show no differences in body build if they were to be compared at the same maturational *status* during adolescent development.

Following through on this rationale, Bayley set up three groups differing in maturation rate (Early, Average, and Late, as determined by CA at skeletal maturity) and, for each group, constructed growth curves for bi-iliac/height in which group means on this index of linearity were plotted against *skeletal* age. This technique was intended to insure that girls of differing maturation rates would be compared at the same maturational status. The same blanket adjustment, based on group mean differences in maturational level, was applied to all cases within each maturity group. For example, all Early girls were regarded as precisely one year in advance of Average girls, the mean difference between the two groups. Thus, only for a girl whose relative maturational status coincided with the mean of her own maturity group would the correction have been an exact one.

Proceeding in this manner, Bayley finds an almost perfect superimposition of the mean bi-iliac/height growth curves for the Early, Average, and Late groups over a five-year age range (skeletal ages 11.7 to 16.7). And it is this result which supports the conclusion that "Differences in hip-width relative to height are *not related to rate of maturing in girls when they are equated for skeletal age*" (2, p. 60; italics in original). Yet we, and others, do find such differences both at age 8, before any significant acceleration in growth rate has

---

[2]Holding PI_{min} constant, the correlations with MFS were: endomorphy, 0.16; mesomorphy, 0.11; ectomorphy, −0.01.

occurred, and at maturity—when, by definition, skeletal age is equated.

We believe the contradiction may be resolved by an analysis of the effects of equating for skeletal age by mean group differences rather than by individual differences. The three maturity groups derive from a tripartitioning of the distribution of age at reaching skeletal maturity. The distributions for the Early and Late groups are, therefore, necessarily sharply skewed, being the tails of a normal curve. (The fate of the Average group is irrelevant to this analysis.) This skewness is maintained, although a bit reduced, in the skeletal age distributions for given CAs at which the two groups have been matched on mean skeletal age. The Early group would be skewed positively; the Late, negatively. Bayley apparently made the simplifying assumption that, if skeletal age means were matched in this manner, then the absence of true body build differences among maturity groups would be demonstrated by a failure of the bi-iliac/height means to show significant between-group variation. This, however, is an incorrect statement of the null hypothesis for the present case. Since bi-iliac/height doubtlessly correlates less than unity with skeletal age, the resultant distributions of bi-iliac/height for the Early and Late groups would, through regression, be less skewed and have their means displaced, in opposite directions, from equality. The Early group mean must shift *downward* towards greater slenderness; the Late group mean, *upward* towards greater broadness. Because of this, extreme groups matched on skeletal age means *necessarily* differ on their bi-iliac/height means; the Late maturing group will appear to be *broader* than the Early group when, in fact, no true relation exists. Under these circumstances, one would expect to find equality of mean bi-iliac/height between groups only if

there were a reliable difference in the *opposite* direction—Late more slender than Early—of a magnitude sufficient to overcome the artificial difference.[3] The fact, therefore, that Bayley finds the Early and Late curves to be superimposed actually demonstrates the existence of a body build difference, and in the expected direction, between girls differing in maturation rate.[4] By this analysis, then, the generalization that earlier maturing women are less linear in build appears to have been made, at least for the moment, unanimous.

Summary

The literature gives considerable, but not unequivocal, support to the proposition that maturation rate and linearity of body build in women are negatively related. The present study re-examines this question, employing highly general measures of both physique and maturation rate, and places special emphasis on evaluating the Bayley hypothesis that such an association is a transient adolescent phenomenon, deriving from differential time of the adolescent growth spurt.

A sample of girls ($N = 68$) from whom adequate longitudinal growth data were available was employed; maturation rate

---

[3]This artifact would have been avoided if, in adjusting groups to a common maturational status, the bi-iliac/height index for each girl had been estimated for the precise time she attained a given skeletal age. This method of controlling for maturational differences on an individual basis is an admittedly cumbersome procedure, but it does make legitimate the direct comparison of group means on bi-iliac/height.

[4]In a recent personal communication, Bayley points out that this general result can be inferred from the mean values of height and weight for groups differing in maturation rate which she reports in a later publication (3).

was assessed by a general factor score, and somatotype provided the primary description of body build. Endomorphy is found to be significantly associated with earlier maturation; ectomorphy is negatively, and less strongly, related; mesomorphy bears no significant first-order relationship to maturation rate. It does, however, contribute significantly to the three-component multiple correlation $(R = 0.49, \ p < 0.001)$ in which endomorphy is the major predictor; ectomorphy makes no independent contribution. The ponderal index (height/cube root of weight) can account entirely for the somatotype-maturation rate covariation. Also, the relation remains undiminished when the index is based on data at age 8 or at skeletal maturity. The latter finding establishes the association between linearity of build and maturation rate as an enduring one, not dependent upon adolescent growth spurt timing.

References

1. Barker, R. G., & Stone, C. P. Physical development in relation to menarcheal age in university women. *Hum. Biol.*, 1936, **8**, 198–222.

2. Bayley, N. Size and body build of adolescents in relation to rate of skeletal maturing. *Child Developm.*, 1943, 14, 47–90.

3. Bayley, N. Growth curves of height and weight by age for boys and girls, scaled according to physical maturity. *J. Pediat.*, 1956, **48**, 187–194.

4. Livson, N., & McNeill, D. Physique and maturation rate in male adolescents. *Child Develpm.*, 1962, **33**, 145–152.

5. Macfarlane, J. W. Studies in child guidance: I. Methodology of data collection and organization. *Monogr. Soc. Res. Child Develpm.*, 1938, **3**, No. 6 (Serial No. 19).

6. Nicolson, A. B., & Hanley, C. Indices of physiological maturity: derivations and interrelationships. *Child Develpm.*, 1953, **24**, 3–28.

7. Reynolds, E. L., & Wines, J. V. Individual differences in physical changes associated with adolescence in girls. *Amer. J. Dis. Child.*, 1948, **75**, 329–350.

8. Richey, H. G. The relation of accelerated, normal and retarded puberty to the height and weight of school children. *Monogr. Soc. Res. Child. Develpm.*, 1937, **2**, No. 1 (Serial No. 8).

9. Sheldon, W. H. *Atlas of men.* Harper, 1954.

10. Shuttleworth, F. K. Sexual maturation and the physical growth of girls age six to nineteen. *Monogr. Soc. Res. Child Develpm.*, 1937, **2**, No. 5 (Serial No. 12).

11. Shuttleworth, F. K. The physical and mental growth of girls and boys age six to nineteen in relation to age at maximum growth. *Monogr. Soc. Res. Child Developm.*, 1939, **4**, No. 3 (Seria. No. 22).

12. Simmons, K., & Greulich, W. W. Menarcheal age and the height, weight and skeletal age of girls age 7 to 17 years. *J. Pediat.*, 1943, **22**, 518–548.

13. Stone, C. P., & Barker, R. G. On the relation between menarcheal age and certain aspects of personality, intelligence and physique in college women. *J. genet. Psychol.*, 1934, **45**, 121–135.

14. Tuddenham, R. D., & Snyder, M. M. Physical growth of California boys and girls from birth to 18 years. *Univer. Calif. Publ. Child Develpm.*, 1954, **1**, No. 2.

3. *Physique and Motivation*

JUAN B. CORTÉS AND FLORENCE M. GATTI

In accordance with the large collection of research findings on *n* Ach published by D. C. McClelland and his associates, it was hypothesized that mesomorphy would correlate positively with *n* Ach. The *Ss* were 100 nondelinquent and 100 delinquent boys with a mean of 17½ yr. They were somatotyped following, not Sheldon's, but Parnell's more recent and objective method. They also took the test that McClelland has used in various countries for measuring *n* Ach as well as other kinds of motivation. A positive and significant correlation between mesomorphy and *n* Ach was obtained in both samples as well as a negative and significant correlation between ectomorphy and *n* Ach. Other types of motivation were also studied.

This paper may be considered as a sequel to one on physique and self-description of temperament we have recently published (Cortés & Gatti, 1965). There we reported a strong and significant association between physique, or body-build, and some temperamental traits. Endomorphs (persons with a predominance of the organs derived from the endodermic layer and who tend to be physically round, soft, circular, and fat) rated themselves significantly more often as being kind, relaxed, warm, soft-hearted; mesomorphs (those with a predominance of organs derived from the mesodermic layer and who tend to be physically strong, hard, athletic, and muscular) rated themselves significantly more often as being confident, energetic, adventurous, enterprising; ectomorphs (individuals with a predominance of the organs derived from the ectodermic layer and who tend to be physically thin, tall, weak, and linear) rated themselves significantly more often as being detached, tense, shy, reserved.

Among other investigators, McClelland, Atkinson, Clark, and Lowell (1953), McClelland (1961, 1964, 1965), and Atkinson (1958, 1964) have been instrumental in creating the current interest in need for Achievement (*n* Ach) and in their publications both of them have accumulated a large collection of research findings on this type of motivation. Other human motives also studied by similar methods in the past years, though not so intensively, have been need for Affiliation (*n* Aff; Shipley & Veroff, 1953), *n* Power (Veroff, 1957) and *n* Sex (Clark,

SOURCE: *Article by Juan B. Cortés and Florence M. Gatti, "Physique and motivation" in the* Journal of consulting psychology, *Vol. 30, pp. 408–414, 1966. Copyright 1966 by the American Psychological Association and reprinted by permission.*

1952, 1955, 1956). With regard to *n* Ach, which will be the main concern of the present study, the results of this large collection of experimental findings afford a composite portrait of a person with high scores in *n* Ach as someone who is concerned over accomplishments, who wishes to do well at what he undertakes, and who is energetic, confident, competitive nonconforming, and enterprising. Such a person is predisposed toward innovations, toward working at tasks which are not safe and traditional and which involve some element of risk — in sum, is a person who possesses and demonstrates great energy, both physically and psychologically. Therefore, a natural outgrowth of our previous study was to hypothesize that persons high in *n* Ach would also be high in mesomorphy, the energetic component of physique.

METHOD

Subjects

In Experiment 1, our subjects (*S*s) were 100 boys of a mean age of $17\frac{1}{2}$ years, seniors of a private high school in Boston. We asked the dean of the school to supply boys between 17 and 18 years of age, and of the eight senior class sections he indicated three with a total of 98 boys. Section A (31 boys) was an Honor Science class made up of the best students, with an average IQ of 136 according to the California Test of Mental Maturity. Section C (32 boys) was among the poorest sections in scholastic grades, with the boys averaging an IQ of 114. Finally, Section H (35 boys) was an intermediate group with an average IQ of 127. To complete the requested 100, two other boys were added from another section. All the *S*s were Catholic, the majority belonged to the middle class, and 92% later attended college. The mean somatotype of these *S*s (obtained by the method to be mentioned below) was 3.91–3.55–3.53. None of the *S*s had ever been involved with the police.

In Experiment 2, we tested 100 delinquents,

again of a mean age of $17\frac{1}{2}$ years. Seventy of these delinquents were institutionalized, and 30 were noninstitutionalized. The criterion for delinquency was conviction and sentence by the court. The noninstitutionalized *S*s were either on probation or under suspended sentence. The institution authorities, or probation officers, selected the *S*s who met the age criterion. Since there were not many delinquents over 17 years of age at the institutions, we tested practically all the boys of the two Massachusetts reform schools to which we applied. The mean somatotype of these 100 delinquents was 3.50–4.40–3.06. No data were collected on the IQ of these *S*s; however, their fathers differed significantly from the fathers of the *S*s in Experiment 1, both in educational and occupational levels.

Procedure

As it is known, somatotyping is an attempt at a quantification of the primary physical components of the human constitution. All *S*s were somatotyped by means of Parnell's method. This particular method was selected for reasons of objectivity, consistency and convenience. A detailed explanation of how somatotyping is done may be found in Parnell's (1958) book, *Behavior and Physique*. According to Parnell, the first physical component or endomorphy, is obtained by measuring the subcutaneous fat in three sites of the body. The second component, mesomorphy, is secured by measuring certain bones and muscles of the arms and legs. These measurements are taken in centimeters, with steel calipers and tapes. The third component, ectomorphy, is obtained by dividing the height over the cube root of weight. Once the measurements are known, and after taking the age and other factors into consideration, the published norms (see Parnell, 1958, p. 21) immediately indicate the somatotype, or individual amount of these three physical components.

To measure the *n* Ach, as well as *n* Aff and *n* Power, we employed the standard set of six pictures (representing men in a variety of common but ambiguous situations) which has been widely used by McClelland and his associates in this and other countries. The set comprises the pictures numbered 5, 28, 83, 9,

24, and 53, respectively, in Atkinson's (1958, Appendix III, pp. 831 ff.) master list. This projective test is similar to Murray's Thematic Apperception Test (TAT). The 200 Ss were asked to write a story for 5 full minutes about each of the six pictures. No instructions were given other than those printed with the test. In order to avoid any danger of bias, the stories of the Ss in Experiment 1 were not scored for *n* Ach by the writers. Instead, this work was done by an expert scorer, one of McClelland's associates, who neither had seen the Ss previously nor had any knowledge of the somatotype or of the hypothesis being tested. After having somatotyped the boys, the senior author, who had also been associated with McClelland for approximately 5 years, scored over 100 of the stories, and a coefficient of agreement was found of +0.93 between both scorers. The stories of the Ss in Experiment 2 were scored by the senior author after estimating the somatotypes of the boys. Furthermore, 10 tests, or 60 stories were rescored by the previous expert scorer. The coefficient of agreement was again very high: +0.95. None of the delinquents classified as high or low in *n* Ach were classified differently by the other experimenter. In the results to be presented below, the scoring of the expert was the only one we have taken into consideration for the 100 nondelinquent Ss. In the case of the 100 delinquent Ss (Experiment 2), the scoring used was that obtained by the senior author. In both instances the norms for scoring have been those published in Atkinson's (1958, pp. 179–204) *Motives in Fantasy, Action, and Society*. Although another type of test was used and other motives were also scored (which will be discussed briefly below), we will now present the results concerning only physique and *n* Ach for both groups of Ss.

Results

Nondelinquents. We obtained a significant and positive association between mesomorphy and *n* Ach, as it was hypothesized, and a significant but negative association between ectomorphy and *n* Ach. The correlations between *n* Ach and mesomorphy and ectomorphy are, respectively, +0.35 and −0.27. Both correlations for a sample of 100 are significant beyond the 0.01 level of probability. Endomorphy also correlates positively with *n* Ach, but the correlation, +0.16, is low and not significant. However, those correlations may underemphasize our findings. According to Sheldon (1954, p. 34), the mean somatotype of 46,000 Americans is 3.3–4.1–3.4. In each component, the same amount, say 4, does not possess the same strength since the 4 would be higher than average in the first and third components but not in the second. If we transform the somatotype of 4–4–4 into its percentile values we obtain 80–55–75 (Sheldon, 1954, p. 33), which indicates that a 4 in ectomorphy is higher than a 4 in mesomorphy for the American male population. Moreover each physical component is influenced by the strength of the other two. In the somatotypes 4–4–2 and 2–4–4, the 4 in mesomorphy probably has a higher strength in the first than in the second example of somatotype because the negative correlation between the second and third components is higher than between the first and second components (−0.63 and −0.29, respectively, in Sheldon, 1942, p. 400).

It is for these reasons that we conducted various chi-square tests. All the results were highly significant. Tables 1 and 2 present two of these tests with the observed frequencies concerning *n* Ach and mesomorphy and ectomorphy in 2 × 2 contingency tables. In Table 1 the entire sample has been classified into two groups: those Ss whose mesomorphy is higher than their ectomorphy (disregarding the first component) and those Ss whose ectomorphy is higher than their mesomorphy. In cases of equal numbers in the somatotype for both components, ectomorphy has been considered as being higher in accordance with the data

TABLE 1   *Mesomorphy, Ectomorphy, and* n
Ach in Nondelinquents

n ACH	Ss HIGHER IN MESOMORPHY THEN ECTOMORPHY	Ss HIGHER IN ECTOMORPHY THAN MESOMORPHY
High	34 (80%)	18 (31%)
Low	8 (19%)	40 (69%)

Note.$-\chi^2 = 22.36, p < 0.0001$.

TABLE 2   *Mesomorphy, Ectomorphy and* n
Ach in Nondelinquents

n ACH	MESOMORPHS	ECTOMORPHS
Above median	30(80%)	6(19%)
Below median	5(15%)	25(81%)

Note.$-\chi^2 = 26.58, p < 0.0001$.

reported above. In Table 2, we have included the Ss who were above average in mesomorphy and ectomorphy (with a rating of 4.0 or better) and above or below the median in *n* Ach (a rating of 7 or higher and a rating of 6 or lower). The Ss who were average in both components, mesomorphy and ectomorphy, have been omitted from Table 2 in order to keep both groups mutually exclusive as required for the chi-square test.

Table 1 shows that of the 42 Ss whose mesomorphy is higher than their ectomorphy, 34, or 80%, are above the median in *n* Ach. Table 2 shows that of the 35 Ss above the class average in mesomorphy, 30, or 85%, are above the median in *n* Ach. Inverse results and percentages were found concerning those Ss whose ectomorphy is higher than their mesomorphy, or who are above average in ectomorphy (31% and 19%, respectively). There can be little doubt that in this sample *n* Ach is both positively and significantly associated with mesomorphy, and negatively and significantly associated with ectomorphy.

Delinquents.   In the sample of delinquents, we obtained a correlation between *n* Ach and mesomorphy of +0.20 which is significant at the 0.05 level of probability. Tables 3 and 4 offer the results for the 100 delinquents following exactly the same criteria used for Tables 1 and 2, respectively.

Although the results are not so significant in this sample (probably due to reasons to be discussed later), there is still a positive and significant association between mesomorphy and *n* Ach, and a negative and significant association between ectomorphy and *n* Ach. In both tables the data are significant beyond the 0.05 level of probability. It should also be added that no significant difference in *n* Ach was found between the institutionalized and noninstitutionalized delinquents.

Decisions Test.   The 100 nondelinquents were also administered another test, the results which may now be mentioned. This test, which we term Decisions

TABLE 3   *Mesomorphy, Ectomorphy, and* n
Ach in Delinquents

n ACH	Ss HIGHER IN MESOMORPHY THEN ECTOMORPHY	Ss HIGHER IN ECTOMORPHY THAN MESOMORPHY
High	43	12
Low	26	19

Note.$-\chi^2 = 3.88, p < 0.05$.

TABLE 4   *Mesomorphy, Ectomorphy, and* n
Ach in Delinquents

n ACH	MESOMORPHS	ECTOMORPHS
Above median	38	4
Below median	20	10

Note.$-\chi^2 = 4.90, p < 0.05$.

Test consists of 22 different situations showing two alternatives and the Ss are asked to decide which one of the two they prefer. Some examples of these situations will clarify our meaning:

10. *A group of boys have planned a farewell picnic at Crane's Beach on Saturday. All of Joe's friends will be there, and it will be the first time he will see some of them for a long time. They are going into the service. Joe wants to go but he has a college entrance examination that he feels he could well do some studying on. What do you think Joe should do?*
    10a. *He should be with his friends. (n Affiliation)*
    10b. *He should stay home and study. (n Achievement)*
19. *George has gotten back from the Army and is thinking about going to college. He is deeply in love with a fine girl whom he wants to marry. If he decides to marry her, however, he will have to give up college.*
    19a. *He should go to College. (n Achievement)*
    19b. *He should marry the girl. (n Sex).*

The test was designed to measure *n* Ach, *n* Aff, and *n* Sex. The type of need that the decisions might reveal was not decided by the writers but was determined by the agreement of two psychologists, one of whom was D. C. McClelland. A score of 1 was given for each positive decision implying *n* Ach. It may be argued

that the test probably measures value judgments rather than motives, or that, to say the least, it measures motives at a more conscious level than McClelland's test. The Ss, however, were asked not to judge the alternatives but to decide between them, perhaps manifesting in their decisions values either influenced by motives or associated with motives to some degree. It is not unlikely that both tests, the above mentioned and that of McClelland, may be measuring elements of a common variable of personality at two different but somewhat interrelated levels. In fact, the *n* Ach scores obtained by both tests correlate $+0.22$ ($p < 0.05$). Some evidence for this assumption is also afforded by the finding that the correlations obtained between physique and *n* Ach follow exactly the same pattern which was found in the previous test.

Table 5 shows the correlations between *n* Ach, as measured by this test, and each of the three components of physique. The table also offers the correlations between *n* Ach and physique found previously in our two samples by means of the projective test. Thus, it may serve as a summary of all the data reported so far.

By means of the Decisions Test, the correlation between *n* Ach and mesomorphy is still higher and more significant than with the projective test. The number of Ss for the second test was only 91 because it was given at the end of the testing session and some Ss did not have time to

TABLE 5   *Correlations between n Ach, as measured by the Two Tests, and each of the Basic Components of Physique in Delinquents and Nondelinquents*

MOTIVE	N	CATEGORY	ENDOMORPHY	MESOMORPHY	ECTOMORPHY	TYPE OF TEST
n Ach	100	Nondelinquent	$+0.16$	$+0.35$†	-0.27†	McClelland's test
n Ach	91	Nondelinquent	$+0.15$	$+0.54$‡	-0.20*	Decisions test
n Ach	100	Delinquent	$+0.01$	$+0.20$*	-0.06	McClelland's test

*$p < 0.05$.
†$p < 0.01$.
‡$p < 0.001$.

complete it. But in Table 5 it appears suggestive that although the samples of delinquents and nondelinquents differed in so many variables, the correlations between mesomorphy and *n* Ach are positive and significant in both samples, and also, that in the sample of nondelinquents, by using both types of tests, positive and significant correlations have been found to exist. In Table 5, mesomorphy appears definitely associated with *n* Ach. Nuttall (1964) has also obtained similar although small and not significant correlations (+ 0.07 between *n* Ach and mesomorphy; − 0.05 between *n* Ach and ectomorphy). His *S*s numbered about 200 Negroes, male and female. However, he used a very rough estimate of the somato-type (merely the height divided by the cube root of weight), and for measuring *n* Ach he used only two pictures which had never been previously employed.

Other Motives. McClelland's test was also scored, following the published norms (see Atkinson, 1958, pp. 205–233) for *n* Aff, *n* Power, and *n* Sex. No significant correlations were found between physique and these needs. As indicated above, the Decisions Test was also designed to measure *n* Aff and *n* Sex. The meaning of this last need was interpreted in a broad sense: those decisions which implied socially accepted relationships with the other sex (to avoid the inhibiting factor which seems to operate when measuring this need) such as marriage, spending time with the girl friend, danc-

ing, etc. were scored for *n* Sex.

In the case of *n* Aff, a significant but low and negative correlation was obtained between ectomorphy and *n* Aff (−0.20). The findings on *n* Sex may be of some interest. In his volume *Varieties of Temperament*, Sheldon (1942) reports significant correlations between physique and *n* Sex. He defines sexuality as "the relative importance and prominence of the sexual impulse in the individual's history" (Sheldon, 1942, p. 286). After long and detailed interviews with each of his 200 *S*s, most of them college students, Sheldon assigned to them ratings of from 7 to 1 in their sexuality thus defined. The significant correlations he obtained between this need and the basic components of physique are presented in Table 6 together with the correlations we obtained by means of the Decisions Test.

Our correlations are not significant, and probably Sheldon's results cannot be accepted at their face value, but it appears suggestive that in both instances the trend is in the same direction, and that ectomorphy is the only physical component that correlates positively with *n* Sex. These results do not warrant any conclusions, but they indicate that the topic might deserve further investigation.

Before discussing the data thus far presented, we should mention in passing that the delinquents of our sample were significantly higher in the mesomorphic component, as other investigators, using less objective methods of somatotyping, have already reported (see Gibbens,

TABLE 6 *Physique and Need for Sex*

MOTIVE	N	AGE RANGE	ENDOMORPHY	MESOMORPHY	ECTOMORPHY	METHOD	INVESTIGATOR
n Sex	200	17–31	−0.43†	−0.16*	+0.54†	Interview	Sheldon
n Sex	91	17–18	−0.10	−0.13	+0.14	Decisions test	Cortés-Gatti

*$p < 0.05$.
†$p < 0.01$.

1963; Glueck & Glueck, 1950; Sheldon, 1949). They were also higher, though not significantly so, in *n* Ach. The means in *n* Ach were, respectively, 7.61 for the 100 delinquents and 7.09 for the 100 non-delinquents. The nonsignificant correlation, reported above, between meso-morphy and *n* Power, was positive. The delinquents, higher in mesomorphy than the nondelinquents, were also significantly higher in *n* Power ($F = 8.699$, $p < 0.01$).

Discussion

The main finding of this study has been a significant relationship between the mesomorphic component and *n* Ach. We have verified such a relationship in three separate instances, by using two tests in Experiment 1 with nondelinquents and by administering one of these tests to a very different sample in Experiment 2. Obviously the relationship found is not one of cause and effect. The results allow us to speak only of an association between *n* Ach and physique, an association which is not due to chance but which cannot be called very strong for the positive correlations between the variables are not high, varying from $+0.20$ to $+0.54$. We cannot even determine which variable comes first, physique or *n* Ach, nor whether both variables are directly influenced by a third common factor.

We have shown, nevertheless, that physique is a relevant variable in the field of motivation, or, more concretely, in the case of *n* Ach. The two samples tested differed in many variables, such as intelligence, socioeconomic status, educational level of the parents, and family background (64% of the delinquents came from broken homes versus only 14% of the nondelinquents). Also,

but to a lesser degree, they differed in race (9 delinquents were Negroes), ethnic origin (most nondelinquents were of Italian or Irish descent), and religion (24 delinquents were Protestant; all nondelinquents were Catholic). Despite all this, the correlations obtained have been consistent.

Veroff, Atkinson, Feld, and Gurin (1960) conducted a nationwide survey to assess motivation. They tested a representative sample of 1,619 adults and found the *n* Ach was significantly related to the number of words in the stories, to education, broken homes (*n* Ach was higher in individuals from intact homes), social class (*n* Ach higher in middle class), and race (*n* Ach lower in Negroes). If these factors were all-important, they would have obscured to a much greater degree the association between meso-morphy and *n* Ach in Experiment 2, for the delinquents were affected by all these significant variables. In particular, the average number of words for the six stories of nondelinquents was 562.1 versus 408.7 for the delinquents. Nevertheless, even without any correction for length of protocol, the mean *n* Ach of delinquents was higher than the mean of nondelinquents. If we were to follow the correction for length of protocol adopted by Veroff et al. (1960), our sample of delinquents would be significantly higher ($t = 3.87$, $p < 0.001$) in *n* Ach than the sample of nondelinquents.

But in interpreting the association between physique and *n* Ach we should proceed with extreme caution. We believe that most motives are learned and that environmental factors do play a very important role in the field of motivation. The lower correlations found in the sample of delinquents give added support to this belief. Moreover, it is not asserted, and cannot be asserted, that physique directly influences needs and motives. However, it seems reasonable to assume that physique, through the organs of the body, glandular secretions, and the particular chemotype, predisposes, together with many other variables, toward some types of motivation more than toward others. It also appears reasonable to assume that if *n* Ach means high degree of psychological energy, which leads individuals toward entrepreneurship, innovations, and calculated risks, those persons who by nature have a high degree of physical energy will possess a better endowment for that type of motivation. We are merely postulating some amount of continuity between physical and psychological energy. Only a biased attitude toward biological factors will deny some degree of probability to this interpretation.

References

Atkinson, J. W. (Ed.) *Motives in fantasy, action, and society*. Princeton, N. J.: Van Nostrand, 1958.

Atkinson, J. W. *An introduction to motivation*. Princeton, N. J.: Van Nostrand, 1964.

Clark, R. A. The projective measurement of experimentally induced levels of sexual motivation. *Journal of Experimental Psychology*, 1952, **44**, 391–399.

Clark, R. A. The effects of sexual motivation on phantasy. In D. C. McClelland (Ed.), *Studies in motivation*. New York: Appleton-Century-Crofts, 1955. Pp. 44–57.

Clark, R. A., & Sensibar, M. R. The relationships between symbolic and manifest projections of sexuality with some incidental correlates. *Journal of Abnormal and Social Psychology*, 1956, **50**, 327–34.

Cortés, J. B., & Gatti, F. M. Physique and selfdescription of temperament. *Journal of Consulting Psychology*, 1965, **29**, 432–439.

Glueck, S., & Glueck, E. *Unraveling juvenile delinquency*. New York: The Commonwealth Fund, 1950.

Gibbens, T. C. N. *Psychiatric studies of Borstal lads*. New York: Oxford University Press, 1963.

McClelland, D. C. *The achieving society*. Princeton, N. J.: Van Nostrand, 1961.

McClelland, D. C. The roots of consciousness. Princeton, N. J.: Van Nostrand, 1964.

McClelland, D. C. N achievement and entrepreneurship: A longitudinal study. *Journal of Personality and Social Psychology*, 1965, **1**, 389–392.

McClelland, D. C., Atkinson, J. W., Clark, R. A., & Lowell, E. L. *The achievement motive*. New York, Appleton-Century-Crofts, 1953.

Nuttall, R. L. Some correlates of high need for achievement among urban northern Negroes. *Journal of Abnormal and Social Psychology*, 1964, **68**, 593–600.

Parnell, R. W. *Behavior and physique: An introduction to practical and applied somatometry.* London: E. Arnold, 1958.

Sheldon, W. H. (with the collaboration of S. S. Stevens). *The varieties of temperament.* New York: Harper, 1942.

Sheldon, W. H. (with the collaboration of E. M. Hartl & E. McDermott). *Varieties of delinquent youth.* New York: Harper, 1949.

Sheldon, W. H. (with the collaboration of C. W. Dupertuis and E. McDermott). *Atlas of men: A guide for somatotyping the adult male at all ages.* New York: Harper, 1954.

Shipley, T. E., & Veroff, J. A projective measure of need affiliation. *Journal of Experimental Psychology*, 1952, **43**, 349–356.

Veroff, J. Development and validation of a projective measure of power motivation. *Journal of Abnormal and Social Psychology*, 1957, **54**, 1–8.

Veroff, J., Atkinson, J., Feld, S., & Gurin, G. The use of thematic apperception to assess motivation in a nationwide interview study. *Psychological Monographs*, 1960, **74** (12, Whole No. 499).

4. *Morphology and Behavior*

GARDNER LINDZEY

The theme of this sermon is that human structure and function are significantly intertwined. In the lines to follow I propose to assert the relative neglect by American students of behavior of the physical person and its components, to suggest some possible determinants of this persistent myopia, to examine some arguments and evidence for the importance of such constitutional parameters for the psychologist, and, finally, to mention a few illustrative areas of potential research interest. Initially I should make clear that I am using the term morphology quite broadly to refer not only to the physical, structural aspects of the organism but also to any externally observable and objectively measurable attribute of the person, thus embracing such variables as hirsuteness, symmetry, color and even esthetic attractiveness.

American Resistance to Constitutional Psychology

It is a commonplace observation that American psychologists have been reluct-

SOURCE. *Chapter by G. Lindzey "Behavior and morphological variation" in* Genetic Diversity and Human Behavior. *Edited by J. N. Spuhler, Chicago: Aldine, 1967, pp. 227–240.*

ant to give serious consideration to the study of morphology and behavior (cf. MacKinnon & Maslow, 1951; Hall & Lindzey 1957) and some of the determinants of this enduring resistance are quite clear. First, it is undeniable that our attention has been devoted primarily to the study of social and behavioral *change*. The modal emphasis among psychologists in America has been upon learning, acquisition, shaping, or the modification of behavior, and not upon those aspects of the person and behavior that appear relatively fixed and unchanging. As has been said elsewhere, "One important by-product of American democracy, the Protestant ethic, and the dogma of the salf-made man has been the rejection of formulations implying that behavior may be innately conditioned, immutable, a 'given.' Because it is commonly accepted that physical characteristics are linked closely to genetic factors, the suggestion that physical and psychological characteristics are intimately related seems to imply a championing of genetic determinism. It is not surprising that such a conception has been unable to muster much support in the face of the buoyant environmentalism of American psychology." (Hall & Lindzey, 1957, p. 337).

A second significant deterrent has been the spectacular failure of the influential formulations of Gall and Spurzheim (1809) concerning body and behavior, coupled with the popularity of morphological variables among such diagnostic charlatans as palmists and physiognomists. These two conditions provide a ready-made cloak of naivete, ignorance or dishonesty for the person interested in working in this area.

Third is the fact that constitutional psychology has in recent decades become so closely associated with the name and work of William Sheldon that attitudes toward the one are scarcely separable from attitudes toward the other. In his research and writing Sheldon is much more the sensitive naturalist, observer and categorizer and much less the hard, quantitative and objective scientist than would be optimal to assure a good press from our colleagues. Moreover, in his writings he has proven to be singularly adept at ridiculing or parodying just those aspects of the scientific posture of psychologists that are most sensitively, rigidly and humorlessly maintained. One might argue convincingly that if Sheldon had conducted the same research but had reported it in an appropriately dull, constricted and affectless manner (consistent, let us say, with *Journal of Experimental Psychology* standards) its impact upon the discipline of psychology might have been much greater. What I am suggesting is that acceptance of Sheldon's work was impaired by a general resistance on the part of American psychologists to the study of behavior in relation to fixed characteristics and, conversely, that his irreverent and unconventional style provided further support for the belief that the study of morphology and behavior was an unsanitary practice. Whatever the determinants, it seems clear that American psychology in the past and present has maintained a suspicious hostility toward formulation and investigation concerned with body and behavior. Perhaps only the

study of behavior in relation to the soul has been equally unpopular among psychologists.

Morphological Dimensions

A word should be said concerning available variables and methods for describing the physical person. It is obvious that we do not yet have agreement concerning those components or dimensions that can be employed most fruitfully to represent morphological variation, although there are three sets of variables and attendant measures that have had a reasonable range of modern application. First, and best known, are Sheldon's (1940, 1954) components of endomorphy, mesomorphy and ectomorphy; with ratings for each dimension derived from a standardized set of photographs by means of a complex rating procedure or through the actuarial use of a small number of relatively objective indices. The full details of the latter procedure have not yet been fully published, but the indices are age, height, ponderal index, and trunk index. Parnell (1958) has devised an alternative method of measuring comparable variables which he labels fat, muscularity and linearity. His ratings are based upon a small number of anthropometric measures of subcutaneous fat, bone length, and girth of arm and calf. Third is Lindegård's (1953; Lindegård & Nyman, 1956) scheme which includes four variables — length, sturdiness, muscularity and fat. His dimensions were identified with the aid of factor analysis and they are rated by means of a combination of anthropometric measurements and performance (strength) tests.

It is clear that much important research remains to be done in further identifying alternative or additional dimensions to represent the body and that the existing dimensions and measures are far from ideal. Indeed there have been a number of publications (e.g., Hammond, 1957a, 1957b; Hunt, 1952) that have been sharply critical of the best known measurement systems. Still the deficiencies that inhere in these particular schemes and measurement operations must be expected to attenuate or obscure attempts to relate these variables to behavior. Thus, whatever well-controlled associations we now observe between morphology and behavior may be considered to represent minimum estimates rather than an upper limit. It is important to note that in spite of diversity in the particular measures or indices investigators have commenced with, and differences in the methods of analysis they have employed, there is a high degree of congruence among the three sets of variables that are currently popular. Finally, and perhaps most important, we do possess a set of existing tools with which one readily can initiate research in this area.

Mechanisms Mediating a hypothetical Relationship Between Morphology and Behavior

Ultimately, justification for increased interest in morphology and behavior must rest upon the provision of compelling empirical evidence for important associations between these two sectors of the person. Before turning to even a glimpse at empirical evidence, however, it seems reasonable to examine the rational and theoretical basis that can be provided to motivate an interest in such relationships. In brief, what we are concerned with here is a specification of the reasonable pathways or mechanisms whereby an important association between physical and behavioral components might be achieved. A crude classification suggests that there are five discriminable means that might lead one to predict such associations.

First is the possibility that a *common experimental* or environmental class of *events* has a characteristic *influence* upon personality or *behavior and*, at the same time, has a regular and detectable effect upon *morphology*. For example, if we accept certain psychoanalytic formulations (Bruch, 1947) concerning the relation between obesity and a particular type of of parent-child relation—maternal overprotectiveness—and assume, moreover, that physical components are influenced by weight and diet factors, we would confidently expect some degree of association between the endomorphic or fat factor and those behavioral consequences that are believed to be associated with maternal overprotectiveness. Or, if we accept the report of Landauer and Whiting (1965) that in societies where noxious and traumatic experiences are a regular part of the socialization practice, "the mean adult male stature was over two inches greater than in societies where these customs were not practiced" and assume, moreover, that such early experiences also have an influence upon behavior, we would once again expect physique and behavior to be importantly linked. There is, of course, a good deal of lower animal evidence (e.g., Denenberg, 1962; Lindzey, Winston & Manosevitz, 1963) to support this same point of view— that early experience influences both morphology and behavior. In brief, this position makes the reasonable assumption (with some supporting evidence) that there are certain important events that serve to determine, both physical and behavioral development in a manner that produces significant associations between outcomes in these two spheres.

Second is the inevitable observation that *behavior is directly limited or facilitated* to some degree *by the physical person*. Even the most dedicated and competitive 145 pound athlete cannot aspire realistically to play first string tackle for a Big Ten university, nor is it likely that the 260 pound tackle could ever compete successfully in a marathon race or as an effective jockey. A male whose maximum height is 5'4" cannot reasonably expect to compete with John Thomas or Valeri Brumel. The frail ectomorph cannot expect to employ physical or aggressive responses with the same effect as the robust mesomorph. Height, strength, weight and comparable dimensions place direct and unmistakable limits upon what responses the individual can hope to make adaptively in a given environmental setting.

A third factor, which is closely related to the second, concerns the *indirect consequences of* a particular set of *physical attributes.* For example, within our society, if an individual's biological makeup places him well above most others in size and strength, it is very likely that he will be recruited early in his life into competitive athletics and that this experience will play an important role in his life. Those who have undergone or studied the impact of four to ten years of varsity athletics upon behavior would scarcely question the profound implications of this experience for many important aspects of the individual's values, dispositions and overt behavior. To take a widely divergent example, it is now carefully documented for women that linearity (ectomorphy) is negatively associated with rate of physical and biological maturation. A study by McNeil & Livson (1963), the only published research with which I am familiar that employs Sheldon's new and presumably more actuarial method of somatotyping, provides compelling evidence for a significant association between a process of great psychological importance and one morphological component. No observer of the adolescent female, or student of the socialization process, would be likely to deny that the age at which a girl becomes, in some sense, a woman, has significance for her psychological development; and here we have clear evidence that the more linear her physique, the slower she will be in undergoing and completing this developmental stage.

The two examples that have been cited could be multiplied endlessly by listing the implications of particular kinds of bodies for particular kinds of environmental events and experiences. Surely there is some degree of regular behavioral impact attendant upon being a handsome man as opposed to an ugly man: a "stacked" girl as opposed to a fragile, linear girl; a large, powerful man in comparison to a small, weak man.

Fourth is a special case of the indirect implications of physique, and relates to *role specification* or the social stimulus-value of particular variations in the physical person. Insofar as a given society includes a number of individuals who hold common expectations in regard to the "fat man," the "lean and hungry person," "the red head," "the receding chin," etc., it is clear that the individuals who fit these physical prescriptions will be exposed to a somewhat different set of learning experiences or environmental events than the person of more modal body or whose physique is extreme in a different manner. Whether the behavior that is expected of the particular physique is grounded in firm empirical observation, casual superstition, or magical thinking, if the expectation is maintained by a sizeable number of persons it creates a different social reality for those who fit the prescription. Whether they conform to social expectation or vigorously oppose it, they are influenced by a common set of experiential determinants that set them off from those of a different morphology and, consequently, we might expect to find some uniformities in their behavior not shared by persons of very different physique.

Finally, we come to the mechanism which is probably most objectionable to the majority of American psychologists — *joint biological determinants of both behavior and physique.* This type of association could be produced by a known set of physiological processes that demonstrably influence both behavior and physique. (in the abstract it is easy to cite endocrine function) or the link might be produced by a common set of genetic determinants, with or without information concerning the process whereby genetic variation is translated into morphological and behavioral variation. To take a simple case, for both man and lower animal it is well known that a large proportion of the morphological variables that have been studied are importantly influenced by genetic variation. For example, the two major twin studies that have examined physical attributes (Newman, Freeman & Holzinger, 1937; Osborne & DeGeorge, 1959) report heritability coefficients for specific morphological attributes that for the most part are above 0.70. Sheldon's physique components are reported by Osborne & DeGeorge to display appreciably lower heritability coefficients (Total Somatotype: Males = 0.36; Females = 0.61) but it remains clear that genetic variation makes a significant contribution to morphological variation.

Given this observation, it seems altogether reasonable to anticipate that the chromosomal loci that influence variation in morphology may have multiple or pleitropic effects, some of which are behavioral. To use an illustration made somewhat remote by phylogenetic regression, my colleague Harvey Winston and I (Winston & Lindzey, 1964), working with mice, have produced tentative evidence suggesting that albinism (which is determined by a recessive gene cc in linkage group 1) is associated with a relative deficiency in escape learning. Whether this particular finding is sustained or not, there is every reason to expect that comparable pleitropic effects linking physical and behavioral components will be found in a variety of behavioral and physical areas. Even at the human level we may expect comparable, although perhaps more complex, examples. Indeed, if we are willing to include the realm of pathology in our discussion, it is clear that there are numerous examples of conditions which, under the normal range of environmental variation, are controlled by genetic variation and include both behavioral and physical deviations. An evident example of this is Down's Syndrome (Mongolism) which as a result of modern cytological advances we now know to be produced by a genetic anomoly, typically involving either trisomy or translocation associated with the 21st chromosome (Jarvik, Falek & Pierson, 1964), and which leads to a variety of dramatic behavioral and physical consequences. Here, then, is a particular kind of genetic variation (objectively identifiable) which leads to profound and undeniable effects in both the physical and behavioral sphere. Numerous other examples could be discussed including Huntingdon's Chorea, Phenlyketonuria, and Infantile Amaurotic Idiocy.

The main generalization I wish to extract from what has just been said is that working within the assumptions that are common to most psychologists (whether learning, developmental, physiological, social, or what not) it appears altogether reasonable for one to expect to observe important associations between morphology and behavior. Or, stated in the ritual terminology of modern psychology, given appropriate information concerning morphology we may expect with reasonable confidence to have some degree of predictive control over the variance of behavior.

Some Illustrative Findings

This is obviously not the place to attempt a serious literature survey, but what I can do is select several areas where there has been a reasonable amount of investigative activity and examine the trend and implications of the data. The two active areas I will discuss are concerned with (1) estimating the direct relation between observer ratings of personality and morphological variables; and (2) relating morphology to a complex achievement variable, in this case criminal behavior.

Personality Ratings. Almost every introductory psychology student has learned to recognize and distrust the striking findings that Sheldon (1942) has reported between dimensions of physique and temperament. Studying 200 male college students individually over a considerable period of time, he assigned ratings to each subject for his three somatotype components and also, on the basis of extensive interviewing and observing, he made ratings for three temperament variables that were intended to represent aspects of behavior associated with each of the dimensions of physique. When the temperament ratings were correlated with ratings for the associated physique component the correlations ranged from +0.79 to +0.83. There are a number of factors that would have to be considered in a full discussion of why so much covariation was observed, but for most psychologists the explanation has seemed to lie in the fact that Sheldon himself executed both sets of ratings. Consequently, one may reason that implicitly Sheldon's

prior convictions or expectations in this area led him to rate both physique and temperament in a consistent manner, whatever may have existed in reality.

There have been many other studies relating morphological variation to ratings of personality and most of them have produced at least some evidence for association between these two domains. Let us here direct our attention upon two studies that have minimized, more successfully than most, the possibility of contamination of data or experimenter bias.

The first investigation was executed by Irvin Child (1950) utilizing 414 male, undergraduate students who were routinely somatotyped as freshmen and who, as sophomores, completed a questionnaire that consisted of multiple-choice questions concerning the subjects' own behavior and feelings. Each item was designed to measure some aspect of behavior that, on the basis of Sheldon's study of temperament, was believed to be related to one or more dimensions of physique. In advance of any analysis of the data a total of 94 predictions were made concerning associations between self ratings and somatotype ratings — these predictions were simple reflections of what Sheldon had already reported. The somatotype ratings were assigned by Sheldon on the basis of the standard photographs and without any knowledge of the questionnaire results. More than three quarters (77%) of the predictions were confirmed in regard to the direction of the relationship between physical component and self rating, and more than one fifth of the predictions were confirmed at the five per cent level; while only one of the findings that reversed the prediction was significant at the five per cent level. When Child combined certain of the items into scales for each of the temperament variables so that they could be correlated with the physique dimensions, he observed positive correlations between the comparable physique and temperament dimensions, the highest of which was +0.38.

The most important observation here is that even when we eliminate the major design and inference shortcomings of Sheldon's study, we still observe a pattern of relations between physique and behavior that resembles in direction, if not degree, the findings reported by Sheldon. The magnitude of association between self ratings and morphology is obviously much less than that reported by Sheldon, but it is difficult to know what proportion of this change is attributable to elimination of experimenter bias and what proportion is due to the relative insensitivity of self ratings.

A similar study was carried out by Walker (1962) working with 125 male and female nursery school children. The somatotype measures were based upon ratings made independently by three different judges which were then combined by an averaging method. Two of these judges never naw the children while the third was acquainted with them. Each of the children was also rated on a one to seven scale for 64 specific behavioral items by two to five judges, none of whom were involved in the morphological ratings and at least two of whom were ignorant of the purpose of the study. Again, the individual score for each item was determined by averaging the judges' ratings. These items also had been selected for their pertinence to Sheldon's findings and a total of 292 specific predictions were made in advance and tested separately for the male and female subjects. Altogether, 73% of the predictions were confirmed in direction and 21% were confirmed at or below the 5% level of significance while only 3% were disconfirmed at the 5% level.

Once again we observe significant and appreciable relations between morpho-

logical variation and behavior which are consistent with Sheldon's findings, even though the major opportunities for systematic bias have been removed. Again, the degree of association is less than that reported by Sheldon but the fact that these observer ratings of behavior might be considered less sensitive than those used by Sheldon, in addition to the use of young children as subjects, makes it difficult to consider these findings as clearly contradictory on this score.

The principal generalization I wish to derive from these findings is that the most firmly based evidence we now possess suggests the existence of important associations between morphology and behavior (just as reason would assert), while the magnitude of this relation, or rather its varying magnitude depending upon the conditions of study, remains to be determined precisely. If, as the climate of current opinion urges, the magnitude of association reported by Sheldon represents in large measure co-variance attributable to experimental error, this fact remains to be demonstrated unequivocally. Moreover, in view of the extensive criticism of his study, it does seem odd that there has not been one single effort at a careful replication eliminating the major defects in Sheldon's study, while at the same time attempting to preserve other relevant conditions as exactly as possible. What we have witnessed, instead, has been the complacent dismissal of a potentially important set of results without any serious attempt at an empirical resolution.

Criminal Behavior. We turn now to a morphological correlate that is far removed from specific ratings of items or components of personality. Here we are concerned with a complex outcome variable, criminal behavior, that includes a wide variety of topographically different forms of behavior and is undoubtedly related to many different antecedent events. Again I will limit my discussion to the initial findings reported by Sheldon and a small number of subsequent investigations involving similar questions and methods.

Over an eight-year period Sheldon and his collaborators (Sheldon, 1949) conducted a study of physique and behavior with the residents of a rehabilitation home for boys in Boston. The findings of this study are largely clinical or descriptive but he does present a graphic comparison of college youths and his delinquent subjects which makes clear that while the college distribution shows a clustering about the mid-range physique (4-4-4), the delinquent youths show a tendency to cluster in the "northwest region." In brief, mesomorphs, particularly endomorphic mesomorphs, are over represented among the delinquents. This generalization, although initially supported by little in the way of convincing empirical data, has been re-examined subsequently in four separate studies that have involved better controls and more objective analysis of data.

The best known of these subsequent studies was conducted by Glueck and Glueck (1950, 1956) and involved the study of 500 persistent delinquents and 500 proven non-delinquents; matched in age, intelligence, ethnic background and place of residence. Independently of any knowledge of the classification of the individual subjects, their physiques were rated in terms of the relative dominance of Sheldon's three components. An examination of the somatotype distributions for the two groups provides a powerful confirmation of Sheldon's findings— approximately 60% of the delinquent youths were classified as mesomorphic while only about 30% of the non-delinquent subjects were so classified. Moreover, less than 15% of the delinquents

were categorized as ectomorphic and almost 40% of the normal subjects were placed in this category. A final item of confirmation was found in the incidence of endomorphic mesomorphs in the delinquent (13%) and non-delinquent (3%) subjects. All in all, under what appear to be very well controlled circumstances, a quantitative analysis of the relation between criminal behavior and morphological variation provides a highly significant and impressive confirmation of Sheldon's rather impressionistic findings.

A study by Epps and Parnell (1952) is of particular interest because it involved both a change in society (England) and in sex (girls) and yet also led to the observation that when female delinquents were compared with female college students they were "shorter and heavier in build, more muscular and fat." (Epps and Parnell, 1952, p. 254.) A more recent study by Gibbons (1963) also employed English subjects, in this case male, and again found a substantial confirmation of the finding that delinquent youth are predominantly of "northwest physique."

Another recent study (Cortes, 1961), involved the use of Parnell's techniques of measurement and the comparison of 100 adolescent boys who had been convicted by courts of violations of the criminal law with a group matched in age but with no record of delinquent behavior. When the subjects were classified according to their dominant physique component, Cortes found 57% of the delinquents to be mesomorphic while only 19% of the normal subjects were so classified. On the other hand, 33% of the normal subjects were dominantly ectomorphic in comparison to 16% of the delinquents. In spite of the different somatotyping method, and other variations in procedure, these results almost exactly parallel the findings of the Gluecks' and provide further confirmation for the original association reported by Sheldon.

Thus, four separate studies involving different methods, different sexes and different societies, some of them employing excellent controls against experimenter bias, have produced findings that are consistent among themselves and congruent with Sheldon's initial report. No one is likely to argue seriously that mesomorphy directly causes (or is caused by) criminal behavior but an association as consistently and strongly observed, and involving as complex and socially important a variable as criminal behavior, obviously warrants further systematic study.

It is even possible to see hints of an interesting association between these findings and those that have been reported in connection with psychopathic or sociopathic traits. Lykken (1957), in an ingenious study, has reported a deficiency in capacity for avoidance learning on the part of the "constitutional psychopath." More recently, Schachter (in press) has replicated this finding and introduced the fascinating additional observation that sociopaths show considerable improvement in avoidance learning when injected with adrenaline, while normal subjects demonstrate no such change in performance. It is interesting to note that Sheldon's (1942) early description of the somatotonic temperament (corresponding to mesomorphy) placed considerable emphasis upon indifference to pain and low anxiety. If it should eventually be shown unequivocally that low anxiety, deficient avoidance learning and an atypical effect of adrenaline upon avoidance learning are all associated with extremes of mesomorphy, there would be the possibility of integrating a variety of discrete and individually important results bearing upon criminal behavior. Such results obviously would have implications extending far beyond study of the psychopath or criminal.

Areas of Potential Research Interest

I have just mentioned several areas of investigation that seem to me to promise significant returns. Before closing, permit me to briefly allude to a few additional topics that may offer similar rewards. It should be clear that these selections are quite arbitrary and in no sense intended to represent the entire range of investigative possibilities.

Effects of Early Experience. A recent consequence of Freud's seminal observations and the findings of ethologists and comparative psychologists has been an intense contemporary interest in the effects of early experience. Numerous studies with both human and lower animal subjects exploring this problem (Beath & Jaynes, 1954; Bowlby, 1951; Denenberg, 1962) have left most observers convinced that variation in early experience has important implications for adult behavior or personality. Unfortunately there are many disagreements concerning the exact nature of the function linking infantile experience and adult behavior. Even in connection with such a seemingly simple question as whether traumatic or strong noxious stimulation in infancy has adaptive or maladaptive effects, or increases or decreases emotionality, the answer seems by no means clear (e.g., Denenberg, 1961; Levine, 1961; Hall & Whiteman, 1951; Lindzey, Lykken & Winston, 1960a, 1961a, 1961b). One significant question here is whether there may not be important differences in the nature (and perhaps even the direction) of effects from the same noxious stimulus when administered to different classes of organisms; whether the same stimulus may not have a quite different impact upon different bodies, with different sensitivities and varying response capacities. It is at least possible that certain kinds of stimulation will have divergent effects upon the fragile, linear, hyper-reactive infant and the heavy, spherical and sluggish infant. Indeed, one might argue that evidence from a variety of lower animal sources (King & Eleftheriou, 1959; Valenstein, Riss & Young, 1955), including our own research (Lindzey, Lykken & Winston 1960; Lindzey, Winston & Manosevitz, 1963; Winston, 1963), indicates that the effects of early experience are influenced by genotype or biological variation, thus providing presumptive support for just such a formulation. All of this implies that introduction of morphological variation as a parameter or variable to be studied when examining the effects of early experience might shed considerable light upon the complexities of this important area.

Psychopharmacology. To select still another fashionable area of research, there is the largely unexamined interaction between morphological variation and effects of psychoactive drugs. One of the major puzzles that plagues research in psychopharmacology is the observation of very large individual differences in reaction to the same doses of the same drug under the same environmental conditions. Undoubtedly there are many factors contributing to this variation but one such class may consist of morphological variables. Indeed, beginning with Sheldon's (1942) temperament descriptions of his polar physical varieties we find a number of hints that observers have believed this to be the case. In fact, the gross morphological variable of weight has always been considered an important parameter in predicting the effects of any drug—psychoactive or not.

Moreover, there is considerable evidence from lower animals for the influence of biological determinants, including genotype, upon response to particular drugs, including alcohol (McClearn & Rodgers, 1951, 1961). All in all, whether concerned with alcohol, narcotic agents, or the more recent hallucinogenic and tranquilizing drugs, there seems every reason to expect morphological variation to play a meaningful role in determining the psychological effects of the drug.

Social Interaction and Morphology. As a final illustrative item it may be appropriate to mention a topic that appears to have little fit with current psychological interest. Modern social psychology has shown very little interest in the physical structure of the persons who are studied in temporary or enduring interaction. Indeed an examination of the index of the *Handbook of Social Psychology* (Lindzey, 1954) reveals no entries for "physique" or "somatotype" and only a single entry for "physical factors."

In spite of this systematic neglect, few, if any, would deny that the physical attractiveness of a person, whether male or female, has a marked influence upon the way in which he is responded to by others. It would come as a shock to most of us if we found that social status, popularity and such had no relation to esthetic appeal. Likewise the question of how big, how strong, how quick, how well coordinated have obvious implications for the way in which the person is perceived by others, as well as the way in which he participates in group functioning.

Many years ago Freud (1914) pointed to a fascinating area of investigation in his remarks concerning the social significance of the narcissism encountered prototypically in the big cats and beautiful women. For a complex of reasons we seem to have shown little professional interest in lions, tigers, or stunning women. Perhaps now is the time to restore beauty and other morphological variables to the study of social phenomena.

References

Bowlby, J. *Maternal care and mental health*. Geneva: World Health Organization, 1951.

Bruch, Hilde. Psychological aspects of obesity. *Psychiatry*, 1947, **10**, 373–381.

Child, I. The relation of somatotype to self-ratings on Sheldon's temperamental traits. *J. Pers.*, 1950, **18**, 440–453.

Cortes, J. B. *Physique, need for achievement, and delinquency*. Doctoral dissertation, Harvard Univ., 1961.

Denenberg, V. H. Comment on "Infantile trauma, genetic factors, and adult temperament." *Psychol. Rep.*, 1961, **8**, 459–462.

Denenberg, V. H. The effects of early experience. In E. S. E. Hafez (Ed.) *The behaviour of domestic animals*. Baltimore: Williams & Wilkins, 1962, pp. 109–138.

Epps, P. & Parnell, R. W. Physique and temperament of women delinquents compared with women undergraduates. *Brit. J. med. Psychol.*, 1942, **25**, 249–255.

Freud, S. On narcissism. In *Standard Edition Vol. XIV*. London: Hogarth Press, 1957. (Originally published in 1914).

Gall, F. J. & Spurzheim, J. G. *Recherches sur le Systeme nerveux*. Paris: Schoell, 1809.

Gibbens, T. C. N. *Psychiatric studies of Borstal lads*. London: Oxford, 1963.

Glueck, S. & Glueck, Eleanor. *Unraveling juvenile delinquency*. New York: Harper, 1950.

Glueck, S. & Glueck, Eleanor. *Physique and delinquency*. New York: Harper, 1956.

Hall, C. S. & Lindzey, G. *Theories of personality*. New York: Wiley, 1957.

Hall, C. S. & Whiteman, P. H. The effects of infantile stimulation upon later emotional stability in the mouse. *J. comp. physiol. Psychol.*, 1951, **44**, 61–66.

Hammond, W. H. The constancy of physical types as determined by factorial analysis. *Human Biol.*, 1957a, **29**, 40–61.

Hammond, W. H. The status of physical types. *Human Biol.*, 1957b, **29**, 223–241.

Hunt, E. A. Human Constitution: an appraisal. *Amer. J. phys. Anthrop.*, 1952, **10**, 55–73.

Jarvik, Lissy F., Falek, A. & Pierson, W. P. Down's Syndrome (Mongolism): the heritable aspects. *Psychol. Bull.*, 1964, **61**, 388–298.

King, J. A. & Eleftheriou, B. E. Effects of early handling upon adult behavior in two subspecies of deermice, *Peromyscus maniculatus. J. comp. physiol. Psychol.*, 1959, **52**, 82–88.

Landauer, T. K. & Whiting, J. W. M. Some effects of infant stress upon human stature. *Amer. Anthrop.* (in press).

Levine, S. Discomforting thoughts on "infantile trauma, genetic factors, and adult temperament." *J. abnorm. soc. Psychol.*, 1961, **63**, 219–220.

Lindegård, B. Variations in human body-build. *Acta Psychiatrica et Neurologica. Supplementum* **86**, 1953, 1–163.

Lindegård, B. & Nyman, G. E. Interrelations between psychologic, somatologic, and endocrine dimensions. *Lunds Universitets Årsskrift*, 1956, **52**, (No. 8), pp. 1–54.

Lindzey, G. *Handbook of social psychology*. Vols. I & II. Reading, Mass.: Addison-Wesley, 1954.

Lindzey, G., Lykken, D. T. & Winston, H. D. Infantile trauma, genetic factors, and adult temperament. *J. abnorm. soc. Psychol.*, 1960, **61**, 7–14.

Lindzey, G., Lykken, D. T. & Winston, H. D. Confusion, conviction, and control groups. *J. abnorm. soc. Psychol.*, 1961a, **63**, 221–222.

Lindzey, G., Lykken, D. T. & Winston, H. D. Trauma, emotionality, and scientific sin. *Psychol. Rep.*, 1961b, **9**, 199–206.

Lindzey, G., Winston, H. D. & Manosevitz, M. Early experience, genotype and temperament in *Mus musculus. J. comp. physiol. Psychol.*, 1963, **56**, 622–629.

Lykken, D. T. A study of anxiety in the sociopathic personality. *J. abnorm. soc. Psychol.*, 1957, **55**, 6–10.

MacKinnon, D. W. & Maslow, A. H. Personality. In H. Helson (Ed.) *Theoretical foundations of psychology*. New York: Van Nostrand, 1951, pp. 602–655.

McClearn, G. E. & Rodgers, D. A. Differences in alcohol preference among inbred strains of mice. *Quart. J. Stud. Alcohol.*, 1959, **20**, 691–695.

McClearn, G. E. & Rodgers, D. A. Genetic factors in alcohol preference of laboratory mice. *J. comp. physiol. Psychol.*, 1961., *54*, 116–119.

McNeil, D. & Levison, N. Maturation rate and body build in women. *Child Develpm.*, 1963, **34**, 25–32.

Newman, N. H., Freeman, F. N. & Holzinger, K. J. *Twins: a study of heredity and environment*. Chicago: Univ. Chicago Press, 1937.

Osborne, R. H. & De George, F. V. *Genetic basis of morphological variation*. Cambridge: Harvard Univ. Press. 1959.

Parnell, R. W. *Behavior and physique: an introduction to practical and applied somatometry*. London: Arnold, 1958.

Schachter, S. Crime, cognition and the automatic nervous system. *Nebraska Symposium on Motivation.* Lincoln, Neb.: Univ. Nebraska Press (in press).

Sheldon, W. H. (with the collaboration of S. S. Stevens & W. B. Tucker). *The varieties of human physique: an introduction to constitutional psychology.* New York: Harper, 1940.

Sheldon, W. H. (with the collaboration of S. S. Stevens). *The varieties of temperament: a psychology of constitutional differences.* New York: Harper, 1942.

Sheldon, W. H. (with the collaboration of E. M. Hartl & E. McDermott). *Varieties of delinquent youth: an introduction to constitutional psychiatry.* New York: Harper, 1949.

Sheldon, W. H. (with the collaboration of C. W. Dupertius & E. McDermott). *Atlas of men: a guide for somatotyping the male at all ages.* New York: Harper, 1954.

Valenstein, E. S., Riss, W. & Young, W. C. Experimental and genetic factors in the organization of sexual behavior in male guinea pigs. *J. comp. physiol. Psychol.*, 1955, **48**, 397–403.

Walker, R. N. Body build and behavior in young children: I. Body build and nursery school teachers' ratings. *Monogr. Soc. Res. Child Develpm.*, 1962, **27**, No. 3 (Serial No. 84).

Winston, H. D. Influence of genotype and infantile trauma on adult learning in the mouse. *J. comp. physiol. Psychol.*, 1963, **56**, 630–635.

Winston, H. D. & Lindzey, G. Albinism and water escape performance in the mouse. *Science*, 1964, **144**, 189–191.

Section IX

Cattell's Factor Theory

The characteristic and impressive productivity of Raymond B. Cattell continues unabated. Together with his students he has published such an amazing array of books and articles that it is difficult to give an adequate representation of his writings within the limited space available here.

The recent writings of Cattell provide a significant and logical extension of his previous work. The technique of factor analysis has remained at the core of his studies, and he has continued to be concerned with fundamental problems of classification or taxonomy. Moreover he has made serious efforts to introduce elements of unity or consistency into the extensive research literature concerned with factor analysis.

The first paper included here, *The Nature and Measurement of Anxiety*, provides a simple discussion of factor analysis and illustrates the application of this technique to the study of anxiety—one of the most important variables in personality. The paper clearly reveals the diversity of subjects and measures with which Cattell is at home, and also suggests the potential merit of factor analysis as an aid to taxonomy, concept formation, and the clarification of personality variables.

The second paper, written with Shotwell and Hurley, demonstrates the possibility of applying factor analysis to the individual case—in this instance, a mentally retarded patient. Once again, the wide variety of data sources (i.e., ratings by schoolteacher, ward technicians, and self, questionnaire data, word association, and paired companions) used by Cattell is clearly demonstrated. The use of the *P*-technique for studying individuals has not been widely exploited, but its potential utility for personality psychologists is clearly shown in the present study.

The third paper in this section is a recent article by Cattell and Gibbons. One question that has been persistently asked by critics of factor analysis is, "Why do different factor analytic studies often produce inconsistent results?" For indeed, if these techniques reveal the underlying structure of personality, then all factor analytic investigators should produce highly similar results. It is this general problem that Cattell and Gibbons address and in the process provide an introduction to a number of important issues and procedural matters involved in factor analytic studies. The paper provides an illuminating comparison between the work of Cattell and J. P. Guilford. The latter is another leading personality investigator who extensively uses factor analysis.

The wide range of Cattell's research interests is nicely illustrated in these last two papers that range from the detailed appraisal of a single hospitalized patient to a large scale study of normal personality structure in undergraduate students.

1. The Nature and Measurement of Anxiety

RAYMOND B. CATTELL

Ours is said to be the age of anxiety, but what exactly is anxiety and how can it be measured? What are its manifestations and how does it affect the functioning of human beings? The initial difficulty in answering such questions—as in so many problems of psychology—is one of definition. A generation has passed since Edward Lee Thorndike replied to critics of psychological measurement with the dictum: Everything that exists, exists in some degree and can be measured. Since then psychometry—the branch of psychology concerned with measurement—has done rather better at inventing scaling systems, units and tests than at defining the entities to be scaled. In Thorndike's own field the proliferation of empirical definitions of intelligence finally reduced many psychologists to the desperate statement: "Intelligence is what intelligence tests measure." What led to a way out of this morass was the development of the technique of factor analysis by Charles E. Spearman, Louis L. Thurstone, Sir Cyril Burt, and other psychologists. In my laboratory at the University of Illinois we have been applying factor analysis to the problem of defining and learning how to measure anxiety.

To seek to define anxiety is to attempt to tie down something recognized by everyone in two distinct ways: as an inner experience known from introspection and as a pattern of behavior observable in ourselves and in others as restlessness, irritability, tremor and so on. Sigmund Freud wrote much about anxiety but was content to fall back largely on introspection and semantics for its definition. He pointed to the solid distinction in his native language between *Furcht* (fear) and *Angst* (anxiety), and most psychologists have followed him in considering anxiety to be quite different from fear. At the very least anxiety is viewed as being a fear triggered by cues or symbols for some remote and uncertain danger rather than one physically or immediately present.

Other definitions go further afield. One U.S. school of learning theorists would have us consider anxiety as being the main drive to action. Almost in polar opposition to this view of anxiety as the effective mover is the clinical view expressed by Frank M. Berger (who discovered the chemical that led to the tranquilizer meprobamate) that anxiety is a disorganizer of effective action. Related to this

SOURCE. *Article by Raymond B. Cattell, "The nature and measurement of anxiety" in* Scientific American, *Vol. 208, pp. 96–104, 1963.*

disorganization concept is the psycho-analytic view that anxiety is the central problem in neurosis. In looser thinking this often degenerates into the notion that anxiety and neurosis are synonymous, with the result that people with a high anxiety level are treated as neurotics. Clearly the various theorists are talking about different things when they mention anxiety, and a heavy preliminary investment of research in simply isolating and measuring anxiety is strongly indicated.

The technique we have worked with, factor analysis, is in principle quite simple, although it does involve some complicated matrix algebra and usually requires the aid of electronic computers. In essence it involves the intercorrelation of a large number of observations to find out what factor or factors control them. The factor—"anxiety," for example—can then be defined and measured in terms of the variables that are its clearest manifestations.

When one looks at a mass of social or biological variables so richly interrelated that one cannot tell which are important and which are incidental, which are dependent on others and which are independent, it is useful to watch their mode of variation under the impact of changing circumstances and see what goes with what and to what extent. So might a hunter peer into a jungle swamp and wait for some telltale movement to show that what looked like two logs is

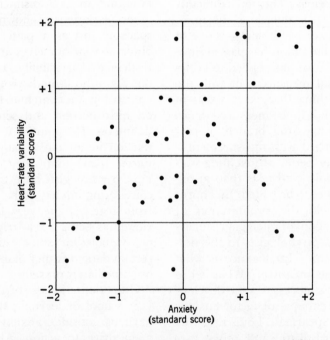

Figure 1. *Correlation between a patient's heart-rate variability and his anxiety as rated by psychiatrists is shown by this "scatter plot." The physiological and psychological measurements are reduced to "standard scores," in which the mean is taken to be zero and the deviation from the mean is independent of the raw scores. When the observations are plotted, their elliptical pattern indicates that the variables correlate positively but moderately.*

VARIABLE	LOADING
High susceptibility ao annoyance	0.56
High willingness to admit common faults	0.47
High tendency to agree	0.38
High heart rate	0.30
Slow reaction time	0.28
Low writing pressure	0.28
Low total physical strength	0.27
High critical severity	0.25
High autonomic conditioning rate	0.25
Low hand-steadiness	0.22
High emotionality of comment	0.20
High self-criticism	0.19
Less alkaline saliva	0.19
Slow speed of perceptual judgment	0.18

"Loading Pattern" for a factor designated as anxiety (U.I. 24 on a Universal Index of factors) shows how highly a number of variables "load" on the factor, or correlate with it. The higher the coefficient at the right, the greater the association with anxiety.

actually one crocodile. The factor analyst uses the correlation coefficient to calculate the precise extent to which two measured variables covary, or move together. The coefficient can range from +1.0 through 0 to −1.0, indicating, respectively, a complete positive correlation, no relation at all and a complete negative, or inverse, correlation. A correlation can be demonstrated visually by a "scatter plot" of the kind illustrated in Figure 1. Each dot on the chart represents an observation of a

	VARIABLE	LOADING
OBJECTIVE TESTS	Raised cholinesterase	0.78
	High hippuric acid	0.74
	High willingness to admit common faults	0.58
	High susceptibility to annoyance	0.46
	High rate of respiration	0.45
	High steroid hormone level	0.43
	High heart rate	0.30
	High systolic pulse pressure	0.29
	Less alkaline saliva	0.23
	Fast reversible perspective	0.19
	High saliva volume	0.13
QUESTIONNAIRE PRIMARIES	Low ego-strength (C−)	0.77
	Low will-control (Q_3−)	0.51
	High ergic tension (Q_4)	0.48
	High guilt proneness (O)	0.37
	High nonconformity (M)	0.31

Anxiety can be measured in an individual over a period of time. This is the loading pattern for anxiety as a fluctuating state rather than as the personality trait U.I. 24.

patient at one session during which psychiatrists rated his anxiety level and a record was made of the degree to which his heart rate was varying. When these dissimilar measurements are reduced to "standard scores" and plotted on two coordinates, their pattern indicates the degree of correlation between "anxiety and heart-rate variability. The fact that most of the dots fall into a rough ellipse (the closest approach to a straight line one can expect when many influences are at work) shows that there is a positive correlation between the two variables. The computation of a correlation coefficient from the actual anxiety ratings and heart-rate measurements gives a value of $+0.49$, which is a fairly marked relation as psychological variables go.

Even when such a relation is obtained it can be interpreted as indicating that variable a influences b, that b influences a or that some as yet unmeasured entity influences both of them. The investigator usually seeks to fix such causal dependencies by observing in time sequences or by forcibly isolating and manipulating one of the variables. The factor analyst, partly because he often deals with unmanipulable things such as the private lives of clinical patients, takes a different approach. Instead of observing a and b alone, he may observe a large number of variables in a group of subjects. With values for, say, 100 variables taken on a large number of subjects, he can work out a square correlation matrix containing the coefficients for all the possible 4,950 relations among the variables. By applying factor-analysis computations to this matrix he can discover the number of independent variables, or factors, that must be at work to account for the complex interrelations represented by the coefficients. And he can learn a good deal about the nature of these factors in terms of their pattern of effects on the dependent variables.

In the undisciplined infancy of psychology theorists often fell into the trap, originally pointed out by Francis Bacon, of assuming that because there is one word there must be one thing. An open-minded investigator must begin by questioning that assumption—by asking, in this field, if there is one thing called anxiety or several distinct and possibly unrelated forms of anxiety response.

At various times a variety of introspective, behavioral and physiological manifestations have been alleged to be signs of underlying anxiety. They include low hand-steadiness, inability to look someone in the eye, sinking feeling in the stomach, dry mouth, high irritability, raised muscle tension, decreased power of concentration, high emotionality in word choice, lack of readiness to try new tasks, tendency to jump at noises, high galvanic skin response, more rapid conditioning and a tendency to see threatening objects in blots or unstructured drawings. Between 1948 and 1960 we measured such objective-test variables as these in groups of from 100 to 500 people—young and old, mentally healthy and mentally ill—and then intercorrelated the hypothesized anxiety manifestations. The correlations turned out to be generally positive and significant. And through factor analysis they pointed to the existence of a single, pervasive factor of anxiety.

Up to this stage the assumption that there is a single entity that can be called anxiety was vindicated. In major respects the factor agreed with what is covered by the semantic concept of "anxiety." But not every popularly alleged manifestation of anxiety was confirmed. For example, in anxiety salivary output turned out to increase rather than to decrease. General muscle tension did not correlate in the way a tense person might expect from introspection. What correlated with the anxiety factor was tension in the trapezius,

VARIABLE	LOADING
Inability to do simple addition and subtraction mentally	0.57
Stuttering and upset of speech with delayed auditory feedback	0.57
Slow and erratic recognition of upside-down forms	0.57
Aspiration-level high relative to performance	0.55
Poor ability to co-ordinate simultaneous spatial cues	0.55
Low metabolic rate change in response to stimuli	0.50
Low readiness to tackle unpleasant activities	0.47
Numerous "indecisive" responses in questionnaires	0.44
Errors in reciting alphabet with prescribed skipping	0.42
Rapid increase of errors when made to hurry	0.31
High motor-perceptual rigidity	0.29
Affected more by color than form in artistic preferences	0.25
High body sway in suggestibility sway test	0.20

"Regression" is one of the factors that distinguish neurotics from other people, and is indexed as U.I. 23. This is the loading pattern for some variables influenced by U.I. 23.

the large muscle that runs from the shoulder to the back of the head; handwriting pressure was actually significantly lower in persons of high anxiety.

Once a factor has been checked in several samples of people and across several ranges of measurement, it provides a "loading pattern" (see top illustration on page 297) that shows the degree of influence of the underlying independent variable on each of the main manifestations in terms of correlation coefficients between the factor — anxiety in this case — and the variable. The loading pattern provides a means of recognizing and identifying the factor and a basis for more developed hypotheses about its nature. It also tells one how to test for the factor. Although anyone is free to affix such names as "anxiety" or "intelligence" to whatever he pleases, there is now an objectively discovered, repeatable response pattern to which one can refer when the label is used. In this case it dictates a particular battery of tests — usually the composite of measurements from the 10 or so most highly loaded manifestations — for anxiety experiments. To avoid merely semantic disputes factors are sometimes indexed simply by number. In a proposed Universal Index of factors that psychologists interested in such matters have been compiling, I have indexed anxiety as U.I. 24. When expert psychiatric diagnosticians rate patients for anxiety level, their estimates correlate more consistently and more highly with the U.I. 24 battery than with any other factor. Although the correlations shown in the U.I. 24 table (which is based on the work of John Hundleby of the University of Illinois and Kurt Pawlik of the University of Vienna) are not high, they are mean values across five experiments, and they have since risen to higher values in longer tests developed after the exploratory research phase.

Although a psychologist feels on firmest ground when he has located anxiety as a behavioral pattern in U.I. 24, he is also interested to see how anxiety emerges in the introspective account the subject gives of himself in responding to a questionnaire. The factoring of questionnaire items is an established branch of psychometrics. Among 16 major factors established by David R. Saunders, Glen F. Stice, Richard Coan, Bien Tsujioka, Rutherford B. Porter, and me there were a number that appeared to have "anxiety content."

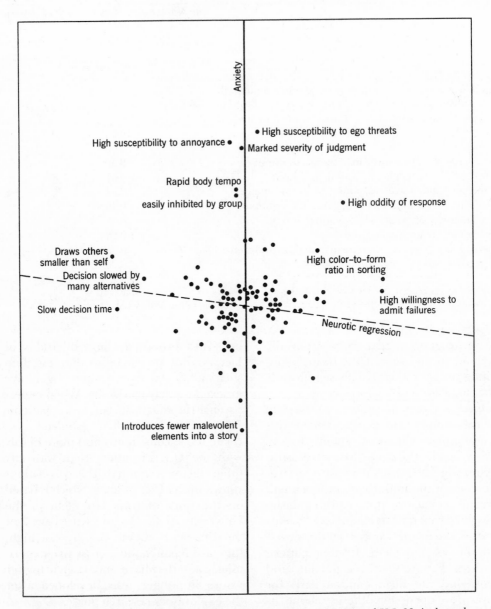

Figure 2. *Independence of the anxiety and regression factors, U.I. 24 and U.I. 23, is shown here in geometric terms. Each dot is the end point of a vector representing a measured variable, its direction and distance from the origin determined by factor-analysis computations. There are as many dimensions in the solid "graph" so produced (from which this is a two-dimensional projection) as there are factors at work on the variables. Tests points tend to coagulate in "hyperplanes," or multidimensional galaxies, which indicate the positions in which to place various factors; these factors emerge as axes of the "graph" placed as perpendiculars to the galaxies. Projected in two-dimensional space, a hyperplane should ideally appear as a line, but it is usually (as in this diagram) a lens-shaped swarm of points. A test like "Marked severity of judgment," lying in the hyperplane of neurotic regression, has zero-projection, or "zero-loading," on it; that is, it does not correlate with regression. On the other hand it loads highly on anxiety; it is, in other words, closely associated with anxiety. The greater the angle between two tests or factor axes, the more independent they are of each other. In this case the anxiety and regression axes are nearly perpendicular to each other; they are independent.*

One, which I called "ergic tension" or "drive tension" and labeled as factor Q_4, came out of such questions as are listed in the illustration on page 303. Another, indexed as O, had items indicating guilt proneness. Still another was the reciprocal of ego strength, or "ego weakness" (C−).

Could the existence of only one functional unity of response in behavior — U.I. 24 — be reconciled with several factors in the area of introspection? It is possible in factor analysis to correlate factors themselves and then to factor-analyze their correlation matrix just as one did the original variables. What comes out of this is a "second order" factor. (General intelligence is a second-order factor among such primary abilities as verbal ability, spatial ability, numerical ability and so on.) When we factored some 20 of the personality factors based on data from questionnaires, precisely those six factors that a psychiatrist would consider to have anxiety content — and no others — fell into a single second-order factor. At that point, therefore, we had one factor in behavioral response and one in introspection, but the possibility remained that they would prove to be not the same thing — that people who measured high on the "mental interior" factor might not show identical scores on the behavioral "exterior" factor. A crucial test with more than 500 Air Force men proved that these two ways of measuring were operating on the same entity: the correlation between them was close to +1.0. This close correspondence can be shown in visual terms (see figure 3 on page 302) by a technique that will be discussed later in this article.

Why should a first-order factor in one medium turn up as a second-order factor in another? Finding six partially distinct influences in introspection corresponding to one in behavior must mean, in the first place, that introspection is more

sensitive. It could also mean that a causal mechanism is being revealed in terms of six different sources of one common pool of anxiety. As usual with purely correlational evidence, one cannot say for sure in which direction the causality acts. But if the anxiety factor represents, as it were, a common reservoir of anxiety to which ego weakness, guilt proneness, frustrated drive and other primary factors contribute, our results would offer striking experimental vindication of some of Freud's theories as to the origin of anxiety in neurotics. At the same time, this experimental approach introduces several concepts beyond any in classical psychoanalysis, because factor analysis, like the microscope, opens up relations that cannot be seen by the unaided eye of the clinician.

The concept of U.I. 24 with which I have dealt so far has rested solely on observations of the individual differences among people, that is, on anxiety as a trait of personality. But anxiety also varies in level in the same person from time to time. The psychologist wants to discover the pattern of anxiety as a fluctuating state and to find out if it is the same as that of the personality trait. This question can be explored through single-person factor analysis, in which one person is measured every day, for perhaps 100 or 200 days, on the various alleged measures of anxiety. When these time series are correlated, a significant positive correlation should exist among variables affected by the same underlying source. For example, if higher systolic blood pressure, irritability, tremor and "Yes" answers to certain questionnaire items are all signs of anxiety, they should vary together as the onslaught of daily events raises and lowers the anxiety level. Investigation showed that the pattern for anxiety as a state is unmistakably the same species of response as that for the trait (see lower illustration on page 297). It differs in some tendency of the physiological variables to load more highly on the state factor. By working with the same subject one could eliminate individual differences resulting from extraneous influences on the variables.

Experiments with individuals have been particularly valuable in locating the physiological concomitants of anxiety and in distinguishing the anxiety pattern from other states, such as stress, fatigue and excitement, with which it has often been confused experimentally and conceptually. Harold Persky and Roy R.

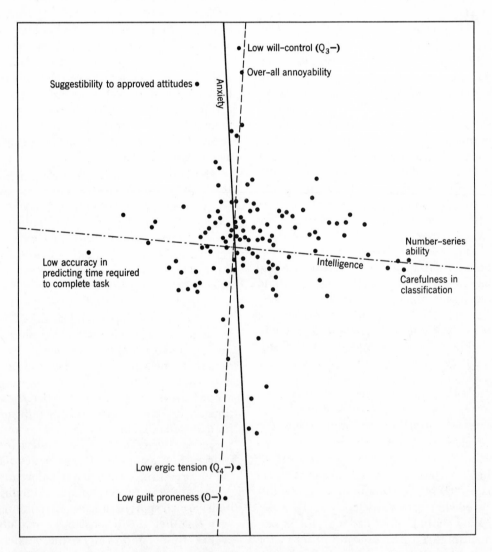

Figure 3. *Close correlation between anxiety as defined by objective tests (U.I. 24) and anxiety as a second-order factor derived from questionnaire data is shown by this diagram: the questionnaire axis (broken black line) is nearly aligned with the U.I. 24 behavioral axis (solid black line). But the axis for intelligence performance (white line) is almost perpendicular to the anxiety axis.*

Grinker of Michael Reese Hospital in Chicago, working with paratroopers in training, found that during what appeared to be anxiety periods the level of hippuric acid in the urine and of adrenal cortical steroids in the blood rose, the white-cell count and electrical skin resistance decreased and breathing speeded up. Ivan H. Scheier of my laboratory, together with Grinker, Sheldon Korchin and others at Michael Reese, studied patients undergoing various stresses and located a specific pattern of physiological upset characteristic of anxiety; the patterns for effort stress, excitement and other states differed both behaviorally and physiologically. Further investigations by Roy B. Mefferd and Louis J. Moran at the University of Texas and by Hudson Hoagland at the Worcester Foundation for Experimental Biology leave little doubt that anxiety and effort stress are two different things. Psychologically the effort-stress pattern usually shows no anxiety or other emotionality, only strong concentration and perhaps awareness of effort. High cholesterol levels, which we found to be completely uncorrelated with anxiety, may really belong to the effort-stress pattern. Anxiety seems to affect metabolism primarily by upsetting anabolic processes, which may account for the weight loss suffered by combat soldiers exposed to unremitting anxiety.

There is even evidence in Scheier's results that effort stress (which has resemblances to Hans Selye's "stress adaptation stage one" and arises from physical as well as mental causes) may have some inverse relation to anxiety. When a person grapples with a difficulty, he shows the stress response; when he retreats and attempts escapist solutions, he shows anxiety. The so-called psychosomatic neurotic, who develops a physical symptom from his encounter with a problem, is in this sense the opposite of a neurotic.

Whether or not anxiety originates as a response to prolonged and remote fear signals, it is quite different from fear as an actual response pattern. Fear is associated with the release of adrenalin; anxiety is not. Fear dries the mouth, whereas anxiety produces increased salivation as well as increased gastric secretion. Fear is sometimes described as *realistic*, whereas anxiety is considered unrealistic and indeed neurotic. Scheier and I found that students showed raised anxiety levels three weeks before an

QUESTIONNAIRE ITEM	LOADING
Do you find yourself with strong moods of anxiety, amusement, sorrow, etc., which you cannot account for by anything that has recently happened?	0.60
Do you frequently get in a state of tension and turmoil when thinking over the day's happenings?	0.57
Do quite small setbacks irritate you unduly?	0.56
Do you, when forced to remain inactive, begin to doodle, draw things on the margin of your paper, etc.?	0.55

Questionnaire items can be factored like behavioral or physiological variables. The coefficients at the right show how well a "Yes" answer to each question correlates with a factor designated as "ergic tension." When this factor and others based on questionnaires are factored in turn, anxiety emerges as a "second order" factor influencing them. Questions are from anxiety scale published by Institute for Personality and Ability Testing.

important examination but lowered anxiety and raised effort stress at the examination itself. The raised anxiety may be "neurotic" in the sense that it does no good, but it is a response to a real-world danger. If such anxiety is neurotic, so also is fear neurotic when it arises from a present danger about which nothing can be done.

Some years ago Hans J. Eysenck of Maudsley Hospital in London demonstrated that a factor I had measured by objective psychological tests and indexed as U.I. 23 powerfully distinguishes neurotics from normals. Some of the manifestations that consistently correlate with what Eysenck then called the neuroticism factor but that we conceive of as "regression" (only one of the components in neuroticism) are set out in the illustration on page 299.

The factor-analysis evidence for the independence of the influences defined as anxiety and regression can be presented visually. The variables are drawn as vectors from a common origin; the more closely correlated the variables are, the closer together they will lie, so that a group of mutually highly correlated variables will look like a sheaf of arrows. The number of dimensions in the space common to these vectors reflects the number of factors required to explain them. Since any set of variables usually involves a number of factors, a plot of the vectors would not be a conventional two-dimensional graph but an imaginary construct in a "hyperspace" of many dimensions. The nature of the experimental results identifies certain variables as factors; these can be treated as the axes of a co-ordinate system. When the end points of the vectors representing variables are projected on these axes in two dimensions, their location represents their loading on the axes.

Because the angles representing the relations among variables are implicit in the correlation results, the whole vector system is rigid. It can, however, be rotated with respect to the axes. The analyst wants to find the one position in which the factors and variables lie in their true relation. For this purpose he depends on the principle of "simple structure," which assumes that in an experiment involving a broad and well-sampled set of variables it is improbable that any single influence will affect all of them. In other words, it is more "simple" to expect that any one variable will be accounted for by less than the full complexity of all the factors acting together. This implies that there should be dense groups, like astronomical galaxies, constituted by variables unaffected by any one factor. In multidimensional space each such galaxy would lie in a "hyperplane"; in three dimensions it would be a disk lying in a plane. Projected in two-dimensional space it should reveal itself as a row of variables lining up with "zero loading"—that is, with no correlation or projection—on some factor axis moved to the correct position.

Such dense disks are indeed found in real data. By placing each chosen axis perpendicularly to a well-defined disk, the analyst rotates his results finally to a unique explanatory position. He thereby establishes the factor to which any set of variables is least related and the one with which it correlates most highly. The illustration on page 300 is a plot, in the plane set by the anxiety and regression factors, of data from a study of 111 variables, covering 18 factors, made by Richard Coan of the University of Arizona on a group of 164 seven-year-old children. The variables fall into two hyperplanes seen as rough ellipses (one rarely gets the galaxies exactly on edge in a row) lying along the axes and intersecting at the origin. The fact that these axes are almost at right angles to each other, with very different kinds of variables projecting close to each of them, shows that they are almost completely independent influences, with very different characteristics.

A similar plot makes clear the close relation, reported earlier in this article, of the behavior-based to the questionnaire-based data on anxiety (see illustration on page 302). The axis of the second-order questionnaire factor aligns itself, within the limits of experimental error, with that of the U.I. 24, or behavioral, factor. This diagram is also of interest in that it shows the psychological and statistical independence of anxiety and intelligence. The direction of the anxiety factor is fixed by the hyperplane oriented largely in intelligence-performance results. The axis representing the intelligence factor is approximately perpendicular to the anxiety axes. In this group of airmen anxiety and intelligence were almost completely independent of each other, and this has proved to be the case in most other experiments.

Factor analysis, then, succeeds in sorting out anxiety from two things with which it is constantly confused: the stress reaction and the neurotic-personality maladjustment. The more precise measurements of anxiety that are now possible also clarify the relation between anxiety and a factor such as intelligence and should help to answer many similar questions about the relation between anxiety and various situations and performances.

During the past decade, for example, almost every theoretically possible relation between anxiety and learning has been reported as being experimentally supported. Our results make it seem probable that those who found better school achievement with higher anxiety were mixing a state measure with a trait measure a few weeks before an examination, and that workers who correlated better achievement with lower anxiety were using an anxiety measurement tainted with neuroticism components. The issue was confused by the inclination of many learning theorists to assume that all

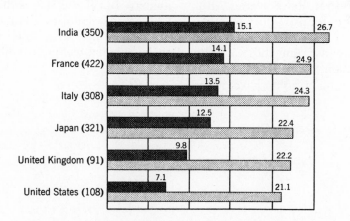

Figure 4. *Intercultural differences in anxiety and neuroticism were revealed by questionnaire data. The anxiety score is shown by the dark bars (possible range, 6 to 30) and the neuroticism score by the light bars (possible range, 6 to 54). The differences between countries were statistically significant except, in anxiety, for the U.K. and U.S. and, in neuroticism, for France and Italy. Numbers at left show size of the group tested in each country.*

learning is conditioning. Our experiments do show more rapid conditioning of autonomic, or involuntary, responses with higher anxiety. On the other hand, learning as reflected by grades is slightly but significantly inversely related to anxiety. It still remains to be seen which is cause and which is effect.

New objective and questionnaire-based anxiety batteries developed by Scheier have already yielded verifiable results showing differences in anxiety level with age, occupation, clinical syndromes and national culture. Anxiety fluctuates in early childhood, rises most consistently in adolescence and declines considerably through adulthood until it rises again after 60 or 65. Among occupations, newspaper editors, artists and air cadets in training have been found to have high anxiety; policemen, clerical workers and engineers have lower levels. Probably both personnel selection and the nature of the jobs are responsible for these differences. Among patients in mental health clinics those diagnosed as anxiety hysterics have the highest scores and alcoholics are also far above average. But the average scores for psychotics, whether schizophrenic or manic-depressive, are not very different from those of the general population.

Some surprising results have come from comparisons across cultures. To obtain data the questionnaire items were translated carefully (often back and forth twice) and checked by working out the factor structure until it was practically identical in each of the nations under study. When the scores were compared, some major differences appeared. Indians and Frenchmen, for example, showed substantially higher anxiety and neuroticism levels than Americans did (see illustration on page 305). This hardly fits the American's treasured view of himself as the most harassed of mortals, or the notion that anxiety is tied up with the pace and complexity of industrialized society. National comparisons are invidious and notoriously tricky, but these results may possibly fit a theory that low anxiety is associated with better economic level and closer political integration. This fits recent data showing still higher anxiety levels in countries that are split culturally and politically and that are low in economic status. Perhaps—and this is a subject for research—the U.S. might head the list in effort stress rather than anxiety. But if the U.S. is the archetypal 20th-century culture, literary psychologists may be far astray when they project their personal feelings to call this the age of anxiety.

2. Motivational Structure of an Hospitalized Mental Defective

ANNA M. SHOTWELL, JOHN R. HURLEY,
AND RAYMOND B. CATTELL

Freud, McDougall, Murray, and others, in attempting to isolate basic dimensions of motivation, did not have the benefit of the factor analytic methods which have enabled Cattell and his co-workers to substantiate the concepts of drive, ego structure, and sentiment. On the assumption that factor analysis of many scores obtained on objective attitude measuring devices would reveal a limited number of motivational components which could account for the multitude of phenomena observed in dynamic behavior, Cattell pioneered three researches: an R-technique study to isolate and identify the basic motivational determinants (Cattell, 1950), another R-technique study to confirm the findings of the first and to develop alternative objective measuring methods (Cattell & Miller, 1952), and a P-technique study to confirm further and to clarify the ideas elicited by the other two studies as well as to investigate the applicability of these ideas to an individual (Cattell & Cross, 1952).

The present case study continues this line of research.

The objective here was to discover the motivational dimensions of an institutionalized mental defective by objective P-technique factor analysis and to ascertain whether the findings were congruent with clinical understanding of the case and with earlier factor analytic results on nondefectives.

METHOD

The subject, a female patient at Pacific State Hospital in California, was a heavy-set 15-year-old Negro mental defective of mild degree who had come from an unfit home. Her mother was sexually promiscuous and probably of retarded intelligence. After the subject's father molested her sexually, her mother killed him with the subject a witness to the killing. The subject was described by the hospital staff as quiet, somewhat withdrawn, and undemonstrative, but usually cooperative. For a period of 100 days (5 days per week for 20 weeks), she was given a series of tests and was rated on various traits by her school teachers, by the technician in charge of her ward, and by herself. The test instruments, constructed on the assumption that drives and sentiments are revealed as patterns among

SOURCE. Article by Anna M. Shotwell, John R. Hurley, and Raymond B. Cattell, "Motivational structure of an hospitalized mental defective" in Journal of abnormal and social Psychology, Vol. 62, pp. 422–426, 1961.

attitudes, were designed to measure attitudes in an objective manner by means of ratings, questions about activities, word association, and paired comparisons. Each previously known dynamic factor in the literature was represented by at least two marker variables, i.e., variables which were strongly loaded in the previously known factor were carried over in some form and used in this investigation.

To distinguish each type of evaluative variable from all other variables in the factor matrix, a letter prefix was assigned as follows: RT, ratings by school teacher; RW, ratings by ward technicians; RS, self-ratings; QA, questions regarding activities; WA, word association; and PC, paired comparisons.

The subject was rated by herself and two others on 14 traits. The best possible score was 10; the worst possible was 0. Of the 42 trait ratings, only 9 proved variant enough to be retained for analysis.

Most of the original 22 questions regarding the subject's daily activities required only a "yes" or "no" answer. A few, such as the question, "How many cigarettes have you smoked?" required a quantitative answer. Of the original group of 22, 9 questions were retained for analysis, the remainder being eliminated because they displayed little or no variance.

Thirty-four word association items were presented to the subject in the format:

top . . . . . . lid____winner____

The second and third words of the series were assumed to represent one of several hypothesized drives and sentiments. From these two words, the subject was to choose the one which she first associated with the first word of the series. It was assumed that the choice of one word over another would be determined by her attitudes. The subject's choices were then pooled to obtain a score for each of the hypothesized drives and sentiments. Since the sequence of items was changed from day to day, there was no chance for the subject to mechanize her responses.

Paired comparisons consisted of having the subject indicate which of a pair of statements, each printed on a separate slip of paper, most strongly represented her present desires. Sixteen statements were constructed so as to define each attitude by in-

clusion of its parts: the stimulus situation, an organism, a need, a course of action, and an object concerned in that course of action. One of the statements was, "I want a good looking boy to make love to me." Since each statement was paired against every other statement, the subject made 120 choices each day for 100 days. Again the sequence of presentation was altered daily to obviate the possibility of the subject repeating responses mechanically. The 16 statements as well as the Word Association test were markers for seven drives and one sentiment. The seven drives were sex-mating, gregariousness, appeal-dependence, escape-fear, self-assertion, parental-protective, and narcissistic play. The eighth motivational component hypothesized was the self-sentiment.

Analysis of Data

As a result of the above procedure, each of the original 98 variables was represented by measures on 100 items. Means, standard deviations, and all possible intercorrelations were computed for each of the 98 variables. Upon inspection of the results, the decision was made to eliminate 56 of the original 98 variables. The major reason for this was that the data displayed little or no variance for these measures. The intercorrelations of the remaining 42 variables were then factor analyzed by the complete simple centroid method (Thurstone, 1947). The diagonal values were set at unity. The resulting factor matrix was then rotated to orthogonal simple structure by the method of quartimax (Neuhaus & Wrigley, 1954). Quartimax failed to disperse fully the main centroid. Consequently, the unrotated factor matrix was again rotated, this time to oblique simple structure. The method used was a combination of oblimax (Pinzka & Saunders, 1954) and Hurley's analytical method.[1] A decent oblique simple

---

[1]The unrotated factor matrix was first rotated by the method of oblimax to give an idea of the oblique structure. Then a rotated matrix V_{ij} was postulated on the basis of the oblimax solution. V_{ij} was constructed to display simple structure. The matrix equation $F_0 t = V_{ij}$ was then solved for t, the transformation matrix. All statistical computations were performed on the University of Illinois digital computer, ILLIAC.

structure was finally obtained, with a total of 11 rotated factors remaining for interpretation.[2]

DISCUSSION

Of the 11 factors found, 7 corresponded to factors found by previous researchers. Of 2 new factors, 1 did not lend itself to precise interpretation, and 1 was a subfactor. The factors are shown below in estimated order of variance accounted for.

Factor I — The Sex Erg

		LOADING
PC 10	I want a good-looking boy to make love to me	0.70
PC 11	I want to go to a good movie every week	0.64
RT 1	Lack of shyness	0.57
PC 25	I don't want to keep good control of my temper	0.53
PC 13	I want to watch games like baseball	0.51
PC 20	I don't want to help people in trouble	0.50
PC 12	I want to take an active part in recreation	0.49
PC 21	I don't want my parents always to have what they need	0.39
WA 35	Sex-mating (word association)	0.12

This component is one which has accounted for the most variance in all of the studies in which it has appeared. Variables PC and PC 11 label this as a sex component. The other variables, in general, contribute to the picture

[2]Tables containing the unrotated factor matrix, the transformation matrix, the rotated factor matrix, and the cosine matrix have been deposited with the American Documentation Institute. Order Document No. 6742 from ADI Auxiliary Publications Project, Photoduplication Service, Library of Congress; Washington 25, D.C., remitting in advance $1.25 for microfilm or $1.25 for photocopies. Make checks payable to: Chief, Photoduplication Service, Library of Congress.

of an uninhibited, amoral drive which has already found expression in sports and recreation. Variable WA 35 is included even though the loading is low, in order to show that its direction lines up with the sense of the factor as illustrated by the other variables.

Factor II — Fear-Anxiety Erg

		LOADING
PC 17	I want there to be fewer deaths	0.54
RT 1	Shyness	0.40
PC 16	I want the U.S. to have better protection against the A-bomb	0.39
RS 8	Amount of worry (high)	0.35
RS 5	Cooperation (low)	0.34
PC 23	I don't want time to enjoy my own company	0.33
QA 30	Did you watch TV yesterday? (Yes)	0.21
WA 38	Escape-fear (word association)	0.08

The general sense here is of a motivational component akin to anxiety. Variable RT 1 indicates withdrawal, whereas Variable PC 23 would seem to leave the subject no alternative but extraversion. Thus, the central problem of almost any anxiety syndrome is seen. This factor also removes any doubt as to one of the most useful functions of the television set, the poor man's Miltown.

Factor III — Self-Regard Sentiment

		LOADING
RW 3	Evenness of temper	0.73
RW 4	Daydreaming	0.71
PC 24	I want to do things to make people respect me	0.37
PC 13	I don't want to watch games like baseball	0.33
PC 11	I don't want to go to a good movie every week	0.31
RS 7	Loneliness	0.31
PC 25	I want to keep good control of my temper	0.24
WA 42	Self-sentiment (word association)	0.22

We have here a pensive, self-regarding quality, coupled with a resolve to perform in a socially acceptable fashion in one's activities. It is thought of as a sentiment rather than the drive of self-assertion (Cattell, 1957) because its pattern more closely fits that of the previously defined sentiment (Cattell, 1950; Cattell & Cross, 1952; Cattell & Miller, 1952). This sentiment is somewhat analogous to what Horney (1950) means in speaking of the "tyranny of the should."

Factor IV — Gregarious Erg

		LOADING
WA 42	Self-sentiment (word association)	0.52
WA 36	Gregarious drive (word association)	0.49
WA 41	Narcissistic-play drive (word association)	0.49
PC 12	I want to take an active part in recreation	0.37
PC 13	I want to watch games like baseball	0.36
PC 11	I want to go to a good movie every week	0.27

"Man is a social animal . . ." is here again restated in factor analytic terms. A drive to be part of the crowd is manifested by the desire for participation in essentially social activities such as baseball and movies. The gregarious erg is not as clear here as in previous research. It seems here to be mixed in with goodly helpings of self-regard and self-love or desire for self-enhancement. Variables WA 36, PC 12, and PC 13 are markers from previous research. This factor demonstrates superb simple structure and has no significantly high correlations with any other factors. Perhaps further research will be able to rotate the confusing Variables WA 42 and WA 41 out of the picture.

The strong appearance here of Variables PC 14, PC 15, and WA 37 leads to the conclusion that this factor represents the dependency drive. It is the "Mama's boy," the homesick child at camp, and the confused neurotic's plea for help. A lack of self-assertion and escape-fear is entirely consistent with this

Factor V — Appeal-Dependence Erg

		LOADING
WA 39	Lack of self-assertion (word association)	0.62
WA 38	Lack of escape-fear (word association)	0.54
RS 9	Poor state of health	0.39
PC 14	I want to feel close to God	0.35
PC 15	I want to have the advice of my parents	0.34
WA 37	Appeal-dependence drive (word association)	0.32

interpretation, as is a poor state of health. Picture the person who has been "down on his luck" for a relatively long period of time.

Factor VI — Menstruation-Depression

		LOADING
PC 10	I don't want a good-looking boy to make love to me	0.43
PC 23	I want time to enjoy my own company	0.41
RS 9	Poor state of health	0.29
QA 34	Are you menstruating? (Yes)	0.25

A more solid, impressive display of the efficacy of factor analysis could hardly be found outside the textbooks of Thurstone and Burt. It naturally follows that a girl who is menstruating considers herself in a poor state of health, wants to be alone, and especially wants no amorous entanglements at this delicate time. This type of factor has not appeared before in factor analytic research.

Factor VII — Self-Assertion

		LOADING
PC 18	I want to earn more money	0.52
PC 15	I don't want to have the advice of my parents	0.48
QA 27	Did you get a letter from home yesterday?	0.40

Factor VIII (cont'd)

		LOADING
WA 40	Parental-protective drive (word association)	0.38
QA 28	Did you write a letter home yesterday?	0.28
PC 23	I don't want time to enjoy my own company	0.27
RT 2	Reduced quantity of work	0.26
RS 7	Loneliness	0.25
PC 19	I want to succeed in my life's work	0.25
PC 22	I don't want to spend more time on smoking or drinking	0.24
RS 6	Happiness	0.24
WA 39	Self-assertion drive (word association)	0.07

This factor has the poorest simple structure in the rotated reference vector matrix. The variance of the factor is spread thin over many seemingly unrelated variables. The presence of Variables PC 18, PC 15, PC 19, and PC 22 lead strongly to the interpretation that this represents a motivational component of self-assertion even though the factor is generally muddy. Perhaps further research will provide the answer to the unsatisfactory pattern found here.

Factor VIII — Sub-Factor: "Good Time Yesterday"

		LOADING
QA 29	Did you spend any money yesterday?	0.54
QA 31	Did you read any books on the ward yesterday? (Yes)	0.49
QA 32	Did you eat between meals yesterday? (Yes)	0.46
QA 33	Did you play any games on the ward yesterday? (Yes)	0.46
PC 22	I want to spend more time on smoking and drinking	0.26
PC 15	I don't want to have the advice of my parents	0.22

This factor correlates highly with Factor IX, Narcissism (0.51), and has no real substance in itself. Therefore, it is interpreted as a sub-factor of Factor IX. This interpretation means that in another experiment, with possibly a larger number of measurements being taken, this "factor" would resolve itself into Factor IX.

Factor IX — Narcissism Erg

		LOADING
QA 31	Did you read any books on the ward yesterday? (Yes)	0.68
QA 33	Did you play any games on the ward yesterday? (Yes)	0.58
PC 22	I want to spend more time on smoking or drinking	0.38
QA 27	Did you get a letter from home yesterday? (No)	0.32
RS 8	Low amount of worry	0.32
PC 23	I want time to enjoy my own company	0.28
QA 26	Did you dream about your boyfriend last night? (Yes)	0.28
WA 41	Narcissistic-play drive (word association)	0.14

As previously mentioned, most of the variables of Subfactor VII are included here as a subset. This component is interpreted as an erg of narcissism, a self-love or desire to make oneself feel better, etc. In Freudian terms, it represents one of the paths along which the self-worshipping libidinal energy may flow. It compels its possessor to have interest investments in sex, drinking, and other "fun" activities. In the realm of clinical diagnosis, the clinician would suspect conflict if this factor and Factor III, the self-regard sentiment, were simultaneously running at relatively high levels in the same person.

There is seemingly no plausible interpretation which can be made of Factor X. It is reproduced here as much as an indication of the writers' bewilderment as for the reader's amusement. An awkward, tentative hypothesis is that this is a component somehow connected

Factor X

			LOADING
RS	7	Low amount of loneliness	0.45
PC	22	I want to spend more time on smoking or drinking	0.36
RS	6	Unhappiness	0.34
RS	8	I don't want to succeed in my life's work	0.32
PC	14	Low amount of worry	0.31
PC	19	I don't want to feel close to God	0.30
PC	20	I want to help people in trouble	0.30

with philanthropy, a sentiment possessed by one with much money (no worry) and many friends (no loneliness) but with an urge to help others. Variables RS 8 and PC 19 may indicate guilt feelings.

Factor XI — Repressed Sex Component

			LOADING
WA	35	Sex-mating (word association)	0.39
WA	40	Parental-protective drive (word association) (negative)	0.35
PC	23	I want time to enjoy my own company	0.34
QA	26	Did you dream about your boyfriend last night? (Yes)	0.31
QA	27	Did you get a letter from home yesterday? (No)	0.31

This is the last factor to be retained from the factor matrix. As such, the variance which it accounts for is necessarily lower than that accounted for by the other 10 factors. It is here interpreted as a component of repressed sex energy. The clash of feelings for one's parents and feelings for oneself comes into sharp focus in this pattern. The rise of this factor in intensity from day to day could be a signal of dammed-up sex energy looking for release. The sense of this factor, even though it correlates 0.37 with the Sex Erg, is not one of a constant flow of sexual vitality. Rather, it suggests the accumulation of sex vitality which has not yet gained expression.

SUMMARY

Objective tests whose motif was structured after that of devices employed by previous researchers were administered to a maladjusted mental defective who was a patient in a mental institution. The scores on the tests were correlated and factor analyzed. On interpretations of the factors after appropriate rotation to oblique positions, the factors so discovered appeared to be essentially congruent with previous research. Further, the factor pattern that emerged was capable of being interpreted as the motivational structure of the subject.

The possibility that not all ergs (drives) and metanergs (sentiments) were found does not detract from the basic fact that with suitable instruments one can measure and reveal the fundamental dynamic structures of a maladjusted mental defective. The implications of this for clinical practice are promising. Further confirmatory research is needed to furnish a valid, reliable instrument which can be successfully and economically used as both a diagnostic and a predictive tool. The hope that such a tool can be produced depends on the degree to which clinicians and psychometrists can work together.

References

Cattell, R. B. The discovery of ergic structure in man in terms of common attitudes. *J. aborm. soc. Psychol.*, 1950, **45**, 598–618.

Cattell, R. B. *Personality and motivation structure and measurement.* New York: World Book, 1957.

Cattell, R. B., & Cross, K. P. Comparison of the ergic and self-sentiment structures found in dynamic traits by R- and P-techniques. *J. Pers.*, 1962, **21**, 250–271.

Cattell, R. B., & Miller, A. A confirmation of the ergic and self-sentiment patterns among dynamic traits by R-technique. *Brit. J. Psychol.*, 1952, **43**, 280–294.

Horney, Karen, *Neurosis and human growth.* New York: Norton, 1950.

Neuhaus, J. O., & Wrigley, C. The quartimax method. *Brit. J. statist. Psychol.*, 1954, **7**, 81–92.

Pinzka, C., & Saunders, D. R. Analytic rotation to simple structure: II. Extension to an oblique solution. (RB-54-31) Educational Testing Service Bulletin, 1954. (Multilithed)

Thurstone, L. L. *Multiple-factor analysis.* Chicago: Univer. Chicago Press, 1947.

3. Personality Factor Structure of the Combined Guilford and Cattell Personality Questionnaires

RAYMOND B. CATTELL AND B. D. GIBBONS

2 major, but different, systems of well-factored personality-measurement scales in the questionnaire medium are currently available. 1 of these systems, developed by Guilford and his co-workers, is an orthogonal series now principally embodied in the Guilford-Zimmerman (G-Z) scale, whereas the other system, developed by Cattell and his co-workers, is an oblique series typified by the 16 PF test. The present study aimed at carrying out an adequate, though not exhaustive, oblique factor analysis jointly upon the 16 PF and G-Z scales to determine (a) if a good, unique simple structure resolution can be attained in correlation matrices obtained jointly from scales originally fitted to orthogonal and oblique factorings and (b) if the natural source traits thus revealed are those conceived in the G-Z or in the 16 PF. Attempts were also made to determine if the 2 series of scales occupy the same or a different personality space and if any meaning could be given to any extra dimensions found. The results of the analysis yielded natural source traits which, in general, were those proposed by the oblique scales. The controversy between proponents of the orthogonal systems and proponents of the oblique systems was discussed. The limitations of the present study and proposals for further, more definitive research were considered.

The Issue of Orthogonal Or Oblique Personality Source Traits

Practicing psychologists are puzzled by being presented with two major, but different, systems of well-factored personality-measurement scales in the questionnaire medium. On the one hand, there is an orthogonal series (at the adult level only) by Guilford and his coworkers (Guilford, 1940; Guilford & Guilford, 1936; Guilford & Martin, 1943; Guilford & Zimmerman, 1956) now principally embodied in the Guilford-Zimmerman scale (1949). On the other, there is the oblique series constituted by the 16 PF (Cattell & Eber, 1966), the HSPQ (Cattell, et al., 1967; Cattell, Coan, & Beloff, 1958), the CPQ (Porter, Schaie, & Cattell, 1966), and the ESPQ (Baker, Cattell, & Coan,

SOURCE. Article by Raymond B. Cattell and B. D. Gibbons, "Personality factor structure of the combined Guilford and Cattell personality questionnaires" in the Journal of personality and social psychology, Vol. 9, pp. 107–120, 1968. Copyright 1968 by the American Psychological Association and reprinted by permission.

1965), by Cattell and his co-workers, aiming to measure the same unitary traits in steps over the developmental age range.

It is not surprising that many have asked "Which factor in the Cattell series corresponds to which in the Guilford-Zimmerman?" and that many correlation matrices have been developed empirically to discover what the relationships may be. For example, French (1953) has attempted a decision at an inspectional level, and Becker (1961) found large correlations of Cattell's H, F, and Q4 with Guilford's S, R and N, respectively, while Michael, Barth, and Kaiser (1961) found much space in common to Cattell's 16 PF and Thurstone's Temperament Schedule (derived from Guilford's factors). However, with the exception of the last study (which aimed at second-order structure), these psychologists have unfortunately thought fit to ask a question which, in the simple form posed, has no systematic answer. This quickly becomes even empirically apparent in the above correlational studies, wherein the Cattell–Guilford-Zimmerman scale correlation matrix can never be arranged as a simple diagonal of near-unity correlations.

While this may be disappointing to anyone seeking an immediate convenient practical translation, in terms of supporting basic principles it is a satisfying and edifying conclusion. For it is exactly what would be expected from the obvious geometrical principle that a system of orthogonal and truly oblique factors can *never* become mutually aligned! The practitioner's demand for some kind of conceptual harmony thus compels psychometrists to face the larger issue which they should have faced before, namely, the theoretical problem of whether simple structure factor resolutions should be orthogonal or oblique. That the importance of this issue for all personality theory is now becoming more widely realized

is evidenced by the recently arranged debate on the topic between Guilford and Cattell.[1]

On behalf of the orthogonal factor position, it is argued that all calculations are simpler, and that scales are—at least theoretically, though not in practice—maximally independent. On the other hand, the argument for allowing simple structure to go oblique, if required by the data, goes back to one's possible preference for the scientific model which claims that the greatest simple structure alone will yield *invariant* unitary source traits. This model rests also on the arguments: (*a*) that unitary influences operating in a common universe would be *expected* to have some interrelation and correlation; (*b*) that in empirical fact, the ideal of simple structure per se is simply not achievable, when evaluated as total hyperplane count, when pursued with the orthogonal restriction as when pursued with the orthogonal restriction as when pursued freely (obliquely) as the sole principle of rotation; (*c*) that even if simple structure factors happened to be orthogonal in one population or sample, statistical laws would cause the same factor scales to be oblique in all others (whence it is inconsistent as a generally sought goal); (*d*) that the practical calculation simplicities hoped for from orthogonal factors are, in practice, never gained, because even if the pure factors *are* made orthogonal, the actual scales, which can never be developed as pure measures, remain oblique, and (*e*) that if the obliquity of the natural structure is accepted, a new explanatory domain of higher order factors is opened up in which we already have evidence of well defined, replicated structure.

---

[1] J. P. Guilford and R. B. Cattell, "Oblique or Orthogonal Factors?" Annual Meeting of the Society for Multivariate Experimental Psychology, University of Colorado, Boulder, 1963.

Regarding the last, that is, ignoring the higher order, by maintaining what seems to us the fiction of orthogonal factors, "personality psychology" is in fact denied a domain of scientific meaning in which many, for example, Cattell and Scheier (1961), Eysenck (1953), Thurstone (1938), have already found useful predictive concepts. For example, extraversion and anxiety are two well-replicated (Cattell & Scheier, 1961) higher order factors scorable from the 16 PF and also from the High School Personality Questionnaire, etc. (HSPQ—Cattell, 1965; Cattell & Nuttall, 1967), which would never be perceived in the orthogonal resolution.

Some of the above issues, notably the argument of essential incompatibility of orthogonality and simple structure, have been pursued within the technical realm of factor analysis *per se* elsewhere (Cattell, 1966). But in the present article, it is planned simply to carry out a first adequate, though not exhaustive, factor analysis jointly upon the Cattell 16 PF and the Guilford-Zimmerman scales to see what simple structure yields. The questions asked are: (*a*) In correlation matrices jointly from scales originally fitted to orthogonal and oblique factorings, can a good, unique, simple structure resolution actually be attained? (*b*) If so, are the natural source traits thus revealed those conceived in the G-Z or in the 16 PF? (*c*) Quite apart from whatever factor resolution is indicated, do the two series of scales *occupy* the same or a different personality space? (For if the answer to the last is that there is considerable overlap, it would at least be possible to supply practicing psychologists with multiple regression equations for predicting scores on Guilford factors from Cattell factors and vice versa.) (*d*) Can any meaning, perhaps distinct from either scale concepts, be given to any extra dimensions that may be found?

Design of the Experiment

The Guilford scale, which we shall generally call the G-Z scales for short, are actually spread over four sources labelled in Table 1, the GAMIN (Guilford & Martin, 1943), the DFOS (Guilford & Zimmerman, 1956), the STDCR (Guilford; 1940), and the GZTS (Guilford & Zimmerman, 1949). It is helpful to give a brief historical resume of the origins of this work. Guilford's interest began with an attempt to define Extraversion-Introversion, in which he and R. B. Guilford selected 35 questionnaire items which represented recognized qualities in that area. These items were administered to a large sample of 302 subjects and tetrachoric correlations were calculated. The centroid factor analysis revealed 5 meaningful factors, named by them, social introversion, emotionality, masculinity, thinking introversion, and rhathymia (Guilford & Guilford, 1936). Two additional studies by the Guilfords resulted in the identification of four additional factors: Depression, Alertness, Nervousness, and General Drive (Guilford & Guilford, 1939a, 1939b).

Using the information from these early studies on Introversion-Extraversion, Guilford (1940) developed the *Inventory of Factors STDCR*, and collaborating with Martin, developed the *Inventory of Factors GAMIN* (Guilford & Martin, 1943). Finally, in order to consolidate factors into a single inventory for obtaining a comprehensive picture of individual personalities, Guilford and Zimmerman selected factors from the Guilford and Guilford-Martin inventories and developed the *Guilford-Zimmerman Temperament Survey* (1949).

By contrast, the 16 PF was based on the concept of a total *personality sphere* of variables, which at first had to rest on the dictionary and therefore on factors found in ratings (Cattell, 1946). A systematic survey of all factors found in questionnaires to that date showed that they occupied only a corner—and largely a clinical corner—of the personality sphere space (Cattell, 1946), so their items were balanced, in the hundreds of items from which the 16 PF was developed, by such rating dimension equivalents as dominance-submission, radicalism, premsia, autia, the self-sentiment, etc. The succession of factor analysis since then (Cattell, 1950, 1956; Cattell & Eber, 1966; Cattell, Pichot, & Rennes, 1961; Cattell & Tsujioka, 1965) have checked the structure, here and abroad, and have extended the measurement basis. However, this work has always recognized (Cattell, 1957) that some 10 further factors need inclusion, some of them in the psychotic behavior area. On historical origins, therefore, one might expect the 16 PF to reach out into somewhat broader space (notably beyond the *exvia-invia* area using exvia for the second order factor at the core of the popular "extraversion" notion), yet still not to be entirely comprehensive of a normal and abnormal personality sphere.

Because only 1.5–2 hours of student time were available, the full Guilford and Cattell scales could not be used, but instead two or three sufficiently representative "packages" of items from each of the Guilford scales and each of the 16 PF scales (1962 edition: see Cattell & Eber, 1966) were made up, of the size and nature shown in Table 1. The plan called for each hypothesized factor to be represented by at least two packages—the theoretically requisite minimum number for marking a common or broad factor—in the case of both the Guilford and the Cattell systems. In some cases, however, the supply of items made it possible to introduce three, and in a few instances, perhaps unfortunately, only one marker was introduced. When the latter was done, it was justified on the high probability,

from psychological meaning ("content"), that other packages existed elsewhere in the series to bring out that factor.[2]

As far as representation of the hypotheses inherent in the G-Z scales and the 16 PF is concerned, the 40 markers averaging five items each from the former and 28 averaging six each from the latter, as shown in Table 1, would seem to be adequate. Incidentally, the above slight discrepancy in items representing the 14 of the 16 PF marked and the 15 G-Z factors cannot be said to give any really heavier representation to one than the other in determining the final common factors, since there is a certainty from previous research that a great deal of common space will emerge so that most markers will do duty in defining the factors of both series of scale.

A factor analysis of the final battery of 424 items, representing the 68 variables of Table 1 (plus a masculine-feminine sex variable), seemed to require a minimum of 250 subjects on Tucker's rule that subjects outnumber variables at least 3 to 1, and the empirical finding of Cattell (1966) and Cattell, Rican, and Jaspers (1968) that with studies of their general size the loadings stabilize with numbers between 250 and 500. Accordingly, a sample of 302 undergraduate students, roughly evenly divided between the sexes, and ranging in age from 17 to 25, were given the whole battery in a single session of $1\frac{1}{2}$ to $1\frac{3}{4}$ hours.

---

[2]From the standpoint of the senior author, it would have been more satisfactory here not to omit Factor N from the 16 PF or to rest the definition of A on only one marker. In explaining this slight difference of valuation it may be helpful to the reader to be informed that the junior author had the "third person" role, highly desirable in a research of this kind, of working on the one hand closely with J. P. Guilford on the thesis designed in this area and on the other, with R. B. Cattell, as a research associate, experimenting with rotational methods.

TABLE 1   *Brief Identification of 69 Variables: Personality Factor Scale Packages Used in This Analysis*

VARIABLE NO.	NAME	NO. ITEMS IN PACKAGE	PERSONALITY TEST	FACTOR SYMBOL
1	Male-Female dichotomy	—	—	—
2	Social interest	5	16 PF	H
3	Social poise	5	16 PF	H
4	Artistic refinement	5	16 PF	I
5	Refinement vs. practicality	5	16 PF	I
6	Refinement vs. practicality	5	16 PF	I
7	Cultural interests	5	16 PF	M
8	Inferiority vs. confidence	5	16 PF	O
9	Emotional immaturity	5	16 PF	O
10	Meditative thinking	5	16 PF	Q_1
11	Disliking activity with others	5	16 PF	Q_2
12	Disliking activity with others	5	16 PF	Q_2
13	Lack of impulsiveness	5	16 PF	Q_3
14	Lack of impulsiveness	5	16 PF	Q_3
15	Persistent effort	5	16 PF	Q_3
16	Emotional immaturity	5	16 PF	Q_4
34	Moral sensitivity	5	16 PF	C
35	Moral sensitivity	5	16 PF	C
36	Lack of hypo-chondriasis	5	16 PF	C
37	Ascendance (Leadership)	5	16 PF	E
38	Confidence vs. inferiority	5	16 PF	E
39	Ascendance	5	16 PF	H
40	Radicalism vs. conservatism	5	16 PF	Q_1
41	Radicalism vs. conservatism	5	16 PF	Q_1
42	Rapid pace	6	GAMIN	G
43	Drive for activity	6	GAMIN	G
44	Masculine vocational preference	6	GAMIN	M
45	Masculine avocational preference	6	GAMIN	M
46	AA – Graphic arts	6	DFOS	AA
47	AA – Drama	6	DFOS	AA
48	AA – Literature	6	DFOS	AA
49	Cultural conformity – conformity	6	DFOS	CC

No.	Trait		Test	Factor
17	Social interest	5	16 PF	A
18	Ascendance (face-to-face)	5	16 PF	E
19	Liking activity and change	5	16 PF	F
20	Lack of moral restraint	5	16 PF	F
21	Rhathymia vs. restraint	5	16 PF	F
22	Confidence vs. inferiority	5	16 PF	G
23	Moral restraint	5	16 PF	G
24	Confidence vs. inferiority	5	16 PF	H
25	Criticalness	5	16 PF	L
26	Criticalness	5	16 PF	L
27	Resentment	5	16 PF	L
28	Cultural sensitivity	5	16 PF	M
29	Cultural sensitivity	5	16 PF	M
30	Inferiority vs. confidence	5	16 PF	O
31	Lack of social interest	5	16 PF	Q_2
32	Inferiority vs. confidence	5	16 PF	Q_4
33	Nervousness vs. composure	5	16 PF	Q_4

No.	Trait		Test	Factor
50	Maintain one's rights	6	GAMIN	A
51	Feelings of acceptance	6	GAMIN	I
52	Lack of restlessness	6	GAMIN	N
53	Lack of nervousness—jumpiness	6	GAMIN	N
54	Lack of fatigueability	6	GAMIN	N
55	Lack of gregariousness	6	STDCR	S
56	Physical depletion	6	STDCR	D
57	Carefreeness vs. restraint	6	STDCR	R
58	Unconcern vs. seriousness	6	STDCR	R
59	Lack of social poise	6	STDCR	S
60	Liking for serious thinking	6	STDCR	T
61	Analysis for self and others	6	STDCR	T
62	Emotional depression	6	STDCR	D
63	Tolerance	6	GZTS	P
64	Thickskinned	6	GZTS	O
65	Lack of hostility	6	GZTS	F
66	Liking social affairs	6	GZTS	S
67	Friends and acquaintances	6	GZTS	S
68	Optimism	6	GZTS	E
69	Even mood	6	GZTS	E

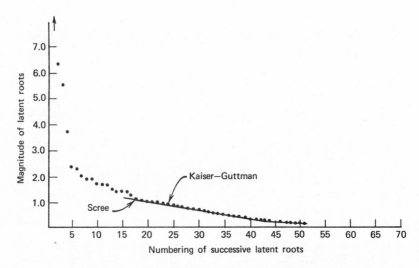

Figure 1. *Application of tests for the number of factors*

Statistical Analysis

Scores on the 69 scales (parcels) were intercorrelated by the tetrachoric correlation coefficient by use of the cosine-pi approximation. To decide on the number of factors, both a Kaiser-Guttman (Kaiser, 1960) and a Scree (Cattell, 1966b) test were applied. Both required that a principal axis factoring with unities in the diagonal first be performed. Since the number of factors is an important issue here, the result of these tests is shown in Diagram 1 [Fig. 1].

The Scree test definitely indicates either 17 or 18 factors, while the Kaiser-Guttman suggests 23 or 24 factors. As shown elsewhere (Cattell, 1966a), the latter test tends to underestimate with few variables and overestimate with many (say, over 50), so the former is supported. In any case, rather than risk factor fission in the rotation, the authors preferred the disadvantage of possibly missing a factor and having somewhat blurred hyperplanes. Accordingly, we compromised

on 18 and returned to the computer to interate the communalities to exact values for this number of factors. The resulting unrotated V_0 matrix is preserved and available from the senior author while the original correlation matrix is obtainable from a thesis (Gibbons, 1966).

Two different rotational solutions, one restricted to orthogonal position and one not so restricted, were tried. The first, using varimax, obtained a total ± 0.10 hyperplane count of 48%. By Bargmann's test (1954), this gives a nonsignificant simple structure of $p > 0.20$. It has accordingly not been reported in detail here, but is available for inspection elsewhere (Gibbons, 1966). The second analysis, for oblique simple structure, used the new topological computer program Maxplane,[3] followed by a very thorough pursuit of simple structure by 11 shifts on

---

[3] R. B. Cattell, J. Ford, and A. Wagner. The flexible and prescribed Maxplane topological program for oblique simple structure. Manuscript in preparation.

the Rotoplot program (Cattell & Foster, 1963). The latter showed the usual climb to a steady hyperplane maximum (plateau on curve), and achieved a hyperplane count (± 0.10 hyperplane) of 63.6%. This reaches a Bargmann significance of $p <$ 0.02, emphatically better than for the alternative orthogonal resolution above, yet not so good as the 81% obtained for the 16 PF alone (Cattell & Eber, 1966). However, regardless of the absolute significance, the very extensive trial and error exploration of the space by the 11 Rotoplot shifts makes it extremely improbable that any substantially better position exists to be found, and that we are close to the unique maximum.

This highest achieved simple structure position is definitely oblique, the correlations among the factors shown in Table 3. The reference vector solution obtained is shown in Table 2, where the numbers of the variables are the same as in Table 1.

Two of the factors in Table 2, namely 16 and 18, can be written off as practically formless residuals (we believed we had overextracted by one factor to allow for such error factors). Also, from a personality standpoint, we can set aside 17 which picks out clearly the interest factor in arts, in Variables 46, 47, and 48 in DFOS. As an interest-motivation factor it is not of the same species as the personality factors. Of the remaining 15 factors, 11 (Numbers 1–7, 9, 10, 12, and 13) turn out to have the markers for the 16 PF factors appearing upon them just as the theory regarding these personality source traits would require, the highest loading of the 16 PFs being higher than for any other variable. In two other factors, 8 and 11, both the 16 PF markers again appear just as they should, as to sign and significance, and the simple structure is good, but a slightly higher loading than that of the legitimate markers is achieved by some seemingly erratic

variable, adequate for marking neither a Guilford nor a Cattell factor in terms of its marker "company." The remaining two factors are relatively obscure: 15 is a split off "half" of Guilford's E factor; 14 has some loading on the 16 PF Ergic Tension (Q_4) and consistently on the two Guilford markers for his General Activity (42, Rapid Pace, and 43, Drive for Activity), but also some seemingly erratic loading on 47 and 58. If the latter could be reconciled it could be reasonably interpreted as a factor combining the meaning of Cattell's Ergic Tension (Q_4) and Guilford's General Activity, which are psychologically consistent in conceptualization.

By contrast with the above extent of consistency, shown by 13 of the 15 submitted 16 PF factors having turned up with their markers on, and essentially *only* on, a given factor here, the G-Z factor markers are mainly scattered. For example, the markers for GAMIN G, though substantially homogeneous (by the verdict of the correlation matrix) split in rotation evenly between the simple structure Factors 6 and 14; the markers for R split between 1 and 12; those for Guilford's T straddle 7 and 9 evenly; those for the G-Z E divide between 10 and 15; while conversely, those for D, P, O and F (Numbers 62–65) lose their independent identity by landing on one and the same factor.

On the other hand, three G-Z factors, M, N, and S, show good consistency both as to consistency of marker placement and goodness of simple structure property. However, they do so by landing on factors already more highly marked by 16 PF factors. Thus M (Masculinity) is seemingly identical with the 16 PF factor I(−) (Harria), while N (Nervousness − 52, 53, 54) aligns with 16 PF O, Guilt Proneness, and S Sociability (Variables 59, 66, 67) coming out clearly in company with Cattell's H factor, Parmia-vs.-Threctia.

Table 2 Primary Factor Pattern: Rotated Factor Matrix

INDENT. BY 16 PF VARIABLE NO. (TABLE I)	1 A	2 C	3 E	4 F	5 G	6 H	7 I	8 L	9 M	10 O	11 Q1	12 Q2	13 Q3	14 Q4 (NEW)	15 RESID.	16 RESID.	17 AA	18 RESID.	14 Q4 (OLD)
Catell Markers:																			
1	19	00	20	−04	−03	−00	−67	13	−07	−02	26	10	08	−07	07	−08	13	08	−07
2	01	−10	−11	−02	−12	62	16	02	−10	−07	−01	−00	07	−02	−04	−13	25	04	01
3	−02	−40	30	−07	04	58	17	−06	−05	−12	12	01	01	−04	−00	41	07	29	01
4	−26	15	15	−03	11	−11	37	01	10	06	−06	08	−02	−05	06	07	06	18	−08
5	02	−11	03	18	05	01	76	−18	12	07	−01	−03	−08	05	−01	04	−17	−05	03
6	16	09	−21	21	01	−08	60	−05	11	01	03	07	08	−01	06	02	07	19	−01
7	03	03	−00	12	−11	−07	47	−25	24	02	−06	22	06	04	−04	01	05	−01	03
8	−02	−10	04	−04	−09	−26	10	03	03	30	−25	−11	15	08	−02	−29	−08	22	−03
9	−04	−14	12	08	15	08	−02	−09	13	49	−29	−02	00	14	−03	01	−04	09	−05
10	24	03	12	06	−03	−06	−25	−09	04	−12	19	−05	−11	−19	38	−10	−10	−05	−16
11	−23	02	−07	24	−13	−10	06	15	03	05	01	67	04	16	−00	15	17	12	15
12	−33	−02	−04	−01	14	05	−23	−47	−01	−10	−01	45	−03	−14	02	−16	06	−06	−11
13	11	−19	−09	−13	21	−11	−19	−00	−11	−22	20	−04	10	−10	28	−16	−11	−05	−02
14	18	09	−24	09	04	−30	−06	−05	03	−35	32	07	21	−14	−00	−02	−09	05	−01
15	13	−02	06	−11	−06	07	−11	−01	21	−01	−00	00	59	32	−17	13	09	−05	35
16	00	01	17	−09	12	−05	03	01	−11	43	−43	00	−09	44	−05	02	06	04	24
17	54	03	−01	09	15	07	04	07	29	03	−05	−23	01	−03	02	00	10	03	−04
18	03	−03	16	16	−10	42	−01	15	−16	34	−07	07	−14	11	−01	04	05	03	−02
19	−11	10	15	04	19	40	02	−30	13	21	33	00	−11	15	03	−20	−01	15	08
20	01	−08	−07	85	05	03	14	27	03	−03	−12	03	03	21	02	−05	−08	02	−22
21	01	−00	01	11	02	49	06	−07	03	13	00	−07	−02	10	−05	06	−07	54	06
22	07	05	−18	−12	49	−01	10	09	−08	−12	−01	11	−02	−08	05	−00	−01	04	−04
23	17	11	−08	01	33	−06	−06	−08	−08	−05	03	−03	32	01	−01	06	−07	−11	03
24	06	−17	−02	−18	05	47	−09	00	41	−18	−12	−02	06	−17	07	28	−03	06	−11
25	−0.	−12	03	−09	28	00	−26	30	19	13	−01	04	−13	06	−04	−01	−05	−05	01
26	03	−10	11	−02	−07	03	−03	36	06	45	−12	02	−01	22	23	02	06	−13	06
27	−04	−03	−08	−18	09	26	10	14	44	29	−08	08	02	10	−33	01	14	05	−01
28	−02	−03	−03	14	06	−03	27	42	45	25	04	00	52	11	30	03	09	07	02
29	−03	−06	−06	−18	−08	04	28	01	50	−09	−06	01	−10	−03	−12	06	02	05	00
30	06	−03	03	03	−04	−19	23	02	−04	61	−04	02	03	34	−21	11	09	07	12
31	−25	−01	−17	−01	32	−36	−05	−01	−02	−02	−05	17	−05	−04	−03	32	05	05	03
32	08	−17	−06	−07	05	06	13	05	12	49	−24	−06	09	23	05	15	13	−14	05
33	−04	09	−03	−05	07	−05	20	06	−08	60	−09	12	00	22	12	09	05	−07	00

Var																			
34	11	43	-02	20	23	-07	-21	30	04	43	05	-03	-10	03	-24	-07	-10	06	
35	-02	28	-05	-12	10	00	11	-04	-02	-32	-07	-03	14	12	05	-03	06	28	
36	-05	35	11	-09	04	-02	-04	-03	-21	-26	-09	-01	01	33	07	10	07	12	
37	-01	02	30	12	-12	01	-01	15	01	09	-03	02	09	29	-01	11	-00	06	
38	09	09	51	01	-01	03	-06	-08	11	-01	06	20	00	02	06	12	01	00	
39	-04	-01	19	-01	44	06	09	-06	06	13	29	13	16	04	19	13	10	12	
40	-14	-24	17	-09	-04	-02	-02	-26	-02	-04	13	02	02	-06	07	-12	-01	04	
41	-08	04	06	21	-12	21	-17	21	33	29	-09	07	37	10	07	01	01	38	
Guilford Markers:																			
42	09	-10	-02	20	-09	-02	02	-09	08	-02	08	-02	37	01	-02	-25	-02	-10	06
43	01	-09	03	-06	05	03	-00	03	-04	07	-04	-06	46	-00	03	-09	-03	06	28
44	30	08	32	-04	-02	16	-70	-02	09	-02	09	11	02	08	24	11	08	07	24
45	-07	11	23	-06	05	23	-42	01	-09	01	-09	-12	00	-09	08	-06	-20	-00	-00
46	-04	03	26	08	-04	-05	59	08	08	02	06	09	-04	08	03	07	-06	-10	04
47	00	08	-08	04	03	-12	57	-01	-01	03	-01	-01	-04	-01	15	02	07	02	-05
48	22	-13	-00	06	-02	11	32	49	-01	01	-10	25	09	06	49	11	-02	13	24
49	-14	-22	11	-13	-03	-02	32	-01	10	-01	20	-04	22	-05	32	02	-06	15	21
50	-06	-19	11	-02	-04	-05	-04	13	20	00	-05	06	15	-10	-04	-13	-05	22	22
51	10	04	08	07	-03	-10	03	-31	10	-10	07	39	09	-00	-03	04	-00	-13	02
52	02	-09	02	11	-08	-09	-05	-41	07	-11	11	13	-13	10	-40	-08	-10	-14	03
53	-03	-01	28	05	06	06	-07	-46	08	-08	05	-12	-14	-08	-07	-03	03	-12	09
54	01	-04	08	04	-11	-00	-28	-55	05	-33	04	08	-03	04	-40	-05	01	03	07
55	07	-01	-05	-01	-11	04	-04	-15	01	01	-27	11	18	01	-03	19	-05	07	-06
56	-11	-01	19	12	-11	03	-12	50	07	-03	-06	13	09	07	12	00	19	-01	-01
57	-44	02	00	09	02	04	-05	04	12	12	-03	-03	46	07	-02	04	-06	02	34
58	05	-06	04	04	-14	-09	06	-13	-06	-02	-06	-03	29	-36	-34	09	-13	-46	58
59	-06	-13	-09	01	03	01	51	30	-03	-07	03	-06	22	-07	-01	-02	09	29	05
60	39	-02	-01	18	03	18	47	-07	25	-00	03	-05	30	25	-04	01	01	22	00
61	-12	-07	09	22	06	03	22	04	03	-02	-07	-31	-12	03	-03	01	18	-40	-07
62	-06	09	-14	05	-09	06	-04	49	-02	-21	-02	-06	-03	-02	-25	-12	22	-02	-07
63	01	12	-03	19	-04	-09	-10	47	-21	-49	-10	-22	-14	-21	-00	09	-04	10	-07
64	09	18	-02	18	-09	00	-00	-37	04	37	-03	-08	-20	-30	18	31	12	05	01
65	01	02	04	-05	16	01	18	03	00	03	13	07	05	07	-25	-05	08	03	02
66	-30	04	-06	01	-05	-02	31	-28	06	04	-02	-09	-04	-12	39	16	01	-04	00
67	-01	02	-11	05	12	-06	05	-53	-12	02	-30	02	06	03	03	-05	-01	10	37
68	07	-11	-02	-11	06	-08	-01	-59	03	-00	-27	-05	-18	-10	07	12	05	-02	17
69	-16	-02	-03	06	-06	11	-12	-10	-10	-14	-05	-05	-35	-10	-06	06	-11	-06	-14

Note.—All decimal points have been omitted. Around loadings fitting final interpretation by these markings. Around loadings not fitting final interpretation by these marking. Around loadings fitting final interpretation by these markings.

Since the last is only one of four distinct components in sociability (i.e., in the second order FI, Exvia-vs.-Invia, in the 16 PF), the restricted technical (auto-nomic) definition given by the term Parmia-vs.-Threctia is perhaps preferable in precise psychological analysis to "Soci-ability."

Description of the total resolution in Table 2 would require some reference also to minor, more detailed points, only briefly discussable in this space. As far as support for the 16 PF factors is concerned, the main weakness here lies in the com-paratively poor definition of the Ergic Tension (Q_4) factor, and the absorption of part of its variance, as well as some of C(–), Ego Weakness, into O factor. We suspect that if anyone cares to carry the notational exploration still further he may find some improvement of the

relative positions of these factors which would exclude the trespass of C and Q_4 on O and of O slightly on Q_1. Since the above table was set up, in fact, a new position was found by a research assistant for Q_4 (Factor 14). It has the original loadings shown at the right of Table 2, as 14, and this position, having slightly better simple structure, has been used in further work in Table 3 and in the mean simple structure count. This slight mu-tual entanglement of C(–), O, and Q_4, which are normally clearly separate, yet productive by their characteristic posi-tive correlations of a common second order factor (Anxiety), will be discussed below.

Since the parcels of items were cut to rather few items each to get into the total $1\frac{1}{2}$ hours of testing, Table 2 shows the defects of some unreliability of loadings

TABLE 3   Structure at The Second Order: Rotated Factor Matrix

FACTORS BY 16PF SYMBOLS	PRIMARY No.	Second-Stratum Numbers								
		1 EXVIA	2 ANXIETY	3 CORTERTIA	4 INDEP.	5	6	7	8	9
A	1	16	−01	35	−25	−05	10	−06	−16	00
C	2	07	−49	−03	−03	01	−01	13	12	−19
E	3	32	−05	14	46	33	06	05	−00	−13
F	4	41	−02	−10	19	−03	−09	−04	02	01
G	5	51	37	−09	09	16	−22	−03	04	01
H	6	10	−46	−12	−12	08	−14	−03	19	06
I	7	02	01	58	−08	08	−08	−01	05	06
L	8	−04	−01	−12	−02	71	14	01	01	−09
M	9	−07	03	−05	63	−01	19	29	−34	−04
O	10	−61	04	−12	−28	−41	01	03	−29	−19
Q_1	11	−46	−02	11	16	09	01	−08	−19	−28
Q_2	12	−20	03	02	10	−13	87	01	02	03
Q_3	13	−02	−21	00	−01	−20	−03	01	78	−00
Q_4	14	09	41	−50	−04	06	−00	01	06	05
(?)	15	−03	−03	−01	02	−03	01	−00	−01	64
(?)	16	34	−31	06	−03	−07	−10	−08	−10	−01
(AA)	17	09	03	−24	38	−02	−04	−11	−08	06
(?)	18	02	−01	02	−00	01	−03	77	−01	04

Note. — all decimal points have been omitted.

(including the random erratics mentioned) and of uneven communalities. Bringing all variables to the same, unit communality as in Alpha factor analysis (Kaiser & Caffrey, 1965) might be a useful step to throw a little light on one question — the estimated degree of factor purity. However, any estimate of what would happen with increased marker reliability simultaneously introduces other errors, so we have not pursued analysis in this direction on the present sample. However, the issue needing to be explored is whether such alternative analyses raise loadings of markers where a true factor match has been asserted without raising their loadings on other, nonrelevant factors beyond the hyperplane level.

The main upshot of the analysis to this point may therefore be described as the appearance, at the maximum simple structure position, of: (*a*) all but possibly one of the 16 PF factors; (*b*) the alignment of three G-Z factors with three of them; M(−) with I in the 16 PF, N with O, and S with H; (*c*) the almost even splitting, as if they were complex variables of four Guilford factors: G, R, T, and E, between just two 16 PF factors each (E *should* split, since it is conceived a composite); (*d*) the absence of evidence of the full supposed dimensionality in the Guilford factors in that, reciprocally to the above splitting, there is coherence of five supposed independent factors—D, P, O, F, and N upon one factor, O in the 16 PF (This could be — except in the case of N—for lack of second markers, i.e., they might have factor dimensionality if split again, but correlate strongly with 16 PF O.); (*e*) a small number of random unexpected projections, not nearly enough to upset simple structure, but indicating that a precise answer on issues above will require scales of longer item count. One hopes that these uncertainties will be cleared up in the larger scale study by Sells (1966) now in progress.

The Higher Stratum Structure

It is now generally recognized that the matching and identification of factors is not to be settled by primary factor loading pattern alone, but also by factor variance size, etc. (Cattell, 1962), and, particularly, by the structure which emerges at the higher order (Cattell, 1962). Accordingly, the present analysis was next carried to the second order, to compare with the now numerous and concordant results on second-order structure in this realm (Cattell, 1956, 1957; Cattell & Eber, 1966; Cattell & Tsujioka, 1965; Gorsuch & Cattell, in press; Karson & Pool, 1958.)

The Scree test (Cattell, 1966b), applied to the latent roots from Table 2, and similarly calculated to that shown in Figure 1 at the first order, showed 9 factors, which, when extracted and rotated by Maxplane plus 10 Rotoplot shifts, finished with the highest attainable simple structure (63.5%) shown in Table 3.

The agreement with the central tendency of other studies is on the whole good, but weak on Factor I, Exvis-vs.-Invia. Characteristically this loads A+, E+, F+, H+, and Q_2−, as here, but in the present instance, Factor I also has some substantial loadings on G, O, and Q_1. Factor II is an excellent anxiety pattern, except perhaps for insufficient loading on O. Factors II and IV behave just as Cortertia and Independence patterns typically do, except here for the large loading on Q_4, while the later smaller factors are compatible with the alternatives which normally arise in rotations of the remainder. The second order thus supports what was suggested at the first: (*a*) that the main 16 PF factors are identifiable, but (*b*) that there is something amiss in the rotation positions of O and Q_4. (Incidentally, the new primary— "graphic arts interest," No. 17 — is shown to be partly a combination of Pathemia, No. 3 (−), opposite of Corteria, and Independence, No. 4, which suggests a promising psychological hypothesis for those concerned with the roots of artistic interest.)

A third, but slighter check on the present identification of the primaries comes from the sex correlation—Row I in Table 2. These again are congruent with the 16 PF source trait findings generally, the associations of masculinity with Dominance (E+), with Harria (I), again and with Radicalism (Q₁), being those typically found. However, again O and Q₄ seem to be poorly located, for the usual correlation of higher score with feminine sex does not appear. For those wishing to examine yet higher orders the correlations of the secondaries are set out in Table 4.

Discussion and Summary

The vital issues which this factor analytic study raises for further discussion turn less on any technical procedures employed in determining number of factors, communalities, etc., which are those ordinarily used and leave little room for dispute, than on the precision of the particular resolution reached by simple structure. A reliable verdict in any simple structure resolution needs to be based on (*a*) use of a sufficiently large and comprehensive (stratified or random) sample of variables; (*b*) blind pursuit of a maximum hyperplane count without regard to subjective ideas of meaning or the preservation of orthogonality; (*c*) demonstration that the position reached is statistically significant or unimprovable. Parenthetically, it is neither a necessary nor a sufficient condition that the position reached by an *automatic* computer program! For most analytic programs are inadequate, and blind rotation, pursued for example by Rotoplot (Cattell & Foster, 1963), can practically invariably reach more significant hyperplane counts than any automatic program.

Elsewhere (Cattell, Coan, & Beloff, 1958) the senior author has pointed out that though rotation by putting axes through homogeneous clusters can very easily be biased by choice of items, it is difficult, by similar artificial choice of items, to create an *n* dimensional hyperplane "cluster," that is, to modify rotation by deliberate choice of items. However, in the *orthogonal* case only, a collection of variables *can* be relatively easily manufactured in which hyperplanes fit an a priori system. It can be done by starting with enough items and retaining, as each factor marker is set up in the next

TABLE 4 R_{fn}: *Correlations Among Second-order Factors*

	1	2	3	4	5	6	7	8	9
1	100	−18	−02	−28	−20	32	−07	−15	−03
2	−18	100	10	−08	04	00	−06	05	−23
3	−02	10	100	−11	−04	10	08	07	09
4	−28	−08	−11	100	−22	−31	−21	09	20
5	−20	04	−04	−22	100	08	01	16	−37
6	32	00	10	−31	08	100	−05	−08	−10
7	−07	−06	08	−21	01	−05	100	−06	−07
8	−15	05	07	09	16	−08	−06	100	−06
9	−03	−23	09	20	−37	−10	−07	−06	100

Note.—All decimal points have been omitted.

research in the area, just those high on other factors (in the orthogonal matrix) which have zero loading on the vector one has arbitrarily chosen to consider a factor. Thus one "purifies" the orthogonal matrix, in favor of items having only highs and zeroes as required, and this could be done even from the first, principal axis *un*rotated matrix.[4]

If one's aim, as in the philosophy of "structured psychological measurement" (Cattell, 1957) is to construct scales which follow the forms of nature, each factor scale or battery being aimed at some meaningful psychological concept which is invariant across experiments, then simple structure has to be found in a random sample of variables, not made. By contrast, the argument for orthogonal scales being functional is akin to that of a forester who lops off from his trees all branches that are not horizontal and then preceeds with his forestry science on the definition of branches as horizontal projections.

Once artificial scales have been set up with certain restrictions (be they, in our analogy, horizontal branches, or, say, only all oblique branches left exactly at 45 degrees to the vertical), simple structure is likely to pull out of research what was put in. Factor analysis so conducted is vulnerable to all the old criticism that "it only gets out what it puts in." There is some gleam of possible discovery, however, even in such procedures, since the

fallible human experimenter, despite himself, in injecting his own a priori structure, may have forgotten to remove some more subtle structure which he failed to see, and which remains as an alternative to his imposed structure. Consequently, when as here, one puts together a set of variables possessing an imposed orthogonal structure, with a set claiming to represent the natural oblique structure originally found in nature in a far larger sample of items representing the personality sphere, it is not a foregone conclusion that the artificial orthogonal structure will determine the rotation. But, almost certainly, problems will arise in the rotation which do not arise in rotating a broad sample of variables for the first time from the personality sphere.[5]

Since a predominance of scales from an artificial orthogonal construction could swamp the natural position, it would seem that in cases of this kind the salvation of the natural resolution lies in (*a*) the fact that those who attempt to construct scales along a priori orthogonal vectors (which are not factor source traits) will fail to get orthogonality in the scales themselves, and the regression from orthogonality will be toward the zones where items are more readily obtained (the hyperplanes); (*b*) attention to the experimental design's retaining a predominance of scales which have not been tampered with, that is, which simply reflect the simple structure found in a far larger sample of variables, and (*c*) the inclusion not just of *one* experimenter's selection of orthogonal scales but of such

---

[4]Scientifically the procedure is no more defensible than was Spearman's "purification" of a correlation matrix by rejecting whatever broke the hierarchy of his general factor, yet oddly enough it has not so far incurred the same criticism. Indeed, Guilford has actually set up this notion of purification as an ideal in scale construction, and practiced it in producing his scales. As pointed out, any corresponding attempt at artificial hyperplane construction with oblique structures would be far more difficult, and it would also (on an arbitrary basis) be pointless, so that as far as the authors know, it has never been invoked.

[5]This was clearly evident in our Rotoplots, which had an unmistakably abnormal appearance relative to those we have seen in several dozens of experiments with representative or random samples of variables. The oddity consisted mainly of an unusual number of variables of high communality (long vectors) fanning out about the central hyperplane tendency instead of settling into reasonably narrow hyperplanes.

orthogonals from at least three or four independent subjective choices of orthogonal systems. For less the investigators all happen to be bewitched by the same concepts in the Zeitgeist, prejudices will tend to cancel and the scales will make the same approach to a comprehensive random sampling of behavior as originally occurred in items. However, even then there will be *some* false concentrations of variables at right angles to the positions in which the concentrations naturally occur, that is, the true obliquity will tend to be reduced.

Fortunately, the solution to this problem is helped here, even with the unusually good workmanship of the Guilford scales, by the above regression of constructed scales from the orthogonality aimed at in the theoretical scales. For the actual G-Z scales, as is well known (see Guilford & Zimmerman, 1963), do not preserve the mutual zero correlation specified in the ideal orthogonal scales of the original factor analysis from which the blue prints were constructed. Whatever natural tendencies there were to concentrate in certain planes which existed in the large sample of original items will to some extent get through. However, our experience with the distortion of the second-order realm here (where slight deviations, as in the O and Q_4 factors, can cause appreciable upset) strongly supports the above theoretical argument that any attempt to decide between factor structures of two scales had best (*a*) include other sources of items carefully chosen as a stratified sample from a representative defined total personality sphere, and (*b*) break down the scales under examination ideally into single items or, if economy forbids this, into a fair number—at least three or four—nonoverlapping, random "parcels" from each scale.

The present study has introduced *a* only to a minor degree, and has gone only

a moderate way toward a sufficiency of *b*. As a pilot study its results suggest that the conditions chosen are perhaps only just within the limits of successful handling of the problem. Certainly a definitive study will need to go further in the direction indicated for ideal conditions.

Meanwhile, our results on the present basis may be summarized:

1. That the simple structure obtainable in a joint sample of variables by oblique resolution, even where one of the two systems has constructed its scales to be orthogonal, is decidedly better than for the corresponding orthogonal resolution.

2. This resolution confirms, by the two or three markers for the hypothesized factor appearing consistently together on one factor, and not saliently on any other, all 14 of the 16 PF factors included (Intelligence, B, and Shrewdness, N, were not used).

3. Further evidence of the present resolution being correct exists, (*a*) in the sex differences on the factors appearing, where they appear, as previously found and, (*b*) more crucially, in the second order structure being consistent in its major features with that usually obtained.

4. Nevertheless, the same criteria agree in suggesting that Factor O, Guilt Proneness, Q_4, Ergic Tension, and C, Ego Strength, suffer from some distortion of their usual rotation position here.

5. Three Guilford factors align as simple structure factors clearly with Cattell factors (M with I; N with O, and S with H). Four (like C, O, and Q_4 above), namely E, G, R, and T, split their loadings and would be considered, by the 16 PF and this analysis, as test-homogeneous —factor-heterogeneous scales. Five G-Z factors seem to be expressions of only one factor here; that usually identified as Guilt Proneness, O.

6. No broad dimensionality not com-

mon to the two series can be clearly recognized except in the "arts interest" factor. It is not easy to make an unqualified condensed quantitative statement of the percentage of space common to the two systems of personality scales. But if we project to a space in which all factors clearly located here could be assumed to be measured with full validity, the extent of overlap could be expressed by saying that the 14 Cattell dimensions and 15 Guilford scales have eight dimensions in common: namely, A, H, I, M, O, Q_2, and Q_4, and less clearly, Q_1 in their 16 PF labels. The 14 dimensions used from the 16 PF retain a dimensionality of 14, while the 15 from the G-Z yield 9. Consequently 6 dimensions—C, E, F, G, L, and Q_3—remain essentially outside the G-Z, and one dimension in the G-Z—

AA, Arts' interest—remains outside the 16 PF. On the eight common dimensions mutual multiple regression coefficients could be set up giving tolerably efficient mutual estimations between the scales of the two series.

7. From a methodological standpoint this pilot study indicates that present experimental design conditions stand within the limits of tolerable effectiveness, but discussion is given to further conditions desirable in a definitive study. These indicate the need to include more than one independent orthogonal choice of scales, and, especially, the need for more numerous "packages," approaching perhaps only two or three items in each, so that sampling is adequate for naturally occuring hyperplanes clearly to express themselves.

References

Baker, R., Cattell, R. B., & Coan, R. B. The Early School Personality Questionnaire. Champaign, Ill.: Institute for Personality and Ability Testing, 1968.

Bargmann, R. Signifikanzuntersuchungen der Einfachen Struktur in der Faktoren Aanalyse. Mitteilungsblatt für Mathematische Statistik. Sonderdruck. Wurzburg: Physica-Verlags, 1954.

Becker, W. C. A comparison of the factor structure and other properties of the 16 P.F. and the Guilford-Martin Personality Inventories. *Educational and Psychological Measurements*, 1961, **21**, 293–404.

Cattell, R. B. *Description and measurement of personality*. Yonkers-on-Hudson, N.Y.: World Book, 1946.

Cattell, R. B. The main personality factors in questionnaire, self-estimate material. *Journal of Social Psychology*, 1950, **31**, 3–38.

Cattell, R. B. *Factor analysis*. New York: Harper, 1952.

Cattell, R. B. Validation and intensification of the Sixteen Personality Factor Question-naire. *Journal of Clinical Psychology*, 1956, **12**, 205–214.

Cattell, R. B. *Personality and motivation structure and measurement*. New York: Harcourt, Brace & World, 1957.

Cattell, R. B. The basis of recognition and interpretation of factors. *Educational and Psychological Measurements*, 1962, **22**, 667–697.

Cattell, R. B. A cross-cultural check, on second stratum personality factor structure—notably of anxiety and exvia. *Australian Journal of Psychology*, 1965, **17**, 12–23.

Cattell, R. B. The meaning and strategic use of factor analysis. In R. B. Cattell (Ed.), *Handbook of multivariate experimental psychology*. Chicago: Rand McNally, 1966. (a)

Cattell, R. B. The Scree Test for the Number of Factors. *Multivariate Behavioral Research*, 1966, **1**, 78–98. (b).

Cattell, R. B., Coan, R., & Beloff, H. A reexamination of personality structure in late childhood, and development of the High School Personality Questionnaire. *Journal of Experimental Education*, 1958, **27**, 73–88.

Cattell, R. B., & Eber, H. W. The Sixteen Personality Factor Questionnaire. (3rd ed.) Champaign, Ill.: Institute for Personality and Ability Testing, 1966.

Cattell, R. B., & Foster, M. J. The Rotoplot program for multiple, single plane, visually guided rotation. *Behavioral Science*, 1963, **8**, 156–165.

Cattell, R. B., & Nuttall, R. The High School Personality Questionnaire. Champaign, Ill.: Institute for Personality and Ability Testing, 1967.

Cattell, R. B., Pichot, P., & Rennes, P. Constance inter-culturelledes facteurs de per-sonalite measures par le test 16 P.F. II. Comparison francoamericaine. *Revue de Psychologie Applique*. 1961, **11**, 165–196.

Cattell, R. B., Rican, P., & Jaspers, J. Gencoal plasmode No. 30-10-5-2 for factor analy-tic exercises and research. *Multivariate Behavioral Research*, 1968, in press.

Cattell, R. B., & Scheier, I. H. *The meaning and measurement of anxiety and neuroticism*. New York: Ronald Press, 1961.

Cattell, R. B., & Tsujioka, B. A cross cultural comparison of second stratum question-naire personality factor structure—anxiety and exvia—in American and Japan. *Journal of Social Psychology*, 1965, **65**, 205–219.

Eysenck, H. J. *The structure of human personality*. London: Methuen, 1953.

French, J. W. *The description of personality measurements in terms of rotated factors*. Prince-ton, N. J.: Educational Testing Service, 1953.

Gibbons, B. D. A study of the relationships between factors found in Cattell's 16 PF questionnaire and factors found in the Guilford personality inventories. Unpub-lished doctoral dissertation, University of Southern California, 1966.

Gorsuch, A. L., & Cattell, R. B. Second strata personality factors defined in the ques-tionnaire medium by the 16 PF. *Multivariate Behavioral Research*, 1967, **2**, 211–224.

Guilford, J. P. *Inventory of factors STDCR*. Beverly Hills, California: Sheridan Supply, 1940.

Guilford, J. P. When not to factor analyze. *Psychology Bulletin*, 1952, **49**, 26–37.

Guilford, J. P. *Personality*. New York: McGraw-Hill, 1959.

Guilford, J. P., Christensen, P. R., & Bond, N. A. *The DF Opinion Survey: Manual of instructions and interpretations*. Beverly Hills, Calif.: Sheridan supply, 1956.

Guilford, J. P., & Guilford, R. B. Personality factors, S, E, and M. and their measurement. *Journal of Psychology*, 1936, **2**, 109–127.

Guilford, J. P., & Guilford, R. B. Personality factors D, R, T, and A. *Journal of Abnormal and Social Psychology*, 1939, **34**, 21–36. (a)

Guilford, J. P., & Guilford, R. B. Personality factors N, G, and D. *Journal of Abnormal and Social Psychology*, 1939, **34**, 239–248. (b)

Guilford, J. P., & Martin, H. G. *An inventory of factors GAMIN*. Beverly Hills, Calif.: Sheridan Supply, 1943.

Guilford, J. P., & Martin, H. G. *Personnel inventory*. Beverly Hills, Calif.: Sheridan Supply, 1943.

Guilford, J. P., & Zimmerman, W. S. *The Guilford-Zimmerman temperament survey*. Beverly Hills, Calif.: Sheridan Supply, 1949.

Guilford, J. P., & Zimmerman, W. S. Fourteen dimensions of temperament. *Psychological Monographs*, 1956, **70** (10, Whole No. 417).

Guilford, J. P., & Zimmerman, W. S. Some variable-sampling problems in the rotation of axes in factor analysis. *Psychology Bulletin*, 1963, **60**, 289–301.

Hammond, S. Personality factors in ratings. In R. B. Cattell (Ed.), *Handbook of modern personality theory*. Chicago: Aldine, 1968, in press.

Kaiser, H. F. Comments on communalities and the number of factors. Unpublished manuscript, University of Illinois, 1960.

Kaiser, H. F., & Caffrey, J. Alpha factor analysis. *Psychometrika*, 1965, **30**, 1–14.

Karson, S., & Pool, K. B. Second order factors in personality measurement. *Journal of Consulting Psychology*, 1958, **22**, 299–303.

Michael, W. B., Barth, G., & Kaiser, H. F. Dimensions of temperament in three groups of music teachers. *Psychological Reports*, 1961, **9**, 601–704.

Porter, R., Schaie, W., & Cattell, R. B. The Child Personality Questionnaire. Champaign, Ill.: Institute for Personality and Ability Testing, 1967.

Sells, S. B. Personal communications on planning of factor study across the Q-data realm, 1966. Texas Christian University, Fort Worth, Texas.

Thurstone, L. L. *Primary mental abilities*. Chicago: Chicago University Press, 1938.

Tupes, E. C., & Cristal, R. C. Stability of personality-trait rating factors obtained under diverse condition. USAF, WADC, Technical Note, 1958, No. 58–61.

Section X

Stimulus-Response Theory

Stimulus-response theory is one of the most rapidly expanding and evolving of personality theories. While many have contributed to the theory, these psychologists are by no means uniform in their approach to the same problem, nor do they necessarily agree upon where the most important problems are located. The enormous amount of resulting conceptual and empirical activity relevant to S-R theory has produced literally hundreds of papers that on theoretical or substantive grounds are well qualified for inclusion in this section.

Faced with such a profusion of excellent material we have selected first a major paper by Neal Miller who has long been a theoretical and empirical leader among stimulus-response psychologists. This article describes an exciting new program of research that involves the application of the methods of conditioning to involuntary or autonomic processes such as heart rate and intestinal responses. The findings of these studies are of great interest both because they are contrary to what many psychologists would have expected and because they suggest the possibility of new approaches to many significant human problems including the psychosomatic disorders. If cardiovascular and digestive functions can be learned they are, in principle, capable of being controlled and thus it should be possible to develop effective new methods of treating many forms of illness.

The paper by Costello is part of a continuing dialogue that has been going on since 1965, dealing with fundamental aspects of the application of learning theory to the modification of behavior. Some of the leading S-R theorists have been involved in these theoretical exchanges and the reader may follow these arguments by referring to the previously published papers cited by Costello in his article and by consulting subsequent issues of the *Psychological Review* in 1971. Although Costello uses a clinical problem—phobias—as the focus of his discussion, the issues he raises involve a number of general questions about the development and modification of conditioned avoidance responses. This is a topic that has been the subject of many laboratory studies using infrahuman subjects, and one can see that the animal data on conditioned avoidance responses from such studies is useful in attempting to resolve issues in personality psychology. Specifically Costello objects to the tendency of most behavior therapists to equate phobias with conditioned avoidance responses as studied in the laboratory. He insists that those responses are not comparable because phobias are maladaptive while conditioned avoidance responses are highly adaptive.

The last paper in this section, by Masters and Morris, is a good example of the type of research many child psychologists raised in the S-R tradition are conducting. The effects of models upon the imitative behavior of young children are being studied from a number of viewpoints. Imitation is a phenomenon that has been of keen interest to personality and social psychologists for many years, and is viewed by S-R theorists as a major factor in socialization and personality development. Recently the model's attributes have been studied to determine the effects of these variables upon the imitative behavior of the observing child. The Masters and Morris study follows in this general tradition (see the Baer and Sherman selection, page 414) but assesses the effects of differential prior experience with a model upon *generalized* imitative behavior. Most previous studies have studied a single disposition or form of behavior, such as aggression, and not the general disposition or tendency to imitate.

1. *Learning of Visceral and Glandular Responses*

NEAL E. MILLER

There is a strong traditional belief in the inferiority of the autonomic nervous system and the visceral responses that it controls. The recent experiments disproving this belief have deep implications for theories of learning, for individual differences in autonomic responses, for the cause and the cure of abnormal psychosomatic symptoms, and possibly also for the understanding of normal homeostasis. Their success encourages investigators to try other unconventional types of training. Before describing these experiments, let me briefly sketch some elements in the history of the deeply entrenched, false belief in the gross inferiority of one major part of the nervous system.

Historical Roots and Modern Ramifications

Since ancient times, reason and the voluntary responses of the skeletal muscles have been considered to be superior,

SOURCE. *Article by Neal E. Miller "Learning of visceral and glandular responses," in* Science, *Vol. 163, pp. 434–445, 1969. Copyright by the American Association for the Advancement of Science.*

while emotions and the presumably involuntary glandular and visceral responses have been considered to be inferior. This invidious dichotomy appears in the philosophy of Plato (*1*), with his superior rational soul in the head above and inferior souls in the body below. Much later, the great French neuroanatomist Bichat (*2*) distinguished between the cerebrospinal nervous system of the great brain and spinal cord, controlling skeletal responses, and the dual chain of ganglia (which he called "little brains") running down on either side of the spinal cord in the body below and controlling emotional and visceral responses. He indicated his low opinion of the ganglionic system by calling it "vegetative"; he also believed it to be largely independent of the cerebrospinal system, an opinion which is still reflected in our modern name for it, the autonomic nervous system. Considerably later, Cannon (*3*) studied the sympathetic part of the autonomic nervous system and concluded that the different nerves in it all fire simultaneously and are incapable of the finely differentiated individual responses possible for the cerebrospinal system, a conclusion which is enshrined in modern textbooks.

Many, though not all, psychiatrists

have made an invidious distinction between the hysterical and other symptoms that are mediated by the cerebrospinal nervous system and the psychosomatic symptoms that are mediated by the autonomic nervous system. Whereas the former are supposed to be subject to a higher type of control that is symbolic, the latter are presumed to be only the direct physiological consequences of the type and intensity of the patient's emotions (see, for example, *4*).

Similarly, students of learning have made a distinction between a lower form, called classical conditioning and thought to be involuntary, and a superior form variously called trial-and-error learning, operant conditioning, type II conditioning, or instrumental learning and believed to be responsible for voluntary behavior. In classical conditioning, the reinforcement must be by an unconditioned stimulus that already elicits the specific response to be learned; therefore, the possibilities are quite limited. In instrumental learning, the reinforcement, called a reward, has the property of strengthening any immediately preceding response. Therefore, the possibilities for reinforcement are much greater; a given reward may reinforce any one of a number of different responses, and a given response may be reinforced by any one of a number of different rewards.

Finally, the foregoing invidious distinctions have coalesced into the strong traditional belief that the superior type of instrumental learning involved in the superior voluntary behavior is possible only for skeletal responses mediated by the superior cerebrospinal nervous system, while, conversely, the inferior classical conditioning is the only kind possible for the inferior, presumably involuntary, visceral and emotional responses mediated by the inferior autonomic nervous system. Thus, in a recent summary generally considered authorita-

tive, Kimble(*5*) states the almost universal belief that "for autonomically mediated behavior, the evidence points unequivocally to the conclusion that such responses can be modified by classical, but not instrumental, training methods." Upon examining the evidence, however, one finds that it consists only of failure to secure instrumental learning in two incompletely reported exploratory experiments and a vague allusion to the Russian literature(*6*). It is only against a cultural background of great prejudice that such weak evidence could lead to such a strong conviction.

The belief that instrumental learning is possible only for the cerebrospinal system and, conversely, that the autonomic nervous system can be modified only by classical conditioning has been used as one of the strongest arguments for the notion that instrumental learning and classical conditioning are two basically different phenomena rather than different manifestations of the same phenomenon under different conditions. But for many years I have been impressed with the similarity between the laws of classical conditioning and those of instrumental learning, and with the fact that, in each of these two situations, some of the specific details of learning vary with the specific conditions of learning. Failing to see any clear-cut dichotomy, I have assumed that there is only one kind of learning(*7*). This assumption has logically demanded that instrumental training procedures be able to produce the learning of any visceral responses that could be acquired through classical conditioning procedures. Yet it was only a little over a dozen years ago that I began some experimental work on this problem and a somewhat shorter time ago that I first, in published articles(*8*), made specific sharp challenges to the traditional view that the instrumental learning of visceral responses is impossible.

Some Difficulties

One of the difficulties of investigating the instrumental learning of visceral responses stems from the fact that the responses that are the easiest to measure—namely, heart rate, vasometer responses, and the galvanic skin response—are known to be affected by skeletal responses, such as exercise, breathing, and even tensing of certain muscles, such as those in the diaphragm. Thus, it is hard to rule out the possibility that, instead of directly learning a visceral response, the subject has learned a skeletal response the performance of which causes the visceral change being recorded.

One of the controls I planned to use was the paralysis of all skeletal responses through administration of curare, a drug which selectively blocks the motor end plates of skeletal muscles without eliminating consciousness in human subjects or the neural control of visceral responses, such as the beating of the heart. The muscles involved in breathing are paralyzed, so the subject's breathing must be maintained through artificial respiration. Since it seemed unlikely that curarization and other rigorous control techniques would be easy to use with human subjects, I decided to concentrate first on experiments with animals.

Originally I thought that learning would be more difficult when the animal was paralyzed, under the influence of curare, and therefore I decided to postpone such experiments until ones on nonparalyzed animals had yielded some definitely promising results. This turned out to be a mistake because, as I found out much later, paralyzing the animal with curare not only greatly simplifies the problem of recording visceral responses without artifacts introduced by movement but also apparently makes it easier for the animal to learn, perhaps because paralysis of the skeletal muscles removes sources of variability and distraction. Also, in certain experiments I made the mistake of using rewards that induced strong unconditioned responses that interfered with instrumental learning.

One of the greatest difficulties, however, was the strength of the belief that instrumental learning of glandular and visceral responses is impossible. It was extremely difficult to get students to work on this problem, and when paid assistants were assigned to it, their attempts were so half-hearted that it soon became more economical to let them work on some other problem which they could attack with greater faith and enthusiasm. These difficulties and a few preliminary encouraging but inconclusive early results have been described elsewhere (9).

Success with Salivation

The first clear-cut results were secured by Alfredo Carmona and me in an experiment on the salivation of dogs. Initial attempts to use food as a reward for hungry dogs were unsuccessful, partly because of strong and persistent unconditioned salivation elicited by the food. Therefore, we decided to use water as a reward for thirsty dogs. Preliminary observations showed that the water had no appreciable effects one way or the other on the bursts of spontaneous salivation. As an additional precaution, however, we used the experimental design of rewarding dogs in one group whenever they showed a burst of spontaneous salivation, so that they would be trained to increase salivation, and rewarding dogs in one group whenever they showed a burst of spontaneous salivation, so that they would be trained to increase salivation, and rewarding dogs in another group whenever there was a long interval between spontaneous bursts, so that they would be trained to decrease salivation. If the reward had any unconditioned effect, this effect might be classically conditioned to the experimental situation and therefore produce a change in salivation that was not a true instance of instrumental learning. But in classical conditioning the reinforcement must elicit the response that is to be acquired. Therefore, conditioning of a response elicited by the reward could produce either an increase or a decrease in salivation, depending upon the direction of the unconditioned response elicited by the reward, but it could not produce a change in one direction for one group and in the opposite direction for the other group. The same type of logic applies for any unlearned cumulative aftereffects of the reward; they could not be in opposite directions for the two groups. With instrumental learning, however, the reward can reinforce any response that immediately precedes it; therefore, the same reward can be used to produce either increases or decreases.

The results are presented in Fig. 1, which summarizes the effects of 40 days of training with one 45-minute training session per day. It may be seen that in this experiment the learning proceeded slowly. However, statistical analysis showed that each of the trends in the predicted rewarded direction was highly reliable (*10*).

Since the changes in salivation for the two groups were in opposite directions, they cannot be attributed to classical conditioning. It was noted, however, that the group rewarded for increases seemed to be more aroused and active than the one rewarded for decreases. Conceivably, all we were doing was to change the level of activation of the dogs, and this change was, in turn, affecting the salivation. Although we did not observe any specific skeletal responses, such as chewing movements or panting, which might be expected to elicit salivation, it was difficult to be absolutely certain that such movements did not occur. Therefore, we decided to rule out such movements by paralyzing the dogs with curare, but we immediately found that curare had two effects which were disastrous for this experiment: it elicited such copious and continuous salivation that there were no changes in salivation to reward, and the salivation was so viscous that it almost immediately gummed up the recording apparatus.

Heart Rate

In the meantime, Jay Trowill, working with me on this problem, was displaying great ingenuity, courage, and persistence in trying to produce instrumental learning of heart rate in rats that had been paralyzed by curare to prevent them from "cheating" by muscular exertion to speed up the heart or by relaxation to slow it down. As a result of preliminary testing, he selected a dose of curare (3.6

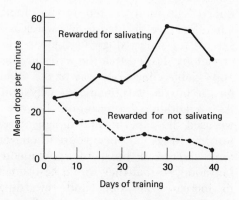

Figure 1. *Learning curves for groups of thirsty dogs rewarded with water for either increases or decreases in spontaneous salivation [From Miller and Carmona (10).]*

milligrams of *d*-tubocurarine chloride per kilogram, injected intraperitoneally) which produced deep paralysis for at least 3 hours, and a rate of artificial respiration (inspiration-expiration ratio 1:1; 70 breaths per minute; peak pressure reading, 20 cm-H$_2$O) which maintained the heart at a constant and normal rate throughout this time.

In subsequent experiments, DiCara and I have obtained similar effects by starting with a smaller dose (1.2 milligrams per kilogram) and constantly infusing additional amounts of the drug, through intraperitoneal injection, at the rate of 1.2 milligrams per kilogram per hour, for the duration of the experiment. We have recorded, electromyographically, the response of the muscles, to determine that this dose does indeed produce a complete block of the action potentials, lasting for at least an hour after the end of infusion. We have found that if parameters of respiration and the face mask are adjusted carefully, the procedure not only maintains the heart rate of a 500-gram control animal constant but also maintains the vital signs of temperature, peripheral vasomotor responses, and the pCO$_2$ of the blood constant.

Since there are not very many ways to reward an animal completely paralyzed by curare, Trowill and I decided to use direct electrical stimulation of rewarding areas of the brain. There were other technical difficulties to overcome, such as divising the automatic system for rewarding small changes in heart rate as recorded by the electrocardiogram. Nevertheless, Trowill at last succeeded in training his rats (*11*). Those rewarded for an increase in heart rate showed a statistically reliable increase, and those rewarded for a decrease in heart rate showed a statistically reliable decrease. The changes, however, were disappointingly small, averaging only 5 percent in each direction.

The next question was whether larger changes could be achieved by improving the technique of training. DiCara and I used the technique of shaping—in other words, of immediately rewarding first very small, and hence frequently occurring, changes in the correct direction and, as soon as these had been learned, requiring progressively larger changes as the criterion for reward. In this way, we were able to produce in 90 minutes of training changes averaging 20 percent in either direction (*12*).

Key Properties of Learning: Discrimination and Retention

Does the learning of visceral responses have the same properties as the learning of skeletal responses? One of the important characteristics of the instrumental learning of skeletal responses is that a discrimination can be learned, so that the responses are more likely to be made in the stimulus situations in which they are rewarded than in those in which they are not. After the training of the first few rats had convinced us that we could produce large changes in heart rate, DiCara and I gave all the rest of the rats in the experiment described above 45 minutes of additional training with the most difficult criterion. We did this in order to see whether they could learn to give a greater response during a "time-in" stimulus (the presence of a flashing light and a tone) which indicated that a response in the proper direction would be rewarded than during a "time-out" stimulus (absence of light and tone) which indicated that a correct response would not be rewarded.

Figure 2 shows the record of one of the rats given such training. Before the beginning of the special discrimination training it had slowed its heart from an

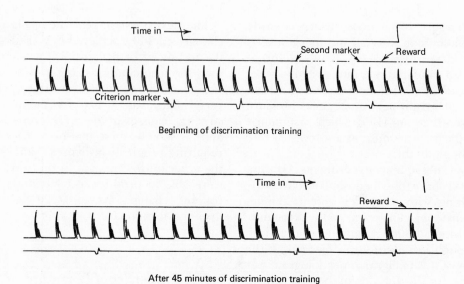

Figure 2.   *Electrocardiograms at the beginning and at the end of discrimination training of curarized rat rewarded for slow heart rate. Slowing of heart rate is rewarded only during a "time-in" stimulus (tone and light). [From Miller and DiCara (12).]*

initial rate of 350 beats per minute to a rate of 230 beats per minute. From the top record of Fig. 2 one can see that, at the beginning of the special discrimination training, there was no appreciable reduction in heart rate that was specifically associated with the time-in stimulus. Thus it took the rat considerable time after the onset of this stimulus to meet the criterion and get the reward. At the end of the discrimination training the heart rate during time-out remained approximately the same, but when the time-in light and tone came on, the heart slowed down and the criterion was promptly met. Although the other rats showed less change than this, by the end of the relatively short period of discrimination training their heart rate did change reliably ($P < 0.0001$) in the predicted direction when the time-in stimulus came on. Thus, it is clear that instrumental visceral learning has at least one of the important properties of instrumental skeletal learning—namely, the

ability to be brought under the control of a discriminative stimulus.

Another of the important properties of the instrumental learning of skeletal responses is that it is remembered. DiCara and I performed a special experiment to test the retention of learned changes in heart rate (*13*). Rats that had been given a single training session were returned to their home cages for 3 months without further training. When curarized again and returned to the experimental situation for nonreinforced test trials, rats in both the "increase" and the "decrease" groups showed good retention by exhibiting reliable changes in the direction rewarded in the earlier training.

Escape and Avoidance Learning

Is visceral learning by any chance peculiarly limited to reinforcement by the unusual reward of direct electrical stimulation of the brain, or can it be reinforced by other rewards in the same way that skeletal learning can be? In order to answer this question, DiCara and I (*14*) performed an experiment using the other of the two forms of thoroughly studied reward that can be conveniently used with rats which are paralyzed by curare—namely, the chance to avoid, or escape from, mild electric shock. A shock signal was turned on; after it had been on for 10 seconds it was accompanied by brief pulses of mild electric shock delivered to the rat's tail. During the first 10 seconds the rat could turn off the shock signal and avoid the shock by making the correct response of changing its heart rate in the required direction by the required amount. If it did not make the correct response in time, the shocks continued to be delivered until the rat escaped them by making the correct response, which immediately turned off both the shock and the shock signal.

For one group of curarized rats, the correct response was an increase in heart rate; for the other group it was a decrease. After the rats had learned to make small responses in the proper direction, they were required to make larger ones. During this training the shock signals were randomly interspersed with an equal number of "safe" signals that were not followed by shock; the heart rate was also recorded during so-called blank trials—trials without any signals or shocks. For half of the rats the shock signal was a flashing light; for the other half the roles of these cues were reversed.

The results are shown in Fig. 3. Each of the 12 rats in this experiment changed its heart rate in the rewarded direction. As training progressed, the shock signal began to elicit a progressively greater change in the rewarded direction than the change recorded during the blank trials; this was a statistically reliable trend. Conversely, as training progressed, the "safe" signal came to elicit a statistically reliable change in the opposite direction,

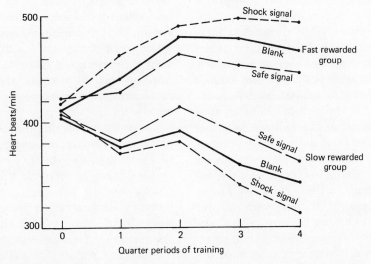

Figure 3.   *Changes in heart rate during avoidance training.* [*From DiCara and Miller (14).*]

toward the initial base line. These results show learning when escape and avoidance are the rewards; this means that visceral responses in curarized rats can be reinforced by rewards other than direct electrical stimulation of the brain. These rats also discriminate between the shock and the "safe" signals. You will remember that, with noncurarized thirsty dogs, we were able to use yet another kind of reward, water, to produce learned changes in salivation.

Transfer to Noncurarized State: More Evidence against Mediation

In the experiments discussed above, paralysis of the skeletal muscles by curare ruled out the possibility that the subjects were learning the overt performance of skeletal responses which were indirectly eliciting the changes in the heart rate. It is barely conceivable, however, that the rats were learning to send out from the motor cortex central impulses which would have activated the muscles had they not been paralyzed. And it is barely conceivable that these central impulses affected heart rate by means either of inborn connections or of classically conditioned ones that had been acquired when previous exercise had been accompanied by an increase in heart rate and relaxation had been accompanied by a decrease. But, if the changes in heart rate were produced in this indirect way, we would expect that, during a subsequent test without curare, any rat that showed learned changes in heart rate would show the movements in the muscles that were no longer paralyzed. Furthermore, the problem of whether or not visceral responses learned under curarization carry over to the noncurarized state is of interest in its own right.

In order to answer this question, Di-

Cara and I (*15*) trained two groups of curarized rats to increase or decrease, respectively, their heart rate in order to avoid, or escape from, brief pulses of mild electric shock. When these rats were tested 2 weeks later in the noncurarized state, the habit was remembered. Statistically reliable increases in heart rate averaging 5 percent and decreases averaging 16 percent occurred. Immediately subsequent retraining without curare produced additional significant changes of heart rate in the rewarded direction, bringing the total overall increase to 11 percent and the decrease to 22 percent. While, at the beginning of the test in the noncurarized state, the two groups showed some differences in respiration and activity, these differences decreased until, by the end of the retraining, they were small and far from statistically reliable ($t = 0.3$ and 1.3, respectively). At the same time, the difference between the two groups with respect to heart rate was increasing, until it became large and thus extremely reliable ($t = 8.6$, d.f. $= 12$, $P < 0.0001$).

In short, while greater changes in heart rate were being learned, the response was becoming more specific, involving smaller changes in respiration and muscular activity. This increase in specificity with additional training is another point of similarity with the instrumental learning of skeletal responses. Early in skeletal learning, the rewarded correct response is likely to be accompanied by many unnecessary movements. With additional training during which extraneous movements are not rewarded, they tend to drop out.

It is difficult to reconcile the foregoing results with the hypothesis that the differences in heart rate were mediated primarily by a difference in either respiration or amount of general activity. This is expecially true in view of the research, summarized by Ehrlich and Malmo (*16*), which shows that muscular activity, to affect heart rate in the rat, must be rather vigorous.

While it is difficult to rule out completely the possibility that changes in heart rate are mediated by central impulses to skeletal muscles, the possibility of such mediation is much less attractive for other responses, such as intestinal contractions and the formation of urine by the kidney. Furthermore, if the learning of these different responses can be shown to be specific in enough visceral responses, one runs out of different skeletal movements each eliciting a specific different visceral response (*17*). Therefore, experiments were performed on the learning of a variety of different visceral responses and on the specificity of that learning. Each of these experiments was, of course, interesting in its own right, quite apart from any bearing on the problem of mediation.

Specificity: Intestinal versus Cardiac

The purpose of our next experiment was to determine the specificity of visceral learning. If such learning has the same properties as the instrumental learning of skeletal responses, it should be possible to learn a specific visceral response independently of other ones. Furthermore, as we have just seen, we might expect to find that, the better the rewarded response is learned, the more specific is the learning. Banuazizi and I worked on this problem (*18*). First we had to discover another visceral response that could be conveniently recorded and rewarded. We decided on intestinal contractions, and recorded them in the curarized rat with a little balloon filled with water thrust approximately 4 centimeters beyond the anal sphincter. Changes of pressure in the balloon were transduced into electric

voltages which produced a record on a polygraph and also activated an automatic mechanism for delivering the reward, which was electrical stimulation of the brain.

The results for the first rat trained, which was a typical one, are shown in Fig. 4. From the top record it may be seen that, during habituation, there were some spontaneous contractions. When the rat was rewarded by brain stimulation for keeping contractions below a certain amplitude for a certain time, the number of contractions was reduced and the base line was lowered. After the record showed a highly reliable change indicating that relaxation had been learned (Fig. 4, second record from the top), the conditions of training were reversed and the reward was delivered whenever the amplitude of contractions rose above a certain level. From the next record (Fig. 4, middle) it may be seen that this type of training increased the number of contractions and raised the base line. Finally (Fig. 4, two bottom records) the reward was discontinued and, as would be expected, the responses continued for a while but gradually became extinguished, so that the activity eventually returned to approximately its original base-line level.

After studying a number of other rats in this way and convincing ourselves that the instrumental learning of intestinal responses was a possibility, we designed an experiment to test specificity. For all the rats of the experiment, both intestinal contractions and heart rate were recorded, but half the rats were rewarded for one of these responses and half were rewarded for the other response. Each of these two groups of rats was divided into two subgroups, rewarded, respectively, for increased and decreased response. The rats were completely paralyzed by curare, maintained on artificial respiration, and rewarded by electrical stimulation of the brain.

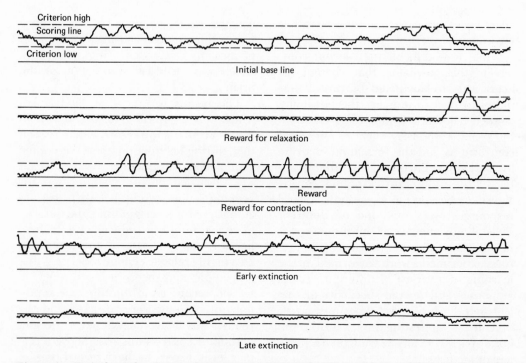

Criterion high
Scoring line
Criterion low

Initial base line

Reward for relaxation

Reward

Reward for contraction

Early extinction

Late extinction

Figure 4. *Typical samples of a record of instrumental learning of an intestinal response by a curarized rat. (From top to bottom) Record of spontaneous contraction before training; record after training with reward for relaxation; record after training with reward for contractions; records during nonrewarded extinction trials. [From Miller and Banuazizi (18).]*

The results are shown in Figs. 5 and 6. In Fig. 5 it may be seen that the group rewarded for increases in intestinal contractions learned an increase, the group rewarded for decreases learned a decrease, but neither of these groups showed an appreciable change in heart rate. Conversely (Fig. 6), the group rewarded for increases in heart rate showed an increase, the group rewarded for decreases showed a decrease, but neither of these groups showed a change in intestinal contractions.

The fact that each type of response changed when it was rewarded rules out the interpretation that the failure to secure a change when that change was not rewarded could have been due to either a strong and stable homeostatic regulation of that response or an inabil-

ity of our techniques to measure changes reliably under the particular conditions of our experiment.

Each of the 12 rats in the experiment showed statistically reliable changes in the rewarded direction; for 11 the changes were reliable beyond the $P < 0.001$ level, while for the 12th the changes were reliable only beyond the 0.05 level. A statistically reliable negative correlation showed that the better the rewarded visceral response was learned, the less change occurred in the other, nonrewarded response. This greater specificity with better learning is what we had expected. The results showed that visceral learning can be specific to an organ system, and they clearly ruled out the possibility of mediation by any single general factor, such as level of activation or central com-

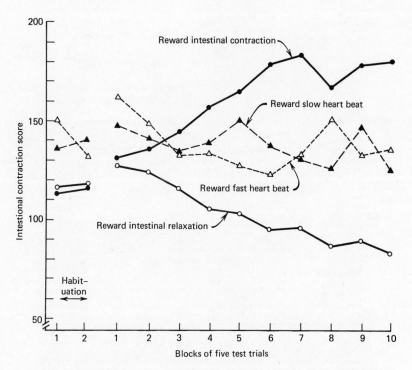

Figure 5. *Graph showing that the intestinal contraction score is changed by re-warding either increases or decreases in intestinal contractions but is unaffected by rewarding changes in heart rate.* [*From Miller and Banuazizi (18).*]

mands for either general activity or re-laxation.

In an additional experiment, Banua-zizi (*19*) showed that either increases or decreases in intestinal contractions can be rewarded by avoidance of, or escape from, mild electric shocks, and that the intestinal responses can be discrimina-tively elicited by a specific stimulus as-sociated with reinforcement.

Kidney Function

Encouraged by these successes, DiCara and I decided to see whether or not the rate of urine formation by the kidney could be changed in the curarized rat rewarded by electrical stimulation of the brain (*20*). A catheter, permanently in-serted, was used to prevent accumulation of urine by the bladder, and the rate of urine formation was measured by an electronic device for counting minute drops. In order to secure a rate of urine formation fast enough so that small changes could be promptly detected and rewarded, the rats were kept constantly loaded with water through infusion by way of a catheter permanently inserted in the jugular vein.

All of the seven rats rewarded when the intervals between times of urine-drop formation lengthened showed decreases in the rate of urine formation, and all of the seven rats rewarded when these in-tervals shortened showed increases in the

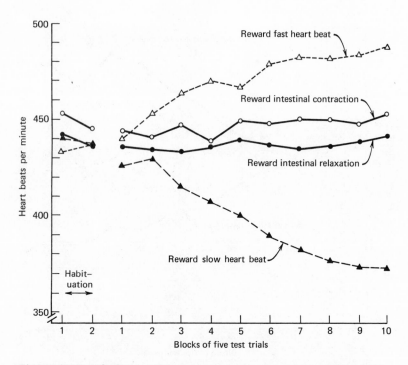

Figure 6. *Graph showing that the heart rate is changed by rewarding either increases or decreases in heart rate but is unaffected by rewarding changes in intestinal contractions. Comparison with Figure 5 demonstrates the specificity of visceral learning. [From Miller and Banuazizi(18).]*

rate of urine formation. For both groups the changes were highly reliable ($P < 0.001$).

In order to determine how the change in rate of urine formation was achieved, certain additional measures were taken. As the set of bars at left in Fig. 7 shows, the rate of filtration, measured by means of ^{14}C-labeled insulin, increased when increases in the rate of urine formation were rewarded and decreased when decreases in the rate were rewarded. Plots of the correlations showed that the changes in the rates of filtration and urine formation were not related to changes in either blood pressure or heart rate.

The middle set of bars in Fig. 7 shows that the rats rewarded for increases in the rate of urine formation had an increased

rate of renal blood flow, as measured by ^{3}H-p-aminohipuric acid, and that those rewarded for decreases had a decreased rate of renal blood flow. Since these changes in blood flow were not accompanied by changes in general blood pressure or in heart rate, they must have been achieved by vasomotor changes of the renal arteries. That these vasomotor changes were at least somewhat specific is shown by the fact that vasomotor responses of the tail, as measured by a photoelectric plethysmograph, did not differ for the two groups of rats.

The set of bars at right in Fig. 7 shows that when decreases in rate of urine formation were rewarded, a more concentrated urine, having higher osmolarity, was formed. Since the slower passage of

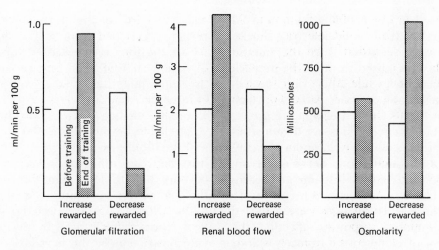

Figure 7. *Effects of rewarding increased rate of urine formation in one group and decreased rate in another on measures of glomerular filtration, renal blood flow, and osmolarity. [From data in Miller and DiCara(20).]*

urine through the tubules would afford more opportunity for reabsorption of water, this higher concentration does not necessarily mean an increase in the secretion of antidiuretic hormone. When an increased rate of urine formation was rewarded, the urine did not become more diluted—that is, it showed no decrease in osmolarity; therefore, the increase in rate of urine formation observed in this experiment cannot be accounted for in terms of an inhibition of the secretion of antidiuretic hormone.

From the foregoing results it appears that the learned changes in urine formation in this experiment were produced primarily by changes in the rate of filtration, which, in turn, were produced primarily by changes in the rate of blood flow through the kidneys.

Gastric Changes

In the next experiment, Carmona, Demierre, and I used a photoelectric plethysmograph to measure changes, presumably in the amount of blood, in the stomach wall (21). In an operation performed under anesthesia, a small glass tube, painted black except for a small spot, was inserted into the rat's stomach. The same tube was used to hold the stomach wall against a small glass window inserted through the body wall. The tube was left in that position. After the animal had recovered, a bundle of optical fibers could be slipped snugly into the glass tube so that the light beamed through it would shine out through the unpainted spot in the tube inside the stomach, pass through the stomach wall and be recorded by a photocell on the other side of the glass window. Preliminary tests indicated that, as would be expected, when the amount of blood in the stomach wall increased, less light would pass through. Other tests showed that stomach contractions elicited by injections of insulin did not affect the amount of light transmitted.

In the main experiment we rewarded

curarized rats by enabling them to avoid or escape from mild electric shocks. Some were rewarded when the amount of light that passed through the stomach wall increased, while others were rewarded when the amount decreased. Fourteen of the 15 rats showed changes in the rewarded direction. Thus, we demonstrated that the stomach wall, under the control of the autonomic nervous system, can be modified by instrumental learning. There is strong reason to believe that the learned changes were achieved by vasomotor responses affecting the amount of blood in the stomach wall or mucosa, or in both.

In another experiment, Carmona (22) showed that stomach contractions can be either increased or decreased by instrumental learning.

It is obvious that learned changes in the blood supply of internal organs can affect their functioning—as, for example, the rate at which urine was formed by the kidneys was affected by changes in the amount of blood that flowed through them. Thus, such changes can produce psychosomatic symptoms. And if the learned changes in blood supply can be specific to a given organ, the symptom will occur in that organ rather than in another one.

Peripheral Vasomotor Responses

Having investigated the instrumental learning of internal vasomotor responses, we next studied the learning of peripheral ones. In the first experiment, the amount of blood in the tail of a curarized rat was measured by a photoelectric plethysmograph, and changes were rewarded by electrical stimulation of the brain (23). All of the four rats rewarded for vasoconstriction showed that response, and at the same time, their

average core temperature, measured rectally, decreased from 98.9° to 97.9°F. All of the four rats rewarded for vasodilatation showed that response and, at the same time, their average core temperature increased from 99.9° to 101°F. The vasomotor change for each individual rat was reliable beyond the $P < 0.01$ level, and the difference in change in temperature between the groups was reliable beyond the 0.01 level. The direction of the change in temperature was opposite to that which would be expected from the heat conservation caused by peripheral vasoconstriction or the heat loss caused by peripheral vasodilatation. The changes are in the direction which would be expected if the training had altered the rate of heat production, causing a change in temperature which, in turn, elicited the vasomotor response.

The next experiment was designed to try to determine the limits of the specificity of vasomotor learning. The pinnae of the rat's ears were chosen because the blood vessels in them are believed to be innervated primarily, and perhaps exclusively, by the sympathetic branch of the autonomic nervous system, the branch that Cannon believed always fired nonspecifically as a unit (3). But Cannon's experiments involved exposing cats to extremely strong emotion-evoking stimuli, such as barking dogs, and such stimuli will also evoke generalized activity throughout the skeletal musculature. Perhaps his results reflected the way in which sympathetic activity was elicited, rather than demonstrating any inherent inferiority of the sympathetic nervous system.

In order to test this interpretation, DiCara and I (24) put photocells on both ears of the curarized rat and connected them to a bridge circuit so that only differences in the vasomotor responses of the two ears were rewarded by brain stimulation. We were somewhat surprised and greatly delighted to find that this experiment actually worked. The results are summarized in Fig. 8. Each of the six rats rewarded for relative vasodilatation of the left ear showed that response, while each of the six rats rewarded for relative vasodilatation of the right ear showed that response. Recordings from the right and left forepaws showed little if any change in vasomotor response.

It is clear that these results cannot be by-products of changes in either heart rate or blood pressure, as these would be expected to affect both ears equally. They show either that vasomotor responses mediated by the sympathetic nervous system are capable of much greater specificity than has previously been believed, or that the innervation of the blood vessels in the pinnae of the

ears is not restricted almost exclusively to sympathetic-nervous-system components, as has been believed, and involves functionally significant parasympathetic components. In any event, the changes in the blood flow certainly were surprisingly specific. Such changes in blood flow could account for specific psychosomatic symptoms.

Blood Pressure Independent of Heart Rate

Although changes in blood pressure were not induced as by-products of rewarded changes in the rate of urine formation, another experiment on curarized rats showed that, when changes in systolic blood pressure are specifically reinforced,

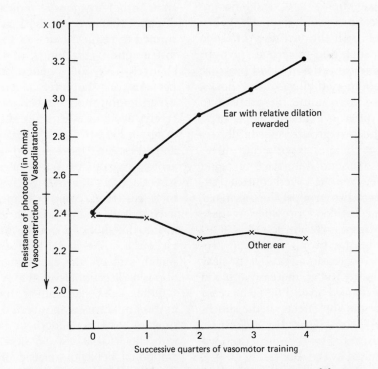

Figure 8. *Learning a difference in the vasometer responses of the two ears in the curarized rat. [From data in DiCara and Miller (24).]*

they can be learned (25). Blood pressure was recorded by means of a catheter permanently inserted into the aorta, and the reward was avoidance of, or escape from, mild electric shock. All seven rats rewarded for increases in blood pressure showed further increases, while all seven rewarded for decreases showed decreases, each of the changes, which were in opposite directions, being reliable beyond the $P < 0.01$ level. The increase was from 139 mm-Hg, which happens to be roughly comparable to the normal systolic blood pressure of an adult man, to 170 mm-Hg, which is on the borderline of abnormally high blood pressure in man.

Each experimental animal was "yoked" with a curarized partner, maintained on artificial respiration and having shock electrodes on its tail wired in series with electrodes on the tail of the experimental animal, so that it received exactly the same electric shocks and could do nothing to escape or avoid them. The yoked controls for both the increase-rewarded and the decrease-rewarded groups showed some elevation in blood pressure as an unconditioned effect of the shocks. By the end of training, in contrast to the large difference in the blood pressures of the two groups specifically rewarded for changes in opposite directions, there was no difference in blood pressure between the yoked control partners for these two groups. Furthermore, the increase in blood pressure in these control groups was reliably less ($P < 0.01$) than that in the group specifically rewarded for increases. Thus, it is clear that the reward for an increase in blood pressure produced an additional increase over and above the effects of the shocks per se, while the reward for a decrease was able to overcome the unconditioned increase elicited by the shocks.

For none of the four groups was there a significant change in heart rate or in temperature during training; there were no significant differences in these measures among the groups. Thus, the learned change was relatively specific to blood pressure.

Transfer from Heart Rate to Skeletal Avoidance

Although visceral learning can be quite specific, especially if only a specific response is rewarded, as was the case in the experiment on the two ears, under some circumstances it can involve a more generalized effect.

In handling the rats that had just recovered from curarization, DiCara noticed that those that had been trained, through the avoidance or escape reward, to increase their heart rate were more likely to squirm, squeal, defecate, and show other responses indicating emotionality than were those that had been trained to reduce their heart rate. Could instrumental learning of heart-rate changes have some generalized effects, perhaps on the level of emotionality, which might affect the behavior in a different avoidance-learning situation? In order to look for such an effect, DiCara and Weiss (26) used a modified shuttle avoidance apparatus. In this apparatus, when a danger signal is given, the rat must run from compartment A to compartment B. If he runs fast enough, he avoids the shock; if not, he must run to escape it. The next time the danger signal is given, the rat must run in the opposite direction, from B to A.

Other work had shown that learning in this apparatus is an inverted U-shaped function of the strength of the shocks, with shocks that are too strong eliciting emotional behavior instead of running. DiCara and Weiss trained their rats in this apparatus with a level of shock that is approximately optimum for naive rats of this strain. They found that the rats that had been rewarded for decreasing their heart rate learned well, but that those that had been rewarded for increasing their heart rate learned less well, as if their emotionality had been increased. The difference was statistically reliable ($P < 0.001$). This experiment clearly demonstrates that training a visceral response can affect the subsequent learning of a skeletal one, but additional work will be required to prove the hypothesis that training to increase heart rate increases emotionality.

Visceral Learning without Curare

Thus far, in all of the experiments except the one on teaching thirsty dogs to salivate, the initial training was given when the animal was under the influence of curare. All of the experiments, except the one on salivation, have produced surprisingly rapid learning—definitive results within 1 or 2 hours. Will learning in the normal, noncurarized state be easier, as we originally thought it should be, or will it be harder, as the experiment on the noncurarized dogs suggests? DiCara and I have started to get additional evidence on this problem. We have obtained clear-cut evidence that rewarding (with the avoidance or escape reward) one group of freely moving rats for reducing heart rate and rewarding another group for increasing heart rate produces a difference between the two groups (27). That this difference was not due to the indirect effects of the overt performance of skeletal responses is shown by the fact that it persisted in subsequent tests during which the rats were paralyzed by curare. And, on subsequent retraining without curare, such differences in activity and respiration as were present earlier in training continued to decrease, while the differences in heart rate continued to increase. It seems extremely unlikely that, at the end of training, the highly reliable differences in heart rate ($t = 7.2$; $P < 0.0001$) can be explained by the highly unreliable differences in activity and respiration ($t = 0.07$ and 0.2, respectively).

Although the rats in this experiment showed some learning when they were trained initially in the noncurarized state, this learning was much poorer than that which we have seen in our other experiments on curarized rats. This is exactly the opposite of my original expectation, but seems plausible in the light of hindsight. My hunch is that paralysis by curare improved learning by eliminating sources of distraction and variability. The stimulus situation was kept more constant, and confusing visceral fluctuations induced indirectly by skeletal movements were eliminated.

Learned Changes in Brain Waves

Encouraged by success in the experiments on the instrumental learning of visceral responses, my colleagues and I have attempted to produce other unconventional types of learning. Electrodes placed on the skull or, better yet, touching the surface of the brain record summative effects of electrical activity over a considerable area of the brain. Such electrical effects are brain waves, and the record of them is called an electroencephalogram. When the animal is aroused, the electroencephalogram consists of fast, low-voltage activity; when the animal is drowsy or sleeping normally, the electroencephalogram consists of considerably slower, higher-voltage activity. Carmona attempted to see whether this type of brain activity, and the state of arousal accompanying it, can be modified by direct reward of changes in the brain activity (*28, 29*).

The subjects of the first experiment were freely moving cats. In order to have a reward that was under complete control and that did not require the cat to move, Carmona used direct electrical stimulation of the medial forebrain bundle, which is a rewarding area of the brain. Such stimulation produced a slight lowering in the average voltage of the electroencephalogram and an increase in behavioral arousal. In order to provide a control for these and any other unlearned effects, he rewarded one group for changes in the direction of high-voltage activity and another group for changes in the direction of low-voltage activity.

Both groups learned. The cats rewarded for high-voltage activity showed more high-voltage slow waves and tended to sit like sphinxes, staring out into space. The cats rewarded for low-voltage activity showed much more low-voltage fast activity, and appeared to be aroused, pacing restlessly about, sniffing, and looking here and there. It was clear that this type of training had modified both the character of the electrical brain waves and the general level of the behavioral activity. It was not clear, however, whether the level of arousal of the brain was directly modified and hence modified the behavior; whether the animals learned specific items of behavior which, in turn, modified the arousal of the brain as reflected in the electroencephalogram; or whether both types of learning were occurring simultaneously.

In order to rule out the direct sensory consequences of changes in muscular tension, movement, and posture, Carmona performed the next experiment on rats that had been paralyzed by means of curare. The results, given in Fig. 9, show that both rewarded groups showed changes in the rewarded direction; that a subsequent nonrewarded rest increased the number of high-voltage responses in both groups; and that, when the conditions of reward were reversed, the direction of change in voltage was reversed.

At present we are trying to use similar techniques to modify the functions of a specific part of the vagal nucleus, by recording and specifically rewarding changes in the electrical activity there. Preliminary results suggest that this is possible. The next step is to investigate the visceral consequences of such modification. This kind of work may open up possibilities for modifying the activity of specific parts of the brain and the functions that they control. In some cases, directly rewarding brain activity may be a more convenient or more powerful technique than rewarding skeletal or visceral behavior. It also may be a new way to throw light on the functions of specific parts of the brain (*30*).

Human Visceral Learning

Another question is that of whether people are capable of instrumental learning of visceral responses. I believe that in this respect they are as smart as rats. But, as a recent critical review by Katkin and Murray (*31*) points out, this has not yet been completely proved. These authors have comprehensively summarized the recent studies reporting successful use of instrumental training to modify human heart rate, vasomotor responses, and the galvanic skin response. Because of the difficulties in subjecting human subjects to the same rigorous controls, including deep paralysis by means of curare, that can be used with animal subjects, one of the most serious questions about the results of the human studies is whether the changes recorded represent the true instrumental learning of visceral responses or the unconscious learning of those skeletal responses that can

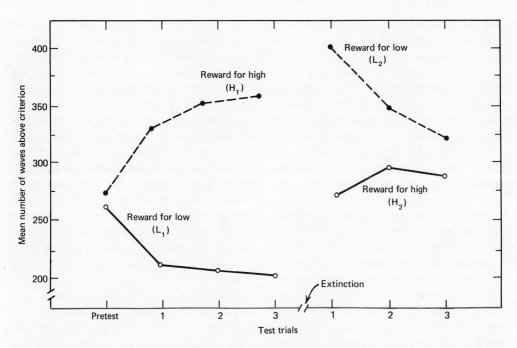

Figure 9. *Instrumental learning by curarized rats rewarded for high-voltage or for low voltage electro-encephalograms recorded from the cerebral cortex. After a period of nonrewarded extinction, which produced some drowsiness, as indicated by an increase in voltage, the rats in the two groups were then rewarded for voltage changes opposite in direction to the changes for which they were rewarded earlier. [From Carmona(29).]*

produce visceral reactions. However, the able investigators who have courageously challenged the strong traditional belief in the inferiority of the autonomic nervous system with experiments at the more difficult but especially significant human level are developing ingenious controls, including demonstrations of the specificity of the visceral change, so that their cumulative results are becoming increasingly impressive.

Possible Role in Homeostasis

The functional utility of instrumental learning by the cerebrospinal nervous system under the conditions that existed during mammalian evolution is obvious.

The skeletal responses mediated by the cerebrospinal nervous system operate on the external environment, so that there is survival value in the ability to learn responses that bring rewards such as food, water, or escape from pain. The fact that the response mediated by the autonomic nervous system do not have such direct action on the external environment was one of the reasons for believing that they are not subject to instrumental learning. Is the learning ability of the autonomic nervous system something that has no normal function other than that of providing my students with subject matter for publications? Is it a mere accidental by-product of the survival value of cerebrospinal learning, or does the instrumental learning of autonomically mediated responses have some adaptive function, such as helping to maintain that constancy of the internal environment called homeostasis?

In order for instrumental learning to function homeostatically, a deviation away from the optimum level will have to function as a drive to motivate learning, and a change toward the optimum level will have to function as a reward to reinforce the learning of the particular visceral response that produced the corrective change.

When a mammal has less than the optimum amount of water in his body, this deficiency serves as a drive of thirst to motivate learning; the overt consummatory response of drinking functions as a reward to reinforce the learning of the particular skeletal responses that were successful in securing the water that restored the optimum level. But is the consummatory response essential? Can restoration of an optimum level by a glandular response function as a reward?

In order to test for the possible rewarding effects of a glandular response, DiCara, Wolf, and I (32) injected albino rats with antidiuretic hormone (ADH) if they chose one arm of a T-maze and with the isotonic saline vehicle if they chose the other, distinctively different, arm. The ADH permitted water to be reabsorbed in the kidney, so that a smaller volume of more concentrated urine was formed. Thus, for normal rats loaded in advance with H_2O, the ADH interfered with the excess-water excretion required for the restoration of homeostasis, while the control injection of isotonic saline allowed the excess water to be excreted. And, indeed, such rats learned to select the side of the maze that assured them an injection of saline so that their glandular response could restore homeostasis.

Conversely, for rats with diabetes insipidus, loaded in advance with hypertonic NaCl, the homeostatic effects of the same two injections were reversed; the ADH, causing the urine to be more concentrated, helped the rats to get rid of the excess NaCl, while the isotonic saline vehicle did not. And, indeed, a group of rats of this kind learned the opposite choice of selecting the ADH side of the maze. As a further control on the effects of the ADH per se, normal rats which had not been given H_2O or NaCl exhibited no learning. This experiment showed that an excess of either H_2O or NaCl functions as a drive and that the return to the normal concentration produced by the appropriate response of a gland, the kidney, functions as a reward.

When we consider the results of this experiment together with those of our experiments showing that glandular and visceral responses can be instrumentally learned, we will expect the animal to learn those glandular and visceral responses mediated by the central nervous system that promptly restore homeostasis after any considerable deviation. Whether or not this theoretically possible learning has any practical significance will depend on whether or not the innate homeostatic mechanisms control the levels closely enough to prevent any deviations large enough to function as a drive from occurring. Even if the innate control should be accurate enough to preclude learning in most cases, there remains the intriguing possibility that, when pathology interferes with innate control, visceral learning is available as a supplementary mechanism.

Implications and Speculations

We have seen how the instrumental learning of visceral responses suggests a new possible homeostatic mechanism worthy of further investigation. Such learning also shows that the autonomic nervous system is not as inferior as has been so widely and firmly believed. It removes one of the strongest arguments for the hypothesis that there are two fundamentally different mechanisms of learning, involving different parts of the nervous system.

Cause of Psychosomatic Symptoms. Similarly, evidence of the instrumental learning of visceral responses removes the main basis for assuming that the psychosomatic symptoms that involve the autonomic nervous system are fundamentally different from those functional symptoms, such as hysterical ones, that involve the cerebrospinal nervous system. Such evidence allows us to extend to psychosomatic symptoms the type of learning-theory analysis that Dollard and I (7, 33) have applied to other symptoms.

For example, suppose a child is terror-stricken at the thought of going to school in the morning because he is completely unprepared for an important examination. The strong fear elicits a variety of fluctuating autonomic symptoms, such as a queasy stomach at one time and pallor and faintness at another; at this point his mother, who is particularly concerned about cardiovascular symptoms, says, "You are sick and must stay home." The child feels a great relief from fear, and this reward should reinforce the cardiovascular responses producing pallor and faintness. If such experiences are repeated frequently enough, the child, theoretically, should learn to respond with that kind of symptom. Similarly, another child whose mother ignored the vasomotor responses but was particularly concerned by signs of gastric distress would learn the latter type of symptom. I want to exphasize, however, that we need careful clinical research to determine how frequently, if

at all, the social conditions sufficient for such theoretically possible learning of visceral symptoms actually occur. Since a given instrumental response can be reinforced by a considerable variety of rewards, and by one reward on one occasion and a different reward on another, the fact that glandular and visceral responses can be instrumentally learned opens up many new theoretical possibilities for the reinforcement of psychosomatic symptoms.

Furthermore, we do not yet know how severe a psychosomatic effect can be produced by learning. While none of the 40 rats rewarded for speeding up their heart rates have died in the course of training under curarization, 7 of the 40 rats rewarded for slowing down their heart rates have died. This statistically reliable difference (chi square = 5.6, $P < 0.02$) is highly suggestive, but it could mean that training to speed up the heart helped the rats resist the stress of curare rather than that the reward for slowing down the heart was strong enough to overcome innate regulatory mechanisms and induce sudden death. In either event the visceral learning had a vital effect. At present, DiCara and I are trying to see whether or not the learning of visceral responses can be carried far enough in the noncurarized animal to produce physical damage. We are also investigating the possibility that there may be a critical period in early infancy during which visceral learning has particularly intense and long-lasting effects.

Individual and Cultural Differences. It is possible that, in addition to producing psychosomatic symptoms in extreme cases, visceral learning can account for certain more benign individual and cultural differences. Lacey and Lacey(34) have shown that a given individual may have a tendency, which is stable over a number of years, to respond to a variety of different stresses with the same profile of autonomic responses, while other individuals may have statistically reliable tendencies to respond with different profiles. It now seems possible that differential conditions of learning may account for at least some of these individual differences in patterns of autonomic response.

Conversely, such learning may account also for certain instances in which the same individual responds to the same stress in different ways. For example, a small boy who receives a severe bump in rough-and-tumble play may learn to inhibit the secretion of tears in this situation since this peer group will punish crying by calling it "sissy." But the same small boy may burst into tears when he gets home to his mother, who will not punish weeping and may even reward tears with sympathy.

Similarly, it seems conceivable that different conditions of reward by a culture different from our own may be responsible for the fact that Homer's adult heroes so often "let the big tears fall." Indeed, a former colleague of mine, Herbert Barry III, has analyzed cross-cultural data and found that the amount of crying reported for children seems to be related to the way in which the society reacts to their tears(35).

I have emphasized the possible role of learning in producing the observed individual differences in visceral responses to stress, which in extreme cases may result in one type of psychosomatic symptom in one person and a different type in another. Such learning does not, of course, exclude innate individual differences in the susceptibility of different organs. In fact, given social conditions under which any form of illness will be rewarded, the symptoms of the most susceptible organ will be the most likely

ones to be learned. Furthermore, some types of stress may be so strong that the innate reactions to them produce damage without any learning. My colleagues and I are currently investigating the psychological variables involved in such types of stress(36).

Therapeutic Training. The experimental work on animals has developed a powerful technique for using instrumental learning to modify glandular and visceral responses. The improved training technique consists of moment-to-moment recording of the visceral function and immediate reward, at first, of very small changes in the desired direction and then of progressively larger ones. The success of this technique suggests that it should be able to produce therapeutic changes. If the patient who is highly motivated to get rid of a symptom understands that a signal, such as a tone, indicates a change in the desired direction, that tone could serve as a powerful reward. Instruction to try to turn the tone on as often as possible and praise for success should increase the reward. As patients find that they can secure some control of the symptom, their motivation should be strengthened. Such a procedure should be well worth trying on any symptom, functional or organic, that is under neural control, that can be continuously monitored by modern instrumentation, and for which a given direction of change is clearly indicated medically—for example, cardiac arrhythmias, spastic colitis, asthma, and those cases of high blood pressure that are not essential compensation for kidney damage(37). The obvious cases to begin with are those in which drugs are ineffective or contraindicated. In the light of the fact that our animals learned so much better when under the influence of curare and transferred their training so well to the normal, nondrugged state, it should be worth while to try to use hypnotic suggestion to achieve similar results by enhancing the reward effect of the signal indicating a change in the desired direction, by producing relaxation and regular breathing, and by removing interference from skeletal responses and distraction by irrelevant cues.

Engel and Melmon (*38*) have reported encouraging results in the use of instrumental training to treat cardiac arrhythmias of organic origin. Randt, Korein, Carmona, and I have had some success in using the method described above to train epileptic patients in the laboratory to suppress, in one way or another, the abnormal paroxysmal spikes in their electroencephalogram. My colleagues and I are hoping to try learning therapy for other symptoms — for example, the rewarding of high-voltage electroencephalograms as a treatment for insomnia. While it is far too early to promise any cures, it certainly will be worth while to investigate thoroughly the therapeutic possibilities of improved instrumental training techniques.

References and Notes

1. *The Dialogues of Plato*, B. Jowett, Transl., (Univ. of Oxford Press, London, ed. 2, 1875), vol. 3, "Timaeus."

2. X. Bichat, *Recherches Physiologiques sur la Vie et le Mort* (Brosson, Gabon, Paris, 1800).

3. W. B. Cannon, *The Wisdom of the Body* (Norton, New York, 1932).

4. F. Alexander, *Psychosomatic Medicine: Its Principles and Applications* (Norton, New York, 1950), pp. 40–41.

5. G. A. Kimble, *Hilgard and Marquis' Conditioning and Learning* (Appleton-Century-Crofts, New York, ed. 2, 1961), p. 100.

6. B. F. Skinner, *The Behavior of Organisms* (Appleton-Century, New York, 1938); O. H. Mowrer, *Harvard Educ. Rev.* **17**, 102 (1947).

7. N. E. Miller and J. Dollard, *Social Learning and Imitation* (Yale Univ. Press, New Haven, 1941); J. Dollard and N. E. Miller, *Personality and Psychotherapy* (McGraw-Hill, New York, 1950); N. E. Miller, *Psychol. Rev.* **58**, 375 (1951).

8. N. E. Miller, *Ann. N.Y. Acad. Sci.* **92**, 830 (1961); _____, in *Nebraska Symposium on Motivation*, M. R. Jones, Ed. (Univ. of Nebraska Press, Lincoln, 1963); _____, in *Proc. 3rd World Congr. Psychiat., Montreal, 1961* (1963), vol. 3, p. 213.

9. _____, in "Proceedings, 18th International Congress of Psychology, Moscow, 1966," in press.

10. _____ and A. Carmona, *J. Comp. Physiol. Psychol.* **63**, 1 (1967).

11. J. A. Trowill, *ibid.*, p. 7.

12. N. E. Miller and L. V. DiCara, *ibid.*, p. 12.

13. L. V. DiCara and N. E. Miller, *Commun. Behav. Biol.* **2**, 19 (1968).

14. _____, *J. Comp. Physiol. Psychol.* **65**, 8 (1968).

15. _____, *ibid.*, in press.

16. D. J. Ehrlich and R. B. Malmo, *Neuropsychologia* **5**, 219 (1967).

17. "It even becomes difficult to postulate enough different thoughts each arousing a different emotion, each of which in turn innately elicits a specific visceral response. And if one assumes a more direct specific connection between different thoughts and different visceral responses, the notion becomes indistinguishable from the ideo-motor hypothesis of the voluntary movement of skeletal muscles." [W. James, *Principles of Psychology* (Dover, New York, new ed., 1950), vol. 2, chap. 26].

18. N. E. Miller and A. Banuazizi, *J. Comp. Physiol. Psychol.* **65**, 1 (1968).

19. A. Banuazizi, thesis, Yale University (1968).

20. N. E. Miller and L. V. DiCara, *Amer. J. Physiol.* **215**, 677 (1968).

21. A. Carmona, N. E. Miller, T. Demierre, in preparation.

22. A. Carmona, in preparation.

23. L. V. DiCara and N. E. Miller, *Commun. Behav. Biol.* **1**, 209 (1968).

24. _____, *Science* **159**, 1485 (1968).

25. _____, *Psychosom. Med.* **30**, 489 (1968).

26. L. V. DiCara and J. M. Weiss, *J. Comp. Physiol. Psychol.*, in press.

27. L. V. DiCara and N. E. Miller, *Physiol. Behav.*, in press.

28. N. E. Miller, *Science* **152**, 676 (1966).

29. A. Carmona, thesis, Yale University (1967).

30. For somewhat similar work on the single-cell level, see J. Olds and M. E. Olds, *in Brain Mechanisms and Learning*, J. Delafresnaye, A. Fessard, J. Konorski, Eds. (Blackwell, London, 1961).

31. E. S. Katkin and N. E. Murray, *Psychol. Bull.* **70**, 52 (1968); for a reply to their criticisms, see A. Crider, G. Schwartz, S. Shnidman, *ibid.*, in press.

32. N. E. Miller, L. V. DiCara, G. Wolf, *Amer. J. Physiol.* **215**, 684 (1968).

33. N. E. Miller, in *Personality Change*, D. Byrne and P. Worchel, Eds. (Wiley, New York, 1964), p. 149.

34. J. I. Lacey and B. C. Lacey, *Amer. J. Psychol.* **71**, 50 (1958); *Ann. N.Y. Acad. Sci.* **98**, 1257 (1962).

35. H. Barry III, personal communication.

36. N. E. Miller, *Proc. N.Y. Acad. Sci.*, in press.

37. Objective recording of such symptoms might be useful also in monitoring the effects of quite different types of psychotherapy.

38. B. T. Engel and K. T. Melmon, personal communication.

2. Dissimilarities Between Conditioned Avoidance Responses and Phobias

C. G. COSTELLO

The behavior therapists have accepted Mowrer's two-factor theory of avoidance as an experimental paradigm of phobia development. The inadequacy of this theory, reviewed in detail by Herrnstein, has been further emphasized. The adaptive nature of conditioned avoidance responses has been contrasted with the maladaptive nature of phobias. Alternative theories to the conditioning one have been briefly noted.

Breger and McGaugh (1965) and Weitzman (1967) have made a number of general criticisms of behavior therapy, the two most important, perhaps, being that (a) contrary to the behavior therapists' belief (e.g., Eysenck, 1960), there is considerable controversy among learning theorists and some of their fundamental notions are being questioned; (b) the techniques used by behavior therapists are probably more complicated than their theoretical formulations would suggest.

The comments of these critics have been important, particularly as starting points for the reevaluation of therapeutic techniques that are becoming increasingly popular. But the lack of specificity in their criticisms has made them vulnerable to countercriticism (e.g., Wiest, 1967). Further reevaluations should perhaps consist of the more specific detailing of discrepancies between the data of learning studies and the practices and formulations of the behavior therapists. It is one such discrepancy that will be discussed here.

One of the best known among the techniques being used is systematic desensitization developed by Wolpe (1958) for the treatment of phobic conditions. It is assumed by those who use this technique that phobias are analogous to experimentally established conditioned avoidance responses. Thus, Eysenck and Rachman (1965) present the essentials of the behavior therapists' theory of phobia development in nine statements, two of which are

8. Neutral stimuli which are associated with a noxious experience(s) may develop

SOURCE. *Article by C. G. Costello "Dissimilarities between conditioned avoidance responses and phobias, in the* Psychological Review, *Vol. 77, pp. 250–254, 1970. Copyright 1970 by the American Psychological Association and reprinted by permission.*

(secondary) motivating properties. This acquired drive is termed the fear drive.
9. Responses (such as avoidance) which reduce the fear drive are reinforced [p.82].

They make the comment that all of the nine statements "are supported by the full weight of almost all the evidence accumulated in research on the learning process [p. 82]."

It is clear that Eysenck and Rachman have accepted Mowrer's (1947) two-factor theory of avoidance learning and consider it to be an acceptable account of the development of phobias. The aim of systematic desensitization treatment is to reciprocally inhibit the conditioned anxiety response which maintains the avoidance (phobic) behaviors. But Herrnstein's (1969) review of the literature shows that the experimental evidence to date is not in support of the two-factor theory. Rather, it shows that termination of a conditioned stimulus (CS) is an unnecessary and insufficient feature of avoidance procedures and that when a CS is introduced into the avoidance learning situation, it appears to function as a discriminative stimulus for the avoidance response rather than as a conditioned aversive stimulus. Herrnstein suggests that some Pavlovian conditioning may be going on during avoidance learning so that the CS does acquire some aversive properties due to its association with shock. But the classically conditioned responses are not a requirement for the instrumental avoidance behavior. As shall be noted below, there is some evidence that even this relatively unimportant classical aversive conditioning of the CS becomes attenuated as a function of the increasing strength of the avoidance response.

In support of the suggestion that the CS in the avoidance situation is a discriminative stimulus for reinforced responding rather than a conditioned

aversive stimulus, Herrnstein refers to the following findings: (*a*) animals do not learn to avoid the CS, as one would expect, if it had become aversive (e.g., Sidman & Boren, 1957); (*b*) avoidance responses are readily learned when they produce a distinctive feedback stimulus instead of CS termination (D'Amato, Fazzaro, & Etkin, 1968); (*c*) rats prefer signaled to unsignaled shock (Lockard, 1963).

As evidence contrary to one or the other of the acquired drive or secondary reinforcement positions or to both of them, the following findings may be added to Herrnstein's list: (*a*) the difficulty of using a CS from an avoidance learning situation to establish higher order avoidance learning (McAllister & McAllister, 1964); (*b*) during the avoidance learning of human Ss, the cardiac response of acceleration extinguishes when avoidance has been well established (Bersh, Notterman, & Schoenfeld, 1956); (*c*) sympathectomized dogs operated on after acquisition of an avoidance response show strong resistance to extinction (Wynne & Solomon, 1955); (*d*) when fear of the CS is measured by its suppressant effects in a Skinner box, the function relating fear to avoidance acquisition is U shaped. In other words,

"To a point, prolonged acquisition training increases fear of the CS; however, when S achieves a long run of consecutive avoidances, fear of the CS diminishes sharply . . . "[Kamin, Brimer, & Black, 1963, p. 501].

One of the attractions of the conditioned avoidance analogue for the behavior therapist is that conditioned avoidance responses like phobias appear to be particularly resistant to extinction. The explanation usually accepted by behavior therapists (e.g., Eysenck & Rachman, 1965) for this slow extinction is one of the two proposed by Solomon and Wynne (1954). It suggests that extinction is prevented because the avoidance response makes "reality testing" (the unreinforced presentation of the CS) impossible. The explanation was derived from two-factor theory and its status as an explanation must therefore be in doubt. It should be noted that Eysenck (1968) more recently has commented on the experimental and clinical evidence indicating that anxiety and fear responses may increase rather than decrease in strength with repeated unreinforced presentation of the CS. He has suggested "a theory of incubation . . . which proposes that CRs are themselves reinforcing [p. 318]." This theory is related to classical aversive conditioning rather than avoidance conditioning. It is not, therefore, subject to the major criticism being made here. On the other hand, it does not appear to have resulted in any proposed changes in the understanding and methods of treatment of phobias and need not be discussed further.

Experimental evidence, then, suggests that the CS in avoidance procedures may have little or no aversive properties and may indeed have some important positive properties related to the *adaptive* instrumental response of avoidance. The adaptive nature of the avoidance response is emphasized in order to contrast it with the unadaptive nature of phobic behaviors. It is interesting, in this connection, to note that though strains of emotionally reactive rats show stronger conditioned emotional responses, measured in the Estes and Skinner (1941) manner, than nonreactive rats (Singh, 1959), they are inferior in avoidance learning (Broadhurst & Levine, 1963; Joffe, 1964; Levine & Broadhurst, 1963). Responses learned in the usual avoidance procedure are adaptive because they enable the animals simply to avoid a noxious stimulus. If this were true also

of the consequences of phobic behaviors, they could not be considered maladaptive and would not come to the attention of clinicians. But phobias are maladaptive because they prevent the occurrence of behaviors desired by the individual (e.g., the claustrophobic person cannot sit in a lecture theatre or a cinema) and/or desired by society (as in the case of a child with a school phobia).

Although Wolpe (1952) demonstrated that one did not need to oppose appetitive and avoidance behaviors to produce "neurotic" behavior in cats, a finding later confirmed by Smart (1965), even the most casual observation of clinical phobias suggests that such an opposition is involved. It is true that phobias for things like snakes may not involve approach—avoidance conflicts, since the avoidance of snakes, at least in North America, probably does not reduce the opportunity to engage in personally and/or socially desirable behavior. In this sense, snake phobias may resemble the conditioned avoidance responses established in the laboratory. But phobias for heights in our increasingly vertical environment, for crowds in our overpopulated world, for traffic in an affluent society, these and similar phobias are generally quite incapacitating.

But even comparisons between the less maladaptive phobias such as snake phobias and conditioned avoidance responses are somewhat strained. The demonstration by Watson and Rayner (1920) that a neutral object could become aversive by association with a noxious stimulus has been made to carry too much weight by the behavior therapists. Such a demonstration by no means establishes that phobias, whether or not they involve approach-avoidance conflicts, develop in a similar manner. It also does not seem to be generally recognized that though Jones (1924) obtained findings similar to Watson and Rayner, Bregman (1934) failed to reproduce Watson and Rayner's findings using more neutral stimuli for the CS.

Before learning accounts of any kind of phobias become too generally accepted, far more data are required on the natural history of phobia development. Furthermore, alternative theories to the learning theories are equally worthy of experimental attention at this time. Some possible alternatives will be mentioned briefly at a later point.

It may be argued that the success of systematic desensitization in the treatment of phobias suggests that the learning account is a correct one. Such a deduction is not, of course, inevitable and not even logically sound. In any case, methods other than systematic desensitization appear to be equally successful: (a) presentation at the first session of the most disturbing scene of an anxiety hierarchy rather than a gradual presentation of the scenes from the least to the most disturbing (Hogan & Kirchner, 1967; Stampfl & Levis, 1967; Weitzman, 1967; Wolpin & Raines, 1965); (b) instructions to tense the muscles rather than relax them during visualizations of scenes (Wolpin & Raines, 1965); (c) graduated practice in facing phobic stimuli with feedback of exposure times (Leitenberg, Agras, Thompson, & Wright, 1968); (d) leading subjects to believe that the phobic stimuli do not affect them by presenting false heart-rate feedback during the exposure to the stimuli (Valins & Ray, 1967). It may be suggested that these are but a variation of systematic desensitization treatment; but such a suggestion implies acceptance of much looser thinking than is usually practiced in the experimental laboratory and increases rather than decreases the distance between the laboratory and the clinic.

Some evidence has been obtained to suggest that relaxation plus the gradual presentation of anxiety stimuli is more effective in reducing phobic behaviors than either of these procedures alone (Rachman, 1967). But the crucial elements involved in the systematic densensitization procedure are far from having been teased out. The findings of Leitenberg et al. (1968), in particular, suggest that the learning of coping behaviors, to use White's (1959) term, is an important factor. Systematic densitization techniques may have a function similar to the play of children as described by Freud:

"The ego, which has experienced the trauma passively, now actively repeats an attenuated reproduction of it with the idea of taking into its own hands the direction of its course. We know that the child behaves in such a manner towards all impressions which he finds painful, by reproducing them in play; through this method of transition from passivity to activity the child attempts to cope psychically with its impressions and experiences [Freud, 1936, quoted in Mowrer & Viek, 1948, p. 193].

To recapitulate—the types of conditioned avoidance responses that have been regarded by behavior therapists as providing adequate experimental analogues of phobic behaviors are dissimilar to such behaviors because (a) the avoidance responses are adequate (coping) behaviors and (b) they do not involve a conflict with approach behaviors and such a conflict appears to be characteristic of clinical phobias.

Phobias might be better regarded as the result of a failure to develop coping behaviors in a situation that is in some respects attractive. The problem for psychologists is to determine why such coping behaviors fail to develop. There is no reason to assume that it is because of the development of conditioned aversive responses, though the lack of coping behaviors is itself presumably aversive. It must be emphasized that though approach-avoidance conflicts appear to be characteristic of clinical phobias, it is not suggested that Miller's (1959) experimental paradigm of approach-avoidance conflict is an adequate one for the understanding of phobias. Pairing of neutral conditioned stimuli with aversive unconditioned stimuli may play no role at all. At least equally plausible, despite the lack of an experimental analogue, is the suggestion that phobias develop in relation to the satisfaction of dependency needs (Andrews, 1966). Another alternative hypothesis, based on Pribam's (1967) analysis of emotion, might be that certain people fail to develop coping responses because of their intolerance of the uncertainty inherent in situations before and during the early stages of the development of coping behaviors. This intolerance may be partly a result of constitutional factors, but not necessarily the autonomic ones proposed by Eysenck (1957). Such an intolerance may, for instance, reflect deficiencies in the inhibitory reactions which Fenz and Epstein (1968) have suggested to be associated with the mastery of stress.

Phobias, though appearing to be among the more simple kinds of maladaptive behavior, are far from having been satisfactorily explained, and a satisfactory explanation is likely to occur only if the premature acceptance of any one theory is obviated and alternative theories are given equal time in the laboratory.

References

Andrews, J. D. W. Psychotherapy of phobias. *Psychological Bulletin*, 1966, **66**, 455–480.

Bersh, P. J., Notterman, J. M., & Schoenfeld, W. N. Extinction of a human cardiac-response during avoidance conditioning. *American Journal of Psychology*, 1956, **69**, 244–251.

Breger, L., & McGaugh, J. L. Critique and reformulation of "learning-theory" approaches to psychotherapy and neurosis. *Psychological Bulletin*, 1965, **63**, 338–358.

Bregman, E. O. An attempt to modify the emotional attitudes of infants by the conditioned response technique. *Journal of Genetic Psychology*, 1934, **45**, 169–198.

Broadhurst, P. L., & Levine, S. Behavioural consistency in strains of rats selectively bred for emotional elimination. *British Journal of Psychology*, 1963, **54**, 121–125.

D'Amato, M. R., Fazzaro, J., & Etkin, M. Anticipatory responding and avoidance discrimination as factors in avoidance conditioning. *Journal of Experimental Psychology*, 1968, **77**, 41–47.

Estes, W. K., & Skinner, B. F. Some quantitative properties of anxiety. *Journal of Experimental Psychology*, 1941, **29**, 390–400.

Eysenck, H. J. *The dynamics of anxiety and hysteria.* London: Routledge & Kegan Paul, 1957.

Eysenck, H. J. (Ed.) *Behavior therapy and the neuroses.* New York: Pergamon Press, 1960.

Eysenck, H. J. A theory of incubation of anxiety/fear responses. *Behaviour Research and Therapy,* 1968, **6**, 309–321.

Eysenck, H. J., & Rachman, S. *The causes and cures of neurosis.* London: Routledge & Kegan Paul, 1965.

Fenz, W. D., & Epstein, S. Specific and general inhibitory reactions associated with mastery of stress. *Journal of Experimental Psychology,* 1968, **77**, 52–56.

Freud, S. *The problem of anxiety.* New York: Norton, 1936.

Herrnstein, R. J. Method and theory in the study of avoidance. *Psychological Review,* 1969, **76**, 49–69.

Hogan, R. A., & Kirchner, J. H. Preliminary reports of the extinction of learned fears via short term implosive therapy. *Journal of Abnormal Psychology,* 1967, **72**, 106–109.

Joffe, J. M. Avoidance learning and failure to learn in two strains of rats selectively bred for emotionality. *Psychonomic Science,* 1964, **1**, 185–186.

Jones, M. C. A laboratory study of fear: The case of Peter. *Pedagogical Seminar,* 1924, **31**, 308–315.

Kamin, L. J., Brimer, C. J., & Black, A. H. Conditioned suppression as a monitor of fear of the CS in the course of avoidance training. *Journal of Comparative and Physiological Psychology,* 1963, **56**, 497–501.

Leitenberg, H., Agras, W. S., Thompson, L. E., & Wright, D. E. Feedback in behavior modification: An experimental analysis in two phobic cases. *Journal of Applied Behavior Analysis,* 1968, **1**, 131–137.

Levine, S., & Broadhurst, P. L. Genetic and ontogenetic determinants of adult behavior in the rat. *Journal of Comparative and Physiological Psychology,* 1963, **56**, 423–428.

Lockard, J. S. Choice of a warning signal or no warning signal in an unavoidable shock situation. *Journal of Comparative and Physiological Psychology,* 1963, **56**, 526–530.

McAllister, D. E., & McAllister, W. R. Second order conditioning of fear. *Psychonomic Science,* 1964, **1**, 383–384.

Miller, N. E. Liberalization of basic S-R concepts: Extension to conflict behavior, motivation and social learning. In S. Koch (Ed.), *Psychology: A study of a science.* Vol. 2. New York: McGraw-Hill, 1959.

Mowrer, O. H. On the dual nature of learning: A re-interpretation of "conditioning" and "problem-solving." *Harvard Educational Review,* 1947, **17**, 102–148.

Mowrer, O. H., & Viek, P. An experimental analogue of fear from a sense of helplessness. *Journal of Abnormal and Social Psychology,* 1948, **43**, 193–200.

Pribam, K. H. The new neurology and the biology of emotion. *American Psychologist,* 1967, **22**, 830–838.

Rachman, S. Systematic desensitization. *Psychological Bulletin*, 1967, **67**, 93–103.

Sidman, M., & Boren, J. J. A comparison of two types of warning stimulus in an avoidance situation. *Journal of Comparative and Physiological Psychology*, 1957, **50**, 282–287.

Singh, S. D. Conditioned emotional response in the rat. I. Constitutional and situational determinants. *Journal of Comparative and Physiological Psychology*, 1959, **52**, 574–578.

Smart, R. G. Conflict and conditioned aversive stimuli in the development of experimental neuroses. *Canadian Journal of Psychology*, 1965, **19**, 208–223.

Solomon, R. L., & Wynne, L. Traumatic avoidance learning: The principles of anxiety conservation and partial irreversibility. *Psychological Review*, 1954, **61**, 353–385.

Stampel, T. G., & Lewis, D. J. Essentials of implosive therapy: A learning theory based psychodynamic behavioral therapy. *Journal of Abnormal Psychology*, 1967, **72**, 495–503.

Valins, S., & Ray, A. A. Effects of cognitive desensitization on avoidance behavior. *Journal of Personality and Social Psychology*, 1967, **7**, 345–350.

Watson, J. B., & Rayner, R. Conditioned emotional reactions. *Journal of Experimental Psychology*, 1920, **3**, 1–4.

Weitzman, B. Behavior therapy and psychotherapy. *Psychological Review*, 1967, **74**, 300–317.

White, R. W. Motivation reconsidered: The concept of competence. *Psychological Review*, 1959, **66**, 297–333.

Wiest, W. M. Some recent criticisms of behaviorism and learning theory with special reference to Breger and McGaugh and to Chomsky. *Psychological Bulletin*, 1967, **67**, 214–225.

Wolpe, J. Experimental neuroses as learned behaviour. *British Journal of Psychology*, 1952, **43**, 243–261.

Wolpe, J. *Psychotherapy by reciprocal inhibition*. Stanford: Stanford University Press, 1958.

Wolpin, M., & Raines, J. Visual imagery, expected roles and extinction as possible factors in reducing fear and avoidance behaviour. *Behaviour Research and Therapy*, 1965, **4**, 25–37.

Wynne, L. C., & Solomon, R. L. Traumatic avoidance learning: Acquisition and extinction in dogs deprived of normal peripheral autonomic functioning. *Genetic Psychological Monographs*, 1955, **52**, 241–284.

3. Effects of Contingent and Noncontingent Reinforcement upon Generalized Imitation

JOHN C. MASTERS AND RICHARD J. MORRIS

After being exposed to a female model who exhibited aggressive behaviors and instructed S to imitate each aspect of the sequence, nursery school Ss were exposed to a male model displaying neutral behaviors, and their subsequent imitation was rated. During the first session, the female model either (a) contingently rewarded S for imitation, (b) provided no rewards for imitation, or (c) gave S rewards in a noncontingent "prepayment" before instructing him to imitate. In a fourth condition, S's imitation was rewarded impersonally by mechanical dispensers. Girls who were contingently rewarded by the female model showed greater subsequent generalized imitation than did girls who received the noncontingent prepayment of nonreward and marginally greater imitation than girls who received contingent reward from mechanical devices. Similar trends were observed for boys.

Theories of imitative learning (Bandura & Walters 1963; Miller & Dollard 1941; Mowrer 1960) have often proposed that the tendency to respond imitatively is enhanced by the administration of reward contingent upon imitative behavior. Studies have indeed shown that a model is more likely to induce imitation if he is rewarded for his behavior (Bandura 1965a; Bandura, Ross, & Ross 1963) and that the performance of behavior which has been observed may be enhanced by rewarding the subject (Bandura 1965b).

Unfortunately, it is difficult to study the effects of reward upon the acquisition of imitative tendencies in the young human organism who has not yet exhibited imitative behavior. Miller and Dollard (1941) examined conditions for the establishment of imitation in rats. These studies, however, left open the question as to whether the rats simply learned to follow another rat in order to obtain food or whether they had in fact learned to attend to the same cues as did the model rat. The question was

SOURCE. *Article by John C. Masters and Richard J. Morris "Effects of contingent and noncontingent reinforcement upon generalized imitation," Child Development, Vol. 42, pp. 385–397, 1971. Copyright 1971 by the Society for Research in Child Development, Inc., and reprinted by permission.*

also left open as to whether any generalization of this imitative tendency would occur. Most theories of imitation hypothesize a tendency or set to imitate in order to account for observed imitation of novel behaviors, the performance of which (imitative or otherwise) has not been previously reinforced.

The literature on the development and generalization of imitation in children is extraordinarily sparse. Baer, Peterson, and Sherman (1967) report the induction of imitation in severely retarded children who exhibited no imitative tendencies at all prior to an experimental manipulation comprised of shaping and fading procedures. In the training procedure, E physically manipulated S's behavior in such a way that it corresponded to the modeled behavior. Following this, S was rewarded. Some imitative behaviors developed during the training period in all three Ss studied, and these behaviors appeared to extinguish following the cessation of reward.

There have been few studies which directly concern themselves with the effects of reinforcement upon generalized imitation. Church (1957) demonstrated that rats which were rewarded for imitation (following another rat) learned to attend to the cues which the model rat was discriminating in the determination of its response. Schein (1954) devised a guessing task in which the imitation of a partner's guess often constituted a correct response by S. In this study, the reward for imitation was simply being told that the response was correct. Schein demonstrated that the imitation rose as a function of this reinforcement and generalized to a new but highly similar task. The generalization of imitation was not apparent for tasks of intermediate and distant similarity. (Imitation in this study appears quite similar to cheating and may have been so construed by some of the Ss.)

In a study utilizing normal children, Baer and Sherman (1964) rewarded children for imitating a variety of responses emitted by a puppet. These responses including nodding, mouthing, and a variety of nonsense statements. After the Ss were consistently imitating responses, the puppet also began pressing a bar, similar to one which the children had at their disposal, at alternating fast and slow rates. Although the children's imitative bar pressing was never rewarded, rewards were administered for their imitation of the nodding, mouthing, and nonsense statement responses. It is unclear in this study whether S was able to discriminate that these later reinforcements were contingent only upon the nodding, etc., responses and not upon his bar pressing, since both types of responses were occurring simultaneously. It was observed, however, that the child's rate of bar pressing did increase over a base rate of imitative bar pressing assessed at the commencement of the experiment. Unfortunately, no statistics were employed, and four of the 11 Ss failed to show any development of imitative bar pressing.

Studies with young children may not reflect directly upon the initial learning of any response system. However, if it could be shown that contingent reinforcement for imitation of one set of responses will increase imitation of a highly divergent set, theorizing that environmental reinforcement is important in the development of imitation would be strengthened. Such findings would certainly indicate that the generalized imitative response tendency remains subject to reinforcement contingencies.

Earlier studies have been concerned primarily with the effects of reinforcement upon a single imitative response or response category. Also, those studies which have been concerned with reinforcement effects upon generalized imitation have typically assessed such imitation with respect to new *responses* only and have not simultaneously varied the *situation* in which the imitation occurs or the *model* who displays the new behaviors.

The present study was designed to create a more stringent test of the hypothesis that reinforcement for imitative responding will result in generalized imitation. In the current study, children were trained to imitate behaviors of one response class (aggressive, high magnitude behaviors) and at a later time tested for their tendency to imitate behaviors of a highly divergent response class (nonaggressive, low-magnitude behaviors) performed by a new model in a completely different experimental setting. To be more specific, nursery school children were first exposed to a female model who exhibited a sequence of aggressive behaviors and instructed the child to imitate each aspect of the sequence. Following a short lapse of time, the children were exposed to a male model who displayed a sequence of neutral behaviors and subsequently left the child alone in a room which included the articles employed in the neutral behavior sequences. The children's behavior was then observed for a period of 3 minutes.

During the training portion with the female model, the experimental manipulation was effected. In one condition, the children were rewarded with tokens worth valuable prizes as well as with social approval when they imitated each portion of the model's aggressive sequence. In a second condition, no rewards of any sort were forthcoming after the child's imitative behavior. In a third condition, designed to control for the acquisition by the model of additional secondary reinforcing characteristics by her being paired with the token rewards, these rewards were dispensed by a token-dispensing machine and the social

reward (positive verbal comments) came from a tape recorder. Finally, in a fourth condition, children were given a noncontingent "prepayment" of tokens, equal to the amount accrued by children in each of the other conditions, *before* they observed the female model and imitated her as she instructed them to do.

Method

Subjects. Subjects were 56 4-year-old children, 28 girls and 28 boys, from two nursery schools in Saint Paul, Minnesota.

Procedure. Subjects were seen individually in two sessions separated by approximately 1 hour. The sessions were conducted in smaller nursery school rooms not typically used by the children. There were two phases to the experiment. In the treatment phase, a female model displayed seven aggressive behavior sequences, instructing the child to imitate each one, and then did or did not dispense rewards according to the experimental condition involved. In the test phase, a series of six neutral behavior sequences were exhibited by a male model who did not reward the child. An initial attempt to counterbalance *E*s had to be discarded when pilot testing indicated that nearly all children were frightened and inhibited by the observation of the male model exhibiting aggressive behaviors.

Treatment Phase. In this phase, the female *E* brought *S*s from the nursery school area to one of the experimental rooms. For all conditions, *E* explained that she and *S* would play a game in which *S* was to watch and then, when it was his turn, to do just what the *E* had done. For all conditions involving reinforcement, *E* then explained that *S* would received some marbles and that they were worth valuable prizes. It was stressed that the more marbles *S* received, the better the prize he would eventually gain, and thus he would want to acquire as many marbles as he could. In the condition involving no reinforcement, *E* went through the typical game explanation but with no mention of the marbles or prizes.

Following the introduction, *E* demonstrated the seven aggressive behavior sequences, taking turns with *S*, who was instructed to imitate each sequence after *E*'s demonstration. In this phase of the experiment, *E* performed the following behaviors: throwing a ball at toy soldiers, hitting a Bobo doll, building a bridge and kicking it down, laying the Bobo doll on the ground and hitting specified areas, making flying motions with a small plane and letting it crash, marching arross the room, and hitting the Bobo doll with a ball. All of these behavior sequences were accompanied by specific verbalization. The behaviors of the child were recorded at the time of occurrence by *E*, using a preestablished set of response categories.

In the reinforcement condition, *E* introduced the game in a warm and friendly manner and explained about the marbles. After each modeled behavior sequence, *E* turned to the child, smiled, and said, "It's your turn now." After every other response, starting with the first response, *E* said with a broad smile, "Good, you did just what I did" and, after every response, *E* counted three marbles into *S*'s hand. The *S* then deposited these rewards in a treasure chest. At the end of the game, *E* turned and said to *S*, "Let's see how many marbles you have. Boy, you sure have a lot. You know what? Because you did just what I did and because you earned so many marbles, I'm going to give you a very special prize." The *S* was then allowed to select a prize from a box containing a number of inexpensive toys.

In the nonreinforcement condition, *E* gave the introduction described above but rendered it "coldly" and did not squat down beside the child in a friendly manner as in the other conditions. No mention was made of the marbles. The *E* then performed the sequence of behaviors and *S* imitated in his turn. After every other response, *E* coldly said, "You did just what I did. It is my turn now."

In the impersonal reinforcement condition, *E* gave the introduction described above in the manner of the reinforcement condition. The marbles, however, were dispensed into a cup from a marble dispenser. To control for the handling of the marbles, *S* was instructed to retrieve the marbles from the cup and place them in his treasure chest. After every other response, a taped voice, controlled by *E*, said, "Good, you did just what she did." At the end of the game, *E* turned and made the same final statement as in the reinforcement condition (see above), specifically noting that, "Because you did just what I did and because you earned so many marbles, I'm going to give you a very special prize."

In the noncontingent reward condition, *E* introduced the game and the marbles in the manner described for the reinforcement condition. Since *S*s in all conditions were instructed to imitate *E*, the amount of reward obtained for each *S* in the reinforcement conditions was a constant. In the present condition, following the introduction, *S*s were given this number of marbles in a lump sum and no mention was made concerning a possible contingency between the receipt of these rewards and *S*'s subsequent imitative behavior.

Test Phase. This phase was similar for all *S*s, and neither the models nor the observing raters were aware of which treatment the S had experienced. A male model (M) took S from the nursery school to a new experimental room approximately 1 hour following the termination of the treatment phase. The S was told that he and M would have an opportunity to play with the toys which were distributed around the room. It would be M's turn first and S was to watch. Afterward, S could play with the toys in any way he pleased.

Following this introduction, M demonstrated six behavior sequences which were judged to be "neutral" in the sense that they were nonaggressive. These sequences included the following: First, M built a tower in a particular way from three blocks and immediately dismantled it. He then walked to and fro with a rattle, saying, "Rattle, rattle, spin, spin." Next, he selected an orange hat and a yellow feather from a display of three differently colored hats and feathers, placed the feather in the hat, and said, "Hat in my hand, hat on my head [while performing the appropriate actions]. This is a special hat. Around and around, around and around." During the latter verbalization, he turned around twice. Next, he commented that there was a baby doll somewhere in the room and that she must be hiding something. The doll was sitting on a small box. The M lifted her up, put her down on the floor, and then peeked into the box, following which he returned the doll to her place on the box. During this sequence, M verbally described what he was doing as he performed. Then, M turned his attentions to some animal stickers and a large pad of paper. From four animals represented, he selected a bear, licked it, and stuck it in the upper right-hand corner of the paper, noting verbally the corners in which he would *not* stick it as well as the one in which he actually did. Finally, M discovered a ball which he tossed up in the air twice, bounced off

the ground twice, and then rolled into a corner, again verbalizing all the while. Following each sequence of behaviors, the items used were returned to their original placements. The only exception was the bear sticker, which remained affixed to the upper right-hand corner of the pad of paper.

After M had completed his various behaviors, he excused himself from the room on the pretext of unfinished work elsewhere and told S that, while M was gone, S could "play with these toys and do anything you want to."

Rating Procedure. During the treatment phase, all Ss were instructed to imitate and no systematic variation among the experimental treatments was expected. During this phase, however, E recorded S's imitative behavior so that this expectation could be verified. During the test phase, all Ss were observed by a rater who recorded incidences of verbal and motor imitation by checking preselected responses on a score sheet. The modeled sequences were broken down into component behaviors and preferences indicated be these behaviors. For example, imitation of the hat and feather sequence contained eight behaviors designated as potentially imitative; selecting any hat, selecting the orange hat (preference), selecting the yellow feather, putting the hat on S's head, saying "hat in my hand," "hat on my head," "around and around," and actually turning around. There were a total of 17 verbal and 17 motor/preference behaviors which could be scored as imitative during the six behavior sequences displayed by M. Only 10 of the 56 Ss imitated any of the verbal behaviors. Analyses were conducted in terms of total imitation scores, but it should be noted that these scores reflect primarily the imitation of motor behaviors and preferences. Thirty-three of the Ss were observed by a second rater for a reliability check. The intercorrelation between these two raters, using total imitation scores, was + 0.974 (Pearson *r*).

Statistical Analyses. For all analyses, it was decided to use 0.05 as the probability level to be considered significant. Analyses and individual group comparisons for which the probabilities that observed differences were due to random variation were 0.10 or less, but still greater than 0.05, will be reported, since they approach an acceptable level of significance and may identify fruitful comparisons for future studies to explore.

Results

Although all children were instructed to imitate during the treatment phase, there were minor variations in the extent of their imitation. A two-way analysis of variance for equal *N*'s (Winer 1962) was conducted on the scores for imitation during the treatment phase. The two dimensions employed were sex of subject and conditions. The analysis, however, revealed neither a significant effect for sex of subject ($F = 2.38$; $df = 1$, 48) nor for conditions ($F = 1.54$; $df = 3$, 48). The interaction of these two variables also failed to reach significance ($F < 1$).

Imitation scores during the test phase were also subjected to a two-way analysis of variance, utilizing sex of subject and conditions as the main dimensions. This analysis revealed a significant effect for sex of subject ($F = 5.03$; $df = 1$, 48; $p < 0.05$), indicating that boys imitated the male model to a significantly greater extent ($\overline{M} = 9.59$) than did the girls ($\overline{M} = 6.64$). The effect for conditions approached significance ($F = 2.43$; $df = 3$, 48; $p < 0.10$), while the interaction between these

two main effects was not significant ($F = 1.13$; $df = 3$, 48).

As figure 1 illustrates, boys showed consistently greater imitation, but the group differences shown by the boys were less striking than those shown by the girls. It was felt that this attenuation may have been due to the boy's tendencies to imitate a male model to a high degree regardless of the prior experimental treatment. It was felt, then, that the data for each sex should be examined separately, even though the sex × conditions interaction had not been significant. This decision was also based on the considerations that the sex of *S* effect had been significant and that the interaction test in a factorial design is not a very powerful one, especially when several levels of one of the variables are employed. Consequently, the imitation scores for children of each sex were subjected to a one-way analysis of variance in order to explore in greater depth the marginal conditions effect reported above. These analyses revealed that the effect of conditions was not significant for the boys ($F = 1.23$; $df = 3$, 24), but reached an acceptable level of significance for girls ($F = 13.26$; $df = 3$, 24; $p < 0.001$). The difference in the magnitudes of the conditions effects is due in part to striking differences in the within-groups variances for each sex. The girls' data showed greater between-groups variation coupled with within-groups variance which was only half that shown by the boys.

Individual group comparisons for the data from girls were conducted via the Duncan Multiple-Range Test. These comparisons, presented in table 1, revealed that girls who had been rewarded for imitating by the first model imitated the new behaviors of the unfamiliar model to a greater extent than did girls who had not been rewarded at all or who had received rewards in a noncontingent "prepayment." Girls who had been

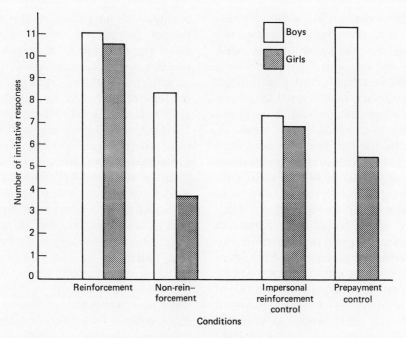

Figure 1. *Mean number of imitative responses for each sex in each condition.*

rewarded by the initial model also imitated to a greater extent than those who had been contingently rewarded by mechanical devices, although this difference only approached an acceptable level of significance.

Discussion

The results for girls indicated that contingent reward dispensed by the model can produce generalized imitation of highly divergent behaviors performed by

TABLE 1   *Generalized Imitation by Girls: Individual Group Comparisons Duncan Multiple-Range Test*

	CONDITIONS			
MEANS	Non-reinforcement (3.71)	Noncontingent Reinforcement (5.43)	Impersonal Reinforcement (6.86)	Reinforcement by Model (10.57)
3.71	—	1.72	3.15	6.86‡
5.43	· · ·	· · ·	1.43	5.14†
6.86	· · ·	· · ·	· · ·	3.71*

Note. — Means in parentheses.
*$p < 0.10$.
†$p < 0.05$.
‡$p < 0.01$.

a different model and in a different situation. It is disappointing, but perhaps not surprising, that the experimental manipulations did not significantly affect the generalized imitative behavior of the boys. In all conditions, boys tended to imitate to a greater extent than did the girls and were much more variable within groups. The tall, bearded male model may have decreased the mean and constricted the variance of imitation by the girls, thus accentuating the differential effects of the experimental manipulations. Consequently, there seems little reason to conclude that contingent reward for imitation increases the generalized tendency to imitate only for girls and not for boys. It is unfortunate that, due to the use of aggressive behavior in the treatment phase, it was not possible to counterbalance *E*s because the male model's performance of aggressive behaviors was a frightening stimulus in a pilot study and inhibited imitation entirely, even in the treatment phase during which *S*s were actually instructed to imitate.

What is perhaps most noteworthy about the present results is that contingent reward for imitation affected generalization only when it was dispensed by the model and not when automatic dispensing devices were employed, even though the same reinforcers were utilized in both instances. A secondary reinforcement theory of imitation (Mowrer 1950, 1960) predicts that the dispensation of rewards by the model will increase his secondary reinforcing properties. Through higher-order conditioning, the model's behaviors should also come to possess acquired reinforcing properties. One might thus expect increased imitation of the model because attention to his behaviors will increase (promoting acquisition) and because performance of the modeled behavior sequences will have become intrinsically rewarding. Although the difficulty in demonstrating the ac-

quisition of secondary reinforcing properties by neutral stimuli (Stevenson 1970) argues against flagrant use of the concept, social-learning oriented studies of model nurturance (Bandura, Grusec, & Menlove 1967) and model power (Mischel & Grusec 1966; Mischel & Liebert 1967) have produced results in line with predictions from a secondary reinforcement theory. Noncontingent reinforcement by the model (nurturance) or the model's potential for future reinforcement, whether contingent or noncontingent (power), have been shown to be effective variables for increasing children's imitation.

It is thus important to note that, in the present study, contingent reinforcers dispensed by mechanical devices were no more effective than noncontingent reinforcement or the complete absence of reinforcement for the promotion of generalized imitation. The finding that these automatically dispensed contingent reinforces were less effective than model-dispensed contingent reinforcers, even though this finding only approached significance, argues further that the contingency of reinforcement is not itself a sufficient factor for increasing generalized imitation. The present study is not the first to demonstrate that the source of reward may be a determinant of its effectiveness. Hartup (1964) has shown that reinforcement by liked peers has a different effect from reinforcement dispensed by peers who are disliked. Experiments by Walters and his colleagues, demonstrating that an increase in social-reinforcer effectiveness following isolation may be due to arousal, have employed strange versus familiar or "warm" versus "cold" or "neutral" adults as reinforcing agents. Results from these studies (Walters & Karal 1960; Walters & Parke 1964) indicate that this variation in source of reward affects the power of the reinforcer employed. Other studies have shown that reinforcement by fathers and mothers has different effects on children of each sex (Patterson et al. 1964), and Stevenson and his colleagues (Stevenson, Keen, & Knights 1963) report that social reinforcement offered by strangers produces significantly higher levels of performance than does such reinforcement when offered by parents.

In the case of the present study, we would argue that the differential effect of personally and impersonally dispensed reinforcers is not necessarily due to changes in the secondary reinforcing properties of the model or his behaviors, or to changes in the inner state of the child (such as arousal), although the fact that E was "cold" toward the child during the impersonal reinforcement condition makes the latter interpretation plausible. It seems likely, rather, that in the complex environment of the child, variables such as the source of reward will come to have discriminative value, especially in the determination of generalized responding. Obviously, the child does not imitate all individuals who have rewarded him nor does he increase the frequency of all imitative behaviors which have been followed by rewarding consequences. He may quickly learn that behaviors which are attended to and rewarded by socializing agents (and here we need not limit ourselves only to imitation) are profitably generalized, while those behaviors which are fortuitously followed by reward do not produce continued positive consequences when performed in new situations. "Superstitious conditioning" is said to have occurred when an organism responds to a random reinforcement as though it were contingent. The young child may have difficulty discriminating reinforcement which is "intentionally contingent" from that which is only "fortuitously contingent," unless he attends to obvious cues such as the source of these rewards.

Bandura (Bandura 1969; Bandura & Barab 1969) has pointed out that generalized imitation in children is highly discriminative, and that discriminated imitative responding, not an indiscriminate, generalized tendency to imitate, is a primary determinant of imitative learning. The initial intent of the present study was to demonstrate that contingent reinforcement could control generalized imitation, the argument being that discriminative responding acts as an "overlay" upon a generalized tendency to imitate. In the demonstration of this point, we interpret the ancillary finding concerning the importance of the source of reward as an affirmation of the importance of discrimination. As argued earlier, attention to the source of contingent reward may provide important information concerning the consequences which are likely to follow imitation of modeled behaviors. Observation that rewards were dispensed contingently by the model or another socializing agent may constitute specific information that the behavior, when observed by socializing agents in the future, will again be rewarded. It is interesting to note, then, that in the present study, generalized imitation was measured in the model's *absence*. It may be that young children often find that they have been observed by adults even when they thought they were alone. Such experiences would encourage the performance of contingently rewarded behaviors in the absence of a socializing agent. A prediction from this argument would be that older children will show less generalization than younger children when observed in the model's absence.

Future research might profitably explore the source of reward in its role as a potential discriminative cue. It has not yet been determined whether the effect of various sources of reward is similar for acquisition, for performance in the presence of the rewarding source, and for performance in the absence of the rewarding source or in different situations (generalization). When impersonal and personal sources of reward are compared, acquisition and generalization may be affected similarly. Reinforcers which are not dispensed by a person may be deemed merely adventitious, with only apparent contingency, and consequently may promote neither acquisition nor generalization of the behavior in question. On the other hand, reinforcers contingently dispensed by socializing agents may promote *both* acquisition and generalization. When two sources, both personal, are compared, the child may *learn* from both sources of contingent reward but *perform* only in the presence of, say, a familiar or liked source. In a generalization task, however, and in the absence of the original source of reward, the rewarded behavior may be performed regardless of the original source of reward (so long as it was a person).

References

Baer, D. M.; Peterson, R. F.; & Sherman, J. A. The development of imitation by reinforcing similarity to a model. *Journal of the Experimental Analysis of Behavior*, 1967, **10**, 405–416.

Baer, D. M., & Sherman, J. A. Reinforcement control of generalized imitation in young children. *Journal of Experimental Child Psychology*, 1964, **1**, 37–49.

Bandura, A. Vicarious processes: a case of no-trial learning. In L. Berkowitz (Ed.), *Advances in experimental social psychology*. Vol. **11**. New York: Academic, 1965. (a)

Bandura, A. Influence of models' reinforcement contingencies on the acquisition of imitative responses. *Journal of Personality and Social Psychology*, 1965, **1**, 589–595. (b)

Bandura, A. Modeling theory: some traditions, trends, and disputes. Unpublished manuscript, Stanford University, 1969.

Bandura, A., & Barab, P. G. Conditions governing nonreinforced imitation. Unpublished manuscript, Stanford University, 1969.

Bandura, A.; Grusec, J. E.; & Menlove, F. L. Some social determinants of self-monitoring reinforcement systems. *Journal of Personality and Social Psychology*, 1967, **5**, 449–455.

Bandura, A.; Ross, D.; & Ross, S. A. Vicarious reinforcement and imitative learning. *Journal of Abnormal and Social Psychology*, 1963, **67**, 601–607.

Bandura, A., & Walters, R. H. *Social learning and personality development*. New York: Holt, Rinehart & Winston, 1963.

Church, R. M. Transmission of learned behavior between rats. *Journal of Abnormal and Social Psychology*, 1957, **54**, 163–165.

Hartup, W. W. Friendship status and the effectiveness of peers as reinforcing agents. *Journal of Experimental Child Psychology*, 1964, **1**, 154–162.

Miller, N. W., & Dollard, J. *Social learning and imitation.* New Haven, Conn.: Yale University Press, 1941.

Mischel, W., & Grusec, J. E. Determinants of the rehearsal and transmission of neutral and aversive behaviors. *Journal of Personality and Social Psychology*, 1966, **3**, 197–205.

Mischel, W., & Liebert, R. M. The role of power in the adoption of self-reward patterns. *Child Development*, 1967, **38**, 673–683.

Mowrer, O. H. Identification: a link between learning theory and psychotherapy. In O. H. *Mowrer* (Ed.), *Learning theory and personality dynamics.* New York: Ronald, 1950. pp. 69–94.

Mowrer, O. H. *Learning theory and the symbolic processes.* New York: Wiley, 1960.

Patterson, G. R.; Littman, R.; & Hinsley, C. Parental effectiveness as reinforcers in the laboratory and its relation to child rearing practices and child adjustment in the classroom. *Journal of Personality*, 1964, **32**, 180–199.

Schein, E. H. The effect of reward on adult imitative behavior. *Journal of Abnormal and Social Psychology*, 1954, **49**, 389–395.

Stevenson, H. W. Learning in children. In P. H. Mussen (Ed.), *Carmichael's handbook of child psychology.* New York: Wiley, 1970.

Stevenson, H. W.; Keen, R.; & Knights, R. M. Parents and strangers as reinforcing agents for children's performance. *Journal of Abnormal and Social Psychology*, 1963, **67**, 183–186.

Walters R. H., & Karal, P. Social deprivation and verbal behavior. *Journal of Personality*, 1960, **28**, 89–107.

Walters, R. H., & Parke, R. D. Emotional arousal, isolation, and discrimination learning in children. *Journal of Experimental Child Psychology*, 1964, **1**, 163–173.

Winer, B. J. *Statistical principles in experimental design.* New York: McGraw-Hill, 1962.

Section XI

Skinner's Operant Reinforcement Theory

The degree of influence of Skinner's research and theory upon our life and times can probably be compared seriously only to that of Sigmund Freud. He is one of a small number of psychologists, living or dead, whose name is likely to evoke a response from almost any educated person as well as from virtually all scholars, whether they are humanists or physicists. It is a testimony to the power of Skinner's ideas that this tremendous influence has been based largely on experiments conducted with rats and pigeons and has been accomplished within the perspective of a relatively simple, if not sparse, theoretical system. Although his principles of behavior have been derived from laboratory experiments, he does not hesitate to generalize and extend them quite freely, because he is convinced the principles are firmly established and can be used in other contexts with no diminution of predictive power. His applications have met with sufficient success so that it is not easy to argue with this position.

With the publication of Skinner's most recent book, *Beyond Freedom and Dignity* (1971), he has widened his sphere of influence and as usual has elicited strong and mixed reactions. For example, shortly after the publication of this book, a congressman argued in a speech to the House of Representatives that although he did not question Skinner's right to publish his ideas, he did question the propriety of spending tax dollars to support Skinner's research, since his ideas were threatening to the United States' system of government! Yet he has received many awards and honors including the National Medal of Science and the 1971 J. P. Kennedy Jr. International Award for Outstanding Scientific Research as well as almost all of the traditional honors that psychologists are able to bestow upon themselves.

Unlike many theories of personality the path from Skinner's operant reinforcement theory to experimentation and application is relatively straightforward. Thus, his theory has generated thousands of unambiguous experiments—most of which are confirmatory—and has led to countless applications ranging from communal living through much of education and therapy to animal training.

Skinner is an unusually lucid and persuasive writer, and this is not altogether surprising in view of his early interest in creative writing. The first two papers we have chosen for this section clearly demonstrate both his writing ability and his wide-ranging interests in pure science and applications. The first selection, "A case history in scientific method," is an essay in which Skinner describes from a personal viewpoint, how one "does science." In it the growth of his ideas is recorded, and he shows how closely the observed regularities (and thus the principles) of behavior are tied to apparatus or available methods. For the student contemplating a research career in psychology, this paper should be of particular value, since it gives a first-hand glimpse, albeit over Skinner's shoulder, of the details of how one eminent psychologist has gone about his research. As one can see from this paper, at least in the case of Skinner, the philosophy of science and the logic of experimentation as usually expounded, are not always the same as that which is practiced.

"Pigeons in a pelican" is a delightful essay describing one of Skinner's more unusual research projects. It is noteworthy that in Skinner's opinion one of the most important features of this project was its contribution to other, and very different, problems in the control and understanding of behavior, thus illustrating the complex and reverberating relationship between pure science and technology. No better illustration could be provided of the unexpected directions that research can take under the guidance of a lively imagination and radical behaviorism. The project and its outcome also exemplify the resistance that Skinner's ideas and research have typically generated in much of the general public. It was not too long ago that people all around the world eagerly followed the activities of chimpanzees orbiting about the earth, and it is clear that at least scientifically those chimpanzees were lineal descendants of the "Pigeons in a pelican."

The concluding paper, by Baer and Sherman, deals with imitative responses in children. The idea that learning, particularly of complex social behavior, can occur through imitation, has been of interest to many psychologists and sociologists over the years. Yet the details of how this process operates, if indeed it does, is far from understood and agreed upon. In this paper, Baer and Sherman analyze imitation from the special perspective of operant conditioning. They cast their analysis, as one might expect, in terms quite different from those usually employed in explanations of imitation, and their approach provides an interesting contrast to that of Masters and Morris (see pp. 367–377).

Reference

Skinner, B. F. *Beyond Freedom and Dignity*. New York: Knopf, 1971.

1. A Case History in Scientific Method

B. F. SKINNER

It has been said that college teaching is the only profession for which there is no professional training, and it is commonly argued that this is because our graduate schools train scholars and scientists rather than teachers. We are more concerned with the discovery of knowledge than with its dissemination. But can we justify ourselves quite so easily? It is a bold thing to say that we know how to train a man to be a scientist. Scientific thinking is the most complex and probably the most subtle of all human activities. Do we actually know how to shape up such behavior, or do we simply mean that some of the people who attend our graduate schools eventually become scientists?

Except for a laboratory course which acquaints the student with standard apparatus and standard procedures, the only explicit training in scientific method generally received by a young psychologist is a course in statistics—not the introductory course, which is often required of so many kinds of students that it is scarcely scientific at all, but an advanced course which includes "model

building," "theory construction," and "experimental design." But it is a mistake to identify scientific practice with the formalized constructions of statistics and scientific method. These disciplines have their place, but it does not coincide with the place of scientific research. They offer *a* method of science but not, as is so often implied, *the* method. As formal disciplines they arose very late in the history of science, and most of the facts of science have been discovered without their aid. It takes a great deal of skill to fit Faraday with his wires and magnets into the picture which statistics gives us of scientific thinking. And most current scientific practice would be equally refractory, especially in the important initial stages. It is no wonder that the laboratory scientist is puzzled and often dismayed when he discovers how his behavior has been reconstructed in the formal analyses of scientific method. He is likely to protest that this is not at all a fair representation of what he does.

But his protest is not likely to be heard. For the prestige of statistics and scientific methodology is enormous. Much of it is borrowed from the high repute of mathematics and logic, but much of it derives from the flourishing state of the art itself. Some statisticians are professional people employed by scientific

SOURCE. *Article by B. F. Skinner, "A case history in scientific method" in the* American Psychologist, *Vol. 11, p. 221–233, 1956. Copyright 1956 by the American Psychological Association and reprinted by permission.*

and commercial enterprises. Some are teachers and pure researchers who give their colleagues the same kind of service for nothing—or at most a note of acknowledgment. Many are zealous people who, with the best of intentions, are anxious to show the nonstatistical scientist how he can do his job more efficiently and assess his results more accurately. There are strong professional societies devoted to the advancement of statistics, and hundreds of technical books and journals are published annually.

Against this, the practicing scientist has very little to offer. He cannot refer the young psychologist to a book which will tell him how to find out all there is to know about a subject matter, how to have the good hunch which will lead him to devise a suitable piece of apparatus, how to develop an efficient experimental routine, how to abandon an unprofitable line of attack, how to move on most rapidly to later stages of his research. The work habits which have become second nature to him have not been formalized by anyone, and he may feel that they possibly never will be. As Richter[1] has pointed out, "Some of the most important discoveries have been made without any plan of research," and "there are researchers who do not work on a verbal plane, but cannot put into words what they are doing."

If we are interested in perpetuating the practices responsible for the present corpus of scientific knowledge, we must keep in mind that some very important parts of the scientific process do not now lend themselves to mathematical, logical, or any other formal treatment. We do not know enough about human behavior to know how the scientist does what he does. Although statisticians and method-

ologists may seem to tell us, or at least imply, how the mind works—how problems arise, how hypotheses are formed, deductions made, and crucial experiments designed—we as psychologists are in a position to remind them that they do not have methods appropriate to the empirical observation or the functional analysis of such data. These are aspects of human behavior, and no one knows better than we how little can at the moment be said about them.

Some day we shall be better able to express the distinction between empirical analysis and formal reconstruction, for we shall have an alternative account of the behavior of Man Thinking. Such an account will not only plausibly reconstruct what a particular scientist did in any given case, it will permit us to evaluate practices and, I believe, to teach scientific thinking. But that day is some little distance in the future. Meanwhile we can only fall back on examples.

When the director of Project A of the American Psychological Association asked me to describe and analyze my activities as a research psychologist, I went through a trunkful of old notes and records and, for my pains, reread some of my earlier publications. This has made me all the more aware of the contrast between the reconstructions of formalized scientific method and at least one case of actual practice. Instead of amplifying the points I have just made by resorting to a generalized account (principally because it is not available), I should like to discuss a case history. It is not one of the case histories we should most like to have, but what it lacks in importance is perhaps somewhat offset by accessibility. I therefore ask you to imagine that you are all clinical psychologists—a task which becomes easier and easier as the years go by—while I sit across the desk from you or stretch out upon this comfortable leather couch.

---

[1]Richter, C. P. Free research versus design research. *Science*, 1953, **118**, 91–93.

The first thing I can remember happened when I was only twenty-two years old. Shortly after I was graduated from college Bertrand Russell published a series of articles in the old *Dial* magazine on the epistemology of John B. Watson's Behaviourism. I had had no psychology as an undergraduate but I had had a lot of biology, and two of the books which my biology professor had put into my hands were Loeb's *Physiology of the Brain* and the newly published Oxford edition of Pavlov's *Conditioned Reflexes*. And now here was Russell extrapolating the principles of an objective formulation of behavior to the problem of knowledge! Many years later when I told Lord Russell that his articles were responsible for my interest in behavior, he could only exclaim, "Good Heavens! I had always supposed that those articles had demolished Behaviorism!" But at any rate he had taken Watson serious, and so did I.

When I arrived at Harvard for graduate study, the air was not exactly full of behavior, but Walter Hunter was coming in once a week from Clark University to give a seminar, and Fred Keller, also a graduate student, was an expert in both the technical details and the sophistry of Behaviorism. Many a time he saved me as I sank into the quicksands of an amateurish discussion of "What is an image?" or "Where is red?" I soon came into contact with W. J. Crozier, who had studied under Loeb. It had been said of Loeb, and might have been said of Crozier, that he "resented the nervous system." Whether this was true or not, the fact was that both these men talked about animal behavior without mentioning the nervous system and with surprising success. So far as I was concerned, they cancelled out the physiological theorizing of Pavlov and Sherrington and thus clarified what remained of the work of these men as the beginnings of an independent science of behavior. My doctoral

thesis was in part an operational analysis of Sherrington's synapse, in which behavioral laws were substituted for supposed states of the central nervous posed states of the central nervous system.

But the part of my thesis at issue here was experimental. So far as I can see, I began simply by looking for lawful processes in the behavior of the intact organism. Pavlov had shown the way; but I could not then, as I cannot now, move without a jolt from salivary reflexes to the important business of the organism in everyday life. Sherrington and Magnus had found order in surgical segments of the organism. Could not something of the same sort be found, to use Loeb's phrase, in "the organism as a whole"? I had the clue from Pavlov: control your conditions and you will see order.

It is not surprising that my first gadget was a silent release box, operated by compressed air and designed to eliminate disturbances when introducing a rat into an apparatus. I used this first in studying the way a rat adapted to a novel stimulus. I built a soundproofed box containing a specially structured space. A rat was released, pneumatically, at the far end of a darkened tunnel from which it emerged in exploratory fashion into a well-lighted area. To accentuate its progress and to facilitate recording, the tunnel was placed at the top of a flight of steps, something like a functional Parthenon (Figure 1). The rat would peek out from the tunnel, perhaps glancing suspiciously at the one-way window through which I was watching it, then stretch itself cautiously down the steps. A soft click (carefully calibrated, of course) would cause it to pull back into the tunnel and remain there for some time. But repeated clicks had less and less of an effect. I recorded the rat's advances and retreats by moving a pen back and forth across a moving paper tape.

The major result of this experiment was that some of my rats had babies.

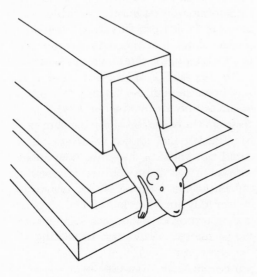

Figure 1.

I began to watch young rats. I saw them right themselves and crawl about very much like the decerebrate or thalamic cats and rabbits of Magnus. So I set about studying the postural reflexes of young rats. Here was a first principle not formally recognized by scientific methodologists: When you run onto something interesting, drop everything else and study it. I tore up the Parthenon and started over.

If you hold a young rat on one hand and pull it gently by the tail, it will resist you by pulling forward and then, with a sudden sharp spring which usually disengages its tail, it will leap out into space. I decided to study this behavior quantitatively. I built a light platform covered with cloth and mounted it on tightly stretched piano wires (Figure 2). Here was a version of Sherrington's torsion-wire myograph, originally designed to record the isometric contraction of the *tibialis anticus* of a cat, but here adapted to the response of a whole organism. When the tail of the young rat was gently pulled, the rat clung to the cloth floor and tugged forward. By amplifying the fine movements of the

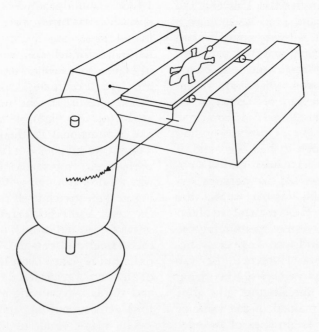

Figure 2.

Figure 3.

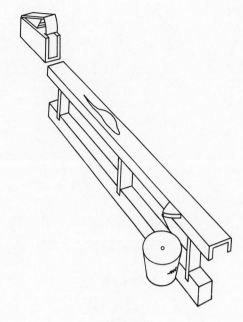

Figure 4.

platform, it was possible to get a good kymograph record of the tremor in this motion and then, as the pull against the tail was increased, of the desperate spring into the air (Figure 3).

Now, baby rats have very little future, except as adult rats. Their behavior is literally infantile and cannot be usefully extrapolated to everyday life. But if this technique would work with a baby, why not try it on a mature rat? To avoid attaching anything to the rat, it should be possible to record, not a pull against the substrate, but the ballistic thrust exerted as the rat runs forward or suddenly stops in response to my calibrated click. So, invoking the first principle of scientific practice again, I threw away the pianowire platform and built a runway, eight feet long. This was constructed of light wood, in the form of a U girder, mounted rigidly on vertical glass plates, the elasticity of which permitted a very slight longitudinal movement (Figure 4). The runway became the floor of a long tunnel, not shown, at one end of which I placed my soundless release box and at the other end myself, prepared to reinforce the rat for coming down the

runway by giving it a bit of wet mash, to sound a click from time to time when it had reached the middle of the runway, and to harvest kymograph records of the vibrations of the substrate.

Now for a second unformalized principle of scientific practice: Some ways of doing research are easier than others. I got tired of carrying the rat back to the other end of the runway. A back alley was therefore added (Figure 5). Now the rat could eat a bit of mash at point C, go down the back alley A, around the end as shown, and back home by runway B. The experimenter at E could collect records from the kymograph at D in comfort. In this way a great many records were made of the forces exerted against the substratum as rats ran down the alley and occasionally stopped dead in their tracks as a click sounded (Figure 6).

There was one annoying detail, however. The rat would often wait an inordinately long time at C before starting down the back alley on the next run.

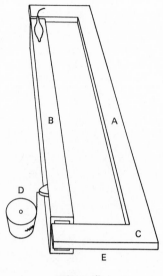

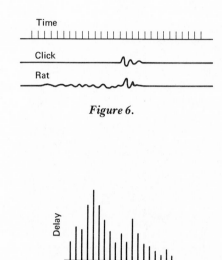

Figure 6.

Figure 5.

Figure 7.

There seemed to be no explanation for this. When I timed these delays with a stop watch, however, and plotted them, they seemed to show orderly changes (Figure 7). This was, of course, the kind of thing I was looking for. I forgot all about the movements of the substratum and began to run rats for the sake of the delay measurements alone. But there was now no reason why the runway had to

be eight feet long and, as the second principle came into play again, I saw no reason why the rat could not deliver its own reinforcement.

A new apparatus was built. In Figure 8 we see the rat eating a piece of food just after completing a run. It produced the food by its own action. As it ran down the back alley A to the far end of the rect-angular runway, its weight caused the

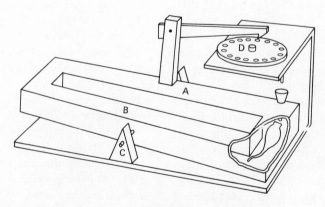

Figure 8.

whole runway to tilt slightly on the axis C and this movement turned the wooden disc D, permitting a piece of food in one of the holes around its perimeter to drop through a funnel into a food dish. The food was pearl tapioca, the only kind I could find in the grocery stores in reasonably uniform pieces. The rat had only to complete its journey by coming down the homestretch B to enjoy its reward. The experimenter was able to enjoy *his* reward at the same time, for he had only to load the magazine, put in a rat, and relax. Each tilt was recorded on a slowly moving kymograph.

A third unformalized principle of scientific practice: Some people are lucky. The disc of wood from which I had fashioned the food magazine was taken from a storeroom of discarded apparatus. It happened to have a central spindle, which fortunately I had not bothered to cut off. One day it occurred to me that if I wound a string around the spindle and allowed it to unwind as the magazine was emptied (Figure 9), I would get a different kind of record. Instead of a mere report of the up-and-down movement of the runway, as a series of pips as in a polygraph, I would get a *curve*. And I knew that science made great use of curves, although, so far as I could discover, very little of pips on a polygram. The difference between the old type of record at A (Figure 10) and the new at B may not seem great, but as it turned out the curve revealed things in the rate of responding, and in changes in that rate, which would certainly otherwise have been missed. By allowing the string to unwind rather than to wind, I had got my curve in an awkward Cartesian quadrant, but that was easily remedied. Psychologists have adopted cumulative curves only very slowly, but I think it is fair to say that they have become an indispensable tool for certain purposes of analysis.

Eventually, of course, the runway was

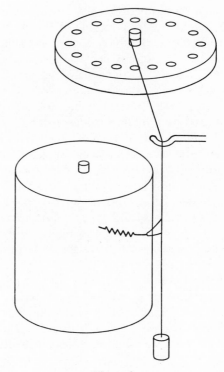

Figure 9.

seen to be unnecessary. The rat could simply reach into a covered tray for pieces of food, and each movement of the cover could operate a solenoid to move a pen one step in a cumulative curve. The first major change in rate observed in this way was due to indigestion. Curves showing how the rate of eating declined with the time of eating comprised the

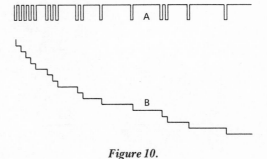

Figure 10.

other part of my thesis. But a refinement was needed. The behavior of the rat in pushing open the door was not a normal part of the ingestive behavior of *Rattus rattus*. The act was obviously learned but its status as part of the final performance was not clear. It seemed wise to add an initial conditioned response connected with ingestion in a quite arbitrary way. I chose the first device which came to hand—a horizontal bar or lever placed where it could be conveniently depressed by the rat to close a switch which operated a magnetic magazine. Ingestion curves obtained with this initial response in the chain were found to have the same properties as those without it.

Now, as soon as you begin to complicate an apparatus, you necessarily invoke a fourth principle of scientific practice: Apparatuses sometimes break down. I had only to wait for the food magazine to jam to get an extinction curve. At first I treated this as a defect and hastened to remedy the difficulty. But eventually, of course, I deliberately disconnected the magazine. I can easily recall the excitement of that first complete extinction curve (Figure 11). It had made contact with Pavlov at last! Here was a curve uncorrupted by the physiological process of ingestion. It was an orderly change due to nothing more than a special contingency of reinforcement. It was pure behavior! I am not saying that

I would not have got around to extinction curves without a breakdown in the apparatus; Pavlov had given too strong a lead in that direction. But it is still no exaggeration to say that some of the most interesting and surprising results have turned up first because of similar accidents. Foolproof apparatus is no doubt highly desirable, but Charles Ferster and I in recently reviewing the data from a five-year program of research found many occasions to congratulate ourselves on the fallibility of relays and vacuum tubes.

I then built four soundproofed ventilated boxes, each containing a lever and a food magazine and supplied with a cumulative recorder, and was on my way to an intensive study of conditioned reflexes in skeletal behavior. I would reinforce every response for several days and then extinguish for a day or two, varying the number of reinforcements, the amount of previous magazine training, and so on.

At this point I made my first use of the deductive method. I had long since given up pearl tapioca as too unbalanced a diet for steady use. A neighborhood druggist had shown me his pill machine, and I had had one made along the same lines (Figure 12). It consisted of a fluted brass bed across which one laid a long cylinder of stiff paste (in my case a MacCollum formula for an adequate rat diet). A

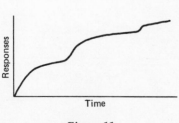

Figure 11.

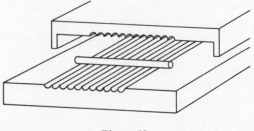

Figure 12.

similarly fluted cutter was then lowered onto the cylinder and rolled slowly back and forth, converting the paste into about a dozen spherical pellets. These were dried for a day or so before use. The procedure was painstaking and laborious. Eight rats eating a hundred pellets each per day could easily keep up with production. One pleasant Saturday afternoon I surveyed my supply of dry pellets and, appealing to certain elemental theorems in arithmetic, deduced that unless I spent the rest of that afternoon and evening at the pill machine, the supply would be exhausted by ten-thirty Monday morning.

Since I do not wish to deprecate the hypothetico-deductive method, I am glad to testify here to its usefulness. It led me to apply our second principle of unformalized scientific method and to ask myself why *every* press of the lever had to be reinforced. I was not then aware of what had happened at the Brown laboratories, as Harold Schlosberg later told the story. A graduate student had been given the task of running a cat through a difficult discrimination experiment. One Sunday the student found the supply of cat food exhausted. The stores were closed, and so, with a beautiful faith in the frequency-theory of learning, he ran the cat as usual and took it back to its living cage unrewarded. Schlosberg reports that the cat howled its protest continuously for nearly forty-eight hours. Unaware of this I decided to reinforce a response only once every minute and to allow all other responses to go unreinforced. There were two results: (*a*) my supply of pellets lasted almost indefinitely, and (*b*) each rat stabilized at a fairly constant rate of responding.

Now, a steady state was something I was familiar with from physical chemistry, and I therefore embarked upon the study of periodic reinforcement. I soon found that the constant rate at which the rat

stabilized depended upon how hungry it was. Hungry rat, high rate; less hungry rat, lower rate. At that time I was bothered by the practical problem of controlling food deprivation. I was working half time at the Medical School (on chronaxie of subordination!) and could not maintain a good schedule in working with the rats. The rate of responding under periodic reinforcement suggested a scheme for keeping a rat at a constant level of deprivation. The argument went like this: Suppose you reinforce the rat, not at the end of a given period, but when it has completed the number of responses ordinarily emitted in that period. And suppose you use substantial pellets of food and give the rat continuous access to the lever. Then, except for periods when the rat sleeps, it should operate the lever at a constant rate around the clock. For, whenever it grows slightly hungrier, it will work faster, get food faster, and become less hungry, while whenever it grows slightly less hungry, it will respond at a lower rate, get less food, and grow hungrier. By setting the reinforcement at a given number of responses it should even be possible to hold the rat at any given level of deprivation. I visualized a machine with a dial which one could set to make available, at any time of day or night, a rat in a given state of deprivation. Of course, nothing of the sort happens. This is "fixed-ratio" rather than "fixed-interval" reinforcement and, as I soon found out, it produces a very different type of performance. This is an example of a fifth unformalized principle of scientific practice, but one which has at least been named. Walter Cannon described it with a word invented by Horace Walpole: *serendipity*—the art of finding one thing while looking for something else.

This account of my scientific behavior up to the point at which I published my results in a book called *The Behavior of Organisms* is as exact in letter and spirit as I can now make it. The notes, data, and publications which I have examined do not show that I ever behaved in the manner of Man Thinking as described by John Stuart Mill or John Dewey or in reconstructions of scientific behavior by other philosophers of science. I never faced a Problem which was more than the eternal problem of finding order. I never attacked a problem by constructing a Hypothesis. I never deduced Theorems or submitted them to Experimental Check. So far as I can see, I had no preconceived Model of behavior—certainly not a physiological or mentalistic one and, I believe, not a conceptual one. The "reflex reserve" was an abortive, though operational, concept which was retracted a year or so after publication in a paper at the Philadelphia meeting of the APA. It lived up to my opinion of theories in general by proving utterly worthless in suggesting further experiments. Of course, I was working on a basic Assumption—that there was order in behavior if I could only discover it—but such an assumption is not to be confused with the hypotheses of deductive theory. It is also true that I exercised a certain Selection of Facts but not because of relevance to theory but because one fact was more orderly than another. If I engaged in Experimental Design at all, it was simply to complete or extend some evidence of order already observed.

Most of the experiments described in *The Behavior of Organisms* were done with groups of four rats. A fairly common reaction to the book was that such groups were too small. How did I know that other groups of four rats would do the same thing? Keller, in defending the book, countered with the charge that groups of four were too *big*. Unfortunately, however, I allowed myself to be persuaded of the contrary. This was due in part to my association at the University of Minnesota with W. T. Heron. Through him I

came into close contact for the first time with traditional animal psychology. Heron was interested in inherited maze behavior, inherited activity, and certain drugs—the effects of which could then be detected only through the use of fairly large groups. We did an experiment together on the effect of starvation on the rate of pressing a lever and started the new era with a group of sixteen rats. But we had only four boxes, and this was so inconvenient that Heron applied for a grant and built a battery of twenty-four lever-boxes and cumulative recorders. I supplied an attachment which would record, not only the mean performance of all twenty-four rats in a single averaged curve, but mean curves for four subgroups of twelve rats each and four subgroups of six rats each.[2] We thus provided for the design of experiments according to the principles of R. A. Fisher, which were then coming into vogue. We had, so to speak, mechanized the Latin square.

With this apparatus Heron and I published a study of extinction in maze-bright and maze-dull rats using *ninety-five* subjects. Later I published mean extinction curves for groups of twenty-four, and W. K. Estes and I did our work on anxiety with groups of the same size. But although Heron and I could properly voice the hope that "the possibility of using large groups of animals greatly improves upon the method as previously reported, since tests of significance are provided for and properties of behavior not apparent in single cases may be more easily detected," in actual practice that is not what happened. The experiments I have just mentioned are almost all we have to show for this elaborate battery of boxes. Undoubtedly more work could

---

[2]Heron, W. T., & Skinner, B. F. An apparatus for the study of behavior. *Psychol. Rec.*, 1939, **3**, 166–176.

be done with it and would have its place, but something had happened to the natural growth of the method. You cannot easily make a change in the conditions of an experiment when twenty-four apparatuses have to be altered. Any gain in rigor is more than matched by a loss in flexibility. We were forced to confine ourselves to processes which could be studied with the baselines already developed in earlier work. We could not move on to the discovery of other processes or even to a more refined analysis of those we were working with. No matter how significant might be the relations we actually demonstrated, our statistical Leviathan had swum aground. The art of the method had stuck at a particular stage of its development.

Another accident rescued me from mechanized statistics and brought me back to an even more intensive concentration on the single case. In essence, I suddenly found myself face to face with the engineering problem of the animal trainer. When you have the responsibility of making absolutely sure that a given organism will engage in a given sort of behavior at a given time, you quickly grow impatient with theories of learning. Principles, hypotheses, theorems, satisfactory proof at the 0.05 level of significance that behavior at a choice point shows the effect of secondary reinforcement—nothing could be more irrelevant. No one goes to the circus to see the average dog jump through a hoop significantly oftener than untrained dogs raised under the same circumstances, or to see an elephant demonstrate a principle of behavior.

Perhaps I can illustrate this without giving aid and comfort to the enemy by describing a Russian device which the Germans found quite formidable. The Russians used dogs to blow up tanks. A dog was trained to hide behind a tree or wall in low brush or other cover. As a tank

approached and passed, the dog ran swiftly alongside it, and a small magnetic mine attached to the dog's back was sufficient to cripple the tank or set it afire. The dog, of course, had to be replaced.

Now I ask you to consider some of the technical problems which the psychologist faces in preparing a dog for such an act of unintentional heroism. The dog must wait behind the tree for an indefinite length of time. Very well, it must therefore be intermittently reinforced for waiting. But what schedule will achieve the highest probability of waiting? If the reinforcement is to be food, what is the absolutely optimal schedule of deprivation consistent with the health of the dog? The dog must run to the tank—that can be arranged by reinforcing it with a practice tank—but it must start instantly if it is to overtake a swift tank, and how do you differentially reinforce short reaction times, especially in counteracting the reinforcement for sitting and waiting? The dog must react only to tanks, not to a refugee driving his oxcart along the road, but what are the defining properties of a tank so far as a dog is concerned?

I think it can be said that a functional analysis proved adequate in its technological application. Manipulation of environmental conditions alone made possible a wholly unexpected practical control. Behavior could be shaped up according to specifications and maintained indefinitely almost at will. One behavioral technologist who worked with me at the time (Keller Breland) is now specializing in the production of behavior as a salable commodity and has described this new profession in the *American Psychologist*.[3]

There are many useful applications within psychology itself. Ratliff and

---

[3]Breland, K., & Breland, Marion. A field of applied animal psychology. *Amer. Psychologist*, 1951, **6**, 202–204.

Blough have recently conditioned pigeons to serve as psychophysical observers. In their experiment a pigeon may adjust one of two spots of light until the two are equally bright or it may hold a spot of light at the absolute threshold during dark adaptation. The techniques which they have developed to induce pigeons to do this are only indirectly related to the point of their experiments and hence exemplify the application of a behavioral science.[4] The field in which a better technology of behavior is perhaps most urgently needed is education. I cannot describe here the applications which are now possible, but perhaps I can indicate my enthusiasm by hazarding the guess that educational techniques at all age levels are on the threshold of revolutionary changes.

The effect of a behaviorial technology on scientific practice is the issue here. Faced with practical problems in behavior, you necessarily emphasize the refinement of *experimental* variables. As a result, some of the standard procedures of statistics appear to be circumvented. Let me illustrate. Suppose that measurements have been made on two groups of subjects differing in some detail of experimental treatment. Means and standard deviations for the two groups are determined, and any difference due to the treatment is evaluated. If the difference is in the expected direction but is not statistically significant, the almost universal recommendation would be to study larger groups. But our experience with practical control suggests that we may reduce the troublesome variability by changing the conditions of the experiment. By discovering, elaborating, and fully exploiting every relevant variable,

we may eliminate *in advance of measurement* the individual differences which obscure the difference under analysis. This will achieve the same result as increasing the size of groups, and it will almost certainly yield a bonus in the discovery of new variables which would not have been identified in the statistical treatment.

The same may be said of smooth curves. In our study of anxiety, Estes and I published several curves, the reasonable smoothness of which was obtained by averaging the performances of twelve rats for each curve. The individual curves published at that time show that the mean curves do not faithfully represent the behavior of any one rat. They show a certain tendency toward a change in slope which supported the point we were making, and they may have appeared to warrant averaging for that reason.

But an alternative method would have been to explore the individual case until an equally smooth curve could be obtained. This would have meant not only rejecting the temptation to produce smoothness by averaging cases, but manipulating all relevant conditions as we later learned to manipulate them for practical purposes. The individual curves which we published at that time point to the need not for larger groups but for improvement in experimental technique. Here, for example, is a curve the smoothness of which is characteristic of current practice. Such curves were shown in the making in a demonstration which Ferster and I arranged at the Cleveland meeting of the American Psychological Association (Figure 13). Here, in a single organism, three different schedules of reinforcement are yielding corresponding performances with great uniformity under appropriate stimuli alternating at random. One does not reach this kind of order through the application of statistical methods.

---

[4]Ratliff, F., & Blough, D. S. Behavioral studies of visual processes in the pigeon. Report of Contract N50ri-07663, Psychological Laboratories, Harvard University, September, 1954.

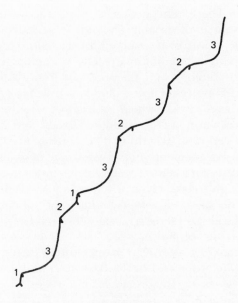

Figure 13.

An early application of the method to the behavior of avoidance and escape was made by Keller in studying the light aversion of the rat. This was brilliantly extended by Murray Sidman in his shock-avoidance experiments. It is no longer necessary to describe avoidance and escape by appeal to "principles," for we may *watch* the behavior develop when we have arranged the proper contingencies of reinforcement, as we later watch it change as these contingencies are changed.

Hunt and Brady have extended the use of a stable rate in the study of anxiety-producing stimuli and have shown that the depression in rate is eliminated by electroconvulsive shock and by other measures which are effective in reducing anxiety in human patients. O. R. Lindsley has found the same thing for dogs, using insulin-shock therapy and sedatives. Brady has refined the method by exploring the relevance of various schedules of reinforcement in tracing the return of the conditioned depression after treatment. In these experiments you *see* the effect of a treatment as directly as you see the constriction of a capillary under the microscope.

Early work with rats on caffeine and Benzedrine has been extended by Lindsley with dogs. A special technique for evaluating several effects of a drug in a single short experimental period yields a record of behavior which can be read as a specialist reads an electrocardiogram. Dr. Peter Dews of the Department of Pharmacology at the Harvard Medical School is investigating dose-response curves and the types and effects of various drugs, using pigeons as subjects. In the Psychological Laboratories at Harvard additional work on drugs is being carried out by Morse, Herrnstein, and Marshall, and the technique is being adopted by drug manufacturers. There could scarcely be a better demonstration of the

In *The Behavior of Organisms* I was content to deal with the over-all slopes and curvature of cumulative curves and could make only a rough classification of the properties of behavior shown by the finer grain. The grain has now been improved. The resolving power of the microscope has been greatly increased, and we can see fundamental processes of behavior in sharper and sharper detail. In choosing rate of responding as a basic datum and in recording this conveniently in a cumulative curve, we make important temporal aspects of behavior *visible*. Once this has happened, our scientific practice is reduced to simple looking. A new world is opened to inspection. We use such curves as we use a microscope, X-ray camera, or telescope. This is well exemplified by recent extensions of the method. These are no longer part of my case history, but perhaps you will permit me to consult you about what some critics have described as a *folie à deux* or group neurosis.

experimental treatment of variability. In a *single* experimental session with a *single* organism one observes the onset, duration, and decline of the effects of a drug.

The direct observation of *defective* behavior is particularly important. Clinical or experimental damage to an organism is characteristically unique. Hence the value of a method which permits the direct observation of the behavior of the individual. Lindsley has studied the effects of near-lethal irradiation, and the effects of prolonged anesthesia and anoxia are currently being examined by Thomas Lohr in co-operation with Dr. Henry Beecher of the Massachusetts General Hospital. The technique is being applied to neurological variables in the monkey by Dr. Karl Pribram at the Hartford Institute. The pattern of such research is simple: establish the behavior in which you are interested, submit the organism to a particular treatment, and then look again at the behavior. An excellent example of the use of experimental control in the study of *motivation* is some work on obesity by J. E. Anliker in collaboration with Dr. Jean Mayer of the Harvard School of Public Health, where abnormalities of ingestive behavior in several types of obese mice can be compared by direct inspection.

There is perhaps no field in which behavior is customarily described more indirectly than psychiatry. In an experiment at the Massachusetts State Hospital, O. R. Lindsley is carrying out an extensive program which might be characterized as a quantitative study of the temporal properties of psychotic behavior.[5] Here again it is a question of making certain characteristics of the behavior visible.

The extent to which we can eliminate sources of variability before measurement is shown by a result which has an unexpected significance for comparative psychology and the study of individual differences. Figure 14 shows tracings of three curves which report behavior in response to a multiple fixed-interval fixed-ratio schedule. The hatches mark reinforcements. Separating them in some cases are short, steep lines showing a high constant rate on a fixed-ratio schedule and, in others, somewhat longer "scallops" showing a smooth acceleration as the organism shifts from a very low rate just after reinforcement to a higher rate at the end of the fixed interval. The values of the intervals and ratios, the states of deprivation, and the exposures to the schedules were different in the three cases, but except for these details the curves are quite similar. Now, one of them was made by a *pigeon* in some experiments by Ferster and me, one was made by a *rat* in an experiment on anoxia by Lohr, and the third was made by a *monkey* in Karl Pribram's laboratory at the Hartford Institute. Pigeon, rat, monkey, which is which? It doesn't matter. Of course, these three species

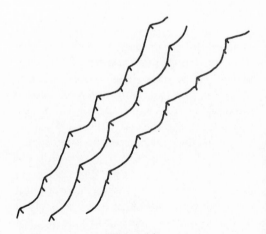

Figure 14.

[5]Lindsley, O. R. "Operant conditioning methods applied to research in chronic schizophrenia," *Psychiat. Res. Rep.*, 1956, **5**, 118–139.

have behavioral repertoires which are as different as their anatomies. But once you have allowed for differences in the ways in which they make contact with the environment, and in the ways in which they act upon the environment, what remains of their behavior shows astonishingly similar properties. Mice, cats, dogs, and human children could have added other curves to this figure. And when organisms which differ as widely as this nevertheless show similar properties of behavior, differences between members of the same species may be viewed more hopefully. Difficult problems of idiosyncrasy or individuality will always arise as products of biological and cultural processes, but it is the very business of the experimental analysis of behavior to devise techniques which reduce their effects except when they are explicitly under investigation.

We are within reach of a science of the individual. This will be achieved, not by resorting to some special theory of knowledge in which intuition or understanding takes the place of observation and analysis, but through an increasing grasp of relevant conditions to produce order in the individual case.

A second consequence of an improved technology is the effect upon behavior theory. As I have pointed out elsewhere, it is the function of learning theory to create an imaginary world of law and order and thus to console us for the disorder we observe in behavior itself. Scores on a T maze or jumping stand hop about from trial to trial almost capriciously. Therefore we argue that if learning is, as we hope, a continuous and orderly process, it must be occurring in some other system of dimensions— perhaps in the nervous system, or in the mind, or in a conceptual model of behavior. Both the statistical treatment of group means and the averaging of curves encourage the belief that we are

somehow going behind the individual case to an otherwise inaccessible, but more fundamental, process. The whole tenor of our paper on anxiety, for example, was to imply that the change we observed was not necessarily a property of behavior, but of some theoretical state of the organism ("anxiety") which was merely *reflected* in a slight modification of performance.

When we have achieved a practical control over the organism, theories of behavior lose their point. In representing and managing relevant variables, a conceptual model is useless; we come to grips with behavior itself. When behavior shows order and consistency, we are much less likely to be concerned with physiological or mentalistic causes. A datum emerges which takes the place of theoretical fantasy. In the experimental analysis of behavior we address ourselves to a subject matter which is not only manifestly the behavior of an individual and hence accessible without the usual statistical aids but also "objective" and "actual" without recourse to deductive theorizing.

Statistical techniques serve a useful function, but they have acquired a purely honorific status which may be troublesome. There presence or absence has become a shibboleth to be used in distinguishing between good and bad work. Because measure of behavior have been highly variable, we have come to trust only results obtained from large numbers of subjects. Because some workers have intentionally or unconsciously reported only selected favorable instances, we have come to put a high value on research which is planned in advance and reported in its entirety. Because measures have behaved capriciously, we have come to value skillful deductive theories which restore order. But although large groups, planned experiments, and valid theorizing are associated with significant scientific results, it does not follow that nothing can be achieved in their absence. Here are two brief examples of the choice before us.

How can we determine the course of dark adaptation in a pigeon? We move a pigeon from a bright light to a dark room. What happens? Presumably the bird is able to see fainter and fainter patches of light as the process of adaptation takes place, but how can we follow this process? One way would be to set up a discrimination apparatus in which choices would be made at specific intervals after the beginning of dark adaptation. The test patches of light could be varied over a wide range, and the percentages of correct choices at each value would enable us eventually to locate the threshold fairly accurately. But hundreds of observations would be needed to establish only a few points on the curve and to prove that these show an actual change in sensitivity. In the experiment by Blough already mentioned, the pigeon holds a spot of light close to the threshold throughout the experimental period. A single curve, such as the one sketched in Figure 15, yields as much information as hundreds

of readings, together with the means and standard deviations derived from them. The information is more accurate because it applies to a single organism in a single experimental session. Yet many psychologists who would accept the first as a finished experiment because of the tables of means and standard deviations would boggle at the second or call it a preliminary study. The direct evidence of one's senses in observing a process of behavior is not trusted.

As another example, consider the behavior of several types of obese mice. Do they all suffer from a single abnormality in their eating behavior or are there differences? One might attempt to answer this with some such measure of hunger as an obstruction apparatus. The numbers of crossings of a grid to get to food, counted after different periods of free access to food, would be the data. Large numbers of readings would be needed, and the resulting mean values would possibly not describe the behavior of any one mouse in any experimental period. A much better picture may be obtained with one mouse of each kind in

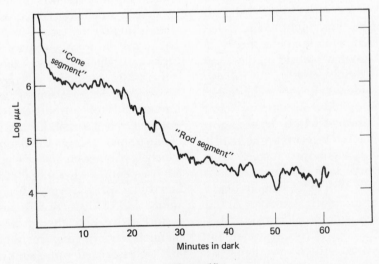

Figure 15.

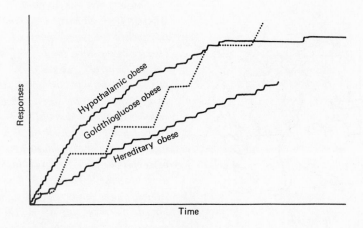

Figure 16.

single experimental sessions, as Anliker has shown.[6] In an experiment reported roughly in Figure 16, each mouse was reinforced with a small piece of food after completing a short "ratio" of responses. The hypothalamic-obese mouse shows an exaggerated but otherwise normal ingestion curve. The hereditary-obese mouse eats slowly but for an indefinite length of time and with little change in rate. The gold poisoned obese mouse shows a sharp oscillation between periods of very rapid responding and no responding at all. These three individual curves contain more information than could probably ever be generated with measures requiring statistical treatment, yet they will be viewed with suspicion by many psychologists because they are single cases.

It is perhaps natural that psychologists should awaken only slowly to the possibility that behavioral processes may be directly observed, or that they should only gradually put the older statistical

and theoretical techniques in their proper perspective. But it is time to insist that science does not progress by carefully designed steps called "experiments" each of which has a well-defined beginning and end. Science is a continuous and often a disorderly and accidental process. We shall not do the young psychologist any favor if we agree to reconstruct our practices to fit the pattern demanded by current scientific methodology. What the statistician means by the design of experiments is design which yields the kind of data to which *his* techniques are applicable. He does not mean the behavior of the scientist in his laboratory devising research for his own immediate and possibly inscrutable purposes.

The organism whose behavior is most extensively modified and most completely controlled in research of the sort I have described is the experimenter himself. The point was well made by a cartoonist in the Columbia *Jester* (Figure 17). The caption read: "Boy, have I got this guy conditioned! Every time I press the bar down he drops in a piece of food." The subjects we study reinforce us much more effectively than we reinforce them. I have been telling you simply how I have been

[6]Anliker, J., and Mayer, J. Operant conditioning technique for studying feeding patterns in normal and obese mice. *J. Appl. Psychol.*, 1956, **8**, 667–670.

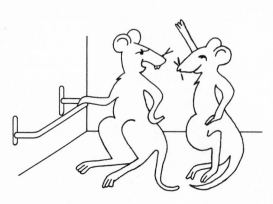

Figure 17.

I have only one important characteristic, Burris: I'm stubborn. I've had only one idea in my life—a true idée fixe . . . to put it as bluntly as possible, the idea of having my own way. "Control" expresses it, I think. The control of human behavior, Burris. In my early experimental days it was a frenzied, selfish desire to dominate. I remember the rage I used to feel when a prediction went awry. I could have shouted at the subjects of my experiments, "Behave, damn you, behave as you ought!" Eventually I realized that the subjects were always right. They always behaved as they ought. It was I who was wrong. I had made a bad prediction."

conditioned to behave. And of course it is a mistake to argue too much from one case history. My behavior would not have been shaped as it was were it not for personal characteristics which all psychologists fortunately do not share. Freud has had something to say about the motivation of scientists and has given us some insight into the type of person who achieves the fullest satisfaction from precise experimental design and the intricacies of deductive systems. Such a person tends to be more concerned with his success as a scientist than with his subject matter, as is shown by the fact that he often assumes the role of a roving ambassador. If this seems unfair, let me hasten to characterize my own motivation in equally unflattering terms. Several years ago I spent a pleasant summer writing a novel called *Walden Two*. One of the characters, Frazier, said many things which I was not yet ready to say myself. Among them was this:

(In fairness to Frazier and the rest of myself, I want to add his next remark: "And what a strange discovery for a would-be tyrant, that the only effective technique of control is unselfish." Frazier means, of course, positive reinforcement.)

We have no more reason to say that all psychologists should behave as I have behaved than that they should all behave like R. A. Fisher. The scientist, like any organism, is the product of a unique history. The practices which he finds most appropriate will depend in part upon this history. Fortunately, personal idiosyncrasies usually leave a negligible mark on science as public property. They are important only when we are concerned with the encouragement of scientists and the prosecution of research. When we have at last an adequate empirical account of the behavior of Man Thinking, we shall understand all this. Until then, it may be best not to try to fit all scientists into any single mold.

2. *Pigeons in a Pelican*

B. F. SKINNER

This is the history of a crackpot idea, born on the wrong side of the tracks intellectually speaking, but eventually vindicated in a sort of middle-class respectability. It is the story of a proposal to use living organisms to guide missiles — of a research program during World War II called "Project Pigeon" and a peacetime continuation at the Naval Research Laboratory called "ORCON," from the words "organic control." Both of these programs have now been declassified.

Man has always made use of the sensory capacities of animals, either because they are more acute than his own or more convenient. The watchdog probably hears better than his master and, in any case, listens while his master sleeps. As a detecting system the dog's ear comes supplied with an alarm (the dog need not be taught to announce the presence of an intruder), but special forms of reporting are sometimes set up. The tracking behavior of the bloodhound and the pointing of the hunting dog are usually modified to make them more useful. Training is sometimes quite explicit. It is said that sea gulls were used to detect submarines in the English Channel during World War I. The British sent their own submarines through the Channel releasing food to the surface. Gulls could see the submarines from the air and learned to follow them, whether they were British or German. A flock of gulls, spotted from the shore, took on special significance. In the seeing-eye dog the repertoire of artificial signaling responses is so elaborate that it has the conventional character of the verbal interchange between man and man.

The detecting and signaling systems of lower organisms have a special advantage when used with explosive devices which can be guided toward the objects they are to destroy, whether by land, sea, or air. Homing systems for guided missiles have now been developed which sense and signal the position of a target by responding to visible or invisible radiation, noise, radar reflections, and so on. These have not always been available, and in any case a living organism has certain advantages. It is almost certainly cheaper and more compact and, in particular, is especially good at responding to patterns and those classes of patterns called "concepts." The lower organism is not used because it is more

SOURCE. *Article by B. F. Skinner "Pigeons in a pelican," in the* American Psychologist, *Vol. 15, pp. 28–37, 1960. Copyright by the American Psychological Association and reprinted by permission.*

sensitive than man—after all, the kamikaze did very well—but because it is readily expendable.

Project Pelican

The ethical question of our right to convert a lower creature into an unwitting hero is a peacetime luxury. There were bigger questions to be answered in the late thirties. A group of men had come into power who promised, and eventually accomplished, the greatest mass murder in history. In 1939 the city of Warsaw was laid waste in an unprovoked bombing, and the airplane emerged as a new and horrible instrument of war against which only the feeblest defenses were available. Project Pigeon was conceived against that background. It began as a search for a homing device to be used in surface-to-air guided missile as a defense against aircraft. As the balance between offensive and defensive weapons shifted, the direction was reversed, and the system was to be tested first in an air-to-ground missile called the "Pelican." Its name is a useful reminder of the state of the missile art in America at that time. Its detecting and servomechanisms took up so much space that there was no room for explosives: hence the resemblance to the pelican "whose beak can hold more than its belly can." My title is perhaps now clear. Figure 1 shows the pigeons, jacketed for duty. Figure 2 shows the beak of the Pelican.

At the University of Minnesota in the spring of 1940 the capacity of the pigeon to steer toward a target was tested with a moving hoist. The pigeon, held in a jacket and harnessed to a block, was immobilized except for its neck and head. It could eat grain from a dish and operate a control system by moving its head in appropriate directions. Movement of the head operated the motors of the hoist. The bird could ascend by lifting its head, descend by lowering it, and travel from side to side by moving appropriately.

Figure 1. Thirty-two pigeons, jacketed for testing.

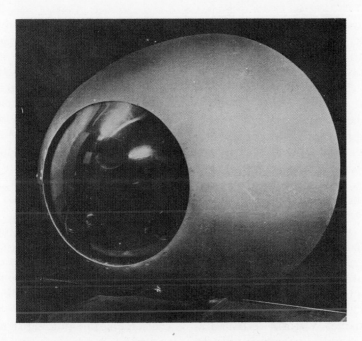

Figure 2. *Nose of the Pelican, showing lenses.*

The whole system, mounted on wheels, was pushed across a room toward a bull's-eye on the far wall. During the approach the pigeon raised or lowered itself and moved from side to side in such a way as to reach the wall in position to eat grain from the center of the bull's-eye. The pigeon learned to reach any target within reach of the hoist, no matter what the starting position and during fairly rapid approaches.

The experiment was shown to John T. Tate, a physicist, then Dean of the Graduate School at the University of Minnesota, who brought it to the attention of R. C. Tolman, one of a group of scientists engaged in early defense activities. The result was the first of a long series of rejections. The proposal "did not warrant further development at the time." The project was accordingly allowed to lapse. On December 7, 1941, the situation was suddenly restructured; and, on the following day, with the help of Keller Breland, then a graduate student at Minnesota, further work was planned. A simpler harnessing system could be used if the bomb were to rotate slowly during its descent, when the pigeon would need to steer in only one dimension: from side to side. We built an apparatus in which a harnessed pigeon was lowered toward a large revolving turntable across which a target was driven according to contacts made by the bird during its descent. It was not difficult to train a pigeon to "hit" small ship models during fairly rapid descents. We made a demonstration film showing hits on various kinds of targets, and two psychologists then engaged in the war effort in Washington, Charles Bray and Leonard Carmichael, undertook to look for government support. Tolman, then at the Office of Scientific Research and Development, again felt that the project did not warrant support, in part because the United States had at that time no missile capable of being guided toward a target. Commander (now Admiral) Luis de Florez, then in the Special Devices Section of the Navy, took a sympathetic view. He dismissed the objection that there was no available vehicle by suggesting that the pigeon be connected with an automatic pilot mounted in a small plane loaded with explosives. But he was unable to take on the project because of other commitments and because, as he explained, he had recently bet on one or two other equally long shots which had not come in.

The project lapsed again and would probably have been abandoned if it had not been for a young man whose last name I have ungratefully forgotten, but whose first name—Victor—we hailed as a propitious sign. His subsequent history led us to refer to him as Vanquished; and this, as it turned out, was a more reliable omen. Victor walked into the Department of Psychology at Minnesota one day in the summer of 1942 looking for an animal psychologist. He had a scheme for installing dogs in antisubmarine torpedoes. The dogs were to respond to faint acoustic signals from the submarine and to steer the torpedo toward its goal. He wanted a statement from an animal psychologist as to its feasibility. He was understandably surprised to learn of our work with pigeons but seized upon it eagerly; citing it in support of his contention that dogs could be trained to steer torpedoes, he went to a number of companies in Minneapolis. His project was rejected by everyone he approached; but one company, General Mills, Inc., asked for more information about our work with pigeons. We described the project and presented the available data to Arthur D. Hyde, Vice-President in Charge of Research. The company was not looking for new products, but Hyde though that it might, as a public service, develop the pigeon system to the point at which a governmental agency could be persuaded to take over.

Breland and I moved into the top floor of a flour mill in Minneapolis and with the help of Norman Guttman, who had joined the project, set to work on further improvements. It had been difficult to induce the pigeon to respond to the small angular displacement of a distant target. It would start working dangerously late in the descent. Its natural pursuit behavior was not appropriate to the characteristics of a likely missile. A new system was therefore designed. An image of the target was projected on a translucent screen as in a camera obscura. The pigeon, held near the screen, was reinforced for pecking at the image on the screen. The guiding signal was to be picked up from the point of contact of screen and beak.

In an early arrangement the screen was a translucent plastic plate forming the larger end of a truncated cone bearing a lens at the smaller end. The cone was mounted, lens down, in a gimbal bearing. An object within range threw its image on the translucent screen; and the pigeon, held vertically just above the plate, pecked the image. When a target was moved about within range of the lens, the cone continued to point to it. In another apparatus a translucent disk, free to tilt slightly on gimbal bearings, closed contacts operating motors which altered the position of a large field beneath the apparatus. Small cutouts of ships and other objects were placed on the field. The field was constantly in motion, and a target would go out of range unless the pigeon continued to control it. With this apparatus we began to study the pigeon's reactions to various patterns and to develop sustained steady rates of responding through the use of appropriate schedules of reinforcement, the reinforcement being a few grains occasionally released onto the plate. By building up large extinction curves a target could be tracked continuously for a matter of minutes without reinforcement. We trained pigeons to follow a variety of land and sea targets, to neglect large patches intended to represent clouds or flak, to concentrate on one target while another was in view, and so on. We found that a pigeon could hold the missile on a particular street intersection in an aerial map of a city. The map which came most easily to hand was of a city which, in the interests of international relations, need not be identified. Through appropriate schedules of reinforcement it was possible to maintain longer uninterrupted runs than could conceivably be required by a missile.

We also undertook a more serious study of the pigeon's behavior, with the help of W. K. Estes and Marion Breland, who joined the project at this time. We ascertained optimal conditions of deprivation, investigated other kinds of deprivations, studied the effect of special reinforcements (for example, pigeons were said to find hemp seed particularly delectable), tested the effects of energizing drugs and increased oxygen pressures, and so on. We differentially reinforced the force of the pecking response and found that pigeons could be induced to peck so energetically that the base of the beak became inflamed. We investigated the effects of extremes of temperature, of changes in atmospheric pressure, of accelerations produced by an improvised centrifuge, of increased carbon dioxide pressure, of increased and prolonged vibration, and of noises such as pistol shots. (The birds could, of course, have been deafened to eliminate auditory distractions, but we found it easy to maintain steady behavior in spite of intense noises and many other distracting conditions using the simple process of adaptation.) We

investigated optimal conditions for the quick development of discriminations and began to study the pigeon's reactions to patterns, testing for induction from a test figure to the same figure inverted, to figures of different sizes and colors, and to figures against different grounds. A simple device using carbon paper to record the points at which a pigeon pecks a figure showed a promise which has never been properly exploited.

We made another demonstration film and renewed our contact with the Office of Scientific Research and Development. An observer was sent to Minneapolis, and on the strength of his report we were given an opportunity to present our case in Washington in February, 1943. At that time we were offering a homing device capable of reporting with an on-off signal the orientation of a missile toward various visual patterns. The capacity to respond to pattern was, we felt, our strongest argument, but the fact that the device used only visible radiation (the same form of information available to the human bombardier) made it superior to the radio-controlled missiles then under development because it was resistant to jamming. Our film had some effect. Other observers were sent to Minneapolis to see the demonstration itself. The pigeons, as usual, behaved beautifully. One of them held the supposed missile on a particular intersection of streets in the aerial map for five minutes although the target would have been lost if the pigeon had paused for a second or two. The observers returned to Washington, and two weeks later we were asked to supply data on (*a*) the population of pigeons in the United States (fortunately, the census bureau had some figures) and (*b*) the accuracy with which pigeons struck a point on a plate. There were many arbitrary conditions to be taken into account in measuring the latter, but we supplied possibly relevant data. At long last, in June, 1943, the Office of Scientific Research and Development awarded a modest contract to General Mills, Inc. to "develop a homing device."

At that time we were given some information about the missile the pigeons were to steer. The Pelican was a wing-steered glider, still under development and not yet successfully steered by any homing device. It was being tested on a target in New Jersey consisting of a stirrup-shaped pattern bulldozed out of the sandy soil near the coast. The white lines of the target stood out clearly against brown and green cover. Colored photographs were taken from various distances and at various angles, and the verisimilitude of the reproduction was checked by flying over the target and looking at its image in a portable camera obscura.

Because of security restrictions we were given only very rough specifications of the signal to be supplied to the controlling system in the Pelican. It was no longer to be simply on-off; if the missile was badly off target, an especially strong correcting signal was needed. This meant that the quadrant-contact system would no longer suffice. But further requirements were left mainly to our imagination. The General Mills engineers were equal to this difficult assignment. With what now seems like unbelievable speed, they designed and constructed a pneumatic pickup system giving a graded signal. A lens in the nose of the missile threw an image on a translucent plate within reach of the pigeon in a pressure-sealed chamber. Four air valves resting against the edges of the plate were jarred open momentarily as the pigeon pecked. The valves at the right and left admitted air to chambers on opposite sides of one tambour, while the valves at the top and bottom admitted air to opposite sides of another. Air on all sides was exhausted by a Ven-

turi cone on the side of the missile. When the missile was on target, the pigeon pecked the center of the plate, all valves admitted equal amounts of air, and the tambours remained in neutral positions. But if the image moved as little as a quarter of an inch off-center, corresponding to a very small angular displacement of the target, more air was admitted by the valves on one side, and the resulting displacement of the tambours sent appropriate correcting orders directly to the servosystem.

The device required no materials in short supply, was relatively foolproof, and delivered a graded signal. It had another advantage. By this time we had begun to realize that a pigeon was more easily controlled than a physical scientist serving on a committee. It was very difficult to convince the latter that the former was an orderly system. We therefore multiplied the probability of success by designing a multiple-bird unit. There was adequate space in the nose of the Pelican for three pigeons, each with its own lens and plate. A net signal could easily be generated. The majority vote of three pigeons offered an excellent guarantee against momentary pauses and aberrations. (We later worked out a system in which the majority took on a more characteristically democratic function. When a missile is falling toward *two* ships at sea, for example, there is no guarantee that all three pigeons will steer toward the same ship. But at least two must agree, and the third can then be punished for his minority opinion. Under proper contingencies of reinforcement a punished bird will shift immediately to the majority view. When all three are working on one ship, any defection is immediately punished and corrected.)

The arrangement in the nose of the Pelican is shown in Figure 3. Three systems of lenses and mirrors, shown at the left, throw images of the target area on

Figure 3. *Demonstration model of the three-pigeon guidance system.*

the three translucent plates shown in the center. The ballistic valves resting against the edges of these plates and the tubes connecting them with the manifolds leading to the controlling tambours may be seen. A pigeon is being placed in the pressurized chamber at the right.

The General Mills engineers also built a simulator (Figure 4)—a sort of Link trainer for pigeons—designed to have the steering characteristics of the Pelican, in so far as these had been communicated to us. Like the wingsteered Pelican, the simulator tilted and turned from side to side. When the three-bird nose was attached to it, the pigeons could be put in full control—the "loop could be closed" —and the adequacy of the signal tested under pursuit conditions. Targets were moved back and forth across the far wall of a room at prescribed speeds and

in given patterns of oscillation, and the tracking response of the whole unit was studied quantitatively.

Meanwhile we continued our intensive study of the behavior of the pigeon. Looking ahead to combat use we designed methods for the mass production of trained birds and for handling large groups of trained subjects. We were proposing to train certain birds for certain *classes* of targets, such as ships at sea, while special squads were to be trained on special targets, photographs of which were to be obtained through reconnaissance. A large crew of pigeons would then be waiting for assignment, but we developed harnessing and training techniques which should have solved such problems quite easily.

A multiple-unit trainer is shown in Figure 5. Each box contains a jacketed

Figure 4. *Simulator for testing the adequacy of the pigeon signal.*

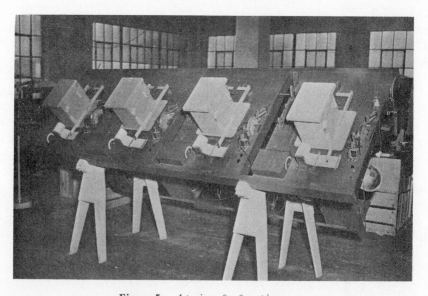

Figure 5. *A trainer for four pigeons.*

pigeon held at an angle of 45° to the horizontal and perpendicular to an 8″ × 8″ translucent screen. A target area is projected on each screen. Two beams of light intersect at the point to be struck. All on-target responses of the pigeon are reported by the interruption of the crossed beams and by contact with the translucent screen. Only a four-inch, disk-shaped portion of the field is visible to the pigeon at any time, but the boxes move slowly about the field, giving the pigeon an opportunity to respond to the target in all positions. The positions of all reinforcements are recorded to reveal any weak areas. A variable-ratio schedule is used to build sustained, rapid responding.

By December, 1943, less than six months after the contract was awarded, we were ready to report to the Office of Scientific Research and Development. Observers visited the laboratory and watched the simulator follow a target about a room under the control of a team of three birds. They also reviewed our tracking data. The only questions which arose were the inevitable consequence of our lack of information about the signal required to steer the Pelican. For example, we had had to make certain arbitrary decisions in compromising between sensitivity of signal and its integration or smoothness. A high vacuum produced quick, rather erratic movements of the tambours, while a lower vacuum gave a sluggish but smooth signal. As it turned out, we had not chosen the best values in collecting our data, and in January, 1944, the Office of Scientific Research and Development refused to extend the General Mills contract. The reasons given seemed to be due to misunderstandings or, rather, to lack of communication. We had already collected further data with new settings of the instruments, and these were submitted in a request for reconsideration.

We were given one more chance. We took our new data to the radiation lab at the Massachusetts Institute of Technology where they were examined by the servospecialists working on the Pelican controls. To our surprise the scientist whose task it was to predict the usefulness of the pigeon signal argued that our data were inconsistent with respect to phase lag and certain other characteristics of the signal. According to his equations, our device could not possibly yield the signals we reported. We knew, of course, that it had done so. We examined the supposed inconsistency and traced it, or so we thought, to a certain nonlinearity in our system. In pecking an image near the edge of the plate, the pigeon strikes a more glancing blow; hence the air admitted at the valves is not linearly proportional to the displacement of the target. This could be corrected in several ways: for example, by using a lens to distort radial distances. It was our understanding that in any case the signal was adequate to control the Pelican. Indeed, one servo authority, upon looking at graphs of the performance of the simulator, exclaimed: "This is better than radar!"

Two days later, encouraged by our meeting at MIT, we reached the summit. We were to present our case briefly to a committee of the country's top scientists. The hearing began with a brief report by the scientist who had discovered the "inconsistency" in our data, and to our surprise he still regarded it as unresolved. He predicted that the signal we reported would cause the missile to "hunt" wildly and lose the target. But his prediction should have applied as well to the closed loop simulator. Fortunately another scientist was present who had seen the simulator performing under excellent control and who could confirm our report of the facts. But reality was no match for mathematics.

The basic difficulty, of course, lay in

convincing a dozen distinguished physical scientists that the behavior of a pigeon could be adequately controlled. We had hoped to score on this point by bringing with us a demonstration. A small black box had a round translucent window in one end. A slide projector placed some distance away threw on the window an image of the New Jersey target. In the box, of course, was a pigeon — which, incidentally, had at that time been harnessed for 35 hours. Our intention was to let each member of the committee observe the response to the target by looking down a small tube; but time was not available for individual observation, and we were asked to take the top off the box. The translucent screen was flooded with so much light that the target was barely visible, and the peering scientists offered conditions much more unfamiliar and threatening than those likely to be encountered in a missile. In spite of this the pigeon behaved perfectly, pecking steadily and energetically at the image of the target as it moved about on the plate. One scientist with an experimental turn of mind intercepted the beam from the projector. The pigeon stopped instantly. When the image again appeared, pecking began within a fraction of a second and continued at a steady rate.

It was a perfect performance, but it had just the wrong effect. One can talk about phase lag in pursuit behavior and discuss mathematical predictions of hunting without reflecting too closely upon what is inside the black box. But the spectacle of a living pigeon carrying out its assignment, no matter how beautifully, simply reminded the committee of how utterly fantastic our proposal was. I will not say that the meeting was marked by unrestrained merriment, for the merriment was restrained. But it was there, and it was obvious that our case was lost.

Hyde closed our presentation with a brief summary: we were offering a hom-

ing device, unusually resistant to jamming capable of reacting to a wide variety of target patterns, requiring no materials in short supply, and so simple to build that production could be started in 30 days. He thanked the committee, and we left. As the door closed behind us, he said to me: "Why don't you go out and get drunk!"

Official word soon came: "Further prosecution of this project would seriously delay others which in the minds of the Division would have more immediate promise of combat application." Possibly the reference was to a particular combat application at Hiroshima a year and a half later, when it looked for a while as if the need for accurate bombing had been eliminated for all time. In any case we had to show, for all our trouble, only a loftful of curiously useless equipment and a few dozen pigeons with a strange interest in a feature of the New Jersey coast. The equipment was scrapped, but 30 of the pigeons were kept to see how long they would retain the appropriate behavior.

In the years which followed there were faint signs of life. Winston Churchill's personal scientific advisor, Lord Cherwell, learned of the project and "regretted its demise." A scientist who had had some contact with the project during the war, and who evidently assumed that its classified status was not to be taken seriously, made a good story out of it for the *Atlantic Monthly*, names being changed to protect the innocent. Other uses of animals began to be described. The author of the *Atlantic Monthly* story also published an account of the "incendiary bats." Thousands of bats were to be released over an enemy city, each carrying a small incendiary time bomb. The bats would take refuge, as is their custom, under eaves and in other out-of-the-way places; and shortly afterwards thousands of small fires would break out practically simultaneously. The scheme was never used because it was feared that it would be mistaken for germ warfare and might lead to retaliation in kind.

Another story circulating at the time told how the Russians trained dogs to blow up tanks. I have described the technique elsewhere. A Swedish proposal to use seals to achieve the same end with submarines was not successful. The seals were to be trained to approach submarines to obtain fish attached to the sides. They were then to be released carrying magnetic mines in the vicinity of hostile submarines. The required training was apparently never achieved. I cannot vouch for the authenticity of probably the most fantastic story of this sort, but it ought to be recorded. The Russians were said to have trained sea lions to cut mine cables. A complicated device attached to the sea lion included a motor-driven cable cutter, a tank full of small fish, and a device which released a few fish into a muzzle covering the sea lion's head. In order to eat, the sea lion had to find a mine cable and swim along side it so that the cutter was automatically triggered, at which point a few fish were released from the tank into the muzzle. When a given number of cables had been cut, both the energy of the cutting mechanism and the supply of fish were exhausted, and the sea lion received a special stimulus upon which it returned to its home base for special reinforcement and reloading.

ORCON

The story of our own venture has a happy ending. With the discovery of German accomplishments in the field of guided missiles, feasible homing systems suddenly became very important. Franklin V. Taylor of the Naval Research Laboratory in Washington, D. C., heard about our project and asked for further details. As a psychologist Taylor appreciated the special capacity of living organisms to respond to visual patterns and was aware of recent advances in the control of behavior. More important, he was a skillful practitioner in a kind of control which our project had conspicuously lacked: he knew how to approach the people who determine the direction of research. He showed our demonstration film so often that it was completely worn out—but to good effect, for support was eventually found for a thorough investigation of "organic control" under the general title ORCON. Taylor also enlisted the support of engineers in obtaining a more effective report of the pigeon's behavior. The translucent plate upon which the image of the target was thrown had a semiconducting surface, and the tip of the bird's beak was covered with a gold electrode. A single contact with the plate sent an immediate report of the location of the target to the controlling mechanism. The work which went into this system contributed to the so-called Pick-off Display Converter developed as part of the Naval Data Handling System for human observers. It is no longer necessary for the radar operator to give a verbal report of the location of a pip on the screen. Like the pigeon, he has only to touch the pip with a special contact. (He holds the contact in his hand.)

At the Naval Research Laboratory in Washington the responses of pigeons were studied in detail. Average peck rate, average error rate, average hit rate, and so on, were recorded under various conditions. The tracking behavior of the pigeon was analyzed with methods similar to those employed with human operators (Figure 6). Pattern perception

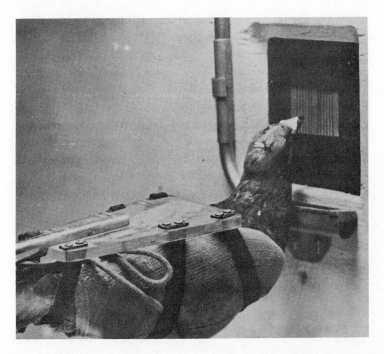

Figure 6. *Arrangement for studying pursuit movements.*

was studied, including generalization from one pattern to another. A simulator was constructed in which the pigeon controlled an image projected by a moving-picture film of an actual target: for example, a ship at sea as seen from a plane approaching at 600 miles per hour. A few frames of a moving picture of the pigeon controlling the orientation toward a ship during an approach are shown in Figure 7.

The publications from the Naval Research Laboratory which report this work[1] provide a serious evaluation of the possibilities of organic control. Although in simulated tests a single pigeon occasionally loses a target, its tracking characteristics are surprisingly good. A three- or seven-bird unit with the same individual consistency should yield a signal with a reliability which is at least of the order of magnitude shown by other phases of guided missiles in their present stage of development. Moreoever, in the seven years which have followed the last of these reports, a great deal of relevant information has been acquired. The color vision of the pigeon is now thoroughly under-

[1]Chernikoff, R., and Newlin, E. P. ORCON. Part III. Investigations of target acquisition by the pigeon. *Naval Res. Lab. Lett. Rep.*, 1951, No. S-3600-629a/51 (Sept. 10). Conklin, J. E., Newlin, E. P., Jr., Taylor, F. V., and Tipton, C. L. ORCON. Part IV. Simulated flight tests. *Naval Res. Lab. lett. Rep.*, 1953, No. 4105. Searle, L. V., and Stafford, B. H. ORCON. Part II. Report of phase I research and bandpass study. *Naval Res. Lab. lett. Rep.*, 1950, No. S-3600-157/50 (May 1). Taylor, F. V. ORCON. Part I. Outline of proposed research. *Naval Res. Lab. lett. Rep.*, 1949, No. S-3600-157/50 (June 17). White, C. F. Development of the NRL ORCON tactile missile simulator. *Naval Res. Lab. Rep.*, 1952, No. 3917.

Figure 7. *Frames from a simulated approach.*

stood; its generalization along single properties of a stimulus has been recorded and analyzed; and the maintenance of behavior through scheduling of reinforcement has been drastically improved, particularly in the development of techniques for pacing responses for less erratic and steadier signals. Tests made with the birds salvaged from the old Project Pigeon showed that even after six years of inactivity a pigeon will immediately and correctly strike a target to which it has been conditioned and will continue to respond for some time without reinforcement.

The use of living organisms in guiding missiles is, it seems fair to say, no longer a crackpot idea. A pigeon is an extraordinarily subtle and complex mechanism capable of performances which at the moment can be equalled by electronic equipment only of vastly greater weight and size, and it can be put to reliable use through the principles which have emerged from an experimental analysis of its behavior. But this vindication of our original proposal is perhaps the least important result. Something happened during the brief life of Project Pigeon which it has taken a long time to appreciate. The practical task before us created a new attitude toward the behavior of organisms. We had to maximize the probability that a given form of behavior would occur at a given time. We could not enjoy the luxury of observing one variable while allowing others to change in what we hoped was a random fashion. We had to discover all relevant variables and submit them to experimental control whenever possible. We were no doubt under exceptional pressure, but vigorous scientific research usually makes comparable demands. Psychologists have too often yielded to the temptation to be content with hypothetical processes and intervening variables rather than press for rigorous experimental control. It is often intellectual laziness rather than necessity which recommends the *a posteriori* statistical treatment of variation. Our task forced us to emphasize prior experimental control, and its success in revealing orderly processes gave us an exciting glimpse of the superiority of laboratory practice over verbal (including some kinds of mathematical) explanation.

The Crackpot Idea

If I were to conclude that crackpot ideas are to be encouraged, I should probably be told that psychology has already had more than its share of them. If it has, they have been entertained by the wrong people. Reacting against the excesses of psychological quackery, psychologists have developed an enormous concern for scientific respectability. They constantly warn their students against questionable facts and unsupported theories. As a result the usual PhD thesis is a model of compulsive cautiousness, advancing only the most timid conclusions thoroughly hedged about with qualifications. But it is just the man capable of displaying such admirable caution who needs a touch of uncontrolled speculation. Possibly a generous exposure to psychological science fiction would help. Project Pigeon might be said to support that view. Except with respect to its avowed goal, it was, as I see it, highly productive; and this was in large measure because my colleagues and I knew that, in the eyes of the world, we were crazy.

One virtue in crackpot ideas is that they breed rapidly and their progeny show extraordinary mutations. Everyone is talking about teaching machines nowadays, but Sidney Pressey can tell you what it was like to have a crackpot idea in that field 40 years ago. His self-testing devices and self-scoring test forms now need no defense, and psychomotor training devices have also achieved a substantial respectability. This did not, however, prepare the way for devices to be used in verbal instruction—that is, in the kinds of teaching which are the principal concern of our schools and colleges. Even five short years ago that kind of instruction by machine was still in the crackpot category. (I can quote official opinion to that effect from high places.) Now, there is a direct genetic connection between teaching machines and Project Pigeon. We had been forced to consider the mass education of pigeons. True, the scrap of wisdom we imparted to each was indeed small, but the required changes in behavior were similar to those which must be brought about in vaster quantities in human students. The techniques of shaping behavior and of bringing it under stimulus control which can be traced, as I have suggested elsewhere to a memorable episode on the top floor of that flour mill in Minneapolis needed only a detailed reformulation of verbal behavior to be directly applicable to education.

I am sure there is more to come. In the year which followed the termination of Project Pigeon I wrote *Walden Two*[2] a utopian picture of a properly engineered society. Some psychotherapists might argue that I was suffering from personal rejection and simply retreated to a fantasied world where everything went according to plan, where there never was heard a discouraging word. But another explanation is, I think, equally plausible. That piece of science fiction was a declaration of confidence in a technology of behavior. Call it a crackpot idea if you

---

[2]Skinner, B. F. *Walden Two*. New York: Macmillan, 1948.

will; it is one in which I have never lost faith. I still believe that the same kind of wide-ranging speculation about human affairs, supported by studies of compensating rigor, will make a substantial contribution toward that world of the future in which, among other things, there will be no need for guided missiles.

3. Reinforcement Control of Generalized Imitation in Young Children

DONAL M. BAER AND JAMES A. SHERMAN

The term "imitation" has seen much use in the literature of child psychology. However, experimental work in this area has often failed to invoke its most powerful meaning. In experimental situations, behavior frequently has been called imitative because it resembled that of a model previously observed by the subject. But there rarely has been any guarantee that the *similarity* of the two behaviors was functional in producing the behavior in the observer. Instead, it has been common to require the observer to learn a reinforced response after having watched a model perform the same response and receive reinforcement for it. The observer often does profit from this observation of a correct performance. However, it is quite possible that he does so because certain stimuli of the situation have been paired with the sight of the reinforcement secured by the model. Since the sight of reinforcement should be a powerful secondary reinforcer, observational learning, not of a similar response, but of the cues which will facilitate that response may very well take place. When the observer is placed in the situation, his learning (of what typically is the only reinforced response in the situation) is speeded by his previously acquired sensitivity to the cues in the situation.

For example, a child may watch a model turn a crank on a green box and receive nothing, then turn a crank on a red box and receive reinforcement consistently and repeatedly. As a result of this observation, the observer subsequently may learn the same discrimination more quickly than a control subject. This may be due simply to the establishment of red as a discriminative cue for reinforcement. The observer is better reinforced for approaching red than green as a consequence of his observation, and thereby is more likely to turn the crank on the red box and be reinforced by it. There is no need in this example to assume that the *similarity* of his crank-turning response and the model's is involved. The similarity may lie in the eye of the experimenter rather than in the eye of the observer, and, in this situation, only a similar response will be

SOURCE. *Article by Donald M. Baer and James E. Sherman* "Reinforcement control of generalized imitation in young children," *in the* Journal of experimental child psychology, *Vol. 1, pp. 37–49, 1964.*

reinforced. Hence the similarity is both forced and (perhaps) irrelevant.

However, there can be a more powerful use of imitation in the experimental analysis of children's learning if it can be shown that similarity per se functions as an important stimulus dimension in the child's behavior. The purpose of the present study is to add another demonstration of this role of similarity to the small body of literature already produced (e.g., Bandura and Huston, 1961) and to show the function of certain social reinforcement operations in promoting responding along the dimension of similarity in behavior. Specifically, a response is considered which is imitative of a model but never directly reinforced. Instead, other responses, also imitative of a model, are controlled by reinforcement operations. The strength of the unreinforced imitative response is then observed as a function of these reinforcement operations. An animated talking puppet, used previously in studies of social interaction with children (Baer. 1962b), serves both as a model to imitate and as a source of social reinforcement.

Method

Apparatus. The apparatus was an animated talking puppet dressed as a cowboy and seated in a chair inside a puppet stage. The puppet was capable of making four kinds of responses: (1) raising and lowering his head, or *nodding*. (2) opening and closing his mouth, or *mouthing*, (3) *bar-pressing* on a puppet-scaled bar-pressing apparatus located beside his chair, almost identical in appearance to a regular-sized bar-pressing apparatus located beside the child; and (4) *talking*, accomplished by playing *E*'s voice through a loudspeaker mounted

behind the puppet's chair, while the puppet's jaw was worked in coordination with the words being spoken. (For a more complete description and a photograph, cf. Baer, 1962b.)

First Sequence of Procedures. *Introduction.* The experiment was conducted in a two-room mobile trailer-laboratory (Bijou, 1958) parked in the lot of a daycare nursery. *E* observed the child and puppet through a one-way mirror from the other room. The child sat in a chair immediately in front of the puppet stage. An adult assistant, *A*, brought the child to the laboratory, introduced him to the puppet, seated him in his chair, and then sat in a screened corner of the room, out of the child's sight. The introduction for the first session was, "This is Jimmy the puppet. He wants to talk to you. And this (pointing) is your bar. See, it's just like Jimmy's bar, only bigger (pointing). Do you know how it works?" The usual answer was "No," in which case *A* demonstrated a bar-press, saying "Now you try it." (Some children pressed the bar without demonstration.) *A* then said, "You can talk to Jimmy now." On all later sessions, *A* said simply, "Hello Jimmy, here's (child's name) to talk to you again," and, to the child, "Now you can talk to Jimmy again."

After *A*'s introduction, the puppet raised his head and began speaking to the child. He followed a fairly standard line of conversation, starting with greetings, and progressing through expressions of pleasure over the chance to talk with the child to alternating questions about what the child had been doing and colorful stories about what the puppet had been doing. This type of conversation was maintained throughout all the sessions; the social reinforcement procedures used as the independent variable in this study were interjected within the conversation according to the experimental design.

Operant Level. The first session was to acquaint child and puppet and to collect an operant level of the child's bar-pressing, imitative or otherwise. Shortly after the puppet began talking to the child, he began to press his bar, alternating between a slow rate of 1 response per 15 seconds and a fast rate of about 3 responses per second. The puppet's bar-pressing was recorded on a cumulative recorder.

The operant level period was interrupted after 5–10 minutes of the puppet's bar-pressing for a special procedure. The special procedure was designed to establish whether the child could generalize from the puppet's bar to his own. After the puppet had stopped bar-pressing, he would nod twice and say, "This is my head. Show me your head." Invariably, the child would move his head or point to it. The puppet then said, "Good," and began mouthing, saying, "This is my mouth. Show me your mouth." The child would move his mouth or point to it. Then the puppet said "Good," and bar-pressing twice, said, "This is my bar. Show me your bar." Some children imitated the response; some pointed to their bar. A few did neither; of these, some appeared puzzled, and others tentatively reached for the puppet's bar. These were the children the procedure was designed to detect. In their cases, the puppet explained that they had a bar of their own and helped them find it, which usually sufficed to produce either a bar-press or a pointing toward the bar. The puppet gave no reinforcement for the bar-pressing response, and instead resumed the conversation about his adventures or the child's. With some subjects there then followed another 5–10 minutes of bar-pressing by the puppet to determine whether this procedure in

itself had promoted imitative bar-pressing by the child. No imitative bar-pressing ever did develop as a result of this procedure alone in the children subjected to it. For the rest of the subjects, this extra portion of the operant level period was dropped.

Still another 5–10 minutes of bar-pressing by the puppet was sometimes displayed. On these occasions, the puppet took up a very approving line of conversation, dispensing a great deal of "Good," "Very good," and "You're really smart" to the child. This was to determine the effect of noncontingent social reinforcement on the child's imitative bar-pressing. However, no child subjected to this procedure ever developed imitative bar-pressing as a result. The other subjects had a similar kind of noncontingent approval incorporated into the earlier portions of their operant level periods.

The typical rate of imitative bar-pressing during operant level periods was zero. In fact, of 11 children seen in this study, only one showed a slight tendency to imitate the puppet's bar-pressing, but this disappeared early in her operant level period. Two others showed a non-imitative bar-pressing rate during the initial session.

Reinforcement of Some Imitative Responses. After collecting the child's operant level of bar-pressing, the puppet stopped bar-pressing and began to present a series of other responses one after another at first, and then at scattered points in his conversation. Each time he would first ask the child, "Can you do this?" These responses consisted of nodding, mouthing, and a variety of nonsense statements (such as "Glub-flub-bug," "One-two-three-four," or "Red robins run rapidly"). In each case, if the child imitated the responses, the puppet reinforced the child's response with approval, consisting mainly of the words "Good," "Very good," and "Fine." Almost without exception, the children did imitate virtually every response the puppet presented in this way, and after a few reinforcements, the puppet stopped asking "Can you do this?" in preface to the response.

After the child was consistently imitating each of these other responses without the prefatory "Can you do this?", the puppet resumed bar-pressing, alternating fast and slow rates. He continued to display nodding, mouthing, and verbal nonsense statements at scattered points in his conversation, and maintained a continuous schedule of reinforcement for every imitation of these by the child. The child's bar-pressing from this point on was the basic dependent variable of the study. An increase over operant level in this never-reinforced[1] bar-pressing by the child, especially insofar as it matched the puppet's bar-pressing, would be significant: It would be attributable to the direct reinforcement of the other responses (nodding, mouthing, and verbal). These responses have very slight topographical resemblance to bar-pressing; they are like it essentially in that they all are imitative of a model's behavior. Thus an increase in imitative bar-pressing by the child would indicate that similarity of responding per se was a functional dimension of the child's behavior, that is, similarity of responding could be strengthened as could responding itself.

This program of reinforcement for all imitative responding (other than bar-pressing) was usually begun during the first session. With some children, it was started early in their second session. Children were seen as many as 7 sessions in the course of the study. These sessions were separated by 3–7 days.

---

[1]On one occasion with one child, a bar-press was accidentally reinforced. This will be noted in the results.

Results

In the design of this study, both individual and group performances are relevant to the central question. If any child showed a significant increase in imitative bar-pressing over his operant level, as a result of direct reinforcement of other imitative responses, this would demonstrate the functional role of similarity in behavior for that child. Hence each child represented an experiment in himself. As a group, the sample allows some estimation of the probability of the effect occurring in children from this population.

Of 11 children studied, 4 failed to show any development of an imitative bar-pressing response during the course of reinforcement of nodding, mouthing, and verbal imitations. Two of these were the only two children showing a high level of non-imitative bar-pressing during their operant level periods. The remaining 7 children showed varying degrees of increase in bar-pressing, as illustrated in Figure 1. This figure shows 4 records, selected to indicate the range of increase in bar-pressing obtained. A fact not always apparent in these records (necessarily compressed for publication) is that virtually every bar-pressing response by the child occurs closely following a response (or response burst) by the puppet, and hence is clearly imitative.

Further Procedure and Results

The increased imitative bar-pressing by some of the children was brought about by reinforcement of other imitative responding by the child (nodding, mouthing, and verbal performances). Further procedures were developed to show the dependence of the generalized imitative bar-pressing on this reinforcement. These procedures were of two kinds: ex-

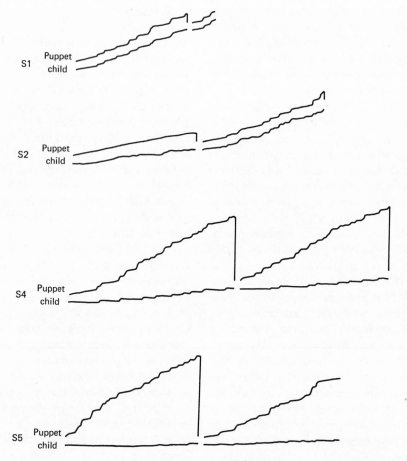

Figure 1. *The development of generalized imitative bar-pressing in four representative SS.*

tinction of the other imitative responding and time-out from the other imitative responding.

Extinction of Imitation

Extinction was instituted with two children, one of whom had developed a near-perfect rate of imitative bar-pressing, the other showing a low rate. After a stable rate of imitative bar-pressing had been established by each child, the puppet stopped giving any reinforcement for imitation of his nodding, mouthing, or verbal nonsense performances (imitation of which in the immediate past he had reinforced continuously). However, he continued performing these actions at the same rate. He also continued to reinforce the child at the same rate, but at appropriate points in the child's conversation rather than for imitation. This continued for several sessions, until the child had shown a stable or marked decrease in imitative bar-pressing. Then reinforcement was shifted back to imitations of nodding, mouthing, or verbal nonsense performances and maintained as before, until the child showed a stable or marked increase in imitative bar-pres-

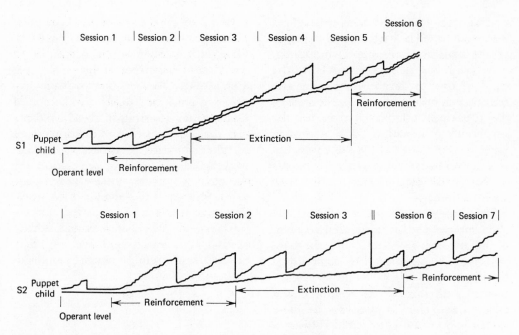

Figure 2.   *The effects of extinction of previously reinforced imitation on generalized imitative bar-pressing in two SS.*

sing. As usual, bar-pressing was never reinforced.

The subjects chosen for this procedure were $S1$ and $S4$ of Figure 1; both were girls. Their records (Figure 2) include the early sessions that show operant level and the development of generalized imitation, already seen in Figure 1, as a baseline against which the effect of extinction of other imitative responding is seen. (Sessions 4 and 5 are omitted from the record of $S4$ because they are virtually identical in procedure and performance to Session 3 and would needlessly enlarge Figure 2 if included.) It is clear that $S1$ was very responsive to the extinction and reinforcement operations: Her near-perfect rate of imitative bar-pressing weakened considerably after nearly one complete session of extinction for other imitative responding, but promptly recovered its near-perfect aspect when reinforcement was resumed.[2] The record

of $S4$ shows the same pattern, but the differences are not so apparent. This may be due to the low rate of imitative bar-pressing induced in $S4$ under the previous reinforcement conditions. Sighting along the curve, however, will make clear the same pattern of rate changes apparent in the record of $S1$.

Time-out from Imitation

Time-out procedures were instituted with two other children, one of whom had a high rate of imitative bar-pressing, and the other only a modest rate. After

---

[2]In the case of $S1$, it can be seen that the effects of

extinction are markedly stronger with the beginning of Session 4, and that the effects of resumed reinforcement, clear in the last half of Session 5, are even more pronounced with the beginning of Session 6. This interaction between session changes and experimental conditions remains an unexplained complication of the data; however, it need not greatly alter the conclusions drawn.

a stable rate of imitative bar-pressing had been established by each child, the puppet ceased providing any nodding, mouthing, or verbal nonsense performances for the child to imitate, hence eliminating any reinforcement of imitation by eliminating the previously established cues for the occurrence of imitation. Social reinforcement was continued at the same rate, but was delivered for appropriate comments in the child's conversation rather than for imitation.

This time-out was continued until the child showed a stable or marked decrease in imitative bar-pressing. Then the puppet resumed performances of nodding, mouthing, and verbal nonsense statements, and shifted his reinforcement back to the child's imitations of these performances until the child showed a stable or marked increase in imitative bar-pressing. Then the whole cycle of time-out and reinforcement was repeated in exactly the same way. Bar-pressing, of course, was never reinforced.

The subjects chosen for this procedure were *S*2 of Figure 1 and *S*3, both girls. Their records are shown in Figure 3. (The early portion of the record of *S*2 has already been seen in Figure 1.) It is apparent that the time-out condition produced a quick and drastic weakening of imitative bar-pressing in these children, and that a resumption of reinforcement of other imitative responses, when these were again displayed by the puppet for the child to imitate, quickly generalized to the nonreinforced imitative bar-pressing. (By accident, *S*3 received one reinforcement for bar-pressing during Session 1. It is assumed that the effect of this single reinforcement was negligible.)

Discussion

In this study, social reinforcement has been used to strengthen a set of behaviors directly. The responses of nodding, mouthing, and saying nonsense syllable

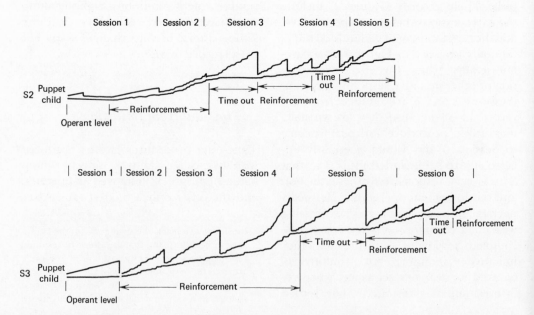

Figure 3. *The effects of time-out from reinforced imitation on generalized imitative bar-pressing in two Ss.*

chains have been established through instructions ("Can you do this?") and reinforcement, and maintained with reinforcement. These responses have in common the fact that they are all imitative of a model's behaviors and that the child does them only when the model does. It is in this context that the strengthening of imitative bar-pressing becomes significant. Bar-pressing was never reinforced directly; nor was the child ever instructed to bar-press imitatively. (The simple instructions dealing with the child's bar— "Show me your bar"— never promoted imitative bar-pressing in the children observed specifically for this possibility.) Bar-pressing has little physical or topographical resemblance to nodding, mouthing, and verbal nonsense chains. What it does have in common with these responses is the fact that it too is imitative of one of the model's performances. Hence its strengthening, following the direct strengthening of nodding, mouthing, and verbal responses, may be attributed to generalization along a dimension of similarity between the child's response and the model's response. In other words, the child is responsive to the stimulus of similarity between responses per se, apparently independently of the particular physical stimuli involved in specific responses.

It can be important to demonstrate that similarity between behaviors of model and child can be a functional stimulus dimension. Such a demonstration would be essential in at least some reinforcement analyses of imitation, especially in any analysis trying to show that imitation should be a strong response in a child, even when it does not produce extrinsic reinforcement. One such analysis might proceed as follows:

In the ordinary course of his early life, a child will form many hundreds of discriminations that involve the sight or sound of a model's behavior as a cue for a response by the child which achieves the same (or a similar) reinforcing outcome. In effect, in all such situations, the child is in a position to learn what response on his part reproduces the effect produced by the model's behavior. Many times, the world will be such that only a response similar in physical make-up or topography will reproduce the same effect. For example, many times a child will need to get through a latched door. He will often observe an older or more skillful model turn the knob and pass through. The child will eventually differentiate his own behavior to the point where it succeeds in opening the door. But doors are such that very few responses will succeed, and consequently the child's behavior will be very similar to the model's. In this situation, and in many others like it, the stimulus of similarity between the child's behavior and the model's is consistently programmed and sets the occasion for reinforcement of the child. Given enough of these situations, of adequate consistency and variety, the stimulus of similarity between behaviors in general may become discriminative for reinforcement. Since a stimulus which is discriminative for reinforcement becomes (secondarily) reinforcing in its own right, then responses which produce similarity between behaviors will thereby be strengthened. Responses of the child which "produce similarity" are those responses which have a topography that the child can compare to the topography of the model's responses, e.g., he can see both his response and the model's or can hear both. Hence the child will become generally "imitative," and, if similarity has great strength as a discriminative and therefore reinforcing stimulus, imitative behavior will be correspondingly more prevalent and apparently autonomous.

Certain details of procedure in this study may be worthy of note. One involves the fact that noncontingent social reinforcement given by the puppet to the child was not sufficient to induce imitation of the puppet. Furthermore, once a generalized imitation had been set up, noncontingent reinforcement was not sufficient to maintain it. Only when other imitative responses were being reinforced would imitative bar-pressing (never directly reinforced) remain at any strength. The puppet would, as the design required, shift his reinforcement from imitative responses to other appropriate moments in the interactions, but the general amount and spacing of this reinforcement remained the same. Hence the effects on imitative bar-pressing noted here cannot be attributed to the simple presence or absence of reinforcement, but rather are related to its contingent or noncontingent use. This is at some variance with the results of other studies (cf. Bandura and Huston, 1961), in which a prior condition of noncontingent social reinforcement from a model evoked more imitation of the model from the child than otherwise. This may be due to the particular response used in this study to observe generalized imitation, which was bar-pressing. Bar-pressing may be an unusual response for a young child and may have relatively little resemblance to the strong responses already in his repertoire. For this reason, it may be a relatively inefficient response with which to demonstrate a generalized imitation of the puppet. On the other hand, it may

be that while similarity between behaviors is reinforcing for children, this reinforcing value is closely dependent on similarity remaining discriminative for at least some reinforcement in the situation. Possibly, when similarity clearly is no longer discriminative for reinforcement, it loses its own reinforcing function rather quickly. It will take an extensive program of research to provide useful data on this question, but the question may well be worth it, since such arguments about imitation can figure heavily in a conceptual account of socialization or "identification."

Another point, possibly important, is that all of the subjects showing imitation were girls. Since the group sampled was composed largely of girls, this may not be unusual. However, the puppet was clearly a male cowboy, and since cross-sex interactions are prevalent where social reinforcement is involved (especially with young children), it may be that later data will demonstrate that the sex of the subject and the model is an important variable. No conclusion is possible from the present data.

Finally, the increased imitative bar-pressing demonstrated here is not simply part of a generalized increase in activity; its clearly imitative nature denies that. Furthermore, it was apparent to the observers that there was no general increase of other observable activities as imitative bar-pressing developed in the child.

Section XII

Rogers' Self Theory

Carl Rogers has not been content to rest on the laurels he has received for his substantial contributions to psychology. He is constantly redefining, sharpening, elaborating, modifying, and interpreting his position. He writes and speaks to many different audiences because he believes with passion that psychology has much to contribute toward understanding and hopefully toward solving many of the problems that vex people today.

The primary source selection made for this book was one written at the request of psychologists to be read by psychologists. It is not, however, couched in professional jargon. The description of the soil from which the theory grew provides the reader with a first-hand view of how personal and professional experiences influence theory construction and research. One important source of stimulation for personality theorists has been clinical practice, and this certainly has been the case with Carl Rogers. Rogers' discussion and elaboration of his "self" construct should provide additional meaning to the reader of how he uses this important concept. One of the most significant features of this selection is Rogers' outline of future research relevant for the theory.

A hallmark of self theory is the significance it attributes to conscious— one might even say—self-conscious reports by the experiencing person. In this respect, it constitutes a third force between psycho-analysis, on the one hand, which seeks out the mind in all of its subterranean hideaways, and behaviorism, on the other hand, which concerns itself largely with overt behavior. It would be hard to imagine self theorists pursuing their empirical activities in an animal laboratory. The consequences for research of the position taken by this third force are far-reaching. It is considerably easier to secure self-reports from conscious human beings than it is to explore the unconscious or to contrive controlled conditions for eliciting overt behavior. Consequently, recent psychological literature is replete with investigations of hypotheses derived from self theory. Most of this literature consists of short articles; many of the investigators make use of Stephenson's Q technique. For a critique of this literature the reader is referred to Ruth Wylie's book, *The Self Concept* (1961).

We have selected as an example of this type of research on self theory a paper by Turner and Vanderlippe. In this study college students were asked to sort 100 statements into self descriptive categories (the Q-sort technique) first under the instructions "describe yourself as you see yourself today," and then using the instructions "describe your ideal self—the kind of person you would most like to be." A diverse set of behavioral indicators was used in an attempt to obtain adequate measures of adjustment. Those students whose ideal self was similar to the way they saw themselves in actuality were compared on the several adjustment measures with students whose ideal self differed markedly from the way they saw themselves. Significant differences between several of the adjustment measures indicated that the more congruence there is between what a person thinks he is and what he would like to be, the better adjusted the person is.

The third paper in this section is an interesting study of psychotherapy using objective and quantifiable methods of assessment. In this area Rogers has been a pioneer. His research on the process of psychotherapy, an enterprise in which he has been joined by a number of coworkers, was virtually unique when it was initiated. The study by Cartwright and Lerner is a well-controlled study of 28 patients seen by client-centered therapists at the University of Chicago Counseling Center. Patients and therapists filled out rating scales at the beginning of therapy and again at the end of therapy. This formed the primary data for the study. Patients that showed a high need for change and had a therapist who could, at the beginning of therapy, accurately understand the way the patient viewed himself were more likely to show improvement, and this improvement would come in relatively fewer treatment sessions. These results are congruent with Roger's formulation of client-centered psychotherapy.

In the last paper of this section we return to college students for our subjects. Vingoe had each subject fill out several objective personality inventories and peer ratings. Peer rating techniques are not widely used in personality research, but they can be an important source of data and probably could be used more frequently. Peer ratings were used in the present study to obtain a measure of self-awareness. The results showed that, as predicted from Rogers' theory, normal subjects were more self-accepting than neurotic female college students as determined by scores on Eysenck's neuroticism scale.

Reference

Wylie, R. C. *The self concept.* Lincoln: University of Nebraska Press, 1961.

1. A Theory of Therapy, Personality, and Interpersonal Relationships, as Developed in the Client-centered Framework

CARL R. ROGERS

Introduction

Being one who has deprecated the use of compulsion as a means of altering personality and behavior, it is no doubt singularly appropriate that I should be forced to acknowledge the value of the gentle compulsion of a formal request. For some time I had recognized the need of a more adequate and more up-to-date statement of the theories which have been developing in the group associated with client-centered therapy. This might well have remained in the realm of good intentions, had it not been for the formal request from the American Psychological Association, on connection with its Study of the Status and Development of Psychology in the United States, to prepare a systematic statement of this developing theory. To join with others who were endeavoring to formulate their own theories and to use, so far as possible, a common outline—this seemed to be both an obligation and an opportunity which could not be refused. It is this softly voiced but insistent pressure from my colleagues which has caused me to write the following pages now, rather than at some later date. For this pressure I am grateful.

The Soil of The Theory. No theory can be adequately understood without some knowledge of the cultural and personal soil from which it springs. Consequently I am pleased that the first item of the suggested outline requests a thorough discussion of background factors. This means, I fear, that I must take the reader through some autobiographical material since, although the client-centered orientation has become very much of a group enterprise in every respect, I, as an individual, carry a considerable responsibility for its initiation and for the beginning formulation of its theories. I shall, therefore, mention briefly some cultural influences which may or may not have relevance to the theory itself. I shall not attempt to evalu-

SOURCE. *Selection from Carl R. Rogers, "A theory of therapy, personality, and interpersonal relationships, as developed in the client-centered framework"* in Psychology: A Theory of Science, *Vol. 3. Edited by Sigmund Koch. New York: McGraw-Hill, 1959.*

ate these influences, since I am probably a poor judge of the part they have played.

I lived my childhood as a middle child in a large, close-knit family, where hard work and a highly conservative (almost fundamentalist) Protestant Christianity were about equally revered. When the family moved to a farm at the time I was twelve, I became deeply interested and involved in scientific agriculture. The heavy research volumes I read on my own initiative in the next few years regarding feeds and feeding, soils, animal husbandry, and the like, instilled in me a deep and abiding respect for the scientific method as a means of solving problems and creating new advances in knowledge. This respect was reinforced by my first years in college, where I was fond of the physical and biological sciences. In my work in history I also realized something of the satisfactions of scholarly work.

Having rejected the family views of religion, I became interested in a more modern religious viewpoint and spent two profitable years in Union Theological Seminary, which at that time was deeply committed to a freedom of philosophical thought which respected any honest attempt to resolve significant problems, whether this led into or away from the church. My own thinking lead me in the latter direction, and I moved "across the street" to Teachers College, Columbia University. Here I was exposed to the views of John Dewey, not directly, but through William H. Kilpatrick. I also had my first introduction to clinical psychology in the warmly human and common-sense approach of Leta Hollingworth. There followed a year of internship at the Institute for Child Guidance, then in its chaotic but dynamic first year of existence. Here I gained much from the highly Freudian orientation of most of its psychiatric staff, which included David Levy and Lawson Lowrey. My first attempts at therapy were carried on

at the Institute. Because I was still completing my doctorate at Teachers College, the sharp incompatibility of the highly speculative Freudian thinking of the Institute with the highly statistical and Thorndikean views at Teachers College was keenly felt.

There followed twelve years in what was essentially a community childguidance clinic in Rochester, New York. This was a period of comparative isolation from the thinking of others. The psychology department of the University of Rochester was uninterested in what we were doing because our work was not, in its opinion, in the field of psychology. Our colleagues in the social agencies, schools, and courts knew little and cared less about psychological ideologies. The only element which carried weight with them was the ability to get results in working with maladjusted individuals. The staff was eclectic, of diverse background, and our frequent and continuing discussion of treatment methods was based on our practical everyday working experience with the children, adolescents, and adults who were our clients. It was the beginning of an effort, which has had meaning for me ever since, to discover the order which exists in our experience of working with people. The volume on the *Clinical Treatment of the Problem Child* was one outcome of this effort.

During the second half of this period there were several individuals who brought into our group the controversial therapeutic views of Otto Rank and the Philadelphia group of social workers and psychiatrists whom he had influenced. Personal contact with Rank was limited to a three-day institute we arranged; nevertheless his thinking had a very decided impact on our staff and helped me to crystallize some of the therapeutic methods we were groping toward. For by this time I was becoming more competent as a therapist, and beginning to sense a discoverable orderliness in this experience, an orderliness which was inherent *in* the experience, and (unlike some of the Freudian theories which had grown so far from their original soil) did not have to be imposed *on* the experience.

Though I had carried on some part-time university teaching throughout the Rochester years, the shift to a faculty position at Ohio State University was a sharp one. I found that the emerging principles of therapy, which I had experienced largely on an implicit basis, were by no means clear to well-trained, critically minded graduate students. I began to sense that what I was doing and thinking in the clinical field was perhaps more of a new pathway than I had recognized. The paper I presented to the Minnesota chapter of Psi Chi in December, 1940, (later chapter 2 of *Counseling and Psychotherapy*) was the first conscious attempt to develop a relatively new line of thought. Up to that time I had felt that my writings were essentially attempts to distill out more clearly the principles which "all clinicians" were using.

The new influence at Ohio State, which continued to be felt in my years at Chicago, was the impact of young men and women —intellectually curious, often theoretically oriented, eager to learn from experience and to contribute through research and theory to the development of a field of knowledge. Through their mistakes as well as their successes in therapy, through their research studies, their critical contributions, and through our shared thinking, have come many of the recent developments in this orientation.

In the past decade at the University of Chicago the new elements which stand out most sharply are the opportunity for and the encouragement of research, the inclusion of graduate students from education, theology, human develop-ment, sociology, industrial relations, as well as psychology, in the ramified activities of the Counseling Center, and the creative thinking of my faculty colleagues, especially those connected with the Center.

The persistent influence which might not be fully recognized, because it is largely implicit in the preceding paragraphs, is the continuing clinical experience with individuals who perceive themselves, or are perceived by others to be, in need of personal help. Since 1928, for a period now approaching thirty years, I have spent probably an average of 15 to 20 hours per week, except during vacation periods, in endeavoring to understand and be of therapeutic help to these individuals. To me, they seem to be the major stimulus to my psychological thinking. From these hours, and from my relationships with these people, I have drawn most of whatever insight I possess into the meaning of therapy, the dynamics of interpersonal relationships, and the structure and functioning of personality.

Some Basic Attitudes. Out of this cultural and personal soil have grown certain basic convictions and attitudes which have undoubtedly influenced the theoretical formulation which will be presented. I will endeavor to list some of these views which seem to me relevant:

1. I have come to see both research and theory as being aimed toward the inward ordering of significant experience. Thus research is not something esoteric, nor an activity in which one engages to gain professional kudos. It is the persistent, disciplined effort to make sense and order out of the phenomena of subjective experience. Such effort is justified because it is satisfying to perceive the world as having order and because rewarding results often ensue when

one understands the orderly relationships which appear to exist in nature. One of these rewarding results is that the ordering of one segment of experience in a theory immediately opens up new vistas of inquiry, research, and thought, thus leading one continually forward.

Thus the primary reason for research and systematic theory in the field of therapy is that it is personally dissatisfying to permit the cumulating experiences of therapeutic hours to remain as a conglomeration of more or less isolated events. It feels as though there is an order in these vents. What could it be? And of any hunch regarding the inherent order, it is necessary to ask the question, is this really true, or am I deceiving myself? Thus slowly there is assembled a body of facts, and systematic constructs to explain those facts, which have as their basic function the satisfaction of a need for order which exists in me.

(I have, at times, carried on research for purposes other than the above to satisfy others, to convince opponents and sceptics, to gain prestige, and for other unsavory reasons. These errors in judgment and activity have only deepened the above positive conviction.)

2. It is my opinion that the type of understanding which we call science can begin anywhere, at any level of sophistication. To observe acutely, to think carefully and creatively—these activities, not the accumulation of laboratory instruments, are the beginnings of science. To observe that a given crop grows better on the rocky hill than in the lush bottom land, and to think about this observation, is the start of science. To notice that most sailors get scurvy but not those who have stopped at islands to pick up fresh fruit is a similar start. To recognize that, when a person's views of himself change, his behaviors changes accordingly, and to puzzle over this, is again the beginning of both theory and science. I voice this

conviction in protest against the attitude, which seems too common in American psychology, that science starts in the laboratory or at the calculating machines.

3. A closely related belief is that there is a natural history of science—that science in any given field, goes through a patterned course of growth and development. For example, it seems to me right and natural that in any new field of scientific endeavor the observations are gross, the hypotheses speculative and full of errors, the measurements crude. More important, I hold the opinion that this is just as truly science as the use of the most refined hypotheses and measurements in a more fully developed field of study. The crucial question in either case is not the degree of refinement but the direction of movement. If in either instance the movement is toward more exact measurement, toward more clear-cut and rigorous theory and hypotheses, toward findings which have greater validity and generality, then this is a healthy and growing science. If not, then it is a sterile pseudo science, no matter how exact its methods. Science is a *developing* mode of inquiry, or it is of no particular importance.

4. In the invitation to participate in the APA study, I have been asked to cast our theoretical thinking in the terminology of the independent-intervening-dependent variable, in so far as this is feasible. I regret that I find this terminology somehow uncongenial. I cannot justify my negative reaction very adequately, and perhaps it is an irrational one, for the logic behind these terms seems unassailable. But to me the terms seem static —they seem to deny the restless, dynamic, searching, changing aspects of scientific movement. There is a tendency to suppose that a variable thus labeled, reamins so, which is certainly not true. The terms also seem to me to smack too much of the laboratory, where one under-

takes an experiment *de novo*, with everything under control, rather than of a science which is endeavoring to wrest from the phenomena of experience the inherent order which they contain. Such terms seem to be more applicable to the advanced stages of scientific endeavor then to the beginning stages.

Please do not misunderstand. I quite realize that *after the fact*, any research investigation, or any theory constructed to relate the discovered facts, should be translatable into the language of independent and dependent variables or there is something wrong with the research or theory. But the terms seem to me better adapted to such autopsies than to the living psychology of scientific work in a new field.

5. It should be quite clear from the foregoing that the model of science which I find most helpful is not taken from the advanced stages of theoretical physics. In a field such as psychotherapy or personality the model which seems more congenial to me would be taken from the much earlier stages of the physical sciences. I like to think of the discovery of radioactivity by the Curies. They had left some pitchblende ore, which they were using for some purpose or other, in a room where they stored photographic plates. They discovered that the plates had been spoiled. In other words, first was the observation of a dynamic event. This event might have been due to a multitude of causes. It might have been a flaw in the manufacture of the plates. It might have been the humidity, the temperature, or any one of a dozen other things. But acute observation and creative thinking fastened on a hunch regarding the pitchblende, and this became a tentative hypothesis. Crude experiments began to confirm the hypothesis. Only slowly was it discovered that it was *not* pitchblende, but a strange element *in* the pitchblende

which was related to the observed effect. Meanwhile a theory had to be constructed to bring this strange phenomenon into orderly relationship with other knowledge. And although the theory in its most modest form had to do with the effect of radium on photographic plates, in its wider and more speculative reaches it was concerned with the nature of matter and the composition of the universe. By present-day standards in the physical sciences, this is an example of a primitive stage of investigation and theory construction. But in the fields in which I am most deeply interested I can only hope that we are approaching such a stage. I feel sure that we are not beyond it.

6. Another deep-seated opinion has to do with theory. I believe that there is only one statement which can accurately apply to all theories — from the phlogiston theory to the theory of relativity, from the theory I will present to the one which I hope will replace it in a decade — and that is that at the time of its formulation every theory contains an unknown (and perhaps at that point an unknowable) amount of error and mistaken inference. The degree of error may be very great, as in the phlogiston theory, or small, as I imagine it may be in the theory of relativity, but unless we regard the discovery of truth as a closed and finished book, then there will be new discoveries which will contradict the best theories which we can now construct.

To me this attitude is very important, for I am distressed at the manner in which small-caliber minds immediately accept a theory — almost any theory — as a dogma of truth. If theory could be seen for what it is — a fallible, changing attempt to construct a network of gossamer threads which will contain the solid facts — then a theory would serve as it should, as a stimulus to further creative thinking.

I am sure that the stress I place on this grows in part out of my regret at the history of Freudian theory. For Freud, it seems quite clear that his highly creative theories were never more than that. He kept changing, altering, revising, giving new meaning to old terms—always with more respect for the facts he observed than for the theories he had built. But at the hands of insecure disciples (so it seems to me), the gossamer threads became iron chains of dogma from which dynamic psychology is only recently beginning to free itself. I feel that every formulation of a theory contains this same risk and that, at the time a theory is constructed, some precautions should be taken to prevent it from becoming dogma.

7. I share with many others the belief that truth is unitary, even though we will never be able to know this unity. Hence any theory, derived from almost any segment of experience, if it were complete and completely accurate, could be extended indefinitely to provide meaning for other very remote areas of experience. Tennyson expressed this in sentimental fashion in his "Flower in the Crannied Wall." I too believe that a complete theory of the individual plant would show us "what God and man is."

The corollary, however, is of equal importance and is not so often stated. A slight error in a theory may make little difference in providing an explanation of the observed facts out of which the theory grew. But when the theory is projected to explain more remote phenomena, the error may be magnified, and the inferences from the theory may be completely false. A very slight error in the understanding of Tennyson's flower may give a grossly false understanding of man. Thus every theory deserves the greatest respect in the area from which it was drawn from the facts and a decreasing degree of respect as it makes predictions in areas more and more remote from its origin. This is true of the theories developed by our own group.

8. There is one other attitude which I hold, which I believe has relevance for the proper evaluation of any theory I might present. It is my belief in the fundamental predominance of the subjective. Man lives essentially in his own personal and subjective world, and even his most objective functioning, in science, mathematics, and the like, is the result of subjective purpose and subjective choice. In relation to research and theory, for example, it is my subjective perception that the machinery of science as we know it—operational definitions, experimental method, mathematical proof—is the best way of avoiding self-deception. But I cannot escape the fact that this is the way it appears to me, and that had I lived two centuries ago, or if I were to live two centuries in the future, some other pathway to truth might seem equally or more valid. To put it more briefly, it appears to me that though there may be such a thing as objective truth, I can never know it; all I can know is that some statements appear to me subjectively to have the qualifications of objective truth. Thus there is no such thing as Scientific Knowledge; there are only individual perceptions of what appears to each person to be such knowledge.

Since this is a large and philosophical issue, not too closely related to what follows, I shall not endeavor to state it more fully here but refer any who are interested to an article in which I have tried to expound this view somewhat more fully (1954). I mention it here only because it is a part of the context in which my theoretical thinking has developed.

A Digression on the Case History of a Construct. Since the abstraction which we term the self is one of the central constructs in our theory, it may be helpful to interpose a somewhat lengthy digression at this point in our list of definitions in order to relate something of the development of this construct. In so doing we will also be illustrating the manner in which most of these defined constructs have come into being in our theory.

Speaking personally, I began my work with the settled notion that the "self" was a vague, ambiguous, scientifically meaningless term which had gone out of the psychologist's vocabulary with the departure of the introspectionists. Consequently I was slow in recognizing that when clients were given the opportunity to express their problems and their attitudes in their own terms, without any guidance or interpretation, they tended to talk in terms of the self. Characteristic expressions were attitudes such as these: "I feel I'm not being my real self." "I wonder who I am, really." "I wouldn't want anyone to know the real me." "I never had a chance to be myself." "It feels good to let myself go and just *be* myself here." "I think if I chip off all the plaster facade I've got a pretty solid self—a good substantial brick building, underneath." It seemed clear from such expressions that the self was an important element in the experience of the client, and that in some odd sense his goal was to become his "real self."

Raimy (1943) produced a careful and searching definition of the self-concept which was helpful in our thinking. There seemed to be no operational way of defining it at that point. Attitudes toward the self could be measured, however, and Raimy and a number of others began such research. Self-attitudes were determined, operationally, by the categorizing of all self-referent terms in interviews preserved in verbatim form by electrical recording. The categories used had a satisfactory degree of interjudge reliability, thus making them suitable scientific constructs for our work. We were encouraged to find that these self-referent attitudes altered significantly in therapy as we had hypothesized they would.

As we focused more upon the concept of the self, clinical experience again gave us further clues as to its nature. For example, in the process of change which appeared to occur in therapy, it was not at all uncommon to find violent fluctuation in the concept of the self. A client, during a given interview, would come to experience himself quite positively. He felt he was worthwhile, that he could meet life with the capacities he possessed, and that he was experiencing a quiet confidence. Three days later he might return with a completely reversed conception of himself. The same evidence now proved an opposite point. The positive new choice he had made now was an instance of silly immaturity; the valid feelings courageously expressed to his colleagues now were clearly inadequate. Often such a client could date, to the moment, the point at which, following some very minor incident, the balance was upset, and his picture of himself had undergone a complete flip-flop. During the interview it might as suddenly reverse itself again.

Consideration of this phenomenon made it clear that we were not dealing with an entity of slow accretion, of step-by-step learning, of thousands of unidirectional conditionings. These might all be involved, but the product was clearly a gestalt, a configuration in which the alteration of one minor aspect could completely alter the whole pattern. One was forcibly reminded of the favorite textbook illustration of a gestalt, the double picture of the old hag and the young woman. Looked at with one mind set, the picture is clearly that of an ugly old woman. The slightest change, and the whole becomes a portrait of an attractive girl. So with our clients. The self-concept was clearly configurational in nature.

Our clinical experience gave us another clue to the manner in which the self functioned. The conventional concept of repression as having to do with forbidden or socially taboo impulses had been recognized as inadequate to fit the facts. Often the most deeply denied impulses and feelings were positive feelings of love, or tenderness, or confidence in self. How could one explain the puzzling conglomeration of experience which seemingly could not be permitted in awareness? Gradually it was recognized that the important principle was one of consistency with the self. Experiences which were incongruent with the individual's concept of himself tended to be denied to awareness, whatever their social character. We began to see the self as a criterion by which the organism screened out experiences which could not comfortably be permitted in consciousness. Lecky's little posthumous book (1945) reinforced this line of thought. We also began to understand other functions of the self in its regulatory influence on behavior, and the like.

At about this juncture Stephenson's *Q* technique (1953) opened up the possibility of an operational definition of the self-concept. Immediately, research burgeoned. Though it has barely made a start in exploiting the possible testing of hypotheses, there have already been measurements and predictions regarding the self as of this moment, the self in the past, "myself as I am with my mother," "the self I would like to be," etc. Probably the most sophisticated and significant of these studies is that completed by Chodorkoff (1954) in which his hypothesis, stated informally, is as follows: that the greater the agreement between the individual's self-description and an objective description of him, the

less perceptual defensiveness he will show, and the more adequate will be his personal adjustment. This hypothesis is upheld and tends to confirm some important aspects of our theory. In general the various investigations have agreed in indicating that the self-concept is an important variable in personality dynamics and that change in the self is one of the most marked and significant changes occurring in therapy.

It should be recognized that any construct is a more or less arbitrary abstraction from experience. Thus the self could be defined in many different ways. Hilgard, for example (1949) has proposed that it be defined in such a way as to include unconscious material, not available to awareness, as well as conscious material. Although we recognize that this is certainly a legitimate way of abstracting from the phenomena, we believe it is not a useful way because it produces a concept which cannot at this point be given operational definition. One cannot obtain sufficient agreement as to the content of the individual's unconscious to make research possible. Hence we believe that it is more fruitful to define the self-concept as a gestalt which is available to awareness. This has permitted and encouraged a flood of important research.

At all times, however, we endeavor to keep in the forefront of our thinking the fact that each definition is no more than an abstraction and that the same phenomena might be abstracted in a different fashion. One of our group is working on a definition of self which would give more emphasis to its process nature. Others have felt that a plural definition, indicating many specific selves in each of various life contexts, would be more fruitful, and this way of thinking has been embodied in, for example, Nunally's (1955) research. So the search continues for a more adequate conceptualization of this area of our therapeutic experience and for more adequate technical means of providing operational definitions for the concepts which are formulated.

This concludes our interruption of the list of definitions. It is hoped that this one example will give an indication of the way in which many of our basic constructs have developed—not only the self-concept but the constructions of congruence, incongruence, defensiveness, unconditional positive regard, locus of evaluation, and the like. Although the process has been irregular, it has tended to include clinical observation, initial conceptualization, initial crude research to test some of the hypotheses involved, further clinical observation, more rigorous formulation of the construct and its functional relationships, more refined operational definitions of the construct, more conclusive research.

A Continuing Program of Theory and Research. The theoretical system and the research program which are connected with client-centered therapy have grown from within themselves. This point can hardly be overemphasized. The thought that we were making a start on a theoretical system would for me have been a most distasteful notion even as little as a dozen years ago. I was a practical clinician and held (*horrible dictu!*) an open scorn of all psychological theory, as my early students at Ohio State can testify. This was true even at the same time that I was beginning to discern the orderliness which existed in the therapeutic process. I like to think that the theoretical system and far-reaching web of research which have developed, have grown in an organic fashion. Each plodding step has simply been a desire to find out this, a desire to find out that, a need for perceiving whatever consistencies, or invariances, or order exists in the material thus far unearthed.

Consequently when I am asked, as I am in the outline suggested for this paper, "the extent to which the systematic program has been realized," I feel it is the wrong question for this system. I have no idea what will be the ultimate realization of the living program which has developed. I can see some of the likely next steps, or the current directions, but have no assurance that these will be taken. We have continued to move in the directions which are *experienced* as rewarding, not necessarily in those directions which logic points out. I believe this has been the strength of the program, and I trust it will continue.

Thus I believe that we are likely to see progress in the following directions, but I am not sure of any of them. It seems likely that further moves will be made toward theory and research in the field of perception, enriching that field by the insights gained in therapy, and being enriched by the wealth of research data and theory in perception which can be brought to bear in the refinement of the theories we are developing. One such study now in progress, for example, is attempting to investigate perceptual changes which occur during therapy. The measures range from those entirely concerned with social perception—of people, of relationships—to those entirely concerned with the physical perception of form, color, and line. Does therapy change only social perception, or does it alter even the most basic perceptual processes? If not, where on this continuum does change cease to occur?

I visualize the same type of *rapprochement* with learning theory, where in my judgement we have much to offer in the way of new directions in that field, as well as being able to use much of the material available there. It also seems likely that a number of the hypotheses we are formulating may be tested in the laboratory, some on human and some on animal subjects, thus linking the field of personality and therapy with so-called experimental psychology. There seems no reason, for example, why research on the establishment and consequences of conditions of worth, as spelled out in this theory, might not be carried out on higher animals, with a wider range of experimental conditions and more adequate controls than could be achieved with human subjects.

I regard it as possible that there may be a closer linking of our theory with the developing interest in creativity in the humanities and social sciences generally, and I trust that this theory may provide a number of relevant hypotheses for testing. I regard it as very likely that the implications of this body of theory for industrial production will be developed much more fully—the beginnings, as described by Richard in Gordon's book (1955), seem very exciting. I believe it is possible that the near future may see a clear linking with the psychiatric group and a testing of the theory in a wider variety of human disorders, with a reduction in the professional parochialism which has thus far kept the medical group largely ignorant of the research in this field.

One direction which appears only theoretically possible is the exploitation in governmental affairs and international relations of some of the implications of this theory. I do not regard this as likely in the near future.

I suspect that the discovery and development of a contextual basis for this theory in some form of existential philosophy will continue. The general orientation of philosophical phenomenology is also likely to continue to have its influence in this respect. These are some of the potentialities for future development—rather grandiose, to be sure—which I see. The extent to which any of them will organically grow is a matter

which demands a gift of prophecy I do not have.

Immediate Strategy of Development. To return, in closing, to the much more immediate issues facing us in the systematic development of the theory, I see several problems which have very high priority if our general systematic thinking is to have a healthy development. I will list these problems and tasks, but the order of listing has no significance, since I cannot determine the priority.

1. We are urgently in need of new and more ingenious tools of measurement. Stephenson's Q technique (1953) has been most helpful and Osgood's method for quantifying semantic space (1954) also seems promising. But most urgently needed of all is a method whereby we might give operational definition to the construct *experience* in our theory, so that discrepancies between self-concept and experience, awareness and experience, etc., might be measured. This would permit the testing of some of the most crucial hypotheses of the theoretical system. To be sure, some attempts have been made to approach such an operational definition, but the instrumentation is exceedingly cumbersome and admittedly inadequate.

2. An increased amount of experience with individuals classed as psychotic, and the testing of a variety of the theoretical hypotheses in therapeutic work with this group and in research with psychotics as subjects, would round out and enrich our systematic thinking in an area in which it is at present inadequate. It would provide the type of extreme reality test which is most helpful in the confirmation, modification, or disproof of a theoretical system. There would seem to be no barriers except practical ones to such a development.

3. An increased amount of experience

and careful studies of hypotheses developed from the theory are needed in the area of group relationships. Hypotheses regarding leadership, facilitation of learning, and reduction of social conflict seem particularly fruitful to study. Here again, the test of the theory at one of its deduced extremes would be most helpful in confirming or revising its core.

4. Still another urgent need — no doubt quite evident to readers of this presentation — is the translation of the present theory into terms which meet the rigorous requirements of the logic of science. Although progress in this direction has been made there is still a woefully long distance to go. Such a development, carried through by competent persons, would greatly sharpen the deductive hypotheses which might be drawn from the system, and hence provide more crucial tests of it.

5. The final need I wish to mention may seem to some very contradictory to the one just voiced. Personally I see it as a possible evolutionary step, not as a contradictory one. I see a great need for creative thinking and theorizing in regard to the methods of social science. There is a rather widespread feeling in our group that the logical positivism in which we were professionally reared is not necessarily the final philosophical word in an area in which the phenomenon of subjectivity plays such a vital and central part. Have we evolved the optimal method for approximating the truth in this area? Is there some view, possibly developing out of an existentialist orientation, which might preserve the values of logical positivism and the scientific advances which it has helped to foster and yet find more room for the existing subjective person who is at the heart and base even of our system of science? This is a highly speculative dream of an intangible goal, but I believe that many of us have a readiness to respond to the persons who can evolve a tentative answer to the riddle.

References

Chodorkoff, B. Self-perception, perceptual defense, and adjustment. *J. abnorm. soc. Psychol.*, 1954, **49**, 508–512.

Gordon, T. *Group-centered leadership*. Boston: Houghton Mifflin, 1955.

Hilgard, E. R. Human motives and the concept of self. *Amer. Psychologist*, 1949, **4**, 374–382.

Lecky, P. *Self-consistency: a theory of personality*. New York: Island Press, 1945.

Nunnally, J. C. An investigation of some propositions of self-conception: the case of Miss Sun. *J. abnorm. soc. Psychol.*, 1955, **50**, 87–92.

Osgood, C. E. The nature and measurement of meaning. *Psychol. Bull.*, 1954, **49**, 197–237.

Raimy, V. C. The self-concept as a factor in counseling and personality organization. Unpublished doctoral dissertation, Ohio State University, 1943.

Rogers, C. R. & Dymond, R. F. (Eds.) *Psychotherapy and personality change*. Chicago: Univer. Chicago Press, 1954.

Stephenson, W. *The study of behavior: Q-technique and its methodology*. Chicago: Univer. Chicago Press, 1953.

2. *Self-ideal Congruence as An Index of Adjustment*

RALPH H. TURNER AND RICHARD H. VANDERLIPPE

Underlying the use of the *Q*-sort technique is the theoretical assumption that the satisfaction or concern of an individual with his phenomenal self is an operationally definable datum of great importance in the area of adjustment. The discrepancy between the placements of a given characteristic on the self scale and the ideal scales has been taken as indicating not only the way in which an individual perceives himself as possessing this characteristic but the degree to which he values this trait. Given these assumptions, then successful therapy should be accompanied by a reduction in the magnitude of self-ideal discrepancies. Further, self concepts should change more as a result of therapy than ideal concepts since the latter are firmly anchored as general societal concepts, whereas the former may be more idiosyncratic. These expectations have been confirmed by Butler and Haigh (3).

Nevertheless, the confirmation of these expectations is not itself a sufficient reason for assuming the adequacy of the basic theoretical framework within which the hypotheses were developed. Dymond (4) has pointed out that the therapist's attitude of satisfaction with a case may be communicated to the individual, who then reflects these attitudes in his self-description. Even if this possible source of contamination did not exist, it would still be necessary to test the assumption that a change of the phenomenal self in the direction of the ideal self may be taken as an indication of better adjustment. Because this is difficult to demonstrate on a before-and-after basis with the same *S*s, an alternative is to select two groups who presently represent the before-and-after conditions as defined by self-referent statements and to obtain behavioral criteria of adjustment for each. The need for such an approach has become even more pressing since Taylor (7) has shown that successive *Q* sorts, without benefit of therapy, reflect changes of the kind reported for successful counseling. Brownfain's study (2) was a step in this direction, but the relationship between his instrument and the conventional *Q* sort requires exploration.

SOURCE. Article by Ralph H. Turner and Richard H. Vanderlippe, "Self-ideal congruence as an index of adjustment" in The *Journal of abnormal and social psychology*, Vol. 57, No. 2, September 1958. Copyrighted 1958 by American Psychological Association.

METHOD

Measurement of Self and Ideal Self

One hundred and seventy-five upper-class students enrolled in introductory psychology at Oberlin College served as subjects (*S*s) on a volunteer basis. The 100 items and general methodology of the SIO *Q* sort developed by Butler and Haigh (3) were selected because of their frequent and systematic use in current research. Each of the items of self-reference was placed on a 3×5 card to facilitate manipulation. The *S*s were seen in groups of 20, each *S* having a set of 100 items, an instruction sheet, and sufficient table space for privacy and easy manipulation of the items. The following instructions were read to the *S*s:

> You are about to take part in a preliminary test in connection with a research project in the department of psychology. It is very important that you follow directions as carefully as possible. You have before you a pile of 100 cards. Each card has a single sentence written upon it. After I have finished reading these instructions, you are to take the cards and sort them into nine piles in such a way as to describe yourself as you see yourself today. The nine piles will range from those statements that are least like you (Pile 1) to those statements that are most like you (Pile 9). There is a specific number of cards to be placed in each pile. This number is shown on page 2 of these instructions. You can interpret the meaning of each statement in any way you think is correct. I will answer no questions concerning meaning during the sorting. It is very important that you sort these cards as honestly as you can. It is not necessary to attempt arranging the cards within each pile. After you have finished sorting the cards, check to make sure you have the correct number of cards in each pile.

When this self sort was concluded, the items were shuffled and directions given for the ideal sort. These were similar to the instructions given previously except for the substitution of the phrase "sort the cards to describe your ideal self—the kind of person you would most like to be."

Following the mode of analysis adopted by Brownfain (2) and by Hanlon, Hofstaetter, and O'Connor (6), the *S*s were divided into two groups, the high comprising the 25 *S*s having the highest correlations between self and ideal sorts and the low comprising the 25 having the lowest correlations. This division permitted an approximation to the differences that have been reported for groups seeking therapy as opposed to groups not seeking therapy. No evidence was found that men and women college students differ significantly in the extent of their self-ideal correspondence. This finding is in agreement with that of Block and Thomas (1), who combined the data for the *S*s. Similar practice was followed here, yielding a high group of 11 men and 14 women and a low group of 10 men and 15 women. It is in terms of the significance of differences between each of these two groups of 25 *S*s on various criteria of adjustment that the validity of the *Q* sort and the theoretical assumptions upon which it rests were tested. For this purpose, Fisher's *t* for small samples was utilized. All values are based upon one-tailed tests of significance since a directional hypothesis governed the original design of the experiment.

The Q-Adjustment Score Criterion

Dymond's (4) procedure was followed in utilizing the 37 items of the SIO *Q* sort that trained clinical psychologists believed a well-adjusted person would say were unlike him (Piles 1–4) and the 37 items they believed a well-adjusted person would say were like him (Piles 6–9). The *Q*-adjustment score for any *S* was the number of these 74 items that were sorted into the "correct" side of the distribution in the course of making a *Q* sort of the self.

Behavioral Criteria of Adjustment

The behavioral criteria against which the *Q*-sort scores were tested were health, extracurricular participation, sociometric indices, and scholastic adjustment. From the files of the student health service, three indices of health were computed: (*a*) mean number of days per college year spent in the hospital, (*b*) mean number of times per college year that assistance for any reason was requested, (c) the total number of negative health items mentioned in the pre-entrance health history as ascertained by a form on which both the student and the family physician had entered appropriate data.

The extracurricular participation score for all Ss in the high and low groups calculated by first compiling a list of 94 extracurricular organizations. Through interviews with officials of each organization, every position within the organizations was given three ratings on five-point scales for the amount of time involved, the status of the position within the particular group, and the status of the position on the campus as a whole. The sum of these three ratings constituted the weight given that position. The number of years a position was held was multiplied by its appropriate weight, and all such products for each activity summed to yield a total score for each S. This was divided by the number of years S had been on the campus to obtain the final participation score.

The sociometric indices involved getting from dormitory housemothers the names of the nine students whose rooms were closest to each S in the high and low groups. Each of the ten students in these living units received a ranking form with the names of the other nine written as column headings to facilitate marking. By entering numbers in the appropriate name column, each student ranked the other nine on each of the following questions: (a) With which person do you spend the most time when you are in a mood to relax? (b) Which person would be best at organizing a group of about 12 people for a particular purpose (such as a clean-up campaign)? (c) If you wanted to talk about a personal problem with a trusted and helpful person, with whom would you be most apt to talk? (d) Which person is the quietest? (e) Which person do you feel has had the most favorable influence upon you? (f) Which person makes friends with others most quickly? (g) Who would most fairly evaluate the circumstances under which an important college regulation had been broken and decide what punishment, if any, should be given? (h) Who is the most cooperative teamworker, working

well with a group and doing his/her share? (i) Who is most apt to handle wisely any situation which calls for quick, clear thinking? (j) Which person is most apt to initiate spontaneous group recreational activities? (k) With whom do you (or would you) especially want to be in a dormitory living group again? The mean rank each S received from other members of his living group was then computed for each of these items.

The comparative scholastic achievement of the two groups was obtained by comparing the mean cumulative academic grades of those in the high and low groups. Because such a comparison might reflect a difference in initial scholastic potential rather than a difference in adjustment, the mean of the raw scores on the American Council Test (8) was computed for each group. This test, taken by all students during the first week of the freshman year, was found to yield a product-moment correlation of 0.51 with cumulative grades for the students on this campus. It thus fulfills the function of providing a moderately valid index of scholastic aptitude. To the extent that the two groups do not differ significantly with respect to scholastic aptitude, any significant difference in scholastic achievement may be interpreted as an indication of a difference in scholastic adjustment.

Standard Tests as Criteria

Although not an original part of the study design, 50 of the original Ss were given the Guilford-Zimmerman Temperament Survey (5) as part of another project. Under standard administration and scoring procedures, scores were obtained for the 10 traits measured. Product-moment correlations were run between raw scores for each of these traits, on the one hand, and the correlations between self and ideal Q sorts, on the other, the latter being first transformed into corresponding z scores.

RESULTS

Table 1 presents the range of the self-ideal correlations in order to facilitate a comparison between the high and the low groups. By use of the z transformation, the mean correlations

TABLE 1   Correlation Between Self Sort and Ideal Self Sort

Group	N	Range	Mean z	Equiva-lent r
All Ss	175	−0.08 to 0.91	0.63	0.56
High	25	0.75 to 0.91	0.08	0.79
Low	25	−0.08 to 0.25	0.11	0.11

for each group were calculated. The correlation of 0.79 indicates reasonably high correspondence between self and ideal ratings for the high group. The corresponding r of 0.11 for the low group does not permit rejection of the hypothesis that the population correlation is zero.

The Q-adjustment scores for the high group yielded a range of 44–59 with a mean of 52.04. The low group yielded a range of 13–43 with a mean of 29.68. This latter mean corresponds closely to that of 28.80 reported by Dymond (4) for a group that had sought therapy. The mean for the high group is somewhat above the 44.96 she reported for her control group. The range of adjustment represented by the present high and low groups, as measured by this criterion, is certainly no smaller than that found between those seeking therapy and those not seeking therapy. Since the distribution of Q-adjustment scores for the high and low groups did not overlap, there is a significant relationship between self ideal Q-sort scores and this external criterion of adjustment.

Table 2 indicates that no evidence was found that the high and low groups differed significantly with respect to the number of days spent

TABLE 2   Mean Group Differences in Health Indices

Health Index	High Group	Low Group	Diff.	t Value	p <
Days in hospital	1.14	0.93	0.21	0.458	0.35
Reports to clinic	3.99	2.71	1.28	0.977	0.20
Health history items	1.24	1.84	0.60	0.470	0.35

in the hospital, the number of times the student sought assistance at the health service, or the number of health items mentioned in the pre-entrance health history.

The mean social participation score for the high group was 20.24, while that for the low group was 13.84. A test of the significance of the difference yielded a t of 2.12, significant beyond the 0.05 level. It appears that those with substantial correlations between self and ideal ratings on the Q sort are significantly more active as measured by this index of social participation than are those whose correlations do not differ significantly from zero.

Table 3 summarizes the data from the sociometric study. The original two groups of 25 each suffered some attrition because of lack of cooperation on the part of some members of the living group. The mean rank received by Ss from those in the living group is indicated for each of the questions and for all items combined. With the combined rank taken as a score for the instrument as a whole, those in the high group achieve a significantly better rating than those in the low group. Examination of the individual items indicates that those in the high group are given preferential ranks without a single exception. Eight of the 11 individual items yielded an acceptable level of significance.

The cumulative academic grade, based upon

TABLE 3   Mean Ranks in Sociometric Items [a]

Item	High Group (N − 24)	Low Group (N − 18)	Diff.	t Value	p <
All	4.2	5.2	1.0	2.38	0.03
a	4.6	5.1	0.5	1.34	0.10
b	3.7	5.1	1.4	2.50	0.01
c	4.4	5.1	0.7	1.75	0.05
d	4.9	4.6	0.3	0.51	0.35
e	4.2	5.3	1.1	2.46	0.01
f	4.4	5.3	0.9	1.67	0.10
g	4.0	5.0	1.0	1.82	0.05
h	4.0	4.7	0.7	1.39	0.10
i	4.1	5.3	1.2	2.17	0.03
j	4.1	5.8	1.7	3.06	0.01
k	4.5	5.3	0.8	1.80	0.05

[a]A low rank is considered an indication of better adjustment except in the case of item *d*.

a point system currently in effect, yielded a mean of 1.78 points for the high group and 1.52 for the low group. This difference, which favors the high group, was found to reach the criterion of significance ($p < 0.05$) with a t of 1.81. The mean raw scores of the high and low groups on the American Council Test were 134.6 and 133.1 respectively. This difference was not significant ($p < 0.40$ with a t of 0.31). The scholastic superiority of the high group thus does not appear to rest primarily upon an initial difference in scholastic potential and suggests somewhat better scholastic adjustment on the part of those whose self-ideal congruence is high.

Table 4 indicates the correlation between self-ideal congruence expressed as z values and the traits measured by the Guilford-Zimmerman Temperament Survey (5). Five of these yielded correlations sufficiently large that the hypothesis of zero correlation could be rejected at the 0.01 level. Those high in self-ideal congruence tended to have high scores in general activity (strong drive, much energy, enthusiasm), ascendance (strong self-defense, leadership, ease in speaking and persuading), sociability (at ease with others, readily established rapport), emotional stability (optimism and freedom from neurotic tendencies),

TABLE 4   *Correlations Between Self-Ideal Congruence Expressed as z Values and Traits Measured by the Guilford-Zimmerman Temperament Survey*

Trait	Correlation with Self-Ideal Congruence
1. General Activity	0.50[a]
2. Restraint	−0.10
3. Ascendance	0.58[a]
4. Sociability	0.36[a]
5. Emotional Stability	0.36[a]
6. Objectivity	−0.03
7. Friendliness	−0.16
8. Thoughtfulness	0.41[a]
9. Personal Relations	−0.25
10. Masculinity	0.10

[a]Significant at the 0.01 level.

and thoughtfulness (mental poise, observation of behavior in others, capability as supervisor of others, reflectiveness). In each instance, the scores for those high in self-ideal congruence are indicative of better adjustment than are those for *S*s low in self-ideal correspondence.

DISCUSSION

Of the criteria of adjustment utilized, a number of significant differences were found between the group high in self-ideal congruence and the group low in this respect. In no instance was a significant difference found in a direction contradictory to the hypothesis. The failure of certain criteria to show a significant difference between the two groups may reflect the inadequacy of these criteria or may indicate that self-ideal congruence is not equally valid as an index of adjustment when applied to all dimensions of adjustment. The possibility of an approach in terms of dimensions of adjustment is suggested by noting that the *Q*-adjustment score was found to be the external criterion of adjustment most closely related to self-ideal congruence. Since this instrument was the only one in the enviable position of having all its items drawn from the same statements used in the *Q* sort, it preserved a close relationship with it in terms of the dimensions tapped.

Health-related behavior can occasionally be shown to reflect personal conflict. It may be questioned that it is an appropriate index of adjustment within the adjustment range of the student population sampled. The overlay of genuine organic complaints constitute determiners of behavior that may effectively mask adjustment-motivated behavior in this area.

Block and Thomas (1), contending that self-satisfaction is not linearly related to the social dimension of adjustment, quite properly suggested that it may, as a consequence, have only very limited relevance as an index of the outcome of psychotherapy. It nevertheless appears that in the context of adjustment defined by the criteria utilized here, the theoretical assumptions upon which the conventional *Q* sort are based received substantial support.

SUMMARY

A test of the theoretical assumptions and the methods upon which the conventional *Q* sort rests was made using several criteria of adjustment. The results tended to support the theoretical assumptions underlying the *Q* sort as currently utilized. Although certain criticisms of the procedures involved are not thereby completely invalidated, it would appear that they are not sufficiently serious to justify abandoning either the method or the assumptions supporting the method.

The emergent composite picture of the college student high in self-ideal congruence (as contrasted with the student low in self-ideal congruence) is that of one who participates more in extracurricular activities, has a higher scholastic average, is given higher sociometric ratings by his fellow students, and receives higher adjustment ratings on both the *Q*-adjustment score and certain traits measured by the Guilford-Zimmerman Temperament Survey.

References

1. Block, J., & Thomas, H. Is satisfaction with self a measure of adjustment? *J. abnorm. soc. Psychol.*, 1955, **51**, 254–259.

2. Brownfain, J. Stability of the self-concept as a dimension of personality. *J. abnorm. soc. Psychol.*, 1952, **47**, 597–606.

3. Butler, J. M., & Haigh, G. V. Changes in the relation between self concepts and ideal concepts consequent upon client centered counseling. In C. R. Rogers & Rosalind Dymond (Eds.), *Psychotherapy and personality change.* Chicago: Univer. of Chicago Press, 1954. Pp. 55–75.

4. Dymond, Rosalind. Adjustment changes over therapy from self-sorts. In C. R. Rogers & Rosalind Dymond (Eds.), *Psychotherapy and personality change.* Chicago: Univer. of Chicago Press, 1954, Pp. 76–84.

5. Guilford, J. P., & Zimmerman, W. S. *The Guilford-Zimmerman Temperament Survey: Manual of instructions and interpretations.* Beverly Hills, Calif.: Sheridan Supply Co., 1949.

6. Hanlon, T. E. Hofstaetter, P. R., & O'Connor, J. P. Congruence of Self and ideal self in relation to personality adjustment. *J. consult. Psychol.*, 1954, **18**, 215–218.

7. Taylor, D. M. Changes in the self concept without psychotherapy. *J. consult. Psychol.*, 1955, **19**, 205–209.

8. Thurstone, L. L., & Thurstone, Thelma G. *Psychological examination for college freshmen: 1947 norms.* Washington, D.C.: American Council on Education, 1948.

3. Empathy, Need to Change, and Improvement with Psychotherapy

ROSALIND DYMOND CARTWRIGHT AND BARBARA LERNER

To study the influence of: the patient's need to change, the therapist's experience level, the empathic understanding of the therapist, the sex of the patient and therapist, and the amount of psychological distance between them, on psychotherapy improvement, 28 patients in client-centered counseling were tested before and after therapy with scales built from the Kelly Role Construct Repertory Test. Patients' initial need to change was found to be directly related to improvement. Therapists' final level of understanding was also directly related. Patient's need and therapist's empathy considered jointly produced a prediction model for therapy length and success. 2 success groups were found: same-sex patients of experienced therapists whose distance from him the therapist initially reduced, and opposite-sex patients of inexperienced therapists whose distance from him the therapist initially increased.

There is a growing body of evidence indicating that improvement in psychoneurotic patients takes place concurrent with psychotherapy, but as yet little consensus concerning the factors responsible for such improvement. To the majority of writers in this field, improvement is a function of specific patient variables, therapist variables, and the interactions among them. However, different writers select different factors as accounting for the major portion of the variance in therapeutic outcome. Since the research evidence is most often unreplicated, or even contradictory, and since there are still large unexplored areas, one can pick and choose among the scraps and fashion a patchwork quilt after one's own heart or theoretic commitment.

Although the various schools of psychotherapy have different views as to what constitutes the necessary and sufficient conditions of the therapeutic process, the studies which compare the respective percentages of successfully treated cases have shown rather similar results for all theoretic approaches. This frequent finding suggests that some common elements exist among the various approaches to psychotherapy and, that they might very well be more significantly

SOURCE. Article by Rosalind Dymond Cartwright and Barbara Lerner, "Empathy, need to change, and improvement with psychotherapy," in the Journal of consulting psychology, Vol. 27, pp. 138–144, 1963. Copyright 1963 by the American Psychological Association and reprinted by permission.

related to improvement than the elements on which the schools differ.

The evidence for two such common elements has been accruing slowly. The studies of Heine (1950) and Fiedler (1950a, 1950b) strongly suggest that one important therapist variable, independent of technique differences, is the therapist's ability to empathically understand his patient. A patient variable which is suggested by the work of Butler and Haigh (1954), Rosenthal and Frank (1956), Cartwright and Cartwright (1958), and Kirtner and Cartwright (1958), as one important to any form of verbal therapy, is the patient's initial recognized need to change. These two promising variables, *the therapist's empathy* and *the patient's need to change*, were selected to form the basic dimensions of this study. However, since we now feel that therapy depends not only on the qualities of the two participants but also on how these affect their relationship, this study attempted to tease out some of the interaction effects of these two major variables.

Part I of the study was undertaken with three primary hypotheses:

1. The degree of need to change on the part of the patient is directly related to improvement with psychotherapy.

2. The empathic understanding of the patient by the therapist is directly related to the degree of improvement in the patient with psychotherapy.

3. These two variables considered jointly will give a better prediction of outcome than either taken singly.

After analyzing the data relative to these hypotheses which had been formulated prior to the data collection, other questions arose concerning the interaction of additional variables with those selected for this study and with the dependent variable, improvement. Part II of this paper considers the sex of the patient in relation to the sex of the therapist,

the "psychological distance" the therapist puts between himself and his patient, and the experience level of the therapist. These additional variables were explored to help clarify some of the interpersonal processes underlying the results obtained from testing the major hypotheses. This study, then, involves the consideration of five variables, some of their interactions, and their relation to improvement with psychotherapy. These five variables can be organized according to a threefold scheme: (*a*) patient characteristics independent of the particular therapist (recognized need to change), (*b*) therapist characteristics independent of particular patient (therapist's level of experience), and (*c*) characteristics dependent upon the particular patient-therapist pair (the therapist's empathy or ability to understand the patient in his own terms, whether or not the patient and therapist are of the same sex, and the therapist's distancing of the patient).

METHOD

Sample

The subjects were 28 patients who voluntarily sought treatment at the Counseling Center of the University of Chicago.[1] Fourteen of the subjects were male, 14 female. They ranged in age from 19 to 43 with a mean age of 27.7. Although these patients were not formally diagnosed, according to their therapists' ratings on "severity of illness" they ranged from "very mild" to "near psychotic." Sixteen client-centered therapists were involved, and the case length varied from 6 to 116 interviews with a mean of 40.

---

[1]No selectivity of patients was exercised. Each new applicant was requested to participate in the study until the quota of 30 subjects was reached. Two patients had not completed treatment at the time the data analysis was begun.

Instruments

The two instruments in this study are referred to as Scale A and Scale B. Scale A provided the data for the improvement criterion and Scale B provided the measure of the patient's need to change, the measure of the therapist's empathic understanding of his patient, and the therapist's distancing of the patient.

Scale A was administered to the therapists on two occasions, after the second interview, referred to as the pretherapy rating, and after the last interview, for a posttherapy rating. The Improvement score was the sum of four components: three change scores between the pre- and posttherapy ratings of: (*a*) the patient's integration; (*b*) his kind of organization (defensive versus open); and (*c*) his present life adjustment. The fourth component of the Improvement score was the therapists' final rating of the outcome of therapy. All ratings were made on nine-point scales.

Scale B differed in content for each subject. Each subject in a sense supplied his own items. This was done in an effort to insure that the scales would be highly personally relevant to each patient. The items were the personal constructs obtained by first administering Kelly's (1955) Role Construct Repertory Test to each subject. From these personal constructs which each patient introduced as constituting the important similarities and differences among the real people in his life, the first 10 discrete ones were selected. Scale B was then made up of the 10 items supplied by each patient arranged as five-point rating scales. On the first testing occasion following interview Number 2, the subject made various ratings of these items: (*a*) to describe himself as he is at present, and (*b*) to describe himself as he wants to be when therapy has been completed. The sum of the squared discrepancies between these two sets of ratings was used as the measure of his felt need to change on the 10 items of particular significance to him. The patient repeated this task at posttherapy to again describe himself as he was then.

Scale B was also the basis for the measurement of the therapist's empathic understanding of his patient. After the second interview the therapist was given a Scale B form containing the 10 items chosen by his patient. He then attempted to describe "the patient as he sees himself." The empathy measure was the squared discrepancy between the patient's self-description and the therapist's attempt to predict the patient's self-description. The therapist repeated this task at posttherapy time. This procedure was used to measure the therapist's empathic understanding after increased contact with the patient.

Results

Part I   *Hypothesis 1: The degree of need to change on the part of the patient is directly related to improvement.* Table 1 shows that Hypothesis 1 is strongly supported.

The mean need to change score was much higher for the improved than for the unimproved group.

Hypothesis 2: The empathic understanding of the patient by the therapist is directly related to the degree of improvement in the patient with psychotherapy. Table 1 shows that there was no significant difference between the improved and unimproved cases on their therapists' ability to understand their pretherapy self-image. However, at the close of therapy, the therapists understood the self-image of the improved patients significantly better than they did those who were unimproved. Also there was a significant gain in the therapists' empathy score between the first (E_1) and second (E_2) occasions—but only for the improved cases. This result showed that there was a significant relation between improvement and increased understanding. For those who were rated unimproved through therapy, the therapists made no significant gain in their understanding of them.

Perhaps the explanation of the relation between high posttherapy empathy and improvement is not the obvious one, that the therapist coming to understand his

TABLE 1   *Mean Scores on Patients' Need to Change and Therapists' Empathy for the Improved and Unimproved Patients*

VARIABLES	IMPROVED[a]	UNIMPROVED[b]	t	df
Need to change	47.26	20.00	3.17†	26
Pre-T empathy (E_1)	15.93	16.69	—	
Post-T empathy (E_2)	9.40	14.46	2.24*	26

Note. — Since the Empathy Score is based on a D^2 measure, the lower the score the greater the empathy.
[a]$N = 15$.
[b]$N = 13$.
*$p > 0.02$.
†$p > 0.01$.

patient's own view of himself contributes to more and better therapeutic work being done. Perhaps, instead of the therapist coming to understand the patient, the patient is adopting his therapist's view of him. This alternate view might well account for the results. Such a change would make it easier for the therapist to predict how the patient "sees himself" and also possibly be valued as a growth in insight making it more likely that the case be rated "improved." We have, then, to test: do improved cases change so that their post-therapy self-description resembles the description the therapist made of them at pretherapy time more closely than their pretherapy self-description did. The chi square test here was significant in the opposite direction. At posttherapy, 11 of the improved cases descriptions of themselves were *less* like the therapists' pretherapy descriptions of them than they had originally been, and only 4 were more like them. For the unimproved group the reverse relationship was found, 9 cases were more like their therapists' pretherapy conceptions of them and only 4 were less like them. Improvement, then, goes with a patient change away from the therapist's early conception of him. Is the therapist's posttherapy conception of the patient then less like his pretherapy self-description and more like the patient's self-conception? The answer, given by a

highly significant chi square, is yes for patients rated improved. The therapists of improved cases have changed their conceptions of the patients in ways that bring them closer to the patients' own view.

Perhaps the improved cases stayed longer and so these therapists had more contact time within which to improve their understanding. Actually, the improved cases had fewer interviews ($M = 37.33$) than the unimproved cases ($M = 43.69$, a nonsignificant difference). Thus neither a change to resemble the therapists earlier views nor the amount of contact alone accounts for the relation found here between improvement in therapy and increase in the level of understanding of the patient by the close of therapy.

Hypothesis 3: The two variables considered jointly will give a better prediction of outcome than either taken singly. By taking the two variables together, improvement and length of treatment, some interesting differences were revealed. Dividing the cases at the median by length into Long (25 or more interviews) and Short (less than 25), and into Improved (Improvement score 10 or greater) and Unimproved (Improvement score 9 or less) four subgroups were formed. Table 2 gives the means for these groups on the two measures.

Schematically, then, the relations be-

TABLE 2 Patients' Need to Change, Therapists' Empathy for Four Improvement
        Subgroups

GROUP	PATIENTS' NEED TO CHANGE		THERAPISTS' E_1		THERAPISTS' E_2		EMPATHY CHANGE $E_1 - E_2$
	M	Rank	M	Rank	M	Rank	M
Short Improved $N = 8$	56.62	1	12.37	1	10.12	2	2.2
Long Improved $N = 7$	36.57	2	20.00	4	8.57	1	11.4
Short Unimproved $N = 6$	17.66	4	19.83	3	18.16	4	1.6
Long Unimproved $N = 7$	22.00	3	14.00	2	11.28	3	2.7

tween the variables were as follows:

Length improvement	Need to change	Empathy (E_1)
Short improved	High	High
Long improved	High	Low
Short unimproved	Low	Low
Long unimproved	Low	High

In terms of the joint consideration of the patient's need to change and the therapist's empathic understanding, several generalizations can now be offered.

Therapy is short when either of two conditions obtains. (*a*) Both the patient's need to change and the therapist's understanding of the patient are high. Although the mean number of interviews is small, these cases leave therapy with high improvement scores. (*b*) The patient's need to change and the therapist's understanding of him are both low. These cases leave therapy in an equally short time but as unimproved.

Therapy is long, on the other hand, under two other conditions. (*a*) The patient's need to change is high but the therapist initially misperceives him. The high degree of patient motivation to change seems to be sufficient to keep him in contact long enough for the therapist to correct his misperception and come to

see the patient in his own terms ($E_1 = 20.00$, $E_2 = 8.57$). These are long term cases but do eventually leave improved. (*b*) The therapist understands the patient's self-conception but the patient doesn't really want to change. The high understanding probably has sufficient reward value to keep the patient in contact but without the internal pressure to change or recognition that change is possible, he eventually leaves therapy unimproved.

Part II. Having reached this stage in the analysis, the study might well have been concluded. However, further questions kept occurring for which some clarification might be reached by searching the available data in new ways.

The finding that therapists varied in their level of understanding of their patients' self-conceptions after an exposure of only two interviews was not surprising. Nor was it surprising to find that some therapists, whose first attempts at understanding their patients were pretty wide of the mark, increased their understanding to a high level by the time therapy had drawn to a close. However, since there was a strong relationship between the therapist's ability to understand his patient's self-conception at the close of therapy and the outcome of the case, there was interest in discovering what characteristics of the relationship made the initial understanding either easy or difficult, and what characteristics were related to an improvement in understanding through time. The first of these characteristics to be investigated was the sex of the therapy pair.

Sex. Therapists obtained significantly higher empathy scores on the first occasion with patients of the opposite sex than with patients of the same sex. By the time therapy had been completed this difference no longer held. It seemed that the therapists had more initial difficulty understanding patients of like sex than of the opposite sex but that this handicap was overcome with time. (Therapists' empathy for clients of like sex did increase significantly $t = 2.37$, $p < 0.05$, df 13.) Perhaps therapists at the beginning of their contacts with patients of the same-sex err in understanding by assuming that they are more like themselves than is warranted. This assumption of similarity would be less likely to occur with patients of the opposite sex, leaving the therapist freer from a projective set and more open to discovering how it is that the patient views himself.

Distance. *"In order to test the suggested explanation of the effect of the sex pairing on empathy, a distance measure was devised. First the actual similarity in the ratings that the therapist and patient each made to describe themselves was calculated. The squared discrepancy between these was called a measure of their "Real Similarity." Next the similarity of the therapist's description of his patient and of himself was calculated. The squared discrepancy between these two was called a measure of the therapist's "Assumed Similarity." The difference between the Real and Assumed similarity scores was used as a measure of the distance the therapist placed between himself and the patient. If he "assumed" more similarity than was "real" he was erring psychologically by bringing the patient closer to himself than was represented by the reality distance between their two self-ratings. These errors were scored with a positive sign and are referred to as errors in the direction of reducing the distance. If the therapist assumed less similarity than was real he erred in the direction of putting the patient farther from him than corresponded to the real difference in their ratings. These errors were scored with a negative sign and referred to as errors of increasing the distance."*

Therapists on the first testing occasion reduced the distance with same-sex patients and increased the distance with opposite-sex patients. This tendency

TABLE 3   *Sex of Therapist–Patient Pairs and Empathy, Improvement, and Distancing*

VARIABLES	SAME SEX[a]	OPPOSITE SEX[b]	t	df
E_1	20.21	12.35	2.278†	26
E_2	12.00	11.50	—	
$E_{1,2}$	8.21	0.85	1.777*	26
Improvement	10.00	9.35	—	
Distancing	+5.21	−6.42	2.211†	26

[a]$N = 14$.
[b]$N = 14$.
*$p < 0.10$.
†$p < 0.05$.

would seem to help to account for the finding of poorer initial empathy with same-sex than with opposite-sex patients. It appears from Table 3 that therapists potentially can understand patients of either sex equally well (E$_2$ 12.00 and E$_2$ 11.50) but that the initial assumption that the self-images of same-sex patients will be more like their own than in fact they are, temporarily delays the full operation of the empathic capacity. Although therapists also err initially with patients of the opposite sex by overemphasizing the differences between them, this negative distancing does not seem to interfere markedly with the empathy score. That is to say, therapists may incorrectly perceive the patient as very different from themselves and still perceive the way he sees himself reasonably accurately.

Distance, Sex, and Improvement. Now what is the effect of this initial distancing of same- and opposite-sex patients on their eventual therapeutic gain? Table 4 shows that the therapist's initial distancing of both same- and opposite-sex patients who were judged improved at termination was considerably more extreme than his distancing of those who were judged unimproved. Although both improved sex groups were subject to large distancing errors, these were in op-

posite directions. The same-sex patients who improved in therapy were initially seen by the therapist as more like himself than their own ratings would suggest. This reduction of distance seems to imply an immediate emotional acceptance of these people. In contrast, the same-sex patients who were subsequently rated as unimproved were held off emotionally at the beginning of therapy and seen by the therapist as more different from him than their own ratings placed them as being. For the opposite-sex patient the relationships were reversed. The opposite-sex patients who improved in therapy were early seen by their therapist as being very different from him — more different than their self-ratings showed them to be. This viewing the opposite-sex patient as very different seemed to imply a classification of, and insistence upon, the sex role distinction. The cross-sex patients who failed to improve were not seen by the therapist as occupying a pattern distinct from his own. They were seen as being about as much like the therapist as their self-ratings showed them to be.

The really big difference was between same- and opposite-sex patients who improved. Same-sex patients who improved were early accepted by the therapist as very like him and opposite-sex patients who improved were early seen as very different.

TABLE 4   Effect of Distancing of Same- and Opposite-Sex Patients on the Improved and Unimproved Cases

	DISTANCING				
SEX PAIRING	Improved	Unimproved	t	df	p
Same sex	+14.00 N = 10	−6.50 N = 4	2.594	12	0.02
Opposite sex	−11.85 N = 6	−1.00 N = 8	2.893	12	0.02
t	4.649	0.797			
df	14	10			
p	0.001	ns			

Experience of the Therapist. The effect of the experience level of the therapist on distancing, empathy, and improvement was investigated next. Eight of the therapists were classified as more experienced, on the grounds of having handled more than five research cases prior to the present one, and eight were classified as inexperienced, having treated fewer than five. For five of the therapists the present case was the first one. The experienced therapists made distancing errors in both directions with about equal frequency. They were as likely to err in the direction of seeing more similarity than actually present as they were to see less. The inexperienced therapists, though, had a significant bias in the direction of the negative errors. Inexperienced therapists tend to see patients as less like them than the patients' own views show them to be. Perhaps what one learns as a result of experience in doing therapy is that nothing human is really foreign to us. Or perhaps it is that the new therapist is more open to threat and more easily made anxious by seeing patients as similar to himself and so does more defensive distancing.

Now to relate these various findings to improvement with psychotherapy, it appears that improvement was rated high for two groups of patients: same-sex patients treated by experienced therapists, and opposite-sex patients treated by inexperienced therapists. In both groups the therapists' posttherapy level of empathy (E_2) was high and the original distancing of the patient by the therapist extreme. The experienced therapist achieved high empathy and improvement with same-sex patients with whom the psychological distance was immediately reduced and the inexperienced therapist achieved high empathy and improvement with opposite-sex patients with whom distance was immediately increased.

Discussion

The study shows that psychoneurotic patients have the best chance for a successful treatment experience with nondirective therapy, if they come to it with a high need to change, and meet a therapist who can accurately understand the way they see themselves. Some patients meet with therapists who have difficulty perceiving them in their own terms. If they have sufficiently high motivation to change they continue in therapy, and the therapist does come to understand more accurately how it is they see themselves.

For the therapist to improve his understanding in this way he must have more access to material relevant to the task. Presumably he misperceives originally because of barriers to this material, either in himself which distort his perceptions, or because of barriers in the patient which prevent him from revealing himself accurately. Barriers of both kinds are, in all likelihood, related to defenses against the potential threat involved in conscious recognition. If threat is reduced in the patient he would be more able to communicate personally relevant material to the therapist. This in turn would enable the therapist to base his view of his patient's self-image on a deeper understanding of him. If threat is reduced in the therapist he would be freer to perceive the patient's communications without distortions.

It would seem that the inexperienced therapist is the more open to threat in this situation than is the experienced therapist, and, in truth, it is he who tends to increase the distance with his patients. This in effect denies some of the similarity between himself and his patients which can be interpreted as a defensive maneuver to reduce his threat. This distancing might well be experienced by his patients as a message to the effect that "you are really very different from me." Such a message would probably raise the threat level of the same-sex patients but reduce it for opposite-sex patients. The experienced therapist who has less personal threat decreases distance between himself and his same-sex patients and conveys by this, "you are really much more like me than you think you are." This message from a prestigeful person of the same sex probably reduces the patient's threat level. This tentative explanation would account for the high improvement and final level of empathic understanding of the same-sex patients treated by experienced therapists and of the opposite-sex patients treated by inexperienced therapists.

References

Butler, J. M., & Haigh, G. V. Changes in the relation between self-concepts and ideal concepts consequent upon client-centered counseling in *Psychotherapy and personality change*. In Carl R. Rogers & Rosalind F. Dymond (Eds.), Chicago: Univer. Chicago Press, 1954. Pp. 55–75.

Cartwright, D. S., & Cartwright, Rosalind D. Faith and improvement in psychotherapy. *J. counsel. Psychol.*, 1958, **5**, 174–177.

Fiedler, F. E. A comparison of therapeutic relationships in psychoanalytic, non-directive, and Adlerian therapy. *J. consult. Psychol*, 1950, **14**, 436–445. (a)

Fiedler, F. E. The concept of the ideal therapeutic relationship. *J. consult. Psychol.*, 1950, **14**, 239–245. (b)

Heine, R. W. An investigation of the relationship between changes and the responsible factors as seen by clients following treatment by psychotherapists of the psychoanalytic, Adlerian, and non-directive schools. Unpublished doctoral dissertation, University of Chicago, 1950.

Kelley, G. *The psychology of personal constructs*. New York: Norton, 1955.

Kirtner, W., & Cartwright, D. S. Success and failure in client-centered therapy as a function of initial in-therapy behavior. *J. consult. Psychol.*, 1958, **22**, 329–333.

Rosenthal, D., & Frank, J. Psychotherapy and the placebo effect. *Psychol. Bull.*, 1956, **53**, 294–302.

4. Rogers' Self Theory and Eysenck's Extraversion and Neuroticism

FRANK J. VINGOE

The present paper presents evidence which supports Rogers' Self Theory. The Ss were 66 freshmen women who rated themselves and their peers on 6 personality variables. Measures of self-awareness were determined by the congruence between self-ratings and mean peer-ratings, while measures of self-acceptance were determined by the congruence between self-ratings and social desirability ratings. Neurotics were found to be less self-aware and self-acceptant than normals, although the former only approached significance. There was no difference between Introverts and Extraverts in self-awareness, but Introverts were found significantly less self-acceptant than Extraverts.

Many psychologists, particularly Carl Rogers, consider that one of the factors necessary for good interpersonal relationships is awareness and acceptance of self (Rogers, 1958). The studies on self-acceptance and acceptance of others (Medinnus & Curtis, 1963; Omwake, 1954; Sheerer, 1949) lend support to Rogers' ideas. Rogers' work strongly suggests that neurotic and stable groups should be significantly different on the variables of self-awareness and self-acceptance. However, in a study (Vingoe, 1966) in which Ss were required to predict their position on

SOURCE. *Article by Frank J. Vingoe, "Rogers' self theory and Eysenck's extraversion and neuroticism in the* Journal of consulting and clinical psychology, *Vol. 32, pp. 618–620, 1968. Copyright 1968 by the American Psychological Association and reprinted by permission.*

the introversion-extraversion continuum it was suggested that neurotics were as self-aware as normals. This study also indicated that introverts were somewhat more aware of their position on the introversion-extraversion continuum than extraverts.

The purpose of this paper is to relate measures of self-awareness and self-acceptance to Eysenck's dimensions of extraversion and neuroticism. The following hypotheses were made: (1) Neurotics will be significantly less self-acceptant than Normals (Rogers, 1958); (2) Extraverts and Introverts will not differ in self-acceptance; (3) Extraverts will be significantly less self-aware than Introverts (Vingoe, 1966); and (4) Neurotics and Normals will not differ in self-awareness.

METHOD

The Ss consisted of 66 freshmen women who resided in the same University of Oregon dormitory. These Ss were told only that E was doing some research in the area of personality and that he needed to see them as a group, for 2 hours of psychological testing (Phase 1) and individually for an hour's interview (Phase 2). The results of Phase 2 are presented elsewhere (Vingoe, 1967). All Ss were unmarried. Their mean age was 18.0 years.

Procedure

The assessment instruments were administered in the following order: (a) the Self-rating Booklet, (b) the California Psychological Inventory (CPI; Gough, 1964), (c) the Eysenck Personality Inventory (EPI; Eysenck & Eysenck, 1963), and (d) the Peer-rating Booklet.

The Ss rated themselves and their peers on the variables of Dominance, Sociability, Responsibility, Psychological-mindedness, Self-acceptance, and Extraversion. Definitions of each variable were given, based upon the descriptions of these variables in the manuals for the CPI (Gouch, 1964, pp. 10–11) and the EPI (Eysenck & Eysenck, 1963, pp. 4–5). The Self-rating Booklet asked four questions in reference to these variables; each S was asked (a) to rate herself in terms of the degree of each trait she felt she had (Self-ratings); (b) how she would like to be rated (on the average) by the girls on her wing (Social Desirability Ratings); (c) if the other girls on her wing were to rate her what average rating did she think she would get (Estimated Mean Peer-ratings; and (d) how she though most University of Oregon girls would like to be rated on the average (Perceived Social Desirability Ratings). The Peer-rating Booklet asked each S to rate her peers, specifically the other girls in their dormitory wing, on the traits indicated above. All ratings were made on a 7-point scale from 1, which indicates the ratee is very low on the characteristic, to 7, which indicates the ratee fits the description of the trait very well. The booklet also asked each rater to rate the degree to which each ratee is known. Only those peer-ratings based on the two highest degrees of acquaintance were used to calculate self-awareness scores. Both the Self-rating and the Peer-rating Booklets were based upon material developed by Goldberg and Rorer (1963). However, for the Peer-ratings a horizontal graphic rating scale was used based on Guilford's suggestions (Guilford, 1959).

Individual measures of self-awareness were determined by the congruence between self-ratings and mean-peer-ratings on the six personality variables indicated above. Congruence was actually measured by discrepancy scores, the lower the discrepancy score, the higher the congruence. The discrepancy scores for each of the six variables were summed to obtain a total measure of self-awareness.

Individual measures of self-acceptance were determined by the discrepancy scores between self-ratings and social-desirability ratings on the six personality variables. As with the self-awareness discrepancy scores, the six discrepancy scores for self-acceptance were summed to obtain a total measure of self-acceptance.

The reliability of the self-ratings was established by having Ss rate themselves on the six variables a second time while completing the Peer-rating Booklet. These second self-ratings were the ones used in the calculation of the self-awareness variables. The test-retest reliability of the self-ratings varied from 0.68 for Self-acceptance to 0.91 for Dominance and were considered adequate. Using recently obtained American norms (Gideon, Gordon, Jense, & Knapp, 1966), Ss were dichotomized at the median of the Extraversion scale in order to obtain Introvert and Extravert groups while the Neurotic and Stable groups were derived in a like manner. To determine if these groups differed in self-awareness and self-acceptance, t tests were calculated.

Results

The results relating to the variable of self-acceptance may be noted by referring to Table 1. Here, it is seen that Extraverts are significantly more self-acceptant than

TABLE 1 Extraversion, Neuroticism, and Self-Acceptance

GROUP	N	M	SD	t
Introvert	20	7.65	3.64	
				2.258*
Extravert	46	5.46	3.56	
Neurotic	38	7.10	4.32	
				2.388†
Stable	28	4.89	2.38	

*$p < 0.05$.
†$p < 0.01$.

Introverts. The obtained t value of 2.258 is significant beyond the 0.05 level. Thus Hypothesis 1 is not supported. This table also indicates that the stable group is significantly more self-acceptant than the Neurotic group, thus supporting Hypothesis 2 as predicted. The obtained t value of 2.388 is significant beyond the 0.01 point.

Table 2 presents data relating to the variable of self-awareness. It can be

TABLE 2 Extraversion, Neuroticism, and Self-Awareness

GROUP	N	M	SD	t
Introvert	20	7.20	2.42	
				1.424
Extravert	46	6.26	2.51	
Neurotic	37	7.04	2.51	
				1.805
Stable	29	5.92	2.38	

seen that Introverts and Extraverts are not significantly different in self-awareness. Therefore Hypothesis 3 must be rejected. The Stable and Neurotic groups are not significantly different in self-awareness, supporting Hypothesis 4.

Discussion

The particular method of measuring self-awareness by the congruency between self- and mean peer-ratings should be borne in mind in interpreting the results of this study. The criterion for individual self-awareness is thus a social one, based on the social stimulus value that the individual has for each of her peers. While Vingoe (1966) suggested that neurotics may be as self-aware as are normals, it should be noted that the measure of awareness used there was the congruency between self-rating and test score. Thus, there may be no conflict in the results of these two studies, but rather differences due to different measures. In summary, it was found that Introverts and Extraverts as defined by the EPI do not differ in self-awareness but the Extraverts are significantly more self-acceptant. In support of Rogers' self-theory, Normals were found to be more self-acceptant and self-aware than Neurotics, although the latter finding only approached significance.

References

Eysenck, H. J., & Eysenck, S. B. G. *Manual for the Eysenck Personality Inventory.* San Diego, Calif.: Educational & Industrial Testing Service, 1963.

Gideon, V. C., Gordon, R. A., Jensen, A. R., & Knapp, R. R. *Eysenck Personality Inventory—American College Norms.* San Diego, Calif.: Educational & Industrial Testing Service, 1966.

Goldberg, L. R., & Rorer, L. G. An intensive study of sociometric measures. Unpublished manuscript, Oregon Research Institute, 1963.

Gough, H. B. *Manual for the California Psychological Inventory.* Palo Alto, Calif.: Consulting Psychologists Press, 1964.

Guilford, J. P. *Personality.* New York: McGraw-Hill, 1959.

Medinnus, G. R., & Curtis, F. J. The relationship between maternal self-acceptance and child acceptance. *Journal of Consulting Psychology,* 1963, **27**, 542–544.

Omwake, K. T. The relationship between acceptance of self and acceptance of others as shown by three personality inventories. *Journal of Consulting Psychology,* 1954, **18**, 443–446.

Rogers, C. R. The characteristics of a helping relationship. *Personnel and Guidance Journal,* 1958, **37**, 6–16.

Sheerer, E. An analysis of the relationship between acceptance of and respect for the self and acceptance of and respect for others in ten counseling cases. *Journal of Consulting Psychology,* 1949, **13**, 169–175.

Vingoe, F. J. Validity of the Eysenck extraversion scale as determined by self ratings in normals. *British Journal of Social Clinical Psychology,* 1966, **5**, 89–91.

Vingoe, F. J. Self awareness, self-acceptance and hypnotizability. *Journal of Abnormal Psychology,* 1967, **72**, 454–456.

Existential Psychology

Existential psychology as a systematic conception of personality is a relative newcomer among personality theories. Although its philosophical roots have a long history, the application of existential thinking to psychology and psychiatry has been recent. The impact of existentialism on contemporary psychology continues to grow, and this growth is having its greatest impact on clinical and personality psychology. To some readers this may seem paradoxical, since much of contemporary personality theorizing and research appears to be moving in a direction opposite to that of existential theory. The foundation of much current research is logical positivism, laboratory experimentation with well-controlled experimental designs, and statistical analyses. The foundation of existential psychology is phenomenology, which examines any phenomenon as it relates to the "being" of the person. Thus existentialism explicitly rejects the philosophy of science upon which most traditional personality experimentation is based.

Existentialism not only questions the philosophical base that most personality theories are built upon, but it also questions and challenges basic tenets of most personality theories. For example, the effort to study personality by referring to a single aspect of personality, such as a biological or a learning component, is antithetical to the phenomenological notion that no one dimension of a person can be understood isolated from his entire existence in the world.

Given the way in which research is characterized by existential writers, it is hardly surprising that it is difficult to distinguish what one can consider as primary sources from research reports. The selections chosen for this section are drawn from Binswanger, Straus, and Boss. Clearly they have been among the most influencial contemporary existential-phenomenological theorists. The writings of Binswanger and Boss were the foundations upon which the chapter on existential psychology was built in *Theories of Personality*.

In the first selection Boss provides an existential analysis of love, and in it the unique flavor of existentialism is displayed. Love has not been the subject of much research in personality psychology, and one can see how Boss rejects the ideas of many previous writers on the topic as he offers his own distinctively phenomenological ideas.

Boss rejects the emphasis placed on the pathology of love relations that have been the subject of most psychological discussions of love. Instead he proposes an analysis of love as manifested in nonpathological instances, and he believes the study of normative love relations must precede the study of pathology. Using the phenomenological method love is viewed quite differently from what has typically been seen by "objective" investigators. As described by Boss, the individual who can be in a love relationship is a person who can experience an existence without barriers.

In the next paper, "Norm and pathology of I-world relations," Straus shows how several major ideas of existentialism are related to Heidegger's *Being and Time*. Men cannot be understood in the same way that "things" are understood, since men are not "objects" in existential psychology. To understand a person, one must know him as a "subject" not as an "object," or in Martin Buber's terms, we must become engaged with a person in an "I-thou" relationship. Existentialism rejects division of man into components such as electrical, chemical, or behavioral. Man must be studied as Being-in-the-world.

Binswanger's discussion of Heidegger's analytic of existence is the topic of the third paper in this section. In it a full discussion is presented of the implications of existential psychology for psychiatry and clinical psychology. This discussion touches upon such topics as the method of psychiatry, one's conception of patients, the unconscious, mind-body dualism, and the patient-therapist relationship. The student can see from these selections what implications existential psychology has for a theory of human behavior.

1. The Norm of Love—Psychologic Comments

M. BOSS

If the perverted love reality has thus been greatly neglected by the "anthropologic" investigators, it also has been mistreated by the psychoanalytic perversion theory, which, in fitting perverted love reality into a libido theory, reduced it to mere instinct. The reason for this violation and neglect is to be found in the fact that prior to Freud psychologic science did not take the phenomenon of love seriously. This is quite in contrary to the deep and ancient knowledge of love, which all poets and mystics have had since time immemorial.[1] Only in these last years psychologic science is beginning to appreciate, to see, and to define again the whole reality of love. It is obvious, though, that an adequate scientific analysis of love is the necessary basis for any investigation which delves into the meaning and content of any kind of love disturbance.

M. Scheler[2]—one of the most important scientific critics of Freud—said: "The great error of the naturalistic-sensual philosophy of A. Schopenhauer and S. Freud is that it regards sexual love as a secondary phantastic super-position of the rude sex drive, which has originated in a repression of instincts." However, Scheler makes a new abstraction from love. He formulates the conception of a "personal act," and since he defines a person as a center of those acts, such things as act centers should then be capable of love. At about the same time Allers offers a more tentative start to an understanding of the essence of love. He writes[3]: "In my opinion the deepest

SOURCE. *Selection from M. Boss, "The norm of love—psychologic comments" in* Meaning and Content of Sexual Perversion, *pp. 27–34. New York: Grune and Stratton, 1949.*

[1]See the Aristophanic story in Plato's symposium on the primal man, who was originally round and whole, and who, as a punishment for his arrogance, was cut in half. Compared to this legend all other hitherto formulated explanations of love seem to be more or less narrowed or differentiated variations of its meaning. It is characteristic for Freud's theory that in his *physical-reducing* thinking he misinterprets this legend as an illustration of the repetition compulsion and the death instinct, which would transfer all organic matter to the dead inorganic world. However, the legend obviously represents love as an endeavor of man to return to the most vivid male-female completeness. (S. Freud: Jenseits des Lustprinzips. Ges. Schr. *VI*:250). Compare also the statements on love made by Boehme and his successor Franz von Baader, and the collection of the most beautiful poems in L. Binswanger's: Grundformen und Erkenntnis menschlichen Daseins.

[2]*Ibid.*, p. 136.

[3]*Ibid.*, p. 469.

meaning of love lies in its moving toward a direction of a *We*-formation, of a higher unity of the *We*, which can exist at peace with itself and be self-sufficient." Jaspers describes the reality of love still more completely as follows: "Love as an 'enthusiastic attitude' is absolutely different from all the other possible attitudes; inasmuch as love's submission is strictly opposed to the limitations and isolations of the worldly everyday, objective, self-reflecting attitudes, for example. Here we have the separation of pathways, the setting-up of boundaries, the activity limited by time and space. In love, on the other side, we find the conquering of all boundaries and the active and visionary comprehension of super-earthly values in the earthiness." Jaspers continues: "Love is a movement within us through all concrete things (into the objective world and returning back to ourselves) into the absolute and the totality. Everything is illuminated by this movement of love." In love the object, be it as variegated in the concrete as it may be, is fixed in a specific way. The object rests in the totality of the world, it is trans-illuminated by a ray of light from the absolute and it is connected with the absolute. In Christian words: The object is seen in God, not isolated; it is realized not as a limited fact, but as imbedded in infinity. The tendency is directed towards the whole. Since this "totality" can never be an immediate object of the human intellectual structure, it is seen through a finite object, which thus assumes a peculiar light, or rather, represents this glimmer of the absolute. Jaspers explains all this as characteristic of the experience and he goes on to say: "This is what it means, it offers no metaphysic explanation. It is justifiable for the psychologic description to take up these metaphysic conceptions from everywhere; they are expression phenomena of experiences, and the experience can

be elucidated best by these conceptions 'as though' it were metaphysically really so, which is never decided in this connection."[4]

These formulations by Jaspers, being no speculative interpretations, but only descriptions of actually experienced facts of love, represent just as much reality as any theory of an exact scientist. Any person thinking in exact scientific terms who scorns these love realities as described by Jaspers succeeds only — without his realizing it — in stressing his own vanity. He turns into an intellectual usurper and finally he forgets that the reality of his own experience can be proven just as much or as little as those of a lover.

L. Binswanger recently presented a still more profound scientific interpretation of the essence and significance of love. He based his work on Jasper's formulations as well as on the fundamental ontology of Heidegger[5]. Binswanger[6] does not any more speak of love as of a "movement," and "act" or a certain "orientation" (Plato, Scheler, Allers, Jaspers), nor does he mistake love for a mere sentiment, a feeling, an affect, or a more or less sublimated impulse, according to the older naturalistic theories. He does not intellectually dissolve and destroy the loving person by way of a unilateral theoretic perspective into the abstractions of such objective psychologic notions. Rather he realizes that love deserves the name of a very special mode of existing. To be man, to exist, also means always, and from the very beginning, to exist within a world and to have a world. Therefore, if the lover is existing in a specific way, his world, his love-world in which he exists and which he owns, corresponds to his spec-

[4] K. Jaspers: *Psychologie der Weltanschauungen*. 3rd edition, Berlin, 1925, p. 118.

[5] M. Heidegger: *Sein und Zeit*.

[6] L. Binswanger: *Grundformen und Erkenntnis menschlichen Daseins*, p. 640.

ific mode of existing. Neither this declaration nor Jaspers' Phenomenology of Love can be called an unrealistic abstraction or speculation. These statements really cover the nearest facts; that they have been so close to us is the very reason that our thinking has overlooked them for so long a time. Nothing is more certain than the fact that a lover experiences himself as well as his surroundings in which he lives and loves, in a completely different manner than he does at times when he lives as a scientific researcher, a merchant, or a soldier, and has to deal with the practical aspects of these worlds.

If we accept this simple and well-known fact seriously, we are forced to discard the naïve philosophic premise of an a priori existing objectivity, the prejudice that all human beings possess only the one objective world of concrete rational thinking as their reality.

However, already the sober biologist, von Uexkuell,[7] in his investigations of the surroundings of animals has demonstrated that "it is nothing but laziness of our mind, if we start out with the existence of a single objective world (psychiatrists call it naïvely *the* reality)." Although, because of some biologic misunderstandings, this author cannot yet fully differentiate between the rigidly prescribed animal world and the more or less free world of man, he has demonstrated that there are vast differences in perceiving one and the same object of the world by various kinds of animals. But he also has pointed out how differently an oak tree in the woods is observed and experienced by a hunter, a romantic young girl or a practical lumber dealer[8]. Even the worlds of lovers are different

among themselves: they are as variegated and manifold as there exist ways and possibilities of love. C. G. Jung[9] was the first among modern psychologists to recognize the precise correlation between the inner structure of the soul and the outer worldly possibilities of love for humans. He has demonstrated the strict relationship between "animus" and "anima" (which are his names for these intrapsychic images of male and female essence) and the chosen empiric concrete love partners of the outer world. This represents a correction of Klages'[10] one-sided misleading definition of love as a lonely idiopathic erotic intoxication. At the same time C. G. Jung developed a clear and decisive insight into the general correlative unity of man's Self and the picture of his world which will become so decisive for our own investigations.

There is no doubt that in the future — and this refers to nuclear physics as well as to psychology and to anthropology — we shall have to learn to see our intrapsychic states and outer world perceptions, our self-structure and our world-image, subjectivity and objectivity, no more as strictly divided independent facts, but as strictly correlated manifestations of our human existence.

Therefore, too, the nature of love in particular can best be interpreted from the special structure and character of the lover's world. This world of the lovers is characterized by the fact that no barriers exist in it, that all intentions towards separate worldly limited finite objects are abandoned. Contrary to this, the world of a person who exists only as a human being of practical purposes, is always

---

[7]Von Uexkuell: *Nie geschaute Welten. Die Umwelten meiner Freunde*, p. 20.

[8]Van Uexkuell: *Theoretische Biologie*, 2nd edition, p. 232.

[9]Compare C. G. Jung: *Die Beziehungen zwischen dem Ich und dem Unbewussten*. Darmstadt, 1928, p. 117. Also: *Psychologie und Alchemie*, Zuerich.

[10]L. Klages: *Vom kosmogonischen Eros*. 3rd edition, Jena 1930, p. 76.

divided into a thousand stubborn, potentially hostile individuals and objects. In this form of existence he experiences only sorrow, worldly limitations and emptiness. The lover, however, existing in the "dual mode of existence" of love (Binswanger) has overcome all anxiety and narrowness, every meaninglessness and nothingness. Human existence reaches it maximum of possibilities in the loving communion of "You and I"; loving man experiences infinity and eternity and he finds himself deeply rooted in the ground of his existence. Binswanger expresses this mode of being in words which are very similar to Jasper's formulation. He states: "Man as a lover is at home and safe in his world and is aware of the abundance of his possibilities. He recognizes himself and his beloved partner no more as limited, concrete, separate fleeting phenomena, but 'You and I' becomes transparent for the primal and eternal image of the perfect human being, at peace with himself and devoid of desire and intentions. Therefore, in the state of love and only then, a person is able to experience as an entity transitory content and eternity, fact and eidos, picture and primal image."

At all times the existential form of love, embracing all human possibilities, its totality and oneness of "You and I" is simultaneously male and female; its essence and being a continuous give and take. Binswanger adds[11]: "The true unity of 'You and I,' the true 'We' is always male and female in the dual meaning that the unity itself is male-female, and that each separate member of it is male-female." Each partner is creative-productive as well as creative-receptive. The inconceivable, incomprehensible quality of love is really a twofold miracle: the miracle of loving and the miracle of being loved. It is incorrect to assume that the male love is identified with loving and the female with being loved. Each love has its own way of experiencing both miracles. Whenever the highest plane of love is attained the difference between male and female love has disappeared.

Von Gebsattel, too, had advocated very strongly this totality and abundance of the male-female unity of love. More than twenty years ago he had already favored the psychologic reality of this image of the "super-individual, sexually undivided eternal man." We quote[12]: "This image is not a pattern of conceptions, it is not an idea without reality, but an existing being, filled with life and substance." A proof for this theory can easily be found in the fact that throughout the ages, from the first idols of the primitives, and the gods and mythologies of antiquity to the Christian images of God of the mystics and the alchemists, all pictures and symbols of the perfection of love and existence which human art and mind has created always refer to this spiritual and eternal image of the bisexual "anthropos." In our days still this bisexual anthropos appears as manifestation of the very effective psychic reality of the indivisible male-female entity in frequent dreams and phantasies.[13] Our present-day scientific psychology has no right to disregard these autochthonous forms of the human mind. We consider it as an unjustly biased act of the positivistic-physical intellect to exclude these manifestations of human life from the sphere of psychic realities. These forms are on an equal level with all other phenomena of human existence and thus have to be used also for a scientific understanding of the total human reality.

---

[11]Ibid., p. 683.

[12]E. v. Gebsattel: "Liebe und Ehe." *Zeitschr. f. Voelkerpsychologie und Soziologie*, vol. *I*, 1925.

[13]See also H. Schulz-Hencke: *Der gehemmte Mensch*, and M. Boss: *Die Gestalt der Ehe und ihre Zerfallsformen*, Bern, 1945.

Therefore, we do not agree with A. Kronfeld[14] who disregards them completely, calling them "pure theory" or "metaphysical premises and empirically not probable speculations." This would be comparable to a scotomization like disregarding an important and constant bodily organ.

[14]Ibid., p. 21, 65.

2. Norm and Pathology of I-World Relations

E. W. STRAUS

Heidegger's *Being and Time* (1962) made its entrance into the world of letters in an austere academic environment. The first edition was not a book in its own right. It was published in 1927 as an essay in Husserl's *Yearbook of Phenomenology*, a philosophical journal written by professionals for professionals. Yet, this newborn stood out from the other "brain children" because of its style, its scope, its themes, its depth, and its approach. The starting point was a consideration of man in everyday life, the goal was to reach an understanding of the meaning of Being, and the road leading from that start to this goal was the "analytic of *Dasein*." It is therefore not surprising that the author, the title, and even the book itself were in a short time enthusiastically accepted by many and rejected with no less passion by others.

Like so many readers, psychiatrists were fascinated by the "analytic of *Dasein*," revealing the basic structure of "existence" as being-in-the-world and being-with, dealing with such topics as authenticity and in-authenticity, thrown-ness and project, dread and care, call of conscience and resolve, finiteness and temporality.

The Swiss psychiatrist Ludwig Binswanger (1958, 1960) became convinced that, with *Being and Time*, the philosophical foundation of psychiatry had finally been established. He tried to apply Heidegger's philosophy of existence to psychiatry, to translate the "analytic of *Dasein*" into *Daseinsanalysen* (existential analyses). Yet, on his way back and down from the ontological level to the ontic sphere he had appalling obstacles to overcome. Care, thrownness, and project in Heidegger's work, just as bad faith, freedom, and choice in Sartre's philosophy, are ontological concepts. How can these existentials be applied to the lives of individuals—to their actions and motions? The crucial point is the exalted position which Heidegger assigns to man. "Concerned about his Being and behaving toward his Being as toward his own possibilities" (Heidegger, 1960, p. 42), man appears to him different from all other beings—not only from inanimate things and man-made machines but also radically different from all other living creatures. For this reason, Heidegger rejects the traditional definition of man as a rational animal. He acknowledges, of

SOURCE. *Selection from E. W. Straus, "Norm and pathology of I-World relations" in* Phenomenological psychology: The selected papers of Erwin Straus, *pp. 255–260. New York: Basic Books, 19X6.*

course, our kinship with the animals, yet he emphasizes that man in his existence is separated from them by a very abyss (Heidegger, 1962, p. 12). One cannot ask, according to Heidegger, What man is; still less can one answer this question. One can only ask for the Who and the How. There is no unchangeable order of natural qualities characteristic for the species, no essence in the traditional meaning of the term, which ultimately characterizes man. Therefore, Binswanger (1947) adds, one cannot make man the object of research. We understand the other only as a partner in an I-thou relation.

These theorems lead to serious consequences when applied to psychiatry. If it makes no sense to ask what man is, we no longer see him as a living creature in health and disease. Heidegger was familiar with these and other facts of life; the problem is whether and how he or his followers can incorporate such themes as physical existence, sexuality, animal nature, or disease into his ontological system. Actually, Binswanger leaves no doubt that his *Daseinanalyse* is by no means a specifically psychiatric method. That he used it primarily for the interpretation of schizophrenic cases is a kind of professional accident. Binswanger's existential analyses of Ellen West, Lola Voss, etc. move between the poles of authenticity and inauthenticity, of floundered and accomplished forms of existence—but not between normal and abnormal, healthy and sick. "Existential analysis," Binswanger wrote in 1945, "is not a psychopathology, nor is it clinical research nor any kind of objectifying research. Its results have first to be recast by psychopathology into forms that are peculiar to it, such as that of a psychic organism, or even of a psychic apparatus, in order to be projected onto the physical organism" (1947, p. 216).

However this may be, I shall make clinical experience my point of departure. In turning my attention to a typical case, I do not regard him as an apparatus but as an experiencing creature. Here, I believe I am entitled to claim Heidegger, if not as my master, at least as an ally, for two reasons: First, we encounter the mental patient as a stranger in our everyday-life world (*Lebenswelt*, Husserl's terminology). Whatever theories we may offer to explain psychotic behavior— whether we accept the thesis that mental diseases are brain diseases or search for a conflict between ego and id, ego and reality, and ego and superego—the frame of reference from which we start and to which we return is the structure of the everyday-life world. When Freud speaks about a break with reality, he refers to the reality familiar and common to all of us— the reality of so-called naïve realism. This is the same for the learned and the illiterate, for the rich and the poor, for Lumumba and Hammerskjold. Its characteristics are not taught in school. We live it, enact it, and respond to it, but we do not know it. Indeed, the failure of the mental patient to conform may cause us to stop and think about the *Lebenswelt*. Psychoses are, so to speak, basic experiments arranged by nature; the clinical wards are the natural laboratories where we begin to wonder about the structure of the *Lebenswelt*. We realize that, in order to account for its breakdown, we have to study its norm first. We suddenly notice that we are beginners in a field where we deemed ourselves masters.

Another obstacle exists. The discovery or rediscovery of the *Lebenswelt* has been blocked by a scientific tradition reaching back into antiquity. The *Lebenswelt* was held in contempt and despised as illusory. Modern science has been even more radical in its censure and its demands. The world as it appears to us in its macroscopic structure and with its sensory qualities must be reduced to atomic events. This reduction supposedly leads from a mere appearance, in the sense of an apparition, to the real core of things. The scientific credo professes as an article of common faith, Lashley said, that "all phenomena of behavior and of mind are ultimately describable in the concepts of the mathematical and physical sciences" (1952, p. 112). The paradoxical consequence is that the science of physics must be understood as groups of physical events. Most psychologists, therefore, refuse to waste time in contemplating physics as a human accomplishment which originates in the *Lebenswelt*. They take the possibility of observing for granted. Satisfied with measurement, they do not inquire into the psychological conditions of measuring. The tables are turned; the physicist himself, or man—in all his activities—is considered as an object of physics, a body among other bodies. Human experience and conduct must forcibly be adapted to the ruling system of physicalistic concepts. But this theoretical bias obscures the very sight of the phenomena. Inadvertently and unintentionally, they are assimilated to the "underlying neural mechanisms." The dogma has it that sensations, perceptions, thoughts, and memories occur *within* a particular organism, accompanying excitations of the nervous system. They are side effects, like sparks flashing with the turn of synaptic switches which transmit afferent impulses to the motorium. Experience, and sensory experience, is supposed to be merely "subjective."

Since the days of Galileo, subjectivity has been interpreted in spatial terms. Sensory qualities do not reside—to use Galileo's terminology—in things themselves; they reside in our minds. Today, we let them reside in our brains. From their supposedly original position, percepts are carried outward—through reality testing, projection, or some other voodoo procedure—and finally located in an external world to which none of us has any direct access. Scientific theory, based on Galileo's, Descartes', and Hobbes' metaphysics, teaches a radical sejunction of subject and object. The experiencing creature is cut off from the world.

In the practice of life, however, we do not place others in an outside world; we meet them on common ground. Obviously, the reduction cannot be unilateral. One cannot reduce qualities to cortical stimulation and then talk about our brain. If the sensory qualities are relative to man, man is relative to them. The reduction does not actually change the appearance of things; it is performed in thoughts and words. The physicist never leaves the shores of the *Lebenswelt*. In fact, the reduction of the *Lebenswelt* silently presupposes its validity. We are *in* the world, not outside. There, we are in contact with all things in sight and in reach. The senses do not provide us with mere sensory data. In seeing, we are confronted with the objects themselves, not with their pictorial representations. The act of seeing demands our presence; it commits us to a definite position in relation to our environment. In sensory experience, we are aware of things *and* ourselves; not one before the other, not one without the other. This is the second point where I am at least in partial agreement with Heidegger, who, in the "analytic of *Dasein*," refutes the traditional subject–object dichotomy. I have avoided his telling term "being-in-the-world," because in *Being and Time* it is understood as an ontological concept. It signifies that mode of being which makes the ontic structure of human life possible and understandable. For this reason, the existential being-in-the-world is limited to *Dasein* and cannot be applied to sensory experience in general, i.e., not to animal experience. But medical anthropology cannot omit life and the animal nature of man, although man can and usually does detach himself from the primary modes of contact which he has in common with the animals.

All scientific observation begins on the level of sensory experience, but not all sensory experience ends on that level. Those who run for safety in a hurricane do not measure its velocity. Science demands a detached observer who projects events on an impersonal frame of reference that can always be identified and reconstructed. In science, observers are exchangeable; they all sit in the audience and watch the events on the stage. In primary sensory experience, however, there is no division of space into stage and auditorium; everyone is in the arena. In sensory experience, we are not neutral observers watching the outcome of remote events through a one-way mirror; we are affected, caught, seized, in an egocentric position. The light, the wind, heat and cold, and sounds and scents are obtrusive; we "realize" their impact. Things appear attractive or repulsive. We respond to their physiognomies rather than to their logical order. That we are beset is decisive; the How and What is secondary. The That of being engaged and seized precedes the What. The scientific observer explores and judges the reality of events. To him, the predicate "real" signifies that something has occurred in accordance with the established laws of nature. In sensory experience, however, "reality" has quite a different meaning; it means that something happens to me. Reality of sensory experience concerns me in my unique, vital existence. It is prior to reflection and doubt, as is so clearly demonstrated by the apodictic powers of hallucinations.

In some of my writings, I have tried to re-open the case of sensory experience, to reclaim a territory lost for a long time. In using the term aesthesiology, I have even made an attempt to reinstitute the forgotten meaning of "aisthesis." In this,

I may appear quixotic because I am compelled to challenge such generally accepted doctrines of neurophysiology as "Mind can only be regarded, for scientific purposes, as the activity of the brain" (Hebb, 1949, p. xiv). To this statement Hebb adds, "Modern psychology takes completely for granted that behavior and neural functions are perfectly correlated, that one is completely caused by the other" (1949, p. xiii). In line with this postulate, perceptions must be considered as perfectly correlated with and caused by afferent conduction and cortical excitation. Indeed, the physiological problem of thought, Hebb explains, "is that of the transmission of excitation from sensory to motor cortex" (1949, p. xvi). If this is so, sensory experience cannot add anything essential to the function of the body machine. But these speculations of a tough-minded empiricist leave us completely at a loss as to how he could account for his knowledge of the activities of the brain. For, in every neurophysiological experiment, two brains are involved: the brain observed and the observer's brain. When someone studies the brain of a man or an animal, his own brain is excited by optical stimuli reflected from the surface of some remote object. The stimuli, on their arrival on the retina, will not tell whence they came. The so-called observations must be considered as activities which are located exclusively within the observer's brain and skull, a mere transmission of excitation from sensory to motor cortex. Not even the magic of projection could transform such intracerebral excitations into an object of observation.

Through sensory experience, a new dimension is opened to the experiencing organism. This is the basic fact on which all science rests, even the denial of the fact itself. In sensory experience, we are related to objects *qua* objects, to an environment in which we can orient ourselves and act. The intentional relation to the other enables us to finally comprehend the order and relation of one object to another in the physical world. The relation of a nervous system to stimuli is not commensurate with that of an experiencing being to objects. The work of neurophysiology and psychology is contaminated by the promiscuous usage of the terms "stimulus" and "object," a confusion unpardonably confounded.

References

Binswanger, L. *Ausgewählte Vorträge und Aufsätze*. Vol. 1. Bern: A. Francke, 1947.

Binswanger, L. *The case of Ellen West*. In R. May, E. Angel, & H. Ellenberger (Eds.), *Existence: a new dimension in psychiatry*. New York: Basic Books, 1958.

Binswanger, L. Existential analysis, psychiatry, schizophrenia. *J. exist. Psychiat.*, 1960, **1** (2), 157–175.

Head, H. *Aphasia and kindred disorders of speech*. Cambridge, Eng.: Cambridge University Press, 1926. 2 vols.

Hebb, D. O. *The organization of behavior*. New York: John Wiley, 1949.

Heidegger, M. *Being and time*. New York: Harper, 1962.

Heidegger, M. *Brief über den Humanismus*. Bern: A. Francke, 1947.

Lashley, K. S. *Cerebral mechanisms and behavior*. New York: John Wiley, 1952.

3. Heidegger's Analytic of Existence and Its Meaning for Psychiatry

L. BINSWANGER

And do you think that you can know the nature of the soul intelligently without knowing the nature of the whole?

PLATO, Phaedrus, 270c

Martin Heidegger's analytic of existence is doubly significant for psychiatry. It affords empirical psychopathological research a new methodological and material basis that goes beyond its previous framework, and its treatment of the existential concept of science places *psychiatry in general* in a position to account for the actuality, possibility, and limits of its own scientific world-design or, as we may also call it, transcendental horizon of understanding. These two aspects are quite closely related, and both have their roots in Heidegger's *Sein und Zeit* and *Vom Wesen des Grundes*.

The purpose of *Sein und Zeit* was the "concrete" working out of the question as to the meaning of *Being*. Its preliminary goal was to interpret time as the possible horizon of any understanding of Being. To this end, Heidegger, as we know, gives us the "concrete" working out of the *ontological structure* of the Dasein as being-in-the-world or trans-

SOURCE. *Selection from L. Binswanger "Heidegger's analytic of existence and its meaning for psychiatry" in* Being-in-the-world: Selected papers of Ludwig Binswanger, *edited by J. Needleman, pp. 206–221. New York: Basic Books, 1963.*

cendence. In thus indicating the basic structure of the Dasein as being-in-the-world, Heidegger places in the psychiatrist's hands a key by means of which he can, free of the prejudice of any scientific *theory*, ascertain and describe the *phenomena* he investigates in their full phenomenal content and intrinsic context. It was Edmund Husserl's great achievement to have shown, after Brentano, just what this "phenomenological" method is, and to have indicated what enormous vistas it opened for research in the various sciences. Husserl's doctrine, however, concerns itself solely with the sphere of *intentionality*, considered as the unitary relation between transcendental subjectivity and transcendental objectivity. The shift from the "theoretical" ascertainment and description of psychic processes or events in a "subject" to the ascertainment and description of the forms and structures of "intentional consciousness," consciousness of something or directedness toward something, was a quite decisive shift for psychopathological research. Nevertheless, this consciousness was still suspended in the air, in the thin air of the transcendental ego. The—in the full sense of the word—"fundamental" accomplishment of Heidegger consisted not only in stating the problematic nature of the transcendental possibility of intentional acts. What he did, in addition, was to solve this problem by showing how the intentionality of consciousness is grounded in the temporality of human existence, in the Dasein. Intentionality in general is only possible on the basis of "transcendence" and is thus neither identical with it nor, conversely, does it make transcendence possible. Only by referring intentionality back to the Dasein as transcendence or being-in-the-world and only, therefore, with the inclusion of the transcendental ego in the actual Dasein, was the ("objective-transcendental") question posed as to the *what-ness* of the beings that we ourselves are.* We may thus say, with Wilhelm Szilazi, that *Sein und Zeit* is the first inquiry into our existence "with regard to its objective transcendence."

Since, in "The Existential Analysis School of Thought,"[1] I have already sketched the path thus taken, we turn our attention now to the second aspect of Heidegger's dual significance for psychiatry—namely, the question as to the actuality, possibility, and limits of the horizon of understanding, or world-design of psychiatry in general. This problem might also be characterized as concerning the awareness by psychiatry of its own essential structure as science, or, again, as the effort of psychiatry *to understand itself as science*. It goes without saying that in this brief space I can only hint at what the answer to this problem might be.

---

*Here is one juncture where the gap separating Sartre and Heidegger reveals itself. Sartre does not refer back in this manner; indeed, he reproaches Heidegger: "that he has completely avoided any appeal to consciousness in his description of Dasein." *Being and Nothingness*, p. 85.

I

A science does not understand itself simply by being clear as to the "object" it studies and the basic concepts and research methods by which it conducts these studies. Rather, a science understands itself only when it—in the full sense of the Greek *lógon didónai*—accounts for its interpretation (expressed in its basic concepts) of its particular region of being upon the background of that region's basic ontological structure. Such an accounting cannot be executed with the methods of the particular science itself, but only with the aid of philosophical methods.

Science is autonomous with regard to what, in its terms, can be *experienced.* Here it justifiably protects itself against any philosophical "encroachment," just as, for its part, any philosophy aware of its own purposes restrains itself from such encroachment. While, as history has shown, science and philosophy share the same roots, this means that whereas science sets the questions by which it approaches that which is, philosophy poses the question as to the nature of proof as ground and foundation—the question, that is, as to the function performed by transcendence, as such, of establishing a ground. This is simply to repeat—in different words—that a science can understand itself only if it accounts for the original formulation of its question within which, *qua* this particular *scientific* mode of grounding, it approaches the things it studies and has them speak to it. To this extent, and only to this extent, is science to be "referred" to philosophy; to the extent that is, that the self-understanding of a science, considered as the articulation of an actual store of ontological understanding, is possible only on the basis of *philosophical*, i.e., ontological understanding, in general.

II

Whereas physics and biology and the humanistic sciences as well rest upon their own particular "actual store of ontological understanding,"[2] the same cannot be said of psychiatry. In its clinical setting, psychiatry views its object, the "mentally ill human being" from the aspect of nature, and, thus, within the natural-scientific—mainly biological—horizon of understanding. Here psychiatry's object is—as it is in all of medicine—the "sick" organism. But in psychotherapy, it views its object from the aspect of "the human being," and thus within an (either prescientific or systematic) anthropological horizon of understanding. Here the object of psychiatry is the "mentally ill" Other, the fellow man. The incompatibility of these two conceptual horizons or reality-conceptions is not resolvable within science and leads not only to endless scientific controversy, but, also, as the present situation in psychiatry shows, to a split into two separate psychiatric camps. This fact alone shows how important it is for psychiatry to concern itself with the question as to what we human beings *are*.

In actual practice, these two conceptual orientations of psychiatry usually overlap—as one quick glance at its "praxis" tells us. The clinician, too, first "relates himself to" his patient or seeks "an understanding with him." And precisely from this relating or understanding he attains his initial perspective from which to ascertain the *symptoms* of the disease. It was, in fact, Hönigswald who expressed the view that psychiatric symptoms are primarily disturbances of communication and thus refer[3] to a "meaning given to human intercourse." One of the basic demands of medical psychotherapy, on the other hand, is to view the prospective patient *also* as an organism, the demand, namely, that what must first be ascertained is whether the patient is intact "as" an organism—especially as regards the central nervous system—and whether the possibility of such a disturbance of intactness sets up certain therapeutic limitations from the outset.

To the extent, now, that the psychiatrist views the organism as a natural object, i.e., "physicalistically," to the extent that he thus views the fellow man before him, with whom he tries to come to an understanding and who is his partner in the community of man and is another "human soul"—to that extent will his ontological understanding be clouded, at the outset, by the *psychophysical problem*. For, the mind-body problem is not an ontological problem, but a problem of scientific knowledge, a purely theoretical problem. "Theory," therefore is called in for help in "solving" this problem. No theory, however, can really "solve" it, but can only seek to bridge mind and body with more or less perfunctory theoretical sham solutions ("auxiliary hypotheses"), or immerse the whole problem in a pseudophilosophical (materialistic, spiritualistic, biologistic, or psychologistic) smoke screen.

The problem of mind and body, though it arises out of urgent practical scientific needs, is incorrectly formulated because science—as it must—fails to see that what is involved are two quite different scientific conceptions of reality which cannot be bridged by any theory nor merged together by any amount of speculation. For as soon as I objectify my fellow man, as soon as I objectify his subjectivity, he is no longer my fellow man; and as soon as I subjectify an organism or make a natural object into a responsible subject, it is no longer an organism in the sense intended by medical science. The situation can be put to rights only if we go *behind* both conceptual horizons or reality-conceptions—that of nature and that of "culture"—and approach man's basic function of understanding Being as the establishing of ground—a transcendental function. Our task, then, is to use philosophical rigor in understanding both the power and the impotence of these two conceptions considered as *scientific*, or even as prescientific or "naïve," modes of transcendental grounding or establishment.

III

Scientific understanding is oriented toward fact and factuality, i.e., toward reality and objectivity. Such a project (or design) separates areas of fact and places the various entities in a factual, real, objective, and systematic interconnection.[4] Heidegger has shown that such a project is not simply a demarcation of regions, but is also the establishing of a ground. That is, in such a project a particular sphere "of being" (beings) are "thematized" and thereby rendered accessible to objective inquiry and determination. If this is so, then such a project must be constantly subjected to a critique that concerns itself with the fundamental issues of all scientific inquiry. It is not *only* philosophy that performs this function of criticism. We find it constantly being effected in the way scientific concepts of themselves break down and undergo transformations—in, that is, the various *crises* of science.

Today psychiatry finds itself in just such a crisis. The "Magna Charta"* or framework that was its guide up to now has been broken down on the one hand by psychoanalysis and by psychotherapy's generally deepened understanding of its own scientific bases, and on the other hand by ever-increasing insight into the game of psychosomatics, and above all by "structural"† and empirical existential-analytic research, which has widened the scope and cast light on psychiatry's horizon of understanding.

Simply as regards this "crisis," Heidegger's phenomenological-philosophical analytic of existence is important for psychiatry. This is so because it does not inquire merely into particular regions of phenomena and fact to be found "in human beings," but, rather, inquires into the *being* of *man as a whole*. Such a question is not answerable by scientific methods alone. The conception of man as a physical-psychological-spiritual unity does not say enough. For, as Heidegger says, the being of man cannot be ascertained by the "summative enumeration" of the rather ambiguous ontological modes of body, mind, and soul. What is needed is the return to (subjective) transcendence, to the Dasein as being-in-the-world, even while constant attention is being accorded its objective transcendence.

It is, of course, true that modern psychiatry also seeks to know the nature of the "soul" by regarding the nature of the whole— as Plato prescribed (see the chapter motto). But psychiatry, as a branch of medicine, primarily views this whole as "life," as a biological whole, and every "consideration" of this whole ordinarily takes place at the level of factual objective "relations." In addition the soul is understood as something neutrally present (*vorhanden*) in or with the body. But even aside from these considerations, what is meant by the Greek expression *to Holon*—in contrast to *to Pan*—is not the totality of the whole, but—as in Aristotle—wholeness as such.

---

*[See "Freud and the Magna Charta of Clinical Psychiatry" in this volume.]

†This term is meant to include those psychiatric schools of thought attached to the names of E. Minkowski, Erwin Straus, and V. E. von Gebsattel.

Heidegger's analytic of existence, by inquiring into the being of the whole man, can provide not scientific, but philosophical understanding of this wholeness. Such an understanding can indicate to psychiatry the limits within which it may inquire and expect an answer and can, as well, indicate the general horizon within which answers, as such, are to be found.

It is incorrect to accuse Heidegger's analytic of existence of failing to deal with nature, for it is through this same analytic of existence that the basis for the problem of nature can be obtained—*via* the approach to the Dasein as situationally attuned (*befindlich-gestimmten*) existence *among beings*. It would be equally incorrect to accuse *Daseinsanalyse* of "neglecting the body." Insofar as a world-design is seen as *thrown*—and this means situationally attuned—then, explicitly or not, attention is being directed to the Dasein in its bodiliness.

In practice, whenever the psychiatrist himself tries to look beyond the limitations of his science and seeks to know the ontological grounds of his understanding and treatment of those placed in his care, it is Heidegger's analytic of existence that can broaden his horizon. For it offers the possibility of understanding man as both a creature of nature, and a socially determined or historical being—and this by means of *one* ontological insight, which thus obviates the separation of body, mind, and spirit. Man as a creature of nature is revealed in the thrownness of the Dasein, its "that-it-is," its *facticity*. "Has the Dasein, as such, ever freely decided and will it ever be able to decide as to whether it wants to come into 'existence' or not?" The Dasein, although it exists essentially for its own sake (*umwillen seiner*), has nevertheless not itself laid the ground of its *being*. And also, as a creature "come into existence," it is and remains, *thrown*, determined, i.e.,

enclosed, possessed, and compelled by beings in general. Consequently it is not "completely free" in its world-design either. The "powerlessness" of the Dasein here shows itself in that certain of its possibilities of being-in-the-world are *withdrawn* because of commitment to and by beings, because of its facticity. But it is also just this withdrawal that lends the Dasein its *power*: for it is this that first brings *before* the Dasein the "real," graspable possibilities of world-design.

Transcendence is thus not only a striding or swinging of the Dasein toward the world, but is, at the same time, withdrawal, limitation—and only *in* this limiting does transcendence gain power "over the world." All this, however, is but a "transcendental document" of the Dasein's *finitude*. The thrownness of the Dasein, its facticity, is the transcendental horizon of all that scientific systematic psychiatry delimits as reality under the name of organism, body (and heredity, climate, milieu, etc.), and also for all that which is delimited, investigated, and researched as psychic *determinateness*: namely, as mood and ill humor, as craziness, compulsive or insane "possessedness," as addiction, instinctuality, as confusion, phastasy determination, as, in general, unconsciousness. Now, whereas the science of psychiatry not only observes and establishes connections *between* these two spheres, but also erects the theoretical bridge of the psychophysical—*Daseinsanalyse*, on the other hand, shows that it is the scientific dichotomization of man's ontological wholeness that gives rise to this postulate in the first place. It shows that this dichotomization results from projecting the whole of human being upon the screen of that which is merely objectively present [*vorhanden*]. It also indicates the general world-design of science as stemming from one and the same Dasein, from, namely, the Dasein's ontological potentiality of scientific being-in-the-world. Here, too, it is true to say that what lends the world-design its (limited) scientific power is obtained only through its powerlessness to understand the being of human existence [Dasein] as a whole.

It is to Heidegger's great credit that he summed up the being of the Dasein under the all too easily misunderstood title of Care (= caring for), and to have phenomenologically explored its basic structures and make-up. Thrownness, in the sense of the facticity of the Dasein's answerability to its that-it-is, is only *one* component ("existential") of this structure, the others, as we know, being existence (project) and fallenness.* Thus what in psychiatry is irreversibly separated into discrete realities of fields of study, namely, the finite human Dasein, is presented here in its basic structural unity. (It cannot be emphasized too often that this presentation signifies something quite different from the approach to man under the aegis of one particular *idea*, such as the idea of the will to power, libido, or any idea involving man as, in general, a creature of nature, or even, indeed, the idea of man as a child of God, as *homo aeternus*, etc.) But where there is structure there can be no dissociation of one structural member from the structural whole. Each, rather, remains implicated in the others, and a change in one structural element involves a change in the others. The Dasein can thus never get "behind" its thrownness and can only project those possibilities into which it is thrown. Only, therefore, as surrendered to its *that*, as thrown, does the Dasein *exist* within the ground of its power-to-be. The self of

existence, although it has to lay its own ground, can therefore never have power over this ground. As a being, it has to be "as it is and can be." Its being is a projection of its own power-to-be, and to this extent it is always already in *advance** of itself. This being in advance of itself also concerns the whole of the Dasein's structure. Corresponding to all that we know of its thrownness (as already-being-in-the-world), the being-in-advance-of itself of the Dasein, its futurity, is through and through implicated with its past. Out of both these temporal "ecstasies" the authentic present temporalizes itself. This is what was referred to in the opening pages as the "way" of *Sein und Zeit:* the attempt to understand the basic structure of the Dasein *via* the unitariness of temporality and its ecstasies.

I have elsewhere[5] tried to indicate the significance of this way for psychopathological knowledge and the understanding of the basic forms of human existence. Here, however, we are concerned with pointing out its significance for psychiatry's understanding of itself. The insight into the temporal essence of the Dasein, or transcendence, not only instructs psychiatry as to its "object" — the various modes of "abnormal" human existence — but also instructs it in its understanding of itself in that it compels it to realize that its dissection of human being into various factual regions with their corresponding conceptualizations cannot be the last word. For, as I have already mentioned, it thereby takes *one* level, that of things objectively present [*vorhanden*] "in time and space," here and

---

*For the significance of fallenness "toward the world" — and not only the *Mitwelt* — see *Schizophrenie.*

*Regarding the extent to which the various psychotic forms of manic depression and schizophrenia are rooted in various modes of this being-in-advance-of-itself of the Dasein (be it from the aspect of attunement [*Gestimmtheit*] or "Extravagant" ideal-formation), see my studies *Über Ideenflucht* and *Schizophrenie.*

now, and projects upon that level what makes the understanding of spatialization and temporalization possible in the first place: the Dasein. But if psychiatry realizes—and this is true for all sciences—how provisional its world-designs, its reality-conceptions, are, it will hold on to its basic concepts less rigidly and will find it easier to deepen and change these concepts. It is obvious, after all we have said, that these conceptual changes can be instigated only within scientific research and its particular crises, and therefore only within psychiatry's efforts in its own proper sphere of activity. A "dogmatic" importation of philosophical doctrines as such has almost always been detrimental to science and research.

IV

It is not enough to realize the necessary limitedness of psychiatry's world-design, which, like all world-designs, derives its power from the *elimination* of other possibilities. The analytic of existence can, in addition, show psychiatry *what, materially,* must be "withdrawn," must be neglected, when man is dissected into body, mind, and soul.

I have already cited Hönigswald's essay on philosophy and psychiatry. In it, he also remarks that it must essentially be expected if the organism "that it call itself *I.*" The analytic of existence indicates the root of this "expectation," namely, the basic anthropological fact that the Dasein is, in its being, concerned essentially with this being itself, in other words, that its whereto and wherefore is always directed toward itself. This being for itself by no means signifies an attitude of the I to itself that gives it the possibility of calling itself *I.* If this potentiality is to be "expected" also of the organism, it is because we realize that if this power to say *I* (and *me* and *mine*) is lost sight of in the reality-conception

wherein man is projected, then the splitting of man into organism and Ego, body and soul, physical and psychic, *res extensa* and *res cogitans*, will never be set aright, and that what will be lost sight of is man as he really is. There may be many "factual" grounds for undertaking this separation. But this should not prevent us from seeing that it is undertaken only "for the sake of the matter" and ceases to be valid once we turn our attention from the particular "circumstances" to the being of the Dasein itself. For, the being for itself also concerns the Dasein *qua* organism or body, the Dasein that *is* organism only as mine, yours, or his, and that, under no circumstances, is purely and simply organism and body as such. It is, consequently, naïve to see the psychophysical problem as a riddle of the universe.

For science, this also means that as biologists, or even as physiologists, we ought not to view the organism only as a natural object, but must keep in mind that the concept of organism results from a natural-scientific *reduction*[6] of man to his bodily existence and the further reduction of this bodily existence to a mere neutrally present, "ownerless," object.

One brief example: the conception of remembering, forgetting, and recollection as Mneme and Exphoresis (Semon, E. Bleuler, among others). Here, memory and recollection are conceived purely as brain functions, as "processes in the brain." As opposed to this, however, it is not hard to show that "the brain," like the organism itself, can still only be my, your, or his brain in its "reality." In other words, the mnemonic "brain-function" can be understood only within the perspective of *my Dasein's* power to be-in-the-world as retentive, forgetful, and recollective. This means, in short, that memory cannot be understood solely within physiology. It means, rather, that retention as well as forgetting involves a retreat by the Dasein to its bodily existence and that recollection means a return of the Dasein from its involvement "in the body" to its psychic existence.[7]

The degree to which both modes of human being are interrelated through their "alliance," through what Plato termed *koinonia*, was recently well shown by Wilhelm Szilazi in his Heideggerian interpretation of Plato's *Philebus*.[8] There we find quite clearly stated that the "elements" of the Dasein's power of being stem from the totality of ontological potentialities (the All), but that corporeality only becomes body *via* the *koinonia* that links "the soul" with that which is corporeal.* Equally clearly drawn is the way in which the Dasein "distances" itself from its bodily involvement, its thrownness, in order first to be fully *free as* "spirit." Wherever one leaves out the *koinonia* of the Dasein's ontological potentialities and their gradations — which Aristotle characterized as *syntheton* — then an understanding of man is unattainable. For then, instead of the facticity of the Dasein, which, though it is an innerwordly being, differs basically from the factuality of the neutrally on-hand (the *Vorhanden*), in place of this facticity, the "universal riddle" of the psychophysical problem rears its head.

Turning now to the concept of *disease* in psychiatry, we must consider Paul Häberlin's excellent essay "The Object of Psychiatry."[9] On the basis of anthropology,[10] Häberlin comes to the conclusion that the pathological character of mental diseases is somatically, rather than psychologically, patterned, and that only the so-called neuroses are really psychic diseases and only they should really be called psychoses. The extent to which this

view approaches the state of affairs in psychiatry is the extent to which it presupposes a *koinonia* of mind and body that is of a *different kind* than that which we ourselves are presenting here. Häberlin understands the body as the *image* of the mind, and he characterizes man as a "mental nation" governed with relative success by its founder, the mind. These two types of disease are distinguished, according to Häberlin, in that in one case the mind is "at odds" with *itself*, while in the other case (what is usually called mental disease), it is primarily the — *central* — organization of the *body* that is disturbed. *Both kinds* of disease necessarily express themselves mentally *and* physically. In the first case, that of the so-called neuroses, the mind cannot uniformly carry out its functions, among which is the function of governing the body, and we therefore, to a greater or lesser extent, find somatic consequences in neurosis. But in the case of the so-called psychoses, the mind, in turn, suffers from the disturbance in the organism because this disturbance hinders its governance of the body and, in its receptive aspect, presents the mind with a distorted image of the world so that it, the mind, reacts abnormally. Thus, in *both* cases, the normal *relation* between body and mind (*koinonia*) is disturbed. Every disease affects both sides, regardless of where the primary conditioning factors lie.

And *we too*, from the perspective of Heidegger's analytic of existence, must conceive of both mental disease (Häberlin's somatosis) and neurosis (Häberlin's psychosis) as a disturbance of *koinonia*, of the functional *unity* of the Dasein's ontological potentialities. On this basis it is, for example, understandable that the mental disease called melancholia can be conceived as a disturbance of the *koinonia* between the bodily and mental being of the Dasein, which manifests itself on the

---

*Thus Häberlin (see below) makes no bones about saying that the isolated body ("body without soul") does not exist.

one hand as a "vegetative" disturbance of the organism, and on the other hand as an "isolated," heightened, and distorted form of the finite Dasein's inherent guilt. It is not surprising, therefore, that melancholia can arise because of family tragedy, loss of power, or concrete guilt on the one hand, or on the other hand, in connection with intestinal diseases or even "for no reason at all." Nor is it surprising, then, that we can "cure" the melancholic with electroshock, or calm him with opium, or comfort him with assurances about his recovery and thus spur him on toward a steadfast endurance of his suffering. In each instance, we seek to restore the *koinonia* of body and mind. That in this case success is easier when the patient is treated from the "physical" side only indicates the nature of the melancholic form of existence that involves the *dominant power* of thrownness as already-being-in-the-world (mood), i.e., pastness (*Gewesenheit*) over existence as being-in-advance-of-itself in the future. It in no way argues against the notion that the mental illness known as melancholia involves the Dasein as a whole. The same, in turn, is true of the "neuroses." No matter how well psychopathology may understand neurosis (in strictly Freudian terms) as "psychic conflict," from the point of view of existential analysis, the neuroses must not *merely* be understood within the perspective of existence. That human beings *can* become "neurotic" at all is *also* a sign of the thrownness of the Dasein and a sign of its potentiality of fallenness—a sign, in short, of its finitude, its transcendental limitedness or unfreedom.

Only he who scorns these limits, who—in Kierkegaard's terms—is at odds with the fundamental conditions of existence, can become "neurotic," whereas only he who "knows" of the unfreedom of finite human existence and who obtains "power" over his existence within this very powerlessness is unneurotic or "free." The *sole task* of "psychotherapy" lies in assisting man toward this "power." It is only the *ways* to this goal that are *various*.

Naturally, the philosophical analytic of existence neither will nor can intrude upon psychiatry's conception of reality, nor doubt its empirically established "psycho-physical" connections. However, what it can do and what it seeks to do is simply to show that what we have cited as psychiatry's dual reality-conception owes its power and meaning to its being limited to particular scientific world-designs and not the being of those beings that it thematizes. All those issues, therefore, that extend beyond the field of this "thematization," i.e., questions as to human freedom, "time and space," relation of "mind and matter," questions of philosophy, art, religion, questions as to the nature of genius, etc.—such questions are not to be answered by the science of psychiatry.

A word, in conclusion, about the psychiatric problem of the *unconscious*. While psychoanalysis, as we know, interprets the unconscious from the perspective of consciousness,* it is clear that a doctrine that does not proceed from the intentionality of consciousness, but that, rather, shows how this intentionality is grounded in the temporality of human existence, must interpret the difference between consciousness and unconsciousness temporally and existentially. The point of departure for this interpretation cannot, therefore, be consciousness. It can, instead, only be the "unconscious," the thrownness and determinateness of the

---

*Whereby there obtains the disproportion between the high methodological esteem given to consciousness—indeed, in this respect the best thing that can be said of the workings of the unconscious is that it approaches consciousness or even excels it—and low esteem accorded its material, psychological significance.

Dasein. A closer examination of this issue would, however, require a separate paper.

From the perspective of psychiatry's transcendental understanding of itself as a science — and only from that perspective — we may now interpret the being of the psychiatrist.† Those whose concern is man's physical health know that they must be not only "medical men," but also physicians. To the extent that diagnostic judgment is rooted not in observations of the patient's organism, but in the "coming to an understanding" with him as a human being, as one who also exists humanly — to that extent what is *essentially* involved is not just the attitude of the "medical man" toward his scientific object. What is involved is his *relation*[11] to the patient, a relation rooted equally in "care" and love. Is is of the *essence* of being a psychiatrist, *therefore*, that he reaches beyond all factual knowledge and the abilities that go with it, and that he reaches beyond *scientific* knowledge found in the fields of psychology, psychopathology, and psychotherapy. This swinging beyond or transcending the factuality, objectivity, and reality-orientation of psychiatry can be understood only from the point of view of transcendence itself as being-in-the-world and being-beyond-the-world.[12]

Not only at the initial interview or examination, but also during the course of the whole *treatment*, being a psychiatrist goes beyond being a medical man (in the sense of knowing and mastering the field of medicine). The being of a psychiatrist — I mean, of course, a psychiatrist, as such, and not what is called a "good" psychiatrist — involves, therefore, the insight that no whole, and thus no "whole man" can be "grasped" with the methods of science. Now, if the psychiatrist is oriented toward encounter and mutual understanding with his fellow man and is oriented toward understanding human beings in their totality, in the *koinonia* of their ontological potentialities and the *koinonia* of this totality with more universal ontological potentialities, then the being of the psychiatrist reaches beyond the purely "theoretical" ontological potentialities of man and is directed toward transcendence itself.

It follows from this that the psychiatrist in his being summons and lays claim to the whole man. Whereas in other branches of science it may, to a greater or lesser extent, be possible to separate one's vocation and existence and, so to speak, find one's "existential center of gravity" in a hobby or in some other scientific activity, or in philosophy, a religion, or art, it is not so in psychiatry. In a certain sense being a psychiatrist also claims the existence of the psychiatrist. For where meeting and mutual understanding furnish the grounds and basis for everything that can be viewed as symptoms or even as disease and health per se, and where, therefore, there can be nothing human upon which — *in a psychiatric sense* — judgment cannot be passed, then hobby, science, philosophy, art, and religion must be capable of being projected and understood from the perspective of personal existence as ontological potentialities and conceptual projects. Where this is not the case — as the history of psychiatry shows — every psychiatric judgment actually is deprived of a solid basis. Consequently, the being of the psychiatrist cannot be understood without understanding transcendence as "the freedom to establish a ground."

---

†It goes without saying that what holds true for the physician in general is also true of the psychiatrist, namely: "For him health is the principle of his profession, and wherever he disregards its recognized limits, he makes himself guilty at every step." See the sharp and unambiguous treatment of "Das Prinzip des ärztlichen Berufs" by Paul Matussek in *Festschrift für Kurt Schneider* (Verlag Scherer, 1947).

This "freedom" now permits us to understand that the scientific concerns and necessities (basic concepts, research methods) of psychiatry must stand not in a rigid, but in a flexible and vital relation to the Dasein as being-in-the-world and being-beyond-the-world. It also permits us to understand why scientific progress in psychiatry is especially bound up with the interaction between research into matters of fact and transcendental reflection upon its nature as science.

Notes

[1] See Rollo May, Ernest Angel, and Henri F. Ellenberger (eds.), *Existence* (New York, 1958), pp. 191–213.

[2] See the (expanded) lecture of W. Szilasi (January 10, 1945) in *Wissenschaft als Philosophie* (Zürich, New York, 1945).

[3] See Richard Hönigswald, "Philosophie und Psychiatrie," *Archiv. f. Psychiatrie u. Nervenkrankheiten*, Vol. 87, No. 5 (1929), and Binswanger, Über die manische Lebensform," *Ausg. Vort. u. Aufs.*, Vol. II.

[4] See Szilasi, *op. cit.*

[5] *Grundformen und Erkenntnis menschlichen Daseins.*

[6] See my "Über die manische Lebensform," and above all the excellent treatment by René Le Senne of "La dialectique de naturalisation" in *Obstacle et Valeur*. See further, T. Haering, *Philosophie der Naturwissenschaft* (1923).

[7] See "Über Psychotherapie."

[8] W. Szilasi, *Macht und Ohnmacht des Geistes.*

[9] P. Häberlin, in *Schweiz. Archiv. f. Psych. u. Neur.*, Vol. 60.

[10] *Der Mensch, eine philosophische Anthropologie* (Zürich, 1941).

[11] See *Grundformen*, Part II.

[12] *Ibid.*

Author Index

Author Index

Subject Index

Subject Index